Marianne C. Saccardi

in Story

Teaching Art History to Elementary School Children

Second Edition

Teacher Ideas Press, an imprint of Libraries Unlimited
Westport, Connecticut • London

Library of Congress Cataloging-in-Publication Data

Saccardi, Marianne.
Art in story : teaching art history to elementary school children / Marianne C. Saccardi. — 2nd ed.
p. cm.
Includes bibliographical references and index.
ISBN 1-59158-359-4 (pbk : alk. paper)
1. Art—History—Study and teaching (Elementary) 2. Activity programs in education. I. Title.
N350.S23 2007
372.5'044—dc22 2006033980

British Library Cataloguing in Publication Data is available.

Library of Congress Catalog Card Number: 2006033980
ISBN: 1-59158-359-4

First published in 2007

Libraries Unlimited/Teacher Ideas Press, 88 Post Road West, Westport, CT 06881
A Member of the Greenwood Publishing Group, Inc.
www.lu.com

Printed in the United States of America

The paper used in this book complies with the Permanent Paper Standard issued by the National Information Standards Organization (Z39.48–1984).

10 9 8 7 6 5 4 3 2 1

Art in Story

Art

To Mom and Dad with love,
and
to the many children who over the years
have taught me how to see

Contents

Acknowledgments

There are many people who have helped me write this book, and I would like to thank them here.

First, always, my wonderful family:

My husband Thomas, who has always believed in this book and my ability to write it and who provided some of the photographs;

My son Christopher, who continues to be my computer mentor and gave his permission to use some of his photographs ;

My son Daniel, who cheerfully helped to carry up and down stairs the hundreds of books used in writing this volume, and who also contributed photographs;

Pat Schaefer, who graciously granted me permission to use the story of Noma which appears in "Prehistoric Art" chapter 1;

Tim Williamson, who graciously allowed me to use his ingenious diagrams of the four-centered arch that appear in chapter 2;

April Greiman who kindly supplied the graphics for her wonderful work for chapter 20;

Sharon Coatney, my patient editor;

Marilyn Jody, who cheered and encouraged from the sidelines;

Marylyn Rosenblum, who suggested many years ago that I write a book about my experiences teaching art history;

The many librarians at the Greenwich Public Library, the Perrot Memorial Library, the Byram-Shubert Library, and the Upper School Library at Greenwich Country Day School, all in Greenwich, Connecticut, for their help, advice, and cheerful goodwill throughout the writing of this book; and

My friends in Storytelling Anon who through the years have convinced me of the power of storytelling and have awed me with their talents.

Introduction

Sometimes I can't remember what I had for breakfast,
but I remember every story I ever heard.

—JAMES SANDY, TOWN PLANNER,
in the *Greenwich Time* (Connecticut), July 5, 1995

One of the delightful benefits of teaching is that one gains as much knowledge as one imparts. During my twenty years as an elementary school teacher, my best teachers were the children themselves. And one of the most important lessons they taught me was their infinite capacity to take in the world, to notice even the smallest details, to look long and hard without tiring. The children helped me notice tiny plants and insects I would have missed on my own. They helped me discover colors and shapes and patterns both inside the classroom and in the wider world outside. They were naturally drawn to beauty and found it in all the most unexpected places. Through their eyes I learned to see anew.

It was natural, then, when I began to reevaluate my curriculum after several years of teaching, that I pondered the value of introducing art history into the classroom. Certainly, art had already been an integral part of our class work. We often expressed our social studies learning through art projects. We drew the insects, animals, and plants we studied in science. We drew storybook characters and scenes. And every Friday afternoon we rolled up our sleeves, donned our oversized shirts, and gave ourselves over to extended art activities involving a variety of media. But we had never studied the great artists of the world or viewed their work. It seemed foolish to defer this study to high school or college years when the young children I taught were so ripe for such an exploration into beauty. So I began to develop an art history curriculum for primary school–age children —a curriculum that was to expand over the years to include drama, writing, poetry, and children's literature.

Components of the Art History Lessons

I taught art history in a self-contained classroom once a week. Each lesson took about an hour and was divided into several components to hold the children's attention.

Story

"When children enter into story, they are transported to other worlds, joining in the adventure and the excitement freed of their own time and place—and somehow changed by the experience. They learn about the lives of others and in doing so develop a better understanding of their own lives" (Barton and Booth 1990, 14).

Children love stories. They are great storytellers themselves, and my classrooms have always been abuzz with stories of weekend trips, after-school activities, family happenings, and the latest in the sagas of various friendships. My approach to art history, then, was through story as a way to children's hearts and minds. When I told stories I could make direct eye contact with my young listeners and capture their interest. Each week I searched through books for facts about the artist or period I wished to introduce to my students, and then wove these facts into stories. I didn't worry excessively about whether the facts I used were 100 percent verifiable or merely apocryphal. I simply wanted the children to connect emotionally with an artist. At the start of the lesson, I gathered the children in a circle and told them a story about the artist or time period we were going to study. The children loved these stories and remembered them years later. I fondly recall a sixth-grader coming back to visit the class in which he had been a "little kid" and reminding me of the time I told the story of Benjamin West, who made a paintbrush out of his cat's tail. I had told him that story four years before!

Viewing the Art

After our story, we viewed artworks of the period or artist. Here I let the children take over, encouraging them to talk about the things they noticed, liked best, or wondered about. They often remarked on the content of an artist's painting and how the artist's subjects sprang from his or her life or time. I used the excellent reproductions available in many large art books written for adults as well as those intended for children. In addition, our public school had mounted traveling art prints that I borrowed often throughout the year. Perhaps your school district has similar materials available. DVDs, slides, and films were also an important part of our classes. Extensive lists of books and audiovisual materials appear at the end of each chapter in this book for your convenience. Although older, out-of-print books have been kept to a minimum, some do appear either because their reproductions are too valuable to ignore or because there would not be enough material on the subject without them. This part of the lesson can be as simple or as complex as you wish, depending on the age of the children.

Journal Writing

"When people write about something they learn it better. That, in a nutshell, is the idea behind asking students to keep journals . . . . [Journals] provide a place in which to write informally yet systematically in order to seek, discover, speculate, and figure things out" (Fulwiler 1987, 9). The children kept a learning journal in which they wrote their questions, the most important facts and ideas they learned, what they liked best about an artist's work, etc. I began each year by giving many demonstrations of how to keep such a journal. For several weeks, we composed a learning journal together, and I wrote the children's ideas on a chart. After a while, even first-graders were able to keep their own journals. Some started their entries with drawings, but as the year wore on, they began to write and to manage longer and longer entries.

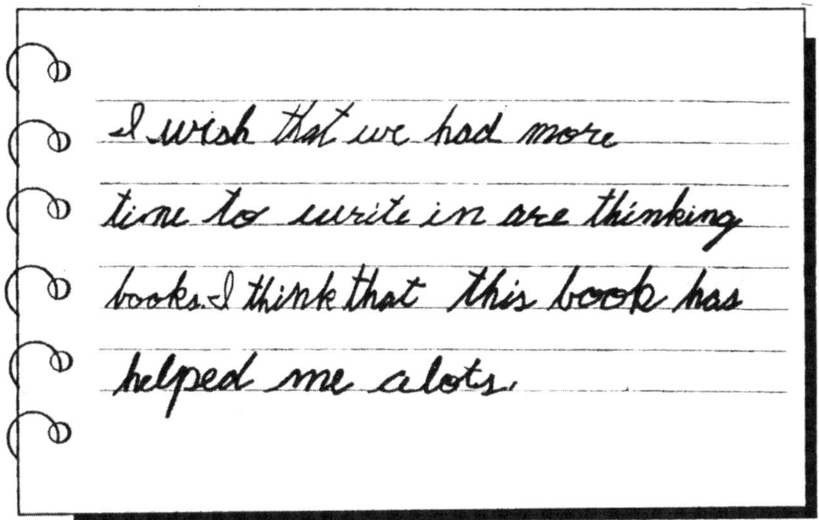

I wish that we had more
time to write in are thinking
books. I think that this book has
helped me alots.

I responded to these journals each week, and it became a great deal of fun to carry on this dialogue about art with my students. I also began to value the journals as a way to discover what worked with the children and what didn't, and where their confusions lay. One second-grader wrote, "It was rely hard for Michelangelo wen he panted the 16 chpl." The children, too, began to look forward to this opportunity to reflect on their learning, and they took their journals home with great pride at the end of the year. In this book I offer suggestions for journal writing for each lesson. These are only meant as suggestions and are, perhaps, most useful for those students who are not sure where to begin. You may want to offer your own prompts in response to class reaction to the lesson, or leave the children completely free to write what they wish.

Art/Drama Activity

Each lesson culminated with an art or drama activity. Sometimes these activities were so involved that they were carried over into the following week. Sometimes the children would role-play something they heard in the story I told. Often they would choose a poem that seemed to fit a particular artist's life or work from the many poetry books in the classroom. Almost always, we engaged in an art activity that required the use of media or technique we had just viewed in the artist's work. For example, after talking about Egyptian art, we assumed the role of palace artists and designed a tomb for the pharaoh. After studying the work of Winslow Homer, we painted pictures using watercolors.

Whenever we engaged in a drama activity, I made certain that the children were truly in character. In other words, if they were making cave drawings for good luck in a hunting expedition, for the duration of the drama they had to really believe they were prehistoric people whose lives depended on the animals they killed. If there were signs that some of the children were not in character, I stopped the activity and began again. Creative drama, along with the stories, helped children remember artists long after we had ceased talking about them. It was commonplace for children to bring in art books their parents have at home to show the class the work of an artist we had studied weeks before.

A Culminating Activity

In the spring I always gave the children the opportunity to put on a play about some of the artists we had studied during the year. The choice was completely theirs. Sometimes they chose Renaissance artists, sometimes American artists or Impressionists. One year they even chose to do picture-book illustrators. The children themselves worked in groups to write the script (which meant they blocked out scenes—first we'll do this, then this, etc.), make props and scenery, and devise costumes. They volunteered for the various acting parts and named their own director and stage crew. Everyone did something. We kept these plays simple, and much of the action and dialogue was improvised, but the children and their parents loved them. The plays became such a high point that new classes would often ask at the first art history session, "Are we going to do a play like your class did last year?"

Changes to the New Edition

This second edition of *Art in Story* contains several changes and additions designed to make the book even more useful in helping teachers bring children to a love of fine art. Most important, the section on ancient Egyptian art has been moved from "Art of the Ancient World" into a newly created chapter, "Art of the Middle East." In addition to Egyptian art, this section features Iranian art. With so much emphasis on the Middle East in today's world, and especially upon the negative view of the region as a training ground for terrorists, it is important for children to hear about the marvels of the Middle East: that it is the birth place of civilization and the ancient seat of learning, and that its people have made enormous cultural, scientific, religious, and artistic contributions to the rest of the world. I hope teachers will draw on this material and that it will be useful in helping them increase their students' appreciation for the incredible artistic achievements of Middle Eastern peoples. Only when our children grow up with a balanced view of those who are different from themselves can we hope to achieve understanding and peace in the world.

The activities in every chapter have now been linked to national standards in every relevant subject. You will note that these standards appear below each section of a lesson, indicating that when teachers use some of the background information with children or engage in the suggested lesson activities with them, they are helping the children toward the achievement of benchmarks indicated by these standards. Of course, doing one lesson on each topic will not mean children have mastered a skill or learned that information perfectly. But throughout the book many activities are repeated: the listening, the writing, looking for countries on a globe, etc. And with this repetition comes increased knowledge and skill levels. The referenced standards indicate that through a study of art as described in this book, students will also be honing their listening and writing skills, learning social studies, music, public speaking and drama, and more. Armed with such information, it should be much easier for teachers to justify to their administration the time spent teaching art history. For a complete listing of the federal curriculum standards for elementary school children, go to http://www.mcrel.org/compendium/browse.asp.

The references at the end of each chapter as well as the general bibliography have been updated. The study of art and artists has become increasingly popular since this book was first published, and fine children's books about art and its creators have come on the market in increasing numbers. All the relevant ones available at this printing have been added to the appropriate chapter resources. New audiovisual and manipulative materials are included as well. The Internet has become an increasingly effective tool for study and research, and Web sites come and go like the wind. All the sites listed for each chapter were viable at the time of publication. If, when you use this book, you are unable to access any of the Web sites suggested either within or at the end of the chapters, it simply means they have been taken out of circulation. However, doing a search on any of the search engines available will surely reap numerous sites on the subjects covered in these pages. Keep in mind that local museums, far too numerous to mention here, usually have a Web page and other materials, and teachers and parents would do well to avail themselves of all the information these institutions readily provide.

Some pictures have been added to this new edition, and it is hoped they enhance the material in the different chapters and are an aid in the viewing portion of the lessons.

How to Use This Book

I began teaching art history armed with only a college survey course. I made no attempt to give the children an in-depth study of art. I simply wanted to build on their natural affinity for beauty and their attention to detail, and to spark their enthusiasm for great works of art. I hoped that what we did together would be the beginning of an interest that would deepen with the years. This book is the culmination of thirteen years of studying art history with children. It is not a scholarly treatise but rather a practical guide to help teachers introduce world-renowned artists to their students. It is meant to make teachers' busy lives easier by eliminating the need for time-consuming research. It is also meant to inspire confidence in those who do not have any training in art studies. The book is organized in a way that makes teaching art history easy and fun. You will find within each chapter background information on the period or artist to be studied; a story to tell the children; suggestions for art and drama activities; ways to integrate art history into other areas of the curriculum; and lists of books, audiovisual, and manipulative materials. In the back of the book there is an index to the works of art by title in each chapter, and a resource directory of companies and institutions that provide audiovisual materials, sometimes free of charge.

I worked with young children, but the lessons here may be adapted for older elementary- and middle school–age children as well. In fact, some of the suggested curriculum activities apply to older students. Because children (and adults) of all ages love stories, the beginning part of the lessons will hold for all grades. It may only be necessary to tell the stories in more sophisticated language. You may wish to use some of the information in the background section to elaborate on the story or to create additional stories of your own. You can also add depth for older students by going into greater detail regarding the artists' styles and works, and by choosing more complex works to view. You can give more scope to the elements of art such as line, form, and color. The children themselves will naturally perform the art and drama activities with greater expertise and complexity. The books suggested cover a wide range of abilities, from picture books for young children to adult art books, and they may be used in a variety of ways. The adult books are a wonderful source of art prints for all children, even though the text will probably be beyond them. You may wish to read some of the children's books aloud, or to make them available for the children to read independently. Groups of children can use some of the books for research while preparing plays. Some of the suggested films have narration that is too difficult for young students;

they are included because they are excellent vehicles for viewing an artist's work, and, in the case of artists living in recent times, to see the artist himself or herself. In cases where books are scarce—about Louise Nevelson, for example—having a film to show is a great help. If the narration is beyond your students, simply turn the sound off and let the children enjoy the artwork depicted. You can show short parts of the films as well. Of course, it is best to see the actual artwork itself, for no reproduction can capture in full the beauty of an artist's creation. If at all possible, try to arrange at least one museum visit during the year. I have found that these visits work best for small groups rather than for a whole class. I usually briefed one or two parents on the exhibits I particularly wanted the children to see and on what we had studied in class, and sent them off with a group of four students. The children prepared for the trips, too, by writing in their journals about the things they hoped to see and learn in the museum. Over a period of several weeks, everyone had a chance to go to the museum, and the trips were truly ventures into the world of art rather than social outings. In today's world of parents and caregivers working outside the home, this may be harder and harder to achieve. It is certainly an ideal to strive for.

As you view the table of contents of this book, you may wonder at some of the choices. Why include Donatello among the Renaissance artists and leave out Titian? Where is Renoir among the Impressionists? Why are some countries not represented at all? Two factors dictated the content of this book. First and foremost was the children themselves. The artists and periods included here are those children have especially loved over the years. The second consideration was space. Many artists and periods I taught successfully had to be omitted here to keep this book within manageable proportions.

Because children, especially the younger ones, have a fuzzy sense of time at best, there is no need to use this book in order. Young children will not really have a sense of when the Renaissance took place—only that it was long ago. Simply teach those artists and time periods you feel your own students would enjoy in whatever order you feel comfortable with. Perhaps the accessibility of materials or museum exhibits in your area will dictate the artists to be studied. Or the children themselves will suggest some names. Once you have used some of the lessons in the book and feel comfortable with the format, you may wish to devise your own lessons about artists you know your students would enjoy.

It is appropriate here to talk briefly about showing prints of nudes to the children. While I would never use blatantly erotic prints, I felt I could not keep such wonderful works as Michelangelo's *David* from the children because they revealed the human body. So I addressed this issue in the very first class each year when we discussed the *Venus of Willendorf* in prehistoric art. We first talked about the wonder of the human body and all the marvelous things it can do and about the fact that there is nothing evil or silly or unlovely about our bodies. I told the children I would from time to time be showing them works of art that celebrate the human form and that we were going to view them as just that—works of art and not "dirty" or forbidden pictures. I made it clear that I would not tolerate snickering, laughing, or jokes. Anyone guilty of this behavior would have to leave the lesson. In all my years of teaching, I never had to ask a child to withdraw. Of course you must make your own decisions about the artwork you discuss with your students and the way you approach parents and school administrators. Only you know them and the community in which you teach.

Because much art up to and including the Renaissance was motivated by belief, it is inescapable that the early chapters of this book present a good deal of religious art. I always told my students that we were not studying a particular work of art because we necessarily shared the belief of the creator, but for the beauty of the artwork itself. The drama activities based on this art, too, often involve religious rituals. There are shamans and enactments of myths involving various gods. These exercises are not meant to capture the belief of a specific people but rather are a blend of traditional stories and folklore passed down through the ages. If you or your community are not comfortable with any of the activities or content of the lessons, simply skip them.

Over the years I've had many moving instances of just how successful teaching art history to young children can be. Parents have talked about being pressed by their children to take them to museums and of being amazed by how much the children were able to say about the various art works they viewed there. A high school student who had just returned from a trip to Italy came back to visit. "You know the stuff you told us about the art in Florence?" he said. "Man, you were right. It's awesome!" So plunge in wherever the water feels fine. You'll love the results.

References

Barton, Bob, and David Booth. *Stories in the Classroom.* Portsmouth, NH: Heinemann, 1990. ISBN 0435085271.

Presents the value of and need for storytelling and addresses some of the ways to make stories come to life in the classroom

Creative Drama and Theater Education Resource Site. http://www.creativedrama.com/ (accessed October 4, 2006).

This excellent site explains what creative drama is and its purpose. It has many links and resources for teachers.

Fulwiler, Toby, ed. *The Journal Book.* Portsmouth, NH: Boynton/Cook, 1987. ISBN 0867091754.

Contains invaluable information on the purpose and characteristics of journals and on how to use them in all subject areas in the classroom.

Part I
Art of the Ancient World

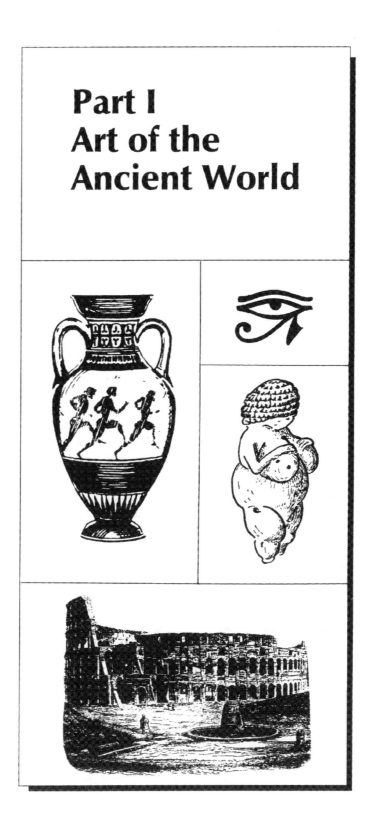

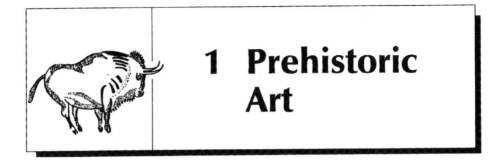

1 Prehistoric Art

"Toros, toros! Bulls, bulls! Father, come and look at the bulls!"
—MARIA DESAUTUOLO

Background Information

The art of the cave dwellers is among the most marvelous art in the world. During the Upper Paleolithic period, which lasted from about 40,000 to 10,000 BC, early humans formed fertility statues of women from bone, ivory, and stone; carved figures of animals on their tools; and painted majestic creatures on their cave walls. While cave art has been found all over the world, some of the most spectacular examples are in the caves of Ventimiglia, Italy; Dordogne, France; and Altamira, Spain. Rock paintings done in the Middle Stone Age from 10,000 to 3,500 BC have been found in North Africa. In the 1960s cave paintings were discovered in Mexico.

The painters and carvers of whom we speak in this lesson were Cro-Magnons, tall people with high foreheads and larger brains than the Neanderthals. The ice was gradually receding, but Cro-Magnon's European home was quite a bit colder than Europe is today. Although we know very little about these people's lives, we can gather some information from the things they left behind: tools of bone, ivory, and stone with which Cro-Magnons hunted wild animals, many of which no longer exist, for food; needles of bone and ivory with which they probably sewed together the skins of those animals for clothing; and their incredible works of art in the form of figurines, decorated tools, and cave paintings. Since there is no evidence of farming tools, and because the climate was still quite cold for crops, we believe the people did not know how to farm but probably gathered nuts, roots, and berries.

The paintings Cro-Magnons did on cave walls are highly sophisticated. These early artists were incredibly successful at rendering three-dimensional objects on a two-dimensional surface. There are bulls that appear to be pawing the ground, ready to charge. One can almost see the steam coming from their nostrils.

The colors are vivid, and gradations of shading are given. Amazing, too, is how the artists use the cave walls themselves in the formation of their pictures. For example, the swollen mound of an animal's belly is placed in just the right position to take advantage of a bulge in the rock.

When we consider Cro-Magnon art, many questions arise. How did the people learn to paint and carve statues? Did they see bear-claw marks on cave walls and then try to carve forms on the walls with stone? How did they come to color in their paintings? The ocher found in the caves themselves gave them yellow, brown, and red colors. Black came from charcoal and lampblack from burning animal fat. White came from rare white marl (Ruskin 1971). Did the people paint their bodies with these colors for religious ceremonies, accidentally smear some color on a cave wall, and like the effect? Why do figures of animals far outnumber figures of people on the cave walls? Why are the animals most often shown in side view rather than head-on? Why are so many of the "Venus" figurines similar—with exaggerated breasts and stomachs?

Life for Cro-Magnons was harsh and dangerous. The people spent much of their time hunting fierce animals and making clothing to protect themselves from the bitter cold. Why, then, did they take the time to create paintings on cave walls or carve figurines? Why, when they probably didn't live in caves anymore but in homes made of animal skins or wood, did they make their paintings in caves? And why did they place them in the darkest recesses of the caves rather than at the entrance where they would be easily seen and enjoyed? The stories that begin the lesson on prehistoric art are an attempt to answer some of these questions.

(Standards: World History 1: 10, 41; Arts and Communication 4-5.20, 24)

LESSON 1: Carved Figurines

The Story

(Tell this story in a very quiet voice and with great drama. Act out sitting alone, picking up a rock, and beginning to carve. If you have drums in the classroom, have a few children beat them softly while you speak.)

It was a time long, long ago in a land we now call Austria that there appeared on the earth the first movable, beautiful thing we now call art. It was a precious thing, which looked like rock and could fit in a person's hand and was formed by the fingers of a woman and it was, in fact, the shape of a woman.

Over 20,000 years ago, early people had a hard life. They lived close to the elements of cold, fire, water, and earth. They ate berries and bark and the animals they could hunt. They treasured children, for their children frequently died before they had a chance to grow. The mothers also died very easily from cold, hunger, or sickness.

Thus it was that an unnamed woman sat alone on a rock on a cold winter day, weeping. In the distance, drums beat a sorrowful sound. Other members of her tribe gathered around the dead body of a woman. The unnamed woman—let us call her Noma—had lost her friend, her sister. How would she carry on? Life was so hard; she needed the help of her friend. She picked up a stone and felt the soft curves in her hand. She reached into her belt and found her flint rock. Slowly she chipped away at the stone. A large round curve in the front of the stone reminded her of her friend, who was pregnant when she died. This was a double sadness for all. That lovely rounded front meant life coming. Noma chipped and chipped. The smoothness comforted her hand. A small head emerged atop the rock body. Noma smiled. Her friend would live again. This lovely rock would bring her to life in a way. It was a promise.

Noma ran with the rock. She stood before the drum-beaters. They looked first at her tear-stained face, then at her tight fist. Slowly she opened her hand to show her treasure. Smiles crept onto the faces of the beaters. "Ah, ah," they said. Noma placed the worked stone figure of her friend softly on the skin wrapped around the dead body. When the sun rose, they would place her body in a hole in the ground, but with it the promise of another life. So beautiful it was.

(Standards: Art Connections 1.7; Listening and Speaking 8.4; World History 1.36, 39)

Viewing the Art

Use some or all of the books that appear in the references below to show pictures of the various figurines carved by prehistoric peoples. It is unfortunate that so many books on the subject are out of print, but your library will surely have some good ones. Include a picture of the *Venus of Willendorf,* the statue that is the subject of the story. Talk about how similar the figurines are even though they were found in different places in Europe. Note how many of them are featureless and are meant to represent the possibility of new life, fertility. Talk about what they were made of. Note the details of hair on some of them. Encourage the children's reactions.

(Standards: Art Connections 1.1-8; Language Arts: Viewing 9.6, 23)

Journal Writing

Have children write about what they have learned—their reactions, questions, etc.—in a learning journal supplied for this course. If this is the first lesson of the year, give the journals out with much fanfare. Talk about them as a wonderful way for the children to think about their learning and express their feelings about art. If the children have never kept a journal, do a class entry on the board or on chart paper. Continue to do this until you feel the children have an understanding of the kind of thing that can go into a learning journal and can make entries on their own. Each journal entry should begin with the date. (If you have a date stamp, you might want to make it available if the children cannot write the date on their own.) Very young children can draw what they have learned if they are unable to write it. It is better for them to draw or write only a word or two rather than dictate their entries for you to write down. Encourage invented spelling and avoid making corrections in any journal writing.

(Standards: Language Arts: Writing 1.7, 23, 33-37; Art Connections 1.3)

Art/Drama Activity: Pantomime

Children truly enjoy pantomiming the story of Noma. You can have a storyteller (or several) tell the story, while some students prepare a body (another student or an imaginary one) for burial, some stand around the grave site, and some drum their sad dirge. Noma, of course, sits apart and carves her figurine, then races to share with the others what she has done.

(Standards: Theater 2.1, 2, 10, 11, 17)

LESSON 2: Cave Paintings

The Story

Over a hundred years ago, in 1879, in Altamira, Spain, there lived a wealthy man named Marcelino de Sautuolo. He had heard about some tools and other objects found by archaeologists in caves in different parts of Europe, and he decided to explore one of the many caves near his home. He was very interested in such things and thought perhaps he would find something marvelous—some tools, a necklace—to show to the world. His little daughter Maria begged to go with him, and he agreed.

But once her father started poking around in the cave, Maria began to get restless. "Let's go home, Daddy. It's dark and cold in here!" Don Marcelino was too busy to pay attention to her. So Maria took a candle and began to move further into the cave. As she went further and further, she came to a place that was so small a grownup couldn't even stand up in it. But little Maria could, and she began to look all around her. All of a sudden she began to yell, "Toros, toros. Papa, toros!" Now "toros" means "bulls" in Spanish. When her father heard Maria yelling, he came running to where she was, but he had to walk in all stooped over. Maria pointed to the ceiling. "Look, papa, toros!" And there Don Marcelino saw paintings of a herd of animals that looked just like bulls. They were painted in shades of red, yellow, and brown. Some were sitting, some were standing, and one was pierced by a spear. Maria's father was amazed. He had never heard of such paintings before. He returned day after day to study them. Finally he wrote an article all about them. He wrote that the paintings had been made by people living over 20,000 years before, in the Stone Age. All the scientists who read the article laughed at him. "Those paintings are not old. Somebody got in that cave and painted them recently." And they called him a faker. Don Marcelino died nine years later, a very sad man.

But finally scientists began to pay attention to cave paintings and to understand that they were very old. In 1940, four young boys in France went rabbit hunting with their dog. The boys went to a hole where they thought rabbits were hiding, and the dog scampered into the hole to scare them out. But no rabbits came out of the hole. And no dog came out either! Then the boys heard barking that seemed to come from deep underground, and one of them decided to crawl down the hole to rescue the dog. He went sliding down, down, down, until he found himself in a deep, dark cave. He shouted to the other boys, and they went sliding down after him. When they lit matches to see where they were, they discovered paintings on the walls.

Since they really couldn't see very much, they decided to come back with flashlights the next day and do more exploring. They explored the caves for five days and found marvelous paintings of animals. This time the scientists paid attention. Now we know about the wonderful art treasures in caves in Spain, France, and other parts of the world, and we can even visit some of those caves ourselves. Because these caves were sealed for thousands of years and no air was able to get in, the paintings are wonderfully preserved. But now we must be careful. Many countries only let a few people at a time into the caves because even our breathing can destroy these precious paintings.

(Standards: Art Connections 1.7; Listening and Speaking 8.4; History 7.1-2, 22; World History 1.36, 39)

Viewing the Art

Use some or all of the reference books following to show pictures of the cave paintings. If you can obtain slides that would be preferable, since the children will be able to see more clearly how the cave artists used the natural formations of the rock in drawing their animals. Discuss the colors the artists used, what they used for paint, the kinds of animals pictured, and which ones are still on the earth and which are extinct. Talk about the positions of the animals and why some are shown with spears in their sides. Patricia Lauber's *Painters of the Caves* (see references) is a fine children's book to use for this viewing in addition to the adult books listed. There is also a wonderful Web site (see references) that shows the paintings in the cave at Lascaux.

(Standards: Art Connections 1.1-8; Language Arts: Viewing 9.6, 23)

Journal Writing

Begin with questions: "When your parents hang pictures in your house, do they hide them, or do they put the pictures where everyone can see and enjoy them? Why do you think the cave artists drew these pictures, and why did they place them deep within the caves instead of right at the entrance where people could see them?" After they have finished writing, discuss the children's responses.

(Standards: Language Arts: Writing 1.7, 23, 33-37; Art Connections 1.3)

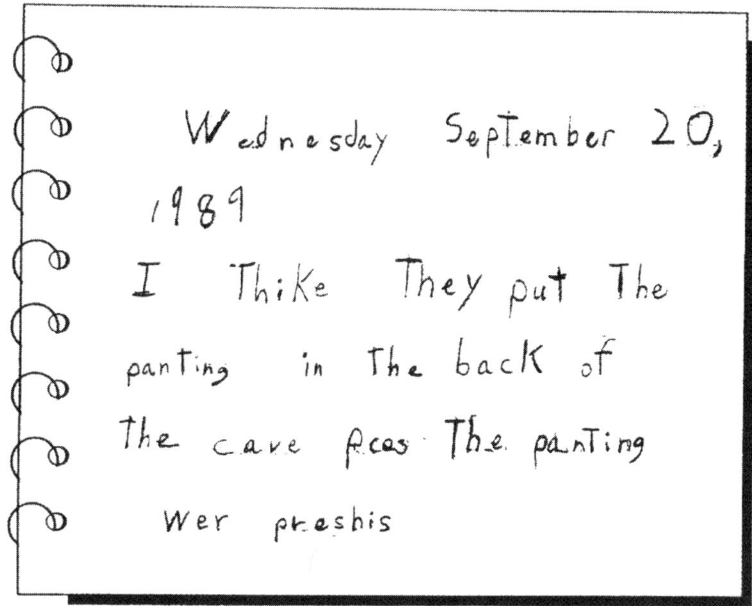

Wednesday September 20, 1989
I Thike They put The
panting in The back of
The cave becas The panting
wer preshis

Art/Drama Activity: Cave Painting Ceremony

If you feel your community might object to the following activity on religious grounds, you can easily make a few changes. Instead of having a child take the role of shaman, have the children gather around their cave animals once they have been taped to the wall. A clan leader can say something like, "Hunters, you see before you the animals that live around us. They are mighty and strong, but we are clever and strong. Go out now and hunt bravely for the sake of your people." The hunters ready their weapons and depart.

(Standards: Theater 2.1, 2, 10, 11, 17; Working with Others 1-5.1-10)

Materials

- Long strip of paper from a roll, preferably brown
- Pastels of the colors used by cave dwellers in their paintings: black, brown, yellow, red
- Drums

One possible explanation of the purpose of the cave paintings is that they were done for religious ceremonies. Perhaps the shaman, or religious leader, went before the pictures and recited special chants so the hunters of these animals would be successful. After all, the people's lives depended on a successful hunting expedition. Assuming that this is a logical explanation, have the children pretend they are a clan of Cro-Magnon people. It is time for another hunt, and the artists have been requested to paint animals on the cave walls in preparation for a special hunting ceremony.

Spread the paper on the floor and allot a space for each child. Distribute the pastels. Ask each child to draw an animal that would have been alive during the Paleolithic period. Dinosaurs are definitely out! These are animals the Cro-Magnon people depended on for their food and clothing. When the drawings are finished, tape the sheet of paper to a classroom or hallway wall so that it resembles a cave wall. If you spray the drawings with fixative, you might even be able to crumple the paper a bit to resemble the bumpy formation of cave walls. Now you are ready to have a special ceremony for the hunt. Have one child volunteer to be the shaman, who will lead the group in a chant, whatever seems appropriate, such as, "O Great Spirits, give us good luck for our hunt!" Some children can beat a drum to this chant while the rest of the class repeats the chant after the shaman.

(Standards: Visual Arts 1.1-5, 4.7-11; Theater 2.1, 2, 10, 11, 17; History 7.36)

Curriculum Connections

Social Studies

- Prehistoric peoples—study how they lived and worked. This Web site may prove useful, as it has many links: http://www.internet-atwork.com/hos_mcgrane/prehistory/eg_prehistory_intro.html. Another Web site that could be useful is this one on Stone Age habitats: http://www.personal.psu.edu/users/w/x/wxk116/habitat/. Also, see *Early Humans* in the references below.
- Study the climate and geography of the areas talked about in the lessons. What continent/country are they in? What was the weather like during the time the cave painters were living? How did they protect themselves from the weather?

- Compare the art in the caves studied in this lesson with the art of the Aborigines in Australia or the ancient artists in Africa. How are they alike? Different?

  (Standards: Geography 1, 2.5, 23, 29-30)

Science

- Study the animals of the Stone Age. See http://geowords.com/histbooknetscape/b06.htm. Also see Jenkins's book *Prehistoric Actual Size,* and *You Wouldn't Want to Be a Mammoth Hunter* (both in references). What animals might still have been alive during the time of the cave painters? Another useful exercise might be to find pictures of animals in real life settings and compare them to the renderings of these animals on cave walls. Margaret Cooper (see references) provides an example of this on page 46 of her wonderful *Exploring the Ice Age.*
- Caves abound with insect and other animal life. Study these creatures.
- How are caves formed? Where are some famous ancient caves in the world? In the United States? Read Siebert's and Gibbons's books (see references). Siebert's exquisite poetry might inspire children to craft their own poems about caves.
- What was medicine like in prehistoric times? Read *Prehistoric and Egyptian Medicine* (see references) to find out.

  (Standards: Science 7.50)

Music

- Make up a melody to accompany the shaman's chant.

  (Standards: Music 1-3.2, 4, 5, 6)

Literature

- Older children might enjoy finding and reading some old creation myths. Talk about why and how these myths came to be told. (See Hamilton's book in the references.)

  (Standards: Literature Reading 5-6.4-5, 13, 23, 28; Listening and Speaking 8)

References

Adult Books

Aujoulat, Norbert. *Lascaux: Movement, Space and Time*. New York: Harry N. Abrams, 2005. ISBN 0810959003.

There are over 200 color illustrations of the most important paintings in the Lascaux Caves in this beautiful book, including a pull-out section.

Bahn, Paul G. *Journey through the Ice Age*. Photographs by Jean Vertut. Berkeley: University of California Press, 2001. ISBN 0520229002.

This beautiful book contains carved objects and wall paintings from 300,000 to 40,000 BC. It is well worth obtaining for whole class viewing.

Chauvet, Jean-Marie, Eliette Brunel Deschamps, and Christian Hillaire. *Dawn of Art: The Chauvet Cave: The Oldest Known Paintings in the World*. New York: Harry N. Abrams, 1996. ISBN 0810932326.

The authors discuss each work of art in the Chauvet cave discovered in 1994. Contains ninety-four full-color illustrations of these amazing works, believed to be over 30,000 years old.

Clottes, Jean. *Chauvet Cave: The Art of Earliest Times*. Salt Lake City: University of Utah Press, 2003. ISBN 0874807581.

Clottes describes the artwork discovered in the Chauvet Cave in France's Rhone Valley in 1994. There are beautiful color photos.

Leroi-Gourhan, André. *Treasures of Prehistoric Art*. Translated by Norbert Guterman. New York: Harry N. Abrams, 1967. o.p. ASIN B0006BR6UK.

A magnificent book filled with large reproductions for viewing.

Ruspoli, Mario. *The Cave of Lascaux*. New York: Harry N. Abrams, 1987. o.p. ISBN 0810912678.

After Lascaux was sealed in 1963, the author was allowed to do a final filming with a crew of six. This book is a record of the wonders within that cave. It includes information on hunting weapons and prehistoric peoples. Marvelous.

White, Randall. *Prehistoric Art: The Symbolic Journey of Humankind*. New York: Harry N. Abrams, 2003. ISBN 0810942623.

Although the text is quite scientific, the 226 color illustrations make this book a worthwhile resource.

Children's Books

Aliki. *Wild and Woolly Mammoths*. Rev. ed. New York: HarperTrophy, 1997. ISBN 0064461793.

After discussing the discoveries of frozen mammoths in recent years, the author tells about these animals and the prehistoric peoples who depended on them for food and clothing.

Banks, Kate. *A Gift from the Sea.* Illustrated by Georg Hallensleben. New York: Frances Foster/Farrar, Straus & Giroux, 2001. ISBN 0-374-32566-9.

A rock that had journeyed from the time of the dinosaurs and on through the ages is found on the beach by a little boy.

Baumann, Hans. *The Caves of the Great Hunters.* Rev. ed. Translated by Isabel McHugh and Florence McHugh. Illustrated by Hans Peter Renner. New York: Pantheon, 1962. o.p. ASIN B0006AXX04.

Baumann recounts the discovery of the great caves in a fictional narrative.

Cooper, Margaret. *Exploring the Ice Age.* New York: Atheneum/Simon & Schuster, 2001. ISBN 0-689-82556-0.

"Let's forget about the Ice Age caveman who keeps popping up in our cartoons," urges the author of this fine book. In narrative style, she presents an account of the lives and artworks of these fascinating people.

Dawson, Ian. *Prehistoric and Egyptian Medicine.* New York: Enchanted Lion/Farrar, 2005. ISBN 1-59270-035-7.

In this carefully researched treatment, readers learn about the practice of medicine in prehistoric and Egyptian societies.

deMagalhaes, Roberto, and Roberto deCarvalho. *Prehistory: From the Dawn of Humanity to the First Towns.* Grand Rapids, MI: Peter Bedrick, 2000. ISBN 087226615X.

This book describes how early peoples lived and provides examples of their art.

Early Humans. New York: DK Children, 2005. ISBN 0756610672.

This is an exploration of how early peoples lived, illustrated with colored photographs.

Gibbons, Gail. *Caves and Caverns.* San Diego: Voyager, 1996. ISBN 0152013652.

Gibbons explains how caves and caverns are formed and what can be found there. Her language is clear and easily understood by young children.

Hamilton, Virginia. *In the Beginning: Creation Stories from Around the World.* Illustrated by Barry Moser. San Diego: Harcourt, 1991. ISBN 0152387420.

These creation stories are beautifully told and illustrated.

Jenkins, Steve. *Prehistoric Actual Size.* Boston: Houghton Mifflin, 2005. ISBN 0-618-53578-0.

The author shows parts of prehistoric animals at their actual size.

Lauber, Patricia. *Painters of the Caves.* Washington, DC: National Geographic Children's Books, 1998. o.p. ISBN 0792270959.

Learn what prehistoric peoples ate, how they clothed themselves, and how they did their artwork. Lauber is such an outstanding author that it is well worthwhile to try to obtain this out-of-print book.

Lessem, Dan. *The Iceman.* New York: Crown, 1994. o.p. ISBN 0517595966.

In large picture-book format, the author tells the story of a 5,300-year-old man found frozen with his clothes, tools, and weapons in an alpine glacier.

Macdonald, Fiona. *The Stone Age News*. Cambridge, MA: Candlewick Press, 2001. ISBN 076361291X.

Written as a newspaper of the time, this book presents readers with information about tool making, animal hunts, food, fashion, and other areas of prehistoric life.

Malam, David. *You Wouldn't Want to Be a Mammoth Hunter: Dangerous Beasts You'd Rather Not Encounter.* Illustrated by David Antram. New York: Franklin Watts, 2004. ISBN 0531163970.

This is a humorous treatment of what prehistoric animals were like and the difficulties involved in hunting them.

Osborne, Mary Pope, and Natalie Pope Boyce. *Sabertooths and the Ice Age.* New York: Random House, 2005. ISBN 0-375-82380-8.

Readers of this simple nonfiction work will learn how humans lived during the Ice Age, who did the cave paintings, and more.

Ruskin, Ariane. *Prehistoric Art and Ancient Art of the Near East.* New York: McGraw-Hill, 1971 o.p. Discovering Art series. ISBN 0070542961.

This overview of prehistoric art, Egyptian art, and art in Mesopotamia is a good source of illustrations for viewing.

Samachson, Dorothy, and Joseph Samachson. *The First Artists.* New York: Doubleday. o.p. ISBN 0385081448.

The authors present the lives and artwork of the first artists of Europe, Africa, and Australia.

Siebert, Diane. *Cave.* Illustrated by Wayne McLoughlin. New York: HarperCollins, 2000. ISBN 068816448X.

Lyrically beautiful language and marvelous illustrations make this a fine read-aloud. The cave itself speaks of its many wonders.

Turner, Ann. *Time of the Bison.* Illustrated by Beth Peck. New York: Macmillan, 1987 o.p. ISBN 0027893006.

An eleven-year-old boy discovers that he is an artist and becomes an apprentice to the cave painter. Fiction. Can be an excellent read-aloud story.

Wheeler, Lisa. *Mammoths on the Move.* Illustrated by Kurt Cyrus. San Diego: Harcourt, 2006. ISBN 0-15-204700-X.

Readers follow a mammoth migration with all its dangers. There is a bouncy refrain youngsters will love repeating. An author's note provides historical context.

Audiovisual Materials

The Caves of Altamira. DVD. Films for the Humanities and Sciences, 1989. ISBN 0-89113-207-4.

This is a lovely, slow-moving film that shows cave paintings of animals and mysterious symbols done thousands of years ago in the Altamira Caves in Spain.

Lascaux: The Prehistory of Art. DVD. Films for the Humanities and Sciences, 2002. ISBN 0-7365-6665-1.

This wonderful film takes viewers inside the caves in Lascaux, France, to view the works of art there.

Mammoths of the Ice Age. Video. WGBH, n.d. ISBN 1-578079-11-X.

This video describes the life cycle of these ancient animals that lived beyond the Ice Age.

Web Sites

Cave Art Lesson. http://www.historylink101.com/lessons/art_history_lessons/cave_art1.htm (accessed January 25, 2006).

This lesson provides pictures of cave art along with follow-up questions.

The Cave of Chauvet Pont D'Arc. http://www.culture.gouv.fr/culture/arcnat/chauvet/en/ (accessed January 25, 2006).

Viewers are able to click on a map and see inside that section of the cave.

The Cave of Lascaux. http://www.culture.gouv.fr/culture/arcnat/lascaux/en/ (accessed February 3, 2006.)

At this spectacular site, students can learn about the discovery of the Lascaux cave and actually take a virtual visit. This is a fine site for the viewing lesson above.

The First Human Creations. http://users.hol.gr/~dilos/prehis/prerm4.htm (accessed January 25, 2006).

A close-up view of the *Venus of Willendorf* is available at this site.

Prehistoric Art. http://www.students.sbc.edu/ogborn03/prehistoricart.htm (accessed January 25, 2006).

This site provides a history of prehistoric art as well as images from different parts of the world.

Witcombe, William L. C. E. *The Venus of Willendorf.* http://witcombe.sbc.edu/willendorf/ (accessed February 3, 2006).

Learn about the discovery of this famous figure as well as about the life of women in prehistoric times.

2 Arts of the Middle East

General Background on the Area

Look at a map and it is easy to see how important the Middle East (a modern term used since World War II and now more widely used than the former "Near East"), a region that extends from the Mediterranean Sea to the Persian Gulf, is to the rest of the world. Its countries connect three continents—Europe, Africa, and Asia—making its location strategic. In addition, this is the area in which human life first began, where the first major civilizations emerged and made enormous contributions to future generations in language, mathematics, and the sciences. Ancient Egyptians gave us many inventions that are essential to our daily lives: paper, the lever, and black ink, to name a few. The countries of the Middle East gave birth to three major world religions—Christianity, Islam, and Judaism—and all three call Jerusalem their Holy City. Huge oil deposits, black gold for an energy-consuming planet, have been discovered here, particularly in Saudi Arabia. Since the United Nations created the state of Israel in 1948, the region has been in a constant state of unrest. Israel has been at war with its Arab neighbors numerous times and is engaged in an ongoing struggle with the Palestinians over land, and especially over control of Jerusalem. Lebanon fought a long civil war; Iran and Iraq fought each other for eight years; Iraq invaded Kuwait in 1990, prompting the United States to go to war in Iraq in 1991. In 2001 the United States invaded Afghanistan to capture terrorist leaders who had attacked the World Trade Center in New York and the Pentagon in Washington, D.C., killing thousands of people. And in 2002, the United States again went to war in Iraq in an attempt to oust the dictator, Saddam Hussein.

Truly, the eyes of the world are on the Middle East, land of contrasts: between its honored position as the seat of antiquity and center of learning and seat of war and unrest; its oil wealth and the poverty of its masses; its promise of democracy for its peoples, male and female, and a religious fundamentalism that threatens to stifle freedom.

Because of the constant movement of borders over hundreds of years of invasions and political strife, there are often differing opinions about exactly what countries comprise the territory we know as the Middle East. According to the *Grolier Multimedia Encyclopedia,* "The modern countries that make up the Middle East, in the most common current usage, can be divided into four groups: Northeast Africa (Egypt and Libya); the Fertile Crescent countries (Syria, Lebanon, Jordan, Iraq, and Israel); the nations of the Arabian Peninsula (Saudi Arabia, Yemen, Kuwait, Bahrain, Qatar, the United Arab Emirates, and Oman); and the Northern Tier (Turkey and Iran)" (Voll 2002). Afghanistan and Sudan are occasionally included as well.

The Middle East is a vast area covering three and a half million miles. Much of the region is mountainous and desert, with its almost 250 million people living in the fertile areas of Egypt, Iran, and Turkey. Although Saudi Arabia is the largest country, it is the most sparsely populated because its land is largely desert. Most of the people in the Middle East are Arabs, Turks, or Iranians (Persians). There are also Jews, Pakistanis, Armenians, and Greeks and small numbers of Kurds. There are three major languages spoken in the Middle East: Arabic (the most widely used), Turkish, and Persian or Farsi. The Kurds speak Kurdish, a language related to Persian, and the Jews in Israel speak Hebrew.

Most of the people in the Middle East are Muslims and practice a religion called Islam, founded by the prophet Muhammad in the seventh century AD. There are five pillars of Islam: (1) to bear witness that no one is worthy of worship except Allah and that Muhammad is his prophet, (2) to pray at least five times a day, (3) to give alms since all that one possesses is a gift from Allah held in trust, (4) to make a pilgrimage (Hajj) to Mecca once in one's lifetime if one is physically and financially able, and (5) to fast from sunrise to sunset during the month-long observance of Ramadan

We focus here on two major countries of this very important and fascinating area of the world. Because Islam is a common thread that binds people throughout the region, Islamic influences will play a major part in the countries' history and artistic output.

(Standards: Geography 2.5; 6.8, 9, 10, 11; 13.22; Arts and Communication 4-5.20, 24)

References

Voll, John O. "Middle East." *Grolier Multimedia Encyclopedia*. CD-ROM,.New York: Scholastic, 2002.

The Great Sphinx, Giza, Egypt

I. ANCIENT EGYPT

"Soldiers, forty centuries are looking down upon you."

—NAPOLEON BONAPARTE to his men as they marched past the Egyptian pyramids

Background Information

The ancient Egyptians were a fascinating people who occupied a prominent place in antiquity for over 3,000 years. The land of Egypt in northern Africa was created by the Nile, which flows north from the center of Africa, forms many branches, and empties into the Mediterranean Sea. Until the Aswan Dam was built in the 1960s, the Nile overflowed each year, bringing rich mud onto the land. The lands bordering the Nile were the most fertile in the world, and Egyptian farmers prospered.

It has been difficult for scholars to determine the chronology of ancient Egypt, because the Egyptians had three calendars: one based on the movements of the star Sothis, one on the flooding of the Nile, and the third on the phases of the moon. Originally, the land of Egypt was divided into two kingdoms: the Upper Kingdom—which, ironically, was the lower half—and the Lower Kingdom, which was the land bordering the Mediterranean. In about 3100 BC, Menes (sometimes called Narmer) united the two kingdoms, and pharaohs thereafter wore a double crown indicating complete authority over the entire land. With Menes began the first of over thirty dynasties, or periods of ruling families, which spanned 3,000 years. The first artist in recorded history was Imhotep, and he built the first Egyptian pyramid for Zoser, a pharaoh who ruled during the Old Kingdom, Egypt's classical era (2686–2181 BC). This period includes Dynasties iii through vi. During this time, King Khufu built the Great Pyramid, the largest pyramid ever built, at Giza. Two other pyramids, for Khufu's successors, stand with it, and the Giant Sphinx stands guard over all three.

During the First Intermediate period (2181–2133 BC), comprising Dynasties vii through x, a social revolution took place in which the pharaohs lost power and the poor claimed possessions and property. Mentuhotep I of Dynasty xi established reunification and ushered in the Middle Kingdom (2133–1786 BC) of Dynasties xi and xii. The pharaohs of the Middle Kingdom strived to recapture the grandeur of the previous centuries, and to revive art and culture, but toward the end of Dynasty xii royal authority again weakened, invaders from Asia called Hyksos overtook the land, and the Second Intermediate period (1786–1650 BC) began.

When the Hyksos were finally driven out, art and culture were reborn, and the country attained its greatest military and political power. The era of the New Kingdom (1650–1085 BC) comprised Dynasties xvii, xviii, xix, and xx. Splendid temples and hundreds of monuments were built. This is the age of the famous pharaoh Ramses II; of Hatshepsut, a capable and powerful ruler who had herself declared "king"; of Akhenaten and his lovely queen, Nefertiti; and of King Tutankhamen, whose tomb was uncovered intact in 1922. Although Tut was a minor pharaoh and ruled for only ten years, he has become very well known in the modern world because the riches found in his tomb give us some idea of the wealth that was buried with the ancient Egyptian pharaohs.

During the Late Dynastic period (945–332 BC), Dynasties xxi through xxx, Egypt began its final decline, with power moving back and forth between Egyptian rulers and their conquering enemies. First the Persians, then the Greeks under Alexander the Great and a succession of Ptolemy pharaohs, and finally the Romans ruled Egypt. Christianity came to the country in the second century AD, and the Arab conquest occurred around 640.

Egyptian art is often referred to as the art of the dead. Ancient Egyptians believed that every person had a soul, or *ka,* which kept on living after the person died. In this life after death, the soul would seek out its body and continue to exist, using all the things it had enjoyed in life. Thus, the Egyptians went to great pains to prepare a body for burial so that it would be preserved for reunification with the soul. They mummified it by removing all the inner organs except the heart and preserving them in jars (they threw out the brain, which they considered of no importance). They washed the body inside and out with wine, stuffed it with cloths to keep its shape, and dried it out in natron, a type of salt, for forty days. The body was then smeared with resin, decorated with jewels, wrapped in linen strips, placed in elaborately decorated nesting coffins, and carried with great ceremony to a tomb. There it was buried with jewels, furnishings, and other treasures to be enjoyed in the next world.

Not every Egyptian had the means for an elaborate funeral, however. Such splendor was usually reserved for the pharaoh, whom the Egyptians believed to be a god and supreme ruler, and for important officials. Ancient Egyptian artists used their talents to decorate the magnificent palaces of their pharaohs, and the pharaohs' pyramids or places of burial. The huge pyramids took years to complete. The stones for these structures were probably quarried, loaded onto barges, and floated down the Nile. Then they were hauled to the building site. It took thousands of workers to accomplish these difficult tasks, and much of the workforce was made up of farmers who built pyramids during the flooding season when they could not plant and tend crops. Since the ancient Egyptians did not use money, they often paid their taxes in labor for the pharaoh.

Egyptian artists made statues of the pharaoh and the royal family, painted their pictures and pictures of their servants on interior pyramid walls, and carved the story of the pharaoh's life and exploits in hieroglyphics on stone walls and pillars. They made magnificent funeral masks, jewelry, furniture, and other artifacts to be entombed with the pharaoh for use in the afterlife.

When we view Egyptian art, we are struck by how stiff it often looks. There is no evident movement, and the position is strange: heads, arms, and legs are in side view, while the eyes and bodies are in front view. That is because the artists had to work in accordance with a strict set of rules. Figures were drawn on a grid, measured out according to an exact formula from which they could not deviate. There was also no perspective or attempt to show depth. But during the reign of Pharaoh Akhenaten, who broke away from the powerful priesthood of the god Amun in the New Kingdom, some of the rules were relaxed, and there was a new movement and fluidity in the artwork.

Egyptian writing, or hieroglyphic, began about 3100 BC. A hieroglyph is an individual symbol in hieroglyphic writing. At first only the names of important people such as pharaohs were written, with their pictures or on statues. But by 2500 BC longer pieces of writing were being done. Only Egyptian professionals such as doctors, lawyers, government officials, or scribes learned how to read and write. A scribe, who could rise to high rank in government if his work pleased the pharaoh, began his studies at about age six and continued for ten years, practicing all day long until he learned about six hundred hieroglyphs. He learned how to paint or carve hieroglyphs on stone and to write on papyrus in hieratic, which was like a cursive in which the hieroglyphic symbols were joined. After many centuries, the hieratic writing became even simpler and was called demotic writing, the writing found on the famous Rosetta Stone discovered by Napoleon's soldiers in 1799. When the brilliant French scientist Jean Champillion later deciphered the writing on this stone, he unlocked the secrets of Egyptian hieroglyphs and in turn many secrets about the ancient Egyptian way of life.

(Standards: Geography: 2.5; 6.8, 9, 10, 11; 13.22; World History: 3.10; Art Connections: 1, 6, 7)

Egyptian Hieroglyphic Writing

LESSON 1: Art for the Afterlife

The Story

Many, many years ago, Osiris ruled over all of Egypt. He was a just and kind king, and he and his wife, Isis, were very happy together. But Osiris had a brother, Seth, who was very jealous. Every time Seth thought about how happy his brother's life was, he became angrier and angrier.

One day, Seth invited Osiris to a banquet.

"How wonderful," thought Osiris. "Perhaps my brother and I can finally become friends." Little did he know that Seth had an evil plan! Seth had made a chest that was exactly his brother's size. During the banquet he said, "Let's have a contest. Anyone who can fit into this chest will win a prize." One by one the guests climbed into the chest. But no one fit—until Osiris tried. Of course, he fit perfectly, and the moment he was inside, Seth slammed the lid shut. Once his brother had suffocated in the chest, Seth cut his body into fourteen pieces and scattered them all over Egypt.

But Isis's love for her husband could not be broken the way his body had been broken by his brother. She wept and wept for him and searched all over Egypt for the pieces of his body. With the help of Anubis, a god with the head of a jackal, she found every piece, and with her own magic, she put them together and brought Osiris back to life. But he could no longer be a king in this world. He became the ruler of the underworld instead. Meanwhile, Isis sent her son, Horus, to avenge his father's murder by Seth.

The ancient Egyptians believed that every pharaoh became the god Horus when he became ruler of Egypt. And when the pharaoh died, he would go to the underworld to be judged. There Anubis would be waiting with a set of two scales. On one scale, he would place the pharaoh's heart. On the other scale, he would place an ostrich feather. If the pharaoh's heart weighed more than the feather because he had lived an evil life, he was eaten by a monster. But if his heart weighed less than the feather because he was honest and good, he then became joined to Osiris and lived happily forever in the underworld, united once again with his soul, or *ka*.

Since his *ka* had to find him, the Egyptians made sure they preserved the pharaoh's body by mummifying it before they buried it in a huge pyramid. (Talk about mummification with the children.) They painted pictures of the pharaoh and his family on the walls of the pyramid and carved into the walls writing telling of all his wonderful deeds. They buried the pharaoh with all the things he would need for his life in the underworld: furniture, tools, weapons, jewelry, etc. Much of the beauty Egyptian artists created was not for this life but for the life they believed was to come.

(Standards: Language Arts Listening and Speaking 8.4)

Viewing the Art

It is a simple matter to make ancient Egyptian artwork available for viewing. There are several videos and some wonderful books with very large prints. Many of these are listed in the references section (see especially *The Quest for Immortality: Treasures of Ancient Egypt*). As you view the work, see if the children notice the unusual position of the figures: the head, arms, and legs appear in side view; the eyes and bodies are in front view. Have the children stand up and try to assume that position. Now have them pretend to be pharaohs, standing with their left feet forward.

Encourage the children's comments and observations. What strikes them? How does this art differ from art with which they are familiar? Explain that Egyptian artists did their art according to a formula on grids, and that much of it appears stiff and flat. Ask the children to note the colors used in the paintings, to observe that the men are always a darker shade (we do not really know why this is so, except that it was one of the conventions of ancient Egyptian painting, which followed strict rules—perhaps it is to make them stand out more in the painting —but it would be interesting to ask the children for their opinions) than the women and that important figures are larger than those of lesser importance. Discuss pyramid-building and the problem of modern grave robbers stealing the wonderful treasures buried in the pyramids.

Talk about Egyptian sculpture and relief carvings. There are three kinds of relief, low, high, and sculpture in the full round. You can demonstrate this very simply with a small piece of modeling clay. Mold the clay into a flat disk. Then, with a pencil point or other sharp instrument, carve a snake into it. This is low relief. Next, remove some of the background clay around the snake so that the snake appears raised on the clay. This is high relief. Finally, carve the entire snake out of the clay disk. This is sculpture in the full round.

An excellent way to culminate this viewing session, if you can, is to visit the Tomb of Perneb at http://www.metmuseum.org/explore/perneb_tomb/index.html, especially if you have access to an LCD projector. Here a guide waits to take the children into the tomb where they can see the different chambers and things the tomb contains. They can do a crossword puzzle to test their knowledge, practice making hieroglyphs, and even make their own papyrus scrolls.

(Standards: Art Connections 1.1-4, 6-7; Visual Arts 1.4-5 3, 4.9-10; Viewing 9.6)

Journal Writing

If you have shown the children any of the films or videos suggested here, they might write about what they have seen. What are some things they noticed about ancient Egyptian art? Would they like to have the job of a scribe in Egypt? Why or why not?

(Standards: Language Arts: Writing 1.7, 23, 33-37; Art Connections 1.3)

1. Art/Drama Activity: Mummy-making and the Arts of Egypt

Materials

- Newspapers
- String
- Masking tape
- Paper, cardboard
- Papier-mâché mix
- Paints, markers

- Beads, macaroni, colored paper
- Roll of paper for a mural

Have the children pretend to be artists hired by the pharaoh to decorate his pyramid and prepare his burial chamber. Divide them into groups to work on several projects. Some can make a papier-mâché mummy. First, ball up old newspapers and form them into a mummy-shaped body. Tape the pieces together. Next, rip sheets of newspaper into strips. Dip each strip into papier-mâché mix and layer the strips over the body. Make many layers until the body is strong and well-formed. Allow it to dry several days. Paint in brilliant colors, using art books for models.

Jewelry makers can make Egyptian necklaces and bracelets from beads, macaroni, etc. They might wish to make jewel-encrusted furniture out of cardboard as well. They can use Egyptian portraits for models.

Painters can work on a mural depicting a scene in the pharaoh's life for the pyramid walls. Illustrations in the books referenced here can provide models. The students may wish to show the pharaoh in his palace with all his family and servants. Or they might like to picture the pharaoh on a hunt. Whatever the scene, they should make sure that the figure of the pharaoh is shown larger and darker than all the rest to indicate his importance.

(Standards: Visual Arts 1.1-4, 5; Working with Others 1-5.1-10)

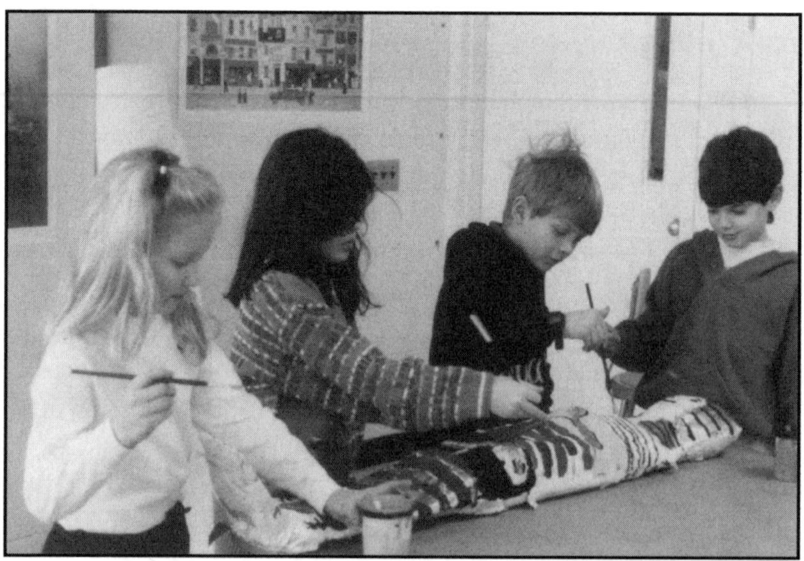

Young Children Working Together to Create an Egyptian Mummy

2. Art/Drama Activity

Children love to act out stories of ancient Egyptian life. *Egyptian Diary: The Story of Nakht* (see references) is the story of a young boy and his family, who are moving to the city of Memphis, where his father is undertaking a new job. If you read sections of this picture book to the children, they might see many opportunities for dramatization. The boy, Nakht, goes to school to learn to be a scribe like his father. Nakht and his sister witness a funeral procession. He visits craftsmen's workshops and tombs. Costumes are extremely easy for this production: large white T-shirts with belts or sheets draped to knee length. Dramatizing some of these scenes from the young boy's life will help children enter into the time of the ancient Egyptians not just with their minds, but with their whole selves.

(Standards: Theater 1.16, 2.1-2, 10; 3, 4.5; Language Arts Listening and Speaking 8.30; Writing 1.34)

LESSON 2: Hieroglyphics

The Story

How many of you like puzzles? If someone were to buy you a 500-piece puzzle, how long do you think it would take you to put it together? Would you try to do it yourself, or would you ask for help? Well, this is the story of an incredible puzzle that took years to solve! It happened long after the ancient Egyptians, whose artwork we have been enjoying, had died. Almost 200 years ago, which is not nearly as long ago as when King Tut was alive, a great French general named Napoleon Bonaparte marched his armies far and wide trying to conquer different countries for France. When he and his men went to Egypt, they took a group of scientists with them. Napoleon loved science, and he couldn't wait for the scientists to study all the wonderful carvings in the Egyptian pyramids and in the museums and to tell him about them.

But when the scientists went into the museums, they could not understand any of the writing they saw there. When they visited the pyramids, they couldn't read any of the writing on the pyramid walls. They had meetings with the Egyptian scientists. "Tell us what these writings mean," they said. But can you believe it? Not even the Egyptian scientists could read the ancient Egyptian writing!

Because so many countries had conquered Egypt since the days of the ancient Egyptians, the new Egyptian people stopped using their old language and spoke the language of their conquerors. By the time Napoleon got there, the people were speaking Arabic. Not a single person or government official or teacher could help the French scientists. Nobody could read or understand ancient Egyptian writing! Napoleon was very disappointed.

But then one day, while his soldiers were digging trenches, they found a large black stone with three kinds of writing on it. One language was Greek, one was Egyptian hieroglyphics, and one was a simpler form of Egyptian writing. They cleaned the stone and sent it to Napoleon, and Napoleon gave it to his scientists. "Now I'll find out about ancient Egyptian writing," he thought. But none of his scientists could figure out what the Egyptian writing said. They could read the Greek writing but not the Egyptian. It was like a secret code they could not break.

Years later, a nine-year-old French boy named Jean Champillion heard about the stone, which was called the Rosetta Stone because it was found in the Egyptian town of Rosetta. "I'm going to be the one to break that code," he said. "I just know I will!"

While he was growing up, Jean studied many languages, and by the time he was in his twenties, he could speak more than ten! He began working on the stone, and after years of effort he finally did crack the code. He figured out what the picture writing called hieroglyphics meant.

Now we know what the ancient Egyptians wrote on their walls and on their statues. And we know a great deal more about their lives. If you want to see the Rosetta Stone, you must travel to a museum in London, England.

(Standards: Language Arts Listening and Speaking 8.4)

Viewing the Art

Show the children pictures of hieroglyphic writing. The ancient Egyptians usually wrote from right to left. But at other times scribes went from left to right. And when they carved on pillars or doorways, the writing went downward! Most ancient Egyptians did not know how to write and employed scribes to write for them. Describe the training and work of a scribe. Show the students the print of the seated scribe (see *Art of Ancient Egypt* by Michalowski). What do the children notice about the hieroglyphs? Which are their favorites? Make certain they observe the oblongs encircling some of the figures. These are called *cartouches* and direct attention to the names of pharaohs and other important personages. Talk about writing on stone and a kind of paper called "papyrus" made from reeds that grow along the Nile.

(Standards: Art Connections 1-8; Visual Arts 1.4-5 3, 4.9-10; Language Arts, Listening and Speaking 8.4, Viewing 9.6)

Journal Writing

What is the children's reaction to the perseverance of Champillion and other scholars? How do they feel about writing? What if they lived in a country in which most people, including themselves, were not able to write? How would their lives be different?

(Standards: Language Arts, Writing 1.23)

Art/Drama Activity: A Cartouche Necklace

Materials

- Plaster of Paris
- Wax paper
- Masking tape
- A sharp instrument such as the point of scissors
- Fine sandpaper
- A copy of the Egyptian hieroglyphs
- Leather strips or string
- Black tempera paint

Have children make cartouche necklaces for themselves or a family member. Give each child a portion of plaster of Paris to shape into a flat oval about one inch thick. Poke a hole through the top for a piece of leather or string to go through. Smooth it out and place it on wax paper to dry over several days. Tape the child's name on the paper. Sand the dry ovals and wipe smooth. Paint with black tempera paint. Have children practice writing their names or a family member's name in hieroglyphics on a piece of paper. They might prefer a description such as "strong one," "wise one," etc. When they can do this well, have them scratch the hieroglyphs vertically onto the cartouches, then string and wear them around their necks.

(Standards: Visual Arts 1.1-4, 5)

Curriculum Connections

See *Pyramids: 50 Hands-On Activities to Experience Ancient Egypt* and *Spend the Day in Ancient Egypt* in the references for many ideas about activities that will connect the study of Egyptian art to other areas of the curriculum.

Social Studies

- Find Egypt on a map. Be certain the children understand that Egypt is part of the huge continent of Africa and is also considered part of the region known as the Middle East.

- Study the history of Egypt and its people. How was life in an ancient Egyptian city different from that in the countryside? (See Hinds's books in the references.)
- Study ancient Egyptian farming and irrigation methods. Compare them to the ways farmers farm and irrigate their crops today.
- Study ancient Egyptian clothing. How do the people dress today? Why do they dress this way?

(Standards: World History 2,3; Geography 14: 23-25)

Mathematics

- Learn about mathematics in ancient Egypt. What symbols did the Egyptians use for writing numbers? (See *Science in Ancient Egypt* in the references.)
- Study Egyptian numerals and counting (read *Of Numbers and Stars*—see references).

(Standards: Mathematics: 9.29)

Science

(See *Science of Ancient Egypt* in the references.)

- Study Egyptian inventions, such as the lever. How many of these inventions do we still use today? How do they make our lives easier?
- What is papyrus? How did the Egyptians use it? Make some papyrus. (See information in the kit in the references.)
- Study Egyptian methods of embalming. There are several books in the references to help with this study. Then, using *Mummies: The Newest, Coolest & Creepiest from around the World* (see references), compare embalming methods in different parts of the world.

(Standards: Science: 29, 39)

Writing

- Have older students use *The Egyptian News* (see references) as a model for creating their own newspaper about ancient Egyptian life.

(Standards: Language Arts Writing: 1-4: 21, 36; World History, Era 2:1)

Literature

- Read some poems in Altman's and Lechner's *Ancient Egypt (Modern Rhymes about Ancient Times* (see references). The children will learn a great deal about ancient Egyptian life through this enjoyable verse.

  (Standards: Language Arts: Reading 6.13, 23, 28)

References

Adult Books

Hawass, Zahi, and Kenneth Garrett. *Hidden Treasures of Ancient Egypt: Unearthing the Masterpieces of the Egyptian Museum in Cairo*. Washington, DC: National Geographic, 2004. ISBN 0792263197.

This book is a presentation of the artifacts that comprised the Egyptian museum of Cairo's centennial exhibit. The pieces were collected from the museum's basement, its permanent exhibitions, and other venues and represent finds unearthed over the last 150 years of excavations. Beautiful color photos.

Hornung, Erik, and Betsy M. Bryan, eds. *The Quest for Immortality: Treasures of Ancient Egypt.* Washington, DC: National Gallery of Art; New York: Prestel, 2002. ISBN 3-7913-2735-6.

This exquisite book has large, color, close-up views of all aspects of Egyptian art: statuary, paintings, carvings, etc. It is a superb choice for viewing. The book was published in conjunction with the film of the same name listed below.

Malek, Jaromir. *Egypt: 4000 Years of Art*. Boston: Phaidon/Time Warner, 2003. ISBN 0714842001

Malek presents Egyptian art from 4000 BC to AD 200. Beautiful full-color illustrations.

Michalowski, Kazimierz. The *Art of Ancient Egypt.* Translated by Norbert Guterman. New York: Harry N. Abrams, 1969, 1986. ISBN 0810900130.

Historical information is interspersed with wonderful large prints suitable for group viewing.

Reeves, Nicholas. 1995. *The Complete Tutankhamun.* New York: Thames & Hudson, 1995. ISBN 0500278105.

There are illustrations depicting the glorious treasures found in Tut's tomb.

Robins, Gay. *The Art of Ancient Egypt*. New Haven, CT: Harvard University Press, 2000. ISBN 0674003764.

This book provides over 300 illustrations, many in full color.

Tiradritti, Francesco, ed. *Egyptian Treasures from the Egyptian Museum in Cairo.* New York: Harry N. Abrams, 1999. ISBN 0810932768.

Noted Egyptologists discuss treasures from the Egyptian Museum in Cairo. Stunning photos.

Children's Books

Aliki. *Mummies Made in Egypt.* New York: Harper Trophy, 1985. ISBN 0064460118

Though this is an older book, it is a classic on the subject and describes in very readable form the process of mummifying bodies in ancient Egypt.

Altman, Susan, and Susan Lechner. *Ancient Egypt: Modern Rhymes about Ancient Times.* Illustrated by Sandy Appeloff. Danbury, CT: Children's Press, 2002. ISBN 0516273728.

Readers learn a good deal about ancient Egypt through the poems in this book.

Bower, Tamara. *How the Amazon Queen Fought the Prince of Egypt.* New York: Atheneum, 2005. ISBN 0689844344.

Based on an actual Egyptian scroll, this is the story of how Amazon women under the rule of Queen Serpot face down an invasion of Egyptian soldiers. Filled with Egyptian hieroglyphs and beautifully illustrated.

Bower, Tamara. *The Shipwrecked Sailor A Tale of Ancient Egypt.* American University in Cairo Press, 1998. ISBN 977424432X.

This tale, based on a story found in ancient papyrus scrolls, is about a sailor who is shipwrecked and finds fortune.

Bunting, Eve. *I Am the Mummy Heb-Nefert.* Illustrated by David Christiana. San Diego: Harcourt Brace/Voyager, 2000. ISBN 0152024646.

In this picture book, the mummified Heb-Nefert speaks from her glass museum case about her life as the daughter of royalty in ancient Egypt.

Clements, Andres. *Temple Cat.* Illustrated by Kate Kiesler. New York: Clarion, 2001. ISBN 0618111395.

A temple cat in ancient Egypt, tired of being pampered, escapes to live with a common fisherman and his family.

Cole, Joanna. *Ms. Frizzle's Adventures: Ancient Egypt.* Illustrated by Bruce Degen. New York: Scholastic, 2003. ISBN 0590446819.

On a routine trip to Egypt, Ms. Frizzle parachutes into the past.

DK Children. *Pyramid.* New York: DK Children, 2006. ISBN 0756614104.

Through panoramic views readers can get inside an Egyptian pyramid.

Egyptology. Cambridge, MA. Illustrated by Emily Sands et al. Cambridge, MA: Candlewick Press, 2004. ISBN 0763626384.

Letters, notes, ticket stubs connected to a trip to Egypt, etc., all supposedly a facsimile of a journal written in 1926.

Fisher, Leonard Everett. *The Gods and Goddesses of Ancient Egypt.* New York: Holiday House, 1997. o.p. ISBN 0823412865.

The author describes thirteen of the most important Egyptian gods, including their parentage, powers, and images. The beautiful art work is inspired by the art and hieroglyphs of ancient Egypt.

Gerrard, Roy. *Croco'nile.* New York: Farrar, Straus & Giroux, 2001. ISBN 0374416117.

Readers get a good glimpse of ancient Egyptian life by following the zany trip Hamut and his sister, Nekatus, take along the Nile.

Giblin, James Cross. *The Riddle of the Rosetta Stone.* New York: Thomas Y. Crowell, 1990. Rebound by Sagebrush in 1999. ISBN 0785704434.

This is the story of how the Rosetta Stone was discovered by Napoleon Bonaparte's men in Egypt and of the work of scholars over the years to decipher it.

———. *Secrets of the Sphinx.* Illustrated by Bagram Ibatouilline. New York: Scholastic, 2004. ISBN 0590098470.

Giblin discusses some of Egypt's most famous artifacts and monuments.

Haeass, Zahi. *Tutankhamun: The Mystery of the Boy King.* Washington, DC: National Geographic, 2004. ISBN 0792283546.

This book has stunning photographs and a re-creation of what Tut might have looked like.

Hart, Avery, and Paul Mantell. *Pyramids: 50 Hands-On Activities to Experience Ancient Egypt.* Illustrated by Michael Kline. Charlotte, VT: Williamson Publishing, 1997. ISBN 1885593104.

This book provides many activities such as forming the Nile River and making pyramids.

Haslam, Andrew, and Alexandra Parsons. *Make It Work: Ancient Egypt.* Minnetonka, MN: Two-Can Press, 2000. ISBN 1587283077.

This wonderful book presents a study of ancient Egypt with accompanying activities, including making clothing, wigs, headpieces, death masks, toys, etc. Includes bibliography.

Hawes, Louise. *Muti's Necklace.* Illustrated by Rebecca Guay. Boston: Houghton Mifflin, 2006. ISBN: 978-0618-53583-5.

This story about a young girl who so treasures a gift from her father that she risks the wrath of the pharaoh is based on an ancient Egyptian tale.

Hinds, Kathryn. *The City.* (Life in Ancient Egypt). New York: Benchmark, 2006. ISBN 076142184X.

Hinds describes life in an ancient Egyptian city. In *Countryside* (Benchmark, 2006. ISBN 0761421858) she talks about life in the country. Both are excellent books.

Hofmeyr, Dianne. *The Star-Bearer: A Creation Myth from Ancient Egypt.* Illustrated by Jude Daly. London: Frances Lincoln, 2001. ISBN 0-374-37181-4.

When Atum begins creating the world, the god of earth, Geb, and the god of sky, Nut, cling to each other until he is forced to separate them. But he creates the stars so they will have enough light to see each other.

Honan, Linda. *Spend the Day in Ancient Egypt: Projects and Activities That Bring the Past to Life.* Hoboken, NJ: Jossey-Bass, 1999. ISBN 0471290068.

Readers follow a fictionalized family throughout the day. Many craft activities are suggested.

Hooper, Meredith. *Who Built the Pyramid?* Illustrated by Robin Heighway-Bury. Reprint, Boston: Candlewick, 2006. ISBN 0763630462.

All the people who played a part in building the pyramid, from the king to the stone mason to the lowly water carrier, describe the roles they played in building this marvelous structure. Even the grave robbers have a say!

Katan, Norma Jean, with Barbara Mintz. *Hieroglyphs.* New York: McElderry, 1981. ISBN 0689501765.

The authors present hieroglyphs found in ancient Egypt and instructions for writing them.

King, David C. *Projects about Ancient Egypt.* New York: Benchmark, 2006. ISBN 0761422587.

The author describes several projects children can do to learn more about ancient Egypt.

Lattimore, Deborah Nourse. *The Winged Cat.* New York: HarperTrophy, 1995. ISBN 0064434249.

The high priest denies killing a cat, though a serving girl has seen him. Both must go to the underworld to be judged. Wonderful story to read in relation to the story of Osiris and Isis.

Levine, Beth. *Write Like an Egyptian.* New York: Scholastic/Tangerine Press, 2003. ISBN 0439549884.

This author provides instructions on how to write with hieroglyphs. The book comes with a plastic template of figures.

Love, D. Anne. *Of Numbers and Stars.* Illustrated by Pam Paparone. New York: Holiday House, 2006. ISBN 0-8234-1621-6.

This picture book biography is the story of Hypatia, a girl who lived in ancient Egypt. Unlike the women of her time, who were usually uneducated, she became famous for her knowledge of mathematics, astronomy, and philosophy.

Macaulay, David. *Pyramid.* Boston: Houghton Mifflin, 1975. ISBN 0395214076.

Macaulay's thorough discussion of the process of building a pyramid in ancient Egypt is a classic!

Malam, John. *Explore It: Ancient Egypt.* Berkeley, CA: Silver Dolphin Books, 2006. ISBN 1592233775.

With this pop-up book, children can see what life was like in ancient Egypt and even go inside pyramids.

Mann, Elizabeth. *The Great Pyramid.* Illustrated by Laura Lo Turco. New York: Mikaya Press/Little Brown, 1996. ISBN 0965049310.

This excellent book discusses Khufu's reign and how his huge pyramid was built. There are many large illustrations and a fictional story at the beginning that is sure to capture children's attention.

Merrill, Yvonne Y., and Jim Tilly. *Hands-On Ancient People, Volume 1: Art Activities about Mesopotamia, Egypt, and Islam.* Illustrated by Mary Simpson. Salt Lake City, UT: Kits Publishing, 2002. ISBN 0-9643177-8-8.

This book has a beautiful, full-page colored illustration for each craft suggested. The object to be made is discussed in the context of the historical period, and clear instructions are given.

Millard, Anne. *The World of Pyramids.* Boston: Houghton Mifflin/Kingfisher, 2004. ISBN 0753457873.

Millard's beautifully illustrated book discusses how and why pyramids were built in several ancient civilizations.

Milton, Joyce. *Hieroglyphs.* Illustrated by Charles Micucci. New York: Grosset & Dunlap, 2000. ISBN 0448419769.

This informative text comes with a stencil for tracing hieroglyphs,

Morley, Jacqueline. *Inside the Tomb of Tutankhamun.* New York: Enchanted Lion/Farrar, 2005. ISBN 1-59270-042-X.

Readers find out what life in ancient Egypt was like during Tut's reign. Different segments of society—priests, tax collectors, etc.—are discussed. How Tut became king and how his tomb was discovered are also treated.

———. *How to Be an Egyptian Princess.* Washington, DC: National Geographic, 2006. ISBN 0792275489.

Readers are treated as if they are preparing to become the next Egyptian princess.

Morley, Jacqueline, and David Salariya. *You Wouldn't Want to Be a Pyramid Builder: A Hazardous Job You'd Rather Not Have.* Illustrated by David Antram. New York: Franklin Watts, 2004. ISBN 0531163962,

Although the title might give the impression that this is not a book of substance, it is actually packed with information about Egyptian pyramid building and the lives of those who did this work.

Nardo, Don. *Ancient Egypt: Daily Life.* New York: Thomson/Kidhaven, 2002. ISBN 0737709553.

This small book describes the lives of various groups of people in ancient Egyptian society such as the wealthy, laborers, women, etc.

Pemberton, Delia. *Egyptian Mummies: People from the Past.* San Diego: Harcourt Brace, 2001. ISBN 0152026002.

The author discusses seven mummies in the British Museum and their lives.

Perl, Lila. *People of the Ancient World: The Ancient Egyptians.* New York: Franklin Watts, 2004. ISBN 0531123456.

This excellent book provides information on many aspects of ancient Egyptian life. Some intriguing chapters are "Farmers, Bakers, and Brewers," and "Warriors and Captives." It includes many study and browsing aids such as an index, a glossary, and ways to find out more.

Platt, Richard. *Egyptian Diary: The Journal of Nakht.* Illustrated by David Parkins. Cambridge, MA: Candlewick Press, 2005. ISBN 0-7636-2756-9.

Nakht and his family move to Memphis so his father can undertake a new position as scribe for his uncle.

Polk, Milbry. *Egyptian Mummies: A Pop-up Book.* Illustrated by Roger Steward and Jose R. Seminario. Collingdale, PA: Diane Publishing1997. ISBN 0756783291.

By pulling tabs, readers get to help embalmers pull organs out of a body to mummify it. There is a good deal of information about what the organs stood for and the process of mummification.

Putnam, James. *The Ancient Egypt Pop-up Book: In Association with the British Museum.* New York: Rizzoli, 2003. ISBN 0789309858.

Seven pop-up spreads illustrate important aspects of ancient Egyptian civilization.

———. *Pyramid.* New York: DK Children's Books, 2004. ISBN 0756607175.

What makes this book different from Macaulay's and others are the beautiful color photographs.

Ross, Stewart, Delia Pemberton, Joann Fletcher, and Edward Bleiberg, consultant. *Egypt in Spectacular Cross-Section.* Illustrated by Stephen Biesty. New York: Scholastic, 2005. ISBN 0439745373

Spectacular is the word for this large book filled with cross-section views of many aspects of ancient Egyptian life.

Rumford, J. *Seeker of Knowledge.* Boston: Houghton Mifflin, 2001. ISBN 0-3995-97934-X.

This is a wonderful picture book biography of Jean-Francois Champillion, the man who first deciphered Egyptian hieroglyphics.

Sabuda, Robert. *The Mummy's Tomb: A Pop-Up Book.* New York: Artists and Writers Guild, 1994. o.p. ISBN 0307176274.

Sabuda offers a very well-designed pop-up book about a tomb in ancient Egypt.

———. *Tutankhamen's Gift.* New York: Atheneum, 1994. ISBN 0689318189.

Although Tut is the youngest of the pharaoh's sons, he does become king and makes an important contribution to Egyptian life. Beautiful linoleum-cut illustrations.

Scieszka, Jon. *Tut Tut.* Illustrated by Lane Smith. New York: Penguin/Puffin, 2004. ISBN 0142400475.

A Time Warp Trio fantasy. The threesome goes back in time to ancient Egypt.

Scott, Henry Joseph, and Lenore Scott. *Egyptian Hieroglyphs for Everyone.* New York: Crowell Junior Books, 1990. o.p. ISBN 0690047533.

This is an excellent introduction to Egyptian hieroglyphs.

Shuter, Jane. *Life along the River Nile.* Chicago: Heinemann Library, 2004. ISBN 1403458359.

Shute describes life along the Nile in ancient Egypt.

———. *Life in an Egyptian Town.* Chicago: Heinemann Library, 2005. ISBN 1403458316.

Photos of objects from ancient Egyptian times along with text give readers an idea of what life was like in an Egyptian town.

———. *Life in an Egyptian Worker's Village.* Chicago: Heinemann Library, 2005. ISBN 1403458324.

This book is about daily life in the ancient Egyptian village of Deir el-Medina.

Stanley, Diane. *Cleopatra.* Illustrated by Peter Vennema. New York: HarperTrophy, 1997. ISBN 0688154808.

Stanley's work is a beautifully illustrated and written biography of the woman who tried to unite Rome and Egypt.

Steedman, Scott. *History News: The Egyptian News.* Cambridge, MA: Candlewick, 2000. ISBN 0763604232.

This humorous book in newspaper format provides a view of ancient Egyptian life, from ads for houses available in the craftworkers' village to news of the death of Ramses II. The book may prompt older students to exhibit their knowledge in a similar way.

Steele, Philip. *The Best Book of Mummies.* New York: Kingfisher, 2005. ISBN 075345873X.

This very colorful book explains why the Egyptians made mummies and the kinds of things needed in the afterlife.

———. *I Wonder Why Pyramids Were Built and Other Questions about Ancient Egypt.* Boston: Kingfisher, 2006. ISBN 0-7534-5963-9.

Questions such as, "Why did women wear cones on their heads?" and "Why is paper called paper?" along with their interesting answers help young children learn a good deal about ancient Egypt.

Stefoff, Rebecca. *The Ancient Near East.* New York: Benchmark, 2005. ISBN 0-7614-1639-0.

Chapters on Mesopotamia, Egypt, and Anatolia (now Turkey), accompanied by fine pictures, make this a valuable resource.

Stewart, David, and David Salariya. *You Wouldn't Want to Be an Egyptian Mummy!* Illustrated by David Antram. New York: Franklin Watts, 2000. ISBN 0531162060.

This is a lighthearted title with information that is anything but light. Details of embalming and Egyptian burial customs are discussed.

Tames, Richard. *Ancient Egyptian Children.* Chicago: Heinemann, 2002. ISBN 1403405131.

Youngsters will enjoy this book about how ancient Egyptian children lived: how they were cared for, their games, and much more.

Tanaka, Shelley. *Mummies: The Newest, Coolest & Creepiest from around the World.* New York: Harry N. Abrams, 2005. ISBN 0-8109-5797-3.

The author talks about mummies that have been discovered in different parts of the world.

van Vleet, Carmella. *Great Ancient Egyptian Projects.* Chicago: Independent Publishers/Nomad, 2006. ISBN 0977129454.

Van Vleet suggests more than two dozen hands-on projects that will help children learn about ancient Egyptians.

Walsh, Jill Paton. *Pepi and the Secret Names.* Illustrated by Fiona French. Kentish Town, London: Frances Lincoln, 2005. ISBN 1845073517.

Pepi lures dangerous animals to serve as models for his father, who is painting decorations for Prince Dhutmose's tomb. Beautifully illustrated, this book contains hieroglyphs for children to decipher.

Winters, Kay. *Voices of Ancient Egypt.* Illustrated by Barry Moser. Washington, DC: National Geographic, 2003. ISBN 0792275608.

Different segments of the ancient Egyptian population—scribe, pyramid builder, etc.—speak in the first person about their lives.

Williams, Brenda. *Ancient Egyptian Homes.* Chicago: Heinemann, 2003. ISBN 1403403104.

Homes of the wealthy, homes of the poor, life in town and in the village, even life in the afterworld—it's all in this interesting book.

Woods, Geraldine. *Science in Ancient Egypt.* New York: Franklin Watts, 1998. ISBN 0531203417.

Mathematics, astronomy, building tips—this book discusses the many contributions the ancient Egyptians have made to the world of knowledge.

Wright, Rachel. *Egyptians: Facts, Things to Make, Activities.* Sea to Sea Publications, 2004. ISBN 1932889000.

Crafts and activities related to the life and customs of ancient Egyptians.

Yates, Philip. *Ten Little Mummies.* Illustrated by G. Brian Karas. New York: Viking, 2003. ISBN 0670036412.

A humorous counting book featuring mummies. Some facts about Egypt appear on the endpapers.

Audiovisual Materials

Ancient Egypt. Video. SR Publications, n.d. Order Code: Al-717363V.

This is a three-segment video that deals with the following topics: ancient Egypt, hieroglyphics, and pyramids of Egypt.

Ancient Egypt. DVD. Library Video Company, 1999. Order Code: V7154.

This video enables children to travel back in time to learn about the lives and accomplishments of ancient Egyptians.

The Art of Ancient Egypt. CD-ROM. Metropolitan Museum of Art/Simon & Schuster, 1997.

This CD-ROM provides maps and a good deal of other information.

Egypt: Inspector Gadget. Video. Library Video Company, 1997. K8176.
Inspector Gadget leads very young children on a journey to ancient Egypt where they can, by viewing the video, enter a burial chamber, visit temples, etc.

Great Egyptians. Video. Library Video Company, 1997. K6273.
This video, divided into three parts, explores the lives of three famous Egyptians: Hatshepsut, Tut, and Cleopatra.

Life in Ancient Egypt. Video. AGC/United Learning, 2000.
This video presents various aspects of life in ancient Egypt. A teacher's guide can be found at http://video1.unitedstreaming.com/videos/Living%20in%20Ancient%20Egypt/1207_TG.pdf.

Mysteries of Egypt. DVD. National Graphic/Imax, 1999. ASIN 6305462534.
This inexpensive film, obtainable on the Internet, brings viewers to ancient Egypt. There is also the discovery of Tut's tomb and other wonders.

Of Time, Tombs, and Treasure: The Treasures of Tutankhamen. Video. National Gallery of Art, n.d. VC132.
This is the story of Carter's discovery of the tomb and presentation of its treasures.

Pyramid. Video. PBS Video/Turner Home Entertainment, 1995. PYRT901.
This is a marvelous video version of David Macaulay's book, with animated elements added.

The Quest for Immortality. Video. National Gallery of Art, n.d. VC168.
This short film presents ancient Egyptian burial practices.

Other Materials

Ancient Egyptian Writing Kit. KingTutShop, 2002. WKIT1001.
This kit contains all the materials children need to engage in ancient Egyptian writing activities.

Immortal Cities: Children of the Nile. Software Program. Metropolitan Museum of Art, 2004. M8040.
For children age eight and up, this is a fascinating, award-winning software program that turns the viewer into a pharaoh who must manage his or her kingdom by satisfying all factions of the population.

Lawson, Jennifer. *Egyptian Symbols: A Hieroglyphic Stamp Kit*. New York: Chronicle, 2000.
This kit contains twenty-nine stamps children can use to write messages in ancient Egyptian hieroglyphs.

Make Papyrus Kit. KingTutShop, 2002. PKIT0500.
This kit provides all the materials necessary to make papyrus.

Old Mummy. Card Game. Palo Alto, CA: Birdcage Press, n.d. ISBN 1-889613-45-2.

Players learn a good deal about ancient Egypt while playing a card game similar to Concentration.

Rosetta Stone. Replica. The Museum Store Company. Item Number 708.

Children will enjoy being able to see and handle this replica of the stone that played a key role in unlocking the mystery of ancient Egyptian writing.

Senet Wooden Board Game. Metropolitan Museum of Art, n.d. M9062.

This board game was a favorite of ancient Egyptian pharaohs. The movement of pieces on the board stand for the movement of the soul in the underworld.

Web Sites

Ancient Egypt. http://www1.pvsd.net/cms/cms-projects/Ancient%20Egypt%20&%20Israeli%20L.htm (accessed January 23, 2006).

There are many, many links here to all aspects of ancient Egyptian life.

Ancient Egypt Teacher Resource File. http://falcon.jmu.edu/~ramseyil/egypt.htm (accessed January 23, 2006).

This is a treasure-trove of information for teachers and includes online print and audiovisual materials. There are many valuable links.

Ancient Egypt Webquest. http://www.iwebquest.com/egypt/ancientegypt.htm (accessed January 23, 2006).

Unless your students are older, they probably will not be able to participate in the actual Webquest. However, there are many fun activities you will be able to do in the classroom.

Egypt. http://witcombe.sbc.edu/ARTHegypt.html#AncEgypt (accessed March 10, 2006).

This wonderful site has many links to information about ancient Egypt and artworks.

Egyptomania: Animals. http://www.clevelandart.org/kids/egypt/animals/index.html (accessed February 26, 2006).

Children have the opportunity to see enlarged pictures of Egyptian animals. If they follow other links on this site, they can view Egyptian artifacts from the Cleveland Museum of Art, find directions for making a pharaoh, and more.

The Great Sphinx. http://interoz.com/egypt/sphinx.htm (accessed May 8, 2006).

Go to this site for a history of this impressive figure as well as pictures.

Hatshepsut's Revenge. http://edweb.sdsu.edu/courses/edtec670/egypt/start.html (accessed April 11, 2006).

This adventure game for older students brings them back into ancient Egypt.

Hieroglyphics, Cartouche, Rosetta Stone. http://ancienthistory.mrdonn.org/AncientEgypt.html#Writing (accessed February 10, 2006).

This is a wonderful page for young children. It has many activities such as making a cartouche.

Hieroglyphs Writing. http://greatscott.com/hiero/hiero_deter.html (accessed January 23, 2006).

This site contains an Egyptian alphabet as well as a pronunciation guide.

National Graphic: Egypt Secrets of an Ancient World/. http://www.nationalgeographic.com/pyramids/ (accessed January 23, 2006).

This site contains lesson plans, cartoons, videos, and more.

II. IRAN

The lives of former generations are a lesson to posterity; that a man may review the remarkable events which have happened to others, and be admonished; and may consider the history of people of preceding ages, and of all that hath befallen them, and be restrained. Extolled be the perfection of Him who hath thus ordained the history of former generations to be a lesson to those which follow.

—*The Thousand and One Nights*, Introduction

Background Information

Iran, formerly known as Persia, is an ancient land, and archaeologists have found proof of humans having inhabited the area now known as Khuzestan as long as 100,000 years ago. This Elamite civilization lasted until the sixth century BC, when two groups of Aryans began coming into Iran from the north and eventually assumed power: the Medes in northwestern Iran and the Parsua, later known as Persians, in the southwest. The king of the Persians, Cyrus the Great, not only defeated the Medes but also conquered most of the known world, creating a Persian empire that stretched from Central Asia to the Egyptian border. Future Persian kings continued to enlarge the empire until the Greek ruler, Alexander the Great, conquered Persepolis in 330 BC. This was the beginning of foreign rule in Persia.

In the fifth century, in the city of Mecca in what is now Saudi Arabia, an Arab named Muhammad received a revelation that, contrary to the many gods the Arabs worshipped, there was really just one God, Allah. He set down Allah's rules in a book called the Qur'an and preached a new way of life in which all peoples are equal and must be committed to helping one another. This new religion, called Islam, spread so rapidly that in little over a hundred years most Persians became Muslims, followers of Islam. The Arabs ruled Iran for about 300 years, followed by the Turks, who came from the northeast (1040–1220), and then the Mongols of eastern Asia.

After Mongol power declined, the great Persian Safavid dynasty was formed by Ismail, who ruled for twenty-three years and declared Shi'ite Islam the official religion. Shah Abbas was the greatest of the Safavid kings, and during his forty-one-year reign he built a new capital at Esfahan, (also spelled Isfahan), complete with an immense Royal Square, two mosques, a drum tower, wide avenues and gardens, and arched bridges. Esfahan was so beautiful that Persians began saying, "Esfahan nesf-e jahan"—"Esfahan is half the world" (Greenblatt 2003, 51).

Iranian art is a product of the many peoples who have ruled the country through the centuries. While the numbers of existing samples are not overwhelmingly vast, the different dynasties and periods spawned distinctive artworks, and to discuss them all would be well beyond the scope of this book. We focus on what is most important in the fascinating history of art in Iran. Among the very earliest works, dating back to the Elamite civilization in prehistoric times and forming a major part of artistic output for over 2,000 years, are pottery and figurines. Many of these pieces are decorated with geometric shapes and stylized animals, especially water fowl, ibexes, bulls, and lions.

"Iranian art *par excellence,* the art which bears the most convincing witness to the artistic sensibility of Iran, has always been architecture," states André Godard (1965, 104). Influenced by the architecture of Mesopotamia (modern-day Iraq), most of the buildings and their furnishings produced by the Elamites centered around worship of their gods, palaces for their rulers—the intermediaries between the gods and humans—and tombs with necessities the dead would need in their afterlife with the gods. They erected temples called ziggurats, built in stages or levels. The ziggurat at Chogha Zanbil, dedicated to the god Inahuahink, is the best preserved of all ancient ziggurats. It was constructed of sun-dried brick with fired brick reserved for facings, in four stages, one inside the other, so that they resemble nesting boxes. Surrounding this temple are palaces and burial chambers from which beautiful artifacts have been unearthed—left there by Elamite artisans so that the dead would have what they needed in the afterlife. Perhaps some of the finest examples of Iranian architecture can be found northeast of Shiraz in what was known as the Persepolis, the City of the Persians. There Darius the Great began building a magnificent stone palace complex, a work that took over 100 years to complete and whose glory was enjoyed by ancient Persians until Alexander the Great destroyed the city 200 years later. The Frieze of Archers that decorated this palace is now in the Louvre Museum in Paris.

The spread of Islam throughout the Middle East in the seventh century had a profound effect on the art of the region, especially its architecture. Muslims are called to pray five times a day, and often these prayers are said in a mosque, especially on Fridays. The mosque is the center of local community life and is usually decorated with Arabic script or the geometric designs often found in Islamic art. Beautiful mosaic tile work also adorns these places of worship. With their massive domes and tall minarets, these structures can be seen from afar and in themselves are a beacon calling Muslims to prayer.

The Savafid Period (1501–1737) is rightly designated by Sheila Canby the "Golden Age" of Persian Art, for under the Savafid Dynasty the arts reached their greatest heights. Shah Abbas's extensive building projects, including palaces and mosques, created a great need for artisans to design and furnish them. Calligraphy flourished. Mer Amad was one of the most famous calligraphers of the Savafid period during the reign of Shah Abas, because his work developed the highest form of Naskhtaliq, a combination of two forms of the Arabic alphabet that is still used today. Persian carpets were at their finest and became so desirable that factories sprang up in the cities of Kerman, Esfahan, Kashan, Tabriz, and Herat, and patterns developed during this time have served as models for carpets produced in other parts of the world even to this day. Persian miniature painting was popular during the Savafid period, and, although there were some wall paintings, was done primarily to illuminate manuscripts. The *Shahnama-yi-Shahi* (*The King's Book of Kings*), with its 258 beautiful miniatures, may be the greatest masterpiece of the age. Miniature painters used intricate brushwork, brilliant colors, and calligraphy in their illustrations, and because their materials—gold and silver leaf—were so expensive, only the wealthy, namely princes and rulers, could afford to sponsor such artwork. Miniatures still play an important part in Iranian artistic expression, and because Islamic law forbids showing the human face or form, miniature paintings are so tiny that human figures could never be identified as actual people. Scenes are secular in nature as well so as to avoid religious conflicts.

(Standards: Geography 2.5; 6.8, 9, 10, 11; 13.22;5; World History 1-4.5, 10-13; Art Connections: 1, 6, 7)

LESSON 1: Early Pottery and Artifacts and Persian Carpets

The Story

Long, long ago in a far away country that was then called Persia and is now called Iran (show map), a new ruler came into power. His name was Shah Abbas, and they called him Shah Abbas the Great because he accomplished great things while he ruled the country. Shah Abbas decided that he would make his capital city one of the greatest cities in the world. To do that, he called together his royal planners and asked their advice. They drew up a plan for the Shah that created a huge new center for the city in the form of a square. The new square had a big open space where caravans of people with camels could come in from the desert and leave their animals while they went to the many bazaars around the square to buy and sell things. Can you imagine a big space with hundreds of camels all standing around or lying down waiting for their owners? It must have been quite a sight, and noisy, too! The Shah loved to sit on the porch of his palace and watch polo matches that took place in the large square. The square also included mosques where the Muslim people could come to pray and gather together for special occasions. One of these mosques, called the Mosque of the Imam, is one of the most beautiful places in the world (show some pictures). And Shah Abbas built himself a palace that was six stories high with a porch that had a roof supported by eighteen tree trunks. (Hobhouse's *Gardens of Persia*—see references —has a wonderful close-up of this palace on page 107.) The palace was surrounded by beautiful gardens because the Persian people loved gardens. They thought gardens were special enclosed places where they could be safe and quiet and enjoy the beautiful plants. In fact, they thought gardens were so wonderful that they were like heaven on earth and they called them paradise. We get our word "paradise" from the ancient Persian people. Like all gardens in Persia, Shah Abbas's garden was divided into four squares, with a large pool of water in the center and channels of water flowing into the other squares. (Show a picture of this garden. Hobhouse has a fine example on page 109. In fact, this book contains gorgeous pictures of gardens in many areas of Persia, and it would be excellent if you could show the children many examples of Persian gardens from this or other sources.) Shah Abbas created such a beautiful city that those who saw it said it must be at least half the world! (Show a picture of the magnificent square Abbas created in Isfahan. Sterlin's *Islamic Art and Architecture*—see references—contains a fine example on pages 136–137.)

Shah Abbas loved to stroll in his gardens and enjoy the beautiful flowers and trees. He loved his gardens so much that he wanted to have them with him all the time—even indoors. And he loved beautiful artwork, too. He spent a great deal of money to support artists, so while he was ruler of Persia many, many wonderful works of art were created. He even had artists living with him in his palace. So he asked his artists to create a work of art that would let him have his beloved gardens and his favorite flowers inside his palace. The artists wove very special carpets that had designs that looked like flowers the Shah especially loved. Some carpets even seemed to have the water in the center of the flowers just like the Shah's garden outdoors. Even today you can buy a carpet that has these special designs. (Show pictures. Hobhouse, on pages 62–63, has a fine example of such a carpet. The Web site http://www.spongobongo.com/her9857.htm has one as well. Also, see Ferrier's *The Arts of Persia*—see References—pages 138–139.) Today artisans in Iran still make beautiful carpets, and people all over the world consider them to be very valuable. Some very old ones are so precious that you have to go to a museum to see them.

(Standards: Language Arts Listening and Speaking 8.4; History 4.1)

Viewing the Art

Be certain to view some early pottery, pointing out the geometric shapes and stylized animals (see Ferrier 1989, 9–11). Can the children find some geometric shapes in the formation of the animal figures? Spend some time viewing the ziggurat at Chogha Zanbil since it is the most impressive example we have of ancient Persian architecture. If you have access to a projector for large screen viewing, the Livius Web site (http://www.livius.org/a/iran/chogha_zanbil/cz.html) has wonderful views of the structure. Ferrier's *The Arts of Persia* is another good source. If you have studied Egyptian pyramids with the children, compare this ziggurat with the pyramids of Egypt. How are they alike, different?

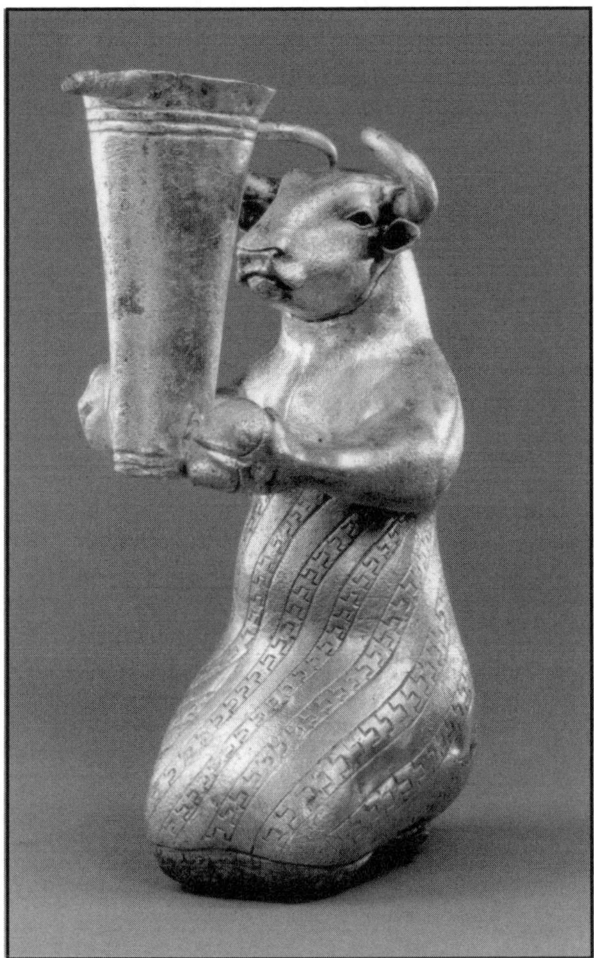

Metalwork-Silver, Iran, southwest region, Proto-Elamite, 3100–2900 B.C.

Silver

H. 6.4 in. (16.2 cm.)

View: ¾ front from left

Kneeling Bull Holding a Spouted Vessel, 3100–2900 BC; Proto-Elamite Period. The Metropolitan Museum of Art, Purchase, Joseph Pulitzer Bequest, 1966 (66.173) Photograph, all rights reserved, The Metropolitan Museum of Art.

Look at some of the tomb statues; the relief carvings; and especially the bowls, vases, and other artifacts found in temples, palaces, and tombs. Children will especially enjoy the silver bull figurine featuring a bull head with a human body holding a silver vase (see page 49). The relief of the Elamite Lady spinning (Ferrier 1989, 19) reveals how robust and honored women appear to have been in Elamite society. The children can view excellent examples of the architecture of Persepolis at http://tehran.stanford.edu/imagemap/perspolis.html. Talk about the tomb of Cyrus and why it might be raised up on a platform, and about the wonderful "Gate of all Nations." You can find excellent slide shows of a reconstruction of Persepolis and the research being done there at http://www.persepolis3d.com/frameset.html. Beautiful large color prints of architecture, reliefs, and artifacts from Persepolis are available in Ferrier (1989) on pages 32ff. Children may especially love the silver rhyton with a griffin head on page 45.

Some students may already be familiar with the term "Persian rugs" and might even have one in their homes. These carpets are marvelous art forms that require great skill and are well worth spending time viewing. Rugs vary in materials, with some being woven of silk and others of wool. The quality of the rug depends on the number of knots used per square centimeter to weave it. The Ardabil Carpet (Ferrier 1989, 120 and Canby 2000 , 48), now in the Victoria and Albert Museum in London, is said to be one of the most magnificent rugs in the world. It has over thirty-two million knots! The patterns seen in ancient carpets may very likely form the basis of patterns the children will see in homes and stores today—even if the rugs come from countries other than Iran. Ferrier has an entire chapter (pp. 118–149) on carpets with many illustrations in full color. Stierlin (2002) has two large beautiful illustrations on pages 123–124. The Web site at http://tehran.stanford.edu/Images/Persian_Carpet/old_jpg1.html has wonderful views of Persian carpets from the Safavid Dynasty.

Finally, look at some Persian miniatures. If you can find the book, it would be good to use Canby's *The Golden Age of Persian Art* since there are many pieces that were created during Shah Abbas's reign. Talk about how small they are—some so small you need a magnifying glass to see the images—and how many were painted to decorate manuscripts. Some of the brushes used have but a single hair. Discuss some of the scenes that are the subject of these paintings. Ferrier (1989) has three chapters on the subject, including one on book arts (pp. 200–245). Children will enjoy seeing the elaborate bindings and illustrations that adorn these books. They will also be interested in the painting of the lady in Persian dress on page 222. If you study medieval illuminated manuscripts, it would be interesting to compare the different illustrations.

(Standards: Art Connections 1.1-4, 6-7; Visual Arts 1.4-5 3, 4.9-10 ; Language Arts, Listening and Speaking 8.4, Viewing 9.6)

Journal Writing

What was the children's favorite figurine, painting? Why? Do they have gardens/plants in their homes? How do they regard these things—as decoration, special spaces? Why do they think carpets are such a special form of art in Iran?

(Standards: Language Arts: Writing 1.7, 23, 33-37; Art Connections 1.3)

1. Art/Drama Activity: Forming Animals with Geometric Shapes

Materials

- Pictures of water fowl and other birds, ibexes, bulls, and lions as they appear in nature
- Pictures of the same animals formed with geometric shapes to use as models (see "Viewing the Art" above)
- Paper
- Pencils, markers, or paint

Make available to the children the pictures of animals the ancient Persians created with geometric shapes shown during the viewing segment of this lesson, to use as models. Show the children pictures of the same animals as they appear in nature. Discuss the similarities and differences. Which shapes might be used to create which animals? Have the children create animals of their choice using these shapes. Make sure the animals they choose are animals that can be found in ancient Persian artifacts: ibexes, birds, water fowl, bulls, lions.

(Standards: Visual Arts 1.1-4, 8)

Man Working on a Fine Carpet

2. Art/Drama Activity: Weaving a Paper Place Mat

Materials

- Colored construction paper
- Pencils
- Scissors
- Glue
- Rulers

Explain to the children that weaving requires two different sets of thread: warp threads, which are held taut, usually on a loom, and weft threads, which are woven over and under the warp threads. They can use this information to weave a simple paper place mat. First have them fold a sheet of construction paper in half to form the warp. Have them place a ruler on the open edge of the paper and draw a guide line along the ruler. This will form a space about an inch wide along the cut edge of the construction paper. The children should then draw five or six lines from that guide line to the folded edge of the construction paper. The lines can be wavy, but not too wavy, or the weaving will be difficult. With the paper still folded, cut along these lines from the folded edge up to the guideline. Don't cut into the guideline. Open out the paper. Then, using a different color, cut strips of about one inch wide, holding the construction paper vertically. Use these strips, the weft, to weave over and under the warp. If a weft strip begins under the warp in the first line, it must begin over the warp in the second to create a pattern. When the weaving has been completed, the children should glue down the loose ends to finish the place mat.

(This lesson was taken from Monaghan and Joyner's book *You Can Weave!*, pages 2–3—see references. There are other marvelous weaving projects in this book, from simple to complex—using all kinds of materials.)

(Standards: Visual Arts: 1-4.1-11)

3. Art/Drama Activity

Students may enjoy acting out some of the scenes from the story of Shah Abbas and his plans for the city of Isfahan (Esfahan). Some possibilities are

- calling in advisors for help planning the huge city square,
- strolling in the garden and asking artisans to create a garden indoors through their art, and
- artisans planning and creating a "garden" carpet.

(Standards: Theater 1.16, 2.1-2, 10; 3, 4.5)

LESSON 2: Persian Mosques

The Story

It was just before dawn and Asif could hear his parents stirring. He groaned and turned over in bed, pulling the covers up over his head. It was cold, so cold on that December morning in Iran. He knew that any minute the call to prayer would be heard coming from the mosque, a building like a church or a temple where he and his family prayed, and he would have to go out even before it was light. And sure enough, there it was. (Here it would be very effective if you could play a recording of a call to prayer. You can go to http://www.isfahan.org.uk/monar/monar.html and record the call to prayer from there. Just be certain that the children are prepared to listen to it quietly and respectfully, since it is very important to Islamic peoples.) In English, this call to prayer was saying:

Allah is Greatest.
I bear witness that there is no other object of worship but Allah.
I bear witness that Muhammad is the Messenger of Allah.
Come to prayer.
Come to success.
Allah is Greatest.
There is no other object of worship but Allah.

Asif dressed quickly and joined his parents, and together they hurried toward the mosque. Other people, families, men and women walking by themselves, were also hurrying to the mosque to make their morning prayer. When they reached the mosque, Asif and his family, along with the others, placed their shoes in a rack so they would keep the mosque clean. They greeted their neighbors and then went to the bathing area to clean themselves, Asif and his father to one room for men and his mother to the room for women. They put on slippers, and before they began to perform *wudu*, a ceremonial washing before prayer, they said: "In the name of God, the Most Gracious, the Most Merciful," and began to wash themselves. They washed their hands, rinsed their mouths and noses, and washed their faces three times each. Then they washed their arms up to their elbows three times, passed their wet hands over their hair and ears once, and washed their ankles three times. They started with the right side and ended with the left. When they finished, they said, "I bear witness that there is no god but God, and Muhammad is the last message of God." They were now ready to go into the large prayer hall, where the huge carpet on the floor had individual prayer rug designs, a separate space for each person. There Asif and his father joined the other men in prayer, all of them facing a carved out section of wall in front of them, called a mihrab, that pointed in the direction of Mecca, the Muslim Holy City. Asif's mother was praying with the women in another prayer hall. Part of the prayer ritual required them to bend down and touch the carpet with their foreheads, and it would be too embarrassing for the women to bend down like that in front of the men. When they had finished their prayers, the family returned to the entrance, put their shoes on, and made their way home. As he walked, Asif thought about what he had just done. He was happy to be a Muslim and begin his day in prayer in the mosque—even though it was hard to get up. His family was so lucky. They lived close to the mosque so they could go there for morning prayer. Other families had to pray in their homes. But on Friday everyone, especially the men, would come at noon from all over the city to pray together in the mosque. Every Friday was a special day of prayer for Muslims, like Saturday is for Jewish people and Sunday is for Christians. On Friday, Asif would hear a special talk given by their prayer leader, and he would go to a class to study the Qur'an, the Muslim holy book. Asif smiled to himself as he walked home.

(Standards: Language Arts Listening and Speaking 8.4)

Viewing the Art

Mosques are among the finest examples of architectural genius in Iran. In addition, they contain important works of Iranian art: carpets, calligraphy, and decorative tiles. Thus this viewing session, following on the heels of a story about an Iranian family at prayer, centers on the mosque. Persian mosques, with their distinctive arches and beautiful tile and calligraphy adornments, are especially beautiful. If and when you study Roman and Gothic arches with the children, it will be interesting to discuss the differences. The Persian arch is four-centered and "combines tight outer curves at the 'shoulders' with much shallower inner curves that meet in a sharp point" (Stierlin 2002, 44). You can find stunning photos of Persian mosques, featuring close-ups of the arches, magnificent domes, minarets, and beautiful tile and calligraphy work, in Stierlin's *Islamic Art and Architecture* (2002, 1–47) and in the section on key monuments. Ferrier's *The Arts of Persia* (1989, 270–293) contains some excellent colored photos of tile work. What color tiles are most frequently used? Talk about the minaret attached to the mosque as a symbol of the link between heaven and earth. If you click on "more pictures of Esfahan" at the bottom of the page at http://www.iranchamber.com/cities/esfahan/esfahan.php, you can view twenty-eight spectacular color pictures of the inside of mosques, the bazaar, and other views of the city. Khan's *What You Will See inside a Mosque* (see references) is a wonderful aid in explaining to children the different parts of the mosque and their function.

David Macaulay's *Mosque* (see references) is just about a "must" for this viewing session. Although the book describes the building of a mosque during the Ottoman Empire in Turkey and not a mosque in Iran (thus, you won't see examples of the Persian arch), the book is marvelous for showing the different parts of the mosque: dome, minaret, mihrab, etc. It discusses construction as well as calligraphy in the mosque, decorative tiles, and more. This gem will surely help your students understand how a mosque is built and what it contains.

(Standards: Art Connections 1.1,3-4, 6-7; Visual Arts 4.8-9; Viewing 9; Mathematics 5.21)

Journal Writing

What features of the mosque do the children find most impressive? How is a mosque different from or the same as the places of worship with which they are familiar? Is there anything that surprised them in this study of the mosque?

(Standards: Language Arts Writing 1.23)

1. Art/Drama Activity: Making Tiles for a Mosque

Undertake this activity if your students are older. Or you can simplify the lesson by using stiff cardboard squares covered with white paper and regular paints. If your school art department has a kiln, this would be a wonderful art project in which the students could actually make a tile mosaic design to decorate an area of the school—a wall in the front lobby, the hall outside their classroom, a border along the midpoint on the hall walls, etc. Or, to connect the activity with something else the children are learning, they could make a tile mosaic that encompasses that subject: murals featuring sea life, insects, etc.

Materials

- Underglaze colors for use on ceramics or regular paint
- Clear glaze
- Unglazed six-inch bisque tiles or cardboard
- Practice paper and pencils
- Kiln

After viewing many examples of designs of Persian tiles, have children select designs that are simple enough for them to copy, for example, simple flower outlines. Ask them to practice their designs on paper before putting them on their tiles or cardboard. The children should then paint the outline of their designs onto their tiles or cardboard with black underglaze paint. If you want a mosaic effect, two or four children could work together with a piece of the design appearing on each tile to make a whole when the tiles are placed together, like puzzle pieces. Next, the children fill in the spaces in their outline with several coats of underglaze colors and go over their black outline again. When the piece is thoroughly dry, apply two coats of clear glaze, allowing each coat to dry before applying the next coat. Finally, if you are using tiles, fire them in a kiln to cone 04 (1400 degrees F, 760 degrees C). Of course, this project will need to be completed over several days. If you are using cardboard, the children simply outline their design in black and fill in colors with paints of their choice.

The Web site http://www.amaco.com/pdfs/Lesson12.pdf has more detailed instructions for this art project.

(Standards: Visual Arts: 1-4.1-11)

2. Art/Drama Activity: Forming the Four-Centered Arch

The students might enjoy seeing how a Persian arch is formed. They can do this individually, or you can demonstrate it for them on a large chart.

Materials

- Compass
- Paper
- Pencil and eraser

Use the instructions on the diagrams on pages 58 and 59 to construct a four-centered arch such as the ones found in Persian architecture.

Curriculum Connections

Social Studies

- Using a map, locate the countries that comprise the area known as the Middle East. Where is Iran? Compare the different sizes of the countries.
- Locate different land forms on a topographic map. Point out the desert areas in Iran and discuss why it would be difficult for people to live in these regions. What would humans need to be able to adapt to such conditions?
- Talk about the different groups of people who ruled Iran (Persia) over the centuries and the influence of each group. Spend time discussing the spread of Islam and what effect that had on the art and culture of the Persian people.
- Talk about clothing. How did the ancient Persians dress? How do the people of Iran dress today? Talk about head scarves and other dress requirements and their meaning.
- Talk about Iranian products and exports, especially petroleum. What is the significance of Iran's oil supply as it affects the rest of the world?

- Enjoy some ancient Persian food. Najmieh Khalili Batmanglij's *New Food of Life* (see references) has many recipes as well as information about different kinds of food. Some of the appetizers are simple enough to prepare in the classroom. Or have a Persian feast and invite parents and other caregivers. (Teachers may enjoy reading *Pomegranate Soup* by Marsha Mehran—see references—and trying some of the recipes the author provides.)

  (Standards: Geography 1.2.30; World History 13.10.130)

Science

- Talk about scientific inventions introduced by ancient Persians, such as the Qanat to bring water to desert areas. This system, devised over 3,000 years ago, is still in use to provide irrigation in Iran today! (See Wulff in references.)
- Ibn Sina was a Persian physician who made enormous contributions to the field of medicine. He was the first to describe meningitis, and discovered that tuberculosis was contagious and that nerves were responsible for muscle pain. What other contributions did he make to the profession? Ibn al-Haytham studied how light travels and how the eye is able to receive light, making sight possible. He also made enormous contributions to the fields of mathematics and astronomy. Try to find out more about these scientists and about science in ancient Persia.
- Study Persian gardens. Have the students compare them to their own gardens or the gardens they know. What kinds of plants do the Persians like to grow? Do any of these plants grow in their part of the country? How are Persian gardens laid out?
- Visit a carpet store and ask to see Persian carpet designs.

  (Standards: Science 6, 11, 12.29, 39, 51)

Mathematics

- Al-Khwarizmi was a Persian mathematician who is considered to be the father of algebra. The word algorithm is derived from his name. Find out more about him and his work.
- Muslims in Arabia recognized the usefulness of the Arabic numerals that had been invented in India. These Arabic numerals are the same ones we use today. Talk about how our number system works. Compare it to other systems.

  (Standards: Mathematics 2, 9.4, 29)

Instructions for Forming

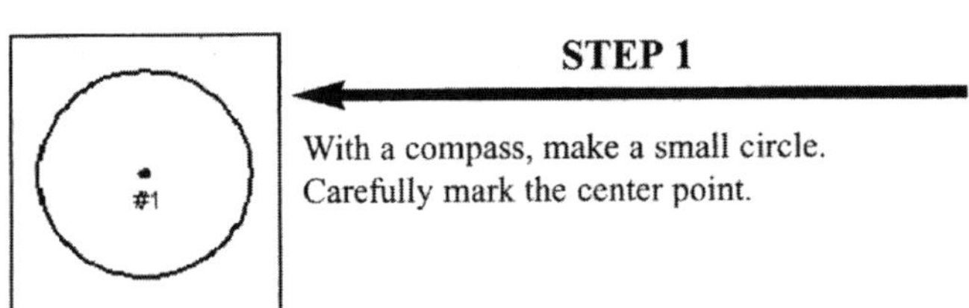

STEP 1

With a compass, make a small circle. Carefully mark the center point.

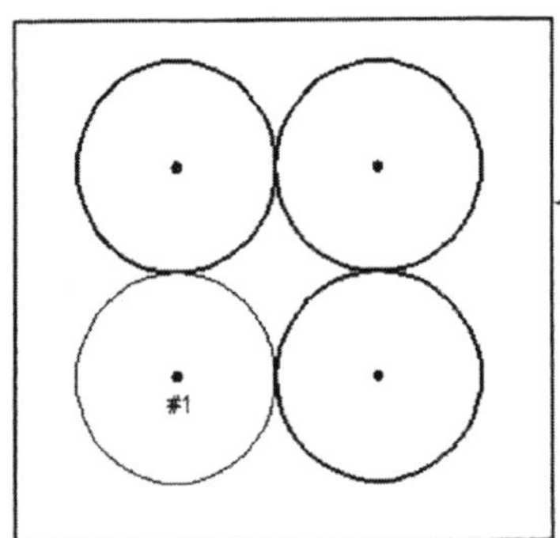

STEP 2

Make three other circles using the same radius. Have all four circles touch as shown. Carefully mark all center points.

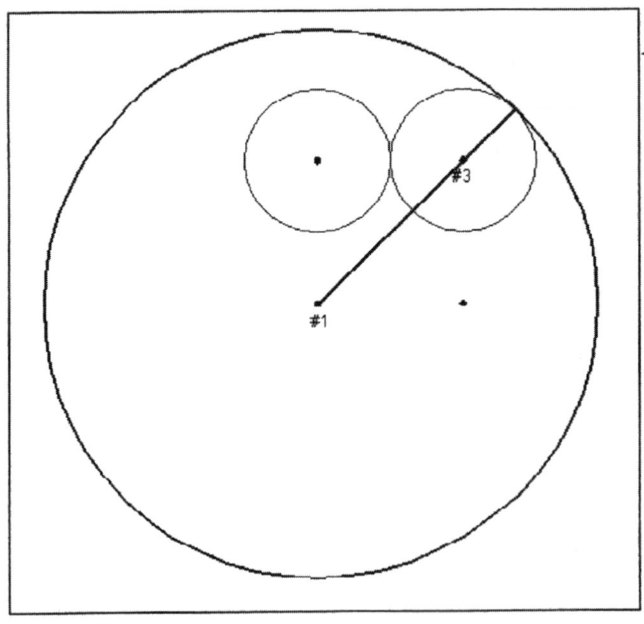

STEP 3

Draw a straight line from circle center #1 through circle center #3 to the outside of circle #3. This forms your large radius. Now with the center point at #1 and your radius as just described, draw another circle.

a Four-Centered Arch

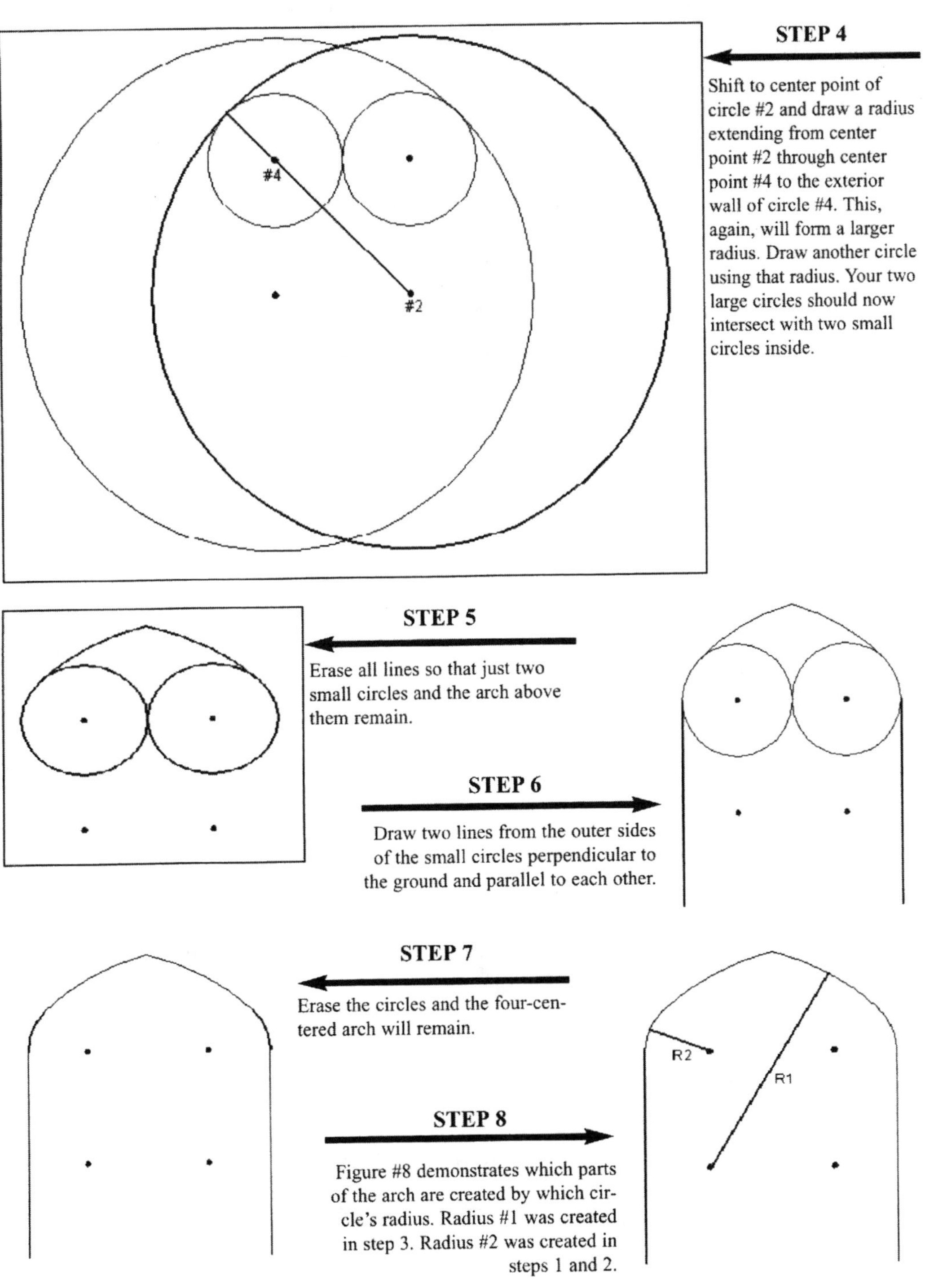

STEP 4
Shift to center point of circle #2 and draw a radius extending from center point #2 through center point #4 to the exterior wall of circle #4. This, again, will form a larger radius. Draw another circle using that radius. Your two large circles should now intersect with two small circles inside.
#4
#2
STEP 5
Erase all lines so that just two small circles and the arch above them remain.
STEP 6
Draw two lines from the outer sides of the small circles perpendicular to the ground and parallel to each other.
STEP 7
Erase the circles and the four-centered arch will remain.
R2
R1
STEP 8
Figure #8 demonstrates which parts of the arch are created by which circle's radius. Radius #1 was created in step 3. Radius #2 was created in steps 1 and 2.

Literature

- Read several Persian folktales to the class (see references). Discuss how these tales reveal aspects of the culture. Compare the Persian version of "Cinderella" with the version the students know. How are they alike, different? Can the students come up with reasons for the differences? If you feel it is appropriate to talk about it with your age group, mention the story of "Sharazad and the 1001 Nights." Point out that Aladdin, a story with which the children are probably familiar, is said to be one of these tales, though this is a subject of controversy. Compare the Aladdin story you read to them with the Disney version. Students may also wish to act out some of the folktales you have shared with them.
- Read some Persian poetry if you think it is appropriate for your class. A good source is *Rumi Birdsong* (see references).

  (Standards: Language Arts Reading 6.13, 14, 23; Listening and Speaking 8)

Writing

- Have fun learning how to write the Arabic alphabet. A useful book is *My First Arabic Alphabet Book* (see references). Compare this alphabet to Egyptian hieroglyphs and to our own Roman alphabet. Talk about Arabic writing used as an art form to decorate books, mosque walls, etc.

  (Standards: Art Connections 1.1, 4)

References

Adult Books

Batmanglij, Najmieh Khalili. *New Food of Life: Ancient Persian and Modern Iranian Cooking and Ceremonies.* Washington, DC: Mage Publishers, 1992. ISBN 0934211345.

This book contains recipes for many Persian dishes, beautiful pictures, and even poems.

Canby, Sheila R. *The Golden Age of Persian Art.* New York: Harry N. Abrams, 2000. ISBN 0810941449.

This book has fine examples of art produced during the important Safavid Dynasty.

Ferrier, R. W., ed. *The Arts of Persia.* New Haven, CT: Yale University Press, 1989. ISBN 0300039875.

This book has large color reproductions of many of the artworks discussed in the lessons above.

Godard, André. *The Art of Iran.* New York: Frederick A. Praeger, 1965. o.p. ASIN B0006BM008.

Although this book is out of print, it is a fine source for ancient artifacts and worth hunting down in a library.

Grabar, Oleg. *Mostly Miniatures: An Introduction to Persian Painting.* Princeton, NJ: Princeton University Press, 2001. ISBN 0691049998.

This is a fine source of beautifully reproduced paintings to use for group viewing.

Hobhouse, Penelope. *Gardens of Persia.* Photography by Jerry Harpur. Carlsbad, CA: Kales Press, 2004. ISBN 0967007666.

The color photographs of Persian gardens in this book are spectacular.

Mahboubian, Houshang. *The Art of Ancient Iran: Copper and Bronze.* London: Philip Wilson, 2003. ISBN 0856674834.

This book is expensive, but if your library has it, it is a treasure trove of ancient copper and bronze works.

Mehran, Marsha. *Pomegranate Soup.* New York: Random House, 2005. ISBN 1400062411.

This is the fictitious story of three sisters who escape from Iran during the revolution and start a restaurant in a small village in Ireland. Recipes are included.

Porada, Edith. *The Art of Ancien Iran: Pre-Islamic Cultures.* New York: Graystone Press, 1969. ASIN BOOO7DTUEC.

This is a fine source for ancient artifacts such as pottery and figurines.

Stierlin, Henri. *Islamic Art and Architecture from Isfahan to the Taj Mahal.* Photography by Anne Stierlin. London: Thames & Hudson, 2002. ISBN 0-500-51100-4.

A well-written text and stunning reproductions make this an excellent book for both background information and viewing.

Wulff, H. E. "The Qanats of Iran." *Scientific American* 219 (1968): 94–105.

In this article Wulff describes how the ancient Persians invented a qanat system more than 3,000 years ago, to bring water from the mountains to desert areas.

Children's Books

Al-Gailani, Noora, and Chris Smith. *The Islamic Year: Surahs, Stories and Celebrations.* Illustrated by Helen Williams. Glos., England: Stroud, 2003. ISBN 1903458145.

Activities and explanations help children understand Muslim holidays and feasts.

Balouch, Kristen. *The King & the Three Thieves.* New York: Viking/Penguin, 2000. o.p. ISBN 0-670-88059-0.

This story features a real king of ancient Persia, King Abbas, who is mentioned in one of the stories in the lessons above. Although it is out of print, this folktale is well worth hunting down and sharing with children.

———. *Mystery Bottle.* New York: Hyperion, 2006. ISBN 078680999-X.

A young boy is sent to America when the revolution breaks out in Iran in 1978 and years later his son receives a mystery bottle that calls him back to Iran to visit his grandfather.

Barnes, Trevor. *Islam.* Boston: Kingfisher, 2005. ISBN 0-7534-5882-9.

Barnes, the religious affairs presenter for BBC-TV, presents the life of Muhammad and the development of Islam and its teachings. This is an accessible book for young people.

Bauer, Brandy, and Akhavi-Pour Hossein. *Iran: A Question and Answer Book.* Mankato, MN: Capstone Press, 2005. ISBN 0736837523.

A very simple book about Iran in which the information is presented in question and answer format.

Beshore, George. *Science in Early Islamic Cultures.* New York: Franklin Watts, 1998. ISBN 0-531-20355-7.

The many scientific and mathematical discoveries made by Muslims throughout the centuries are discussed in this book.

Brown, Tricia. *Salaam: A Muslim-American Boy's Story.* Photographs by Ken Cardwell. New York: Henry Holt, 2006. ISBN 978-0-8050-6538-1.

Inram, a young Muslim American boy, talks about his life in San Francisco.

Bunting, Eve. *One Green Apple.* Illustrated by Ted Lewin. New York: Clarion, 2006. ISBN 978-0-43477-0.

In her second day at school in the United States, a young Muslim girl feels different because she can't speak English and her headdress stands out. But she soon discovers that differences can be an advantage.

Clark, Charles. *Islam.* San Diego: Lucent Books, 2001. ISBN 1-56006-986-4.

This book for older students is good background reading for teachers. The extensive information provided includes both the politics and challenges of Islam. Contains a helpful glossary.

Climo, Shirley. *The Persian Cinderella.* Illustrated by Robert Florczak. New York: Harper Trophy, 2001. ISBN 0064438538.

In this version of Cinderella, a young girl purchases a jug instead of using her money to buy a dress for the prince's celebration.

Conover, Sarah, and Freda Crane. *Ayat Jamilah: Beautiful Signs.* Illustrated by Valerie Wahl. Spokane: Eastern Washington University Press, 2004. ISBN 0-910055-94-7.

This is a wonderful collection of Islamic tales. Although it will be too difficult for younger children to manage themselves, many stories are suitable for reading aloud or for your own retelling.

Demi. *Muhammad.* New York: Margaret McElderry, 2003. ISBN 0689852649.

Demi tells the story of Muhammad and accompanies it with her marvelous illustrations. The prophet himself is not depicted.

dePaola, Tomie. *The Legend of the Persian Carpet.* Illustrated by Claire Ewart. New York: Putnam, Whitebird, 1993. ISBN 0-399-22415-7.

When the king's diamond is stolen, his artisans create a carpet to replace the diamond's brilliance.

Ellabbad, Mohieddin. *The Illustrator's Notebook.* Toronto: Groundwood Books, 2006. ISBN 0888997000.

If you use no other children's book from this chapter, try to get this one. Addressing readers directly, an Egyptian illustrator talks about how he creates his work. The book opens from right to left and is filled with Arabic writing. This is a true treasure!

Fox, Mary Virginia. *Enchantment of the World: Iran.* Chicago: Children's Press, 1991. ISBN 0516027271.

This is a thorough discussion of the history of and current life in Iran. Suitable for older children.

Ghazi, Suhaib Hamid. *Ramadan.* Illustrated by Omar Rayyan. New York: Holiday House, 1996. ISBN 0-8234-1275-X.

Young Hakeem explains how he and his family celebrate the month of Ramadan. This is a simple book for young children.

Greenblatt, Miriam. *Iran: Enchantment of the World.* New York: Children's Press/Scholastic, 2003. ISBN 0-516-22375-5.

Greenblatt describes the geography, history, culture, art, and others aspects of the lives of the people of Iran.

Heide, Florence Parry, and Judith Heide Gilliland. *The House of Wisdom.* Illustrated by Mary Grandpré. New York: DK Children, 1999. ISBN 0789425629.

This story describes how books were held in high esteem in ninth-century Bagdad.

Henderson, Kathy. *Lugalbanda, the Boy Who Got Caught up in a War.* Illustrated by Jane Ray. Cambridge, MA: Candlewick Press, 2006. ISBN 0-7636-2782-8.

This amazing story, perhaps the oldest written story in the world, comes from clay tablets written in ancient Iraq. It tells of Lugalbanda, who followed his brothers into war but with the help of a giant Anzu bird and a goddess brought peace to the land. It is beautifully told and illustrated.

Hickox, Rebecca. *The Golden Sandal: A Middle Eastern Cinderella Story.* Illustrated by Will Hillenbrand. New York: Holiday House, 1999. ISBN 0823415139.

This is an Iraqi version of the Cinderella tale.

Hoyt-Goldsmith, Diane. *Celebrating Ramadan.* Photographs by Lawrence Migdale. New York: Holiday House, 2001. ISBN 0-8234-1581-3.

The author and photographer chronicle Ibraheem and his family during the month of Ramadan.

Jungman, Ann. *The Most Magnificent Mosque*. London: Frances Lincoln, 2004. ISBN 1-84507-012-7.

Three boys grow to love their mosque in Cordoba and as adults work to prevent its destruction.

Khan, Aisha Karen. *What You Will See Inside a Mosque*. Photography by Aaron Pepis. Woodstock, VT: Skylight Paths Publishing, 2003. ISBN 1-8933 61-60-8.

This simply written book describes all the different sections of the mosque and what takes place in each.

Kimmel, Eric A. *The Three Princes: A Tale from the Middle East*. Illustrated by Leonard Everett Fisher. New York: Holiday House, 1994. ISBN 0-8234-41115-X.

A princess who is courted by three princes sends them all on a quest to find the greatest wonder of the world.

Koven, Rosalind. *Id-ul-Fitr*. Austin, TX: Raintree Steck-Vaughn, 1998. ISBN 0-8172-4609-6.

In this book Kerven describes some of the customs of Muslim peoples, especially the feast of Id-ul-Fitr. Includes foods and recipes.

Macaulay, David. *Mosque*. Boston: Houghton Mifflin/Walter Lorraine, 2003. ISBN 0-618-24034-9.

Macaulay, a genius at explaining to young readers the construction of important structures, describes the building and decorating of a mosque. This is a beautiful book.

Manson, Christopher. *A Gift for the King*. New York: Henry Holt, 1989. o.p. ISBN 0-8050-0951-5.

A king takes no pleasure in all the lavish gifts his subjects offer him, until he is in need of a simple drink of water.

Matze, Claire Sidhom. *The Stars in My Geddoh's Sky*. Illustrated by Bill Farnsworth. 1999. Reprint, New York: Albert Whitman, 2002. ISBN 0807553328.

On a visit to the United States, Alex's grandfather teaches him some things about his Middle Eastern culture.

McCaughrean, Geraldine. *One Thousand and One Arabian Nights*. New York: Oxford University Press, 2000. ISBN 01992750135.

The author's fine translation of these tales makes them enjoyable to read aloud.

Merrill, Yvonne Y., and Jim Tilly. *Hands-On Ancient People, Volume 1: Art Activities about Mesopotamia, Egypt, and Islam*. Illustrated by Mary Simpson. Salt Lake City: Kits Publishing, 2002. ISBN 0-9643177-8-8.

This book has a beautiful, full-page, color illustration for each craft suggested. The object to be made is discussed in the context of the historical period, and clear instructions are given.

Mobin-Uddin, Asma. *My Name Is Bilal.* Illustrated by Barbara Kiwak. Honesdale, PA: Boyds Mills, 2005. ISBN 1590781759.

When his sister's head scarf is pulled off, Bilal, defends her by explaining some Muslim customs to their classmates.

Monaghan, Kathleen, and Hermon Joyner. *You Can Weave! Projects for Young Weavers.* Worcester, MA: Davis Publications, 2000. ISBN 087192-493-5.

The authors provide many interesting weaving projects for children, ranging from very simple to more difficult.

Morris, Neil. *The Atlas of Islam: People, Daily Life and Traditions.* Hauppauge, NY: Barrons Educational Books, 2003. ISBN 0764156314.

Although the text in this large book is choppy at times, it provides a good deal of information, including on current terrorist activities.

Osborne, Mary Pope. *Season of All Sandstorms.* New York: Random House, 2005. ISBN 0-375-83031-6.

In this simple novel, Jack and Annie travel to ancient Baghdad to help the caliph disseminate wisdom to the world.

Penney, Sue. *Islam.* Chicago: Reed Educational & Professional Publishing/Heinemann, 2001. ISBN 1-57572-357-3.

This attractive overview of Islam provides color pictures, informational sidebars, and a glossary.

Pullman, Philip. *Aladdin and the Enchanted Lamp.* New York: Scholastic/Arthur Levine, 2005. ISBN 0-439-69255-5.

Despite the inconsistency of the story being set in China and there being minarets and camels in the illustrations, this is a large, colorful book with a lively text.

Rumford, James. *Traveling Man: The Journey of Ibn Battuta, 1325–1354.* Boston: Houghton Mifflin, 2001. ISBN 0618083669.

In 1325, at age twenty-one, Ibn decided to leave Morocco to go on pilgrimage to Mecca and then proceeded to travel for the next twenty-nine years through Africa, across the Asian steppes, into India and China, and back to Morocco.

Rumi, Jelaluddin. *Rumi Birdsong: Fifty-three Short Poems.* Translated by Coleman Barks. Athens, GA: Maypop Books, 1993. ISBN 096189167-X.

This book contains some short poems, many of which are suitable to give even young children a taste of Persian poetry.

Shepard, Aaron. *Forty Fortunes: A Tale of Iran.* Illustrated by Alisher Dianov. New York: Clarion, 1999. ISBN 0395811333.

Ahmed's wife forces him to work as a diviner. But when the king asks him to catch thieves or face prison, he fears the worst.

Taus-Bolstad, Stacy. *Iran in Pictures.* Minneapolis, MN: Lerner, 2004. ISBN 0-8225-0950-4.

This treasure trove of information about Iran lists numerous Web sites and books for additional reading as well as famous people, sites to see in the country, and more.

Yip, Dora, and Maria O'Shea. *Welcome to Iran.* Milwaukee, WI: Gareth Stevens, 2001. ISBN 0-8368-2525-X.

A simple introduction to Iran for young children.

Audiovisual Materials

Ancient Mesopotamia. DVD. Library Video Company, 1998. V7158.

This film takes children to ancient Mesopotamia to learn about the people's lives and customs.

Islam: A Closer Look. Video. SoundVision, 1998. ISBN 1-59011-079-X.

This documentary explains basic Islamic beliefs and practices.

Islamic Art and Culture. Slides, prints, CD, booklet. National Gallery of Art, n.d.. TP317.

This packet of material centers on twenty works of architecture, calligraphy, manuscript illumination, and the decorative arts. It is available for a nine-month loan period.

Jim Weiss, Storyteller—Arabian Nights. CD. Rabbit Ears, 1989.

Weiss tells several stories from the Arabian Nights.

Ramadan. DVD. LibraryVideo, 2004. V7142.

Suitable for children as young as preschool, this film mixes live action with animation to explain the observance of Ramadan.

Other Materials

Islamic Art and Geometric Design: Activities for Learning. Metropolitan Museum of Art Store, n.d. M4379.

This set includes a brief overview of Islamic art, an introduction to related masterworks in the Museum's collection, and a series of pattern-making activities.

Lap Loom. The Metropolitan Museum of Art Store, n.d. M8099.

Children can use this loom to weave many different articles.

Tiles and ceramic paints. American Art Clay Company, Inc., n.d. (800) 374-1600.

This is an excellent source for obtaining tiles and paints for the art activity in the lesson above.

Web Sites

Contemporary Arabic Calligraphy Designs. http://www.ndukhan.com/ (accessed January 23, 2006).

Calligraphy for such words as hope, peace, and angel are drawn simply enough for children to copy.

Frost, Gregory. *The Tale of the Puzzle of the Tales.* http://www.endicott-studio.com/rdrm/forpuzl.html (accessed January 23, 2006).

Gregory discusses some of the controversies surrounding the tale of the Arabian Nights and whether Aladdin actually belongs to this group of stories.

Fundamental Concepts. http://www.isfahan.org.uk/glossary/glossary.html (accessed January 23, 2006.)

Basic fundamental concepts of Islamic art are discussed through a series of links.

Islamic Calligraphy. http://www.islamicity.com/Culture/Calligraphy/default.HTM (accessed January 23, 2006).

This site gives many examples showing how calligraphy is part of the figure itself.

Persian Art through the Centuries. http://www.artarena.force9.co.uk/hpart.html (accessed January 23, 2006).

This marvelous site discusses Persian art throughout the centuries. The home page provides some Persian music.

Persian Carpet. http://www.iranchamber.com/carpet/brief_history_persian_carpet.php (accessed May 8, 2006).

Visitors to this site can view a slide show featuring various Persian carpet designs.

The Persian Carpet Gallery. http://tehran.stanford.edu/Images/Persian_Carpet/carpet.html (accessed May 8, 2006).

This site provides a history of Persian carpets as well as wonderful pictures of weavers at work.

Persian/Iranian World Wide Web Resources. http://www.farsinet.com/persianweb/history.html (accessed January 23, 2006).

This is a marvelous site that has links to many other sites involving all aspects of life and art in Iran as well as its history.

Sexton, Professor Kim S. *Isfahan—Half the World.* http://depts.washington.edu/uwch/silkroad/cities/iran/isfahan/isfahan.html (accessed February 26, 2006).

Professor Sexton discusses the city of Isfahan. There are many fine thumbnail pictures that can be enlarged by clicking on them.

Talk Islam. http://www.talkislam.com/ (accessed January 23, 2006).

This site contains a good deal of information about Islam, including links to other Islamic Web sites and Muslim organizations.

Zurkus, Judith. *Islamic Art; Exploring the Visual Arts of the Middle East.* http://www.cis.yale.edu/ynhti/curriculum/units/2002/2/02.02.03.x.html (accessed January 23, 2006).

Zurkus provides many links to several kinds of Islam art along with lesson plans for creating calligraphy, Persian carpets, and more.

3 Ancient Greek Art

The Parthenon, Athens, Greece

"Future ages will wonder at us, as the present age wonders at us now."

—PERICLES, ruler of Athens, 431 BC

Background Information

The life and art of the ancient Greeks have had a profound effect on humankind. The Greeks were lovers of beauty, philosophers and thinkers, mathematicians, champions of physical fitness and the human body. They gave us the *Iliad* and the *Odyssey*, Homer, Plato, Socrates, and Aristotle. The Greeks developed the first, albeit imperfect, democratic system of government. They loved drama and performed hundreds of plays, several of which survive to this day. Long before Columbus sailed the seas, Greek scholars knew that the earth was round, and

Eratosthenes measured the earth's diameter with remarkable accuracy centuries before the sophisticated instruments we now use for this purpose were invented. The ancient Greeks initiated many of the disciplines we take for granted today: Herodotus wrote about the wars and other events in the lives of his people, and thus became the Father of History; Thales has been called the first scientist; Hippocrates, who tried to find cures for illness, is considered the Father of Medicine (Even to this day, doctors take the Hippocratic Oath promising to do no harm.), and Euclid, the Father of Geometry. The Spartans with their vigorous training and austere way of life became geniuses at waging war, while most Greeks took honing and exercising the body seriously. The Olympic Games originated in Greece in 776 BC, and legend has it that the first marathon was run by Miltiades, who ran twenty-six miles at high speed to bring news that the Athenians had defeated the Persians. Greek sculpture and architecture, frequently created to pay homage to one or more of their many gods, have been unsurpassed by the work of any group of people before or since.

Although there were tribes of peoples speaking Greek in the lands surrounding the Mediterranean Sea as early as 1100 BC, we take up their history in this lesson around 750 BC, with Homer's writing of the *Iliad* and the *Odyssey*. At this time, the tribes formed city-states, the most famous of which was Athens. The Greek statues sculpted around this time, the Archaic Period, were very much like those of the Egyptians. They were mostly of naked young boys, with the wide shoulders and narrow waists of the Egyptian statues, who stood stiffly with one leg forward. During this period, artists painted black figures on the natural clay color of jugs and vases. The lines inside the figures were made by scratching away some of the black paint. This pottery, and the pottery of later eras, is the only record we have of ancient Greek painting, since all the wall paintings have been destroyed.

The classical period (500–323 BC) ushered in a noticeable change in Greek art. Sculptors began to have a better grasp of the human form, and statues took on a new grace, beauty, and sense of movement. Greek sculptors emphasized perfection, giving their figures refined features and perfectly proportioned bodies. Painters left the figures on their pottery in the natural clay color and painted the background black, so they could draw interior lines and features with a brush rather than painstakingly scratching them in.

In ancient Greece, art and individual achievement were honored, and for the first time artists began to sign their works. We know the names of some of the pottery painters, and we know about the work of such marvelous sculptors as Praxiteles, Skopas, and Lysippos. During the classical period the Greeks fought and defeated the invading Persians, and though the Persians destroyed the Acropolis, a hill in Athens on which stood temples to the gods, the Athenians pledged to rebuild their city and to clothe it in even greater splendor. Under its ruler, Pericles, Athens entered into a golden age, or the Age of Pericles. Although this golden age did not last long because of Athens's devastating defeat at the hands of the Spartans in the Peloponnesian War, for the next forty years the city of Athens devoted itself to the arts.

To replace the temple to Athena, goddess of wisdom and patron of Athens, which had been under construction when the Persians destroyed it, Pericles hired two great architects, Iktinos and Callicrates. Greek temples were constructed in different styles, or orders, determined by the type of capital, or head, of the columns that supported them. The orders are the Doric, the Ionic, and most elaborate, the Corinthian. Athena's temple, the Parthenon, constructed in the Doric order, is considered to be one of the most beautiful buildings in the world. The architects built it in only fifteen years.

Designed to compensate for all possible optical illusions, there is not a straight line in the building, though to the observer it is perfectly proportioned. The great sculptor Phidias sculpted the enormous statue of Athena that was to be placed in the Parthenon. Standing on a twelve-foot base, the statue, made of wood overlaid with gold and ivory, rose another thirty-nine feet and held a six-foot statue of Nike, the Greek goddess of victory, in one hand, and a huge shield in the other. She was so grand she actually cost more than the temple that housed her! Unfortunately this statue, as is true of most ancient Greek statues, has been lost or destroyed, and all we have are Roman copies to apprise us of their splendor.

Marble Copy of Statue of Athena by Phidias
http://harpy.uccs.edu/greek/SCULPT/varvakei.jpg

Alexander, called the Great, finally destroyed the much-hated Persian empire and extended Greek rule into Egypt and India. The period following his death in 323 BC is called the Hellenistic Age. It is during this time that Greek portrait statues began to shed their idealistic features and take on more individual characteristics. Finally, from 31 BC to AD 330, Greece fell under Roman rule.

(Standards: World History 6-8.8-10; Geography 13.21-22)

The Story

Long, long ago, there lived a group of gods high on a mountaintop called Olympus. These gods were very interested in what went on in the world of humans living far below them, so when the gods received news that a new city was going to be created, they had a big contest to see which god would be in charge of it. Two of the gods, Poseidon, who ruled the seas, and Athena, goddess of wisdom, led all the others in trying to gain control. Finally, the gods decided to act as judges. Both Poseidon and Athena were ordered to prepare a special gift for the people of the new city. Whoever thought of the best gift would win the contest. The other gods gave Poseidon and Athena time to think of what to offer the people. At last the day arrived for them to stand before the judges.

Poseidon strode proudly forth, and with one wave of his hand he created a thundering earthquake. The earth split at his feet, and out of the enormous crack rose a salt spring. "You see, I have created a body of water for the people. And since I rule the seas, I will make sure that these people are always powerful on water. They will have a mighty navy and defeat any enemies who come to attack them with ships."

The judges looked very pleased. "That is surely a fine gift, Poseidon. It is important that the people have the power to defend themselves. And you have shown yourself to be powerful enough to be their protector. Perhaps we should award you the city immediately. What could this woman do to compare with your gift?" Poseidon laughed in agreement.

Meanwhile, Athena kept silent. She simply bent down and began to dig a hole in the earth. "Ha!" said Poseidon. "She digs a hole with the labor of her hands, while I was able to blast the earth apart. Is there any doubt who is more powerful?" But Athena again said nothing. She just continued to dig. Then she pulled a small bush out of a sack and planted it in the hole.

"That is your gift?" roared Poseidon. "A scruffy-looking little plant? How can that compare with my spring and with my power over the sea? Judges, you see for yourselves that I am the winner of this contest!"

Then Athena rose to her full height, though she was not nearly so tall as Poseidon, and looked her judges right in the eye. She spoke for the first time. "Honorable judges," she said, "this is no ordinary bush. It is an olive plant. When it grows into a fine tree, it will produce flavorful olives that will benefit all the people of the new city. They can use it as food for themselves. They can press the olives into oil to flavor their food and light their lamps when the day grows dark. They can travel across the sea and trade the olives and the oil for money or for the goods of other peoples. This plant will enable the people of the city to feed and support themselves for years and years to come. It will bring them gladness and joy." So saying, Athena stepped back to await the judges' decision.

The judges were truly surprised by Athena's gift. "This gift shows how very wise you are," they said. "Might on the seas is unimportant if the people are starving. So we award the new city to Athena. She will be a wise and helpful patron for the humans who will live there."

Athena called her new city Athens after herself, and the people remained her loyal and loving citizens. They built a marvelous temple called the Parthenon in her honor. It is one of the most famous buildings in the world, and we will look at pictures of it soon. When I show you those pictures, I want you to look closely at the statues the ancient Greek artists carved to decorate the temple. In the triangles formed by the roof, you can see statues of Athena and Poseidon having their contest. And all around the top of the building, artists carved a relief showing the procession the people of Athens had every four years to honor their goddess. Greek artists created statues of Athena and painted her picture on jugs and pottery. So let's enjoy some of the artwork of the ancient Greeks. It is among the most beautiful art ever created.

(You can use this story as an introduction to two lessons, one that has to do with painting and the other with architecture and sculpture.)

(Standards: Language Arts: Listening and Speaking 8.4; History 7.1-2);

LESSON 1: Greek Vase Painting

Viewing the Art

Point out to the children that since wall paintings have been destroyed, the only examples we have of Greek painting are what we have recovered from pottery and vases. Actually, many of the vessels we call "vases" are amphora, jugs the ancient Greeks used for carrying oil. Show several pottery paintings, being sure to include *The Banquet of Heracles with Athena* from the Andokides painter, *The Banquet of Heracles with Athena* from the Lysippides painter, and the beautiful painting of Athena herself by the Berlin painter (all three included in Charbonneaux et al. 1971). The *History of Greek Vases* provides wonderful reproductions of vases, as does the Drees book (1968, 63–87). *The Centaur's Smile* also has outstanding reproductions of vases (see references).

The children should note that some paintings are done in black on red backgrounds, while others are the reverse. Point out the advantages of painting the figures in red so that the black outlines show up more vividly and can be applied with paint. Talk about the different kinds and shapes of jars. Note the subjects of the pottery paintings: Greek gods and heroes, battles, animals. So much of what the ancient Greeks held dear is evident in these paintings—bathing, care of the body, physical prowess. Do the children have particular favorites? Can they tell a story from the paintings? Contrast the earlier forms done in black with the later ones, helping the children to see the increased movement and delicacy of the figures. If the children seem particularly interested, read some children's versions of the Greek myths and talk about the more well-known gods. How many of these gods can the children find in the pottery paintings?

(Standards: Art Connections 1.1-8; Visual Arts 4.8-11)

Journal Writing

What have the children learned about Greek paintings? They can contrast the style of the older paintings with that of the new, talk about their favorite paintings, or recall stories of the gods they particularly enjoy.

(Standards: Language Arts: Writing 1.7, 23, 33-37; Art Connections 1.3)

Art/Drama Activity: Vase-painting and Myth-playing

Materials

- Several copies of outlines of each of different kinds of Greek jugs (or blank paper for the children to draw their own shapes from copies you provide)
- Black and reddish-brown colored pencils
- Scissors

Have the children assume the role of ancient Greek painters and draw stories of the gods or scenes of Greek life on their jug shapes. Perhaps they would enjoy drawing their favorite parts of the Athena myth they heard at the beginning of the lesson. They will either have red figures on a black ground or the reverse. If their figures are black, they should not make them too dark so that they can draw the interior lines in red. The children may wish to draw decorative borders around the top and/or bottom of their jugs. Have art books available so that the class can view the work of the original Greek vase painters.

If your students are older or especially capable, they might want to make their own Grecian vases, as suggested in Wright's *Greeks* (see references).

(Standards: Visual Arts 1.1-4; 5)

Children love enacting Greek myths. I have been especially successful with stories of Athena, Perseus and Medusa, and Persephone. As with the Egyptian dramas, costuming is extremely simple: T-shirts and draped sheets. Enacting Greek myths is especially beneficial for children who might not wish to assume solo parts, since they can be part of a Greek chorus. The chorus sits off to the side and, speaking together, either warns or encourages the main characters or tells the audience what is happening. For example, in an enactment of Perseus and Medusa, when Perseus is about to slay Medusa, the chorus can chant, "Beware, Perseus. Do not look upon Medusa!" (See Marzollo 2006a.)

(Standards: Theater 1-3.1-2, 9-17)

LESSON 2: Greek Sculpture and Architecture

Viewing the Art

Architecture

Show the children pictures of the three Greek capitals (Doric, Ionic, Corinthian) and show samples of each in Greek buildings. Have the children ever seen copies of these three orders in buildings or homes in their neighborhood? In public buildings? Discuss this and other ideas we have copied from the Greeks. Talk about the construction of the Parthenon by Iktinos and Callicrates and show as many pictures as you can of this marvelous structure. (Connolly 2001 has a wonderful painting of the statue on page 31. Also see Curlee in the references.) Mention that the triangles formed in the corners of the building by the roof are called pediments and contain scenes in the life of Athena, while circling the top of the building are statues depicting the marvelous procession the people of Athens had every four years in honor of their goddess. If the children were to visit Greece now, they would not see these statues on the Parthenon. In the nineteenth century, Lord Elgin had them moved to England to protect them from damage, and they can now be seen in the British Museum. Show close-ups of these beautiful "Elgin Marbles." (Papaioannou's *The Art of Greece*—see references—has breathtaking, large views of some of these statues.) Do the children see figures they recognize, such as centaurs?

(Standards: Visual Arts 1.1-4; 5; History 7.36)

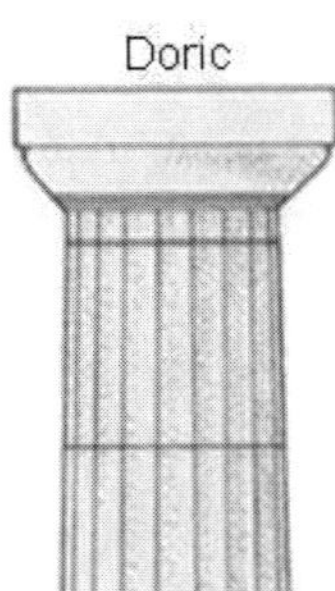

Three Orders of Greek Columns

Sculpture

Show the children early Greek statues of the mid-seventh century BC, known as kouroi, naked male youth possibly representing Apollo, and korai, their female counterparts. *Ancient Art from Cyprus* and *The Oxford History of Classical Art* (see references) provide excellent pictures. Note how rigid and Egyptian-like these statues are in contrast to the work of later periods. Do the children notice the mysterious smiles on the faces of these statues?

Later sculptors began to realize that the human body does not always stand at complete attention and that any action such as putting forth a foot affects the muscles and position of other parts of the body. They began to consider how clothing is draped on the body and the shape of the body beneath the clothing. Have the children take various stances. What is the position of their hips when they take a step? What about the muscles in their arms when they reach back to throw something? How does their clothing move when they walk across the room?

Now look for these things in later Greek sculpture. We have no actual statues from this classical period, but there are Roman copies available for viewing. Show Myron's *Discus Thrower* and the revolutionary leaning ("hip-shot") stance in Praxiteles' *Hermes Holding the Child Dionysos* and his *Aphrodite.* Note the Greek emphasis on beauty in the perfect features, like the "Greek nose," which begins from the forehead and is finely shaped. Talk about how Greek sculptors, in their desire to portray perfection, avoided showing flaws like wrinkles or warts or crooked noses. View the work of Phidias, especially his colossal statue of Athena, created for placement in her special temple, the Parthenon.

(Standards: Visual Arts 1.1-4; 5; History 7.36; Thinking and Reasoning 3.3)

Journal Writing

What are some of the most important things the children have learned about Greek sculpture and architecture? Which is their favorite statue? Why?

(Standards: Language Arts: Writing 1.7, 23, 33-37; Art Connections 1.3)

Art/Drama Activity: Athena's Feast Day

Have the children pretend to be ancient Athenians ready to celebrate a feast in honor of their goddess, Athena. They are making preparations for their great procession, which takes place every four years. What gifts will they bring to her temple? Perhaps they will write poems in her honor and recite them before her statue. Create music for the occasion. The book *A Greek Temple* (see references) would be very useful in planning this procession.

(Standards: Theater 1-3.1-2, 9-17; Music 2-3.2, 4; History 7.36)

Curriculum Connections

Social Studies

- Study the history of ancient Greece and how people lived and worked in ancient times. Compare ancient Greece to Greece today. Kotapish's *Daily Life in Ancient and Modern Athens* (see references) would be especially helpful for this study.
- Study the climate and geography of the Mediterranean region. What countries make up this region? What effect does the climate have on the way people live, the crops they produce, etc.?
- Go to http://www.sikyon.com/Athens/Coins/coins_eg01.html and look at some ancient Greek coins.
- Study Greek production of olives and olive oil. How are olives grown? How is olive oil made? How do we use these products today? A helpful site to visit is http://www.zingermans.com/Article.pasp?ArticleID=article27.
- The ancient Greeks developed the first democracy. What aspects of our government are modeled on the Greek system?

(Standards: Geography 1-2.5, 30; History 7.15; World History 8.34; Civics 8.1, 28)

Science

- Study the life and achievements of Thales, the first scientist, and Hippocrates, Father of Medicine. What other Greek scientists can the students discover?
- Research and discuss what the early Greeks knew about astronomy.

(Standards: History 7.45; Mathematics 9; Grades K-4 History: 8.45)

Physical Fitness

- Research the first Olympics in Greece in 776 BC. See *You Wouldn't Want to Be a Greek Athlete!* (references). In connection with a study of the Olympics, read *The First Olympic Games* (see references), which recalls the chariot race that ushered in the games that would be held every four years in Greece. The children will also enjoy *The First Marathon: The Legend of Pheidippides* by Reynolds (see references). The site http://www.perseus.tufts.edu/Olympics/ has extensive information on the Greek Olympics and a comparison of the ancient games with today's Olympic events.
- Hold your own Olympic games or a physical fitness class in honor of the ancient Greeks. Discuss ways to keep our bodies strong and healthy.

  (Standards: Physical Education 1-5.4. 11, 21, 23,26, 28-29, 36)

Mathematics

- Talk about everyday uses of some of Euclid's geometric principles, such as angles.
- Construct some geometric shapes.
- Go to http://www.math.wichita.edu/history/topics/num-sys.html#greek to practice making Greek numerals.

  (Standards: Mathematics 5, 9.4, 29, 43, 49)

Writing

- Practice making the letters of the Greek alphabet. A copy of the alphabet is available in DuBois's *Greece* (see references). The children could also have fun writing a note in Greek. Go to http://www.teachingideas.co.uk/history/files/ccgreeks.pdf to find out how.

  (Standards: K-4 History 7.30)

Literature

- Read biographies of famous Greeks. *The Librarian Who Measured the Earth* by Lasky is especially accessible for young readers.
- The Greeks loved plays. Use Chrisp's book (see references) to study what theater was like in ancient Greece.
- Read some Greek myths. The references below provide several book suggestions.

- Older children will thoroughly enjoy performing some of the wonderful poems in *Ancient Voices* (see references). The personalities and quirks of the ancient Greek gods shine through these poems.

  (Standards: Language Arts: Reading 6.13, 23, 28)

References

Adult Books

Belozerskaya, Marina, and Kenneth Lapatin. *Ancient Greece: Art, Architecture, and History.* Los Angeles, CA: Getty Trust Publications, 2004. ISBN 0892366958.

This fine book has over 300 illustrations and includes Greek sculptures and vase paintings. It is a good resource for viewing.

Boardman, John. *The History of Greek Vases.* New York: Thames & Hudson, 2001. ISBN 0500237808.

This book provides wonderful reproductions for viewing Greek vases.

Boardman, John, ed. *The Oxford Illustrated History of Classical Art.* New York: Oxford University Press, 2001. ISBN 0192854437.

Written by different experts, each chapter discusses a different period of ancient Greek and Roman art.

———. *The Parthenon and Its Sculptures.* Austin: University of Texas Press, 1985. ISBN 0292764987.

The pictures in this book are well worth hunting down. They provide excellent views of the Parthenon and close-ups of its sculptures.

Charbonneaux, Jean, R. Martin, and F. Villard. *Archaic Greek Art.* Translated by James Emmous and Robert Allen. New York: George Braziller, 1971. o.p. ISBN 0807605875.

Although it is out of print, try to obtain this book from a library for its marvelous discussion and pictures of ancient Greek art from 620 to 480 BC.

———. *Hellenistic Art.* Translated by Peter Green. New York: George Braziller, 1973. o.p. ISBN 0807606669.

The authors discuss ancient Greek art after Alexander the Great (330–50 BC), and provide wonderful pictures for viewing.

Drees, Ludwig. *Olympia: Gods, Artists, and Athletes.* London: Pall Mall, 1968. ISBN 0269670157.

This book provides marvelous reproductions of Greek vases and close-up views of friezes.

Karageorghis, Vassos. *Ancient Art from Cyprus.* New York: Harry N. Abrams, 2000. ISBN 0-87099-944-3.

This book provides large pictures for group viewing.

Liberman, Alexander. *Greece, Gods and Art.* New York: Viking, 1968. o.p. ISBN 0002112949.

This discussion of Greek religious beliefs and their influence on art provides stunning close-up photographs.

Padgett, J. Michael, William A. P. Childs, and Despoina Tsiafakis. *The Centaur's Smile.* New Haven, CT: Yale University Press, 2004. ISBN 0-300-10163-5.

With large pictures of Greek vases, this is an extremely valuable book for group viewing.

Papaioannou, Kostas. *The Art of Greece.* Translated by I. M. Paris. New York: Harry N. Abrams, 1972. o.p. ISBN 0-8109-0634-1.

Papaioannou covers all the periods of ancient Greek art and includes very large pictures.

Children's Books

Ackroyd, Peter. *Ancient Greece.* New York: DK Children, 2005. ISBN 075661368X.

Although the content is meant for older readers, this excellent book is valuable background reading for teachers, and the pictures are well worth sharing.

Altman, Susan, and Susan Lechner. *Ancient Greece.* (Modern Rhymes about Ancient Times). Illustrated by Deborah Schilling. CT: Children's Press, 2002. ISBN 0516273736.

Learn about the ancient Greeks through these wonderful rhymes.

Chrisp, Peter. *A Greek Theater.* Illustrated by Adam Hook. Portsmouth, NH: Raintree/Heinemann, 2000. ISBN 0739823795.

Readers can look inside an ancient Greek theater and see some of the props used.

Connolly, Peter. *Ancient Greece.* New York: Oxford University Press, 2001. ISBN 0-19-910810-2.

This very informative book provides information on ancient Greek clothing (very useful for preparing plays), houses, and much more. The building of the Parthenon is described in detail.

Craft, M. Charlotte. *Cupid and Psyche.* Illustrated by K. Y. Craft. New York: Morrow Junior Books, 1996. ISBN 0688131638.

This is a beautiful picture-book retelling of the Greek myth about the god Cupid who, pierced by his own arrow, falls in love with the beautiful mortal, Psyche.

Curlee, Lynn. *The Parthenon.* New York: Atheneum, 2004. ISBN 0689844905.

Curlee provides thorough coverage of the Parthenon, enriched by acrylic paintings. This is a great source for group viewing of the frieze around the Parthenon and the statue of Athena.

Demi. *King Midas: The Golden Touch.* New York: Margaret McElderry, 2002. ISBN 0689832974.

The familiar story of King Midas is accompanied here by spectacular illustrations.

DuBois, Jill. *Greece.* 2d ed. New York: Benchmark, 2003. ISBN 0761414991.

The author presents many aspects of Greek life, including religion, food, leisure activities, and festivals.

Fleischman, Paul. *Dateline Troy.* Cambridge, MA: Candlewick Press, 1996. Reissue, 2006. ISBN 1564024695.

Fleischman juxtaposes the legend of Troy with twentieth-century news stories. A tour de force!

Ford, Michael, and David Salariva. *You Wouldn't Want to Be a Greek Athlete!: Races You'd Rather Not Run.* Illustrated by David Antran. New York: Franklin Watts, 2004. ISBN 0531163946.

With humorous text and illustrations, the authors provide a good deal of information about athletic training and life in ancient Greece.

Frank, Nicole, and Yeoh Hong Nam. *Welcome to Greece.* Milwaukee, WI: Gareth Stevens Publishing, 2000. ISBN 0-8368-2509-8.

This is a less complex look at Greece for younger children.

Ganeri, Anita. *Athletes and Actors and Other Jobs for Ancient Greeks.* New York: Peter Bedrik, 2001. ISBN 0872266648.

Readers learn about ancient Greece through the eyes of various segments of society.

Hart, Avery, and Paul Mantell. *Ancient Greece!: 40 Hands-On Activities to Experience This Wondrous Age.* Illustrated by Michael Kline. Minneapolis, MN: Sagebrush, 1999. ISBN 0613163184.

The authors suggest engaging activities and projects that are related to ancient Greek life and art. There is even a Greek rap number!

Heinrichs, Ann. *Greece: Enchantment of the World.* New York: Scholastic/Children's Press, 2002. ISBN 0-516-22271-6.

Heinrichs provides information about both ancient and modern Greece.

Hodge, Susie. *Art in History: Ancient Greek Art.* Portsmouth, NH: Heinemann, 1998. ISBN 0431056064.

Hodge presents a fine overview for children.

Hovey, Kate. *Ancient Voices.* New York: Simon & Schuster, 2004. ISBN 0-689-83342-3.

Ancient Greek gods speak through the poems in this book.

Kotapish, Dawn. *Daily Life in Ancient and Modern Athens.* Illustrated by Bob Moulder. Minneapolis, MN: Lerner Publishing Group/Runestone, 2001. ISBN 0822532166.

Readers watch Athens grow from a village in ancient times to the present capital of Greece.

Langley, Andrew. *Athens.* Milwaukee, WI: World Almanac Library, 2004. ISBN 0836850211.

Readers learn about the history of Athens as well as about life in Athens today.

Lasky, Kathryn. *The Librarian Who Measured the Earth.* Illustrated by Kevin Hawkes. Boston: Little, Brown, 1994. ISBN 0316515264.

Lasky describes how Eratosthenes, a Greek astronomer, measured the circumference of the earth.

Macdonald, Fiona. *A Greek Temple.* Illustrated by Mark Bergin. New York: Peter Bedrick Books, 1992. ISBN 0872263614.

Macdonald describes the design and construction of the Parthenon and the ancient Greek feasts surrounding the worship of the goddess Athena. There are wonderful cut-away views.

———. *Inside Ancient Athens.* New York: Enchanted Lion Books, 2005. ISBN 1-59270-044-6.

A fine writer provides information about life in ancient Greece.

Marzollo, Jean. *Let's Go, Pegasus!* Boston: Little, Brown, 2006a. ISBN 0316741361.

This story of Pegasus, who was formed by Perseus after he killed Medusa, is very simply told for young children. An owl takes on the role of the Greek chorus and there are directions for turning the story into a play.

———. *Pandora's Box.* Boston: Little Brown, 2006b. ISBN 0-316-74133-7.

When Pandora opens a box against Zeus's orders, she unleashes a flurry of trouble bugs. This fine picture book is suitable for young readers.

Mayer, Marianna. *Pegasus.* Illustrated by K. Y. Craft. New York: William Morrow, 1998. ISBN 0-688-13382-7.

This is a picture-book version of the story of Pegasus.

McCaughrean, G., reteller. *Greek Myths.* Illustrated by Emma Chichester Clark. New York: Orchard Books, 1992. ISBN 1852133732.

These are delightful retellings of sixteen well-known Greek myths, accompanied by humorous illustrations.

Merrill, Yvonne Y., and Mary Simpson. *Hands-On Ancient People, Volume 2: Art Activities About Minoans, Mycenaeans, Trojans, Ancient Greeks, Etruscans, and Romans.* Illustrated by Mary Simpson. Salt Lake City, UT: Kits Publishing, 2002. ISBN 0964317796.

This book has a beautiful, full-page, color illustration for each craft suggested. The object to be made is discussed in the context of the historical period, and clear instructions are given.

Osborne, Mary Pope. *Favorite Green Myths.* Illustrated by Troy Howell. New York: Scholastic, 1989. ISBN 0-590-41338-4.

This wonderful book contains twenty-five Greek myths.

———. *Tales from the Odyssey: The One-Eyed Monster*. Illustrated by Troy Howell. New York: Hyperion, 2002. ISBN 0786807709.

This is the story of Odysseus's encounter with the Cyclops. This author has written several other books of tales from the Odyssey.

Pearson, Ann. *Ancient Greece*. New York: DK Children, 2004. ISBN 0756606497.

Beautiful illustrations enhance this presentation of ancient Greek life.

Powell, Anton, and Sean Sheehan. *Ancient Greece*. 2d ed. (Cultural Atlas for Young People). New York: Facts on File, 2003. ISBN 0816051461.

Maps, charts, illustrations, and text trace the history and culture of ancient Greece.

Reynolds, Susan. *The First Marathon: The Legend of Pheidippides*. Illustrated by Daniel Minter. New York: Albert Whitman, 2006. ISBN 0807508675.

Reynolds tells the story of Pheidippides, who ran 140 miles round trip to get help for the Greeks, who were fighting the Persians on the plain of Marathon, and who even helped fight the battle before dying of exhaustion. A section for older readers provides research information, and there are helpful maps as well. The fine illustrations in this picture book add to the enjoyment.

Richards, Jean. *The First Olympic Games: A Gruesome Greek Myth with a Happy Ending*. Illustrated by Kat Thacker. Brookfield, CT: Millbrook Press, 2000. ISBN 0-7613-1311-7.

In this myth, Pelops wins a chariot race against the king and thus receives the king's daughter in marriage.

Roberts, Jennifer T., and Tracy Barrett. *The Ancient Greek World*. New York: Oxford University Press, 2004. ISBN 0-19-515696-X.

The authors discuss all aspects of life in ancient Greece.

Rockwell, Anne. *The One-Eyed Giant and Other Monsters from the Greek Myths*. New York: Greenwillow, 1996. ISBN 0688138101.

These ten simple retellings of Greek myths featuring fabulous monsters would make an excellent read-aloud, even for young children. There are delightful illustrations, a pronunciation guide, and source notes.

Ross, Stewart. *Tales of the Dead: Ancient Greece*. Illustrated by Richard Bonson. New York: DK Children, 2004. ISBN 0756605547.

This very informative book contains directions for creating a Parthenon.

Shuter, Jane. *Life in a Greek Temple*. Chicago: Heinemann Library, 2005. ISBN 1403464421.

Readers discover how the ancient Greeks worshipped their gods and goddesses.

———. *Life in Ancient Athens*. Chicago: Heinemann Library, 2005. ISBN 140346443X.

This book explains what life was like in various ancient Greek city states.

Stein, Conrad. *Athens*. Chicago: Children's Press, 1997. ISBN 0516261428.

This book provides close-up views of vases, statues, the Parthenon, and more.

Usher, M. D. *Wise Guy: The Life and Philosophy of Socrates.* Illustrated by William Bramhall. New York: Farrar, Straus & Giroux, 2005. ISBN 0-374-31249-4.

This fun-filled biography is based entirely on ancient sources that are listed in endnotes (with the exception of Socrates's youth, about which almost nothing is known). It can be read on two levels: there is brief text for young children and more detailed information about ancient Greece in text boxes for older children. Children of any age will love the cartoon illustrations.

Williams, Marcia. *Greek Myths for Young Children.* Cambridge, MA: Candlewick Press, 1995. o.p. ISBN 1564024407

How unfortunate that the humorous retellings of eight myths in this oversized book with illustrations resembling comic strips is out of print, since children will love them. Try to obtain a copy if you can.

Wright, Rachel. *Greeks: Facts, Things to Make, Activities.* New York: Franklin Watts, 1992. o.p. ISBN 0531142469.

Craft activities revolving around the lives and beliefs of the ancient Greeks are suggested. There is a glossary and a list of some museums containing Greek art.

Audiovisual Materials

Ancient Civilizations: Athens and Ancient Greece. DVD. Questar Video, 2002. ISBN 1568557647.

This film shows the daily life and customs of ancient Greece as well as twenty-five of the most significant buildings. It would make an excellent source for group viewing.

Ancient Civilizations for Children: Ancient Greece. DVD. Library Video Company, 1998. K6725.

This award-winning film presents life in ancient Greece, including artwork, mythology, government, and more. It would make an extremely valuable addition to this study. The child apprentice detective unearthing information in the film will attract young children.

Ancient Greece. DVD. Library Video Company, 1998. V7155.

This film helps children learn about the lives of the ancient Greeks by taking them to the Acropolis and the Parthenon and including Greek myths.

D'Aulaires Book of Greek Myths. CD. The Metropolitan Museum of Art, 2000. M3978.

The myths contained in this classic book are read by famous stars such as Paul Newman and Sidney Poitier.

The Greek Miracle. 8 study prints, 20 slides, and a booklet. The National Gallery of Art, n.d. TP5.

The many achievements of classical Greece are revealed in this film.

The Measure of All Things. Video. The National Gallery of Art, n.d. VC154.

This short film traces the development of architecture, vase painting, and sculpture in the fifth century BC. An added bonus is the inclusion of major archaeological sites.

Seven Wonders of Ancient Greece. DVD. Discovery Channel, n.d. #710954.

See the statue of Zeus, the Theater at Epidaurus, the Parthenon, and more in this great film.

Web Sites

The Acropolis Museum. http://www.culture.gr/2/21/211/21101m/e211am01.html (accessed February 3, 2006).

By clicking on the images, students will see large-size views of many of the works in the Acropolis Museum, one of the most important museums in the world.

Ancient Greece. http://www.bbc.co.uk/schools/ancientgreece/findout.shtml (accessed February 3, 2006).

By clicking on the many links, students can learn about all aspects of ancient Greek life.

Ancient Greece. http://witcombe.sbc.edu/ARTHgreece.html#Greek (accessed March 10, 2006).

This site has many links, including links to museums and artworks.

The Ancient Greeks. http://www.arwhead.com/Greeks/index.html#Athenians (accessed February 3, 2006).

This site, accompanied by music, provides a good deal of information about the ancient Greeks. The links are especially useful.

Classical Greek Architecture. http://harpy.uccs.edu/greek/classgrkarch.htm (accessed February 3, 2006).

This site provides wonderful views of the buildings of the Acropolis.

Greek Architecture. http://www.crystalinks.com/greekarchitecture.html (accessed February 3, 2006).

Learn about the different Greek columns from this site.

The Greeks: Crucible of Civilization. http://www.pbs.org/empires/thegreeks/ (accessed February 6, 2006).

See an animated view of the Parthenon and more at this site.

Meet the Greeks. http://ancienthistory.mrdonn.org/Greeklife.html (accessed February 3, 2006).

Very young children will enjoy this look at ancient Greek life. They will learn about toys, hairstyles, Greek houses, and much more.

4 Ancient Roman Art

"Go, proclaim to the Romans it is heaven's will that my Rome shall be the capital of the world."

—ROMULUS, legendary founder of Rome, as quoted in *Imperial Rome* by Moses Hadas

Background Information

Rome was founded in 753 BC, when the various settlements of peoples living in the hill country of Italy united to form a city. Built on seven hills, Rome was originally ruled by a succession of Etruscan kings. By 509 BC, the people, unhappy with the king's absolute power, had established a republic ruled by consuls elected by the people of two political parties: the Patricians, representing the rich, and the Plebians, representing the common folk.

This Republican Age, which lasted until Octavian defeated Mark Antony around 27 BC, was a time of great expansion under the mighty Roman army, which knew no equal. After three wars with the Phoenicians in Carthage, North Africa, fought over many years, Rome finally destroyed that city in 146 BC. It was from Carthage that Hannibal crossed the Alps with thousands of men and some elephants to defeat Rome, but he received no help from the surrounding cities, which were prospering under Roman rule, and was himself vanquished. Roman armies also conquered Gaul (now France), Macedonia, Greece, and various provinces in Asia Minor.

The Romans learned from and enriched the art and ideas of the peoples they conquered. Fascinated by Greek sculpture, Roman artists made hundreds of copies of these works. But while the Greeks created generalized or idealized portraits in stone, Roman sculptors of this period were able to capture the personalities of their subjects. Often portraits of venerated ancestors, these busts with their wrinkles and crooked noses seemed almost to speak! Romans experimented with Greek architecture as well, using the Greek orders to create temples to their gods, and they began working with a new material called concrete. Wall paintings and mosaics, many of which were recovered in the excavations of Pompeii and

Herculaneum, cities buried in volcanic ash in AD 79, adorned the homes of the wealthy and reveal a fine knowledge of anatomy and an attempt to convey depth on a two-dimensional surface. Artists painted pictures of the gods, battles, the occupants of the house, still lifes, and, for the first time, landscapes.

The Republic finally dissolved, and the age of the Roman Empire began with the assassination of Julius Caesar and the rise to power of Octavian (called Augustus) in 27 BC. For the next 500 years, Rome was ruled by emperors. "From this point on, Roman art and architecture were to be intimately bound up with propaganda for the state as guided by the imperial family" (Ramage and Ramage 2004). Augustus's reign ushered in a Golden Age similar to that of Pericles in Greece, and he initiated an ambitious building program. The emperors who followed Augustus continued to use the arts to proclaim their own accomplishments and to win the support of the people. The Romans' skill with concrete and their perfection of the use of the arch enabled them to erect massive arenas for the sports and games the populace loved so well; public buildings in the heart of the city, known as the Forum; temples to the gods; and aqueducts, theaters, and bath houses. Roman architects developed the basilica, a rectangular, covered building of many uses. To rid the city of the spectacle of the emperor Nero's "House of Gold" in the midst of Rome's poor housing, his successor, Vespasian, built the Colosseum on its site. Infamous for the bloody gladiator fights and animal killings that took place there, the Colosseum even today is an imposing edifice in the city of Rome.

The emperor Hadrian built the Pantheon, a beautiful temple perfectly preserved to this day, to honor all the Roman gods. A round building surmounted by a dome, the Pantheon's height equals its diameter. The Romans—unlike the Greeks, whose temples were meant to be seen only from the outside—paid great attention to interiors, and the interior of the Pantheon with its golden dome is magnificent.

Roman reliefs on triumphal arches, and especially the column of the emperor Trajan, under whom Rome achieved her greatest expansion, told the stories of their namesakes' victories. Many emperors ruled Rome, some of them well and for long periods of time, and some of them badly or for only six months. In AD 330 Constantine transferred his palace to Constantinople, in what is now Turkey, and after the reign of Emperor Theodosius I the empire was ruled by two separate emperors, one in Rome and the other in Constantinople. With its power divided and its empire far flung, Rome could no longer govern or defend itself and eventually fell victim to the attacks of barbarians from Russia and Hungary.

The Roman Empire ceased to exist in AD 476, but its influence continues to our own day. Our alphabet is Roman, and over 60 percent of our words come from Latin, the language spoken by the ancient Romans. We use the calendar devised by Julius Caesar. Roman numerals play an important part in our documentation. Our system of law, trial by jury, and republican form of government come from Roman traditions. Ancient Rome has given us such wonderful writers as Virgil, Horace, and Cicero. We look to Rome for its marvelous feats of engineering, its development of the arch, its massive structures made possible by the use of concrete. Truly, "All roads lead to Rome!"

(Standards: World History 7-8.10; Art Connections 1.1-8; Geography 2, 14.12, 23-25)

The Story

It was August 24 in the year AD 79 in the Roman city of Pompeii in Italy. (Show it on a map.) And it was hot—very hot. Ten-year-old Marcus was not anxious to get out of his bed, and the slave who came to his door with water for washing had to coax the sleepyhead to start moving. Father would be offering an early morning sacrifice in just a few minutes, and Marcus had to be ready. The boy stretched, splashed some water on his face, pulled a fresh tunic over his head, and left his bedroom. He went out into the atrium, a courtyard inside his home where there was a hole in the roof so light and air could come in. A small pool in the center captured the rainwater. Marcus took a few deep breaths of the early morning air and looked fondly at several portrait statues of his ancestors placed around the room. Then he went to join his parents and older sister before the shrine of the household gods.

"Bless this house. Protect all its people and let no harm come to anyone this day," prayed Marcus's father as he lit the incense before the shrine. After the short service, Marcus and his father left the house and headed for the Forum, the business center of the busy city. There Marcus was planning to watch the trials in the basilica and speak on behalf of a man accused of stealing. The more practice he got speaking in public, the more fit he would be to serve in the government when he grew to be a man. On the way, they passed some merchants opening their shops. Some were selling wine. Others were selling meat. The bakers had already prepared their dough, and the delicious smell of bread baking in the huge round ovens reached Marcus's nostrils. It made him hungry, and he looked forward to having a meal later in the day and a refreshing bath at the public bath house.

Just as they were coming within sight of the Forum, the earth began to shake and they heard a tremendous roar. Marcus screamed in terror. The sky darkened and black ash began to fall everywhere. Marcus put his hand over his face to try to protect himself from the ash and fumes all around him, while his father picked him up and started racing back to the house. "We have to get your mother and sister and the servants out," he cried. Hundreds of people all around them were running, too. Bakers left their bread in their ovens and fled into the streets. Wool dyers left their cloth in the dying vats. Shopkeepers left their food on the shelves and didn't even bother to lock up. Everyone was looking for a safe place to escape the lava and ash spouting from the nearby volcano, Mt. Vesuvius.

When Marcus and his father finally fought through the crowd and reached their home, they found everyone in the household huddled in the cellar. "You'll be buried alive down there! Come, get the horses and wagons quickly!" cried Marcus's father. The servants ran to do his bidding, and in a few minutes everyone had climbed into wagons and was heading out of town. They passed neighbors on foot clutching the few valuables they could lay their hands on. Ash rained down so hard that it seemed black as night even though it was still early in the morning. The ash became so thick and heavy that it caved in roofs and piled deeper and deeper in the streets. It became harder and harder for the horses to pull the wagons through it. But Marcus and his family were among the lucky ones. They had enough money to have wagons and horses, so they were able to get out of Pompeii in time. They drove until they had gone far enough to escape the falling ash and lava. As soon as they reached safety, Marcus and his family gave thanks to the gods for their protection.

But thousands of people weren't so lucky. Some were greedy and stayed behind too long, trying to collect jewelry and other valuable things to take with them. Others couldn't run fast enough and were buried in the ash. Others choked to death on the poisonous fumes seeping out of the earth. Still others made the mistake of seeking shelter in their cellars and were buried there.

Marcus and his family never did go back to Pompeii to live. They never saw their house or the buildings and temples they loved again. The entire city and even a city nearby called Herculaneum were buried by the ash from the volcano. And believe it or not, they stayed buried for more than 1,500 years! Then, one day in 1594, a man named Count Muzzio Tuttavilla wanted to get water from the river to water his land. When he began to dig a tunnel, he cut right through the hidden city of Pompeii. It wasn't until 200 years later that archaeologists began to dig carefully in the area and to uncover the lost city. What they found was simply amazing. The ash and lava had preserved many things just as they were. The archaeologists actually found bread still in the ovens. In the cellars they found the skeletons of people who had tried to escape. They found jewelry and marvelous artworks—wall paintings and mosaics in the homes of the rich, the Forum where Marcus and his father were heading on that terrible morning, temples, shops, public bath houses, theaters.

All the things the scientists found in Pompeii help us to know how the ancient Romans lived 2,000 years ago! The Romans had builders, architects, sculptors, painters, and makers of mosaics. They gave us ideas about making laws and deciding whether people are guilty or innocent of committing crimes. They showed us how to use concrete and a very special architectural form called an arch for large buildings. They even gave us our calendar and our alphabet! We're going to look at some pictures of ancient Roman artwork and buildings now.

Some of the art I'm going to show you was found in the buried city of Pompeii, and you can see the original work in the uncovered city yourself if you travel to Italy some day.

(Standards: Geography 15.19, 25; Language Arts: Listening and Speaking 8)

LESSON 1: Roman Engineering and Sculpture

Viewing the Art

Begin by mentioning that the Romans copied many artistic ideas from the Greeks, whose country they conquered with their mighty army. But the Romans had some ideas of their own as well. Discuss the Romans' engineering genius, emphasizing their use of concrete and their development of the arch, which enabled them to build structures several stories high. Ask the children to hold their arms over their heads in the shape of a Roman arch so that they can experience its shape with their bodies. Using blocks, construct a simple arch. Then press down on it. The arch can withstand a great deal of weight and pressure, but push it sideways, and the arch tumbles over. The Romans solved this problem by covering their structures with a strong material called concrete and then putting a layer of stone or marble over them to make them look beautiful.

Show several pictures of structures that make use of the arch, especially the aqueduct Pont du Gard in Provence, and explain the use of the aqueduct and what an incredible feat it was to span such vast distances. Show the Colosseum (wonderful pictures of the Colosseum can be found in Connolly's *The Ancient City,* pages 190–210—see references). Mann's *The Roman Colosseum* (see References) also provides drawings that make the construction and the activities that were engaged in in the Colosseum come to life. (Some fun reading along with this viewing would be *You Wouldn't Want to Be a Roman Gladiator*—see references.) Be sure to view triumphal arches, and a Roman theater as well. Discuss the purpose of the Colosseum. What similar structures do we have today (baseball and football stadiums)? Do the children have any arches in their own homes (over doorways, for example), or have they seen arches in churches or other public buildings? Show Roman temples and talk about the similarity of Roman and Greek gods. What ideas did the Romans copy from the Greeks in building their temples? Show the Pantheon and talk about its dimensions and its interior—a point of departure from the Greeks. Talk about the marvel of creating a dome, which is really a series of arches, that could enclose such a large space and how church builders in years to come would learn how to do this by studying Roman art. Depending on the children's interest, show pictures of Roman baths and talk about the buildings in the Roman Forum.

Romans honored their ancestors by having busts of them made for display in their homes. Show the children some Roman busts. (See Ramage's *Roman Art* in the references.) How do they differ from Greek statues? (They are not perfect—they contain crooked noses, wrinkles, etc.) The Romans told their heroes' stories in relief sculptures. Show the class pictures of the magnificent Column of Trajan (Ramage's book has excellent detail prints), on which Roman sculptors carved the tale of their emperor's deeds.

(Standards: Art Connections 1.1-8; Language Arts: Viewing 9; Visual Arts 4.5-11)

Journal Writing

What are some differences between Greek and Roman sculpture and architecture? Some similarities? Do the children prefer the more realistic Roman busts to the idealistic statues of the Greeks? Why or why not? If they were having their own portraits done, which would they prefer? In what ways have the children seen arches used even today?

(Standards: Language Arts: Writing 1.7, 23, 33-37; Art Connections 1.3; Thinking and Reasoning 3.3)

January 9, 1991
I think it's great
to that the used the
arches. at home I
have a romen puzzle
it is inside a roman's
house. I have a roman
and greek book two.
But I'm wondering
why did they attack
all those contwes.
I think it must
have been wonderfull.
In ancit rome,
I also think it
still looks wonderfull.

Art/Drama Activity: Trajan's Column

Materials

- Three or four sheets of poster board rolled and taped to form a column (wider at bottom, narrower at top)
- Strips of paper about six inches high and long enough to go around the column (these will be of different lengths, as the column decreases in width)
- Pencils

Divide the children into groups and have them create a column similar to Trajan's that tells the story of their class, or their school, or their town. Discuss the different things they would like their column to say. For example, if it is to represent their class, some ideas might be depicting students doing various academic tasks such as reading or working on a science experiment, taking care of a class pet, planting a garden, playing during recess and/or sports, singing or playing instruments, doing artwork, etc. Give each group a strip of paper and have the children work together to create scenes around one of the topics agreed upon. When the groups have finished their work, tape the various strips around the column and display it in the room.

(Standards: Visual Arts 1, 4-5.1-11; Working with Others 1-5.1-10)

LESSON 2: Roman Wall Painting and Mosaics

Viewing the Art

We know a great deal about Roman painting and mosaics because of the art found in a wonderful state of preservation in Pompeii and Herculaneum. Many of the rich commissioned artists to cover their walls with paintings. Often their floors were covered with beautiful mosaics. Public buildings such as the baths also contained such artwork. Show the children examples of both (see especially Panetta 2004 and Wilkinson 2004). Peter Connolly's *Pompeii* (see references) re-creates the ancient city beautifully. Be sure to include artwork from the House of the Fawn, the Villa of the Mysteries, and the House of the Vettii, all in Pompeii. What colors are most often used by the Roman artists? Can the children describe how mosaics are made? What are the subjects of the paintings and mosaics? *Pompeii Lost and Found* (see references) would be especially helpful during this viewing session.

(Standards: Art Connections 1.1-8; Language Arts: Viewing 9; Visual Arts 4.5-11)

Journal Writing

What have the children learned about Roman painting and mosaics? Have they seen mosaics in use today? If so, where? What are some things they notice about Roman wall paintings? How do the Roman paintings compare to the Greek pottery paintings?

(Standards: Language Arts: Writing 1.7, 23, 33-37; Art Connections 1.3)

Art/Drama Activity: Mosaics

Materials

- Large sheets of white paper
- Package of colored construction paper cut up beforehand into hundreds of small shapes
- Paste or glue

Have the children pretend they are Roman artists commissioned by a rich person to make a mosaic for a diningroom floor. They must submit copies of their pictures or designs for approval. Give each child a large piece of white paper, a pile of colored shapes, and a dollop of glue or paste on a piece of scrap paper. Have them work individually to create a mosaic. Make sure they understand that there should be a tiny white space between the pieces of colored paper and that they should use only the merest speck of glue or it will ooze out all over their paper. It helps to have a sample to show the children before they begin. (See *Creating with Mosaics* in the references below for more ideas about mosaic projects.)

(Standards: Visual Arts 1-5.1-11)

Curriculum Connections

The books *Ancient Rome: Projects and Activities That Bring the Past to Life* and *The Crafts and Culture of the Romans* (see references) contain many projects and activities that will help children learn more about ancient Romans. Children can make wax tablets, build a temple, or create jewelry for their Roman togas. There are even directions for making the togas themselves.

Social Studies

- Study the history and customs of ancient Rome. Several books in the children's book references will be useful for this study. See especially *Rome in Spectacular Cross-Section, The Best Book of Ancient Rome, The Ancient Roman World, Your Travel Guide to Ancient Rome,* and Hinds's books for excellent information.

- Find out about the foods and recipes of ancient Romans. Go to http://www.pbs.org/wgbh/nova/lostempires/roman/recipes.html for some recipes (also see *Roman Cookery* in the references).
- Using a map, find the areas of the world conquered by the Romans. What are these areas called today? Older students might like to connect this with a study of the Roman army, the building of forts, etc. (See Johnson 2001 and Blacklock 2004 for wonderful books on the subject.)
- Study agriculture and farm implements in ancient Rome. If you have studied Egypt with the children, compare Roman and Egyptian farming methods. Harris's *Science in Ancient Rome* (see references) will be helpful in this study.

(Standards: Geography: 1.29–30; Grades K–4 History 1.15; World History 7)

Government

- Older students may enjoy studying how government in ancient Rome worked. A very helpful book for this study is Lassieur's *The Ancient Romans* (see references), which devotes several chapters to the subject and is very interesting reading.

(Standards: Grades K–4 History 4; Civics 1.28)

Science

- Who created the Roman calendar? What does it have to do with the calendar we use today? (See Maestro 1999 and Harris 1998.) Talk about the gods after whom each month was named and how the names of the months of our year are taken from the Roman calendar.
- What was the practice of medicine like in ancient Rome? See Harris (1998) for a picture of some medical instruments as well as names of famous physicians.
- Study Roman engineering feats. What made Roman builders so unique? What do builders today copy from the ancient Romans? (See Nardo's *Roman Amphitheaters* in references.) The Romans built aqueducts, marvels of engineering that carried water from the hills of Rome into the city. Without these aqueducts, the pleasures the Romans enjoyed would have been impossible. Roman engineers also built aqueducts in the countries they conquered. Many are still in use today! Students will have an opportunity to read a manual on how to construct an aqueduct and then assume the role of engineers to actually build one by going to http://www.pbs.org/wgbh/nova/lostempires/roman/aqueductjava.html. To see how a Roman road was built, go to http://www.teachingideas.co.uk/history/romanrd.htm.

(Standards: Grades K–4 History 8.28)

Roman Aqueduct, Spain

Mathematics

- Study Roman numerals. An excellent Web site to visit for this purpose is http://mathforum.org/dr.math/faq/faq.roman.html#basics.

  (Standards: Mathematics 9.4, 29, 49)

Physical Fitness

- Learn about the games Roman children played.
- Learn about Roman sports such as chariot racing and gladiator combat.
- Talk about the Roman baths. How did these baths contribute to the health of the ancient Romans? What were some of the exercises the Romans did during their time at the baths? Can the children do some of these exercises as well? At http://www.pbs.org/wgbh/nova/lostempires/roman/day.html children can take a virtual visit to these wondrous places of long ago by entering all the rooms of an ancient Roman bathhouse.

  (Standards: Physical Education 1-5.4. 11, 21, 23,26, 28-29, 36)

Literature

- Find quotes from famous Roman poets and orators and copy them for display around the room. (See *Words of the Ancient Romans* in the references.)
- Read some Roman myths (see Usher 1983).

- Read biographies of famous Romans and emperors. Make a game similar to Concentration in which you write the person's name on one card and a sentence describing something the person did on another. Players have to match the cards correctly.

  (Standards: Language Arts: Reading 5-7.5, 10, 13; Listening and Speaking 8)

References

Adult Books

Beard, Mary, and John Henderson. *Classical Art: From Greece to Rome.* New York: Oxford University Press, 2001. ISBN 0192842374.

The authors show the art of these two great civilizations in relationship to one another. There are good reproductions for group viewing.

Bussagli, Marco. *Rome.* Konigswinter, Germany: Konemann, 2004. ISBN 3833112328.

There are 500 color illustrations of Rome's most important buildings and works of art, including details of mosaics and paintings.

Connolly, Peter, and Hazel Dodge. *The Ancient City: Life in Classical Athens & Rome.* New York: Oxford University Press, 1998. ISBN 0-19-917242-0.

The first part of this book describes life and art in ancient Greece, while the second part deals with ancient Rome. The pictures are wonderful for viewing.

Grant, Mark. *Roman Cookery: Ancient Recipes for Modern Kitchens.* London: Serif, 1999. ISBN 1897959397.

The author offers a history of ancient Roman cooking as well as recipes.

Hadas, Moses. *Imperial Rome.* 2d ed. New York: Time-Life UK, 1965. ISBN 0809403420.

This is a good overview of this ancient civilization.

Onians, John. *Classical Art and the Cultures of Greece and Rome.* New Haven, CT: Yale University Press, 1999. ISBN 0-300-07533-2.

This book is a good source of pictures of Roman sculpture.

Panetta, Marisa Ranieri. *Pompeii: The History, Life and Art of the Buried City.* Vercelli, Italy: White Star, 2004. ISBN 8854400300.

This book is a collaboration by the staffs of the two organizations charged with excavating and preserving the ancient city of Pompeii. It provides wonderful information.

Ramage, Nancy H., and Andrew Ramage. *Roman Art: Romulus to Constantine.* 4th ed. Upper Saddle River, NJ: Prentice Hall, 2004. ISBN 0131896121.

This book presents Roman art spanning 1,300 years and provides wonderful illustrations for viewing.

Wilkinson, Paul. *Pompeii: The Last Day*. London: BBC Books, 2004. ISBN 0563522399.

This exciting, hour-by-hour account of the events of the day Vesuvius erupted is the companion piece to the Discovery Channel's documentary *The Last Days of Pompeii*. It is filled with wonderful pictures.

Children's Books

Altman, Susan, Susan Lechner, and Sue Hughes. *Ancient Rome: Modern Rhymes about Ancient Times*. Danbury, CT: Children's Press, 2002. ISBN 0516273744.

Children learn about ancient Rome through the many rhymes in this book.

Balit, Christina. *Escape from Pompeii*. New York: Henry Holt, 2003. ISBN 0805073248.

When Mount Vesuvius erupts in AD 79, Tranio and his friend Livia flee from their homes in Pompeii and run to the harbor.

Baxter, Nicola. *Romans*: *Facts, Things to Make, Activities, New Edition*. 1992. Reprint, New York: Franklin Watts, 2001. ISBN 0531141438.

The author offers suggestions for crafts and activities related to the life and history of ancient Romans.

Blacklock, Dyan. *The Roman Army*. Illustrated by David Kennett. New York: Walker & Company, 2004. ISBN 0-8027-8896-3.

This book shows the Roman empire in AD 117, the different components of the army, their equipment, and more.

Clare, John D., ed. *Classical Rome*. San Diego: Gulliver Books, 1993. ISBN 0-15-200513-7.

Photographs featuring modern-day actors depict life in ancient Rome.

Connolly, Peter. *Pompeii*. New York: Oxford University Press, 1994. ISBN 0199171580.

The detailed drawings of such things as baths, theaters, and temples help students understand daily life in Pompeii in the first century.

Corbishley, Mike. *Ancient Rome*. New York: Facts on File, 2003. ISBN 081605147X.

This is an atlas history of Rome that enables children to see where events took place.

———. *Growing Up in Ancient Rome*. Illustrated by Chris Molan. New York: Troll Associates, 1993. ISBN 0816727228

The author presents different aspects of life in ancient Rome, including going to school and getting married.

Deem, James M. *Bodies from the Ash: Life and Death in Ancient Pompeii*. Boston: Houghton Mifflin, 2005. ISBN 0-618-47308-4.

In this page-turning book, the author recounts the events that occurred when Vesuvius erupted and presents the artifacts that have been unearthed from that ancient city.

DuTemple, Lesley. *The Colosseum.* Minneapolis, MN: Learner, 2003. ISBN 0822546930.

This book is a good source of information about the building and history of the Colosseum.

Freixenet, Anna. *Creating with Mosaics.* San Diego: Blackbirch Press, 2000. ISBN 1567114407.

The author presents many easy crafts even young children can undertake.

Guittard, Charles. *The Romans: Life in the Empire.* Translated by Mary Kae LaRose. Illustrated by Annie-Claude Martin. Brookf ield, CT: Millbrook Press, 1992. ISBN 076130097X.

This book describes the creation of the Roman Empire and discusses such topics as table manners, travel, and entertainment. Dates to remember, glossary.

Harris, Jacqueline L. *Science in Ancient Rome.* New York: Franklin Watts, 1998. ISBN 0531159167.

Chapters on Roman building, medicine, mining, and more make this a valuable resource.

Hicks, Peter, et al. *In the Daily Life of the Ancient Romans.* New York: Peter Bedrick, 2001. ISBN 0872265951.

The authors explore the traditions and religious beliefs of the ancient Romans.

Hinds, Kathryn. *The City.* (Life in the Roman Empire). New York: Benchmark, 2004. ISBN 0761416552.

This is one of an excellent four-part series, all published by Benchmark, in which the author describes life for different segments of ancient Roman society. The other books are *The Countryside* (2005, ISBN 0761416560), *The Patricians* (2004, ISBN 0761416544), and *Religion* (2004, ISBN 0761416579).

Honan, Linda. *Spend the Day in Ancient Rome: Projects and Activities That Bring the Past to Life.* Illustrated by Ellen Kosmer. New York: Wiley, 1998. ISBN 0-471-15453-9.

The activities in this book are wonderful, and many are suited to very young children.

James, Simon. *Ancient Rome.* New York: DK Children, 2000. ISBN 0789457881.

Readers see many levels of society, from slaves to emperors, in this exploration of ancient Rome.

Johnson, Stephen. *A Roman Fort.* Illustrated by Mark Bergin. New York: Peter Bedrick, 2001. ISBN 0872266508.

This book provides information on how a fort is built and the life within that fort.

Jovinelly, Joann, and Jason Netelkos. *The Crafts and Culture of the Romans.* New York: Rosen Publishing Group, 2002. ISBN 0-8239-3513-2.

The authors offer a good deal of information about ancient Roman life in addition to the interesting crafts they suggest.

Lassieur, Allison. *The Ancient Romans.* New York: Scholastic/Franklin Watts, 2004. ISBN 0-531-12338-3.

Children will absolutely love the little-known facts treated in this book. The writing is lively and fun.

Macaulay, David. City: *A Story of Roman Planning and Construction.* Boston: Houghton Mifflin. ISBN 0395349222.

Macaulay re-creates the building of an imaginary Roman city. Some excerpts would make fine reading while viewing Roman engineering feats.

Macdonald, Fiona. *How to Be a Roman Soldier.* Illustrated by Nick Hewetson. Washington, DC: National Geographic Children's Books, 2005. ISBN 0792236165.

Readers discover what life was like for a Roman soldier.

Maestro, Betsy. *The Story of Clocks and Calendars: Marking a Millennium.* Illustrated by Giulio Maestro. New York: HarperCollins, 1999. ISBN 0688145485.

This is a fascinating history of calendars.

Malam, John, David Salariya, and David Antram. *You Wouldn't Want to Be a Roman Gladiator!* (You Wouldn't Want To!). New York: Franklin Watts, 2001. ISBN 0531162044.

The authors describe the superiority of the Roman army and how its captives were brought to Rome to be trained as gladiators.

Markel, Rita J. *Your Travel Guide to Ancient Rome.* Minneapolis, MN: Lerner Publications Company, 2004. ISBN 0-8225-3071-6.

A great deal of information about ancient Rome is presented in the form of a travel guide: what to wear, what to eat, where to stay, where to find recreation, etc.

McCaughrean, Geraldine. *Romulus and Remus.* New York: Orchard, 2001. ISBN 1841215228.

This is the myth about the twins who founded Rome.

Mellor, Ronald, and Marni McGee. *The Ancient Roman World.* New York: Oxford University Press, 2004. ISBN 0-19-515380-4.

This is a wonderfully written account of life in ancient Rome.

Merrill, Yvonne Y., and Mary Simpson. *Hands-On Ancient People, Volume 2: Art Activities About Minoans, Mycenaeans, Trojans, Ancient Greeks, Etruscans, and Romans.* Salt Lake City, UT: Kits Publishing, 2002. ISBN 0964317796.

This book has a beautiful, full-page, color illustration for each craft suggested. The object to be made is discussed in the context of the historical period, and clear instructions are given.

Morley, Jacqueline, and John James. *A Roman Villa.* New York: Peter Bedrick, 1992. ISBN 0872263606.

This very readable account of life in a wealthy person's villa outside Rome includes a time chart and glossary.

Murrell, Deborah. *The Best Book of Ancient Rome*. Boston: Kingfisher, 2004. ISBN 0-7534-5756-3.

Large text and many illustrations make this a good source of information for young students.

Nardo, Don. *The Ancient Romans*. San Diego: Lucent Books, 2001. ISBN 1-56006-706-3.

Older students and teachers will find this book a good source of information. Black-and-white photos.

———. *Roman Amphitheaters*. New York: Franklin Watts, 2002. ISBN 0-531-12036-8.

Nardo describes the building and use of Roman amphitheaters.

———. *Women of Ancient Rome*. New York: Lucent Books, 2003. ISBN 1-59018-169-7.

Nardo discusses the different roles women played in ancient Rome.

———. *Words of the Ancient Romans: Primary Sources*. San Diego: Lucent Books, 2003. ISBN 1590183185.

Although not all the words quoted are from primary sources, this is a great resource for studying some of the speeches and other writings of early Romans.

Osborne, Mary Pope. *Pompeii Lost and Found*. Illustrated by Bonnie Christensen. New York: Knopf, 2006. ISBN 0-375-82889-3.

This book is especially valuable for its focus on what life was like in Pompeii before the volcanic eruption. The large illustrations mimic the frescoes that were on the walls of the villas in this doomed city.

Osborne, Mary Pope, and Natalie Pope Boyce. *Ancient Rome and Pompeii*. New York: Random House, 2006. ISBN 0-375-83220-3.

Readers of this easy nonfiction book will learn about life in ancient Rome and what happened to the city of Pompeii.

Sabuda, Robert. *Saint Valentine*. New York: Aladdin, 1999. ISBN 0689824297.

This is a simple biography of Valentine, a Roman physician who lived in the third century AD. Exquisite mosaic illustrations by the author.

Shuter, Jane. *Life in a Roman Villa*. Chicago: Heinemann Library, 2005. ISBN 1403458308.

Shuter describes life in a villa in Roman times.

Solway, Andrew. *Rome in Spectacular Cross-Section*. Illustrated by Stephen Biesty. New York: Scholastic, 2003. ISBN 0-439-45546-4.

Life in the street, in the temple, in the forum, and much more is presented in this beautiful book.

Steward, David. *Inside Ancient Rome*. New York: Enchanted Lion, 2005. ISBN 1-59270-045-4.

Find out what life was like in ancient Rome.

Tanaka, Shelley. *Buried City of Pompeii.* Illustrated by Greg Ruhl. New York: Hyperion, 2000. ISBN 0-7868-1541-8.

The story of the destruction of Pompeii is told by the caretaker of a wealthy family's villa. Readers see modern Pompeii as well as the city in ancient times.

Usher, Kerry. *Heroes, Gods & Emperors from Roman Mythology.* Illustrated by John Sibbick. New York: Schocken Books, 1983. ISBN 0-8052-3880-8.

These are stories about Roman gods and heroes.

Winterfield, Henry. *Detectives in Togas.* Illustrated by Charlotte Kleinert. San Diego: Odyssey Classics, 2002. ISBN 0152162925.

By reading this fictional mystery set in ancient Rome, students will find out a great deal about the lives of children at that time. Winterfield has also written *Roman Ransom*, another mystery.

Audiovisual Materials

Ancient Civilizations for Children: Ancient Rome. DVD. Library Video Company, 1998. V7159.

This is an easy-to-understand film that takes viewers inside ancient Rome to explore many aspects of life there.

Ancient Mysteries: Pompeii—Buried Alive. DVD. A&E Home Video, 2005. ASIN B000BKVL9I.

This film chronicles the day Vesuvius erupted in Pompeii.

Ancient Rome. DVD. Library Video Company, 1998. V7159.

Viewers visit Pompeii, the Coliseum, and other ancient Roman sites.

Life in Ancient Rome. DVD Library Video Company, 1997. K6276.

Viewers will learn what ancient Romans wore, what they ate, and more.

Roman City. DVD. Library Video Company, 1994. A7904.

This Emmy-award-winning video examines how the Roman Empire linked Western Europe, the Middle East, and North Africa and is based on David Macaulay's book. It uses animation and live footage.

Seven Wonders of Ancient Rome. DVD. The Discovery Channel Store, n.d. Item # 702233.

See the Pantheon, the aqueducts, the baths, the Appian Way, and more in this wonderful film.

Unsolved History: The Roman Coliseum. DVD. The Discovery Channel Store, n.d. Item # 684209.

Both the building of the Coliseum and the events that took place there are depicted in this film.

Other Materials

Gladiator Survival Kit. Metropolitan Museum of Art, n.d. M7006.

Students can find out what it was like to be a Roman gladiator. The kit contains a poster, cards, and other materials.

Web Sites

Ancient Rome. http://ancienthistory.mrdonn.org/Romelife.html#INTRO (accessed February 3, 2006).

This is a wonderful site, even for very young children. After reading the Introduction, they can click on any number of links to find out all about life in ancient Rome: games, food, clothing, etc.

The Romans. http://www.bbc.co.uk/schools/romans/, (accessed February 4, 2006).

This amazing site has numerous links, activities for students to do, information for teachers, and more.

Watering Ancient Rome. http://www.pbs.org/wgbh/nova/lostempires/roman/watering.html (accessed February 3, 2006).

Read how the ancient Romans built their aqueducts.

Part II
Arts of the East and Africa

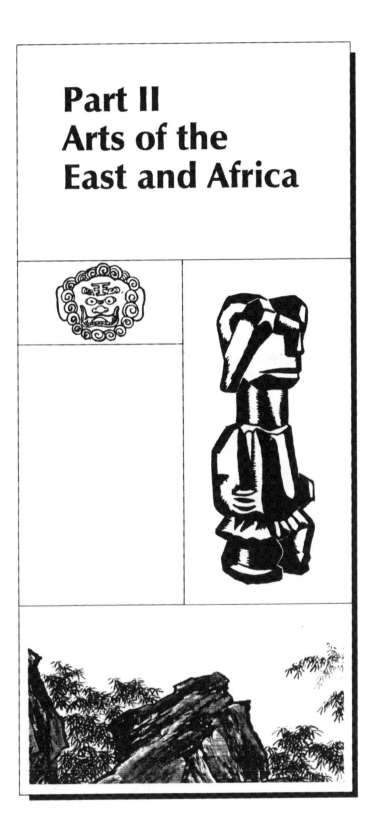

5 The Art of China

"Human eyes are limited in their scope.
Hence, they are not able to perceive all that is to be seen;
Yet with one small brush I can draw the universe."

—WANG WEI, painter, in *Treasures of China* by Annette Juliano

Background Information

The Chinese civilization is one of the oldest on earth. The ancient Chinese were, in many ways, centuries ahead of the rest of the world. They invented paper and printing long before Gutenberg developed his movable type. They used herbs and acupuncture to treat illnesses. By the end of the Han Dynasty (AD 220), the Chinese were able to measure earthquakes and had come to the conclusion that a year was about 365 days long. They had accurate measuring tools and farm implements that were superior to those in the West.

While humans began populating China as early as half a million years ago, the first period in recorded history was that of the Shang Dynasty in 1500 BC. During this dynasty, or period ruled by one family, the Chinese developed a system of writing, begun as questions carved on bones. Many years later Chinese writing became standardized, which enabled the Chinese to maintain unity and continuity in a vast country inhabited by people who spoke numerous dialects. The actual formation of the characters of Chinese writing became prized as an art form in itself, called calligraphy. Chinese paintings were often accompanied by characters drawn in calligraphy, and works of literature were valued as much for the care with which the characters were set down as by the content of the pieces. It was during the Shang Dynasty as well that the Chinese developed bronze, a mixture of copper and tin, and their bronze figures, made in molds, are lovely works of art. Many bronze and pottery models of ritual vessels, furniture, farms, houses, servants, and animals were buried with the dead, for the Chinese, like the Egyptians, believed that the dead person would need them in the afterlife. Archaeological digs have uncovered exquisite bronze and pottery pieces.

Jade, prized by the Chinese even above gold, appeared in Neolithic times and continues to hold a special place in their art today. First used in the making of tools, jade became a favorite material for creating ornaments such as jewelry and figurines. Because of its hardness it is difficult to carve, and jewelry pieces are often formed by constant rubbing and polishing.

The first Zhou king overthrew the Shang Dynasty around 1027 BC, ushering in the longest period of dynastic rule in Chinese history. During this feudal period, the iron and salt industries developed, and the Chinese began to use lacquer, made from the sap of a tree, to coat their artworks. Even the lacquer itself, hardened when exposed to air, was carved and decorated with paint. Ancient lacquer-coated objects, unearthed by archaeologists, are as brilliant today as when they were first created. Two of the greatest Chinese philosophers, Confucius and Lao-tze, were born during the Zhou Dynasty.

In 221 BC, Ying Zheng, the king of the feudal state of Qin, conquered the neighboring states, united them into the first Chinese empire, and declared himself the first emperor. Using half a million workers, he built the Great Wall of China to protect the empire from the hordes of nomads to the north. He used even more workers to construct an elaborate tomb for himself, complete with a terra-cotta army of thousands of life-sized soldiers to protect him in the afterlife. The terra-cotta army was unearthed by farmers digging a well in a field in 1974, and new treasures are continually being excavated from the site, although Zheng's actual burial chamber has yet to be found. (See *The Emperor's Silent Army* and *Chinese Sculpture* in the references for information and excellent pictures of these amazing figures.)

Emperor Qin's Terra Cotta Army, Xi'an, China

The short-lived Qin empire gave way to the Han Dynasty in 206 BC. A civil bureaucracy grew up during this time, and the creation of civil service exams led to the development of an elite educated class that ruled the country. For centuries one of the few peoples who knew how to raise silkworms, the Chinese developed a bustling silk trade during this period. In AD 220, central authority gave way to three kingdoms: Wu, Wei, and Shu. These then split into the northern and southern kingdoms, with one dynasty after another coming into power, until the country was reunited under the Sui Dynasty in AD 581. Buddhism as a religion took firm hold among the people, and many Buddhist sculptures and temples appeared. Wall paintings in palaces, tombs, and temples began to flourish at this time.

The Tang Dynasty, one of China's most glorious eras, began in AD 618. Comparable to the Golden Age of Athens, it is the era of great works of art. During this period the empress Wu Hou, although treating her competitors cruelly and even murdering her own daughter, generously supported the arts. Although the Chinese had been working in pottery since prehistoric times, it was during the Tang dynasty that they developed porcelain by combining kaolin, a fine white clay, with feldspar, a crystalline rock. The famous Blue-and-White porcelain dates from the early Tang Dynasty. Chinese porcelain figures and bowls eventually became so famous that their name has become synonymous with fine tableware—china. Increased production of silk and paper contributed to the development of painting and the rise of landscape artists like Wang Wei.

The Tang Dynasty collapsed in 907, and after a series of dynasties, the Song emperors reigned in the south. Under them, art became softer, more delicate, and rendered in more muted tones, and painting flourished as an art in itself rather than simply as a means of decoration. The Mongol leader Khublai Khan defeated the Songs, taking the dynastic name Yuan. It is to Khan's court that the Venetian trader Marco Polo made his historic visit, linking East and West for the first time.

In 1368 a monk named Chu Yuan-chang drove the Yuan Dynasty out of Peking and became the first Ming emperor. China turned inward in rebellion against foreign influences and, like the Renaissance artists in the West, looked back to ancient art for inspiration. Sixteen Ming dynasties ruled until 1644, when the Manchu or Qing Dynasty took over.

The Qing Dynasty lasted 268 years, until 1912, when a period of unrest began that lasted until World War II, after which the Communists gained control of the country. In all that time—almost 600 years—it was the art and thought of the ancients that held sway. China's worship of ancestors; its Great Wall, which locked traditions in and foreigners out; its symmetrical Forbidden City, with its unchanging Imperial Palace as the home of an emperor whose task it was to maintain harmony between his people and all of nature; its temples to Confucius and Buddha—all reflect China's everlasting link to its past. All have spawned China's art: masterpieces of pottery and bronze buried with the dead; figures of porcelain, lacquer, jade, and ivory; palaces and temples with their distinctive sloping roofs; and exquisitely delicate paintings and calligraphy.

(Standards: Art Connections 1.1, 4, 6-7; Grades K–4 History 7; World History 9.10-13)

The Story

The emperor of China had a pet nightingale. After a long day governing his kingdom, he loved to listen to it sing in the evening The people called the emperor the Son of Heaven, for he was their bridge between earth and heaven. It was his job to preserve harmony among his people and all of the earth, to keep drought and famine and war from them. All day long he listened to the reports of his ministers, judged disputes, made decisions. It was exhausting work! No wonder, then, that he prized his gentle, sweet-singing nightingale above all his possessions.

"What would I do without the soothing song of my nightingale?" he thought as his servant brought the bird in her gilded cage to him. The more the emperor considered his nightingale, the more he loved her and wanted to show others what a marvelous creature she was. So one day he issued a decree to all the painters in his kingdom. "I wish to have a painting of a nightingale to place in the main hall of the palace. Whoever of you paints the most perfect picture of this glorious creature within one year's time will be declared official artist to the emperor and rewarded with a fine silk robe embedded with jewels."

You can imagine that when they heard this news, all the artists of the kingdom were very excited, for each hoped he would be the one appointed artist to the emperor. They spent hours studying nightingales. They viewed nightingales sitting on tree branches, nightingales in cages, nightingales flying through the sky, nightingales singing, nightingales sleeping. Day and night they practiced their brush strokes, searching for the perfect line, the perfect shape, the perfect proportion to create a bird to the emperor's liking.

There was activity everywhere—except on the work table of one artist. Oh, his helpers were working. They showed their master pictures of nightingales. They captured nightingales and brought them as models for their master to paint. They talked about the shape of a nightingale's body, the color of its feathers, the length of its beak. But the master never picked up his brush. After six months had gone by like this, his helpers began to worry and to question their master.

"Sir," they said, "time is passing swiftly while you sit here idly. Are you ill? Is there any way we can help you that we have not already considered? Perhaps we should fashion new brushes for you out of the finest animal hair and wood. Shall we get you new inks?"

But the master painter assured them all was well, and he continued to sit quietly at his work table day after day. No ink touched paper or silk scroll. And the helpers waited, growing more impatient with every passing day. When the master's work table remained empty even through the last month of the contest, his helpers spoke out again. "Master, there are but a few weeks remaining. Would you like one of us to try a painting in your name?"

But the master painter replied, "There is still much time left. When the hour is upon us, the emperor will have his painting." So they continued to wait, trying not to show him how uneasy they were, for he was a kind and thoughtful master and they did not wish to show distrust.

Finally, on the morning all the artists were due at the palace, the master painter bathed in water scented with sweet lotus blossoms. He put on his finest robe and smoothed his topknot. At last he sat at his work table, and with a few strokes of his brush, painted a nightingale. When the ink was hardly dry on the page, he left for the palace accompanied by two of his helpers.

When the master painter and his helpers arrived, the palace guards placed them in a large room where they waited with all the other artists to appear before the emperor. Each painter kept his painting rolled in a long scroll, to be revealed before the eyes of the emperor alone. One after the other the artists went into the throne room, but each one came out as quickly as the last. None of their paintings had been found pleasing. At last, the master artist appeared before his ruler and slowly unrolled his scroll. There on the paper was the most perfect of all nightingales. The emperor was stunned into silence. The two helpers could hardly believe their eyes.

"This is the finest painting I have ever seen!" exclaimed the emperor. "From this moment forward, you are appointed special painter to the emperor." Then, turning to his servants, he said, "Come, bring the ceremonial robe here." And he placed the robe over the artist's own garments and bade him go home to pack his belongings so that he could move into the palace. Bowing low, the delighted painter and his helpers left.

While they walked back, the two helpers questioned their master. "Surely, sir, you painted that bird long ago after many attempts and kept it hidden to surprise us. No one could have painted such a perfect picture in so brief a time." The master replied, "Of course I did not just paint the nightingale in the moments before we left for the palace. I have been painting it in my mind all year. I have been studying nightingales—their song, their flight. I have seen nightingales in my sleeping, in my waking, in my eating. The few strokes I put on the paper today are the result of my working hard all year long, of my finally being one with the nightingale so that I could imagine it as perfectly as it is in nature."

The artist's fame spread throughout the kingdom from that day on, and when he came to live in the emperor's palace and to paint pictures there, the emperor learned never to scold him for appearing lazy, but to wait for the artist to become one with his subject.

We are going to study the work of Chinese artists who believed that there is a harmony, a oneness, between people and nature. We will try to discover that harmony as we view their work. Like the artist in our story, these artists did not paint with an object in front of them but held a picture of the object in their heads. Then they painted quickly, using ink that could not be erased, so they had to be quite sure of their subject before they began.

(Standards: Art Connections 1.1, 4, 5-7; Language Arts: Listening and Speaking 8.4)

LESSON 1: Chinese Painting

Viewing the Art

Try to show examples of the three kinds of Chinese painting: figures, landscapes, and birds and flowers. (Painting on vases, bowls, etc., is the subject of the following lesson.) Many Chinese paintings were done on silk or paper scrolls. The earliest painter to whom specific works can be attributed is Gu Kaizhi of the fourth century. Show several scenes from his *Nymph of the Lo River* and his *Admonitions of the Instructress to the Court Ladies*. The *Admonitions* ushered in Chinese classical painting, and it is an important piece to share with the class. If at all possible, try to obtain McCausland and Gu's excellent book *First Masterpiece of Chinese Painting* (see references) for this purpose. The children might also enjoy Wu Tsung-yuan's *Procession of Taoist Immortals to Pay Homage to the King of Heaven, Duke Wen of Chin Recovering His State* by Li Tang, Hongzhong's *The Night Revelry of Han Xizai* , *Herding Horses* after Wei Yan, and *Eighteen Songs of a Nomad Flute* by an unknown artist. (These can be found in *The Palace Museum;* see references.) Thorp and Vinograd (2001) also have wonderful reproductions of Chinese paintings.

After viewing several landscape paintings with the children, ask them what they see in almost every painting. They should notice mountains and water. Tell them that the Chinese word for landscape means "mountain water" pictures. The Chinese painter does not try to paint an actual scene as a Western painter might. Rather, the painter works from memory and is more interested in depicting the forms of things. Observe the minimal use of color in these paintings. Finally, show some scenes of flowers, birds, and other animals. What kinds of animals appear in the paintings? Observe how some paintings have fine delicate lines while others consist of broad, smudged brush strokes.

While you view the different types of paintings, point out that Chinese characters often appear on them, for calligraphy is directly related to painting. Both use a brush, require prior contemplation, and are done quickly. Often the characters on a painting are a poem related to the scene depicted. The Chinese have thousands of characters, and the art of calligraphy is an exacting one. The children might enjoy this admonition from the calligrapher Wang Hse-chih to his pupils:

> The shape of the character should not be too wide at the top [nor] too narrow at the base. The strokes should not be crowded together or the character will look as though it is plagued by a hundred ailments. The strokes should not be too elongated or it will look like a dead snake hanging from a tree. It should not be too squat or it will look like a frog floating on a pond. (Froncek 1969, p.120)

Both *The Splendors of Imperial China* and Wan-go Weng's *Chinese Painting and Calligraphy* (see references) have wonderful reproductions to use with this lesson. You can also use Ed Young's exquisite *Beyond the Great Mountains* (see references) as inspiration as you view some Chinese paintings. Young's book deals with many of the things the children will see in these paintings.

Children age eight and older would enjoy getting inside a Chinese painting at http://www.metmuseum.org/explore/Chinese/html_pages/index.htm, a site provided by the Metropolitan Museum of art. Here several questions about the Chinese paintings depicted are answered and children have the opportunity to do a related activity, such as making a bamboo painting. They will learn about the lettering on paintings, why paintings have red stamps, and more.

(Standards: Art Connections 1.1-8; Language Arts: Viewing 9.6)

Journal Writing

Of the three kinds of paintings viewed, which did the children like best, and why? What did the children learn about observation from the Chinese artist? Encourage the children to write about the Chinese method of contemplating the subject beforehand and then painting from memory to capture the essence of the thing. Have they ever studied anything for a long period of time in order to be able to picture it in their heads? Would they like to try? What advantages do they think this would have over copying the object as it appears before them?

(Standards: Language Arts: Writing 1, 3.7, 23, 34, 36; Thinking and Reasoning 3.3)

Art/Drama Activity: Chinese Painting

Older children may enjoy using Hsu's Chinese Brush Painting kit (see references) for this activity.

Materials

- Thin brushes
- Black ink (if you are concerned that the ink will stain clothing, substitute watered-down black tempera paint)
- Long pieces of paper that can be rolled horizontally into scrolls
- Newspaper to cover work surfaces
- Books containing scenes of mountains, water, birds, and flowers (if it is not possible to view these outdoors)
- Examples of Chinese characters (if children are interested in trying to draw them)

Although Chinese figure painting may be too difficult for the children, they can probably succeed very well with the other subjects in this lesson. Give them a choice of painting a landscape, a bird, or a flower/plant. If weather permits, take the class outdoors and invite them to choose a scene, a bird, or a flower to study intensely and silently. Give them as much time to do this as possible. How many ways can they see the object they are viewing: its size, shape, weight, color? If it is not possible to go outside, provide books for the children to study. After they have studied their subject sufficiently, invite them to paint it from memory on the paper provided. Talk about the experience after the children have finished their painting. What was it like trying to capture an object in their minds and put it on paper? How was the experience different from the times they copied an image onto paper?

In another lesson, the children might wish to learn the Chinese characters for bird, flower, etc., and to add those characters to their scroll.

(Standards: Visual Arts 1, 4-5.1-11)

LESSON 2: Chinese Porcelain

Viewing the Art

Explain to the children that the Chinese made pottery from the very earliest times, in the Neolithic era (5000–2000 BC), and that many marvelous pieces have been found in tombs uncovered by archaeologists. Then gradually they began to develop a new kind of ceramic called porcelain, 700 years before Europeans figured out how to do so. Porcelain is made by combining kaolin, a fine white clay, with feldspar, a crystalline rock. It is shaped on a potter's wheel and then fired at very high temperatures. It can be very thin, as in delicate cups and dishes, and you can actually see through many of the pieces when they are held up to the light. If you have a piece of fine porcelain, it would be wonderful to hold it up to the light to demonstrate this. Porcelain is really quite strong, and very beautiful. (See McArthur's *The Arts of Asia* in the references for a chapter on porcelain.) The Chinese formed statues, vases, and dishes from porcelain. (Children may especially enjoy seeing the porcelain figures on pages 200–204 in Watt 2004).

Through the centuries, the Chinese experimented with many styles and glazes, reaching a height of production and perfection during the Ming Dynasty (1368–1644). During that time porcelains reached enormous proportions and included huge vases five and six feet high, large dishes, and tall statues. Probably among the best known are the blue-and-white porcelain patterns, called simply Blue-and-White. During this time, the Chinese discovered a fine white clay that did not have a grayish tinge, as did the clay they had formerly been using, and this made all the difference. To make Blue-and-Whites, the Chinese artists painted designs in blue, made from expensive cobalt, on their unfired pieces of white clay. Sometimes they even carved flowers and designs in paste and stuck them onto the figures. Then they covered them with a glaze that was almost colorless and resulted in a shiny, smooth appearance, and fired them in ovens reaching more than 1250 degrees centigrade. Show as many of these pieces as you can (see several exquisite examples in Weng and Boda, *The Palace Museum: Peking*). Many European countries, such as Holland with its Delft, have imitated these Blue-and-Whites. Two hundred years ago, the British developed the famous Willow pattern, which is still popular today. Read Drummond's *The Willow Pattern Story* (see references) aloud as you show the children this pattern.

Also show porcelains of different glazes. Ask the children to note the patterns painted on the porcelain. What kinds of borders do the plates have (often intertwining leaves and flowers)? What are the subjects painted on the pieces (birds, fish, dragons, flowers, water plants)? A trip to a museum to see some porcelain pieces firsthand would be an excellent way to truly appreciate their beauty.

(Standards: Art Connections 1.1-8; Language Arts: Viewing 9.6)

Journal Writing

If the children have had an opportunity to visit a museum, encourage them to write about the experience. Otherwise, ask them to respond from their experience of the art in books. Which pieces did they like best, and why? What figures did the Chinese artists paint on their pieces? What might some of these figures mean to the Chinese?

(Standards: Language Arts: Writing 1, 3.7, 23, 34, 36; Thinking and Reasoning 3.3)

Art/Drama Activity: Pottery Design

Materials

- Paper
- Brushes
- Blue paint or colored pencils
- Newspapers to cover work surfaces

The Chinese prized porcelain, and during the Ming Dynasty, when porcelain pieces proliferated, everyone used it. Chinese emperors collected porcelain pieces: "In the year 1544 . . . the imperial household alone ordered 26,350 bowls with 30,500 saucers to match, 6,000 ewers with 6,900 wine cups, 680 large garden fish bowls, and 1,340 table services of 27 pieces each" (Burling 1953, 153).

Have the children pretend that they work for a famous potter, and the master has just received an enormous order from the emperor. Their job is to design a set of Blue-and-White tableware for the emperor's household. What design will go around the border of the plates? What figures will be painted on the porcelain? Have them work in groups or alone to design a pattern, being faithful to the types of figures found on Chinese porcelain: dragons, birds, flowers, etc. When the children have finished, either discuss which design they like best, or allow them to decide to make the dishes in several different patterns.

(Standards: Visual Arts 1, 4-5.1-11)

Curriculum Connections

Social Studies

- Find China on a world map. Then use a map of China to locate principal cities.
- China is a huge country. Compare its size to that of the United States. Study the different land forms and places of interest. A very helpful book that will give children a sense of the variety and beauty found in China is *Treasures of China* (see references).
- Who are the Chinese people today? There are fifty-six different minority groups in China, with the Han people making up the greatest percentage of the population. Research one or more of these minorities. Where and how do they live? Do they follow the same customs as their ancestors, or have they changed the way they live over time? The Web site http://chineseculture.about.com/library/china/ethnic/blsethnic.htm provides information on several Chinese minorities.

- Bring in a bag of objects purchased in local stores: articles of clothing, household goods, etc. Ask children to place objects made in China in a separate pile. Discuss why so many of the things we use each day are made in China. Research how one of these objects is made—the factory in which it was produced, the kinds of workers who made it, etc.
- Study Chinese farming methods, tools, and crops. Talk especially about how rice is grown and the different ways in which this crop is used. The Web site http://www.kenrahn.com/China/Nanjing/Village/AG.html has wonderful pictures of Chinese rice paddies. Find out about citrus growing in China. Read *Ma Jiang and the Orange Ants* (see references) aloud.
- Discuss Chinese food and prepare a Chinese feast. (See Simonds and Swartz's *Moonbeams, Dumplings & Dragon Boats* and Lin's *Dim Sum for Everyone* in references.) Compestine's *The Story of Chopsticks* and *The Story of Noodles* (see references) are enjoyable books to read aloud. Make the recipe for noodles.

Great Wall of China

- Research the Great Wall of China, the only structure on Earth visible to astronauts in space. Why and how was it built? (See DuTemple 2002.)

- Study the growth and care of silkworms and their contribution to Chinese life and economy. Use *The Silk Route* by John S. Major (see references) to discuss the production and trade of silk. The Web site http://www.pclaunch.com/~kayton/Silkworms/teacher.htm provides many helpful links for an interesting study of silkworms. Also see the Web site and the kit mentioned in "Other Materials" below.
- Kite making and flying is very important to Chinese people. Read Compestine's *The Story of Kites,* Grace Lin's *Kite Flying,* and *Henry and the Kite Dragon* (see references). Divide the children into groups and have them make a kite. Go to http://www.skratch-pad.com/kites/make.html for simple instructions. Fly the kites on a windy day.
- The Chinese use a different calendar than that used by countries in the West. Why? Read Demi's *The Dragon's Tale* (see references), about the animals of the Chinese zodiac. Do the children know which animal year is currently being celebrated? New Year's celebrations are very important in Chinese culture. Read some books from the references about Chinese New Year. What are some customs attached to this celebration? If you study this chapter during the time of the Chinese New Year, have a New Year celebration in the classroom. Invite parents and friends.

(Standards: Grades K–4 History 1.8; Thinking and Reasoning 2-3.8-10; World History 1.10-12, 36-38; Geography 1-2, 10, 14-15, 17.4-5, 15, 23-26, 30, 43)

Civics

- Discuss Chinese government today and Communist rule.
- Discuss some broad principles of Confucianism and Buddhism. Invite a parent or other speaker of Chinese origin to talk to the class.

(Standards: Civics 1)

Mathematics

- Learn to count from one to ten in Chinese. Learn to write some of the numbers in Chinese characters. Go to http://www.newton.mec.edu/Angier/DimSum/Numbers%20to%20Ten%20Lesson.html for information.
- Demonstrate the use of the abacus. Students may enjoy making their own.

(Standards: Mathematics 9.1, 29)

Science

- Study plants and animals native to China. Students may particularly enjoy learning more about the panda. Read *The Year of the Panda* by Miriam Schlein (see references).
- Study Chinese inventions, such as paper, a system of printing, gunpowder, and fireworks.
- Study the contributions of archaeology in revealing information about the ancient Chinese. Children might enjoy reading *The Emperor's Silent Army* (see references).
- Although today they also practice Western medicine, the Chinese have for centuries practiced their own form of medicine, which includes herbs, acupuncture, and other remedies. Find out about these healing arts.

(Standards: Science: Life Science 6-7, 29, 39, 45)

Language Arts

- Read some Chinese poetry. Use *Maples in the Mist,* transalted by Ho Minfong (see references). Encourage the children to write poems to accompany some of the paintings viewed during the art lesson or the paintings they made during the art activity.
- Study Chinese characters and practice making them. (See *Beyond the Great Mountains, Chinese Calligraphy Made Easy,* and *The Simple Art of Chinese Calligraphy* in the references.) In imitation of Huy Voun Lee's books (see references), go outdoors and try to find Chinese characters formed by objects in nature.
- Read biographies of famous Chinese such as Confucius and Buddha (see references). Read some sayings of Confucius at http://pages.prodigy.net/jmiller.cb/pra305.html. The children might like to copy their favorites, decorate them, and display them around the room.
- Read some Chinese folktales. Several are listed in the references, and many more are available. Compare a Chinese version of "Cinderella" with a version the children know. How are they the same? Different? The children may wish to dramatize one or more tales or learn to tell them for a storytelling event.
- Turn a Chinese folktale into a play. Enter the Dragon is a company that provides scripts and production guidelines for three children's plays adapted from Chinese folktales. You can order them from Main Street Arts Press, PO Box 100, Saxtons River, VT 05154, (802) 869-2960, e-mail info@mainstreetarts.org.

(Standards: Language Arts Reading 5-6.13-14, 28, 33; Listening and Speaking 8)

Art

- In addition to the art already viewed and studied, the children might enjoy undertaking a special project: the study of symbols in Chinese art. *Symbols and Rebuses in Chinese Art* (see references) would be especially helpful, and the illustrations are wonderful. What do some of the beasts and flowers, etc., used in Chinese art mean? Do we use symbols in art today (for example, Uncle Sam; symbols on traffic signs; the heart, which is the "I love" symbol on so many bumper stickers)? Compare some of our symbols with those the Chinese used. Do the children wish to create some symbols of their own?
- Study jade making in China. Read *The Jade Necklace* (see resources) aloud.
- Try some traditional Chinese paper cut work. *Lao Lao* (see references) has instructions.
- Visit a potter at work.
- Make tangrams (see references).

  (Standards: Visual Arts 1.1-11)

Music

- Listen to Chinese music. How is it different from what the children are used to hearing? What accounts for that difference? What instruments are particular to China?
- What is Chinese opera? How is it different from opera in other countries? Go to see a Chinese opera or listen to some Chinese opera pieces. Read aloud Paul Yee's *A Song for Ba* (see references).

  (Standards: Music 7.4, 7, 12, 15)

References

Adult Books

Barnhart, Richard M. *Along the Border of Heaven.* New York: Metropolitan Museum of Art, 1983. o.p. ISBN 0870992910.

This is an excellent source of large reproductions suitable for viewing the different kinds of Chinese painting. Accompanied by poetry and sayings.

Burling, Judith. *Chinese Art.* New York: Bonanza Books, 1953. o.p. ASIN B0006D95X4.

Fine reproductions enhance this discussion of Chinese art.

Farrer, Ann, Jane Portal, Shelagh Vainker, and Carol Michaelson. *The British Museum Book of Chinese Art.* Edited by Jessica Rawson. New York: Thames & Hudson, 1996. ISBN 0500279039.

The authors explain various kinds of Chinese art and provide excellent chapters on ceramics, calligraphy, and painting.

Fong, Wen C., and James C. Y. Watt. *Possessing the Past: Treasures from the National Palace Museum, Taipei.* New York: Harry N. Abrams, 1996. ISBN 0810964945.

Issued in conjunction with the exhibition of Chinese art at the New York Metropolitan Museum of Art in 1996, this huge book contains essays and beautiful color reproductions of Chinese art treasures, including many porcelains and paintings.

Froncek, Thomas. *The Horizon Book of the Arts of China.* New York: American Heritage Publications. 1969. ASIN B000EMBU58.

The author presents an overview of the different arts of China.

Hearn, Maxwell K. *Splendors of Imperial China: Treasures from the National Palace Museum, Taipei.* New York: Rizzoli International Publications/Metropolitan Museum of Art, 1996. ISBN 0-87099-766-1.

The illustrations of Chinese paintings are especially useful for group viewing. Also available on CD-ROM (ISBN 0300086865).

Ho, Chuimei, and Bennet Bronson. *Splendors of China's Forbidden City.* New York: Merrell, 2004. ISBN 1-85894-203-9.

The treasures housed in the royal complex in Beijing are presented in large color pictures. This is a treasure in itself.

Howard, Angela Falco, et al. *Chinese Sculpture.* New Haven, CT: Yale University Press/Beijing: Foreign Language Press, 2006. ISBN 0300100655.

This is a gorgeous book and is excellent for viewing the terra-cotta army.

Juliano, Annette. *Treasures of China.* New York: Richard Marek, 1984. ISBN 0399901051.

Juliano discusses China's art and thought as seen through its walls, gardens, temples, tombs, and art treasures.

Kerry, Rose, ed. *Chinese Art and Design: Art Objects in Ritual and Daily Life.* New York: Viking, 1992. ISBN 087951437X.

There are full-page photos of nearly 7,000 years of sculpture, ceramics, painting, and weaving, including objects made of porcelain, jade, lacquer, and silk.

Kleiner, Robert L. *Chinese Snuff Bottles.* New York: Oxford University Press, 1994. ISBN 0195857569.

Illustrations of various kinds of snuff bottles fill this book.

Kwo Da-wei. *Chinese Brushwork.* Mineola, NY: Dover Publications, 1990. ISBN 0486264815.

The author discusses the history, esthetics, and techniques of Chinese brushwork, accompanied by examples.

Ledderose, Lothar. *Ten Thousand Things: Module and Mass production in Chinese Art.* Princeton, NJ: Princeton University Press/Bollingen, 2001. ISBN 069-100957-0.

This book has an interesting chapter on Chinese calligraphy, some good reproductions of Chinese figure painting, and a chapter on the terra-cotta army.

Loehr, Max. *The Great Painters of China.* New York: Harper & Row, 1980. o.p. ISBN 0064353265.

Master painters of the different periods of Chinese history are discussed. There are examples of the three categories of painting mentioned in the viewing section of this chapter.

Mason, Lark E. *Asian Art.* Woodbridge, Suffolk, England: Antique Collectors' Club, 2002. ISBN 1-85149-415-4.

The art of several Asian countries is discussed together in each chapter, and the illustrations of Chinese art are beautiful and well worth using for group viewing.

McArthur, Meher. *The Arts of Asia.* New York: Thames & Hudson, 2005. ISBN 978-0-500-23823-3.

McArthur has a chapter on porcelain in which pictures and text demonstrate how porcelain is made.

McCausland, Shane, and Kaizhi Gu. Foreword by Wen C. Fong. *First Masterpiece of Chinese Painting: The Admonitions Scroll.* New York: George Braziller, 2003. ISBN 080761517X.

This wonderful treatment of a milestone piece of Chinese art is enhanced by eighty-five illustrations, thirty-five of which are in full color.

Morton, W. Scott, et al. *China: Its History and Culture.* New York: McGraw-Hill, 2004. ISBN 0071412794.

The authors present China's history as well as its current position on the world stage.

Pei, Fang Jing. *Symbols and Rebuses in Chinese Art: Figures, Bugs, Beasts, and Flowers.* Berkeley, CT: Ten Speed Press, 2004. ISBN 1-58008-551-2.

There are beautiful illustrations of many symbols used in different kinds of Chinese art.

Qu, Lei Lei, and Lei Lei Qui. *The Simple Art of Chinese Calligraphy: Create Your Own Chinese Characters and Symbols for Good Fortune and Prosperity.* New York: Watson-Guptill, 2005. ISBN 0823048381.

The authors suggest many projects involving Chinese characters.

Reader's Digest. *Treasures of China.* New York: Reader's Digest, 2005. ISBN 0762105658.

With over 400 beautiful color photos, this is a perfect vehicle for introducing children to some of the beauty to be found in China.

Sullivan, Michael. *The Arts of China.* 4th ed. Berkeley: University of California Press, 2000. ISBN 0-520-21876-0.

This edition has more than 380 illustrations, almost half of which are in color.

———. *The Three Perfections: Chinese Painting, Poetry and Calligraphy.* Rev. ed. New York: George Braziller, 1999. ISBN 0807614521.

Sullivan explains why the Chinese write on their paintings.

Thorp, Robert L., and Richard Ellis Vinograd. *Chinese Art & Culture.* New York: Harry N. Abrams, 2001. ISBN 0-8109-4145-7.

A treasure for group viewing, this book contains large reproductions and a time line of Chinese art.

Watt, James C. Y. *China: Dawn of a Golden Age, 200–750 AD.* New Haven, CT: Yale University Press, 2004. ISBN 0-300-10487-1.

Produced in conjunction with an exhibit held at the Metropolitan Museum of Art, this book contains beautiful pictures. The pottery and jewelry are very impressive.

Weng Wan-go. *Chinese Painting and Calligraphy.* New York: Dover, 1978. o.p. ISBN 0486237079.

There is a brief discussion of Chinese painting and calligraphy styles throughout the ages, followed by wonderful full-page reproductions.

Weng Wan-go, and Yang Boda. *The Palace Museum: Peking.* New York: Harry N. Abrams, 1982. o.p. ISBN 0810914778.

Art treasures of the Forbidden City, including architecture, paintings, and figurines, are discussed. Although this book is out of print, the gorgeous, large reproductions make it worth the hunt.

Yue, Rebecca. *Chinese Calligraphy Made Easy.* New York: Watson-Guptill, 2005. ISBN 0823005569.

Yue shows readers how to form Chinese characters.

Zhu Jiajin, comp. *Treasures of the Forbidden City.* New York: Viking, 1986. ISBN 0670807958.

This book traces the origins, development, and characteristics of Chinese bronzes, painting, ceramics, minor arts, and textiles as well as providing descriptions of 100 pieces chosen to represent them. Beautiful, large pictures for group viewing.

Children's Books

Alexander, Lloyd. *Dream-of-Jade: The Emperor's Cat.* Illustrated by D. Brent Burkett. Peterborough, NH: Cricket Books, 2005. ISBN 0812627369.

A cat befriends the emperor and teaches him how to enjoy life and rule well.

Anderson, Dale. *Ancient China: History of Art.* Portsmouth, NH: Raintree/Heinemann, 2005. ISBN 1410905195.

This is a fine presentation of ancient China and Chinese art for young children.

Bateson-Hill, Margaret. Chinese text by Manyee Wan. *Lao Lao of Dragon Mountain.* Illustrated by Sha-Liu Qu. New York: Stewart, Tabor & Chang, 1996. ISBN 1899883649.

A greedy emperor demands that Lao Lao, a peasant woman who makes beautiful shapes from paper, perform an impossible task. The book includes instructions for making traditional Chinese paper cuts.

Cole, Joanna. *Ms. Frizzle's Adventures: Imperial China.* Illustrated by Bruce Degen. New York: Scholastic, 2005. ISBN 0590108220.

The indomitable Ms. Frizzle leaves Chinatown in a huge paper dragon and visits eleventh-century China.

Compestine, Ying Chang. *The Story of Chopsticks.* Illustrated by Yongsheng Xuan. New York: Holiday House, 2001. ISBN 0823415260.

Using his knowledge of Chinese customs and traditions, the author tells how chopsticks might have been invented.

———. *The Story of Kites.* Illustrated by Yong Sheng Xuan. New York: Holiday House, 2003. ISBN 0-8234-1715-8.

This is a story about how kites may have come to be in China. There is an author's note about the history of kites, directions for making a kite, and instructions for flying it safely.

_____. *The Story of Noodles.* Illustrated by Yong Sheng Xuan. New York: Holiday House, 2002. ISBN 0-8234-1600-3.

Three young Chinese boys accidentally invent noodles. A recipe for noodles is included.

Cotterell, Arthur. *Ancient China.* Illustrated by Laura Buller. New York: DK Children, 2005. ISBN 0756613825.

In this treasure trove of information, readers will find out about ancient Chinese emperors, inventions, art, medicine, and much more.

Davol, Marguerite. *The Paper Dragon.* Illustrated by Robert Sabuda. New York: Atheneum, 1997. ISBN 0-689-31992-4.

An artist confronts the dragon that is threatening to destroy his village. Beautifully illustrated.

Demi. *Buddha.* New York: Henry Holt, 1996. ISBN 0805042032.

This is a beautifully illustrated, short biography of the spiritual leader.

———. *Buddha Stories.* New York: Henry Holt, 1997. ISBN 0805048863.

Each of these ten tales from Buddha ends with a moral. The outstanding illustrations are done in Chinese gold ink on vellum.

———. *The Dragon's Tale.* New York: Henry Holt, 1996. ISBN 0-8050-3446-3.

Demi tells a fable about each of the twelve animals of the Chinese zodiac. Demi's wonderful illustrations were rendered with paints made from plants, minerals, and a touch of powdered jade.

———. *The Greatest Power*. New York: McElderry, 2004. ISBN 0-689-84503-0.

The emperor challenges the children to tell him what the greatest power in the world is.

———. *Happy, Happy Chinese New Year*. New York: Crown, 2003. ISBN 0375810080.

Demi describes the many festivities that take place during the Chinese New Year.

———. *Kites: Magic Wishes That Fly up to the Sky*. New York: Dragonfly/Random, 2000. ISBN 0375810080.

A mother asks a painter to make her a magic kite that will carry a wish to the gods to make her son strong.

———. *Su Dongpo: Chinese Genius*. New York: Lee & Low, 2006. ISBN 978-1-58430-256-8.

Su Dongpo, who grew up to be a leading eleventh-century Chinese scholar and statesman, began writing stories and poems as a young boy. This is a beautiful picture-book story of his life.

Drake, Ernest, and Dugald Steer. *Dragonology: The Complete Book of Dragons*. Cambridge, MA: Candlewick, 2003. ISBN 0763623296.

This faux nonfiction book is a real treasure sure to be a hit with children. It contains a complete history of dragons, including Chinese dragons, fold-out illustrations, information about setting up a dragonology lab, and much more. The fun continues in Steer's *Dragonology Handbook*, 2005.

Drummond, Allan. *The Willow Pattern Story*. New York: North South, 1995. ISBN 1558584137.

A young girl is kept from the man she loves, so the two of them flee and eventually end up trapped in an underground passage. At their death they become two doves hovering over the garden they love—and this is the willow pattern that can be found on dinnerware.

DuTemple, Lesley. *The Great Wall of China*. Minneapolis, MN: Learner, 2002. ISBN 0822503778.

The author provides a history of the wall and its building as well as a history of China and its people.

Fang, Linda. *The Ch'i-Lin Purse*. Illustrated by Jeanne M. Lee. New York: Farrar, Straus & Giroux, 1997. ISBN 0374411891.

This is a collection of nine ancient Chinese stories.

Freedman, Russell. *Confucius: Golden Rule*. Illustrated by Frederic Clement. New York: Arthur A. Levine, 2002. ISBN 0439139570.

This is a beautifully written biography by a master of the genre, and the illustrations mirror Chinese-style painting.

Hall, Bruce Edward. *Henry and the Kite Dragon*. Illustrated by William Low. New York: Philomel, 2004. ISBN 0399237275.

A conflict over the Italian children's pigeon raising and the Chinese children's kite flying in New York's Chinatown and Little Italy in the 1920s is satisfactorily resolved.

Ho, Minfong, transl. *Maples in the Mist*. Illustrated by Jean Mou-sien and Tseng Mou-sien. New York: Lothrop, Lee & Shephard, 1996. ISBN 0688147232.

This collection of poems from the Tang dynasty (618–907) and the brush paintings that accompany them are certain to appeal to children.

Hosking, Wayne. *Asian Kites: Asian Arts & Crafts for Creative Kids*. North Clarendon, VT: Tuttle Publishing, 2005. ISBN 0804835454.

The author presents stories and legends associated with kites and provides directions for making and decorating fifteen Asian kites.

Lee, Huy Voun. *At the Beach*. New York: Henry Holt, 1998. ISBN 0805058222

A mother and son enjoy their day at the beach by drawing Chinese characters, many of which resemble the objects for which they stand, in the sand. Lee has written several other books along the same lines, with just a change of venue. All are very simple and would be excellent for encouraging children to try making Chinese characters. The other books are *In the Snow* (2000, ISBN 0805065792); *In the Park* (1998, ISBN 0805041281); and *In the Leaves* (2005, ISBN 0805067647).

Lee, Jeanne M. *The Song of Mulan*. Arden, NC: Front Street, 1997. ISBN 1886910006.

Based on a Chinese folk song, this is the story of a young Chinese girl who rides off to war in her father's stead. Filled with Chinese characters and artwork.

Lee, Milly. *Landed*. Illustrated by Yangsook Choi. New York: Farrar, Straus & Giroux, 2006. ISBN 0-374-34314-4.

Sun comes to America from China with his father, but before he can be pronounced "landed," that is, allowed to come into the country, he must pass a series of tests to prove he is his father's son.

Lin, Grace. *Dim Sum for Everyone*. New York: Knopf, 2001. ISBN 037581082X.

Through the experiences of a family that goes to a Chinese restaurant, readers learn about making dim sum, in this attractive picture book.

———. *Kite Flying*. Cambridgeshire, England: Dragonfly Books, 2004. ISBN 0553112546.

Three girls buy supplies, then make and fly a dragon kite. Lin provides a list of supplies for making kites, some Chinese kite characters and their significance, and a history of kite flying.

———. *The Year of the Dog*. Boston: Little, Brown, 2006. ISBN 0316060003.

In this easy fiction work, young Grace hopes the Year of the Dog will be a special one for her.

Major, John S. *The Silk Route*. Illustrated by Stephen Fieser. Minneapolis, MN: Sagebrush, 1999. ISBN 0613003322.

Major discusses the trade route between China and Byzantium during the Tang Dynasty.

Mak, Kam. *My Chinatown*. New York: HarperCollins, 2001. ISBN 0060291907.

Four lovely poems reveal to readers what life in New York's Chinatown is like.

Marsden, Carolyn, and Virginia Shin-Mui Loh. *The Jade Dragon.* Cambridge, MA: Candlewick, 2006. ISBN 0763630128.

Ginny longs for a best friend but wonders if she should try to win Stephanie's friendship by lending her her family's precious jade dragon heirloom. A novel for grades two and up.

Merrill, Yvonne Y., and Jim Tilly. *Hands on Asia: Art Activities for All Ages.* Illustrated by Mary Simpson. Salt Lake City, UT: Kits Publishing, 2002. ISBN 0-9643177-8-8.

This book has a beautiful, full-page, color illustration for each craft suggested. The object to be made is discussed in the context of the historical period, and clear instructions are given.

Mochizuki, Ken. *Be Water, My Friend: The Early Years of Bruce Lee.* Illustrated by Dom Lee. New York: Lee & Low, 2006. ISBN 978-1-58430-265-0.

This picture-book biography of Bruce Lee describes how he developed an interest in martial arts and eventually became a pioneer of martial arts cinema.

O'Connor, Jan. *The Emperor's Silent Army.* New York: Viking, 2002. ISBN 0670035122.

O'Connor documents the discovery of the terra-cotta army the first emperor of China had made in Xi'an to protect him in the afterlife. The story of these life-sized figures is fascinating.

Poole, Amy Lowry. *The Pea Blossom.* New York: Holiday House, 2005. ISBN 0-8234-1864-2.

Poole sets this Hans Christian Andersen tale, about five peas from the same pod who land in different places, in Beijing.

Porte, Barbara Ann. *Hearsay: Strange Tales from the Middle Kingdom.* Illustrated by Rosemary Feit Covey. New York: Fordham University Press, 2004. ISBN 0823224104.

This collection of Chinese tales is beautifully illustrated with woodcuts.

———. *Ma Jiang and the Orange Ants.* Illustrated by Annie Cannon. New York: Orchard, 2000. ISBN 0-531-30241-5.

MaJiang figures out how to use honey to trap the ants that eat pests that threaten orange trees.

Roome, Diana Reynolds. *The Elephant's Pillow.* Illustrated by Jude Daly. New York: Farrar, Straus & Giroux, 2003. ISBN 0-374-32015-2.

A young boy tries to console the emperor's elephant after the emperor's death.

Schlein, Miriam. *The Year of the Panda.* New York: HarperTrophy, 1992. ISBN 0064403661.

When a Chinese boy rescues a panda, he learns more about these rare bears and the efforts to prevent their extinction.

Simonds, Nina, and Leslie Swartz. *Moonbeams, Dumplings & Dragon Boats: A Treasury of Chinese Holiday Tales, Activities & Recipes*. Illustrated by Meilo So. San Diego: Harcourt/Gulliver, 2002. ISBN 0152019839.

Five Chinese holidays are celebrated in this attractive book.

Tompert, Ann. *Grandfather Tang's Story*. Illustrated by Robert Andrew Parker. New York: Dragonfly/Random House, 1997. ISBN 0517885581.

A grandfather tells a story about shape-changing fairies. Tangrams, ancient Chinese puzzles, are woven into the story, and directions for making them are included.

Tucker, Kathy. *The Seven Chinese Sisters*. Illustrated by Grace Lin. Morton Grove, IL: Albert Whitman, 2003. ISBN 0-8075-7309-4.

Tucker takes off on the familiar Chinese tale and describes very enterprising women who find a way to rescue their baby sister.

Williams, Brian. *Ancient China*. New York: Viking, 1996. ISBN 0670871575.

Double-page, see-through spreads reveal the customs and daily lives of the ancient Chinese. Key dates and glossary.

Williams, Suzanne. *Made in China: Ideas and Inventions from Ancient China*. Illustrated by Andrea Fong. Berkeley, CA: Pacific View Press, 1997. ISBN 1881896145.

Williams includes information on paper making, agriculture, medicine, and much more.

Yee, Paul. *The Jade Necklace*. Illustrated by Grace Lin. New York: Crocodile Books, 2002. ISBN 1-56656-455-7.

When her father is lost at sea during a typhoon and her family no longer has enough to eat, Yanyee travels to Vancouver as a servant.

———. *A Song for Ba*. Illustrated by Jan Peng Wang. Toronto: Groundwood, 2004. ISBN 0-8899-492-3.

A Chinese family who has a long tradition of singing in the Chinese opera find that people in the New World prefer other kinds of entertainment.

———. *Tales from Gold Mountain*. Illustrated by Simon Ng. Vancouver, BC: Douglas and McIntyre, 1999. ISBN 0888990987.

There are eight stories about Chinese immigrants to America and their role in the gold rush, the building of the transcontinental railway, and the settling of the West Coast.

Yep, Laurence. *The Rainbow People*. Illustrated by David Wiesner. New York: HarperTrophy, 1992. ISBN 0064404412.

This is a collection of twenty Chinese folktales.

———. *Tongues of Jade*. Illustrated by David Wiesner. New York: HarperCollins, 1991. ISBN 0-06-022470-3.

Yep retells seventeen Chinese folktales from various Chinese communities around the United States.

Yolen, Jane. *The Emperor and the Kite.* Illustrated by Ed Young. New York: Putnam, 1998. ISBN 0698116445.

The emperor's smallest daughter rescues him from his jailers.

Young, Ed. *Beyond the Great Mountains.* San Francisco: Chronicle Books, 2005. ISBN 0-8118-4343-2.

Young creates beautiful artwork to celebrate the things he loves in his beloved China.

———. *Lon Po Po.* New York: Putnam. 1996. ISBN 0698113829.

This Caldecott award–winning book is a Chinese version of "Little Red Riding Hood" in which three sisters outwit the wolf. Stunning illustrations.

———. *Voices of the Heart.* New York: Scholastic, 2003. ISBN 0439456932.

Using collage art, award-winning artist Ed Young explores twenty-six Chinese characters, each describing a feeling or emotion, and each containing a symbol for the heart.

Zheng, Zhensun, and Alice Low. *A Young Painter.* New York: Scholastic, 1991. ISBN 0590449060.

This is the fascinating story of a young Chinese woman who began painting at the age of three.

Audiovisual Materials

Ancient China. DVD. Library Video Company, 1998. V 7153.

Children will learn about the first four dynasties in ancient China. The film includes information on the terra-cotta army and comes with a teacher guide.

Beyond the Yellow River: Discoveries from Ancient China. Video. National Gallery of Art. n.d. VC161.

This film focuses on archaeological discoveries that have given us insight into the art of ancient China from 500 BC to the tenth century.

The Chinese Past: 6000 Years of Art and Culture. Slides and audiocassettes. National Gallery of Art, n.d. 043.

The slides show objects from the Neolithic period through the Yuan Dynasty. The program is divided into four units: Two units contain narration to accompany the forty-eight slides, and two units contain traditional music, poetry, and a discussion of Chinese philosophies.

The First Emperor of China. DVD. The Library Video Company, 1989. V0068.

This film reveals the spectacular art treasures of the first emperor of China. Film footage of the original archaeological dig, tour of museums, Great Wall. In English and Chinese.

Splendors of Imperial China. CD-ROM. National Gallery of Art, n.d. CD320.

This CD presents more than 475 of the finest works of art in the National Palace Museum, Taipei. Special features include close-up details, audio pronunciations of Chinese terms and names, and the opportunity to unroll precious handscrolls.

Other Materials

The following eleven items, redesigned in 2006, are all available from Rice Paper Kite, Denver, CO. Go to www.DragonExpressKits.com and click on "Chinese Culture for Kids."

Celebrate Chinese New Year.

Discover the fun and excitement of Chinese New Year while making glittery luck posters, a New Year's lantern, and more! This kit includes posters, greeting cards, red envelopes, a paper lantern, glitter glue, a Chinese yo yo, and an activity booklet with instructions.

Celebrate the Dragon Boat Festival.

Children discover how Chinese people celebrate this major summer holiday, make their own dragon boats, have chopsticks races, and more! This kit includes chopsticks, fun chop chopstick helpers, modeling compound, festive lantern, and an activity booklet with instructions.

Chinese Creation Myth: Pan Gu and the Creation of the World Storybook with CD.

This classic Chinese myth tells how Pan Gu created the world. The set includes a color-your-own storybook, CD recording of the story in English, and colorful markers.

Create a Chinese Fan.

Children can create a fan while they learn all about Chinese language and culture. The kit includes one bamboo and paper fan, a set of watercolors, markers, and a *Dragon Express Discovery Booklet.* Ages five and up.

Dancing Dragon Mini Craft Kit.

Children learn what makes Chinese dragons unique. The kit includes a paper dragon, craft sticks, decorations, and instructions.

Discover Chinese Kites.

Fly a kite and learn about Chinese culture! This kit includes a white plastic kite, plastic sticks, kite tail, a handle with kite string, three permanent markers, and a *Dragon Express Discovery Booklet.* Ages five and up.

Discover Chinese Animals.

This kit enables children to discover the important role animals play in Chinese culture while they engage in crafts. It includes animal puppet supplies, a magnifying glass, a pouch of decorations, and instructions.

Explore Chinese Calligraphy.

Students can make beautiful calligraphy cards as they learn about Chinese calligraphy. The kit includes a Chinese sumi brush, black watercolor ink, authentic Chinese calligraphy practice paper, blank cards with envelopes, fancy rice paper, and a *Dragon Express Discovery Booklet.* Ages six and up.

Make Your Own Chinese Paper Cuts Mini Kit.

With this kit, students find out about Chinese paper cuts and make their own. The kit includes a *Mini Discovery Booklet* about paper cuts, three patterns to cut out, and a Chinese paper cut decoration.

Play Chinese Hopscotch Mini Kit.

Children can learn how to play tiao fangzi, the Chinese version of hopscotch. The kit includes two pieces of colorful sidewalk chalk and complete game instructions.

The Tiger and the Frog Storybook with CD.

How can a little green frog frighten a big hungry tiger? By using his wits, of course! This set includes a color-your-own storybook, CD recording of the story in English, and a set of colorful markers.

From Other Sources

Chinese Calligraphy Set. Metropolitan Museum of Art, n.d. M7017.

This set contains everything a child would need to do calligraphy: brushes, inks, and more.

Hsu and Ching. *Chinese Brush Painting: A Beginner's Guide*. New York: Metropolitan Museum of Art, n.d. 14-011506.

Silkworm City. Kit. Kababee, Inc., n.d. #SW-City.

This kit enables a class to raise silkworms and watch them grow.

Web Sites

China the Beautiful. http://www.chinapage.org/main2.html (accessed February 10, 2006).

This site provides numerous links to a plethora of information about China. Students can listen to Chinese opera and Chinese poetry, learn to make Chinese characters, and much more.

Chooey, Colette, *Chinese Tea Stories*. http://firehorseportfolio.com/tea/index.html (accessed September 9, 2006).

This excellent site contains many short Chinese tales for your students to enjoy.

Daily Life in Ancient China. http://members.aol.com/Donnclass/Chinalife.html (accessed February 10, 2006).

Find out all about life in ancient China and the people who lived it.

Dragon Express Kits. www.DragonExpressKits.com (accessed September 11, 2006).

This site provides helpful resources for teachers, including a suggested reading list for ages toddler to adult and free printable Chinese language and culture activities.

The Great Wall of China. http://www.newton.mec.edu/Angier/DimSum/Great%20Wall%20Pix.html (accessed February 10, 2006).

This site provides stunning photos of the wall.

The Great Wall of China. http://www.newton.mec.edu/Angier/DimSum/Great%20Wall%20Background.html (accessed February 10, 2006).

This site provides background information on the Great Wall.

Lifecycle. http://www.pclaunch.com/~kayton/Silkworms/lifecycle.htm (accessed February 6, 2006).

This site provides many stunning pictures of the life cycle of a silkworm.

6 The Art of Africa

"Listen, then, Children of Africa, we have had a glorious past and it presages a promising future."

—HERB BOYD, *African History for Beginners*

Background Information

Africa, the second largest continent, is a land of great beauty and harsh contrasts, of deserts and rain forests, of intense tropical heat and bitter cold, of level plains and steep snow-topped mountains, of busy cities and dense jungles, of wild game preserves and cultivated farmland. There is archaeological evidence that the first humans appeared in eastern Africa about two and a half million years ago. The first art to arise in Africa, as discussed briefly in chapter 1, were the rock paintings, begun over 8,000 years ago and discovered in 2,000 sites throughout the continent. Often pictures are superimposed on one another, and the scenes, while containing some human figures, are, like the cave art found in Europe, overwhelmingly of animals. Prehistoric African artists painted their pictures on rock walls or incised outlines into the rock, either with dots or a solid line.

Egypt, in northern Africa, whose art and culture we discussed at length in chapter 2, was established and prospered as early as 4500 BC. South of Egypt, a kingdom called Kush arose about 2000 BC and lasted until about the fourth century AD. Kush became a major center of trade, learning, and art and developed one of the world's earliest alphabetical scripts. In the eighth century BC, Phoenician traders from the region that is present-day Syria established the city of Carthage, and Africans living in Numidia (now Algeria) and Mauretania (now Morocco) opposed them. By the end of the first century, Rome controlled the northern coast of Africa, and when, in the third century, Christianity became the official Roman religion, it spread to North Africa as well. As the rivers in the Sahara region gradually began to dry up, converting the area into desert, the people living there traveled south, bringing with them two advances that were to have a dramatic effect on the development of the continent: knowledge of farming and raising cattle, and the production of metal tools and weapons. Some of the kingdoms formed by this resettlement of peoples became so famous or spawned leaders so legendary that they remain fascinating to us hundreds of years later.

Much has been written about the kingdoms of Ghana, Mali, and Songhy in West Africa. There were such rich gold deposits in Ghana that entire houses were made of the metal and the area became known as the Gold Coast. The Ashanti in Ghana made gold weights in the shape of animals and birds, which they used for trade. Sundiata, a Mali hero, was once a cripple who overcame his infirmity, became king, and united his kingdom. Although he ruled harshly, he was fair, and he led his people to prosperity. Mali rose to even greater glory under the reign of its greatest ruler, Mansa Musa, between 1307 and 1332. In Timbuktu in Songhy, a university was founded in the thirteenth century that attracted noted Muslim scholars from as far away as India. Some of the most ancient art in all of Africa was produced in early Nigeria. Nok pottery sculptures date from 500 to 200 BC and evince great imagination and beauty. The British brought almost 2,000 bronze, ivory, and wood pieces from Benin in southern Nigeria to Europe in the nineteenth century. The people of the sacred city of Ife in southwest Nigeria created bronze statues using the lost-wax technique. For an explanation of this technique, go to http://www.metmuseum.org/toah/hd/wax/hd_wax.htm.

Trade with other countries for needed commodities, especially salt, introduced the Muslim religion into northern Africa, where it spread into the western kingdoms below the Sahara. The creation of abstract bronze statues and masks was the result, in part, of the Muslim prohibition against exact likenesses. Muslim influence was also felt in education, for the Muslims taught reading and writing in Arabic to many Africans and established religious schools that attracted students from many parts of the continent.

Bantu-speaking peoples moved southward from what is now the Nigeria-Cameroon border region into the forests of central Africa, eventually settling throughout central and southern Africa. Population increased rapidly in the Congo forests, and the kingdoms of Kongo and Ngola became powerful rivals. The kingdom of Bakuba in the Congo was said to have had 124 kings in its long history, and artists carved a seated statue in honor of each king during his lifetime.

Great Zimbabwe, the largest of a series of stone-walled enclosures built in one of the wealthiest kingdoms of southern Africa, is so spectacular that it now gives its name to the country. The outer wall of the enclosure is 16 feet thick, 825 feet long, and 32 feet high. The stone was fitted together without mortar. These structures are so sophisticated and magnificent that early nineteenth-century explorers refused to credit them to the African people. Archaeologists have since proved that Great Zimbabwe is the work of the ancestors of the people who still live in the area.

The first Europeans to land in Africa were the Portuguese, when Vasco da Gama traveled around the southern tip of the continent in 1497. Traders and missionaries soon followed. By the sixteenth century, slave traders from Spain, Portugal, and England were capturing Africans with the cooperation of some African rulers and sending them to work as slaves on the plantations of the Caribbean and the Americas. This slave trade continued into the nineteenth century, and the capture of millions of Africans led to the decline of many of the ancient kingdoms. In the mid-seventeenth century, Dutch farmers went to the Cape of Good Hope as employees of the Dutch East India Company and settled in Cape Town. After the Cape became a British colony in 1806, tensions between the Dutch farmers, or Boers, and the British increased and escalated into a war. The Union of South Africa was created in 1910.

In the nineteenth century, European countries, especially England, France, Portugal, and Germany, entered Africa's interior regions and carved her lands into colonies that they exploited for their rich mineral deposits and natural resources. Only Liberia and Ethiopia escaped this foreign domination, which lasted for eighty years. Today Africa is made up of fifty-two independent countries, and its story is still being written. Ethnic wars are still taking their toll in African nations, resulting in the loss of thousands of lives, and these struggles may create still different borders. One of the greatest triumphs of the African people has been the establishment, after years of agonizing struggle, of majority black rule in South Africa.

It is a mistake to think of the African people as a single group. There are many different tribes and races, and they speak over 1,000 different languages. Each tribe has its own distinct culture, beliefs, and customs. Even occupation, dress, adornment, and housing are different. The people of Africa range from the small Pygmies living in the tropical rain forests of Zaire to the incredibly tall Tutsi living in Burundi and Rwanda. Their skin colors vary from a yellowish tan to light brown to rich ebony. It is into this amazingly diverse world with its ancient and rich heritage that we enter when we study the art of Africa, for African art is intimately connected to the lives and religious beliefs of its creators. "To appreciate it fully, we need to 'read' these works of art as we would read a book, for in the absence of written documents, Africans often preserved their beliefs and values and conveyed them from generation to generation through their art. The significance of each work, therefore, derives not merely from its tangible form or its esthetic merit, but equally from the concepts and beliefs that it embodies" (Robbins and Nooter 1989, p. 11).

As we view these works, we will come to know why they had a powerful place not only in the lives of their creators but also in the art world beyond the borders of Africa, where they have influenced the work of Picasso, Brancusi, Modigliani, and many others and spawned such art movements as Cubism, Expressionism, Fauvism, and Surrealism.

(Standards: Art Connections 1.1, 4, 7; K-4 History 7.1-2, 9, 22; Geography 12, 13:6-12)

The Story

(This story is meant to describe no particular tribe but is the combination of the initiation rites of several different groups of people. Some of the more graphic details of the pain inflicted on initiates in some cultures have been eliminated so the story can be told to young children.)

Koti could hardly keep his mind on his duties. The more he tried to focus on the cattle that his family depended on for their food, clothing, and even their ranking in the tribe, the more his mind wandered. For in a few days he would leave his tasks behind and gather with other boys his age to prepare for one of the most important events of his life. Koti was twelve years old, and if he could prove himself worthy to leave behind the ways of childhood, he would enter into a special ceremony to make him an adult member of the tribe. He was excited, but also a little frightened, because he would have to show his elders he could bear responsibility and even pain. Koti shivered as the sun began to sink on the horizon and streaks of pink stretched across the sky overhead.

Five days later Koti's father led him to the outskirts of the village. As they walked, other boys Koti had played with all his life and their fathers met them on the path, so that before long they formed a solemn procession. There was no running or teasing now, only whispered comments among the boys while their fathers walked tall and proud before them. Soon they came to a round, thatched hut set apart from everything else. Three tribal elders stood there to welcome the boys and send the men away. Koti watched his father leave, and a lump formed in his throat. He would not see any members of his family again until seven days had passed and he performed the special ceremonial dance that announced to everyone that he was an adult member of the tribe.

The boys gathered on the ground while the elders turned toward the altar set in front of them. The altar was a wooden table covered with a cloth woven and dyed in beautiful colors by the women of the village. On the cloth were placed several large statues. Koti knew those statues well. They were images of his ancestors, the great ones who had governed his tribe wisely in past generations. "Oh, fathers," prayed the elders when quiet had settled over the group, "send your spirit into these young people. Open their ears so that they may hear and receive instruction during these special days. Open their minds that they may know and understand the ways of our people. Open their hearts that they may be filled with the courage to accept the pain and challenges that lie before them." As the elders prayed, Koti could feel a deep peace come over him. Yes, his ancestors were with him. He could feel their presence, and he was anxious to join himself to them and to the members of his tribe still living so that he could contribute his strength and his talents for the good of everyone. And so evening came that first day.

Every morning after that, the boys were awakened early and made to cleanse themselves in a nearby stream. Then they spent the rest of the day listening to instructions. They were told what was expected of them as adult men and husbands. They heard of the deeds of those who had gone before them, and the statues of the ancestors surrounded them with their spirit and life. Koti and his friends were allowed food only once a day, a thin gruel that did not fill them but enabled them to keep their strength up. With each passing day, they grew leaner and more determined to succeed. Finally the test of bearing pain came. The skin of each boy's forehead and cheeks was cut in a design that was the special mark of the tribe. Koti stood with his fists clenched during the cutting, neither flinching nor crying out when he felt the knife sting his flesh. Then tree sap was rubbed into the cuts so they would stand out in relief and reveal the decorative pattern. How proud Koti felt to be wearing the mark of his tribe! From this moment onward, everyone who saw him would know to whom he belonged. He was no longer only an individual but part of a group of people all living and working together. Koti felt like jumping and shouting for joy, but he knew he must remain serious and calm before the elders. This was his last night as a child. He would spend it in quiet meditation before the altar of the ancestors.

At dawn on the seventh day, the whole tribe gathered before the thatched hut while the young boys filed out in front of them. The sky was just beginning to fill with color. "My people," said the first elder, "behold these young men. They have proven themselves intelligent and brave. They have been instructed in our ways and have promised to remain faithful to them all their days. Witness now their final movement away from the days of childhood and welcome them into the tribe with open hearts. Share with them your wisdom and courage and allow yourselves to receive their strength when your limbs become weak with age. They are our future and our glory!"

One by one, the elders placed a beautiful ceremonial mask on each boy's head. The masks were heavy and completely covered their faces, for they were no longer only single individuals but joined to each other and to everyone else in the tribe. Slowly the musicians began to play their instruments. Koti could hear his uncle play the *sansa*, an instrument with wooden strips his uncle plucked. He could hear the drummers playing on animal skins and gourds and the trumpeters blowing through animal horns. His feet began to move. Around and around he twirled, while the beat became faster and faster. Koti's feet became a blur as he kept up with the music. He soon forgot where he was and who he was. He knew only that he must dance and dance and that he could not stop even if his body cried out for rest.

On and on the musicians played, until finally, with a loud blast of the horn, they stopped. Koti and the others threw down their masks as a sign that they were throwing away the days of their childhood. The elders came forward and stripped the boys of their clothes and made them wash one more time in the stream. "Wash away your old ways and put on the new life of a man," they said to each boy as they gave him a colorful new cloth to wear. Then they piled the old clothes in the center of the group and set them aflame, for those who wore them were boys no longer. They were men. There followed a big feast, for the women had been preparing for this special day all week. Koti joined his parents and his younger brothers and sisters, proud of his special face markings and his new adult clothing, and there was great rejoicing all that day.

Now we are going to enjoy some of the statues Koti and his people made representing their ancestors and some of the masks they used for their special ceremonies. When we look at them, it is important to remember that most of these works of art were not made as decorations. They were made because of the beliefs of the people about a Higher Power and their own place in the world. So we must think about the ways these things were used and what they stood for, and not judge them according to our old familiar ideas about what makes art beautiful.

(Standards: Language Arts: Listening and Speaking 8.4 Art Connections 1.1, 4, 6-8)

LESSON 1: African Masks

Viewing the Art

African art is often called primitive art. This does not mean it is crude or substandard. It simply means that it is art created by peoples who have had little or no access to machinery or formal training, except by apprenticeship. Most African masks are made of wood. In humid areas of the continent, most wood pieces last only about 200 years, but in arid regions, artworks made of wood are many centuries old.

Some masks are made using the pole style, that is, the mask takes on the long shape of the tree trunk from which it is made. There is no attempt by the artist to make the finished piece smooth. Rather, sharp angles and features emphasize the fierce or frenzied nature of the ceremony for which the mask was intended. Other masks are made in the round style, the finished piece being rubbed smooth and even soaked in oils or other materials to give it a rich tone. Some masks are painted. White often represents death or ghosts. Red is a celebratory color.

Show the children a variety of masks. You may wish to show the art by region—western Sudan, West African coast, Central Africa, eastern Africa, southern Africa—or simply to show a series of African masks. Whatever you decide, be sure to point out that African peoples live in many different countries and regions, where climate and natural resources for creating artwork differ. Their customs differ as well. By discussing this with the children, you help them avoid lumping all Africans into a single group, and thereby increase the children's respect for these talented and diverse peoples. Some of the masks shown in *The African Kings* by Mary Cable (see references) are quite unusual. Or you may wish to view videos or slides (see references), which are particularly effective for showing African art. Try to include a variety of different masks in your viewing: animal as well as human forms, round and pole styles, painted and unpainted examples. The children may especially enjoy the small but incredibly beautiful ivory mask carved for the king of Benin.

(Standards: Art Connections 1.1-8; Visual Arts 4.5-11; Language Arts: Viewing 9.23)

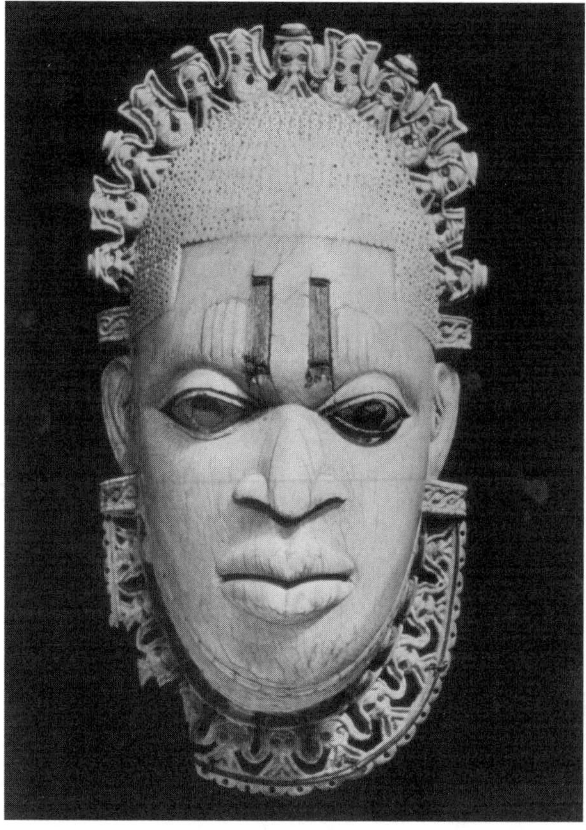

Sculpture, Africa, Nigeria; Edo, Court of Benin, 16th century

Pendant Mask: Iyoba

Ivory, iron, copper (?)

H. 9 ⅜ in. (23.8 cm)

Pendant Mask: Iyoba, Sixteenth Century. The Metropolitan Museum of Art, The Michael C. Rockefeller Memorial Collection, Gift of Nelson A. Rockefeller, 1972 (1978.412.323). Photograph, all rights reserved, The Metropolitan Museum of Art.

Journal Writing

How do the masks make the children feel? Are some frightening to look at? Why do they think the artist made them that way? Perhaps some children would like to choose one particular mask and write about a ceremony in which they think that mask played an important part.

(Standards: Language Arts: Writing 1.7, 23, 33-37; Art Connections 1.3)

Art/Drama Activity: Mask-Making

Materials

- Pictures of African masks to serve as models
- Paints and brushes
- Glue
- Tape
- Newspapers (whole sheets and sheets cut or torn into strips)
- Fabric scraps (or anything else the children may wish to put on their masks)
- Papier-mâché mix
- Large paper plates

Wrap several pieces of newspaper into a round or elongated oval shape (depending on the kind of mask) around a paper plate (or anything else you wish to use as a form) and tape in place. If the mask is an animal with horns, or if it has any other special characteristics, form those shapes with crushed newspaper and tape onto the original shape. Cut or tear the remaining newspaper into strips and coat them with papier-mâché. Cover the newspaper shape with several layers of strips, taking care to smooth them into place after each application. Allow to dry overnight or for several days. Paint the mask, adding eyes, mouth, and other features. Glue on beads, fabric, feathers, etc., as appropriate.

Hands-On Africa: Art Activities for All Ages Featuring Sub-Saharan Africa and *Cut & Make African Masks* (see references) will provide more suggestions for making masks as well as for other interesting activities involving a study of African art.

(Standards: Visual Arts 1, 4-5.1-11)

LESSON 2: African Sculpture

Viewing the Art

Sculptures are made of various materials, including terra-cotta, wood, ivory, and bronze. Some depict a tribe's ancestors, some represent spirits, and still others are fetishes believed to have magic powers to ward off evil and protect people from sickness. Often statues will exaggerate breasts and reproductive organs, bearing witness to the African emphasis on fertility. Show some examples of different kinds of statues. You may wish to show the artwork by region as previously suggested, or simply to show a variety of statues. Some figures you may want to include are the statues of kings from the kingdom of Bakuba in the Congo, the double male and female figures of the Dogon, the Nigerian leopard figures, Nigerian stone and bronze heads, the Bidjugo carved figures from the coast of Guinea; Dogon ancestor figures, Ashanti gold weights, Baluba ancestor figures, Baule figures, the guardian figures from the Congo, or stools from the Hemba and Zela of Zaire. Bassani's *Arts of Africa* (see references) has outstanding reproductions of African statues and some masks.

The children might find it interesting to contrast art currently being created in Africa with the ancient masks and sculptures they've seen thus far. An excellent book to use for this comparison is *African Art Now* (see references). While the older works discussed above are anonymous, the contemporary works in *African Art Now* have known artists, and the children can learn something about them.

(Standards: Art Connections 1.1-8; Visual Arts 4.5-11; Language Arts: Viewing 9.23)

Journal Writing

Ask the children to pick one statue as their favorite out of those they have seen. Why did they choose it? What do they especially like about the statue? Does it give them any ideas about the people who created it?

(Standards: Language Arts: Writing 1.7, 23, 33-37; Art Connections 1.3)

Art/Drama Activity: Initiation Ceremony

Act out an initiation ceremony similar to the one described in the story above. The children can assume the parts of elders, parents, initiates, and musicians. Use the masks created in the first lesson for a ceremonial dance. The children can use some of the text from *Dancing Masks of Africa* by Christine Prince in choral reading to accompany the dance. They may also wish to make instruments and devise a melody to use in the ceremony.

(Standards: Dance 1, 3,5.1, 7, 12, 16-19; Music 2-3.4-5, 16)

Curriculum Connections

Social Studies

- Using a map, show the continent of Africa, locate different countries, find countries where the artworks viewed originated, or where children about whom you read in some of the fiction stories listed in the resources live. Are there children in the class who can trace their ancestry to Africa? If so, to which countries? Locate these countries on a map.
- Locate different natural wonders such as Mt. Kilimanjaro, Victoria Falls, Sahara Desert, etc.
- Older children may wish to talk about African history: the ancient kingdoms, European colonialism, the struggles for independence, the abolition of apartheid in South Africa, or Africa's struggles for survival today. Also talk about the problem of HIV/AIDS in many African countries and what is being done to help curb the spread of this disease.
- Pick a particular African tribe and discuss the different tribal customs, dress, housing, and ways of life of these people. For example, you could use the book *Papa, Do You Love Me?* to initiate a discussion of the traditions and customs of the Masai, *For You Are a Kenyan Child* to discuss life for a Kalenjin child in Kenya, or *Faces of Africa* to view a variety of peoples (see references for these and other helpful books). What is the main occupation in which these people are engaged? What are their houses like? If the children are older, you might read *Our Secret Siri Aang* (see references) aloud and discuss the dilemma of trying to preserve ancient customs in a modern world.
- Help children to understand that Africa has major cities where life is very much like their own, as well as remote villages where life has not changed for centuries.
- Talk about Africa's vast natural resources—metals such as gold, and valuable stones such as diamonds. What kinds of wood do Africa's jungles provide?
- Learn about some African foods. From what African countries do these foods come? How are they prepared there? Have an African feast. Use the recipes in *Mama Panya Makes Pancakes* and *One Child, One Seed* (see references). Also see the Web site listed in the references for recipes and ideas.
- Read *I Lost My Tooth in Africa* (see references) to spark a discussion of family traditions. Are there African American children in the class who can trace some traditions to their roots in Africa?
- If your students are older, you may want to discuss the taking of African peoples as slaves. Tom Feelings's *Middle Passage* (see references) very poignantly tells the story of the journey into slavery. Although they are too numerous to list here, there is an abundant variety of picture books, novels, and nonfiction

books about slavery, life in the American South, and the American Civil War to enrich such a study. A search of your library's catalog will turn up many books that will suit your students' interests and abilities. You might want to connect this study of African art with the transportation of Africans to the Americas and the art these African Americans created throughout the years of their slavery and beyond.

(Standards: Geography 1-2, 10, 17.1, 4-6, 8, 29-30; Grades K-4 History 1, 5-7.2, 22, 32; World History 6.3-4, 10, 25)

Mathematics

- Present some different kinds of African counting. Use *We All Went on Safari: A Counting Journey through Tanzania* (see references) and similar books.

  (Standards: Mathematics 2.3, 29)

Music

- Play tapes or CDs of African music (see references). In what countries did the particular pieces originate?
- Learn some African folksongs using *African Roots* by Jerry Silverman (see references).
- Study African musical instruments. Make some simple instruments to accompany your singing. (See Bingham's *African Art & Culture* and *African Beginnings* in references).
- Read *Imani's Music* and *Drumbeat in Our Feet* (see references).

  (Standards: Music 2-3.4-5, 16)

Science

- For zoology, study some of the wildlife living in Africa. Make a book or calendar featuring African wildlife. Which species are endangered? What can the children do about it?
- What medicines are obtained from African rain forests? How are these valuable areas being used? Preserved? Destroyed?

  (Standards: Science: Life Sciences 6-7.1, 10, 22, 35, 50)

Literature

- Folklore is rich in stories from the different countries of Africa. Anansi the Spider is a famous African trickster. Read many African folktales. (The books listed in the references are only a sampling of the hundreds that are readily available in picture-book format.) Encourage the children to learn some for a storytelling fest. Dramatize a few favorites.

- Study some African proverbs. Are any of them similar to other proverbs the children know? (See *The Night Has Ears* in the references.)
- Read some biographies of famous Africans: Nelson Mandela, Shaka, Sundiata, etc. (See the references for some suggested books.)
- Read some poems by African Americans. (See *Soul Looks Back in Wonder* by Tom Feelings and other poetry listed in the references.)
- Read aloud some of the fiction stories featuring Africans and African Americans (see references).

(Standards: Language Arts: Reading 5-7.4-5, 13, 28)

References

Adult Books

Bacquart, Jean-Baptiste. *The Tribal Arts of Africa: Surveying Africa's Artistic Geography*. New York: Thames & Hudson, 2000. ISBN 0-500-28231-5.

Bacquart has divided Africa into forty-nine geographical areas and discusses representative art from each area. This is a beautiful book for group viewing.

Bassani, Ezio, Ed. *Arts of Africa: 7,000 Years of African Art*. New York: Skira, 2005. ISBN 8876242848.

Over 400 works of African art are reproduced in full color.

Beckwith, Carol, and Angela Johnson. *Faces of Africa*. Washington, DC: National Geographic, 2004. ISBN 079226830X.

This beautiful book is filled with pictures of different tribes of African peoples and their customs and ceremonies.

Boyd, Herb. *African History for Beginners*. Illustrated by Shey Wolvek-Pfister. New York: Writers and Readers Publishing, 1991. o.p. ISBN 0863161448.

This is a poetic exploration of the history of Africa.

Cable, Mary. *The African Kings*. Chicago: Stonehenge Press, 1983. ISBN 0867060891.

This book contains beautiful color reproductions of art created for the African kings and is excellent to use for group viewing.

Courtney-Clarke, Margaret. *African Canvas: The Art of West African Women*. New York: Rizzoli, 1990. ISBN 0847811662.

This beautiful book presents the art of contemporary women living in West Africa who still live in the traditional way of their ancestors.

Magnin, André, et al. *African Art Now: Masterpieces from the Jean Pigozzi Collection.* London/New York: Merrell, 2005. ISBN 1858942896.

Readers can view a wide range of contemporary African art and learn about the artists.

Newton, Douglas. *Masterpieces of Primitive Art.* Photographs by Lee Boltin. New York: Knopf, 1982. o.p. ISBN 0394500571.

Douglas presents the works in the Rockefeller collection of primitive art, among which are many African pieces. Excellent for viewing.

Phillips, Tom, Ed. *Africa: The Art of a Continent.* New York: Prestel Publishing, 1999. ISBN 3791320041.

Phillips covers the art of the continent, from the oldest art to art of the present day.

Robbins, Warren M., and Nancy Ingram Nooter. *African Art in American Collections.* Washington, DC: Smithsonian Institute Press, 1989. ISBN 0874747449.

This introduction to African art and reproductions of pieces housed in the United States is excellent for viewing.

Shillington, Kevin. *History of Africa.* Rev. ed. 1989. Reprint, New York: Macmillan, 1995. ISBN 0312125984.

This history of Africa covers the earliest times to the present. There are discussion questions at the end of each chapter.

Visoná, Monica Blackmun, et al. *History of Art in Africa.* Upper Saddle River, NJ:: Prentice Hall, 2003. ISBN 0131833561.

This impressive book covers the art of the entire continent of Africa, including Egypt. There are over 700 illustrations, many in full color.

Willett, Frank. *African Art.* New York: Thames & Hudson, 2002. ISBN 0500203644.

Willett discusses the art of many African peoples and its impact on artists such as Picasso. There are many colored illustrations.

Children's Books

Altman, Susan, and Susan Lechner. *Ancient Africa: Modern Rhymes about Ancient Times.* Illustrated by Donna Perrone. Danbury: CT: Children's Press, 2002. ISBN 051627371X.

Through the poems in this book, readers learn about life in ancient African kingdoms. Suggested activities are included.

Araujo, Frank P. *The Perfect Orange: A Tale from Ethiopia.* Illustrated by Hsiao-Chun Li. Windsor, CA: Rayve Productions, 1994. ISBN 1877810940.

When Tshai offers the king a perfect orange and accepts no gift in return, the king finds a way to reward her with riches. But trickster hyena is not so lucky.

Ayo, Yvonne. *Eyewitness: Africa.* New York: DK Children, 2000. ISBN 0789460300.

This book in the Eyewitness series discusses African history, beliefs, and customs. Ayo's excellent treatment of many aspects of African life also includes a section on masks.

Badoe, Adwoa. *The Pot of Wisdom: Ananse Stories.* Toronto: Groundwood, 2001. ISBN 088899429X.

Ten Ananse stories are beautifully told and illustrated.

Bingham, Jane. *African Art & Culture.* Chicago: Raintree, 2004. ISBN 073986606-0.

Among the many excellent features of this attractive book is a listing of African ethnic groups. There is also a fine section on African musical instruments.

Browne, Philippa-Alys. *African Animals ABC.* Cambridge, MA: Barefoot Books, 2001. ISBN 1841483192.

Twenty-six African animals, one for each letter of the alphabet, are introduced, with lovely drawings.

Bryan, Ashley. *Ashley Bryan's ABC of African American Poetry.* New York: Aladdin, 2001. ISBN 0689840454.

Bryan beautifully illustrates the poems of such famous poets as Eloise Greenfield and Langston Hughes.

———. *Beautiful Blackbird.* New York: Atheneum, 2003. ISBN 0689847319.

This *pourquoi* tale from Zambia explains why birds have a touch of black coloring.

———. *The Night Has Ears: African Proverbs.* New York: Atheneum, 1999. ISBN 0689824270.

Bryan presents twenty-six African proverbs, each beautifully illustrated on its own page.

Cave, Kathryn. *One Child, One Seed: A South African Counting Book.* Photographed by Gisele Wulfsohn. New York: Henry Holt, 2003. ISBN 0805072047.

A seed grows into a pumpkin in this gorgeous counting book that features information about an extended family living in South Africa. A recipe for isijingi, pumpkin stew, a map, and other facts are included.

Chamberlin, Mary, and Richard Chamberlin. *Mama Panya's Pancakes: A Village Tale from Kenya.* Illustrated by Julia Cairns. Cambridge, MA: Barefoot Books, 2005. ISBN 1841481394.

Mama Panya plans to make pancakes for dinner, but her son has invited so many people she fears she will not have enough food. This book provides a good deal of information about Kenya, including a map and a recipe for the pancakes.

Corwin, Judith Hoffman. *African Crafts.* New York: Franklin Watts, 1990. ISBN 0531108465.

Corwin supplies directions for making several items related to African life and customs.

Cummings, Pat. *Ananse and the Lizard.* New York: Henry Holt, 2002. ISBN 0805064761.

This West African tale explains why lizards stretch their necks.

Cunnane, Kelly. *For You Are a Kenyan Child.* Illustrated by Ann Juan. New York: Atheneum/Ann Schwartz, 2006. ISBN 068986194X.

This lovely story follows a Kalenjin boy through his day in Kenya. It is a perfect story to springboard discussions of different African tribal lives and customs.

Daly, Niki. *Jamela's Dress.* New York: Farrar, Straus & Giroux, 2004. ISBN 0374437203.

Jamela is in charge of taking care of the material for a wedding dress, but distractions cause disaster. There are other delightful books about Jamela by this author.

———. *Not So Fast Songololo.* London: Frances Lincoln, 2001. ISBN 0711217653.

Set in South Africa, this is the picture-book story of a young boy who receives a new pair of shoes from his grandmother as a surprise.

Diakite, Penda. *I Lost My Tooth in Africa.* Illustrated by Baba Wague Diakite. New York: Scholastic, 2006. ISBN 0439662265.

When a young African American girl leaves Oregon with her family to visit relatives in Mali, West Africa, she longs to lose her tooth there so she can leave the tooth under a gourd and receive a chicken from the African Tooth Fairy.

Ellis, Veronica Freeman. *Afro-Bets: First Book About Africa.* Illustrated by George Ford. Orange, NJ: Just Us Books, 1990. ISBN 0940975033.

Young children will appreciate this simple history of Africa.

Feelings, Tom. *Middle Passage: White Ships/Black Cargo.* Introduction by Henrik Clarke. New York: Dial, 1995. ISBN 0803718047.

Incredibly beautiful illustrations tell the painful story of the transportation of Africans to the New World as slaves. For older children.

———. *Soul Looks Back in Wonder.* New York: Puffin, 1999. ISBN 0140565019

This beautifully illustrated, award-winning book contains poems celebrating African Americans by thirteen African American poets.

Gerson, Mary Joan. *Why the Sky Is Far Away.* Illustrated by Carla Golembe. Boston: Little, Brown, 1995. ISBN 0316308749.

This Nigerian *pourquoi* tale explains why the sky moved from being close to the earth to being so far away.

Gilber, Carol. *Masks Tell Stories.* Brookfield, CT: Millbrook Press, 1993. ISBN 1562942247.

Gilber describes the use of masks in ancient and contemporary societies throughout the world. Includes African masks.

Green, Robert. *Nelson Mandela: Activist for Equality.* Chanhassen, MN: Child's World, 2002. ISBN 1567666485.

This is a fine biography of Mandela.

Grifalconi, Ann. *The Village That Vanished.* Illustrated by Kadir Nelson. New York: Dial, 2002. ISBN 0803726236.

The people in an African village erase all traces of themselves and their village to escape being captured by slavers.

Habeeb, William Mark. *Africa: Facts and Figures.* Broomall, PA: Mason Crest Publishers, 2004. ISBN 1590848179.

Although the text is meant for older children, teachers will find this a valuable source of information about the many countries of Africa and a good source of pictures.

Haskins, James. *African Beginnings.* Illustrated by Floyd Cooper. New York: HarperCollins, 1998. ISBN 0688102565.

This beautifully illustrated book discusses, in chronological order, eleven ancient African kingdoms. There is a separate chapter on music and dance.

———. *African Heroes.* San Francisco: Jossey-Bass, 2005. ISBN 0471466727.

Haskins presents the stories of African heroes, both those of long ago and those still living.

Hoffman, Mary. *The Color of Home.* Illustrated by Karin Littlewood. New York: Dial, 2002. ISBN 0803728417.

A young boy from Somalia finds it difficult to adjust to life in the United States.

Joosse, Barbara M. *Papa, Do You Love Me?* Illustrated by Barbara Lavallee. San Francisco: Chronicle Books, 2005. ISBN 0811842657.

A young Masai boy discovers how much his father loves him through the father's explanation of many Masai traditions.

Keeler, Patricia A., and Júú T. Leitão. *Drumbeat in Our Feet.* New York: Lee & Low, 2006. ISBN 158430264X.

This picture book discusses the origins and traditions of African dance, kinds of dances done in different African countries, musical instruments, and more. Outstanding!

Kessler, Cristina. *The Best Beekeeper of Lalibela: A Tale from Africa.* Illustrated by Leonard Jenkins. New York: Holiday House, 2006. ISBN 0823418588.

In this picture-book story, a young girl is determined to produce the best honey in her village, despite jeers from those who think this is a man's work.

———. *Our Secret, Siri Aang.* New York: Philomel, 2004. ISBN 0399239855.

Namelok, a Masai girl, tries to persuade her traditionalist father to delay her initiation and marriage because they will restrict her freedom and keep her from the black rhino mother and baby she is protecting from poachers. For older children.

Kimmel, Eric. *Anansi and the Magic Stick.* Illustrated by Janet Stevens. New York: Holiday House, 2002. ISBN 0823417638.

Anansi tries to save himself work by stealing hyena's magic stick, but the idea backfires on him.

Knight, Mary Burns. *Africa Is Not a Country.* Brookfield, CT: Millbrook Press, 2002. ISBN 0761316477.

Children of fifty-three different African nations are represented here, with a brief amount of information on each country

Krebs, Laurie. *We All Went on Safari: A Counting Journey through Tanzania.* Illustrated by Julia Cairns. Cambridge, MA: Barefoot Books, 2003. ISBN 1841484784.

A group of Masai children lead readers on a journey through Tanzania. There are facts about the country in the back of the book and numbers in Swahili.

Kroll, Virginia. *Jaha and Hamil Went Down the Hill: An African Mother Goose Book.* Boston: Charlesbridge, 1995. ISBN 0-88106-866-7.

Familiar nursery rhymes have their counterparts in this interesting book. An added bonus is that readers will learn a good deal about African foods and customs.

Kurtz, Jane. *Fire on the Mountain.* Illustrated by E. B. Lewis. New York: Aladdin, 1998. ISBN 0689818963.

This Ethiopian tale is about a shepherd boy who stays warm overnight by viewing the fire on a far-off mountain.

Kurtz, Jane, ed. *Memories of Sun: Stories of Africa and America.* New York: Amistad/Greenwillow, 2004. ISBN 0-06-051050-1.

These stories for older children reveal what life is like in different parts of Africa today and how children coming from Africa fare in the United States.

Kurtz, Jane, and Christopher Kurtz. *Water Hole Waiting.* Illustrated by Lee Christiansen New York: Greenwillow, 2002. ISBN 0060298502.

In lovely language, Kurtz writes about animals in Africa who take turns coming to drink at the water hole. A wonderful book to use for a discussion of African animals.

Lekuton, Joseph, with Herman J. Viola. *Facing the Lion: Growing up Massai on the African Savanna.* Washington, DC: National Geographic, 2003. ISBN 0792251253.

A young man who grew up as a Massai in Africa talks about how he came to study in the United States and is now teaching in Virginia.

Masks. Mineola, NY: Dover Publications, 1992. ISBN 0486269191.

There are instructions for making six authentic African masks.

McKissack, Patricia. *Porch Lies : Tales of Slicksters, Tricksters, and Other Wily Characters.* Illustrated by Andre Cahrillo. New York : Schwartz & Wade Books, 2006. ISBN 0375836195.

These African American folktales are retold by a master.

Merrill, Yvonne. *Hands-On Africa: Art Activities for All Ages Featuring Sub-Saharan Africa.* Salt Lake City, UT: Kits Publishing, 2000. ISBN 096431777X.

Information about Africa and interesting activities go hand-in-hand in this fun-filled book.

Mollell, Tololwa. *Ananse's Feast: An Ashanti Tale.* Illustrated by Andrew Glass. Boston: Clarion Books, 2002. ISBN 061819598X.

Ananse uses trickery to keep Turtle from sharing his feast, but Turtle finds a way to outsmart Ananse as well.

Murray, Dr. Jocelyn. *Africa: A Cultural Atlas for Young People.* Rev. ed. Updated by Sean Sheehan. New York: Facts on File, 2003. ISBN 0816051518.

Murray and her contributors explain African history and describes the different tribes and countries in the continent. There are sections on religion, music, and more.

Nelson, Julie. *West African Kingdoms.* Oxford: Raintree, 2001. ISBN 0739835815

This is an introduction for young children to the ancient kingdoms of Mali, Ghana, and Songhay.

Onyefulu, Ifeoma. *Here Comes Our Bride! An African Wedding Story.* London: Frances Lincoln, 2005. ISBN 184507047X.

Readers learn about the customs associated with a wedding in Benin, Nigeria.

———. *Ogbo: Sharing Life in an African Village.* San Diego: Harcourt Brace Jovanovich, 1996. o.p. ISBN 015200498X.

In words and pictures, a young boy tells about his life in Nigeria. Excellent!

———. *Welcome Dede! An African Naming Ceremony.* London: Frances Lincoln, 2005. ISBN 1845073118.

In this story about a Ghanian baby's naming ceremony, children learn about the meaning and importance of a name in this culture.

Paye, Won-Ldy, and Margaret H. Lippert. *Head, Body, Legs: A Story from Liberia.* New York: Henry Holt, 2002. ISBN 0805065709.

This story stresses the importance of working together to succeed.

Prince, Christine. *Dancing Masks of Africa.* New York: Scribner's, 1975. o.p. ISBN 0684143321.

This is a marvelous book in which poetical text describes the role of the many different kinds of masks used in West Africa. It is a perfect accompaniment to the dance activity suggested in the lesson.

Richardson, Hazel. *Life in Ancient Africa.* New York: Crabtree, 2005. ISBN 0778720438.

The author discusses daily life, art, religion and other information about ancient Africa.

Sayre, April Pulley. *Good Morning, Africa!* Brookfield, CT: Millbrook Press, 2003. ISBN 076131993X.

This is a fine introduction to the continent for young children.

Stanley, Diane, and Peter Vennema. *Shaka, King of the Zulus.* Illustrated by Diane Stanley. New York: HarperTrophy, 1994. ISBN 068813114X.

This is a wonderful picture-book biography of the powerful Zulu military leader. Glossary and bibliography.

Tadjo, Véronique, ed. *Talking Drums : A Selection of Poems from Africa South of the Sahara.* New York: Bloomsbury, 2004. ISBN 1582348138.

The delightful poems in this book represent sixteen African countries.

Tchana, Katrin. *Sense Pass King: A Story from Cameroon.* Illustrated by Trina Schart Hyman. New York: Holiday House, 2002. ISBN 0823415775.

In this West African folktale, a king is so jealous of a young girl's talents that he tries to dispose of her.

Uzo, Unobagha. *Off to the Sweet Shores Africa: And Other Talking Drum Rhymes.* Illustrated by Julia Cairns. San Francisco: Chronicle Books, 2005. ISBN 081185101X.

These African-inspired Mother Goose rhymes reveal a great deal about life in West Africa. This is a delightful, award-winning book.

Williams, Karen Lynn. *When Africa Was Home.* Illustrated by Floyd Cooper. 1991. Reprint, New York: Orchard/Scholastic Books, 1994.

When Peter and his family return to the United States, they long for the life they had in Africa, and eventually go back.

Williams, Sheron. *Imani's Music.* Illustrated by Jude Daly. New York: Atheneum, 2002. ISBN 0689822545.

Imani the Grasshopper is given the gift of music, in this African folktale.

Winter, Jeanette. *Elsina's Clouds.* New York: Farrar, Straus & Giroux, 2004. ISBN 0374321183.

Just like Basotho women of southern Africa have always done, young Elsina wants to paint the outside of her family's house with designs that will prompt her ancestors to send much-needed rain.

Wisniewski, David. *Sundiata: Lion King of Mali.* Boston: Clarion, 1999. ISBN 0395764815.

Breathtaking cut-paper illustrations and text tell the story of Sundiata, ruler of Mali in the thirteenth century.

Note: Gareth Stevens publishes a series called Countries of the World. In this series there are several individual books about different African countries.

Audiovisual Materials

Africa. Video. Clearvue & SVE, 1990. W5BVHS850X/W598307-HAVTX.

This tour of Africa allows children to view the history, geography, and customs of many of its people.

Africa: Land and People. Video. Clearvue & SVE, 1990. W5BVHA580X/W598305-HAVTX.

This film examines four major regions of Africa and the people who live there.

African Art. Slides and audiocassette. National Gallery of Art, n.d. 015.

Seventy-seven slides present an overview of works of African art in terms of their ritual usage and regional tribal characteristics.

African Cultures for Children: African American Heritage. Video. Clearvue & SVE, 1997. W56VH3701/W592644-HAVT.

African Tribal Music and Dances. Audio CD. Delta Label, 1993. ASIN B000001V3X.

Ancient Africa. DVD. Library Video Company, 1998. V7152.

Some ancient African kingdoms such as Ethiopia, Ghana, Mali, and others are the subject of this fine film.

Arts of Ghana. DVD. Customflix, n.d. 204781.

Viewers see Ghanian artists make Kente cloth, wooden stools, and other kinds of art.

Children's Stories from Africa. DVD. Monterey Media, Inc, 2004. ASIN B0000YEEKS.

Nandi Nyembe tells twelve stories based on tales about African animals.

A Day in the Life of a Village in Africa. DVD. Customflix, n.d. 204951.

Viewers follow people in a small African farming village through their day.

Families around the World: My Family from South Africa. Video. Clearvue & SVE, 2003. W58VH4879.

This film enables children to see a typical day in the life of a South African child.

How the Leopard Got His Spots. Video. Rabbit Ears, 1989.

This "Just So" story introduces students to Kipling as well as the people and wildlife of Africa,

Ladysmith Black Mambazo, et al. *Exotic Voices from Africa: 30 of the Best African Vocal Groups.* Arc Music, 2000. ASIN B00004UDDA.

Children will have the opportunity to hear thirty African songs in this two-disc set.

Sub-Saharan Africa: Peoples Past and Present. Video/DVD. Clearvue & SVE, 1990. W595423-HAVTX.

Through this film, children have the opportunity to see Africa as it was before colonial occupation and Africa today.

Vieux Diop. CD. Triloka, 1995. ASIN B0000057QT.

Music by African composer Vieux Diop.

West Africa. Video. Library Video Company, 2001. K 4944

This film introduces children to life in West Africa, including a look at life in Mali, Ghana, the Ivory Coast, on the River Niger, in Senegal, Timbuktu, the Cape Verde Islands, and more.

Web Sites

Africa: One Continent, Many Worlds. http://www.nhm.org/africa/index.htm (accessed February 19, 2006).

This is an outstanding, must-visit site. It contains a database of artifacts such as masks and figures to view, African stories, classroom ideas, and much more.

African Art: Aesthetics and Meaning. http://www.lib.virginia.edu/clemons/RMC/exhib/93.ray.aa/African.html (accessed February 19, 2006).

This explanation of African art comes from the University of Virginia and is accompanied by examples.

African Art Museum. http://www.zyama.com/baga/index.htm (accessed February 19, 2006).

Click on the name of the tribe and receive information about that tribe's art, and examples.

The African Cookbook. http://www.africa.upenn.edu/Cookbook/about_cb_wh.html (accessed February 19, 2006).

Click on a country and find out about that African country's food: how it is served, recipes, etc.

African Crafts. http://africancrafts.com/ (accessed February 19 2006).

Meet African craftspeople, obtain lessons on making Kente paper and weaving on a loom, and much more.

Museum for African Arts. http://africanart.org/index.htm (accessed February 19, 2006).

This marvelous site has a link to masks that explains African masks, their uses, and how they're made, and provides examples. There are other links as well, including a link to the museum store, which has artifacts from Africa.

Part III
Art of the Middle Ages and the Renaissance

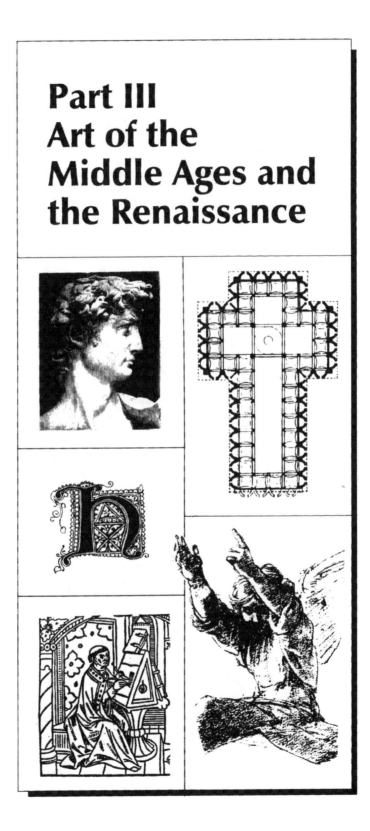

7 Art of the Middle Ages

As the third year that followed the year One Thousand was approaching, almost over the whole earth, but above all in Italy and Gaul, the churches were rebuilt. One might have thought that the earth was shaking itself to shed it skin, and was everywhere re-clad in a white coat of churches.

—RAOUL GLABER (eleventh century) in Sabbagh, *Europe in the Middle Ages*

Background Information

The period from the fall of Rome in AD 476 to AD 1400–1500 is sometimes referred to as the "Dark Ages" of Europe, for most people lived in ignorance, while education was the prerogative of the clergy and the rich. The term "Middle Ages" means the period between between AD 1000 and the birth of the Renaissance in Europe in the mid-fifteenth century. This is the era of building magnificent churches, crafting brilliant mosaics, and writing illuminated manuscripts. Universities, businesses, banking, and trade and commerce among different cities and countries all flowered during the Middle Ages.

But life during this time was harsh and difficult. While some people lived into old age, most did not see their fortieth year. Peasants and serfs worked long hours to eke meager harvests from infertile soil. Women had few rights and often died in childbirth, and noble women were pressed into marriage without their consent to increase the family holdings. There were wars such as the Crusades, initiated by Pope Urban II in 1095 to wrest the Holy Land from the Turks, and the Hundred Years' War, between England and France; the Black Plague, which wiped out a third of the population of Europe and even entire villages; and widespread famine. Indeed, life in the Middle Ages was not for the faint of heart!

The Catholic Church dominated medieval life, and religion was intimately connected to everyday existence. After the Roman persecution of Christians ceased with Constantine's conversion and the proclamation of Christianity as the official religion in AD 392, Christianity spread. Charlemagne, called "Charles the Great" as much for his stature (almost seven feet) as for his exploits, forced the conversion of all of Europe by the sword. Almost all the medieval art we celebrate is religious. Pagan temples were converted to Christian churches, and numerous cathedrals were built in the large cities with financing from clerics and nobles. Each village had its own less elaborate church, supported by the lord of the manor and the peasants, and its bell called the people to prayer throughout the day and to church services on Sundays and Holy Days. Church interiors were decorated with statues and paintings on the walls and ceilings, or beautiful mosaics such as those that adorned the Church of San Vitale in Ravenna.

In the first half of the Middle Ages, education was restricted largely to the wealthy or to boys destined for the priesthood, and books were rare. Priests taught in schools connected to the cathedrals. St. Benedict initiated monastic life for those priests who wished to live apart from the world in monasteries and follow a special rule, or way of life. Monasteries sprang up all over Europe, and some of the monks performed the invaluable service of copying and illustrating the Bible and classical writings by hand. "Books of Hours" containing the prayers the monks and priests said at different times of the day were also copied and lavishly illustrated. Many of these, such as the *Book of Kells*, are works of art in their own right. Thousands of pilgrims made arduous journeys to Rome, the seat of the papacy (in 1309 the papacy moved to Avignon, France, but it returned to Rome once again in 1378), and to shrines to venerate the bones and relics of popular saints. Truly religion was the heart blood of all classes of medieval society.

The dangers of medieval life gradually gave rise to the feudal system, which began in France and, along with the Church, controlled Europe almost into the Renaissance. Under this system, the king granted land or a fief to his most influential lords or barons. They in turn promised to fight for him personally and with knights they supplied and equipped. Powerful lords built castles to protect their fiefs and might, in turn, have lesser lords also under their rule who managed the different parts of their fiefdom and supplied men and arms when they were needed. These lords or barons were in charge of peasants who worked the land and gave to their lord a portion of their produce and livestock. The peasants, who lived in small cottages, often with their animals under the same roof, received protection from their lord in return. When crops were good, peasants were able to sell the surplus at market and to enter into trade. This gradually led to the rise of towns, especially in Italy, and the dissolution of the feudal system. Merchants and tradespeople populated the towns and lived comfortable lives, overseeing workers and apprentices. Some merchants became more prosperous than the lords in their fiefdoms! Trade with other lands, new inventions like the plow, new methods of irrigating the land, and most important of all, the printing press and the spread of education, led eventually to a new birth in art and thought called the Renaissance. But until this revolution took place, Europe was one in a common faith and an organization in which the rules were very clearly defined. Never again would this be so!

While we will concentrate only on church building and the illumination of manuscripts here, there is much about medieval life to capture children's interest and imagination. They may wish to study the construction of castles and to make their own models. This is the age of kings and knights and castles, of King Arthur and his Round Table, of armor and jousts, of fairs, jugglers, magicians, mummers' plays, crusades, and pilgrimages. There are a wealth of books of varying difficulty on this period and many possible activities to keep your students involved in an extended unit if you so choose.

(Standards: Art Connections 1.1-8; K-4 History 1.1; World History 15.14, 48, 52, 64, 70, 110)

The Story

Almost a thousand years ago in France, in a time we call the Middle Ages, two baby boys were born. One baby's father was a poor peasant who had to work in the fields all day on land that was not his own. He had to give part of everything he grew to a great and powerful lord who lived in a castle and owned all the surrounding lands. In return, the lord would protect him and the other peasants on the property if enemies came waging war. The little baby was born in a thatched hut, kept warm by the bodies of the animals that shared the hut with his parents and brothers and sisters.

The child, whose name was Suger, grew to be strong and very clever—so clever, in fact, that his father began to consider something quite out of the ordinary: He would send his son to school. Now, almost no peasants at that time went to school, nor could they read and write. The only exceptions were those boys who were to become priests of the Christian church—and that is what his father determined that Suger would be. So when his son reached the age of nine, he took the lad to a monastery near Paris, a special place where priests, called monks, lived, and asked that he be educated.

Next to the monastery was a church that was a shrine to St. Denis, a special patron saint of France. The monks took care of this shrine and welcomed visitors, who came from great distances to pray there. Because the monks were among the few people who could read and write, they also spent time each day copying the Bible and other important books by hand and painting lovely pictures in them. These books were so beautiful that they were really works of art. And they were very precious, because there were so few books in the land. The monks created a wonderful library filled with the books they copied and started a school next to their monastery. They agreed to educate Suger and to train him in the things he must know to be a priest of God. Suger learned to read so quickly and worked so diligently that the monks were delighted that they had decided to take him in.

The other baby, named Louis Capet, was born in a palace and was the son of a king, King Philip I. He grew up attended by servants. He wore fine clothes and, of course, it was understood that he would be sent to be educated. For when his father died, Louis was destined to take his place as the next king. Certainly he would have to know how to read important documents and to write. When Louis turned nine, he was sent to the same monastery of St. Denis to be educated. He and Suger became best friends and remained so all their lives.

When both boys grew into manhood, Louis was crowned king on the death of his father, and Suger became a monk and lived at the monastery of St. Denis. Suger was the new king's adviser throughout the rest of the king's life and helped him gain power over enemies who tried to take away his throne. He was also elected to a special position as leader, or abbot, of the monastery when the old abbot died. As abbot, Suger had one great desire—to rebuild the Church of St. Denis, because it was crumbling with age and was definitely too small for all the pilgrims who came to pray there each year. He saved as much money as he could from the donations the pilgrims made, and when he finally had enough, he gathered stonecutters and carpenters and artists and began work on the church.

Those of us here probably belong to many different religions. Some of us may be Jewish. Others may be Lutherans or Baptists or Methodists or Muslims. But when Suger lived, most people in the countries of Europe were Catholics, living under the authority of the pope in Rome. When the Roman Empire fell, the temples to the Roman gods were turned into Catholic churches, and many more churches were built. At first, the churches followed the ideas of the Roman builders. They used arches and had very thick walls to support those arches. But Suger had a new idea. He wanted to build a more graceful church, with tall windows that would bathe the interior with light, and he wanted the spires of the church to reach up to the heavens like hands praying to God. No one knew how to build such a church, but Suger and his workers figured out some new designs that made it possible.

We're going to look at some of the marvelous churches built during the Middle Ages, churches that copied the ideas of the Romans, and churches built in the new style of the Church of St. Denis. We'll even see the church of St. Denis itself. And we'll also be looking at some of the marvelous books copied by the monks in their monasteries. For most of the art of the Middle Ages was done not simply to create beauty—it was Christian art done to honor God and the saints.

(Standards: Art Connections 1.1-8; Language Arts: Listening and Speaking 8.4; World History 15.14, 48, 52, 64, 70, 110)

LESSON 1: Medieval Churches

Viewing the Art

While the churches in small medieval towns and villages were simple structures, huge cathedrals were often built in the large cities or where saints lay buried. Help the children understand that constructing such tall structures was an incredible feat at a time when most of the work was done by hand and architects were not always certain how to support them. It was not unheard of to have a church come crashing down several years after its construction. Ask the children to hold their hands over their heads in the shape of a Roman arch. This semicircular arch is very strong, for it can withstand a great deal of downward pressure. But it also requires very thick walls to support it. View some churches constructed with arches in the Roman style. This architectural style is called "Romanesque."

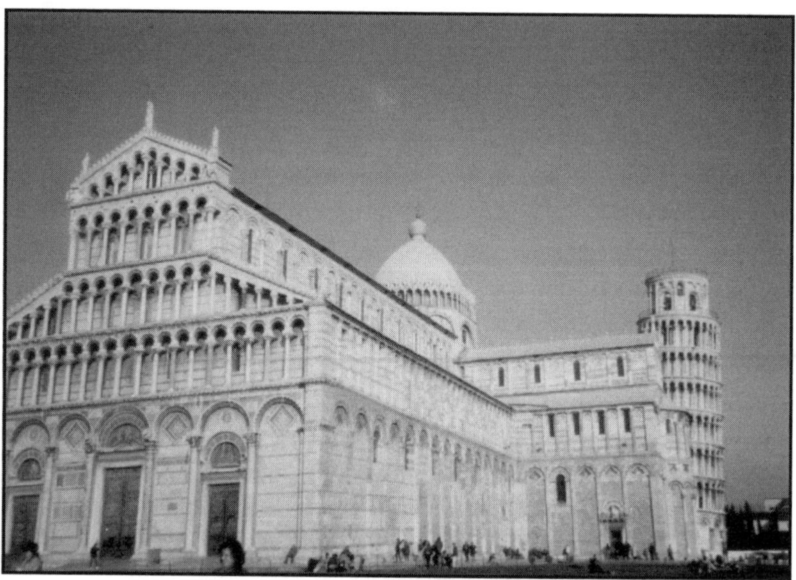

Romanesque Cathedral of Pisa, Italy

Some examples of Romanesque churches are Saint Magdalene of Vezelay, the Church of St. Stephen at Nevers, the Church of St. Michael at Hildesheim, Worms Cathedral, Durham Cathedral, and the Church of St. Stephen at Caen (see Batterberry 1971). What are some things the children notice as they view these churches (arches, small windows, solid-looking walls)? View some church interiors. Note that the main apse, the side transepts, and the center nave form a cross. Invite the children to stand and form a cross-shaped church interior. Abbé Suger's Church of St. Denis ushered in a new architectural style called "gothic." (See http://www.abelard.org/france/cathedral-construction.php#construction for some outline views of the parts of a gothic cathedral.) Show pictures of the Church of St. Denis (See *Great Cathedrals*, pages 23–25) and other gothic churches such as Notre Dame in Paris, Chartres Cathedral, Canterbury Cathedral, and Westminster Abbey. An absolutely gorgeous book for showing cathedrals, especially those of gothic style, is Judith Dupré's *Churches* (see references). It is huge, with the front cover opening in the middle. The book has excellent views of Notre Dame, Chartres Cathedral, Westminster Abbey, and many others, including some the children might know from modern times. What differences do the children notice (pointed arches, bigger windows filled with stained glass, flying buttresses, ribbed vaults)? The pointed arch placed less stress on the walls and enabled architects to use thinner and higher walls. The flying buttresses kept the thinner walls from collapsing under the weight of the roof, and since such solid masses of wall were no longer needed, the builders could create tall, stained-glass windows within those walls to light and beautify the structure. The ribbed vaults were a series of attractive intersecting arches on the underside of the roof. The film *Cathedral* (see references) explains all of these gothic innovations and enables children to follow the long cathedral-building process from beginning to end.

Have the children put their arms over their heads in the shape of a gothic arch, then a Roman arch. (If you have studied Middle Eastern art, recall the Persian arch and point out the differences.) Intersperse pictures of Romanesque and gothic churches and see if the children can tell the difference. Talk about the creation of stained-glass windows: making the glass from sand, lime, and potash; cutting and coloring the glass; and fitting the glass together with lengths of lead to form a picture. Show examples of stained-glass and rose windows. *The Rose Window* and *Medieval and Renaissance Stained Glass* (see references) are wonderful resources for this viewing. Do any of the churches the children attend contain stained glass? Where else have they seen stained glass used?

Since so many people in medieval times could neither read nor write, the interior of the church, where they spent a good deal of their time, served to instruct them in their religion. It was a "book" everyone could read. Stained-glass windows, beautiful wall paintings, and statues told stories about God and the saints. If you wish, you can show the children pictures of some of the church paintings and statuary.

The children may especially enjoy hearing a few excerpts from the writings of medieval bishops and others regarding the building of churches. (See *Chartres Cathedral: Illustrations, Introductory Essay, Documents, Analysis, Criticism,* in references.)

(Standards: Art Connections 1.1-8; Language Arts: Viewing 9.6, 23)

Journal Writing

What are some things the children have learned about Romanesque and gothic churches? Which do they prefer? Why? Do they have any opinions about the huge sums of money spent building and decorating churches?

(Standards: Language Arts: Writing 1.7, 23, 33-37; Art Connections 1.3)

Art/Drama Activity: Stained Glass

Materials

- Sheets of brightly colored cellophane
- A large sheet of black construction paper, folded in half, for each child
- Scissors
- Glue or paste

It is helpful, especially if the children are very young, to have a model of a stained-glass construction to show the children. Have them cut shapes through both thicknesses of their black paper, keeping the fold intact and without going to the edges of the paper. In other words, they must poke a hole through the paper to cut their shapes. Demonstrate this, since it is difficult for some children to grasp. Some children may want to cut figures; others may simply want designs. It is important to have some black between the different shapes. Once this is completed, the children can cut pieces of colored cellophane to fit behind the cut-out shapes. They glue these pieces on the back of one half of the black paper, so that they are sandwiched between the folded halves. Finally, glue the black construction paper closed. Tape the finished pieces to the classroom windows so that the light comes through the cellophane the way that light comes through stained-glass windows in a church.

(Standards: Visual Arts 1, 4.1-11)

LESSON 2: Illuminated Manuscripts

Viewing the Art

It is quite effective to have a Gregorian chant playing softly in the background while viewing the art in this lesson.

Explain to the children what monks are and their role in medieval life. Do the children know of any monasteries near their homes? Have they ever visited one? Show pictures of a typical medieval monastery, pointing out the cloister and garden where the monks could walk and pray, the attached church, the workrooms, and especially the scriptorium. *A Walk through the Cloisters* and *The Cloisters:*

Medieval Art and Architecture (see references) would be especially helpful here. One of the most important functions the monks performed was the creation and preservation of books, rare treasures in the days before the printing press made multiple copies of books feasible. Explain how the monks drew beautiful pictures and designs in the books they copied so that these books became precious works of art. We call these books illuminated manuscripts, because the art seems to light them with beauty. Show as many examples of illuminated manuscripts as you can. (See *The Trés Riches Heures of Jean, Duke of Berry, Calligraphy & Illumination, The Duke and the Peasant: Life in the Middle Ages,* and *A History of Illuminated Manuscript,* in the references.) Note that there are full pages of illustrations as well as decorative borders and even decorative letters—the first letter of a paragraph, for example. What colors are used? What are the subjects of the illustrations? Read *The Sailor Who Captured the Sea* (see references) so that the children can learn that it took 100 years to create the *Book of Kells*! Also view reproductions from the *Book of Kells* itself (see Cirker 1982). Mention that the libraries established by the monks were about the only places in Europe where books were available during medieval times.

(Standards: Art Connections 1.1-8; Language Arts: Viewing 9.6, 23)

Journal Writing

Have the children imagine a world without books, their own lives without books. What would life be like? What are their feelings about the heritage medieval monks have passed on to us? What do they think of the illuminated manuscripts they have viewed?

(Standards: Language Arts: Writing 1.7, 23, 33-37; Art Connections 1.3)

Art/Drama Activity: Illumination and Dramatization

As mentioned in the background notes, the art of the Middle Ages was mostly religious. Monks in their monasteries spent their days copying the Bible by hand and illuminating its pages with their exquisite artwork. However, depending upon your student population and the community in which you teach, the Bible need not be the subject of this activity. A selection from any important document would do just as well.

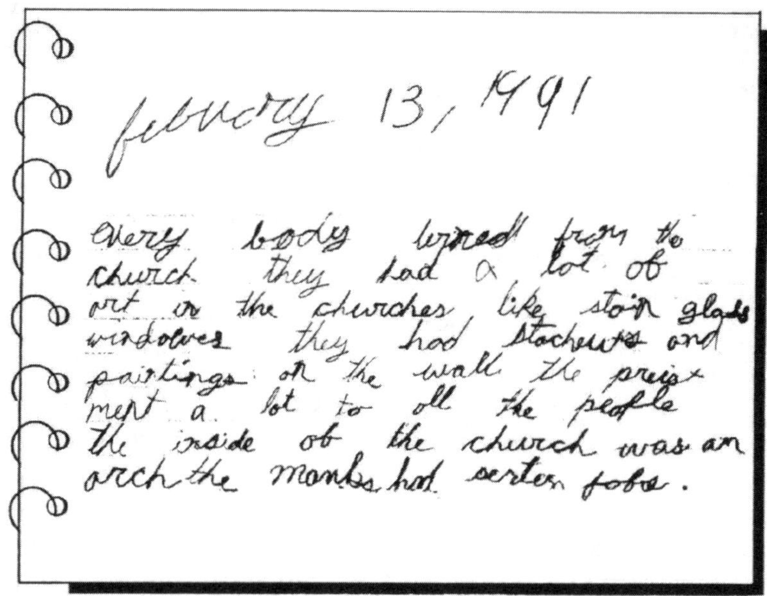

febuary 13, 1991
every body lerned from the church they had a lot of art in the churches like stain glass windows they had stachuets and paintings on the wall the preist ment a lot to all the people the inside of the church was an arch the monks had serten jobs.

Materials

- Samples of illuminated manuscripts, including decorative first letters of a paragraph
- Copies of a selection from the Bible, a government document, or a famous quotation, printed in the center of one side of a large sheet of paper. Leave ample borders and the other half of the sheet blank so children can paint a larger picture there. Leave out the first letter of the selection so children can paint in a decorative one.
- Small paintbrushes
- Paints (make sure you include gold)

Invite the children to "illuminate" the excerpt with their painting. Have samples of illuminated manuscripts available so the children can see where the monks placed their paintings and borders. The children might wish to copy some border patterns or create their own.

Another project the children might enjoy is decorating the initials of their name, a parent or friend's name, etc. Grafton's *Illuminated Initials in Full Color* (see references) provides excellent examples.

(Standards: Visual Arts 1, 4.1-11)

Children love to dramatize medieval life, assuming the different roles of the king, lords, knights, peasants, merchants, monks, cathedral-builders, or artisans. In a series of scenes, have them move through a typical day: knights training for combat, the king and his court seeing to affairs of state, a lord visiting his peasants and overseeing the running of his fiefdom, monks in their scriptorium, merchants in their shops, etc. This can be a very simple way of summing up some discussions of medieval life, or a more elaborate play with costumes, scenery, and an audience.

(Standards: Theater: 2-3.1, 2, 10, 11)

Curriculum Connections

Social Studies

- Study the history of the Middle Ages. What brought about this period of history? (See *Medieval Panorama* as well as Hanawait 1998 and Caselli 1988.)
- Using a map or globe, locate some of the European countries in which the art discussed during the viewing sessions originated or remains at present in churches, museums, etc.
- Make a time line of important events that occurred during the Middle Ages, such as the invention of the printing press, the discovery of America, etc. (See *What Life Was Like in the Age of Chivalry* in the references.)
- What was it like to go to school during the Middle Ages? Who went to school? Woolf's book, *Education,* is a delightful treatment of this topic. Orme's *Medieval Children* has a section about education as well (see references).
- Find out about food during the Middle Ages: how it was grown, what people ate, what feasts were like, etc. Prepare a food that would have been served during this period. (See *Medieval Feasts and Banquets* in the references).
- Find out about medieval clothing. (See *Medieval Clothing and Costumes* in the references.) What were the fashions like for different groups of society? Have some fun making medieval hats.
- Find out what life was like during the Middle Ages for the following people:
  - women (See *Damsels Not in Distress* and *Women in Medieval Times* in the references.)
  - merchants (See *Walter Dragun's Town* and *What Life Was Like in the Age of Chivalry* in the references.)
  - monks, nuns, and other clergy (See *What Life Was Like in the Age of Chivalry* and *Archers, Alchemists, and 98 Other Medieval Jobs You Might Have Loved or Loathed* in the references.)
  - peasants (See *Archers, Alchemists, and 98 Other Medieval Jobs You Might Have Loved or Loathed* in the references.)
  - a person on pilgrimage (See *Pilgrim* in the references.)

- artists (See *Archers, Alchemists, and 98 Other Medieval Jobs You Might Have Loved or Loathed* in the references.)
- knights (See the books by Hinds and the many books about knights and castles in the references.)

(Standards: Geography: 1, 2.30; Grades K–4 History: 1, 7.1-2, 14, 38; World History 15, 20.20-21)

Science

- Research medical practices of the time such as bleeding and herb medicines. What herbs are still in use for healing today? (See *What Life Was Like in the Age of Chivalry* in the references.)
- Talk about illness and disease such as the Black Plague in medieval times. What caused these illnesses? What was sanitation like during this period? (See *The Black Death* in the references.)
- What inventions, military weapons, etc., were used during the Middle Ages? (See "Medieval Technology" in Caselli 1988.)
- Astronomy of the time: Find out what people believed about the earth, sun, and other heavenly bodies.
- Farming methods: Find out whether there were methods more advanced than those of ancient peoples like the Greeks, Egyptians, and Romans.

(Standards: K-4 History 1, 8.15; Science 11.29, 39, 51; World History 15, 20.14)

Music

- Instruments: Find out what instruments were used. Some, such as the recorder and tambourine, are easily obtained in a school. Work with the music teacher to play or invent some medieval tunes, or have older students play for the class. (See *Medieval Music, A Young Person's Guide to Music,* and *Medieval Myths, Legends, and Songs,* in the references.)
- Gregorian chant was the reigning church music of the time. Listen to some pieces. (See audiovisual materials in the references.)
- Learn a maypole or other medieval dance. See Rooyackers (2003) for instructions.

(Standards: Dance: 1, 5.1,7, 17; Music: 2-3, 7.5-7, 16; Arts and Communication: 4-5.29)

Literature

- Older children might enjoy some of Chaucer's *Canterbury Tales,* as adapted by Barbara Cohen (see references).
- After enjoying Barbara Cooney's award-winning version of Chaucer's *Chanticleer and the Fox* (see references), invite the children to perform the story as a puppet show.
- Read some rhymes and songs enjoyed by children during the Middle Ages (see Orme (2001, 137–161).
- Read aloud some of the tales in Bodger's *Tales of Court and Castle* (see references).
- Read biographies of some famous people of the period, such as Marco Polo, St. Benedict, St. Bernard, Dante, and others. (See references for some examples.)
- Read a version of King Arthur's tales suited to class abilities.
- Practice medieval script using Henry Shaw's *Medieval Alphabets and Decorative Devices* (see references).
- Unicorns are well-known medieval mythological creatures and hold a lasting fascination for just about everyone. If an actual visit is not possible, the children will enjoy taking a virtual visit to the unicorn tapestries at the Cloisters Museum in New York. *The Unicorn Tapestries at the Metropolitan Museum of Art* (see references) is an excellent book to use for this purpose. In addition, the museum has a wonderful Web site that enables the children to see the tapestries up close, to learn about hunting in medieval times, and to learn how tapestries are woven: http://www.metmuseum.org/explore/Unicorn/unicorn_splash.htm. Also, see the video in the references.

(Standards: Language Arts: Listening and Speaking 8.4, 13; Reading 5-7)

Older children might enjoy learning about Shakespeare and his plays and the Globe Theatre, in which they were performed, and actually performing some scenes. See references for some suitable books.

References

Adult Books

Barnet, Peter, and Nancy Wu. *The Cloisters: Medieval Art and Architecture.* New York: Metropolitan Museum of Art, 2006. ISBN 0300111428.

The holdings of the Cloisters Museum of the Metropolitan Museum of Art in New York as well as views of the cloister area itself make this a valuable resource for viewing.

Bartlett, Robert, ed. *Medieval Panorama.* Los Angeles: The J. Paul Getty Museum, 2001. ISBN 0-89236-642-7.

Bartlett discusses eight aspects of the medieval world, among them daily life and the legacy of medieval art, and illustrates them with art of the period. This is an invaluable resource.

Batterberry, Michael, adapter. *Art of the Middle Ages.* New York: McGraw-Hill, 1971. o.p. ISBN 07-004082-6.

Batterberry presents an overview of the art of this period, including statuary and painting.

Branner, Robert . *Chartres Cathedral: Illustrations, Introductory Essay, Documents, Analysis, Criticism.* New York: W. W. Norton, 1996. ISBN 0393314383.

This book is valuable for the primary documents it provides as well as the discussion of Chartres and the illustrations.

Cavallo, Adolfo Salvatore. *The Unicorn Tapestries at the Metropolitan Museum of Art.* New York: Metropolitan Museum of Art, 2005. ISBN 0300106300.

The unicorn tapestries are among the most popular holdings at the Cloister Museum, and this book allows readers to see them up close and learn the stories behind them.

Cirker, Blanche. *The Book of Kells: Selected Plates in Full Color.* Mineola, NY: Dover, 1982. ISBN 0486243451.

This book contains thirty-two full-color reproductions from the beautiful *Book of Kells.*

Cowen, Painton. *The Rose Window.* New York: Thames & Hudson, 2005. ISBN 0500511748.

There are over 300 photographs of the most famous rose windows in the world in this outstanding book.

DeHamel, Christopher. *A History of Illuminated Manuscript.* New York: Phaidon Press, 1997. ISBN 0714834521.

Along with a history of illuminated manuscripts, DeHamel provides beautiful examples in full color.

Duby, Georges. *History of Medieval Art, 980–1440.* New York: Rizzoli International, 1986. o.p. ISBN 084780710X.

Duby's history is especially useful for a section on medieval monks and the function of the monastery.

Dupré, Judith, with Mario Botta. *Churches.* New York: HarperCollins, 2001. ISBN 0-06-019438-3.

This stunning book is excellent for group viewing of churches, with excellent views of interiors, rose windows, and more.

Favier, Jean. *The World of Chartres.* Photography by Jean Bernard. New York: Harry N. Abrams, 1990. ISBN 0810917963.

Originally published in French under the title *L'univers de Chartres,* this is an exquisite collection of large photos of the interior and exterior of the cathedral. Especially useful for viewing vaults, flying buttresses, and stained glass.

Grafton, Carol Belanger. *Illuminated Initials in Full Color: 548 Designs.* Mineola, NY: Dover, 1995. ISBN 0486285014.

All the letters of the alphabet are beautifully decorated. This book would provide excellent examples for an art project.

Longnon, Jean, and Raymond Cazelles. *The Trés Riches Heures of Jean, Duke of Berry.* Translated by Victoria Benedict. 1969. Reprint, New York: George Braziller, 1989. ISBN 0-8076-1220-0.

This book contains breathtakingly beautiful, full-page reproductions of the illuminations from the *The Trés Riches Heure.* A must!

Lovett, Patricia. *Calligraphy & Illumination: A History & Practical Guide.* New York: Harry N. Abrams, 2000. ISBN 0-8109-4119-8.

The second half of this book is especially useful for information about how books are illuminated and for the excellent examples provided.

Luttikhuizen, Henry, and Dorothy Verkerk. *Snyder's Medieval Art.* 2d ed. Upper Saddle River, NJ: NJ: Prentice Hall, 2005. ISBN 0131929704.

Wonderful color plates of stained glass and cathedrals make this an extremely valuable resource for group viewing.

McClendon, Charles B. *The Origins of Medieval Architecture.* New Haven, CT: Yale University Press, 2005. ISBN 0300106882.

This book provides excellent examples of Romanesque architecture.

Nees, Lawrence. *Early Medieval Art.* New York: Oxford University Press, 2002. ISBN 0192842439.

Nees discusses the development of art from AD 300 to 1000.

Orme, Nicholas. *Medieval Children.* New Haven, CT: Yale University Press, 2001. ISBN 0-300-09754-9.

Orme treats all aspects of life for children in the Middle Ages.

Rooyackers, Paul. *101 More Dance Games for Children: New Fun and Creativity with Movement.* Alameda, CA: Hunter House, 2003. ISBN 0897933834.

The author provides instructions for many kinds of dances and games, including the maypole.

Schütz, Bernhard. *Great Cathedrals.* New York: Harry N. Abrams, 2002. ISBN 0-8109-3297-0.

More than 250 oversized color plates show gothic cathedrals from every aspect.

Stokstad, Marilyn. *Medieval Art.* 2d ed. Jackson, TN: Westview Press, 2004. ISBN 0813341140.

This edition focuses on all the major works of the period and provides more than ninety full-color reproductions.

Williamson, Paul. *Medieval and Renaissance Stained Glass in the Victorian and Albert Museum.* London: Victoria and Albert Museum, 2004. ISBN 0810966131.

The stained glass holdings of the Victorian and Albert Museum are displayed in more than 100 color plates. Excellent for viewing.

Children's Books

Aliki. *A Medieval Feast.* New York: HarperCollins, 1983. ISBN 0690042469.

Readers follow the preparations at Camdenton Manor for the visit of the king, the queen, and their retinue. This simple picture book gives children an idea of the kind of food eaten in medieval times.

Ardley, Neil. *A Young Person's Guide to Music.* Music by Poul Ruders. New York: Dorling Kindersley, 2004. ISBN 0-7566-0540-7.

There is a section on medieval music in this book.

Arnold, Joan. *Medieval Music.* London: Oxford University Press, 1982. o.p. ISBN 019321332X.

Arnold describes the music and instruments of the day.

Beckett, Sister Wendy. *The Duke and the Peasant: Life in the Middle Ages.* New York: Prestel-Verlag, 1997. ISBN 3-7913-1813-6.

Sister Wendy uses twelve beautifully illuminated pages of the Duc de Berry's *Book of Hours* to describe life in the middle ages.

Bhote, Tehmina. *Medieval Feasts and Banquets: Food, Drink, and Celebration in the Middle Ages.* New York: Rosen Publishing, 2003. ISBN 0-8239-3993-6.

Find out about food and feasts in the Middle Ages through this book.

Bodger, Joan. *Tales of Court and Castle.* Toronto: Tundra Books, 2003. ISBN 0-88776-614-5.

The seven tales retold here were once told in castles and huts, all the way back to the Middle Ages.

Caselli, Giovanni. *The Middle Ages.* New York: Peter Bedrick, 1988. ISBN 087226176X.

Caselli explains everyday life in the Middle Ages, including pilgrims and hospices, and trade fairs and markets.

Cels, Marc. *Arts and Literature in the Middle Ages.* New York: Crabtree, 2004. ISBN 0-7787-1355-5

Chapters on music, dance, and how stained glass was made in the Middle Ages make this a worthwhile resource.

Chaucer, Geoffrey. *Chanticleer and the Fox.* Illustrated by Barbara Cooney. New York: HarperTrophy, 1982. ISBN 0064430871.

Proud Chanticleer, ruler of the roost, is grabbed by a fox and must figure out a way to save himself.

Clare, John D., ed. *Fourteenth-Century Towns.* San Diego: Gulliver Books, 1996. ISBN 0152013202.

Photographs of live actors reveal life in a medieval town, including a look into a merchant's home and apprenticeships.

Cohen, Barbara, adapter. *Canterbury Tales.* Illustrated by Trina Schart Hyman. New York: Lothrop, 1988. ISBN 0688062016.

Four of Chaucer's tales are translated from Middle English and adapted, with delightful illustrations.

Cushman, Karen. *Catherine, Called Birdy*. New York: Clarion, 1994. ISBN 0395681863.

This is a humorous novel for older children in which Catherine, through her diary, tells of her efforts to avoid an arranged marriage.

Forward, Toby. *Shakespeare's Globe : An Interactive Pop-up Theatre*. Illustrated by Juan Wijngaard. Cambridge, MA: Candlewick Press, 2005. ISBN 0763626945.

Children will love the opportunity to interact with this book. It has an actual stage, quotes from plays, punch-out characters from twelve of Shakespeare's plays, and more.

Freedman, Russell. *Adventures of Marco Polo*. Illustrated by Magram Ibatouline. New York: Arthur A. Levine/Scholastic, 2006. ISBN 043952394X.

A master biographer tells Marco Polo's story. The illustrations are wonderful.

Galloway, Priscilla. *Archers, Alchemists, and 98 Other Medieval Jobs You Might Have Loved or Loathed*. Illustrated by Martha Newbigging. New York: Annick Press, 2003. ISBN 1-55037-811-2.

Humorous cartoon drawings accompany this witty book filled with information about all strata of medieval society.

Gravett, Christopher. *Castle*. Photos by Geoff Dann. New York: DK Publishing, 2004. ISBN 0-7566-0660-8.

Readers become eyewitnesses to life in a medieval castle.

Gross, Gwen. *Knights of the Round Table*. New York: Random House Books for Young Readers, 2004. ISBN 0394975790.

This short, simple book tells about Arthur pulling the sword from the stone, Sir Lancelot, and other events featuring Arthur and his knights.

Hanawait, Barbara A. *The Middle Ages: An Illustrated History*. New York: Oxford University Press, 1998. ISBN 0-19-510359-9.

Older children will find this an interesting and complete history of the time.

Hart, Avery, and Paul Mantell. *Knights & Castles: 50 Hands-on Activities to Experience the Middle Ages*. Illustrated by Michael Kline. Charlotte, VT: Williamson Publishing, 1998. ISBN 1885593171.

As they engage in the suggested activities, children will learn a good deal about life in the Middle Ages.

Hinds, Kathryn. *The Castle*. (Life in the Middle Ages). New York: Benchmark, 2000. ISBN 0761410074.

This is one book in an excellent four-part series in which the author describes life for different segments of society in the Middle Ages. These books are beautifully illustrated and provide a great deal of information. The other books are *The Church* (ISBN 0761410082), *The City* (ISBN 0761410058), and *The Countryside* (ISBN 0761410066). All of the books were published by Benchmark in 2000.

Hooper, Meredith. *Stephen Biesty's Castles*. New York: Enchanted Lion Books, 2004. ISBN 1-59270-031-4.

Large illustrations present ten real castles.

Hopkins, Andrea, Ph.D. *Damsels Not in Distress: The True Story of Women in Medieval Times.* New York: Rosen Publishing, 2004. ISBN 0-8239-3992-8.

Were women educated in medieval times? What were marriage and motherhood like? Hopkins answers these questions and many more.

Lattimore, Deborah Nourse. *The Sailor Who Captured the Sea.* New York: HarperTrophy, 2002. ISBN 0064421538.

This picture book shows the incredible work involved in creating the beautiful *Book of Kells.*

Lewis, J. Patrick, and Rebecca Kai Dotlich. *Castles: Old Stone Poems.* Illustrated by Dan Burr. Honesdale, PA: Wordsong, 2006. ISBN 1590783808.

Exquisite poems tell of different castles throughout the world. If the poems are too difficult for younger children, they will certainly enjoy the lovely illustrations.

Lilly, Melinda, Cheryl Goettmoeller, and Patti Rule. *Pilgrim.* Vero Beach, FL: Rourke, 2002. ISBN 1589522303.

The authors introduce the life of a pilgrim during the Middle Ages.

Llewellyn, Claire. *Saints and Angels.* Boston: Kingfisher, 2006. ISBN 0-7534-5906-X.

In this small, gold-edged book, Llewellyn presents short biographies of a number of saints and a discussion of different kinds of angels. Each entry is accompanied by a beautiful work of art in color.

Macaulay, David. *Castle.* Boston: Houghton Mifflin, 1977. ISBN 0395257840.

Macaulay describes the planning and construction of a medieval castle.

———. *Cathedral.* Boston: Houghton Mifflin, 1973. ISBN 0395175135.

Macaulay describes the planning and construction of a medieval cathedral.

Macdonald, Fiona. *How to Be a Medieval Knight.* Illustrated by Mark Bergin. Washington, DC: National Geographic Children's Books, 2005. ISBN 079223619X.

Readers discover what life was like for a medieval knight.

———. *Women in Medieval Times.* Chicago: Peter Bedrick/NTC Contemporary Publishing, 2000. o.p. ISBN 0872265692.

Women and work, women and the church, and women and widowhood are just some of the aspects of women's lives in the Middle Ages discussed in this book.

MacDonald, Fiona, and David Salariya. *You Wouldn't Want to Be a Medieval Knight: Armor You'd Rather Not Wear.* Illustrated by David Antram. New York: Franklin Watts, 2004. ISBN 0531163954.

This humorous look at medieval knighthood gives readers a glimpse of the difficulties of such a life.

Martin, Alex. *Knights & Castles: Exploring History through Art.* Chanhassen, MN: Two-Can Publishing, 2005. ISBN 1-58728-441-3.

Actual paintings by medieval artists help reveal what life was like for knights of the time. A treasure!

Mason, Antony. *If You Were There in Medieval Times*. Illustrated by Richard Berridge. New York: Simon & Schuster, 1996. ISBN 0689809522.

Readers experience firsthand what life was like in the Middle Ages. Includes a fold-out maze.

Morley, Jacqueline. *A Shakespearean Theater*. Illustrated by John James. Columbus, OH: Peter Bedrick, 2004. ISBN 1-57768-979-8.

The author discusses the building of the theater, what goes on back stage, tours, and more in this fine book.

Morressy, John. *The Juggler*. New York: HarperTrophy, 1998. ISBN 0064471748.

This is a fascinating novel for older readers about a juggler living in medieval times, who gives everything he has to perfect his craft.

Murrell, Deborah. *The Best Book of Knights and Castles*. Illustrated by Chris Molen. Boston: Kingfisher, 2005. ISBN 0-7534-5935-3.

How to become a knight, armor and weapons, engaging in a tournament; readers will find out about all this and more in this interesting book.

Norris, Kathleen. *The Holy Twins*. Illustrated by Tomi dePaola. New York: Putnam, 2001. ISBN 0399234241.

Norris presents a fictionalized biography of Saints Benedict and Scholastica.

Olman, Kyle. *Castle*. Illustrated and engineered by Robert Sabuda, Matthew Reinhart, and Tracy Sabin. New York: Orchard Books, 2006. ISBN 0-439-54324-X.

Besides excellent text that describes life in a medieval castle, this outstanding pop-up book features an entire castle, a knight in shining armor, a banquet scene, and much more.

Osborne, Mary Pope. *Favorite Medieval Tales*. Illustrated by Troy Howell. New York: Scholastic, 1998. o.p. ISBN 0590600427.

Try to find this out-of-print collection of nine beautifully illustrated medieval tales, such as "Beowulf" and "Robin Hood." Contains notes on the stories and illustrations, a bibliography, and an index.

Osborne, Will, and Mary Pope Osborne. *Knights and Castles*. Illustrated by Saul Murdocca. New York: Random House, 2000. ISBN 0-375-90297.

Two young children find out the true facts about the Middle Ages and living in a castle.

Peters, Stephanie True. *The Black Death*. New York: Benchmark Books, 2005. ISBN 0761416331.

Peters describes the outbreak of the plague that killed one out of every three people in Europe during the Middle Ages.

Poole, Josephine. *Joan of Arc*. New York: Knopf, 2005. ISBN 0679990410.

In this beautiful picture-book biography, Poole describes the calling of Joan of Arc to save the French king during the Hundred Years' War.

Ross, Stewart. *Medieval Realms: Art and Architecture.* New York: Lucent, 2004. ISBN 1-59018-534-X.

This valuable book covers illuminated manuscripts, churches, stained glass, and other topics, for young people.

Sabbagh, Antoine. *Europe in the Middle Ages.* New York: Silver Burdette, 1988. ISBN 0382094840.

This is a large-format book in which information about the Middle Ages is presented through double-page spreads.

Sancha, Sheila. *Walter Dragun's Town.* New York: Thomas Y. Crowell, 1989. ISBN 0-690-04804-1.

Readers discover what life was like for craftspeople and tradespeople in the Middle Ages.

Scott, Margaret. *Medieval Clothing and Costumes: Displaying Wealth and Class in Medieval Times. New* York: Rosen Publishing, 2004. ISBN 0-8239-3991-X.

Scott discusses different kinds of clothing worn in the Middle Ages and what these clothes meant.

Shaw, Henry, ed. *Medieval Alphabets and Decorative Devices.* Mineola, NY: Dover, 1999. ISBN 0486404668.

Shaw provides models of letters and ornaments from the Middle Ages.

Shuter, Jane. *Life in a Medieval Castle.* Chicago: Heinemann Library, 2005. ISBN 1403464456.

Shuter describes what life was like for all the people living in a medieval castle.

Skurzynski, Gloria. *The Minstrel in the Tower.* Illustrated by Julek Heller. New York: Random House Books for Young Readers, 2004. ISBN 0394895983

Because their father died in the Crusades and their mother is seriously ill, young Roger and Alice set off on a perilous journey to find their uncle, a powerful baron. A short, simple novel.

Stanley, Diane, and Peter Vennema. *Bard of Avon: The Story of William Shakespeare.* Illustrated by Diane Stanley. New York: HarperTrophy, 1998. ISBN 0688162940.

This beautifully illustrated biography of the Bard is one of the very best available.

Steele, Philip. *The Medieval World.* Boston: Kingfisher/Houghton Mifflin, 2006. ISBN 0-7534-5503-7.

The author presents the medieval world with text suitable for primary age children. They will learn about medieval hunts, wearing armor, life in a castle, and much more. Enhanced with colorful illustrations.

Tanaka, Shelley. *In the Time of Knights.* Illustrated by Greg Ruhl. New York: Hyperion, 2000. ISBN 0786806516.

William Marshal was one of the most famous knights in history. Taken captive as a boy, this tells how he eventually rose to knighthood.

Time-Life Books. *What Life Was Like in the Age of Chivalry.* Alexandria, VA: Time-Life, 1997. ISBN 0783554516.

This invaluable book discusses various groups of medieval society: church men and women, peasants, merchants, etc.

Trembinski, Donna. *Medieval Myths, Legends, and Songs.* New York: Crabtree, 2006. ISBN 0778713598.

This book has chapters on medieval troubadours, dance, and more. Readers learn how stories and myths affected people's lives and even found their way into artworks such as tapestries.

Vivian, E. Charles. *Robin Hood.* Compiled by Cooper Edens. San Francisco: Chronicle Books, 2002. ISBN 0811833992.

More than thirty illustrations taken from classic editions beautify this large book.

Walker, Jane. *100 Things You Should Know about Knights & Castles.* Great Bardfield, Essex, England: Miles Kelly, 2004. ISBN 1-59084-450-5.

This is a thoroughly enjoyable presentation of the lives of knights. The "I don't believe it" sections will especially capture children's interest.

Williams, Marcia. *King Arthur and the Knights of the Round Table.* Cambridge, MA: Candlewick Press, 1996. ISBN 074454792X.

Williams presents a comic-strip retelling of the tales of Camelot.

Wilson, Elizabeth B. *Bibles and Bestiaries: A Guide to Illuminated Manuscripts for Young Readers.*. New York: Farrar, Straus & Giroux, 1994. ISBN 0374306850.

This is a marvelous presentation of illuminated manuscripts, how they were made, and the best-selling books of the time. Glossary.

Woolf, Alex. *Education.* New York: Lucent Books, 2004. ISBN 1-59018-532-3.

Woolf describes various methods of education during the Middle Ages.

Wright, Rachel, and Anita Ganeri. *Castles: Facts, Things to Make, Activities.* New York: Franklin Watts, 1995. ISBN 0531141381.

Wright talks about castles of the Middle Ages and describes various activities for children, such as making pulp and paper castles and tapestry.

Young, Bonnie. *A Walk Through the Cloister.* Rev. ed. Photographs by Malcolm Varon. New York: Metropolitan Museum of Art, 1989. ISBN 0300107846.

Young presents the buildings and art collections at the Metropolitan Museum of Art's Cloisters Museum.

Zannos, Susan. *The Life and Times of Marco Polo.* Hockessin, DE: Mitchell Lane Publishers, 2004. ISBN 1584152648.

Zannos describes Polo's journeys to China.

Audiovisual Materials

Castle. DVD. PBS Video, 2000. CAST601.

This DVD tours the castles of Edward I and explores medieval life through an animated story of the castle. Based on Macaulay's book.

Cathedral. DVD. PBS Video, 2006. CADT601.

This DVD is based on the book by David Macaulay, with animation.

Chant. CD. Angel Records, 1994. ASIN B000002SKX.

The Benedictine monks of Santa Domingo de Silos sing Gregorian chants. Simply beautiful! Comes with program notes.

Chant II. Compac Disc. Angel Records, 1995. ASIN B000002SLS.

More beautiful Gregorian chant is sung by the Benedictine monks of Santa Domingo de Silos.

Glories of Medieval Art: The Cloisters Video. Video. Metropolitan Museum of Art, 1989. M2432.

Philippe de Montebello, director of the museum, takes viewers on a tour of the Cloisters, focusing on the Unicorn Tapestries.

Life in the Middle Ages Video Series. Video. Library Video Company, 2002. #D6840.

This is an eight-video set, each video focusing on one segment of medieval society: noble, serf, doctor, knight, merchant, and others.

My Make-Believe Castle. CD-ROM for Mac and Windows. LCSI, 1995. 89317232214.

Children can manipulate medieval characters such as knights, princesses, dragons, etc. They can also design family crests, experiment with a catapult, and play songs on a harp.

A World Inscribed: The Medieval Manuscript. Video. Films for the Humanities and Sciences, 1996. ISBN 1-4213-1661-7.

Meet the scribes and others who copied manuscripts as you learn how manuscripts were illuminated in medieval times and what materials were used.

Other Materials

Medieval Art: A Resource for Educators. Metropolitan Museum of Art, n.d. M4378.

This boxed set includes a binder with 192 pages and 199 illustrations (35 in full color); two full-color posters, forty 35mm slides, and two CD-ROMs. There is an interactive feature involving the Unicorn Tapestries.

Shepard, Mary B., and Fifi Weinert. *Fun with Stained Glass.* New York: Viking, 1996. ISBN 0870998145.

This kit contains everything needed to create colorful stained-glass panels. It comes with a sixty-four-page book that explores the history of stained glass.

Thomson, George. *The Illuminated Lettering Kit : Materials, Techniques, and Projects for Decorative Calligraphy.* San Francisco: Chronicle Books, 2004. ISBN 0811844889.

This kit provides an explanation of how the medieval monks illuminated manuscripts and has directions and materials for users to try four projects on their own.

Web Sites

Gothic Field Guide. http://www.newyorkcarver.com/Glossary.htm (accessed April 10, 2006).

Visit this page for a helpful glossary of terms connected with gothic churches.

Life in the Middle Ages. http://www.kyrene.org/schools/brisas/sunda/ma/mahome.htm (accessed February 27, 2006).

Fourth- and fifth-graders have done research on the Middle Ages and have posted information on such subjects as jousts, food, monks, and much more. This might inspire children to do their own research as well and create a Web site.

Medieval Weddings. http://www.medieval-weddings.net/index.htm (accessed February 22, 2006).

Find out about medieval wedding traditions such as what clothing to wear, what food to eat, and more.

Websites on the Middle Ages. http://themiddleages.net/websites.html (accessed February 27, 2006).

This site has many links to Web sites about the Middle Ages, such as the medieval child, Gregorian chant, etc.

8 Art of the Renaissance

Thank God that it has been permitted to be born in this new age, so full of hope and promise, which already rejoices in a greater array of nobly-gifted souls than the world has seen in the thousand years that have preceded it.

—MATTEO PALMIERI (fifteenth century) in Hale, *Renaissance*

Background Information

As we have seen, Europe during the Middle Ages was in a state of almost constant war and deprivation. Most people worked so hard to survive that they had time for little else. The Church dominated life and thought, and its members obeyed almost without question. But by the fourteenth century, a number of changes had begun to occur that gradually ushered in a new era called the Renaissance, from the French word that means "rebirth."

Artists and scholars began to look back to the glorious days of the Greeks and Romans for inspiration and enlightenment. What they found in the ancient writings gave rise to a new movement called humanism, in which the talents and worth of people in their own right were celebrated. Instead of yielding control solely to the Church, people began to question the Church's practices and to nourish a desire to control their own destinies. The clergy's amassing of wealth and selling of indulgences, believed to shorten a person's punishment after death, eventually gave rise to increased criticism. The monk Savonarola preached repentance and stricter morals in the Church and urged Florentines to burn anything that hinted of the secular world. In 1517 another monk, Martin Luther, published a list of grievances against the Church and caused a split in its ranks. Never again would all of Europe worship with one voice.

The increasing population of the cities and towns and the rise of a merchant class created a need for more widespread education, and the newly invented printing press made such education possible. Libraries—located mainly in the monasteries of Europe where the monks, often poorly educated themselves and prone to make mistakes, painstakingly copied books by hand—gave way to universities where businessmen could learn the intricacies of law they needed to enter into contracts and arrange trade agreements.

Increased trade, in turn, opened the door to new ideas and ways of life and created a need for more direct trade routes. Some countries sent brave men such as Prince Henry the Navigator, Christopher Columbus, Bartholomew Diaz, Vasco da Gama, Ferdinand Magellan, and Sir Francis Drake to seek such routes. What these men found were not only new passages, but entire continents! Such time-honored ideas as a flat world and the earth as the center of the universe shattered in the face of these explorations and the writings of astronomers like Galileo. Machiavelli's *The Prince* revolutionized ideas about governing, while Luca Pacioli's *Arithmetic, Geometry, and Proportion* introduced double-entry bookkeeping to Italian merchants. There were important advances in medicine such as the establishment of hospitals, the quarantine of contagious diseases, and the recognition of typhus by the physician Girolamo Fracastoro.

It is not surprising that the Renaissance began in Italy, where a system of independent city-states had long before replaced the subservient system of feudalism in effect in the rest of Europe. Rich merchants and trading organizations called guilds often wielded great power in these states. In Florence, the Medici, a wealthy merchant and banking family that ruled for three generations, poured immense amounts of money into the arts. Although they suffered at the hands of the rival Pazzi family and Giuliano de Medici was assassinated, his brother Lorenzo spent the family fortune in commissioning artists to beautify not only his palace and gardens, but the city of Florence as well.

Under Medici patronage, artists flourished, and Florence embarked on a golden age similar to that of Athens under Pericles. Giotto, Botticelli, Brunelleschi, Fra Angelico, Luca della Robbia, Donatello, Ghiberti, Michelangelo, and Paolo Uccello are among the marvelous artists who were born and worked in Florence. And numerous others, not native to the city, were attracted there by the generous support and commissions of Lorenzo de Medici. The marvelous painter Masaccio, whose works showed a realism and skill with perspective that made them worthy of study by such artistic giants as Leonardo da Vinci, Michelangelo, and Raphael, spent time in this glorious city. Popes, too, supported the arts, and some gave more thought and money to the building and adornment of churches than to the care and instruction of the faithful.

Although he was born before the fifteenth and sixteenth centuries, which mark the Renaissance proper, Giotto is credited with initiating an artistic renaissance that was to gain momentum and culminate in the work of da Vinci, Michelangelo, and Raphael. Giotto's work, while lacking the sophistication and knowledge of anatomy and perspective of artists who would come after him, is filled with a realism unknown to his contemporaries, who were used to the stiff, decorative figures of the medieval world. His paintings were so revolutionary that he became famous in his own lifetime and raised the vocation of "artist" to a new dignity. Following in Giotto's footsteps, Renaissance artists continued on a revolutionary path, learning more about anatomy, the human figure, realism, and perspective. Sculptors moved from the low-relief sculptures in medieval churches to life-sized statues in the full round, and Donatello created the first nude since Greek times. Della Robbia developed the process of glazing terra-cotta so that less expensive sculptures could be made available to those who wanted them. Architects worked on such magnificent structures as the church of St. Peter in Rome, the church of San Lorenzo and the baptistery, and the cathedral in Florence.

From Florence, the Renaissance gradually spread to northern Italy and then to the rest of Europe, but in no place did it take such a hold as in the glorious "city of the flowers." Even today, almost every street of that city bears witness to the genius of the Renaissance artists who built buildings, sculpted statues, and painted pictures within her walls. Eventually the city-states became weaker, and toward the end of the fifteenth century France invaded Italy. Italian nobility and prominent families could no longer afford to support the arts, and the era of the Renaissance came to a close. But its effects are felt even to our own day, and art will forever be judged by the standards set down in that incredible time.

To make study of this period more manageable, it can be divided into the Early Renaissance and the Late, or High, Renaissance, although this is an artificial division. Giotto, Filippo Brunelleschi, Donatello, and Sandro Botticelli are Early Renaissance; Leonardo da Vinci, Michelangelo Buonarotti, and Raphaello Sanzio are High Renaissance.

(Standards: Art Connections: 1.1-8; K-4 History 7.1; World History 27, 29, 31.20)

LESSON 1: Giotto (1266–1337)

The Story

Once there was a young boy about eight years of age who lived with his family on a farm outside the city of Florence in Italy. Every day his task was to watch the sheep as they grazed on the hillside. Now the boy was happy to help his family in this way, but it was boring work. So to keep himself amused, every day after he had finished his lunch of bread and cheese the boy would pick up a sharp stick and draw pictures on the ground. He drew the sheep, the trees, and the other things he saw around him.

One day, while the boy was packing his lunch and getting ready to set off for the hills with the sheep, an artist named Cimabue was getting ready to take a walk in the countryside. He was the most famous artist in all of Florence—so famous, in fact, that he was exhausted from all the jobs he was given to do. Wealthy people paid him to paint pictures in churches throughout the city. Cimabue had his own workshop, where he taught young boys called apprentices how to paint and gave them small jobs to do on the pictures he painted. But on this day, Cimabue was sick of working. "Some fresh country air will do me a world of good," he told his apprentices. "Take care of things until I return." And off he went.

After walking awhile, Cimabue came to the young boy's farm. The boy had just finished his lunch and was beginning a new drawing on the ground. He was so absorbed in his work that he did not hear the artist come up behind him. Cimabue watched for a long time without making a sound. Finally, he could stand it no longer. "Boy," he said, "who taught you to draw like that?"

Startled, the boy looked up and saw the man, but did not know who he was. He only knew that the man's clothes were much finer than any clothing he had ever seen, and he was afraid. But he answered with courage, "No one, sir."

"Come, come," replied Cimabue. "Someone must have taught you, for you show a good deal of skill. Who is your teacher?"

Again the boy answered, "No one, sir. I am a poor shepherd boy. My father could certainly not afford a teacher for me. I simply draw to pass the time while I guard the sheep."

Cimabue was amazed, for not even the boys he taught in his workshop every day did work as fine as this. "Take me to see your father," he said. So the boy led the sheep back to their corral and took Cimabue to the fields where his father was plowing.

As soon as he saw such a well-dressed man from the city on his property, the boy's father began to worry. Did he owe money on his taxes? Was he about to lose his land? Had his son done something to offend the man? For although Cimabue was famous, the boy's father did not know who he was either.

Then Cimabue spoke. "My good man, I am Cimabue, a painter in the city. My paintings appear in churches throughout Florence, and boys come from far off to study in my workshop. I have watched your son draw, and he has talent. You must allow him to come with me to Florence and live as an apprentice with the other boys. I will teach him all I know about drawing and painting."

The boy's father was deeply troubled by this. How could he afford to pay Cimabue to teach his son? And who would take care of the sheep if his boy were no longer there? "Sir, you flatter us," he said. "But I cannot afford to send my son to you. I am a poor man. And besides, I need him to care for the sheep."

"Sheep!" cried Cimabue. "Do you put sheep before art? Do you put your little farm before the glory of Florence? You must send the boy to me. A talent like his cannot be wasted! I will teach the boy for nothing and will provide his room and board. You need only free him from his work here."

And so the boy's father agreed to send him to Florence the very next day to study with Cimabue. The boy worked for the artist for several years, until he became even better at drawing than his master. Everyone was amazed by his pictures, for the people he drew actually seemed real. After a time he left Cimabue and started a workshop of his own with his own apprentices. Wealthy people and even popes gave him money to paint pictures in churches. One time a pope asked for a sample of his work and the artist, with one stroke of his brush, drew a perfect circle. The pope hired him immediately.

That boy's name was Giotto, and he started a whole new kind of art that was to change forever the way artists painted pictures. Painters came from all over Europe to study his work, and they still do today. When Giotto died, he was buried in the cathedral in Florence, where years before he had designed the baptistery tower. This was an honor reserved only for very important people. More than 100 years after he died, the people of Florence put a special medallion in the cathedral showing Giotto working on a mosaic. They considered him the grandfather of Italian art. The ruler of the city, Lorenzo de Medici, ordered that a plaque be placed under the medallion reading, "I am he through whose merit the lost art of painting was revived; whose hand was as faultless as it was compliant. What my art lacked nature herself lacked; to none other was it given to paint more or better. But what need is there for words? I am Giotto, and my name alone tells more than a lengthy ode."

Giotto's paintings were mostly Bible stories, for they decorated the walls of churches. We're going to enjoy some of them together now, and as I show them to you, see if you know any of the stories the pictures tell.

(Standards: Language Arts: Listening and Speaking 8.4)

Viewing the Art

(For the viewing sessions in all the lessons in this chapter, the two-volume set entitled *The Art of Florence*—see references—is without parallel. If your library does not have this set, it is well worth requesting that it be obtained on loan. Also, for viewing Giotto's work, see *Italian Frescoes: The Age of Giotto*.)

Show some medieval paintings and some work of Cimabue. (See *Cimabue* in the references.) Then show some of Giotto's paintings. His frescoes from the Scrovengi (or Arena) Chapel are especially appropriate, and their reproductions in Madeleine L'Engle's *The Glorious Impossible* are large and very fine. The reproductions in Basile's *Giotto: The Arena Chapel Frescoes* are even larger, and there are many close-up details. (Also see *The Art of Florence,* Volume I, and Bellinati 2005, in the references) What differences do the children see? Quote from Eimerl, *The World of Giotto*:

> Representations of the human face in earlier paintings had given it an expressionless stare; he [Giotto] invested it with grief, fear, pity, joy or other emotions to which the viewer could respond with instant understanding. Above all, Giotto endowed his people with flesh and blood. (1978, 9)

Do the children agree with this statement? Are they able to feel with his characters? The frescoes in the Scrovengi tell a story from the birth of Christ to the Ascension and the Last Judgment. Do the children know any of the stories these paintings tell?

Explain how a fresco was made. (You might want to read *Antonio's Apprenticeship* aloud; see references.):

1. The artist makes an outline, often called a cartoon, of the painting on a piece of paper. Small holes are pierced at intervals along the outline.
2. The cartoon is divided into squares, each square representing one day's work.
3. The whole wall on which the painting will be placed is plastered roughly to cover over bricks or other matter on the wall.
4. When the first coat of plaster is dry, a small portion of the wall, enough for one day's work, is plastered smoothly.
5. One square of the cartoon is placed over the wet plaster, and a bag containing charcoal is rubbed over it. The charcoal seeps through the holes pierced along the cartoon, leaving a black outline on the wet plaster. The dots of charcoal are then joined with paint and the underlying charcoal is brushed away.
6. The picture is painted in using paints mixed beforehand. The painting process must be completed before the plaster dries so that the paint dries into the plaster, thus making a long-lasting work.

Making frescoes is very difficult, because the artist must know how long the plaster will take to dry under various weather conditions, and how long it will take to complete the painting. If he or she makes a mistake, the whole section has to be scraped off and replastered.

Show pictures of the bell tower of the Florence cathedral, designed by Giotto (see page 180). A wonderful story to tell in connection with this bell tower is "The Rose of Midwinter" from the book *Elves and Ellefolk* by Natalia Belting (see references). This story is guaranteed to keep Giotto's bell tower in the children's minds for a considerable time to come.

Whenever we do something for the first time, whether it's riding a bike or learning to write our alphabet, we do it imperfectly. It was the same for Giotto. No artist since the days of the Romans had done what he had. And so even though we know that Giotto's paintings do not have the movement and perspective of later works, he is important because he forged a new beginning and led the way for those who would come after him.

(Standards: Art Connections 1.1-8; Language Arts: Viewing 9.6, 23)

Giotto's Bell Tower, Florence, Italy

Journal Writing

What kinds of emotions do the children see on the faces of Giotto's characters? How does viewing these characters make the children feel? Invite the children to imagine that they are living in Florence in Giotto's time and seeing his work for the first time. They are not used to such pictures. What is their reaction? What do they like or dislike about Giotto's work, and why?

(Standards: Language Arts: Writing 1.7, 23, 33-37; Art Connections 1.3)

Art/Drama Activity: A Fresco Mural

Materials

- Four very large sheets of paper, cut from a roll if possible
- Colored markers

Divide the children into four groups and invite them to make a mural depicting how frescoes, a popular art form during the Renaissance, were made. Each group draws and labels a part of the mural. In their drawings, which can be as simple as stick figures, the children should draw the artist and his apprentices working together. When the groups have finished their work, tape the pieces together to form a large mural for the classroom or hall wall. Keep the mural up throughout your study of the Renaissance. Suggestions for the group divisions and labels:

- Making the cartoon
- Plastering the wall
- Rubbing the cartoon with charcoal
- Painting in the picture

(Standards: Visual Arts: 1-4.1-11; Working with Others: 1.1, 5)

LESSON 2: Filippo Brunelleschi (1377–1446) and Donatello (1386–1466)

The Story

Over 600 years ago in Florence, a boy named Filippo Brunelleschi was born, who would one day become one of the most famous architects who ever lived. His father was a notary. That meant that he witnessed the signing of documents for the wealthy and important businessmen in Florence. So Filippo's family had a good deal of money and were able to give him a fine education. His father hoped that Filippo would work for the government as he did, but Filippo was more interested in art, so the boy was sent to be an apprentice to a goldsmith. It wasn't long before people began to see that he was a sculptor of talent, and Filippo set up a workshop of his own. One day a young boy came and asked to be his apprentice. The boy's name was Donato, but everybody called him Donatello. Donatello's father was not as wealthy as Filippo's, for he was a wool comber. The wool trade was one of the most important businesses in Florence. Donatello was ten years younger than Filippo, but they quickly became good friends.

Now the Florentines loved contests, and they often gave jobs to artists who won them. When the city leaders decided the Baptistery of St. John needed new doors, Filippo and a sculptor named Ghiberti entered a contest to see who would be hired. The doors would be filled with golden squares, each square containing a sculpture of a scene from the Bible. Both Filippo and Ghiberti were told to do the same scene: the story of Abraham being stopped by an angel from sacrificing his son to God. Filippo and Ghiberti worked hard for months to make their bronze carvings as perfect as possible. But when the judges looked at the results, they gave the job to Ghiberti. Filippo was discouraged, but he had to admit that Ghiberti's work was better. (If you go to http://www.bluffton.edu/~sullivanm/ghibertinorth/ghibertinorth.html, you can see wonderfully enlarged, detailed pictures of Ghiberti's sculptures.) And besides, he really didn't want to be a sculptor. His real love was designing buildings. So he decided to go to Rome, the land of the master builders, and learn all he could by studying the buildings of those ancient architects. Although Donatello was only about fourteen at the time, Filippo invited him to go, too.

Both artists loved Rome. Filippo spent hours and hours in the Pantheon looking up at the dome. "How did the Romans get that huge dome up without having it come crashing down?" Filippo asked himself over and over again. In his city of Florence, there was a problem with the cathedral, Santa Maria del Fiore, St. Mary of the Flower. The builders had so enlarged it from its original design they could not figure out how to put a dome over it. No one had been able to solve the problem, and for years the cathedral stood unfinished. Filippo wanted to be the architect who would design a dome for one of Florence's greatest treasures. Donatello, meanwhile, studied the ruins of ancient sculptures. He saw how the Romans formed arms and legs and bodies so that they looked real. Never had he seen anything like these works of art!

When they finally arrived back in Florence, Filippo was given some very important jobs. He designed a hospital for orphans and some churches, and they were all quite wonderful, but he continued to think about a dome for the cathedral. The more he thought, the more convinced he was that he could design a dome that would work, and he began to make a model. His friend Donatello helped him.

Soon the Florentine officials held another big contest, inviting artists from all over Europe to bring their models for the cathedral dome. Filippo's model was finished, but he refused to show it to the judges. Only Donatello knew what it looked like. The judges became very angry and demanded that he present his model the way all the other architects had. But Filippo decided to teach them a lesson. He took a hard-boiled egg from his cloak and asked if they could stand it up without having it fall over. Of course, none of the judges could. Then he banged the egg on the table to flatten one end, and the egg stood perfectly without falling.

"Well, anyone could stand up that egg by smashing one end," said a judge.

"Of course," said another. "If we had only known that's what you were going to do, we could have done it ourselves."

"That's just my point," replied Filippo. "If you see my model, then anyone can copy my idea and build the dome. You must trust that I can do it and give me the job without seeing my model."

The judges didn't like that answer, but none of the other architects had come up with an idea that would work, so Filippo was hired. Filippo's idea was to make two domes, one inside the other, so the two domes would strengthen each other and stay up without a central support until the building was complete. And he made the domes in the shape of a gothic arch so that they wouldn't exert so much pressure on the walls. The dome was so high that Filippo designed special machinery to help the workers get up there safely and haul their materials up as well. What a celebration there was when Florence finally had its finished cathedral! In fact, even now, when Florentines leave their city or go away on vacation, they often say, "I miss my cathedral!"

Filippo's Dome, Florence Cathedral, Italy

Meanwhile, Donatello worked on his own sculptures and amazed the city of Florence by his accomplishments. He carved marble statues of people in the Bible for churches in the city, and he made a bronze statue of David the giant killer that was the first nude statue since the time of the ancient Greeks and Romans! The people of Florence loved their sculptor, and they were sad when he spent a long time in Padua doing sculptures there. While he was in Padua, he carved the first person on horseback since the days of the Romans. When the people began to complain that he was taking too long, Donatello threatened to crack the statue's head.

"If you do that, we will break *your* head," the people said.

"I don't mind," answered Donatello, "as long as you fix my head as beautifully as I will fix the head of your statue" (Bennett and Wilkins , p. 31).

Filippo and Donatello remained friends all their lives. Filippo died at the age of sixty-nine and Donatello was an old man of eighty when he died—most unusual at a time when so many people did not live past forty. The Florentines loved him so much that even though he was too sick to make beautiful statues for them any longer, they rented a house for him and gave him money until his death. Today, if you go to Florence, you can see Filippo's dome rising gloriously above all the other buildings, and you can see Donatello's beautiful statues in churches and museums throughout the city.

(Standards: Language Arts: Listening and Speaking 8.4)

Viewing the Art

(Some Renaissance sculpture recommended for viewing are nudes, as in Donatello's *David* here and some of Michelangelo's works further on. They are mentioned because they are masterpieces and well worth studying. Children who are prepared beforehand can usually handle themselves well. However, if you feel your community might object, simply omit them.)

Battisti's *Filippo Brunelleschi* and Poeshke's *Donatello and His World* (See References) are both incredibly rich sources of large, detailed reproductions of these two artists' work. Be sure to show Donatello's marble *David* and then his very famous bronze *David* (you may want to compare it to Michelangelo's *David* later if you teach that artist); his *Cantoria* for the Duomo (the children should especially love this); his wooden statue of *Mary Magdalene*; his bronze *Judith*; his equestrian *Monument of Gattamelata*; and his crucifix for Santa Croce. Tell the children that when Brunelleschi saw that crucifix, he told Donatello he didn't like it, and Donatello challenged him to make a crucifix himself and see if he could do better. Brunelleschi did, and the crucifix hangs in Santa Maria Novella (Bennett and Wilkins 1985, 31).

After you show both crucifixes (both are in Poeschke 1993), ask the children which they prefer, and why. Mention how unusual it is for a sculptor to work in marble, bronze, and wood. Show Brunelleschi's and Ghiberti's sculptures of *Abraham* for the baptistery doors. Which do the children like best, and why? Also view the foundling hospital. Spend the rest of the time on the dome of the cathedral. Show individual views of the dome and then of Florence, with the dome towering above all else. (A spectacular view of Florence with the dome at its heart can be seen in Volume I of the *Art of Florence*—see references.) It stands as a tribute to Brunelleschi's genius even to this day. (Many books in the references have excellent views of the dome. Children will especially enjoy the pop-up version in *Waiting for Filippo*.)

(Standards: Art Connections 1.1-8; Language Arts: Viewing 9.6, 23)

Journal Writing

Why was Donatello such an important sculptor? Of all the statues they studied, which is the children's favorite, and why? After viewing Brunelleschi's *Abraham* sculpture and his crucifix, do the children think he should have continued sculpting, or was he wise to switch to architecture? If he had remained a sculptor, do they think he and Donatello would have remained friends? Why or why not? In what ways was the friendship of these two men beneficial to themselves and the world of art?

(Standards: Language Arts: Writing 1.7, 23, 33-37; Art Connections 1.3)

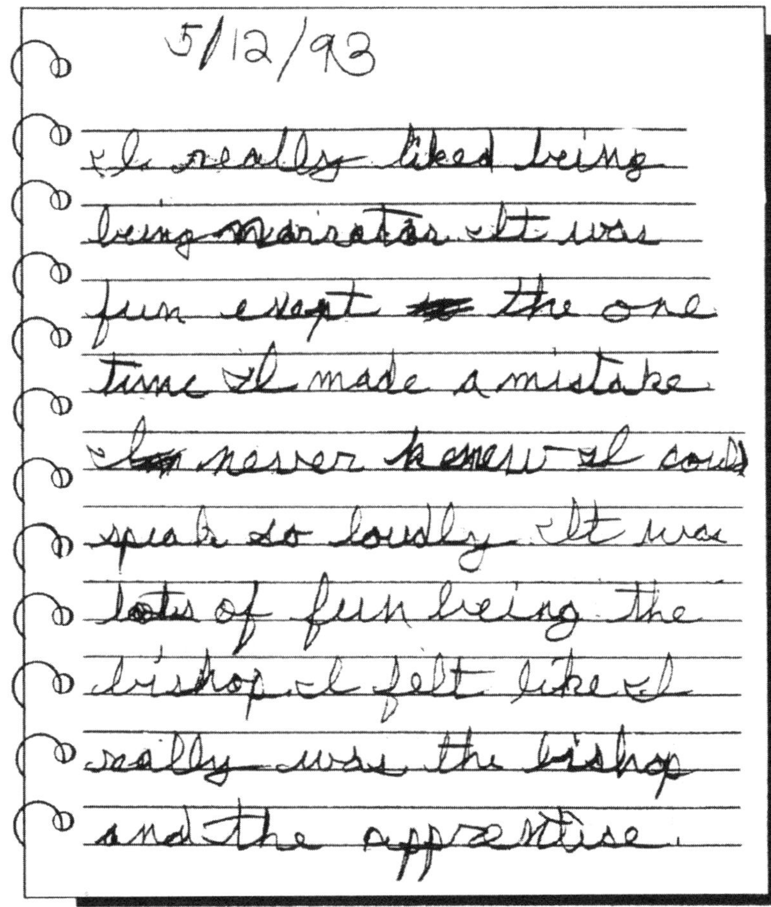

5/12/93

I really liked being
being narrator. It was
fun exept the one
time I made a mistake.
I never knew I could
speak so loudly. It was
lots of fun being the
bishop. I felt like I
really was the bishop
and the apprentise.

Art/Drama Activity: Writing a Book

Materials

- Large sheets of paper
- Pencils
- Markers

Divide the children into groups and invite them to make a book about the lives and work of the two friends, Brunelleschi and Donatello. Each group can work on one phase of the artists' lives, writing a bit of text on one page with an illustration on the opposite page. When the work is complete, bind the pages together for a class book. Decide together on a title and a cover page. Some suggestions for book "chapters":

- Brunelleschi and Ghiberti showing their sculptures for the baptistery doors to the judges
- Brunelleschi and Donatello journeying to Rome and studying there

- Donatello sculpting in his studio; mention some of his statues
- Several architects showing their models to the judges for the dome competition
- Brunelleschi and his workers building the dome
- The cathedral of St. Mary of the Flower

(Standards: Visual Arts: 1, 4-5.1-11; Language Arts: Writing: 1-3.2, 8, 9, 15, 23, 28, 33, 37; Working with Others: 1.1, 5)

LESSON 3: Sandro Botticelli (1444–1510)

The Story

Over 500 years ago, a baby was born in Florence. He was the last of seven children, and his parents named him Sandro. Sandro's father was a tanner, which means that he turned animal skins into leather to be made into shoes, belts, saddles, and other objects. Because there were so many children to feed, the family did not have much money. But when his older brothers and sisters left home to make their own way in the world, Sandro's parents were able to give him an education.

You would think Sandro would be grateful for the opportunity to learn and to have what his parents could not afford to give his brothers and sisters. But he was a grumpy child, often sick, and a nuisance. His father was glad to be able to send Sandro off to his older brother's goldsmith shop as an apprentice, where he learned the skills of an artist. Sandro also studied for eleven years with a famous artist named Fra Filippo. "Fra" means "brother," for Filippo was a monk. Soon Sandro was doing paintings of his own, and his work was so good that the pope heard about him and invited him to Rome to paint some frescoes on the wall of a new chapel, called the Sistine Chapel, which he had just built. Other people began to hear about Sandro, too. One day he received a message from one of the most important men in Florence, Lorenzo de Medici. Lorenzo lived in a palace, and he spent a great deal of money paying artists to paint and do sculptures for the churches and buildings of the city. It was a great honor to be given a job by him, and Sandro went to the palace right away. He did many pictures for Lorenzo and remained his friend until Lorenzo died.

Remember what a cranky child Sandro was? He didn't change when he grew up. He lived by himself and never married. One day he went to the house next door and complained to the weaver who lived there that the noise from his looms was driving him crazy. "I can't think. I can't even paint my pictures"! Sandro complained.

The weaver paid no attention to him. "I can do what I feel like in my own house," he replied.

You can imagine how angry that made Sandro. He thought and thought about a way to get even with the weaver, and finally he had an idea. He got a ladder, climbed up to the roof of his house, and put a big boulder right on the edge. Sandro's roof was very high, higher than the weaver's next door, and slanted. If anything happened to shake the walls of the house, that boulder would roll off and go crashing into the weaver's house. When the weaver looked out his window and saw what his neighbor was doing, he became very frightened and went running to Sandro's house.

When Sandro answered his knock, the weaver said, "You can't keep that boulder on your roof. It could roll off and damage my house. It could even kill me!"

Can you guess Sandro's reply? Of course he said, "I can do what I feel like in my own house!" And from that day on, he never heard the weaver's looms again! (Vasari 2006; Burroughs 1946, pp. 148–149).

As Sandro got older, he became very sick and could no longer paint. He even had to walk with crutches. He received no more jobs and was very poor. After he died at the age of sixty-six, people forgot about his work for 300 years. But now we realize that he was one of the great artists of his time.

(Standards: Language Arts: Listening and Speaking 8.4)

Viewing the Art

Botticelli painted not only religious pictures but secular ones as well. His *Primavera* and *Birth of Venus* are two of his most famous secular paintings. Be sure to show them to the children. (The books about Botticelli in the references contain plates of these paintings.) Help the children to see that Botticelli's figures are elongated, or longer than figures would be in reality. Note his graceful lines and the exquisite features on the faces. Tell the children that "primavera" means "spring." What signs of spring does Botticelli put in his picture? Tell the children the story of the *Birth of Venus* as you view the picture. Show some of Botticelli's portraits (*Giuliane de'Medici, Man with a Medal, Head of a Young Man*) as well as some of his religious paintings (*The Magnificat, Madonna of the Book, Madonna with the Pomegranate, The Annunciation,* and *Adoration of the Magi,* in which the tall figure in the gold cloak on the right is thought to be a self-portrait of Botticelli).

(Standards: Art Connections 1.1-8; Language Arts: Viewing 9.6, 23)

Journal Writing

Which of Botticelli's pictures do the children like best? Why? Why do they think he elongate his figures? What are some words the children can think of to describe Botticelli's paintings? Why do they suppose people neglected his work for 300 years?

(Standards: Language Arts: Writing 1.7, 23, 33-37; Art Connections 1.3)

Art/Drama Activity: Botticelli's *Primavera or Allegory of Spring*

Materials

- Paper
- Colored pencils (make sure to have colors the children will need to represent spring)

Recall for the children your viewing of Botticelli's *Primavera*, and show it to them once again. In addition to the things the artist put in his picture to represent spring, ask the children for some other signs of this season. Make a list that might include robins, insects, gardens, spring sports, etc. After this discussion, invite the children to draw a picture to represent spring. Talk about the kinds of colors that might be used. Botticelli used pastels, not brilliant reds or blues, because in spring most colors in nature are not at their deepest hues. Give the children time to think about how they might incorporate their symbols of spring into a picture before they begin their artwork.

(Standards: Visual Arts: 1-4.1-11)

LESSON 4: Leonardo da Vinci (1452–1519)

The Story

"Andrea, my good friend, how are you?" asked Ser Piero da Vinci as he entered the shop of the great artist Andrea del Verrocchio.

"Ah, fine, Piero, but so busy! Commissions for madonnas, portraits of our rich citizens here in Florence, sculptures . . . so busy. My apprentices and I can hardly keep up with the work."

"Well, look at these, then," said Piero. "They are a few drawings done by my son, Leonardo. You wouldn't believe that boy! Such talent! One day a friend of mine came in with a shield he wanted decorated with a painting. Leonardo took it and assembled dozens of creatures: bats, crawling reptiles, locusts—ugh, such ugly things! He studied them for days. Then he made a painting of one fantastic creature out of all of them. When I saw the shield with that hideous creature painted on it, I thought I was being attacked and nearly fainted. It was so real! Ever since we have moved here from our little town of Vinci, I have dreamed of apprenticing my Leonardo to a master like you. What do you think? Leo can learn much from you, and he would be a help with all the work you have here."

"Hmmm. These are good. Quite good for one so young," said Andrea as he looked at the boy's work. "Send him to me, and we'll see what can be done with him."

And so Leonardo da Vinci came to Verrocchio's workshop and learned how to grind pigments for paints and how to prepare walls for frescoes. He even got to paint in some clothing on the people Andrea drew.

Then one day Andrea said, "Leonardo, paint two angels in the corner of this picture of the baptism of Jesus I've just finished." Leonardo was delighted with this chance to paint real figures. He spent all his spare time walking the streets of Florence studying people—even ugly people, for he was fascinated with faces of all kinds. He would follow a person all day, sketching on the pad he always carried with him. But he did not make these angels ugly. He made them very delicate and graceful, and when he had finished, they were better than the figures his master had painted. "Never again will I work with paints," Andrea declared. "You can do it for me, while I turn my hand to sculpture, which I love much more." Leonardo was only twenty years old when he painted those angels, and they were not perfect. He still had much to learn, but his reputation as a painter spread. And because he was so gentle, kind, and even handsome, people followed him and loved to be near him.

Since he started painting so young and lived a long life for those times, you would think that Leonardo did hundreds of paintings. But actually, he did very few—probably fewer than twenty. And even some of these are not completed. Can you imagine that? Do you think it was because he was lazy? Actually, Leonardo never stopped working, but he worked at so many things, he never spent a long time in one single occupation. He was brilliant—some say one of the smartest people who ever lived—and he was interested in everything. Leonardo da Vinci was a musician who played the lyre, a popular instrument at that time, and sang beautifully. He wrote poetry. He was a scientist who studied the heavens, the muscles and organs of the human body, the movement of water, medicine, and flowers and plants. He also studied mathematics. Leonardo invented many things, including the parachute, weapons, a machine that was like our submarine, and even a flying machine, though it was not very successful. His mind was way ahead of the thinkers of his time, and we still use many of his ideas today.

Drawings, Italian, 16th century, 1508-1512

Leonardo da Vinci (Vinci 1452-1519 Clos-Lucé (Cloux; near Amboise))

Head of the Virgin.

Black chalk, red chalk, traces of white chalk (?); some remains of framing outline in pen and brown ink at upper right (not by Leonardo).

8 X 6 ⅛ in. (20.3 X 15.6 cm)

Head of the Virgin in Three-Quarter View Facing Right, 1508–1512. The Metropolitan Museum of Art, Harris Brisbane Dick Fund, 1951 (51.90). Photograph, all rights reserved, The Metropolitan Museum of Art.

Although we only have a few of Leonardo's paintings, we have hundreds of drawings that he made during his studies. He filled many notebooks with these drawings and notes, and we have about 5,000 pages of these still in existence. But if you tried to read them, you would have a hard time, because he wrote from right to left and reversed his letters. Some people say he did this because he wrote with his left hand and it was easier for him to write like that. Others think he was trying to keep his notes secret.

Leonardo was always conducting experiments. Some worked, but many were failures, and that is why some of his paintings did not survive. Once he was asked to paint a battle scene on the walls of a public building in Florence. He worked for months making beautiful drawings to get ready for the painting. But instead of doing a fresco the way the other painters of his day did, he used a new, thick paint mixture. Before he even got the painting finished, the paint began to run down the walls onto the floor, and he abandoned the project. While he was in the northern Italian city of Milan designing weapons for the ruler there, some monks asked him to do a painting in their monastery. He worked for years on that painting, and some say it is one of the greatest paintings in the world. It is called *The Last Supper* and shows Christ eating with his friends before he died. But again, Leonardo experimented with the paint, and the painting began to flake off the walls even in his own lifetime. The king of France loved that painting so much he tried to have the wall cut out of the monastery and brought to France, but it is still in Milan, and visitors still go to see it.

When Leonardo became old and ill, King Francis I invited him to come to France as his special painter. He gave Leonardo a beautiful house and paid him well. Leonardo's right hand was paralyzed, but since he could paint equally well with both hands, he could still work and teach. He lived for four years in France and died there at the age of sixty-seven. He once said, "As a well-spent day brings happy sleep, so a life well used brings happy death" (McLanathan 1990, 83). Truly, Leonardo had used his life well.

You might want to consider reading *Leonardo's Horse* (see references) to the children to emphasize da Vinci's insatiable thirst to try new things and his penchant for moving from project to project. They will be fascinated by the story of the bronze horse conceived by Leonardo but finished by Charles Dent almost 500 years later!

(Standards: Language Arts: Listening and Speaking 8.4)

Viewing the Art

Mention that since Leonardo was so greatly admired, many artists copied his work, and it is only after careful study that scholars have been able to determine which pictures were actually done by him. Since so few of Leonardo's paintings exist, be sure to show the children as many of them as you can collect. A good place to begin is with Leonardo's angels in Verrocchio's *Baptism of Christ*. Then show *The Annunciation*, Leonardo's first complete work. This does not compare with the wonderful work of his later years. The children may enjoy hearing how someone else enlarged the angel's wings. Talk about the pyramid created by the figures in *Madonna of the Rocks* and *The Virgin and Child with St. Anne*. Note the many different hand positions in the *Madonna of the Rocks*. Show some of Leonardo's portraits: *Ginevra de Benci, Lady with an Ermine, Portrait of a Musician,* and of course his famous *Mona Lisa.* Tell the children that she may be smiling because Leonardo hired musicians to amuse her while he painted her picture. Discuss *The Last Supper* (see especially *Leonardo: The Last Supper* in the references), showing details if you can so that the children can focus on the different faces of the disciples. In Leonardo's unfinished *St. Jerome* and *Adoration of the Magi*, note the expressions on the faces and the multitude of characters in the *Adoration of the Magi*. Perhaps here is where all of Leonardo's studies of people in the streets bore fruit.

As you view all of Leonardo's paintings, a major point to discuss is his use of light and shadow to produce depth, called *chiaroscuro*. The children love pronouncing this musical Italian word. Have them note examples of Leonardo's use of chiaroscuro in his work. From the paintings, move on to the notebooks and drawings. Zöllner's *Leonardo da Vinci: The Complete Paintings and Drawings* is an excellent source. Also mention that Leonardo was one of the first to depict realistic landscape as an integral part of a painting. Be sure to show some of Leonardo's drawings of horses and cats, and mention his love of animals—he loved them so much he became a vegetarian. How many different areas of interest can the children find in the drawings?

(Standards: Art Connections 1.1-8; Language Arts: Viewing 9.6, 23)

Journal Writing

Which of Leonardo's paintings are the children's favorites, and why? Because the artist was interested in so many things, he did not produce a great deal of work in any one field. How do the children feel about that? Would it have been better, in their opinion, to stick to one thing for a lifetime, or to investigate many as Leonardo did? What do they feel is his greatest contribution?

(Standards: Language Arts: Writing 1.7, 23, 33-37; Art Connections 1.3)

Art/Drama Activity: Inventions, Geometry, and Mirror Writing

Materials

- Paper
- Pencils

Ask the children to think about the many conveniences we have now—all the result of people like Leonardo da Vinci, who experimented and asked such questions as "What if we could . . . ?" Or "What if we had . . . ?" We now have machines that wash our dishes and our clothing, fly us around the world and even into space, build our buildings, plow our fields, and harvest our produce. But we still need people to continue asking questions and dreaming dreams. Invite the children to do that very thing—to come up with a need we still have and to invent a machine to answer that need. You may want to brainstorm some ideas as a class to get the children started in their thinking. Allow time for them to share their inventions at the end of the session. They may want to bind them all into a book of fantastic ideas.

(Standards: Thinking and Reasoning: 5.14)

Recall for the children those da Vinci paintings in which the figures form the shape of a pyramid: *Madonna of the Rocks* and *The Virgin and Child with St. Anne*. As an art activity, the children may also wish to draw a picture in which the figures, buildings, or other objects form a pyramid shape.

(Standards: Visual Arts: 1, 3-5.1-11)

Print some information about Leonardo da Vinci's life in mirror writing and have the children decipher it. They love this "secret code" activity, and it helps them remember his work.

LESSON 5: Michelangelo Buonarroti (1475–1564)—Painting and Architecture

The Story

"I don't care what you want to do! Art is for lazy good-for-nothings. You have only been in school three years and you want to quit already. You can barely read and write Italian, let alone Greek and Latin as other boys your age can. You will finish school, become a merchant, and bring some money into this family. If I have to beat art out of you, I will do it," yelled Michelangelo's father.

The young thirteen-year-old boy had asked his father once again if he might go and study art with the master, Ghirlandaio, in the city. Even though he was tired of begging and feared his father's repeated beatings, Michelangelo refused to give up. He was the most stubborn boy you could ever imagine!

"My father gave me up to the stonecutter's family when I was a baby. I grew up with marble dust in my veins. What did he expect? Of course I would want to carve marble for the rest of my life. And right now I want to study drawing like my young friend Granacci," Michelangelo thought to himself.

Finally, his father gave in and brought the young boy to Ghirlandaio's workshop, where he promised that his son would work for the next three years. Michelangelo was already so fine an artist that the master agreed to pay him instead of the other way around. While he worked for Ghirlandaio, Michelangelo also had all of Florence as his school. The greatest artists in the world worked there, and Michelangelo studied their paintings. He made drawings of the frescoes Giotto had done many years before and the frescoes of other Renaissance artists we've talked about.

While Florence was a beautiful city of churches and buildings filled with wondrous artworks, Rome, a city south of Florence and home of the ancient Roman artists, was falling apart. Cattle and sheep grazed in what was once the beautiful forum, and even some of the churches were falling down. So when Julius II became pope in 1503, he decided to do something about it. He wanted to create new works of art for the city, including a magnificent tomb for himself. He wanted to rebuild St. Peter's church, the main cathedral of Christians throughout the world. It was over a thousand years old, and it was crumbling. Julius not only wanted to fix it, he wanted to make it even bigger. And he wanted to improve the Vatican, the special palace in Rome where the pope lives even now.

Julius was a warrior pope, often leading men into battle. He was filled with energy and determination, and when he said he was going to do something, he did it. He didn't care who stood in his way. He was already sixty years old, so he was in a hurry. And he wanted Michelangelo to be one of the artists involved in the work.

Now Michelangelo had already been working, carving statues for the pope's tomb. It was hard work, and there were many statues to be done. But in the middle of the job, the pope told him to stop, and he refused to pay Michelangelo the money he owed him. One thing we know about Michelangelo is that he could get angry and stubborn. He packed his bags and headed back to Florence in the middle of the night. Pope Julius sent messengers after Michelangelo, but they couldn't catch him. The artist was back in his beloved Florence.

Do you think Julius gave up so easily? Of course not! He sent a letter to the leaders of Florence saying that if they did not send Michelangelo back immediately, he would start a war! So back Michelangelo went, and when he got to Rome, he received quite a surprise. Instead of being asked to work on statues, which he loved doing, the pope took him into his own church in the Vatican, called the Sistine Chapel. He pointed to the ceiling, which was covered with blue paint and stars. "I want you to paint frescoes of Bible stories all across this ceiling," the pope said.

"But your holiness, I'm not a painter. I'm a sculptor. There are many fine fresco painters you could ask. How about Raphael? He is here in the city and is very talented. He has done other frescoes for you."

"I said I want *you*!" shouted the pope. "And I want you to begin immediately. I'm in a hurry to get the job done!"

Michelangelo had to obey, so he began making drawings to get ready for the tremendous work—5,800 square feet to be covered with more than 300 figures! No wonder he called for assistants from Florence! But when he saw their work, he yelled, "No, no, this is terrible—not what I had in mind at all. Out, out all of you. I'll do it myself!" Michelangelo was left in the big chapel by himself to perform a task that seemed impossible. Every day he climbed a huge scaffold, where he had to lie on his back to paint the large figures. If he was working on the head, he could not even see where the feet would be. Paint dripped onto his face and into his eyes. And still he kept on.

Every day Pope Julius would visit. "Have you finished yet?" he would ask.

Michelangelo moved his bed into the chapel and slept only a few hours a night. The rest of the time he painted. He even ate his meals up on the scaffold. The pope continued to press him "Are you finished yet?" Sometimes they would get into arguments, but Michelangelo kept working. "I'll have you thrown from that scaffold if you don't tell me you're finished," shouted the pope one day.

That's when Michelangelo finally declared the work completed. It had taken him four years, an incredibly short time. The pope called for a big celebration. For years people had been trying to get a look at what Michelangelo was doing, but he would allow no one into the chapel. Now at last the big moment had arrived. The crowd was amazed at what they saw. "This cannot be the work of a single artist," they declared. "Truly, his gifts are from God!" Pope Julius II died just four months after the ceiling was finished.

Many years later another pope appointed Michelangelo as the chief architect of St. Peter's, because work on the church was still going on even after the death of Pope Julius II. Michelangelo was seventy-two years old! He studied the dome Brunelleschi had designed for his beloved cathedral in Florence. "I can't possibly make one more beautiful," Michelangelo said. "But it will be even larger." Today, St. Peter's is the largest church in the world, and Michelangelo's dome can be seen for miles around. It is a reminder of what an incredibly talented artist he was. Artists of every age study and marvel at his work.

(Standards: Language Arts: Listening and Speaking 8.4)

Viewing the Art

Talk about how being a sculptor influenced Michelangelo's painting. His figures almost have the look of carved marble. Show the *Doni Tondo*, one of Michelangelo's early works. View scenes from the Sistine Chapel. (Try to find Stefano Zuffi's book—every page is a glorious fold-out of scenes from the chapel —see references.) Also, see the Visit to the Sistine Chapel Web site in the references to see different sections of the ceiling in detail. Do the children know some of the Bible stories represented on the chapel ceiling? Mention that dirt and smoke from burning candles in the chapel had made the frescoes so dark you could hardly appreciate Michelangelo's colors. The ceiling was restored several years ago. You may want to show the film about the restoration that is listed in the references . What feelings does the picture of Adam and God evoke? Show the *Last Judgment* (*Michelangelo: The Last Judgment*—see the references—has large pictures of all the figures in the painting and is perfect for viewing.) Concentrate on the different positions of the figures, the expressions on the faces. This is an enormous cast of characters to ponder. Show some of Michelangelo's drawings. He believed that the best way to learn art is to draw as much as possible. Finally, show some pictures of St. Peter's, concentrating on the magnificent dome designed by Michelangelo. Show close-ups of the dome, both inside and out, and compare it to Brunelleschi's in Florence.

(Standards: Art Connections 1.1-8; Language Arts: Viewing 9.6, 23)

Journal Writing

Do the children feel Michelangelo should have listened to his father and pursued a career as a merchant? What do they think of Michelangelo's feat in painting the Sistine Chapel? Should he have accepted help? Is it good to dedicate almost every waking minute to a task? What is their favorite painting? Why? Compare the domes of St. Peter's and Santa Maria del Fiore in Florence. What did Michelangelo learn from Brunelleschi? How are the domes similar and different?

(Standards: Language Arts: Writing 1.7, 23, 33-37; Art Connections 1.3; Thinking and Reasoning 3.3)

Art/Drama Activity: Scaffold Painting

Materials

- Large boards or pieces of corrugated cardboard covered on both sides with art paper—enough for half the class
- Tempera paint
- Paintbrushes
- Paper to cover the floor

Have the children imagine that they are Michelangelo, just given the enormous task of painting the Sistine Chapel. They are going to experience what it feels like trying to paint in such an awkward position. Cover the floor with paper, and divide the children into pairs. Have one child hold a board or cardboard high off the floor, while the other lies on his or her back on the floor (scaffolding) with paint and tries to paint a picture on it. After a few minutes, turn the board over and reverse roles. Then discuss the experience. What does it feel like to paint in that position? How would it feel hour after hour? Day after day? Year after year?

(Standards: Visual Arts: 1-4.1-11)

LESSON 6: Michelangelo Buonarotti (1475–1564)—Sculpture

The Story

If you had the most precious and rare seed in all the world—not another one like it anywhere—where would you plant it? (Invite children's responses.) Of course, you would prepare the richest, best soil you could. You would mix into that soil the best fertilizers and nutrients. You would choose the very best spot to put that soil, where it would receive just the right amount of sunlight and water, and then you would carefully plant that seed at just the right depth. You would probably even build a fence around it so no animals would dig it up or eat it. For if something happened to that seed, there would be no other to replace it. You would watch over it and nourish it and wait patiently for it to grow.

Well, Michelangelo was like that seed. Many people say he was the greatest artist who ever lived, even up to our own day. True, his father didn't care for his son. He beat Michelangelo often. He never understood the boy's art, he never encouraged his art, and he never thought it was good, even when kings and popes were so amazed they knelt down in awe in front of Michelangelo's statues.

But Michelangelo had the good fortune to be born at the perfect time in the perfect city—glorious Florence. The Florentines loved art and were happy to support artists. Michelangelo learned about painting from Ghirlandaio, one of Florence's greatest artists, and when Lorenzo de Medici saw Michelangelo's work, he invited the boy to live in his palace as his own son, to become the pupil of the great sculptor Bertoldo, and to create sculptures for the palace garden.

Lorenzo gave Michelangelo money for his work and treated him well, and Michelangelo produced some beautiful sculptures. After Lorenzo died only three years later, Michelangelo went to a monastery where the prior allowed him to cut open dead bodies and study the shape of muscles and tissues. This study would make him an even greater sculptor, but it was dangerous work, for it was against the law. To thank the prior for his kindness, Michelangelo carved a beautiful crucifix for the monastery.

Once Michelangelo carved a small cupid and sold it to a man for a very low price. The man knew that in Rome, people were very interested in the ancient art of the Greeks and Romans. So he took Michelangelo's little cupid and buried it for several weeks to make it look old. Then he sold it to a cardinal for more than six times what he gave Michelangelo. The cardinal thought he was buying an ancient statue, but some time later he discovered the truth. However, he still knew the statue was very good work, and he hunted and hunted until he found the artist who had carved it, Michelangelo. He invited Michelangelo to live with him, and that's how the artist came to the second city in which he found jobs. All his life he would work mostly for art collectors in Florence and Rome.

While Michelangelo was in Rome, he did such wonderful carvings that another cardinal heard of his work. Now that cardinal wanted to give a work of art to St. Peter's church before he returned to his homeland in France, and he asked Michelangelo to carve a statue for him. It had to be a statue of the Virgin Mary holding the body of Jesus when he was taken down from the cross. This kind of statue is called a *pietà*, an Italian word that means "pity." The cardinal wanted the statue to be life-sized, and he wanted Michelangelo to finish it in exactly one year! Michelangelo was only twenty-three years old, and no one believed he could really do it. But he did—and on time, too!

One day a big crowd was gathered in St. Peter's looking at the *Pietà*, and Michelangelo was hiding behind a pillar. "This work is so perfect, I know it was carved by our great artist in Milan. Only an old man with much experience could perform such a miracle with marble!" said an onlooker. Michelangelo was very angry when he heard that, so he came back to the church with his chisel in the middle of the night and on Mary's sash he carved the words, "Michelangelo Buonarroti the Florentine made it." It is the only work he ever signed. Today people still travel across the world to see that incredible statue.

Near the cathedral in Florence there stood a huge block of marble. The Florentines used to laugh every time they saw it. "What good is that silly piece of marble?" they said. "It is very beautiful, but it is so narrow that nothing useful could ever be carved from it. It is good for nothing, perhaps, but to become a pillar."

"Give it to me," said Michelangelo, "and I will work wonders with it." So the leaders of the city gave Michelangelo the marble, and he built a wooden rectangle around it, hiding it from everybody. Then he set to work carving a statue of David, the young boy in the Bible who killed the giant Goliath with a simple slingshot. David reminded Michelangelo of Florence itself, like a small child defending itself successfully against larger city-states that were always trying to wage war against it. He knew the Florentines would love a statue of David for their city. For almost three years he chiseled away at the statue, and when it was finished, the Florentines couldn't believe their eyes. They placed it outside the palace of the city leaders where everyone could see it. Now it has been moved into a museum to protect it from the weather.

Michelangelo carved many other statues throughout his lifetime. When he died, just before his ninetieth birthday, his body, just as he had wished, was brought back to his beloved Florence. Michelangelo was a painter, a sculptor, an architect, and a poet. He had outlived the other two giants of the Renaissance, Leonardo and Raphael. He had accomplished incredible feats of art, many of which we cannot see because they have disappeared. People say he was the greatest artist who ever lived. What do you think?

(Standards: Language Arts: Listening and Speaking 8.4)

Viewing the Art

(Most books on Michelangelo have some plates of his sculptures. An excellent book devoted especially to the sculpture of this artist is Hodson's *Michelangelo: Sculptor.* It has large pictures for viewing. A most exquisite book is *Michelangelo: Paintings Sculpture Architecture.* The plates are large and amazingly detailed and represent ALL of his work. There are many individual pictures of the paintings on the Sistine Chapel. Unfortunately, they are in black and white, but these close views are wonderful. See the references for both books.)

Show the two works Michelangelo did as a teenager working for Lorenzo: *Madonna of the Stairs* and *Battle of the Centaurs*. What do the children think of such work being done by one so young? Note the twisted bodies of the centaurs and point out that Michelangelo loved to do such forms. Spend time on the first *Pietà*. What emotions does this sculpture evoke? Do the children notice Michelangelo's carving on the Virgin's sash? Talk about Italy's lending the statue, one of its most prized possessions, to the United States for a World's Fair exposition in the 1960s. What do the children think of the *David*? Discuss how Michelangelo's knowledge of anatomy is evident in this statue. What do they think of David's expression? Try to show close-ups of the face and hand. Call attention to the hand holding the slingshot. It is much larger proportionally than it should be because Michelangelo intended viewers to look up to his *David*. The hand is seen in the foreground by one looking up. Recall for the children what a difficult piece of marble Michelangelo had to work with. What is their opinion of the results?

View the statues that make up Julius II's tomb, especially the *Moses*. (See *Michelangelo: The Medici Chapel* in the references.) Note that the horns on Moses's head are the result of a mistake in the Bible translation (instead of light coming from Moses's head, the translation was "horns") . Moses is so real he almost seems to speak his anger at the disobedience of his people. In what ways do Michelangelo's statues *Day* and *Night* reveal those two times of day, or of life? Show Michelangelo's last works, especially the last two *Pietàs*.

Point out that Michelangelo did not do the figure on the left. Can the children note any difference between that statue and the other three? Call their attention to the fact that Joseph is a self-portrait and that Michelangelo smashed the statue in anger but allowed an assistant to repair it.

(Standards: Art Connections 1.1-8; Language Arts: Viewing 9.6, 23)

Journal Writing

If you have taught Donatello, the children might wish to compare his *David* with Michelangelo's. What kind of a person is each *David*? How does the artist show this? Which one do the children like best? Why? Invite the children to compare Michelangelo's three *Pietàs*. How are they alike? Different? What feelings do they arouse?

(Standards: Thinking and Reasoning 3.3; Language Arts: Writing 1.7, 23, 33-37; Art Connections 1.3)

Art/Drama Activity: Biographical Drama

Invite the children to dramatize a scene in the life of Michelangelo. Some possibilities might be:

- Michelangelo begging his father to let him study art
- Michelangelo's being invited by Lorenzo to live in his palace and work in the sculpture garden
- Michelangelo obtaining the narrow piece of marble from the Florentines and carving the *David*
- Michelangelo and Pope Julius II arguing over the ceiling of the Sistine Chapel

(Standards: Theater: 2-4.1-2, 10-11, 14, 17)

LESSON 7: Raphaello Sanzio (1483–1520)

The Story

"Papa, show me how to mix the paints. I know I can do it. Let me help you!" Young Raphael stood by his father, Giovanni, as he painted frescoes on the walls of the duke's palace in the town of Urbino, where Raphael and his parents lived. Raphael's father was a kind man, and realizing his son was interested in art, he taught him all he knew. But the boy was very talented, and before long, he became a better artist than his father.

"My dear," Giovanni said to his wife, "I am going to take our son to Perugia to work in the shop of the famous artist Perugino."

"Oh, you mustn't do that. He is so young, and he is our only child. I shall miss him so."

"But the boy has talent," replied Giovanni. "I have nothing left to teach him. He must go." So Raphael became Perugino's apprentice, and in a very short time his work was as good as his master's. In fact, many people could hardly tell them apart!

While Raphael was studying with Perugino and doing a great deal of artwork on his own, he heard that many artists were traveling to Florence to study drawings made by two special artists, Leonardo da Vinci and Michelangelo. Everybody was buzzing about the battle scenes they had drawn for the walls of a building in Florence. The frescoes never were painted, but the drawings were available for study. Raphael said goodbye to Perugino and went to study in another workshop, the city of Florence.

When Raphael saw Leonardo's and Michelangelo's drawings, he could hardly believe them! He copied them over and over again until he got them right. Then he began to study the other works of those two artists. He loved the way Leonardo used light and shadow in his paintings. He loved how Michelangelo showed nude people in different twisted positions. He drew Michelangelo's *David* many times. He copied Leonardo's *Mona Lisa*. Even though Raphael had been famous in

Urbino, he was a student all over again. And he learned fast, not only from Leonardo and Michelangelo, but from many other great Florentine artists.

Raphael actually stayed in Florence for a few years, and although he never mastered painting nude people as well as Michelangelo, he learned so much that people loved his work. Pope Julius II heard about him. You remember that Julius was busy fixing up the special place in Rome called the Vatican where the pope lives? He had already given Michelangelo the job of painting the Sistine Chapel. Now he ordered Raphael to paint frescoes on the walls and ceiling of one room in the pope's special apartments.

Other artists were already busy painting frescoes in the other rooms. Raphael made many drawings to get ready for this tremendous job, and then he began work. Meanwhile, he kept wondering what was going on in the chapel, because Michelangelo wouldn't let anyone in except the pope, and he didn't even want the pope to bother him. But one day Michelangelo wasn't there, and Raphael sneaked in to see his work. He liked what he saw so much that he repainted one of his own frescoes in the pope's apartment. When the pope saw Raphael's work, he was so happy that he gave him two other rooms to do as well. "Paint over the other artists' frescoes," he ordered. "Your painting is much better than theirs."

Raphael's painting in the pope's chambers made him so famous that many rich people gave him jobs. They wanted their portraits painted. They wanted paintings for their chapels and their palaces. He painted many portraits and over forty pictures of Mary, the mother of Jesus. These paintings are called *Madonnas*. All of them are different and very beautiful. Raphael had so much work that he had many apprentices to help him. People followed him around wherever he went because he was so kind and handsome. Women especially liked him, and he had many girl friends, but he never married.

One day, just before his thirty-seventh birthday, Raphael became ill. In those days, when people became sick doctors drained some of their blood, believing that if they got the bad blood out of the person's body, the person would get better. But that's just what Raphael didn't need. He needed strength, and draining his blood just made him weaker. He became so weak that he died a few days later, on his birthday. Some people say that when Raphael died, painting died with him. Leonardo was a genius at ideas, Michelangelo was a genius at sculpture, and Raphael, they say, was a genius at painting. After we look at some of Raphael's paintings, you can decide for yourselves.

(Standards: Language Arts: Listening and Speaking 8.4)

Viewing the Art

The children might enjoy seeing Raphael's self-portrait. It will certainly give them an idea of how gracefully handsome he was and why he attracted so much attention. (See Chapman et al. 2004, 71.) Spend some time viewing Raphael's famous *School of Athens,* painted in the Vatican apartments. Note how well-balanced the painting is, with the two figures in the middle flanked by almost equal numbers of people on each side. Point out that some say the figure in red in the middle is Leonardo da Vinci, while the man writing in the foreground with his head in his hand is Michelangelo. Raphael has placed himself and his teacher Perugino on the extreme right. Notice the color and movement in this and all Raphael's works. If you have studied Greek art with the children, connect this painting to what they know of the ancient Greeks.

Study Raphael's *Deliverance of St. Peter from Prison.* Point out that since Raphael had to paint this in an alcove, he worked the alcove shape into his painting. Three parts of the story are told in this one painting: Peter's chains being released by the angel, the angel leading Peter out of prison, and the guards discovering Peter's escape. Notice Raphael's use of light and shadow, how the stairs appear to be part of the wall. Show Raphael's last painting, *The Transfiguration,* which was placed near his body at his death. Note the story taking place below—the boy being brought to Christ for a cure. Spend time viewing as many *Madonnas* as you can. Do the children recognize the triangular form in these pictures? From whom did Raphael learn this? (Leonardo.) Notice how well-balanced and graceful these paintings are, how beautiful the *Madonnas'* faces are. Finally, study some of the portraits, especially *Baldassare Castiglione, Angolo Doni, La Gravida,* and *Pope Leo X.* Note the Renaissance clothing and the position of the subjects.

(Standards: Art Connections 1.1-8; Language Arts: Viewing 9.6, 23)

Journal Writing

Raphael fit an enormous amount of work into a very short lifetime. What are some things he learned from other Renaissance painters and even surpassed them in doing? What is the children's favorite work, and why? Do they agree that Raphael is a greater painter than Leonardo or Michelangelo? Why or why not?

(Standards: Thinking and Reasoning 3.3; Language Arts: Writing 1.7, 23, 33-37; Art Connections 1.3)

Art/Drama Activity: Living Portraits

Divide the children into groups and give them several tasks that will allow them to experience in their bodies some of the things they have learned about Raphael's work. For example, encourage the children to use various objects in the room and pose themselves for a portrait so that they form a triangular shape. Or ask them to design themselves into a picture that shows the kind of symmetry evident in Raphael's paintings: the same number of children or objects on one side as on the other. Another possibility might be to encourage them to consider motion in their poses: freeze-frame themselves walking, talking, reaching out to someone, etc.

Additional Activities as an Overview of Renaissance Art

My students have often chosen the Renaissance as the subject for their year-end play. There is such a cast of colorful characters from whom to choose, and it is a wonderful way for them to recall some of the things they have learned about this important period in art history. Some possibilities for dramatization are

- Giotto's discovery by Cimabue
- Brunelleschi's defeat in the contest for the baptistery doors
- Brunelleschi's and Donatello's trip to Rome
- Brunelleschi's designing of the dome and his fight to keep his model secret
- Leonardo inventing new machines
- Leonardo following people to study different kinds of faces
- Michelangelo convincing the Florentines that he can carve something wonderful from the narrow block of marble
- Michelangelo arguing with Pope Julius II and painting the Sistine Chapel in secret, on his back
- Raphael sneaking into the Sistine Chapel to view Michelangelo's work

There are ways to simplify Renaissance dress to make costuming easy. For male parts, a long-sleeved shirt belted at the waist and worn over tights works well. If they can make a money pouch to hang from the belt, that is even better. They can wear ballet slippers or go without shoes. For female parts, it is easy to cut a long tunic with a scoop neck from material. Very little sewing is involved. Again, ballet slippers or feet in tights are fine. Those who are playing the parts of wealthier people can show this by wearing an elaborate hat. Make these by wrapping a pillowcase to resemble a turban. Wear it at a jaunty angle. Consult a book of costumes like the one listed in the references for additional ideas.

(Standards: Theater: 1-4.1-2, 5, 19-11, 14, 17)

Draw a large outline map of Italy on a piece of paper and display it to the children. With their help, put in some of the cities studied in the lessons on the Renaissance: Florence, Vinci, Rome, Urbino, Padua, Milan. Then put in the names of the artists who were born and/or worked in those cities. You could also list some of the artworks created in those cities.

(Standards: Geography: 1-2.30)

Curriculum Connections

Social Studies

- Read a history of the Renaissance. (See *The Atlas of the Renaissance World* in the references.)
- On a large world map, trace the routes of some leading explorers; locate on a map the various Italian cities in which Renaissance artists worked. (See the references for some biographies of explorers.)
- Study the culture of the time of the Renaissance. What was life like for people in different segments of society? (See *Women of the Renaissance, Renaissance People,* and *The Renaissance and the New World* and the Hinds books in the references.)
- Find pictures of clothing of the time and point out its features. Why did people dress as they did? How does it compare with clothing today? (See *Your Travel Guide to the Renaissance* and *Clothing* in the references.)
- Create a time line of important events.
- Create a Renaissance town complete with a palace for the duke or leader, a guild, some apprentice shops, etc.

(Standards: Geography: 1, 17.4, 30, ; Grade K-4 History: 7.1, 4, 8, 11; World History: 26-27.48, 55)

Science

- What were some inventions and medical practices of the time? How did they work? Do we still use them? Focus especially on the inventions of Leonardo da Vinci. (See Anderson 2006, Scjeszka 2006, Dawson 2005, Herbert 1998, and Krull 2005.)
- Study the work of men such as Galileo. What did Galileo have to say about the relationship of the earth and sun, and how did he suffer for his ideas? (See *Starry Messenger* in the references.)
- What were modes of transportation? Make a model of one of Columbus's ships.

(Standards: Geography: 6.43-45; Grade K-4 History: 8.28, 38, 41, 45)

Music

- Listen to Renaissance music: study polyphony, sacred music. Explain that polyphony means many different voices singing and coming in at different times in the music. By going to the Web site listed in the references, you can listen to some of the glorious music composed by Palestrina, a master of polyphony.

- What instruments were popular at the time? Draw them on a chart for display in the room. (See the excellent *Guide to Medieval and Renaissance Instruments* site listed in the references.)

  (Standards: Music 7.3-4, 7; Arts and Communication: 4-5.29)

Mathematics

- Discuss double-entry bookkeeping and its influence on the way records are kept today.

  (Standards: Mathematics: 9.4, 49)

Literature

- Read biographies of some famous people of the time: Galileo, Dante, explorers, Lorenzo de Medici, etc. (see references for titles).
- Find some quotes from the poet Dante that the children can understand and post them on charts around the room. Go to http://www.quotationspage.com/quotes/Dante_Alighieri/ for some suggestions.
- Read some of Michelangelo's poetry. (See *Michelangelo: Life, Letters, and Poetry* in the references.)

  (Standards: Language Arts: Reading: 6, 8.4-5, 13, 23, 28)

References

Adult Books

Andrew, Glenn M., John M. Hunisak, and A. Richard Turner. *The Art of Florence I and II.* Photography by Takashi OIkamura. New York: Artabras/Abbeville, 1988. ISBN 0-89660-111-0.

This is THE viewing source for all the Florentine artists in this chapter. This box set is huge—over 1,000 pages—and the illustrations are gorgeous.

Basile, Giuseppe. *Giotto: The Arena Chapel Frescoes.* London: Thames & Hudson, 1992. ISBN 0500236674.

This is an absolutely beautiful book filled with commentary and large reproductions of the frescoes.

Basta, Chiara. *Botticelli.* New York: Rizzoli, 2004. ISBN 0-8478-2676-7.

Although this is a little book, it is suitable for small group or individual viewing.

Battisti, Eugenio. *Filippo Brunelleschi.* Translated by Robert Erich Wolf. New York: Phaidon, 2002. ISBN 1904313124.

This is a marvelous source of large, detailed reproductions of all of Brunelleschi's works. It contains a large picture of his death mask.

Beck, James. *Raphael: The Stanza della Segnatura.* New York: George Braziller, 1993. ISBN 0807613142.

Beck discusses Raphael's frescoes in the Stanza della Segnatura in the Vatican Palace.

Beck, James, Antonio Paolucci, and Bruno Santi. *Michelangelo: The Medici Chapel.* Photos by Aurelio Amendola. New York: Thames & Hudson, 2000. ISBN 0500236909.

This gorgeous book has huge pictures of the statues on the Medici tombs.

Bellinati, Claudio. *Giotto: Map of The Scrovegni Chapel.* Ponzano Veneto, Italy: Vianello, 2005. ISBN 8872001447.

The paintings on each wall of the chapel are reproduced and discussed.

Bellosi, Luciano, and Giuliana Ragionieri. *Cimabue.* New York: Abbeville Press, 1998. ISBN 0789204665.

The authors discuss Cimabue's work and provide many reproductions for viewing.

Bennett, Bonnie A., and David G. Wilkins. *Donatello.* New York: Abaris Books, 1985. o.p. ISBN 0898352614.

The authors discuss Donatello's life and works.

Brambilla, Pinin, and Pietro C. Marani. *Leonardo: The Last Supper.* Translated by Harlow Tighe. Chicago: University of Chicago Press, 1999. ISBN 0-226-50427-1.

This beautiful book has over 300 large plates of individual parts of the painting.

Brown, David Allan. *Leonardo da Vinci: Origins of a Genius.* New Haven, CT: Yale University Press, 1998. ISBN 0-300-07246-5.

This fine book has large pictures for viewing.

Bull, George. *Michelangelo: Life, Letters, and Poetry.* New York: Oxford University Press, 1999. ISBN 0192837702.

An entire chapter of this book is devoted to Michelangelo's poems.

Burroughs, Betty, ed. *Vasari's Lives of the Artists: Biographies of the Most Eminent Architects, Painters, and Sculptors of Italy.* New York: Simon & Schuster, 1946. o.p. ASIN B000HF1G4M.

Burroughs selects stories from Vasari's original biographies of Renaissance artists.

Chapman, Hugo. *Michelangelo Drawings: Closer to the Master.* New Haven, CT and London: Yale University Press/British Museum Press, 2005.

The author discusses more than ninety of Michelangelo's drawings and shows how they shaped his evolution as an artist.

Chapman, Hugo, Tom Henry, and Carol Plazzotta. *Raphael from Urbino to Rome.* London: National Gallery Company/Yale University Press, 2004. ISBN 1-85709-994-X.

This very beautiful book recounts Raphael's life and contains large color illustrations for viewing.

Cocke, Richard. *Raphael.* London: Chaucer Press, 2004. ISBN 1-904449-38-7.

Cocke describes the work of Raphael. The plates are suitable for viewing.

Cole, Bruce. *Giotto: The Scrovegni Chapel, Padua.* New York: George Braziller, 1993. ISBN 080761310X.

Cole provides commentary on Giotto's work and on each of the plates in the book. The plates are not overly large but are suitable for group viewing.

d'Arcais, Francesca Flores. *Giotto.* New York: Abbeville Press, 1995. ISBN 1558597743.

This book has nearly 400 large color reproductions of Giotto's frescoes and panel paintings.

De Vecchi, Pierluigi. *Michelangelo: The Vatican Frescoes.* Photography by Takashi Okamura. 1997. Reprint, New York: Abbeville Press, 2006. ISBN 0-7892-0142-9.

The paintings of the Sistine Chapel are shown after their restoration.

Eimerl, Sarel. *The World of Giotto.* New York: Time-Life, 1978. o.p. ISBN 0809402106.

This is a thorough discussion of Giotto's contribution to art. It contains many color reproductions, including a large selection of medieval works for comparison.

Franklin, David. *Painting in Renaissance Florence 1500–1550.* New Haven, CT: Yale University Press, 2001. ISBN 0-300-08399-8.

Franklin discusses twelve important Florentine artists. There are many large pictures for viewing.

Graham-Dixon, Andrew. *Renaissance.* Berkeley: University of California Press, 2000. ISBN 0520223756.

Fine reproductions and writing that exhibits a sense of humor make this a good resource.

Hale, J. R., et al. *Renaissance.* New York: Time-Life UK, 1920. ISBN 0900658282.

Hale discusses the causes of the Renaissance, provides an illustrated map of Florence, and discusses some important artists of the period.

Hall, Marcia. *Michelangelo: The Frescoes of the Sistine Chapel.* Photos by Takashi Okamura. New York: Harry N. Abrams, 2002. ISBN 0-8109-3530-9.

This beautiful book has very large photographs of the frescoes.

Hartt, Frederick. *History of the Italian Renaissance.* 5th ed. New York: Harry N. Abrams, 2003. ISBN 0-8109-1230-9.

From the late Middle Ages through the high Renaissance, this is a marvelous history of some of the greatest art in the world. It is useful for viewing the work of all the artists in this chapter.

Hodson, Rupert. *Michelangelo: Sculptor.* London: Philip Wilson, 2003. ISBN 0856675156.

This book contains large pictures for viewing.

King, Ross. *Michelangelo and the Pope's Ceiling.* Reissue. New York: Viking, 2003. ISBN 0142003697.

Ross presents the drama behind the excruciating years it took to create the Sistine Chapel ceiling.

Labella, Vincenzo. *A Season of Giants.* Boston: Little, Brown, 1990. ISBN 0316856460.

Labella discusses the works of the three giants of the Renaissance: Leonardo, Michelangelo, and Raphael. Tied in to a four-hour miniseries on Turner Network.

Legouix, Susan. *Botticelli.* London: Chaucer Press, 2005. ISBN 1904449-212.

The author discusses the life and work of Botticelli. This book is especially useful for viewing the artist's portrait paintings.

Lightbown, Ronald. *Sandro Botticelli: Life and Work.* Rev. ed. New York: Abbeville Press, 1989. ISBN 0896599310.

Lightbown describes the artist's early life and apprenticeship and relates his paintings to the culture of fifteenth-century Florence. More than 217 color plates.

Marani, Pietro C. *Leonardo da Vinci: The Complete Paintings.* New York: Harry Abrams, 1999. ISBN 0-8019-3581-3.

This is an exquisite book with all the paintings in large format available for viewing.

McCarthy, Mary. *The Stones of Florence.* Illustrated by Evelyn Hofer. San Diego: Harcourt Brace, 2002. ISBN 0156027631.

McCarthy discusses art in Florence, with wonderful pictures of Florentine buildings and churches and large reproductions of the work of many Florentine artists.

Michelangelo: Paintings Sculpture Architecture. New York: Phaidon, 1953. Reprint, New York: Phaidon, 1999. ISBN 0-7148-3296-0.

This magnificent book has all of Michelangelo's works in exquisite detail.

Musée de Luxenbourg, ed. *Raphael: Grace and Beauty.* Milan, Italy: Skira, 2001. ISBN 88-8491-027-7.

The very large plates of the artist's work are fine for viewing.

Paoletti, John T., and Gary M. Radka. *Art in Renaissance Italy.* 3d ed. New York: Harry N. Abrams, 2005. ISBN 0131935100.

The authors discuss how the great artworks of the Renaissance came to be. Many pictures are suitable for group viewing.

Partridge, Loren, et al. *Michelangelo: The Last Judgment.* Photos by Takashi Okamura. New York: Harry N. Abrams, 2000. ISBN 0810981904.

This gorgeous book has large pictures of each of the figures in Michelangelo's *Last Judgment.*

Pietrangeli, Carlo, ed. *The Sistine Chapel: A Glorious Restoration*. 2d ed. Translated by Lawrence Jenkens. New York: Harry N. Abrams, 1994. ISBN 0810938405.

This large book is filled with close-ups of all the paintings in the Sistine Chapel. Marvelous for viewing. The book is a companion to the video mentioned below.

Poeschke, Joachim. *Donatello and His World.* Translated by Russell Stockman. Photos by Albert Hirmer and Irmgard Ernstmeier-Hirmer. New York: Harry N. Abrams, 1993. ISBN 0810932113.

This book contains very large photos of all of Donatello's works and of some of Brunelleschi's as well.

———. *Italian Frescoes: The Age of Giotto, 1280–1400.* Photographs by Antonio Quattrone and Ghigo Roli. New York: Abbeville Press, 2005. ISBN 0789208636.

This is a beautiful book with large photographs of the frescoes.

Stubblebine, James H, ed. *Giotto: The Arena Chapel Frescoes : Illustrations, Introductory Essay, Backgrounds and Sources, Criticism.* Reissue. New York: W. W. Norton, 1996. ISBN 0393314065.

This book provides over 120 reproductions of Giotto's frescoes in the Arena Chapel, along with commentary on the art.

Vasari, Giorgio. Philip Jacks, ed. *The Lives of the Most Excellent Painters, Sculptors, and Architects.* Translated by Gaston du C. de Vere. New York: The Modern Library/ Random House, 2006.

Filled with anecdotes and interesting information, these biographies can be sources of stories for students.

Venturi, Lionello. *Sandro Botticelli.* New York: Oxford University Press, 1962. o.p. ASIN B0007JD7VI.

Commentary and large reproductions of Botticelli's work, including wide pull-out reproductions of *Primavera* and *The Birth of Venus,* make this a valuable resource.

Walker, Paul Robert. *The Feud That Sparked the Renaissance: How Brunelleschi and Ghiberti Changed the Art World* New York: HarperCollins, 2002. ISBN 0380977877.

Walker discusses the lives and works of these artists and provides nineteen black-and-white reproductions.

Wasserman, Jack. *Leonardo Da Vinci.* New York: Harry N. Abrams, 1984. ISBN 0810912856.

Wasserman's discussion of Leonardo's life is accompanied by 139 reproductions.

Zöllner, Frank. *Botticelli.* Munich: Prestel, 2005. ISBN 3791332724.

Although Zöllner's writing is rather dry, the glorious reproductions are well worth asking your library to acquire this huge book.

———. *Leonardo da Vinci: The Complete Paintings and Drawings.* Cologne, Germany: Taschen, 2004. ISBN 0681165855.

In addition to all of the artist's paintings, there are 663 of his drawings, all arranged by subject. This is an excellent source for viewing.

Zuffi, Stefano, ed. *Michelangelo: The Sistine Chapel.* New York: Rizzoli, 2003. ISBN 0-8478-2310-5.

Every page is a fold-out of scenes from the Sistine Chapel.

Children's Books

Anderson, Maxine. *Amazing Leonardo da Vinci Inventions You Can Build Yourself.* White River Junction, VT: Nomad Press, 2006. ISBN 0974934429.

In this interactive book, readers can build some of Leonardo's inventions using simple materials. They will also learn about the science of the era.

Anholt, Laurence. *Leonardo and the Flying Boy.* Hauppage, NY: Barrons, 2000. ISBN 0-7641-5225-4.

Zoro, Leonardo's pupil, watches as his master struggles to invent a flying machine. A brief biography of da Vinci is included.

Avery, Charles. *Donatello: An Introduction.* New York: HarperCollins, 1994. ISBN 006430311X.

Avery examines Donatello's sculpture. Many illustrations, including four color plates.

Belting, Natalia M. *Elves and Ellefolk.* New York: Holt, Rinehart & Winston, 1961 o.p. ASIN B0007DQZA4.

This book contains some wonderful tales that can be used for storytelling while studying the Renaissance. Note especially "The Marvelous Doors" and "The Rose of Midwinter."

Bender, Michael. *Waiting for Filippo.* San Francisco: Chronicle Books, 1995. ISBN 0811801810.

This delightful pop-up book tells the story of Filippo Brunelleschi and the building of the dome over the cathedral in Florence.

Brighton, Catherine. *Five Secrets in a Box.* New York: E. P. Dutton, 1987. ISBN 0525443185.

Galileo's daughter, Virginia, tells about the secrets she finds in her father's special box. Very simple re-creation of the world of the Renaissance accompanied by beautiful illustrations.

Byrd, Robert. *Leonardo: Beautiful Dreamer.* New York: E. P. Dutton, 2003. ISBN 0525470336.

This is a beautiful biography accompanied by lively pictures and text, with sidebars for additional information.

Caselli, Giovanni. *The Renaissance and the New World.* New York: Peter Bedrick, 1986. ISBN 0872265641.

Caselli describes the everyday life and culture of Europe during the Renaissance and its spread to the New World.

Corrain, Lucia. *Art of the Renaissance.* New York: Peter Bedrick, 2001. ISBN 0872265269.

Thirty different aspects of life during the Renaissance are discussed through the art of the period.

Dawson, Ian. *Renaissance Medicine.* New York: Enchanted Lion Books, 2005. ISBN 1592700381.

Readers learn about medical procedures such as treatments with leeches, surgery, and more in this informative book.

Day, Nancy. *Your Travel Guide to the Renaissance.* Minneapolis, MN: Learner/Runestone Press, 2001. ISBN 0822530805.

The author gives readers the opportunity to experience life during the Renaissance—its clothing, customs, modes of transportation, etc.

Dorling Kindersley. *Giotto: The Founder of Renaissance Art—His Life in Paintings.* New York: DK Publishing, 1999. ISBN 0789448513.

This wonderful book presents the historical context in which the artist lived and an analysis of his works. There is an abundance of illustrations.

Douglas, Vincent. *The Atlas of the Renaissance World.* New York: Peter Bedrick, 2001. ISBN 0872266923.

Using maps and illustrations, this book provides an overview of the Renaissance period.

Fitzpatrick, Anne. *The Renaissance.* North Mankato, MN: Creative Editions, 2006. ISBN 1-58341-349-9.

The author provides information on the period and the important artists of the time. There are beautifully reproduced artworks as well.

Fritz, Jean. *Leonardo's Horse.* Illustrated by Hudson Talbott. New York: Putnam, 2001. ISBN 0-399-23576-0.

Leonardo made a clay model of a giant horse for the duke of Milan, but it was never cast in bronze until Charles Dent did the work 500 years later.

Greenblatt, Miriam. *Lorenzo de Medici and Renaissance Italy.* New York: Benchmark, 2003. ISBN 0761414908.

Greenblatt discusses Lorenzo's life and role as a patron of the arts and includes poems and rules of the time.

Guarnieri, Paolo. *A Boy Named Giotto.* Translated by Jonathan Galassi. Illustrated by Bimba Landmann. New York: Farrar, Straus & Giroux, 1999. ISBN 0374309310.

This beautifully written biography is suitable even for very young children.

Hart, Tony. *Leonardo da Vinci.* Hauppauge, NY: Barrons, 1994. ISBN 0812018281.

This biography is part of Barrons's Famous Children series.

———. *Michelangelo.* Hauppauge, NY: Barrons, 1994. ISBN 0812018273.

This is a readable biography for children.

Herbert, Janis. *Leonardo da Vinci for Kids: His Life and Ideas.* Chicago: Chicago Review Press, 1998. ISBN 1-55652-298-3.

This fun-filled book has twenty-one activities that center around the work and ideas of Leonardo da Vinci.

Hinds, Kathryn. *City.* (Life in the Renaissance). New York: Benchmark Books, 2003. ISBN 0761416781.

This is part of a four-volume set of books about different aspects of life during the Renaissance. All of the books were published in 2003 by Benchmark. The others are *The Church* (ISBN 076141679X), *The Court* (ISBN 0761416765), and *The Countryside* (ISBN 0761416773).

Howarth, Sarah. *Renaissance People.* Brookfield, CT: Millbrook Press, 1992. ISBN 1562940880.

Howarth describes thirteen types of professions from the Renaissance, including craftsman, artist, banker, and mercenary. Includes glossary, bibliography, and index.

Krull, Kathleen. *Leonardo da Vinci.* Illustrated by Boris Kulikov. New York: Viking Juvenile, 2005. ISBN 067005920X.

Krull's books are wonderfully witty and informative, and this one is no exception. This book provides a wealth of information about the artist and his scientific mind.

Langley, Andrew. *The da Vinci Kit: Mysteries of the Renaissance Decoded.* Philadelphia: Running Brook, 2006. ISBN 0762427876.

This kit contains a book about the artist, a model of his flying machine, a Last Supper restoration simulator, and much more. Great fun!

L'Engle, Madeleine. *The Glorious Impossible.* New York: Simon & Schuster, 1990. ISBN 0671686909

The story of Christ's life is beautifully illustrated with large reproductions from Giotto's frescoes in the Scrovegni Chapel.

MacDonald, Fiona. *You Wouldn't Want to Sail with Christopher Columbus!: Uncharted Waters You'd Rather Not Cross.* Illustrated by David Antram. New York: Franklin Watts, 2004. ISBN 0531160602.

Readers learn about the rigors of Columbus's voyage in this humorous book.

Mayhew, James. *Katie and the Mona Lisa.* New York: Orchard, 1999. ISBN 1860397069.

After entering into a painting of the *Mona Lisa* while visiting a museum, Katie meets the subjects of several Renaissance paintings.

McCarthy, Meghan. *Steal Back the Mona Lisa!* San Diego: Harcourt, 2006. ISBN 0-15-205368-9.

Have fun with this detective caper and help solve the theft of the famous Mona Lisa.

McLanathan, Richard. *First Impressions: Leonardo da Vinci.* New York: Harry N. Abrams, 1990. ISBN 0810912562.

This is a very readable life of Leonardo from his birth to his death in France. Some reproductions.

———. *First Impressions: Michelangelo.* New York: Harry N. Abrams, 1993. ISBN 0810936348.

This is a thorough discussion of Michelangelo's life for children, including a pull-out of the Sistine Chapel.

Molzahn, Arlene Bourgeois. *Ferdinand Magellan: First Explorer Around the World.* Berkeley Heights, NJ: Enslow, 2003. ISBN 0766020681.

Although there is some information about the explorer's childhood, the main thrust of this book is his trip around the world.

Morrison, Taylor. *Antonio's Apprenticeship.* New York: Holiday House, 1996. ISBN 082341213X.

After reading this excellent fictional picture-book story, children will have a good idea of the steps involved in painting a fresco in Florence during the Renaissance.

———. *The Neptune Fountain.* New York: Holiday House, 1997. ISBN 0823412938.

A companion book to *Antonio's Apprenticeship.* In seventeenth-century Rome, young Marco convinces a famous sculptor to take him on as apprentice. Readers will learn a great deal about Renaissance art in this picture-book story.

Muhlberger, Richard. *What Makes a Leonardo a Leonardo?* New York: Viking, 1994. ISBN 0670857440.

An exploration of twelve major works by Leonardo reveals the elements that make his art different from all others.

———. *What Makes a Raphael a Raphael?* New York: Viking, 1993. ISBN 067085204X.

An exploration of twelve major works by Raphael in terms of color, composition, and subject matter reveals what makes his work unique.

Peacock, John. *Costume 1066–1990's.* London: Thames & Hudson, 1994. ISBN 0500277915.

Clothing of different eras is pictured and labeled. Includes bibliography.

Pinguilly, Yves. *Da Vinci: The Painter Who Spoke with Birds.* Translated by by John Goodman. New York: Chelsea House, 1994. ISBN 0791028089.

Leonardo's life is told through letters between a young girl and her uncle.

Provensen, Alice, and Martin Provensen. *Leonardo Da Vinci.* New York: Random House/Arrow, 1984. ISBN 0091591104.

This is an ingenious pop-up book showing the various talents of the artist.

Sabuda, Robert. *Un-Oh, Leonardo.* New York: Atheneum, 2002. ISBN 0-689-81160-8.

Readers learn a good deal about life in Florence in Leonardo's time when they are transported back in time with Providence mouse through this entertaining picture book.

Scieszka, Jon. *Da Wild, Da Crazy, Da Vinci.* Illustrated by Adam McCauley. New York: Puffin, 2006. ISBN 0142404659.

The Time Warp Trio meet Leonardo da Vinci, who threatens to execute them for spying on his inventions, in this romp back in time.

Sis, Peter. *Starry Messenger.* New York: Farrar, Straus & Giroux, 1996. ISBN 0374371911.

This picture-book biography traces Galileo's life from childhood to his days as a prisoner of the Church. The story is enhanced by a great deal of sidebar information. A 1997 Caldecott Honor Book.

Skira-Venturi, Rosabianca. *A Weekend with Leonardo Da Vinci.* Translated by Ann Keay Beneduce. New York: Rizzoli, 1993. ISBN 0847814408.

In a first-person narrative, the artist tells the reader about his life and work.

Somervill, Barbara A. *Michelangelo: Sculptor and Painter.* Minneapolis, MN: Compass Point Books, 2005. ISBN 0-7565-0814-2.

This fine biography for older readers is well written and offers some examples of the artist's work.

Stanley, Diane. *Leonardo da Vinci.* Reprint, New York: HarperTrophy, 1996. ISBN 0688161553.

Stanley, an award-winning author of marvelous biographies for children, here gives a lively account of da Vinci's life. Wonderful illustrations.

———. *Michelangelo.* New York: HarperCollins, 2000. ISBN 0-688-15085-3.

This beautifully illustrated biography has a lengthy text for older readers.

Thomson, Melissa, and Ruth Dean. *Women of the Renaissance.* New York: Lucent Books, 2005. ISBN 1-59018-473-4.

The authors describe the lives of every strata of female society during the Renaissance.

Venezia, Mike. *Botticelli.* Danbury, CT: Children's Press, 1991. ISBN 051642291X.

Although this simple biography is too brief as a sole reference, the reproductions are excellent.

———. *Da Vinci.* Danbury, CT: Children's Press, 1989. ISBN 0516422758.

Venezia provides a brief biography of this amazing artist.

———. *Giotto.* Danbury, CT: Children's Press, 2000. ISBN 0516215922.

Venezia tells the story of the shepherd boy turned artist.

———. *Michelangelo.* Danbury, CT: Children's Press, 1991. ISBN 0516422936.

Venezia offers a brief biography of Michelangelo.

Willard, Nancy. *Gutenberg's Gift.* Illustrated by Bryan Leister. San Diego: Harcourt Brace, 1995. ISBN 0152007830

This clever pop-up book shows how Gutenberg made the first book using movable type.

Wood, Tim. *The Renaissance*. New York: Viking, 1993. ISBN 0670851493.

Wood discusses the achievements of the Renaissance. Plastic overlays give inside views of a Florentine townhouse, the Santa Maria, St. Peter's, and a printer's workshop.

Audiovisual Materials

Britten, Benjamin. *Britten: Songs*. Audio CD. Hyperion, 2001. ASIN B00005JJ3P.

Among the songs on this CD is "The Sonnets of Michelangelo" for voice and piano.

Castellani, Renato. *Leonardo da Vinci: The Most Brilliant Mind in History*. DVD. Questar, 2003. ISBN 1568559372. Order #QD3395.

Shot with over 500 extras in locations actually traversed by Leonardo himself, this wonderful film presents the life and work of the artist and his rivalry with Michangelo.

DaVinci. Video. gettingtoknow.com, 2003. VINC0103.

Winner of the 2004 ALA Notable Children's Video Award, this video is based on the book by Mike Venezia. It combines animation and presentation of actual works by the artist. Young children will love it.

Donatello: The First Modern Sculptor. DVD. Video Universe, 2001. Cat. #9294.

Several modern sculptors comment on Donatello's work. The film was shot on location in Italy.

Kloss, William. *Great Artists of the Italian Renaissance*. DVD. The Teaching Company, 2004. No. 7140.

This series of six thirty-minute DVDs is divided into thirty-six lectures about forty great artists of the Italian Renaissance period. It contains more than 500 images, and even if the lecture content is beyond your students' comprehension, this would be an excellent source of pictures for viewing without the sound.

Leonardo: To Know How to See. Video. National Gallery of Art, n.d. VC107.

This video depicts the accomplishments of the artist, including his best-known paintings. It introduces viewers to some of Leonardo's contemporaries and to the Italian countryside.

Leonardo da Vinci. Video. gettingtoknow.com, 2002. VINC0103.

This animated video of the artist's work will be enjoyed by young children.

Michelangelo. gettingtoknow.com, 2004. MICH0104.

This video is based on the book by Mike Venezia. It combines animation and presentation of actual works by the artist. Young children will love it.

Michelangelo: Artist and Man. DVD. New Video Group, Inc., 1994. ISBN 1-56501-425-1. Cat. #AAE-10461.

Art historians and other experts discuss Michelangelo's life and work.

Raphael and the American Collector. Video. National Gallery of Art, n.d. VC145.
Following a survey of Raphael's work, this film discusses the pieces collected in the United States.

Thompson, Molly, and Alan Goldberg. *Leonardo da Vinci: Renaissance Master.* Video. New Video Group, Inc., 1997. ISBN 0-7670-0256-3. Cat # AAE-14209.
Through extensive use of the artist's own notebooks, this film follows his life from birth to death.

The Treasures of Italy: Florence—Video Portrait of a City. Video. amazon.com, 1988. ASIN 1556250096.
This film presents the works of Michelangelo, Brunelleschi, Botticelli, Giotto, and da Vinci. Compares the *Davids* created by Michelangelo, Verrocchio, and Donatello.

Other Materials

The Art of Renaissance Europe: A Resource for Teachers. Metropolitan Museum of Art, n.d. M3994.
This tote box features Renaissance art contained in the museum. It includes five posters, a CD-ROM, slides, a time line, original fifteenth- and sixteenth-century writings, lesson plans, and suggested additional resources.

Renaissance Go Fish for Art. Card Game Palo Alto, CA: Birdcage Press, n.d. ISBN 1-889613-12-6.
Players learn a good deal about Renaissance artists while they have fun playing "Go Fish."

Web Sites

Giovanni da Palestrina. http://www.dovesong.com/MP3/MP3_Palestrina.asp (accessed March 9, 2006).
Visitors to this site can listen to the glorious music of Palestrina, one of the masters of Renaissance music.

A Guide to Medieval and Renaissance Instruments. http://www.music.iastate.edu/antiqua/instrumt.html (accessed March 9, 2006).
By clicking on the name of any instrument on this page, visitors to the site can see an image of the instrument and hear it being played. This is an excellent site!

Raphael. http://www.artcyclopedia.com/artists/raphael.html (accessed March 10, 2006).
Viewers can see Raphael's works in many museums throughout the world.

Sandro Botticelli. http://www.artcyclopedia.com/artists/botticelli_sandro.html (accessed March 10, 2006).
Viewers can see Botticelli's works in many different museums.

16th Century Art Italy: The High Renaissance and Mannerism. http://witcombe.sbc.edu/ARTH16thcentury.html#Italy16 (accessed March 10, 2006).

This site is well worth visiting as it has links to the artworks of most of the artists discussed in this chapter.

Visit to the Sistine Chapel. http://www.wga.hu/tours/sistina/index.html (accessed May 10, 2006).

Visitors to this excellent site can click on the frescoes, the *Last Judgment*, and more to see different sections in close-up views.

Web Museum, Paris. http://www.ibiblio.org/wm/paint/glo/renaissance/it.html (accessed March 10, 2006).

In addition to learning general information about the Renaissance, viewers can click on any artist's name and see his artworks.

Part IV
Five European Masters

9 Jan van Eyck in Flanders

Here lies Jan, famous through his unparalleled talent.
In whom the art of painting was wonderful.

—FUNERARY MARKER

Background Information

Flanders (present-day Belgium) in the time of the late gothic period (fourteenth and fifteenth centuries) was the scene of an artistic movement away from decorative art to a new realism that endeavored to present pictures as the eye saw them. Flemish artists set their subjects in landscapes of real vegetation. They showed the effects of air, which filters what the eye sees, and of light, which is absorbed by some surfaces and refracted or reflected from others. Although Giotto, in Italy, was experimenting with realism and making some attempt to use perspective, his work was unknown to Flemish artists, who struggled with perspective on their own. Even though there were many commissions for religious paintings in the still-Catholic country, painters introduced landscape and still life. In addition, the growth of mercantilism meant that a good segment of the population had the means to acquire portraits, causing portraiture to gain a new importance. Flemish artists also used oil in a new way. Instead of working with the thick, egg-based paints used by the Italians, they thinned their paints with turpentine and mixed them with clarified oil. They then painstakingly applied their paints in layers, using a transparent glaze as the final coat. The oil permitted the rich colors underneath to shine through, producing a more brilliant work.

The cities of Ghent and Bruges, in Flanders, were two of the busiest in Europe, centers of trade between the north and the south. Rich merchants populated these cities, and many were avid patrons of the arts. Add to this the fact that the Flemish court was the richest in Europe and employed many artists in its decoration, and it is little wonder that the arts flourished in Flanders at this time.

Jan van Eyck was born not only among a populace ready and willing to honor his talent but also into an entire family of gifted artists. His older brother

Hubert, with whom he probably worked on the famed *Ghent Alterpiece,* was a painter of renown. It is generally believed that Hubert also painted four pages in the *Book of Hours of Turin* and the small painting *Marys at the Sepulcher.* Two other siblings—Lambert, and a sister, Margaret—were also painters.

The date of Jan's birth is uncertain, but he was probably born around 1390 in Maaseyck. In 1425 he entered the service of Philip the Good, Duke of Burgundy, and remained in the duke's employ until his own death in 1441. Jan undertook many journeys on behalf of the duke, one of them to Portugal to paint Philip's bride-to-be, the Infanta Isabella, and bring her home to Flanders. As with many of Jan's paintings, this one of Isabella has been lost. In addition to his work for the duke, Jan did several religious commissions, the most famous being the altarpiece at Ghent, and some portraits. He married a woman named Margaret, whose portrait he painted, and had one, or possibly two, children. Jan van Eyck died in Bruges on July 9, 1441, and was buried in the church of St. Donatian. He is considered by many to be one of the greatest Flemish painters and to have contributed enormously to the movement toward realism in painting.

(Standards: Art Connections: 1,1-2, 4, 6-7)

LESSON: Jan van Eyck (1390?–1441)

The Story

(While oil painting probably did not originate with Jan van Eyck, he did work wonders with oil. This story is meant to convey the contribution of the northern painters to the perfection of oil painting.)

It seemed to young Jan van Eyck that as far back as he could remember, he could crinkle his nose and smell the wonderful aroma of paint in the house. He knew the feel of brushes in his hands, thick brushes and thin, delicate ones. His older brother Hubert painted the most wonderful pictures, and Jan loved to watch him work. As he grew to manhood, Jan knew that he wanted to be an artist too, and he worked hard with his brother to learn all he needed to know to earn his living. Early each morning, he began work on his painting. He painted pictures of the things in his house: his room, his bed, bowls of fruit, tables. He painted pictures of his sister, Margaret, and his two brothers. He painted madonnas and saints. The more he worked, however, the more discouraged he became.

"What is wrong, brother?" asked Hubert one day. "Your painting is coming along nicely. Why don't you look more pleased with yourself?"

"Look at the sleeve of Margaret's dress," Jan replied, pointing to his sister, who was sitting on a chair across the room. "Do you see the delicate flowers in the pattern? Do you see the way the folds of the material hang just so?"

"Well, of course I do," replied Hubert. "What is the problem? Are you having trouble drawing Margaret's dress?"

"Oh, no. I love to draw such details. I try to notice everything just as it is and to put each thing I see into my painting. But the paint dries so fast that I do not have the time I need to capture every little detail! I need a different kind of paint. This egg we mix our paints with just doesn't work. The Italians living in their sunny country may like it, but in our cold climate, it is no good at all!"

From that moment on, Jan was determined to find a new way to mix paints. Day after day he experimented. He made his mixtures thicker, then thinner. He tried more egg, then less egg. But nothing pleased him. Frustrated, he decided to mix his paints with something completely different, and he chose oil. The results were amazing.

"Hubert," Jan cried, "come here. Look at what oil allows me to do. I can make my colors glossy and put them on in layers. I can take my delicate little brushes and paint in all the tiny details I wish—and the paint stays wet for a long time!"

Hubert was just as excited as his brother. From that day on, the brothers mixed their paints with oil, and their fame spread throughout the city. Rich wool merchants, who thanked God for their prosperity by giving paintings to the Church, hired the van Eyck brothers to do artworks for them.

When the duke of Burgundy heard about Jan's fine work, he asked him to become his special painter. Jan loved working for Duke Philip. Not only was he asked to paint pictures, but he was also sent on some secret trips. Once he even went all the way to Portugal to bring the duke's new bride back to Flanders. But only a year after Jan began working for the duke, his beloved brother Hubert died. Hubert had been working on a magnificent altarpiece, showing Jesus as the Lamb of God with crowds of people coming to worship him. Jan finished that work, and today it is one of the most famous artworks in the world. Whole books have been written about just that one picture. We will look at it and some of the other pictures painted by Jan van Eyck. Many of his pictures have been lost or destroyed, but the ones we have can show us what a marvelous painter he was.

(Standards: Language Arts: Listening and Speaking 8.4)

Viewing the Art

In viewing van Eyck's work, it is important to choose books that provide details of the larger pictures, since it is the artist's exquisite rendering of the most minute facets of his subjects—the hairs on a dog, the fibers in a garment, the blades of grass in a field—that give such pleasure. The CD-ROM *The Age of van Eyck* is extremely useful for this purpose. Try to show as many of van Eyck's paintings as you can since there are so few, but be sure to focus on two in particular: *The Adoration of the Lamb* altarpiece (Ghent) and *Wedding Portrait*

(Giovanni Arnolfini and His Wife). In the *Adoration of the Lamb*, call attention to the details in the vegetation, the buildings in the background, and the clothing on the crowds of people, especially the magnificent, jewel-encrusted robes of the Christ. The Web site http://keptar.demasz.hu/arthp/html/e/eyck_van/ghent/ has whole and detailed views of the altarpiece in full color and is excellent for viewing, especially if you have an LCD projector. See also http://www.wga.hu/tours/flemish/eyck/index.html for more magnified views. Children especially love the Arnolfini portrait. A detailed discussion of this painting can be found in *What Great Paintings Say, Volume 2* (see references). Many of the details in this picture are symbolic. For example, one candle in the chandelier represents Christ; the dog stands for faith, etc. (See "Curriculum Connections: Literature" in chapter 11 for suggestions for a discussion on symbolism.) How many things can the children notice? Point out the clothing, the oranges by the window and the shrub outside, the shoes the couple have removed from their feet, the chandelier, the mirror with the ten scenes from the Passion and the two witnesses (one possibly the artist) reflected within, the rosary on the wall, the artist's signature, the chair with the statue of St. Margaret, and many other details. How many can the children find on their own? If you show the portrait of the *Man in a Red Turban*, point out that this is possibly a self-portrait.

(Standards: Art Connections 1.1-8; Language Arts: Viewing 9.6, 23)

Journal Writing

Ask the children to choose one person or object from the pictures they have seen and try to list as many details as they can remember about it. For example, if they were to choose Arnolfini's wife, they might mention the lace bordering her veil, her necklace and other jewelry, the bands of gold around her wrists and waist, the folds of her dress, the fur around her mantle, etc. How do these details add to the overall effect of the picture?

(Standards: Language Arts: Writing 1.7, 23, 33-37; Art Connections 1.3)

Art/Drama Activity: Tiny Details

Materials

- Large pieces of paper
- Pencils
- Oil pastels

Ask the children to choose an area of the classroom such as a shelf, or a single object such as a chair or a book, and draw it large enough to fill their paper. They should include as many details as they can in imitation of the Flemish artists of Jan van Eyck's day. While oil paints are not a suitable medium for young children, they can color their pictures with oil pastels to create a brilliant effect if they wish.

(Standards: Visual Arts: 1-4.1-11)

Note: Curriculum connections and references are at the end of chapter 11.

10 Rembrandt and Vermeer in Holland

LESSON 1: Rembrandt (1606–1669)

With the threefold skills of draughtsman, etcher and painter, Rembrandt created three separate worlds, each self-contained and autonomous.

—F. SCHMIDT-DEGENER

Background Information

Rembrandt van Rijn, the ninth child of ten, was born into an era of prosperity and growth in Holland on July 15, 1606. Although the Netherlands was soon to wage a war with Spain for her independence—a war that would last for eighty years—the northern provinces, of which Holland was a part, formed an independent republic in 1609. The north differed from the Catholic south, too, in embracing the Reformation then spreading across Europe, but it was the doctrine of John Calvin rather than that of Martin Luther that held sway. Because Calvin forbade the use of images in church, the wealthy Dutch, who made their living predominantly from the sea around them, lavished their funds on artwork for their own pleasure: portraits of individuals as well as of members of the important guilds, landscapes that celebrated their beautiful countryside, and still lifes. Commissions abounded for artists of talent and industry, and Rembrandt was to profit enormously from this widespread largess.

Rembrandt's father was a miller, and because he had a good income, he was able to send his son to an excellent school. But when it became evident that Rembrandt's interest lay in art, he left school at the age of thirteen and worked as an apprentice to the artist Jacob van Swanenburgh. A few years later he moved to the bustling city of Amsterdam, where he continued his study of art under Pieter Lastman. It was from Lastman that Rembrandt developed a love of painting the Bible scenes that were to become the subjects of his numerous etchings later on.

When he was ready to strike out on his own, Rembrandt teamed up with another young artist, Jan Lievens. They worked so hard and so well that they soon built up a fine reputation. Rembrandt came to the notice of the prince of Orange, and his work for the court made him one of the best known artists in the country, enabling him to charge far more than his contemporaries for his paintings. He did portraits of many Amsterdam notables, and group portraits for important organizations such as the Surgeons' Guild and the Amsterdam Civic Guardsmen. By his twenty-fifth birthday, Rembrandt was famous and wealthy. He married Saskia, cousin of an art dealer with whom he worked, and they had four children. Unfortunately three of the children died before the age of two, and the fourth, Titus, died a year before his father at age twenty-six. Saskia herself died before she turned thirty. Rembrandt's second wife, Hendrickje, also died young.

Rembrandt's years of prosperity and success did not last. He spent his money foolishly, collected artworks and other extravagances, and purchased a large house beyond his means, and his debts soon outweighed his income. In addition, he refused to accommodate his art to popular taste and moved from the flamboyant baroque style favored by his contemporaries to a more somber, introspective vision. His works were dark (though recent cleaning reveals they were not so dark as formerly thought), filled with the unexpected, and required thoughtful study in the face of the current penchant for predictable, uncomplicated scenes. Rembrandt also persisted in etching biblical scenes when the Dutch of the Reformation were increasingly looking for secular art. This fall from favor, coupled with debt and the death of all those close to him, marked Rembrandt's later years with sorrow. (While he continued to receive some important commissions, his star never rose to the heights of his early career.) Yet Rembrandt never ceased working, and he left an incredible legacy: 600 paintings, over 1,400 surviving sketches (he probably did countless more), and 290 etchings. His mastery of chiaroscuro, "with a skill no other artist has ever surpassed" (Wallace 1974, 25), and his poignant portrayal of human character, place Rembrandt at the top of almost anyone's list of the world's greatest artists. He has been so admired and so copied that historians are constantly separating "real" Rembrandts from imitations, and works once thought to be his are still being discredited. (See *Rembrandt/Not Rembrandt* in the references.) But when authentic Rembrandt works are identified, they sell for incredible sums. In 1995, his *Abduction of Europa* sold for $35 million! Rembrandt needs no last name. His genius is simply enough.

(Standards: Art Connections: 1, 1-2, 4, 6-7)

The Story

One day over 300 years ago in Holland, a small crowd gathered outside the town hall, where a special notice had been posted. Everyone was trying to read what it said, and there was much pushing and shoving. Finally, one of the burghers, or citizens, spoke above the crowd.

"Quiet down. Quiet down. I'll read it to all of you." And clearing his throat, he began. "On Friday next, the possessions of one Rembrandt van Rijn will be sold at auction to the highest bidder. Among the items available are one book bound in black leather with the best sketches of Rembrandt; one *St. Jerome* by Rembrandt; one small painting of hares by the same; one small painting of a hog by the same . . ." (Wallace, p. 137). The voice droned on and on.

In all, seventy works of the painter known as Rembrandt would be auctioned off. His house—even some of his handkerchiefs—were on the list! The good citizens of Amsterdam were shocked. Rembrandt had not died. And even if he had, there was his son Titus to inherit his belongings. What had happened to the master painter?

The people were right to be asking such questions, for Rembrandt was one of the most famous painters in Holland. Rich Dutch businessmen paid him more money to paint pictures for them than they paid most other artists. He painted marvelous portraits of individual people and of members of important organizations. Some of his paintings were hung in places where they could be seen by almost everybody in the city. Why, he even painted pictures for the prince!

So what had happened? Well, Rembrandt spent his money even faster than he earned it, if you can believe that. He collected works of art from all over Europe, including some by important Italian Renaissance artists. He bought a house that was much too big and expensive. He bought fine clothes for himself and his wife. He ate fine food. Finally the day came when he owed people so much money that he had to sell things to pay them. Art collectors today, who would gladly pay millions of dollars for just one Rembrandt painting, are shocked at the small amount of money all of Rembrandt's paintings together raised—just 5,000 guilders or about $5,000—not even enough to pay all his debts!

Rembrandt rented a small apartment for himself, his wife, his son, Titus, and his daughter, Cornelia. Not only was he struggling with money problems, but his wife, and a few years later his son, both died. When he was a young man, Rembrandt's first wife and three other children had also died! In fact, his daughter Cornelia was the only one in his family to survive him. His life was certainly filled with sorrow, but he never quit working. He continued to do portraits and etchings of scenes from the Bible right up until his death.

And Rembrandt continued to paint in his own way, even though he could have earned more money if he had done what was popular at the time. The Dutch wanted pictures that were easy to understand. They wanted pictures of themselves, and scenes of their beautiful country. But Rembrandt used light and dark in his pictures the way the Italian painters of the Renaissance did. In fact, he did it even better! The Dutch were not used to such pictures. So Rembrandt never again enjoyed the wealth he had had as a young man. He would even do a portrait for free if he found someone with a face he really wanted to paint! When you look at a portrait by Rembrandt, you can see not only what the person really looked like but what the person *was* like inside.

Today, people say Rembrandt was one of the greatest artists who ever lived. And they say he was the greatest etcher in history. We are going to look at some of his paintings and etchings now. You can decide whether you agree.

(Standards: Language Arts: Listening and Speaking 8.4)

Viewing the Art

In showing Rembrandt's art, it is important to include some paintings, drawings, and etchings. Explain to the children how an etching is made. Geisert's *The Etcher's Studio* (see references) would be a perfect book to use to help the children understand the etching process.

1. Coat one side of a metal plate, usually copper or zinc, with a layer of acid-resistant wax.
2. Coat the other side of the plate with varnish to protect it from the acid.
3. Draw the picture by carving it into the wax with an etching needle or other sharp instrument, exposing the metal beneath the wax.
4. Place the plate with its completed drawing in nitric acid. The wax protects the copper plate from the acid, except for the lines that have previously been carved out.
5. Remove the plate from the acid and take off the remaining wax.
6. Put ink on the plate.
7. Wipe the plate. Ink will remain within the lines "bitten out" by the acid.
8. Place the inked plate in a heavy press and lay a sheet of damp paper over it. Move the plate steadily through the press. When it emerges on the other side, ease the paper off the plate. The drawing will have been transferred to the paper.

Many critics feel Rembrandt has no equal in the art of etching, so be certain to show the children several of his etched works. (See White's *Rembrandt as an Etcher* and Schwartz's *The Complete Etchings,* in the references.) Some you may want to consider are *Three Trees; Jan Six, Reading; Thomas Jacobsz. Haaring; The Descent of Christ from the Cross;* and *Christ Healing the Sick* (or the *Hundred Guilder Print*).

In discussing and viewing Rembrandt's oil paintings, mention his mastery of chiaroscuro (if you have studied Leonardo da Vinci in the chapter on Renaissance painters, you can mention once again his use of chiaroscuro) in such paintings as *The Night Watch*, a portrait of some Amsterdam civic guardsmen. (Its correct title is *The Company of Captain Frans Banning Cocq and Lieutenant Willem van*

Ruytenburch.) The children might be interested in the controversy surrounding this picture. When it was finished, those who had asked Rembrandt to do the painting were not pleased with it because he did not give all of them prominent places in the portrait and had put extra people in it. Some other oil paintings you may wish to view are *Rembrandt and Saskia* (his first wife), *Hendrickje Bathing* (his second wife), *The Anatomy Lesson of Dr. Sebastiaen Egbertsz, The Anatomy Lesson of Dr. Tulp* (see *What Great Paintings Say, Vol. 2),* and *Titus at His Desk.* Show some individual portraits of people outside Rembrandt's family as well. *Rembrandt's Women* (see references) has many large reproductions of his female subjects. (See also Bonafoux 1991.) The children may also find it interesting to view some of Rembrandt's self-portraits. He did more of these than perhaps any other artist. An interesting exercise is to show them in chronological order, for they are an incredible testament to the successes and trials of Rembrandt's life. The Web site *Rembrandt: Self-Portraits* (see references) is an excellent source for these prints.

Although Rembrandt produced a wealth of drawings during his lifetime, only twenty-five that bear his signature are known. View some drawings with the children. An excellent source is Bisanz-Prakken's *Rembrandt and His Time* (see references).

(Standards: Art Connections 1.1-8; Language Arts: Viewing 9.6, 23)

Journal Writing

Have the children choose one portrait and write about it. What kind of a person do they think the subject was? What makes them think so? Why do they think Rembrandt wanted to paint that particular portrait?

(Standards: Language Arts: Writing 1.7, 23, 33-37; Art Connections 1.3)

Art/Drama Activity: A Scratch-work "Etching"

While the children cannot make etchings (it would be wonderful if they could observe an artist working in that medium), doing a scratch-work project may at least give them an idea of what it is like to create a picture using a sharp instrument.

Materials

- Paper
- Black crayons
- Sharp instruments such as scissor points or compass points

1. Have the children cover their papers with a thick layer of black crayon to simulate the wax-covered copper plate.

2. Using the point of a scissor or other instrument, have them scratch lines through the crayon to create a picture. They may wish to create scenes reminiscent of Rembrandt's Holland: ships at sea or in the harbor, windmills, etc. They may even want to scratch in a person wearing the clothing in vogue in seventeenth-century Holland.

(Standards: Visual Arts: 1-4.1-11)

LESSON 2: Jan Vermeer (1632–1675)

With apparent effortlessness he snatched an instant of reality and lifted it out of a static realism to preserve it in a dynamic world of space, light and color.

—HANS KONINGSBERGER, *The World of Vermeer*

Background Information

Jan Vermeer was born in Delft, Holland, in October 1632, the same year Rembrandt's *Anatomy Lesson* became known in Amsterdam. His father was a weaver and later took to inn-keeping and dealing in art. However, he never made much money at either, and after his death in 1652 it took his family years to pay off his debts.

Not much is known about Jan's early art training, but he could have studied in Utrecht, where he may have learned of the work of Caravaggio, the Italian realist painter, and where he met his future wife, Catharina Bolnes, a woman from a well-off Catholic family. Jan converted to Catholicism to obtain permission to marry Catharina. By the time he turned twenty-one, Jan was a member of the Guild of St. Luke and a master painter, an indication that he had served an apprenticeship for several years. In addition, he probably learned much from the pictures his father handled as an art dealer, and from leading artists of the day.

While he began his career doing historical and biblical paintings using a rather dark palette, it is for his interior scenes of young women engaged in ordinary household tasks, his subjects flooded with light, usually from a nearby window, that Vermeer is well known. He and Catharina had fifteen children, eleven of whom survived. Even though Jan worked as an art dealer as well as a painter, the burden of providing for a large family; his country's war with France, which drained the coffers so that even the well-to-do had no money to buy paintings; and the constant haranguing of debtors took their toll. Jan Vermeer died in 1675 at the age of forty-three. His widow, left with large debts and eight children at home, was forced to sell his paintings and other family assets.

Jan Vermeer produced only about forty paintings in twenty-one years, and although he was never quite forgotten, he did not achieve fame until the nineteenth century. Today he is recognized as one of the truly great Dutch masters, and some scholars consider the pearl a perfect symbol for his work, not only because of the radiance of the young girls in his paintings or because so many of them wear pearl earrings or other pearl jewelry. "The paintings themselves suggest pearls. Each of them is a perfect world, closed within itself, secret, softly lit, full of luster" (Koningsberger 1983, 126).

(Standards: Art Connections: 1,1-2, 4, 6-7)

The Story

(Although the camera was not invented until the nineteenth century, artists as early as Leonardo da Vinci's time had been using its precursor, the camera obscura—a device that allowed light to pass through a tiny hole and project an inverted image on the walls of a darkened room. When the camera obscura became small enough to be easily portable, its use increased. By reproducing a scene exactly, the camera obscura saved the artist from the tedious calculations, first devised by Brunelleschi, necessary to obtain the correct perspective. The artist simply had to trace the outlines of the scene projected by the camera obscura. In addition, by reflecting the scene exactly, the camera obscura saved the artist from the tricks his eyes might play on him. The camera obscura also showed "the 'circles of confusion' that occur around points of intense illumination when not every ray in a beam of light is brought into the sharpest focus" (Pollack 1977, 13) Art historians generally agree that Jan Vermeer made wonderful use of the camera obscura, and this story describes the joy he might have had upon discovering it for the first time. A perfect book to use to learn more about the camera obscura is Philip Steadman's *Vermeer's Camera : Uncovering the Truth Behind the Masterpieces.* While the book is not accessible to children, it provides wonderful background information for adults. Students will enjoy the fine picture of the camera obscura on page 9—see references. More abbreviated information and some pictures can be found at http://brightbytes.com/cosite/what.html .)

Over 300 years ago, during the same time that Rembrandt lived and even in the same country, Holland, there lived in the city of Delft a painter named Jan Vermeer and his family. One afternoon, Jan came bursting through the front door.

"My dears, come and see what wonderful device I purchased when I went into town today!"

Jan's wife, Catharina, and his five daughters (in the years to come, he would actually have eleven children) gathered around him as he carefully placed a large object on the table.

"What is it, father?" asked Maria, the oldest.

"This," said her father, "is called a camera obscura." Maria wrinkled her nose at the strange-sounding words. But her excited father continued, "It is just what I need to help me paint wonderful pictures."

"How can a box help you paint? That's silly, father!" laughed Maria.

You must remember that this family lived in the days before the camera was invented, so they had never seen anything like what their father had brought home. And it wasn't a camera like the ones we have now.

"This is not just a box," Jan explained. "It is a special instrument that can actually show me things as they really are, not just as I think they look. Most important of all, it can show me how light hits objects and seems even to dance or bounce off them. Light. It is so wonderful and so mysterious." Jan became very quiet, and his wife and children somehow knew to keep silent, too, for they were used to seeing him sit for hours thinking while he watched daylight stream through the windows of their house.

Finally, Jan remembered that his family was still waiting. "Elisabeth, bring me that candle and I will show you how it works."

Elisabeth gave the candle to her father, who placed it in front of the box. Right before their very eyes, the image of the candle appeared on the glass screen on top of the box.

They all began to talk at once. "Oh, it's magic, father!" "Let me try it." "Can we play with it?"

"No, it is not magic, children," replied Jan. "It is a scientific instrument that shows us how our eyes work. It makes pictures the way our eyes do. And it is not a toy, so you may not play with it. I must use it to help me understand more about light. Run along now so that I can begin my observations."

Day after day Jan studied light. He arranged a few objects in many different ways in the two rooms he used for his painting. "Will the room look bigger if I move the table back here?" he wondered. "What if I drape the cloth this way? Will the light reflect off the folds of material? "Maria," he called, "put on these pearl earrings and come stand by this window. Ah, yes. Now turn your head a little this way. Open your mouth ever so slightly. Perfect!" Jan began to paint his daughter's picture.

Day after day he arranged and thought and painted. You would think that in the twenty-one years he was an artist, Jan Vermeer would have painted hundreds of pictures, for he was a very hard worker. But he only painted about two pictures a year, because each one had to be perfect. His camera obscura showed him how light sparkled in tiny specks. When he painted, Jan tried to get those sparkles just right. He layered his paints so that sometimes there were strokes that were barely the thickness of a single hair!

Some experts say no one has ever mastered light as well as Jan Vermeer did. We are going to look at some of his paintings now. Try to find the shimmering light in them. Notice how he arranged people and objects in his pictures. Then decide whether you agree with what people say about his work.

(Standards: Language Arts: Listening and Speaking 8.4)

Viewing the Art

Since there are so few of Vermeer's works in existence today, try to show as many of them as you can, especially his two outdoor scenes, the magnificent *View of Delft* (see Adda 2005) and *The Little Street*, and his renderings of women engaged in ordinary household tasks. When viewing Vermeer's interior scenes, show several to the children without saying anything. After a while, ask them what they have noticed. Among the things they should say are that all the scenes have women in them, either alone or with others; there is usually a window or source of light; the women are doing ordinary domestic chores; many of the women are wearing and/or holding pearls; the same tile floor, drapery, wall paintings, and globe appear in many pictures; Vermeer uses blue and yellow often. It would be helpful to use books that provide details of the larger reproductions. (There are several excellent titles in the references.) Then you and the children can concentrate on the play of light in the pictures. Find the sparkles of light in such pictures as *Maidservant Pouring Milk, Officer and Laughing Girl*, and *Girl with a Red Hat*. (See *Vermeer and the Delft School* in the references.) These sparkles are achieved with dabs or points of paint and were Vermeer's attempt to paint the sparkles of light he saw in his camera obscura. Point out that although war was raging around him as France invaded Holland, Vermeer never made this violence the subject of his paintings. Nor did he ever paint young children, although he had eleven of his own.

(Standards: Art Connections 1.1-8; Language Arts: Viewing 9.6, 23)

Journal Writing

Which picture is the children's favorite? Invite the children to write as much as they can about that picture—what do they think is happening, what did they notice, how does the painting make them feel, etc.? Does the picture tell them anything about the kind of man Jan Vermeer might have been? Explain.

(Standards: Language Arts: Writing 1.7, 23, 33-37; Art Connections 1.3)

Art/Drama Activities: Pose a Vermeer and Make a Camera Obscura

Materials

- Props to help the children pose pictures Jan Vermeer might have painted. Some suggestions are
  - Material for draping
  - Bowls, pitchers, fruit
  - Table
  - Musical instruments
  - Paper and writing instruments (no pencils or ballpoints!)
  - Pearl jewelry

Divide the children into groups (as many groups as you have materials to support the activity) and invite them to set up a picture for Vermeer to paint. Can they pose by a classroom window to have a source of light? How many people will be in the picture? What will they be doing? How will the scene look? Give each group time to work with the materials, and then to pose their "picture" for each other.

(Standards: Thinking and Reasoning: 6.4, 12, 14; Working with Others: 1-5.1-10)

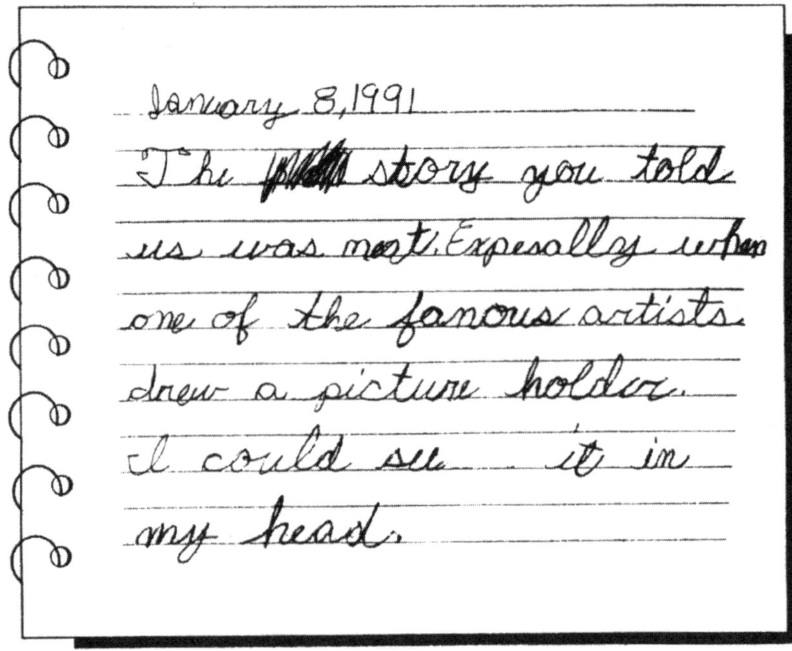
January 8, 1991

The story you told
us was neat. Expesally when
one of the fanous artists
drew a picture holder.
I could see it in
my head.

You could also make a camera obscura and demonstrate how it works.

Materials

- A convex lens
- Scissors
- A mirror
- Tape
- A flashlight
- A cardboard box, the top of which is translucent (use a piece of clear plastic or glass) (An inexpensive lens may be obtained from: Edmund Scientifics, 60 Pearce Ave., Tonawanda, NY 14150, 1-800-728-6999, http://scientificsonline.com/default.asp or Edmund Optics, 101 East Gloucester Pike, Barrington, NJ 08007-1380, Phone: (800) 363-1992, Fax: (856) 573-6295, http://www.edmundoptics.com/us/AboutUs/).

1. Cut a hole in the center of one side of the box just large enough for the lens to fit in snugly.
2. Place the mirror inside the box on a slant.
3. Tape the glass or plastic onto the top of the box.
4. Place an object in front of the lens a short distance from the box.
5. Darken the room and shine only the flashlight near the lens.
6. The object should appear right side up on the glass or plastic.

In addition to Steadman's book, you might also want to look at a lengthy article in *The New York Times,* January 14, 1996, p. E3, for more information about the camera obscura.

(Standards: Visual Arts: 2.2, 5-6, 11; Science: 12.43)

Note: Curriculum connections and references are at the end of chapter 11.

11 Velázquez and Goya in Spain

LESSON 1: Diego Velázquez (1599–1660)

I would rather be the first painter of common things than second in higher art.

—DIEGO VELÁZQUEZ

Background Information

In the fifteenth century, Spain was a dominant power in Europe. It had sent its explorers out to the New World to claim territories rich in gold and other resources. Its armada boasted over a hundred galleons and seemed invincible. Its coffers were filled. But in 1588 the English admiral Francis Drake defeated the Spanish armada, and Spain began a period of devastating decline. The Thirty Years' War fought in alliance with Austria, a war with France, and the eighty years' war to stamp out Protestantism in the Netherlands weakened the country still further.

It was into this dismal scene that Diego de Silva Velázquez was born in Seville in 1599, the oldest of seven children. His parents were of low nobility but had sufficient funds to provide him with a good education. His early desire to become a painter was fulfilled with an apprenticeship to Francisco Pacheco, one of Seville's most prominent artists. He married Pacheco's daughter, Juana, in 1618 and they had two daughters, only one of whom survived to adulthood.

Velázquez was so talented that his work soon outshone the lifeless canvases of his master. Although he distinguished himself early on with his religious paintings and pictures of ordinary people eating and making merry, it is for his work in the Spanish court of Philip IV that Velázquez is most famous. When Velázquez was only twenty-four, the king's advisor, Count Olivares, invited him to court, where he quickly became the young king's chief painter. Over the years, and throughout the mounting vicissitudes of the king's forty-three-year reign, the painter became his friend and confidant as well, until eventually Philip refused to allow any other artist to paint portraits of him or the members of his household.

During his years at court, Velázquez made two trips to Italy, stopping in Venice to study the work of Titian and other Venetian painters, and in Rome, where he was welcomed into the pope's own apartments and allowed to copy the works of Michelangelo and Raphael. While he was there, he painted one of his most famous portraits, that of Pope Innocent X. From his studies in Italy, he perfected his mastery over space and three-dimensionality.

Velázquez served Philip until his own death in 1660, receiving ever-higher ranks and promotions, culminating in his knighthood in the Order of Santiago in 1659. He was the only major artist of his time who painted primarily secular subjects in the face of a highly charged religious atmosphere (Brown 1988, 92). His works are a chronicle of the Spanish working man, and of court life and fashion in the seventeenth century. Famous and respected in his own lifetime, Diego Velázquez today is considered one of Spain's greatest painters.

(Standards: Art Connections: 1,1-2, 4, 6-7)

The Story

Diego Velázquez, the artist, worked for King Philip of Spain. He lived in a beautiful house with his wife and little daughter. He had fancy clothes and fine food, and the king usually paid him well, though not always on time. All day long he worked on pictures of the king and the king's family. And he did other jobs, such as making sure rooms were ready for the king when he needed them.

It sounds like a great life, doesn't it? It was, most of the time, but Diego was restless. He wanted to see the work of other painters and learn new things. So he asked the king for permission to go to Italy and study the great Italian master painters. The king didn't want to let Diego go, but he wanted his favorite artist to be happy, so he finally agreed.

Diego had a wonderful time in Italy. He went to the museums and copied famous paintings. He visited Venice and Rome. And because he was such a famous painter, the Italians treated him well. But one day he received an urgent message from King Philip's special counselor. The poor messenger who delivered it was exhausted from hours and hours of riding. "Come back to Madrid as soon as possible," the message read. "I am building a new palace for the king, and you must fill the huge Hall of Realms with pictures of the royal family and battle scenes that show Spain's victories over her enemies. King Philip is feeling sad about all the things that have been going wrong in the kingdom lately, and this new palace will cheer him up. Hurry! There is much work to be done!"

He packed his things and set off the next morning. When he saw the size of the room he was to decorate, he just shook his head back and forth. It was enormous! How would he ever finish in time for the grand opening of the palace? Quickly he called his assistants together. "The king wants pictures of twelve battle scenes," he said. "That is far too many for me to be able to finish in time. I will draw up a list of the scenes I would like done, and you will do eleven of them. The twelfth I will do myself. In addition, we will need portraits of the royal family."

Diego's assistants scurried to obey, while the painter sat and thought about what scene he would do. Recently he had heard an interesting story. Spain had been fighting with the Netherlands for many years. Finally, to put an end to the war, which was costing lives and a great deal of money, King Philip sent one of his best generals, Ambrosio Spinola, to fight the Dutch general, Justin. Spinola and his men cut off the Dutch army's food supply. But Justin and his soldiers didn't give up for almost a year. You can imagine how the Spanish felt when the Dutch finally surrendered! "Spinola will show them," said the soldiers. "He'll think of some cruel punishments." But Spinola did not. He admired the bravery of the Dutch commander and his men and asked only that they surrender. He didn't even want them to feel embarrassed.

He was very impressed by the way Spinola acted and decided to paint this story. In the picture, Justin is handing the key to the city of Breda to the victorious Spanish general. But instead of showing Spinola looking proud and haughty, Diego painted him putting his hand on Justin's shoulder. It seems as if he's saying, "You put up a good fight. You should be proud of yourself. My men and I will not make you suffer any longer."

Diego was worried that perhaps the king and the Spanish people would think the painting made Spain look weak. But he was wrong. The king and everybody who saw it loved the painting because it showed how dignified and noble a Spanish general could be. In fact, the king liked this work so much he gave Diego a promotion. Diego also worked on some wonderful pictures of the king and his family for the Hall of Realms. In all of them he gave the country and the world an honest picture of the rulers of Spain. The king made Diego a knight, and the Spanish people consider him to be one of their greatest painters.

We are going to look at some of Velasquez's paintings now. As you look at them, see if you can figure out some of the things the artist was trying to tell us about the people whose pictures he painted.

(Standards: Language Arts: Listening and Speaking 8.4)

Viewing the Art

Show the children some portraits of the royal family, making sure to include several of King Philip. (There are several excellent examples in Brown's *Velázquez: Painter and Courtier* in references.) What changes in the king do the children notice as he ages and as the fortunes of the country continue to deteriorate? Show the equestrian portraits of the king, Queen Isabel, and young Prince Balthasar Carlos. Notice the brushwork evident in the horses' manes, the detail in the queen's dress. Study the outlandish dress and wig in the portrait of King Philip's second wife, Queen Mariana, and the dresses on the Infanta Margarita and Prince Felipe Prospero. Spend considerable time on Velázquez 's most famous royal portrait, *Las Meninas* (*The Maids of Honor*). (See *What Great Paintings Say,* Vol. 2, in the references). You may wish to read *The Princess and the Painter* (see references) as you show this marvelous painting. This picture book gives children an idea of what the Infanta Margarita's day might have been like and her possible friendship with Velazquez. In *Las Meninas*, the young princess has just announced that she does not wish to pose. Point out that Velázquez has put himself in the painting on the left. Show the children the portrait of the king and queen in the mirror. Where does this reflection come from? Choose, if you can, a book that includes details of this picture. (See Brown 1988 in the references.) The royal family loved to surround themselves with dwarfs. One is evident in *Las Meninas*. Show Velázquez's portraits of other dwarfs. Is he making fun of them or treating them sympathetically? Finally, show some paintings Velazquez did of people outside the palace, especially the subject of the story above, the *Surrender of Breda*. What do the children think the Spanish soldiers on the right and the Dutch soldiers on the left are saying among themselves? What are the two generals saying? Show the portrait of Juan de Pareja. (Older students may enjoy reading or hearing the novel, *I, Juan Pareja,* in the references. It is based on this real-life servant of the painter.) In the portrait of *Pope Innocent X,* look at the pope's eyes. What kind of a man was he?

(Standards: Art Connections 1.1-8; Language Arts: Viewing 9.6, 23)

Journal Writing

King Philip was not a very handsome man, yet Velázquez always showed him looking kingly and dignified. What are some things the children noticed in the portraits that give them the impression Velázquez wanted people to be proud of their king when they saw his portrait? Are there portraits of other people the children would like to write about?

(Standards: Language Arts: Writing 1.7, 23, 33-37; Art Connections 1.3)

Art/Drama Activity: Costume Design

Materials

- Paper
- Crayons
- Costume books

The costumes of the Spanish court in the seventeenth century were incredibly elaborate and impractical by today's standards. Have the children pretend they are royal tailors commissioned to create clothing for the rulers to wear to the grand opening of their royal palace. First, the tailors must put their designs on paper and present them to the king's counselor for approval. Using Velázquez's portraits and/or costume books as models, ask the children to design clothes for a member of the royal family: the king, queen, prince, or princess. Some may wish simply to design a wig for the queen. When the children have finished their designs, one of them might assume the role of the counselor surveying the results.

(Standards: Visual Arts: 1.1-3, 8-9)

LESSON 2: Francisco Goya (1746–1828)

I am still learning.

—FRANCISCO GOYA, captioned sketch

Background Information

Spain's lengthy wars for European dominance squandered the riches brought in from her North and South American colonies and left her monarchs with little energy to manage affairs at home. The country had no basic services such as education, waste removal, road systems, or effective police. The Catholic Church was a major force in Spanish society, but it used its power more heavily on the side of evil than good, stamping out any who disagreed with its tenets through the Inquisition and bleeding the poor dry. Industry hearkened back to feudal days, and farming methods were so bad that the soil barely yielded a living. Francisco Goya was born in a poor farming village, Fuendetodos, in the province of Aragon on March 30, 1746. The family had gone to the village because his mother had inherited her family's land, but conditions were so severe that they could not eke out a living, and they moved to Saragossa around 1760. There Goya's father took up his trade as a master gilder.

Not much is known about Goya's early years. He studied drawing with a third-rate painter named Luzan for a time, and after a brief stay in Madrid he returned to Saragossa to establish his reputation before beginning his painting career in earnest. He married Josefa Bayeu and the couple had numerous children, only one of whom survived to manhood. While Goya was drawn to the ornate and energetic Baroque style of painting, his desire for success and acceptance forced him at first to conform to the styles of Giambattista Tiepolo and Anton Mengs, then popular painters in Madrid. Later Goya developed his own style, based in part on the principles of the Enlightenment, which emphasized truth in nature. Many of Goya's patrons were leading proponents of Enlightenment philosophy.

Goya began his career in Madrid painting cartoons the weavers used as designs for their work in the royal tapestry manufactory. Over his lifetime he did sixty-three of these paintings, which celebrate the Spanish people engaged in pastimes and festivities. He also painted many portraits of wealthy patrons and was so successful that he finally attained the position for which he longed: first painter to the king. Unlike the king he admired, Charles III, who had ushered in a period of peace after many devastating wars and was intelligent and likable, his successor, Charles IV, was dull-witted and incompetent. Goya did not hide his disdain for this royal family in any of his portraits of them, but they kept him in their employ.

Charles IV's ineptitude, coupled with the ferment generated by the revolution in France, left Spain vulnerable. When Napoleon invaded the country, he met with little resistance from the royal family, who were too busy quarreling over power to realize what was happening. Napoleon seized the throne, but the Spanish people resisted and plunged into a six-year war. The horrors of this war were to transform Goya from portrait artist to the rich to chronicler of disaster.

When the war ended, Charles IV's evil and incompetent son, Ferdinand, took the throne. Conditions did not improve in Spain, and a disillusioned Goya moved from Madrid to a house in the country, where he painted his famous "black paintings" on the walls. In 1824 he left Spain for France and died there in 1829, an old man of eighty-two who had remained an active painter until his brief final illness. Painter of frescoes on church walls, portrait painter of royalty and the rich, etcher of society's foibles, lithographer—in his long lifetime, Goya never ceased to experiment both with media and styles, and to express his inner vision and even his torment in his work. His astonishing accomplishments have rightfully earned him the reputation of being one of Spain's greatest artists, and his daring and innovative brush work have gained for him the title of Father of Modern Art.

(Standards: Art Connections: 1,1-2, 4, 6-7)

The Story

Francisco was in a good mood. He had just finished painting the portrait of his friend Sebastian Martinez, and Sebastian had liked his work. Now he was on his way back to the city of Madrid, where he was First Painter to the king. An artist couldn't get a higher position than that, and Francisco Goya was proud.

Just as he sat back in the carriage pulled by two big black horses, the artist began to get dizzy. "I guess I've been working too hard," he thought. He wanted to get out his handkerchief to wipe his sweating forehead, but he couldn't move his hand! He began to pound on the floor of the carriage with his right foot, the only foot he could move.

The coachman stopped the horses. "What is the matter, sir," he asked, looking into the carriage.

What he saw really frightened him. Francisco sat slumped over, unable to speak. The driver quickly covered him with a blanket, got back up on his seat, and turned the horses around.

"Faster, faster!" he called to them, cracking his whip as he raced back to Señor Martinez's house.

Of course Sebastian was surprised when he heard his friend's coach return, and he ran outside, only to see the coachman trying to lift Francisco out of the carriage. The two men carried him up to bed. For weeks he lay there, visited by the doctor every day.

"Will he recover, doctor?" asked the worried Sebastian.

"Only time will tell," replied the doctor, shaking his head. "This is a very strange illness, and I don't know its cause."

Weeks went by, then months, and slowly Francisco began to gain strength. Some days he would be able to move his hands. But on other days he could hardly move his head. And every day he heard nothing but loud buzzing in his ears. Sebastian came to talk to him. Other friends came. But he could hear none of them. He had become completely deaf! Francisco lay in his bed and thought about his career. He remembered the days when he painted pictures for the weavers to copy when they made rugs for the royal tapestry factory. He thought about the beautiful paintings he had made on the walls and ceilings of churches. He thought about the wealthy families who asked him to paint portraits for them. But most of all, he thought of his work for the king of Spain. He was the king's First Painter, his most important painter. Would he ever be able to paint again? Would he lose his job? How would he support his wife and son?

Francisco did get better. That is, he could move and talk again. But he could never hear from that time on. His deafness didn't stop him from painting, though. He didn't even lose his job as the king's First Painter. But after his deafness, the way he painted did change. His paintings began to show more and more of the foolishness and the suffering of the people of Spain, his beloved country. When war broke out between Spain and France, Francisco did not paint pictures of soldiers and generals as heroes. Instead he showed the horror of war, and how war makes people suffer.

When he was an old man, he became tired of life in Madrid and moved to the country. There he painted pictures on the walls of his house. People call them his "black paintings," because they are filled with strange creatures and nightmarish scenes, grotesque and frightening. It is as if Goya finally believed the world was full of terror.

Francisco Goya lived a long life, even though he suffered some serious illnesses. In all that time, he produced many different kinds of art and became one of the most famous artists Spain has ever had. We are going to view some of his artwork now.

(Standards: Language Arts: Listening and Speaking 8.4)

Viewing the Art

Goya was a prodigious artist who worked in several different forms, and it would be wonderful to give the children a sampling of this variety. You may wish to avoid some of his more graphic works, depending on the age of your students. You should surely include some of his portraits. (Both *I, Goya* and *Francisco de Goya y Lucientes: Goya* have excellent large reproductions—see references.) If you have studied Velázquez, compare his portraits of the royal family to Goya's, especially Goya's *Family of Charles IV*, a work that is almost scurrilous. (See *What Great Paintings Say,* Vol. 2, in the references. A double-page spread of this painting appears in Licht 2001, 96–97.) The queen who dominates this picture dominated the king in actual life as well. She is shown as an angry woman. (Notice that she even seems to scowl or sneer.) King Charles appears fat and dull-looking, hardly a figure of royal competence. The royal children actually appear scared. Ferdinand, the one in blue on the left, will become the future king. Notice that like Velázquez, Goya has placed himself in the back on the left in this royal portrait. View Goya's portrait of his wife, Josefa, and his son, Xavier—the only one of his many children to survive. Goya loved children and painted many portraits of them, both alone and with their families. Show some of these, especially the portrait of young Don Manuel Osorio Manrique de Zuniga. The children may also enjoy some of his self-portraits.

Goya's cartoons for the tapestry works show the Spanish people in celebration and diversionary games. Enjoy a sampling of these. (See Wilson-Bareau and Mena Marqués 1994.) Show some of Goya's etchings, *Los Caprichos* or *The Caprices*, in which he satirizes social foibles such as the idleness of the rich. *The Sleep of Reason* is actually a self-portrait. If you have studied Rembrandt, compare his etchings with Goya's. Finally, view whatever war paintings, such as *The Third of May, 1808,* and black paintings you are comfortable with. (See Guillaud and Guillaud 1988 for magnificent reproductions of the black paintings.) What is Goya saying in these works? Is he glorifying war?

(Standards: Art Connections 1.1-8; Language Arts: Viewing 9.6, 23)

Journal Writing

What do the children think of Goya's work? What do they like or dislike about it, and why? Of the different subjects and styles—portraits, etchings, etc.—which do the children like best, and why? They may wish to concentrate on a single work, especially one that is enigmatic, and discuss their own interpretation of it. Perhaps in this instance you might want to write a group journal on that work of art.

(Standards: Language Arts: Writing 1.7, 23, 33-37; Art Connections 1.3)

Drama/Art Activity: Playing Goya

Goya's colorful life affords many opportunities for dramatization. Divide the class into groups. Either give each group a scene to dramatize or have them decide on one themselves. Some possibilities are

- Goya posing the king and his family for portraits
- Goya becoming ill and going deaf
- Goya painting scenes on the walls of his house

Curriculum Connections

Social Studies

- Study the history and customs of the people living at the time of any of the artists in this section. (See Heinrichs 2003 and Hintz 2004.)
- Locate the different artists' countries of origin on a map.
- Study the clothing of the different times and places and draw some of it for a fashion bulletin board. (See *Clothing through the Ages* in the references for examples.)
- Study the shipping and trading industries in the Netherlands. With what countries did they trade? What goods were bought and sold?
- Several wars were fought during the lifetimes of the artists discussed. Investigate those that interest the children.
- Find out what is meant by the Enlightenment.

(Standards: Geography: 1-2.30; World History: 28-29.30, 55; Grades K-4 History: 1, 7.10, 49)

Science

- One of Rembrandt's paintings shows the medical profession at work. Compare medicine in his time with ours, with medical practices 100 years before him in van Eyck's time, more than 100 years later in Goya's time. Read about the work of William Harvey, who in 1627 explained how blood circulates in the body. (See Yount 1994.)
- Read about the development of the microscope, which was first used in Holland. Relate this to the lens in the camera obscura of Vermeer. How does a lens work? (See *World of the Microscope* in the references.)
- Research Goya's illness. What was it? Is there a cure for it today?
- All objects absorb light, some more than others. Experiment with objects of various kinds: frosted glass, cellophane, clear glass, a piece of paper, etc. Shine

the beam of light from a flashlight on each of the objects. Which absorb so much light that no light gets through? Which allow some light to shine through? Which allow the most light to shine through? Why did Vermeer position the people in his paintings so that light from a window shone on them? (See the Discovery Box listed in the references.)

(Standards: Grades K-4 History: 8.45; Science 11-13.29, 42-45)

Music

- Listen to some baroque music, a style prevalent during this time. Find some artworks that seem to fit this ornate musical style. Go to the Web site listed in the references for information on baroque music, baroque composers, and the opportunity to listen to some music.
- Talk about Beethoven, a German composer who was a contemporary of Goya and also suffered from deafness. Find a Beethoven piece that seems to fit one of Goya's more somber paintings.
- Play some of Mozart's music. How is it like Beethoven's? How is it different?

(Standards: Arts and Communication: 4-5.29; Music 6;7, 9)

Literature

- Read biographies of people who made an impact during the time these artists lived. Some you might want to consider are Descartes, Voltaire, and Louis XIV. (See *The Palace of Versailles: France's Royal Jewel* in the references.)
- Van Eyck's *Wedding Portrait* contains symbols of marriage and domestic life. What is a symbol? Give some present-day examples of "things that stand for other things." Did any of the other painters use symbols in their work?

(Standards: Language Arts: Reading: 5-7.4-5, 23)

References (for chapters 9 through 11)

Adult Books

Ackley, Clifford S., et al. *Rembrandt's Journey: Painter Draftsman Etcher*. Boston: MFA, 2003. ISBN 0878466770.

While Rembrandt's paintings and drawings are included here, this book is especially valuable for the large sampling of his etchings.

Adda, Roberta. *Vermeer*. New York: Rizzoli, 2005. ISBN 0-8478-2680-5.

This small book has an excellent reproduction of Vermeer's *View of Delft* and also his pictures of women.

Ainsworth, Maryan W., and Keith Christiansen, eds. *From Van Eyck to Bruegel: Early Netherlandish Painting in the Metropolitan Museum of Art.* New York: Metropolitan Museum of Art/Harry N. Abrams, 1998. ISBN 0-87099-870-6.

This book is an overview of early painting in the Netherlands featuring works owned by the Metropolitan Museum of Art.

Bisanz-Prakken, Marian. *Rembrandt and His Time: Masterworks from the Albertina, Vienna.* New York: Hudson Hills Press/Milwaukee Art Museum, 2005. ISBN 1555952577.

This book contains the greatest drawings and prints ever produced by Netherlandish artists. An entire section is devoted to Rembrandt and is an excellent source of his drawings for viewing.

Bonafoux, Pascal. *Rembrandt: Master of the Portrait.* Translated by Alexandra Campbell. New York: Harry N. Abrams, 1992. ISBN 0-8109-2813-2.

The author discusses Rembrandt's portraits and provides large reproductions.

Borchert, Till-Holger, et al. *The Age of Van Eyck: The Mediterranean World and Early Netherlandish Painting.* New York: Thames & Hudson, 2002. ISBN 0-500-23795-6.

This book provides a large selection of works by Van Eyck and his followers, with 370 illustrations in color.

Brown, Christopher, Jan Kelch, and Pieter van Thiel. *Rembrandt: The Master & His Workshop.* New Haven, CT: Yale University Press, 1991. ISBN 0300051514.

The authors separate genuine Rembrandts from copies of his style. Many reproductions suitable for group viewing.

Brown, Jonathan. *Velázquez: Painter and Courtier.* New Haven, CT: Yale University Press, 1988. ISBN 0300038941.

Brown brings some interesting new ideas to the study of the artist.

Brown, Jonathan, and Carmen Garrido. *Velázquez: The Technique of Genius.* New Haven, CT: Yale University Press, 2003. ISBN 0300101244.

The authors examine thirty of the artist's works and show how his technique developed.

Brown, Jonathan, and Susan Grace Galassi. *Goya's Last Works.* New York: Frick Collection; New Haven, CT: Yale University Press, 2006. ISBN 0300117671.

Fifty-one works, including miniatures on ivory, done during the last four years of Goya's life, are included in this book.

Brusati, Celeste. *Johannes Vermeer.* New York: Rizzoli, 1993. ISBN 0847816494.

This is a brief discussion of Vermeer's life and work, followed by large reproductions of fifteen of his works.

De Vos, Dirk. *The Flemish Primitives: The Masterpieces.* Princeton, NJ: Princeton University Press, 1997. ISBN 0-691-11661-X.

Van Eyck is included in this beautiful book, with reproductions that show the exquisite details of Flemish painting.

Giorgi, Rosa. *Velázquez: The Genius of the Spanish School—His Life in Paintings.* Edited by Fergus Day and Louise Candlish. Translated by John Gilbert. New York: DK Publishing, 1999. ISBN 0-7513-0781-5.

Although this is a small book and not suitable for large group viewing, it offers many detailed plates of the artist's paintings and would be good to use with individual children or small groups.

Goya, Dagmar Fegheim, et al. *I, Goya.* New York: Prestel, 2004. ISBN 3-7913-3071-3.

If you cannot obtain any other book for viewing, this one will more than suffice. The reproductions are large and beautiful. Especially wonderful are the quotes from Goya himself that fill the book.

Gudiol, José. *Francisco de Goya y Lucientes: Goya.* New York: Harry N. Abrams, 1985. ISBN 0810909928.

This book has large reproductions for group viewing.

Guillaud, Jacqueline, and Maurice Guillaud. *Goya: The Phantasmal Vision.* Paris-New York: Crown, 1988. ISBN 0517568861.

This book focuses on the "black paintings" Goya did on the walls of his home. Double-spread reproductions make this a treasure.

Hagen, Rose-Marie, and Rainer Hagen. *What Great Paintings Say.* Vol. 2. Amsterdam: Taschen, 2002. ISBN 3822813729.

The works of several artists in chapters 9 through 11 are discussed in detail in this book.

Harbison, Craig. *Jan van Eyck: The Play of Realism.* London: Reaktion Books, 1995. ISBN 0948462795.

The author discusses such masterpieces as the Arnolfini portrait.

Klepper, Erhard. *Costume through the Ages.* Mineola, NY: Dover, 1999. ISBN 0486407225.

This book with over 1,400 illustrations will help children learn what people wore in other centuries.

Koningsberger, Hans. *The World of Vermeer.* Rev. ed. 1967. Reprint, New York: Time-Life Books, 1983. o.p. ISBN 0809402084.

Vermeer's life and work are seen in the context of his milieu.

Licht, Fred. *Goya.* New York: Abbeville Press, 2001. ISBN 0-7892-0727-3.

Perfect for group viewing, this book has large color reproductions and a wide sampling of the artist's work.

Liedtke, Walter, et al. *Vermeer and the Delft School.* New York: Metropolitan Museum of Art, 2001. ISBN 0-87099-9737-7.

There are wonderful large reproductions of Vermeer's paintings of women in this beautiful book.

Munz, Ludwig, and Bob Haak. *Rembrandt.* New York: Harry N. Abrams, 1984.

Examines Rembrandt's life and work. Some large reproductions.

Philip, Lotte Brand. *The Ghent Altarpiece and the Art of Jan van Eyck*. Princeton, NJ: Princeton University Press, 1971 o.p. ASIN B0006Y7TDG.

This lengthy discussion of the Ghent altarpiece includes a bibliography and black-and-white reproductions.

Pollack, Peter. *The Picture History of Photography from the Earliest Beginnings to the Present Day*. New York: Harry N. Abrams, 1977. ISBN 0810920565.

The author provides some information on the camera obscura.

Ragusa, Elena. *Velázquez*. New York: Rizzoli, 2006. ISBN 0847828123.

Part of a series of books that introduce famous painters, this volume, while slim, provides information on the artist's most important paintings. The beautiful illustrations are suitable for group viewing.

Schwartz, Gary. *The Rembrandt Book*. New York: Harry N. Abrams, 2006. ISBN 0810943174.

The author, a leading Rembrandt scholar, examines the artist's life and work. There are 700 full-color illustrations.

Schwartz, Gary, ed. *The Complete Etchings of Rembrandt*. Mineola, NY: Dover, 1994. ISBN 0486281817.

Rembrandt's etchings are reproduced in original size. A key volume for this artist given the suggested art activity.

Serullaz, Maurice. *Velázquez*. New York: Harry N. Abrams, 1987. ISBN 0-8109-1729-7.

This volume on the painter's life and work has beautiful, large, color reproductions.

Sonnenburg, Hubert von. *Rembrandt/Not Rembrandt in the Metropolitan Museum of Art*. New York: Metropolitan Museum of Art/Harry Abrams, 1995. ISBN 0-87099-754-8.

The author discusses, with examples, the difficulties involved in identifying true Rembrandts.

Steadman, Philip. *Vermeer's Camera: Uncovering the Truth Behind the Masterpieces*. New York: Oxford University Press, 2002. ISBN 0192803026.

The author describes how a camera obscura works and how Vermeer used it. He has even created miniatures of the rooms in which Vermeer painted .

Sutton, Peter C., et al. *Love Letters: Dutch Genre Paintings in the Age of Vermeer*. Greenwich, CT: Bruce Museum, 2003. ISBN 0-9720736-6-3.

Vermeer's paintings of women writing are included in this beautiful book.

Sweet, Christopher. *The Essential Johannes Vermeer*. New York: Harry N. Abrams, 1999. ISBN 0810958015.

The author does a fine job of discussing Vermeer's works and what makes them unique.

Tomlinson, Janis. *Francisco Goya y Lucientes*. 1994. Reprint, London: Phaidon Press, 1999. ISBN 0714838446.

Goya's life and works are presented with absolutely beautiful reproductions for group viewing.

Van de Perre, Harold. *Jan Van Eyck.* France: Gallimard, 1997. ISBN 2070150410.

This book has large pictures for group viewing.

Wallace, Robert. *The World of Rembrandt, 1606–1669.* New York: Time-Life, 1973. ASIN B0007I0VAY.

The author provides a clear study of the artist's work accompanied by fine reproductions.

Westermann, Mariët. *Rembrandt.* London: Phaidon, 2000. ISBN 0-7148-3857-8.

This is a small book, and while not suitable for large group viewing, it would be fine for small groups or individual children. There are many portraits to view.

Wheelock, Arthur, Jr. *Vermeer: The Complete Works.* New York: Harry N. Abrams, 1997. ISBN 0-8109-2751-9.

This beautiful book contains all the paintings known to be by Vermeer.

Wheelock, Arthur K., Jr., et al. *Johannes Vermeer.* Washington, DC: National Gallery of Art, 1995. ISBN 0300065582.

This marvelous book discusses Vermeer's life and work. Color reproductions.

White, Christopher. *Rembrandt as an Etcher: A Study of the Artist at Work.* 2d ed. New Haven, CT: Yale University Press, 1999. ISBN 0300079532.

White describes Rembrandt's techniques in the creation of his marvelous etchings. This is THE book to use when viewing the artist's etchings.

Williams, Julia Lloyd. *Rembrandt's Women.* New York: Prestel, 2001. ISBN 3-7913-2498-5.

There are many large reproductions of portraits of Rembrandt's female subjects.

Wilson-Bareau, Juliet, and Manuela B. Mena Marqués. *Goya Truth and Fantasy: The Small Paintings.* New Haven, CT: Yale University Press, 1994. ISBN 0-300-05863-2.

This is a good source of examples of Goya's cartoons.

Children's Books

Balliett, Blue. *Chasing Vermeer.* Illustrated by Brett Helquist. New York: Scholastic, 2004. ISBN 0439372941.

Two youngsters try to discover what happened to a missing Vermeer painting in this exciting mystery novel for older readers. There are sequels.

Bonafoux, Pascal. *A Weekend with Rembrandt.* New York: Rizzoli, 1991. ISBN 0847814416.

Rembrandt speaks to the reader about his life and work. Includes a list of museums in which Rembrandt's art is to be found.

Brust, Beth Wagner. *The Great Tulip Trade.* Illustrated by Jenny Mattheson. New York: Random House, 2005. ISBN 0-375-82573-8.

This is an easy reader discussion of the Dutch people's craze for tulips in the seventeenth century and the extremely high prices these flowers would fetch. An author's note is included.

Comora, Madeleine. *Rembrandt and Titus: Artist and Son*. Illustrated by Thomas Locker. Golden, CO: Fulcrum Books, 2005. ISBN 155591490X.

Titus talks about his father's life and work. The illustrations are done in Rembrandt's style.

De Bie, Ceciel, and Martijn Leenen. *Rembrandt: Children's See and Do Book*. Los Angeles: J. Paul Getty Museum, 2001. ISBN 0892366214.

Children learn about several of Rembrandt's artworks through related activities.

De Trevino, Elizabeth Borton. *I, Juan de Pareja*. Reprint, New York: Farrar, Straus & Giroux, 1987. ISBN 0374435251.

Juan, a slave of Velázquez, helps the artist in his studio and himself learns much about art, in this novel for older readers.

Geisert, Arthur. *The Etcher's Studio*. Reprint ed. Boston: Houghton Mifflin/Walter Lorraine, 1997. ISBN 0618556141.

Although this story is not gripping, the author provides a wonderful step-by-step explanation of the technique of etching. A perfect picture book to read when discussing Rembrandt's work.

Heinrichs, Ann. *The Netherlands*. Danbury, CT: Children's Press, 2003. ISBN 0516277502;

This is a very simple history of the Netherlands and its customs.

Hintz, Martin. *Spain*. Danbury, CT: Children's Press, 2004. ISBN 0516228153.

This is a simple history of Spain and its people, for young children.

Hodges, Margaret, adapter. *Don Quixote and Sancho Panza*. Illustrated by Stephen Marchesi. New York: Scribner's, 1992. ISBN 0684192357.

This is an absolutely beautiful picture-book version of selected incidents from the lives of the famous Spanish knight and his squire.

Johnson, Jane. *The Princess and the Painter*. New York: Farrar, Straus & Giroux, 1994. ISBN 0374361185.

This is a picture-book story about Infanta Margarita, the main subject of Diego Velazquez's masterpiece, *Las Meninas*. A wonderful picture of court life in fifteenth-century Spain.

Locker, Thomas. *The Boy Who Held Back the Sea*. New York: Dial, 1987. ISBN 0140546138.

In this old Dutch tale, a young boy saves his village by plugging a hole in the dike. Locker's beautiful oil paintings are done in the style of the old Dutch masters.

———. *The Young Artist*. New York: Dial, 1989. ISBN 0803706251.

In this picture book, a young apprentice in the Netherlands is ordered to paint a portrait of the nobles at court when he would really rather do landscapes.

Muhlberger, Richard. *What Makes a Goya a Goya?* New York: Viking, 1994. ISBN 0670857432.

The author discusses twelve major works by Goya and what makes them different from any other artist's work.

———. *What Makes a Rembrandt a Rembrandt?* New York: Viking, 2002. ISBN 0670035726.

The author discusses what makes Rembrandt's work different from that of other artists.

Noyes, Deborah. *In the Time of the Tulips.* Illustrated by Dagram Ibatoulline. Cambridge, MA: Candlewick Press, 2004. ISBN 0763618756.

Hana is upset by her father's preoccupation with a possible failure of the tulip crop in Holland during Rembrandt's time. The beautiful illustrations are done in Rembrandt's style, and the artist plays a peripheral role in the story. Based on historical fact.

Oxlade, Chris, and C. Stockley. *The World of the Microscope.* Tulsa, OK: E.D.C. Publishing, 1989. ISBN 0746002890.

This book provides a wealth of information about the microscope and how to use it.

Pescio, Claudio. *Rembrandt and Seventeenth-Century Holland.* Illustrated by Sergio. New York: Peter Bedrick, 2001. ISBN 0872263177.

There are twenty-nine double-page spreads containing a great deal of information on the artist and his times.

Rodari, Florian. *A Weekend with Velazquez.* Translated by Ann K. Beneduce. New York: Rizzoli, 1993. ISBN 0847816478.

The reader is invited to spend a weekend with the artist to learn about his life and work. Full-color reproductions.

Schwartz, Gary. *First Impressions: Rembrandt.* New York: Harry N. Abrams, 1992. ISBN 0810937603.

This wonderful biography examines the most significant events in Rembrandt's life.

Spence, David. *Rembrandt and Dutch Portraiture.* Hauppauge, NY: Barrons, 1997. ISBN 0764102907.

Although the illustrations are very small, this book is packed with information about the artist.

Spier, Peter. *Father, May I Come?* New York: Doubleday, 1993. ISBN 038530935X.

Two ships are rescued off Holland, one 300 years ago, the other in the present. Readers learn something about Dutch life and the ever-present sea.

Stanley, Diane. *The Gentleman and the Kitchen Maid.* Illustrated by Dennis Nolan. New York: Dial, 1994. ISBN 0803713215.

A young girl visits an art museum and makes up a story about a kitchen maid and a young gentleman from two paintings by Dutch masters. This picture book can encourage children to imagine the lives of the people in paintings they enjoy.

Sturgis, Alexander. *Introducing Rembrandt.* New York: Little, Brown, 1994. ISBN 0316820229.

This is a wonderful life of the artist for children, including a brief history of Holland at the time, and the art materials available to Rembrandt.

Tagliaferro, Linda. *The Palace of Versailles: France's Royal Jewel.* Edited by Stephen F. Brown. New York: Bearport Publishing, 2005. ISBN 1597160032.

Learn about this magnificent building and King Louis XIV.

Terry, Patricia. *Reynard the Fox.* Berkeley: University of California Press, 1992. ISBN 0520076842.

This is a Dutch folktale about a fox who is so tricky even King Lion cannot match wits with him.

Venezia, Mike. *Diego Velázquez.* Danbury, CT: Children's Press, 2004. ISBN 0516269801.

This is a simple biography of the artist for young children.

_____. *Goya.* Danbury, CT: Children's Press, 1991. ISBN 0516422928.

This is an excellent simple biography suitable for very young children.

_____. *Johannes Vermeer.* Danbury, CT: Children's Press, 2002. ISBN 0516222821.

The author recounts Vermeer's life and work in a simple way for young children.

_____. *Rembrandt.* Danbury, CT: Children's Press, 1988. ISBN 0516422723.

This very simple biography is suitable for very young children.

Wright, Patricia. *Goya.* New York: DK Children, 1999. ISBN 0789448777.

Brief text for each two-page spread covers Goya's life in chronological order. Photos of Goya's and other artists' works.

Yount, Lisa. *William Harvey: Discoverer of How Blood Circulates.* Berkeley Heights, NJ: Enslow Publishers, 1994. ISBN 0894904817.

This biography discusses Harvey's life and work.

Audiovisual Materials

The Age of Rembrandt: Dutch Painting of the Seventeenth Century. Slides and audiocassette. National Gallery of Art, n.d. 052.

This is a selection of works by leading artists in Holland including Rembrandt and Vermeer.

The Age of van Eyck. CD-ROM. CDAccess.com, n.d. Item #VANEYCKDR.

This film is invaluable for showing children the exquisite details in Van Eyck's paintings.

Goya: Reality & Invention. DVD. Homevision, 2001. ASIN B00005NFYE.

After recounting Goya's early career, the film concentrates on the period between 1796 and 1828.

Paintings of the Great Spanish Masters. Slides and audiocassette. National Gallery of Art, n.d. 004.

The slides include paintings by several masters, including Velazquez and Goya. Narration in English or Spanish.

Rembrandt. Video. gettingtoknow.com, 2002. REMB0102.

A finalist in the Chicago International Children's Film Festival, this video is based on the book by Mike Venezia. It combines animation and presentation of actual works by the artist. Young children will love it.

Rembrandt. Video. Kultur International Films, 2000. Catalog #1324.

This film is in two parts. The first part features many of Rembrandt's works, including his wonderful self-portraits. The second discusses the restoration of his painting, *The Night Watch.*

Rembrandt's Masterly Brushstrokes. Video. Kultur International Films, 2001. Catalog #2206.

This film reveals the secret ingredients Rembrandt put into his paints to achieve his special effects.

Velazquez: The Painter of Painters. DVD. Homevision, 2000. ASIN 630299442X.

This film explores the relationship between the artist and the king for whom he worked.

Vermeer: The Magical Light. Video. Kultur International Films, 1999. Catalog #2052.

This film provides an in-depth look at Vermeer's incredible paintings.

Other Materials

Scholastic Books. *Light.* New York: Scholastic, 1997. ISBN 0590926756.

This Discovery Box, accompanied by a thirty-two-page book, contains a convex lens, prism, and a magnifying glass for experimenting with light.

Web Sites

Essential Vermeer. http://essentialvermeer.20m.com/ (accessed on March 16, 2006).

This site provides a multitude of links to every aspect of Vermeer's life and work.

Francisco de Goya. http://www.ocaiw.com/catalog/index.php?lang=en&catalog=pitt&author=410&page=1 (accessed March 16, 2006).

View many of Goya's paintings located in museums throughout the world.

Francisco de Goya. http://www.ibiblio.org/wm/paint/auth/goya/ (accessed March 16, 2006).

In addition to a brief biography of Goya, this site affords visitors the opportunity to see enlarged reproductions of some of his paintings.

Kenneth Clark: Velazquez' "Las Meninas". http://www.artchive.com/meninas.htm (accessed March 16, 2006).

See an enlarged view and an analysis of the artist's famous painting.

Rembrandt: Self Portraits. http://www.ibiblio.org/wm/paint/auth/rembrandt/self/ (accessed March 16, 2006).

This site affords a wonderful look at Rembrandt's portraits.

Tour: Francisco de Goya. http://www.nga.gov/collection/gallery/gg52/gg52-main1.html (accessed March 16, 2006).

View nine of Goya's paintings owned by the National Gallery of Art.

WebMuseum, Paris. Welcome to the Wonderful World of Baroque Music. http://www.baroquemusic.org/index.html (accessed March 15, 2006).

At this wonderful Web site, you can learn about baroque music and its composers and even listen to some baroque works.

Part V Impressionism and Post-Impressionism

12 The Impressionists

Whether for good or bad, for long or for short [Impressionism] is the active influence in the art of today. It has resulted in an added brilliance of light and color that is refreshing . . .

—KATZ AND DARS, *The Impressionists in Context*

Background Information

Impressionist paintings are among the most popular works of art today. The Musée d'Orsay in Paris is a museum devoted exclusively to Impressionist artists, and it is almost always crowded with visitors. Because we find such artworks so accessible and pleasing, it is sometimes difficult to believe that when the Impressionist style first came on the scene in Paris in the late nineteenth century, it represented a radical departure from the art in vogue at the time and was greeted with hostility. "A monkey who has got hold of a box of paints" (Sabbeth 2002, 7) is how one reviewer put it in 1875.

In 1862 four unknown painters—Claude Monet, Frederic Bazille, Auguste Renoir, and Alfred Sisley—met while studying with the Swiss artist Charles Gleyre. Their penchant for painting outdoors, an uncommon pursuit at the time, drew them together. Gradually, other painters of like mind, among them Paul Cézanne, the two friends Edouard Manet and Edgar Degas, Camille Pissarro, and Berthe Morisot, joined the group. Each grappled with ways to "capture nature as she is, which is to say solely by means of colored vibrations" (Jules Laforgue, quoted in Katz and Dars 1991, 62). Their works were refused by the all-powerful Salon, the main exhibitor of artworks in Paris, and the artists, who later came to be known as "Impressionists" after a Monet painting entitled *Impression: Sunrise* (see Sabbeth 2002, 24 for an interesting activity inspired by this painting) were forced in 1863 to hold their own exhibit, the Salon des Refusés, to bring their works before the public. Art critics, who were used to the polished, careful attention to details evident in pieces produced by artists trained in the French Academy system, scorned this exhibition of Impressionist works. In these paintings they saw only "blotches, strokes and scrapes of compacted pigment, which viewed from a 'safe' distance would then coalesce into meaningful shapes" (Katz and Dars 1991, 21).

Impressionism, a revolution in the art world between traditionalism and modernity, came on the Paris scene amid a number of other European revolutions: revolutions among the people to protest foreign invasions and poor economic conditions; revolutions in government as kingdoms gave way to republics and the lives of ordinary people assumed a new importance; revolutions in industry with the advent of new inventions and factory machinery; revolutions in architecture as Paris was modernized and narrow medieval streets made way for wide boulevards. Two developments that had a great impact on the Impressionists, most of whom championed painting outdoors where they could see firsthand the ever-changing effects of light on objects, were the invention of tin tubes for storing oil paint and the expansion of the railroad. Tubes enabled artists to take their paint, now in stable, nonperishable form, beyond their studio walls and to capture immediately on canvas the scenes before them. Railroads made it easy to leave the city to paint in the countryside. The first official Impressionist exhibition was held in 1874, and several others followed, but they were not financial successes. By 1886 most members of the group had embarked on their own, hoping to have their works accepted by the Salon and reap some monetary gain.

Although the Impressionist period lasted a mere ten years, its impact was felt throughout Europe and even as far as the New World, where it found a more accepting public and attracted such American painters as Mary Cassatt and James McNeill Whistler. While it would seem at first glance that Impressionist painting is a simple affair of broad brush strokes and shimmering, luminous color, it is much more complex than that, and many pictures took weeks to complete. Many Impressionists were influenced by Japanese prints, which were becoming popular in France at the time. Such Japanese touches as asymmetrical compositions and cutting figures off at the edges of a painting, and Japanese designs in wallpaper and other objects, are evident in Impressionist works. Individual Impressionist painters were not swallowed up into one style, but each tried to present his or her own vision of the world. Together they created a new way of seeing, a new reverence for color and light, a new emphasis on scenes of everyday life so prevalent among Dutch painters a century earlier, and ushered in the art of the modern world.

(Standards: Art Connections: 1,1-2, 4, 6-7)

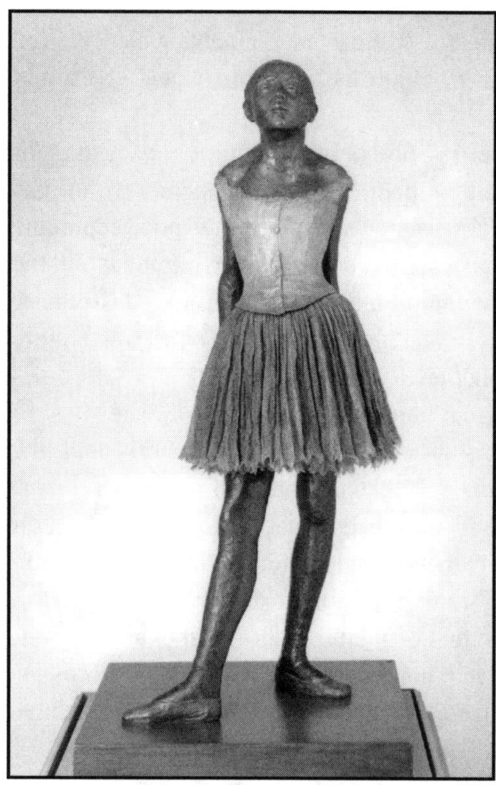

Sculpture, French, Paris, 19th–20th century (executed ca. 1880; cast in 1922)

Edgar Degas (1834–1917)

The Little Fourteen-Year-Old Dancer

Bronze, partially tinted, with cotton skirt and satin hair-ribbon; wood base

H. (w/out base) 39 in. (99.1 cm)

View: overall, front

The Little Fourteen-Year-Old Dancer, 19th–20th Century (executed ca. 1880; cast in 1922). The Metropolitan Museum of Art, H.O. Havemeyer Collection, Bequest of Mrs. H.O. Havemeyer, 1929 (29.100.370). Photograph, all rights reserved, The Metropolitan Museum of Art.

LESSON 1: Edgar Degas (1834–1917)

The Story

Over a hundred years ago, as the artist Edgar Degas emerged from a Paris shop, he saw a woman and a young girl hurrying in the direction of the Opéra, a concert hall where the ballet performed for admiring audiences. The girl held pink ballet shoes by their ribbons, and they bounced against her side as she almost ran to keep up with her mother. The woman looked over at her daughter.

"Now remember to stand straight and answer politely. No fidgeting. When they ask you to dance for them, remember everything Madame has taught you."

That was all Degas could hear, for the two scurried past him and up the Opéra steps. At the top, the woman paused and looked down at the child.

"Gracious, pull up those sagging stockings," she said. Then the mother pushed the stray hairs that had escaped their hairpins off the girl's face, adjusted the girl's dress, and finally led her into the building.

"Poor child," thought Degas. "That mother obviously wants her daughter to be accepted into the ballet school. She will have to perform for Jules Perrot, the ballet master, and endure his cane pounding the floor and his harsh criticisms. I wonder if the girl really wants such a life, or whether it's the mother's idea entirely."

All the way home Degas pondered the matter. He had often attended the ballet and enjoyed it immensely. He loved the way the dancers moved gracefully across the stage and leaped into the air. He had even taken his sketchpad along and tried to capture on paper what he saw during performances. But noticing how obviously tense that young girl looked made Degas think about the lives of the ballet dancers when they were not on the stage. What were the hours of rehearsal like? What about their fatigue? Their stage fright?

The very next day Degas went to see Monsieur Perrot and asked permission to attend rehearsals. Almost every day after that the artist spent time visiting the dance classes at the Opéra. Sketchbook in hand, he drew the dancers not only as they practiced their dance positions at the barre but also as they slumped down to rest, chatted among themselves, or worked on their costumes. He saw nervous girls and their mothers waiting in the hall for auditions. He saw girls tying their shoes or the bows on their costumes. The dance master and the dancers got so used to him they hardly looked up when he came in.

Edgar Degas painted many, many pictures of ballet dancers, and they are among the best known of his works today. When he did not go to the Opéra, girls posed for him in his studio. One fourteen-year-old named Marie became the subject of several wonderful sculptures. Degas even put real clothing on a sculpture of Marie, for he was always trying out new and surprising ideas. In fact, he joined a group of painters who were trying methods no other painters had used before. These artists were called "Impressionists," named because they were more interested in painting their impressions of a scene than painting the scene exactly as it was in real life. They used bold colors and quick brush strokes—perfect for Degas, who was trying to capture the movement and grace of ballerinas.

One day his friend Edouard Manet came to visit Degas in his studio. "Why, Edgar, what have you done here?" asked Edouard as he held up a painting. "This appears to be done with oil, but I know it isn't."

"I've colored this ballerina with pastel chalks, then sprinkled boiling water on the colors, and now I'm using my brushes to brush the color in. So it's not pastels and not oil, but it gives the appearance of oil without all the layers of paint. What do you think?" asked Degas.

"I like it, Edgar. Visiting you is always a surprise. I never know what I will find."

Edgar worked on and on for years, always trying new things. He did etchings, like Rembrandt. He became interested in photography, for the camera had just been invented. He went to the race track, where he sketched the horses and jockeys. He painted portraits of his family and other people he liked.

"What will Degas come up with next?" asked the Parisians.

Edgar Degas painted until a few years before his death at the age of eighty-three. You would think that he died a happy man, but he did not. You see, he was never really satisfied with his work. Why, he once said, "If you'd given me a hat full of diamonds, it wouldn't have made me as happy as destroying this work and starting all over again" (Loumaye 1994, 57). When we look at his art, you'll be able to see just how well he succeeded at making it perfect.

(Standards: Language Arts: Listening and Speaking 8.4)

Viewing the Art

(If this is the children's first introduction to Impressionist painting, give them some background on the Impressionist movement and how revolutionary this type of art was when it first appeared on the Paris scene. An excellent book for helping your students understand this is Salvi's *The Impressionists*—see references. He presents a cast of characters, the place, what artists had been doing up until Impressionism came on the scene, etc. In order for the students to appreciate how different and shocking Parisians found Impressionist works, it is helpful to show them the paintings of some artists working around the same time whose works were more conventional. In the mid-nineteenth century, two of the most powerful figures in French art were Jean-Auguste-Dominique Ingres and Eugène Delacroix. Delacroix championed warm color and romantic passion, while Ingres's works harkened back to the cool lines and subjects of classical art. Although the Impressionists embraced Delacroix's bright colors, they moved dramatically away from the clearly delineated lines and the subject matter found in both Delacroix and Ingres. It was a break the French art world could not easily accept. Jobert's *Delacroix*—see references—contains large color prints you can show the children for comparison, for example, *Women of Algiers, Arab Saddling His Horse,* and *The Sultan of Morocco and His Entourage.* Show some of Ingres's classical paintings. Among those you might choose are *Antiochus and Stratonice; Mademoiselle Rivière;* and *Luigi Cherubini and the Muse of Lyric Poetr*—see Vigne 1995.)

In conjunction with viewing Degas's work, you may wish to read from *Degas: The Painted Gesture* (see references). In this book, eight children attend a weekly art workshop at the Musée d'Orsay in Paris, where they discover Degas's work. They even act out scenes depicted by Degas, and your own students may want to do the same.

It would be wonderful to include at least three areas of Degas's work: the portraits, the ballet dancers (including some sculptures), and the racehorses. When viewing the portraits, point out that Degas often painted family members in groups rather than individually. Show the portrait of the Bellelli family, Degas's Italian relatives. What do the children think is going on in the picture? Why are the mother and daughters wearing black? Why is one girl turning aside? Why is the father separated from them in the picture?

While viewing *The Cotton Market, New Orleans* (see *Degas and New Orleans* in the references), talk about Degas's brothers running a cotton-exporting business in America. Imagine the difficulty of placing fourteen people in a picture so they could all be seen! In *The Orchestra of the Opéra,* Degas placed his friend, the bassoon player, in front, in the center of the picture, even though bassoonists would not really have had that position in an orchestra. Why did Degas do this? Show some self-portraits. What kind of a man does Degas appear to be? The children might also enjoy Degas's portrait of Manet and his wife. Point out that Manet colored over a portion of the picture because he didn't like it.

There are numerous paintings of ballerinas and racehorses to choose from. Point out that Degas worked with these themes because he loved both music and racing and because they gave him an excellent opportunity to draw figures in motion. (The slides for *Degas: The Dancers* and *Degas at the Races* in the resources are excellent resources for this portion of the viewing session.) What are some of the activities going on in *The Dance Class* and *The Dance Class at the Opéra?* Remind the children of Jules Perrot, the dance master, from the story. Be certain to show the sculpture of Marie, the young ballet dancer. You may also wish to read *Marie in Fourth Position* (see references), a fictional story about the girl who served as a model for Degas. *The Carriage at the Races* is actually a portrait of the family in the carriage. In whatever pictures you select, discuss how Degas created the impression of motion. Also point out the looser brush strokes that place his works with that of the Impressionists rather than with the more traditional artists who came before them.

(Standards: Art Connections 1.1-8; Language Arts: Viewing 9.6, 23)

Journal Writing

Degas captured not only the movement of ballerinas across the stage but also their emotions: their anticipation of a performance, their fatigue, their joy in the dance. Invite the children to choose one such picture previously viewed and write about it. What emotions are being expressed in the dancers' faces and bodies? How does Degas show movement in the picture? What is the story of that particular picture?

(Standards: Language Arts: Writing 1.7, 23, 33-37; Art Connections 1.3)

Art/Drama Activity: Pastels and Poetry

Materials

- Pastel paper
- Enough boxes of pastels for children to share
- Brushes
- Water
- Fixative (optional)

Have children draw pictures of ballet dancers or racehorses (or, if this is too difficult, a scene from everyday life—but not a landscape) and color them with pastels. Then they may wish to dip their brushes sparingly in water and go over their work lightly in imitation of Degas's technique. Finally, spray the finished pictures with fixative if you wish.

An interesting activity is to have the children choose horse and dance poetry to go with some of Degas's pictures and do choral recitations while displaying the artwork. This is particularly effective if you use any of the slide programs listed in the references. See Haas 2004, Isadora 2003, Springer 1994, and Hubbell 1990 for poetry selections.

(Standards: Visual Arts: 1-4.1-11; Language Arts: Reading 6.13)

LESSON 2: Claude Monet (1840–1926)

(It is most effective to do this lesson in the spring when you can actually plant a garden as a follow-up to the art/drama activity. Or if you cannot plant a garden outdoors, try planting one or two kinds of flowers in Monet's garden under grow-lights indoors.)

The Story

Young Claude Monet, who lived in Le Havre, France, was smiling to himself as he walked along, for he was on his way to Monsieur Gravier's shop to display some very funny drawings. He had made pictures of his teachers and even some important people in the town, but each picture exaggerated something about the person, such as an extra-big nose or a very long cigar. "Surely these pictures will bring me many francs," Claude thought to himself.

When he arrived at the shop, another artist was already there having frames made for his pictures. "Good morning, Claude," said the painter. "What do you have there?"

Claude showed him the drawings.

"You draw well, but why waste your considerable talent on such foolishness? Come paint outdoors with me. Learn about light and color. Work on landscapes. That's what you should be doing."

"Outdoors! What a silly idea," replied Claude. "Why would I ever want to freeze myself in the cold wind by the water or roast myself in the hot afternoon sun, or drown myself in pouring rain? You must be mad! Besides, I am earning good money with my drawings. Of what use to me are colors and paint? You see, Monsieur Gravier sold four of my drawings just this week and is coming from behind the counter now to give me my money." Claude put the money the shopkeeper handed him in his pocket and left.

But three weeks later, the painter, whose name was Eugene Boudin, came to visit. Eugene had a pack on his back and an easel in his hand.

"Come on, Claude. Let's go outdoors together and do some painting. I promise you, you won't regret it."

"But I've already told you I'm quite content as I am."

"That's only because you don't know what you're missing! Come with me just this once, and if you're not convinced it is right for you, I will never bother you again," said Eugene.

"Oh, all right, I'll come just for today. At least then you will leave me in peace."

So Claude, grumbling, put paper, pencils, and paints in a knapsack, snatched up an easel, and hiked with Boudin into the countryside. They set up their easels, and Claude started to sketch the scene in front of him.

"No, no," said Eugene. "Don't draw. Paint what you see quickly before the light changes. Watch me."

Monet put down his pencils and stood looking over Eugene's shoulder. Suddenly he saw what Eugene meant. Painting right on the spot was so different from sketching and then finishing a picture in a studio indoors! It was as if the painter were an eye to help people see nature as it is, but also a heart to help them feel the beauty of the scene.

"I want to do this for the rest of my life," declared Claude.

Claude's father was not happy with his son's decision and did not want to give him money to study in Paris. But his aunt talked Monsieur Monet into giving Claude an allowance. When Claude began his studies, however, he realized that he did not agree with his teachers. They were talking about painting indoors, using dark colors and making sure that the strokes made with the paintbrush were invisible. Even though leaving his teachers meant receiving no money from his father, Claude went off on his own to paint from nature. He even built himself a boat so he could travel up and down the River Seine, painting.

Painting outdoors wasn't easy. Once he had to tie his easel to a rock to keep it from blowing away. Another time he even had to tie himself down for protection from the wind! His beard became filled with icicles in the freezing cold. He hurt his leg badly. He developed rheumatism in his hands from painting in terrible weather. And even after all that hardship, the public hated his paintings because they were not what people were used to. The judges at the Salon, the most important art exhibition in Paris, refused to hang most of his pictures, and Claude, his wife, and two sons were often so poor they were in danger of starving. They had to move often to escape landlords who kept asking for the rent money.

There were other artists in Paris who thought as Claude did, and Monet gathered them into a special group that art critics called "Impressionists" after one of Claude's paintings named *Impression: Sunrise*. These painters held their own exhibitions, lent each other money, and encouraged each other through the difficult years. Edgar Degas, Auguste Renoir, and Mary Cassatt were members of this group. Eventually people got used to Impressionist paintings, and Claude began to sell his work and to become famous. In time he had enough money to buy his own home. He bought a farm in Giverny, about forty miles from Paris, where he settled with his own two boys and six stepchildren. There he planted a beautiful garden and built a Japanese bridge over a pond filled with water lilies. For the rest of his life, he painted the flowers and scenes in his garden. And for the last ten years of his life, he painted huge pictures of the water lilies. He gave these pictures to France when he died at the age of eighty-six.

Claude Monet was one of the first Impressionist painters. He suffered poverty and hardship to paint the way he believed was right, and he gave the world some of its most beautiful landscape paintings. He once said, "My work belongs to the public, and people can say what they like about it; I've done what I could."

(Standards: Language Arts: Listening and Speaking 8.4)

Viewing the Art

If at all possible, try to see a Monet painting firsthand in a museum. Have the children look at it close up. They will see what appear to be mere globs of paint on a canvas. But when they step back, they can see that these globs are actually figures or parts of a scene. If you cannot visit a museum, try this exercise using a picture in a book. Venezia's *Monet* (see references) offers a similar experience.

Monet painted hundreds of seascapes, for having grown up in the harbor city of Le Havre, he loved the water. Show the children as many of these pictures of the sea as you can. (See *Impressionists on the Seine* in the references.) Some you might choose are *Waterloo Bridge: Sun through the Mist*, *Zaandam*; *The Thames below Westminster*; *The Bridge at Argenteuil*; *The Seine at Lavacourt*; and *The Seine at Vetheuil.* The children may also enjoy seeing Manet's picture of Monet in his boat on the Seine.

Monet loved to paint in series so that he could capture the effect of sunlight on an object at different times of the day. (Stuckey's' *Claude Monet*—see references—is an excellent source.) Show the students some works from his haystacks series: *Haystacks*; *Haystacks in the Snow: Overcast Day*; *Haystack, Sunset*; and *Haystacks: Snow Effect*. Among the paintings in the Rouen Cathedral series you might choose: *Rouen Cathedral*; *Rouen Cathedral: The Portal and the Tower of Saint-Romain, Full Sunlight—Harmony in Blue and Gold*; *Rouen Cathedral in Full Sunlight; Rouen Cathedral: The Portal Seen from the Front—Harmony in Brown*; *Western Portal of Rouen Cathedral—Harmony in Blue*; and *Rouen Cathedral, West Facade, Sunlight*. Before you do, however, it would be wonderful for the class to share Monet's experience of changing light.

Take the class outdoors at different times during the day to view a familiar object in the playground—a slide, a tree, a plant, etc. How does it look in the morning? At noon? In the afternoon? Now view Monet's series paintings. How are they different? At what time of day do the children suppose each was painted?

Finally, concentrate on some of the Giverny paintings: *Garden at Giverny*; *The Flowering Arches: Giverny*; *The Japanese Footbridge*; *The Water-Lily Pond*; and, of course, the numerous paintings of water lilies. *Monet's House* (see references) has beautiful pictures of every room inside Monet's house—even the clothes in his closet!—as well as the gardens. *Monet at Giverny* (see references) has wonderful photographs of Monet and his family at Giverny. The children may enjoy seeing them as they view the paintings Monet did there. Tucker's *Monet in the 20th Century* (see references) has twelve fold-outs of the water lilies. *Monet's Garden in Art* and Russell's *Monet's Water Lilies* (see references) are also excellent sources for the water lily paintings.

(Standards: Art Connections 1.1-8; Language Arts: Viewing 9.6, 23)

Journal Writing

Review with the children the different characteristics of Impressionist painting: luminous colors; painting from nature, often outdoors; using color to define form, including shadows; using quick strokes rather than fine details to capture the essence of the subject, etc. Invite them to choose one of Monet's paintings and write about how he used some of these techniques in creating the work.

Language Arts: Writing 1.7, 23, 33-37; Art Connections 1.3)

Art/Drama Activity: Monet's Garden

Read *Linnea in Monet's Garden* (see references) with the children. As you read, talk about Linnea's experiences: her preparation for the trip, the places she visited, etc. Display a large map of France and invite the children to trace Linnea's journey by placing small cut-out drawings on the map to represent the museums she visited, including, of course, Monet's house and garden at Giverny. (Remind the children that Monet's house is now a museum that was restored through money raised by Americans and that it can be visited even today.) You may also wish to show children the glorious pictures of the interior of Monet's house in Heide's *Monet's House* (see references). Follow-up by re-creating Monet's house and garden on a mural.

Materials

- Large roll of paper
- Poster paints
- Books with pictures in color of Monet's house and garden to use as reference

Divide the children into groups to paint different scenes from Giverny on a mural. For example, one group can work on the house, another on the bridge and lily pond, another on the flowers surrounding the house, etc. When the mural is completed, display it in the classroom or hall. Use it as a guide for planting a garden.

(Standards: Science: 11.1; Working with Others: 1-4.1, 5, 6)

LESSON 3: Mary Cassatt (1844–1926)

The Story

If you were a young girl growing up in a well-off family in the United States in the 1850s, you could look forward to getting married, raising children, and taking care of a house. Or you could get married, raise children, and take care of a house. Or, if you really wanted to, you could get married, raise children, and take care of a house!

I suppose you can guess that girls didn't have the opportunities back then that they have now. A girl couldn't consider being a doctor or a lawyer or having almost any other profession. Most women remained at home taking care of their families for their whole lives. So when a young American teenager named Mary Cassatt finally worked up the courage to tell her father that she wanted to be an artist, he said, "I would rather see you dead!"

Mary's father was not a cruel man. He loved all his children and was kind to them. But he had no hopes that his daughter could actually earn a living as an artist in a world that thought only men could do such things well.

But do you think her father's anger stopped Mary? Not at all! She just kept begging and begging even more until he finally gave in and agreed to send her to one of the finest art schools in the country at the time, the Pennsylvania Academy of Fine Arts. The family lived not far away, in Philadelphia, and Mr. Cassatt did not want his daughter to travel any distance, especially since the Civil War between the North and the South over slavery had just begun.

Mary was so excited she could hardly believe it, but when she began her studies, she was in for some disappointments. Unlike men, women were not allowed to paint live models, and women were not taken seriously as artists. They were not even allowed into the same classes as the men.

"How can I ever learn to paint the human body if I can't see live models?" Mary complained. "They bring us cows to paint! I must go to Europe. Our country is so young there are not very many paintings to study in our museums. I must get to the Louvre in Paris."

Well, you can imagine that Mary's parents did not want to hear this. They had been hoping that she would get painting out of her system and settle down and get married like other young girls. But when they saw that she would not change her mind, they helped her get settled in Paris. Mary loved the city, even though women were not even accepted into art schools there! Artists were everywhere, and Mary studied with them and on her own. Her greatest teachers were the dead artists whose paintings she copied in the Louvre.

Finally, one of Mary's pictures was accepted by the judges of the Salon, the most important art exhibit in the city! "What an incredible honor," she thought. But there were some artists who were angry because these judges criticized their work and would not display it. These painters, called Impressionists, used brighter colors and broader brush strokes than people were used to and painted pictures of the everyday things around them. Mary especially liked the work of Edgar Degas, and he admired hers as well—although he hated to admit that a woman could really paint! When he saw her painting in the Salon, he said, "At last, a woman who feels as I do." Degas asked Mary to enter some paintings in a special Impressionist exhibit, and she agreed. They became good friends and shared ideas with one another until Degas died forty years later.

Mary learned many things from Degas and the Impressionists. She brightened her colors and blurred details. She used pastels the way Degas did. She went into the countryside to paint the people she found there. But she also experimented on her own. She never married, but she loved her nieces and nephews and painted many pictures of them. She also did many paintings of mothers and children. These pictures do not look posed but rather show a special, tender moment between a mother and child. Mary made prints and copied some ideas from the Japanese after she visited an exhibition of Japanese prints in Paris. One of her prints was of a woman washing herself.

"Look at how you've gotten the whole shape of the woman's back with just a few simple lines. You really can draw, and I admire good drawing so much!" said Edgar Degas when she showed it to him.

Mary Cassatt actually became famous in her own lifetime. Her pictures were sold in Europe, and some were even bought by Americans. She also helped her American friends choose good Impressionist paintings for their collections. Even though her parents and all her brothers and sisters died before she did, they lived long enough to see her success and were very proud of her.

"Imagine, my daughter—a woman—and a successful painter!" her father said with pride. Today, Americans are proud of Mary Cassatt, too. She was brave enough to begin a career in painting at a time when women were supposed to remain at home, and she proved that she had great talent. Her paintings are admired throughout the world, and many consider her one of our greatest American artists.

(Standards: Language Arts: Listening and Speaking 8.4)

Viewing the Art

Mary Cassatt's paintings of mothers and children are very appealing to young children, so be sure to spend a good deal of time on them. (Gallati 2004 and Todd 2005 are good sources.) *Little Girl in a Blue Armchair* (see the fiction story by Sweeney [1995]), *Two Children at the Seashore*, *Baby's First Caress*, *The Bath*, *Young Mother Sewing*, *Sleepy Baby*, *The Boating Party*, *Patty Cake*, and *Child in a Straw Hat* are some good choices. Note how natural and unposed the children look. Can the students tell any stories that might go with the pictures? They will probably also enjoy meeting members of Cassatt's family through her paintings. Include *Mrs. Cassatt Reading to Her Grandchildren*; *Lydia Working at a Tapestry Frame*; and *Alexander J. Cassatt and His Son, Robert*. In the latter painting, notice how Cassatt shows the close relationship of father and son by painting their clothing almost as if it is one garment. View some prints as well, especially *Woman Bathing*, *The Letter*, and *Mother's Kiss*. (*Mary Cassatt Modern Woman* is an excellent source—see references.)

(Standards: Art Connections 1.1-8; Language Arts: Viewing 9.6, 23)

Journal Writing

Mary Cassatt went against the customs of her day and struggled to become an artist. What thoughts does her story inspire in the children? Do they have aspirations that may be difficult to achieve? What are they, and what steps can they take to accomplish their goals?

(Standards: Language Arts: Writing 1.7, 23, 33-37)

Art/Drama Activity 1: Mothers and Children

Materials

- Paper
- Paintbrushes
- Paints, especially colors used by Cassatt

Invite the children to imagine some everyday scenes involving mothers and children. Brainstorm together and make a list of such activities: eating, getting dressed, playing with toys, reading, etc. Perhaps they can come up with some not treated by Cassatt. If any of the children have younger siblings at home, invite them to share some ideas. Or perhaps the class can visit a daycare center or nursery in the school or nearby. Have the children create a gallery of pictures of mothers and children in imitation of Cassatt's work. Are there lullabies or other such songs that may go with some of their or Cassatt's paintings? The children may wish to donate their paintings to the daycare or nursery they have visited. *Baby Loves* (see references) may serve as inspiration. If the children are too young to manage such paintings, another idea might be to collect a picture of each child in the class doing an activity with a parent or parents. Bind them all into a book and have the children write a simple caption for their picture, such as, "Mommy is reading me a story".

Art/Drama Activity 2: Print-Making

Although the children are too young to use the kinds of chemicals necessary to imitate the kind of print-making done by Cassatt, Raimondo (2004, 44) describes an interesting activity that will give children an idea of how prints are made.

Materials

- Water-based printing ink
- Brayer (roller)
- Paper
- Pencil
- Clean plastic tray from the purchase of meat or produce

Use the pencil to create a simple drawing on the plastic tray. Press so that the lines form an indentation in the tray. Roll the roller into the printing ink and then roll it across the tray, starting at the top and working as smoothly as possible. Do not use too much ink or it will fill in the lines of the drawing. Children then place a sheet of paper on top of the tray and rub gently with their hands. When they lift the paper, they should have a picture with the background the color of the paint on the roller and the white lines of the drawing. This is called a print. They can press another sheet of paper to make another print so that they understand each print is not individually drawn.

(Standards: Visual Arts: 1-4.1-11; Language Arts: Writing: 1-4.36)

Note: Curriculum connections and references are at the end of chapter 13.

13 The Post-Impressionists

It was necessary to throw oneself heart and soul into the struggle,
to fight against all schools without exception,
not by disparaging them but by something different.
To learn afresh, then, though you know, learn again.
To overcome all fears, no matter what ridicule might be the result.

—PAUL GAUGUIN

Background Information

According to art historian H. W. Janson, it is possible to ascribe the term "Post-Impressionist" to any artist of significance working after 1880, the date that marks the end of the brief but far-reaching Impressionist era. More specifically, the term applies to those artists who once numbered themselves among the Impressionists and then moved outside the tenets of the Impressionist movement. That is certainly the case with the artists whose lives and work make up this chapter. Two of them, Cézanne and Seurat, brought Impressionism back to a more classical form. Van Gogh and Toulouse-Lautrec, on the other hand, moved forward to a new and even looser form. In both cases, form had become important.

Early in his career, Paul Cézanne linked himself to the Impressionists, and especially to Camille Pissarro, his mentor (see *Cézanne & Pissarro* in the references), who taught him to paint directly from nature and to use brighter colors. Although he exhibited his work with the Impressionists, it became clear to Cézanne early on that he was more interested in revealing the solid shapes of things than the Impressionists were, and he struggled throughout his life to give form on canvas to the world around him.

Vincent van Gogh learned about the wonders of color when he stayed with his brother Theo in Paris and met the Impressionist painters working there. He admired their work and joined them for a time, but for him, Impressionism did not allow enough artistic freedom to express emotions. Van Gogh's later works, with their vibrant color and energetic movement, reflect his surging emotion and troubled spirit.

Georges Seurat used the bright colors advocated by the Impressionists, and even some of the subjects favored by them. But rather than give a brief "impression," he followed a painstaking system of juxtaposing dots of colors in such a way that they fused into coherent forms when viewed from a distance. He would spend a year or more on one painting, perfecting this exacting technique, called "Pointillism." Although his theory does not quite work in practice—one can still discern individual dots—Seurat's colors do seem to vibrate and dance off the canvas.

Henri de Toulouse-Lautrec studied the work of the Impressionists as a young art student in Paris. His favorite was Degas, who taught him to capture the small moments of everyday life: a ballet dancer tying her shoe, a woman seated in a café, ladies scrubbing in a laundry, jockeys awaiting a race. Lautrec, ever the keen observer, realized after a while that unlike the Impressionists, who strove to record their emotional reactions to a scene, he wished to record facts—exactly what he saw before him. Soon he developed his own style: outlining his figures, using longer, more sweeping strokes and larger, more brilliant areas of color.

The Impressionists, who were among the first to move away from the accepted and expected forms of classical art and historical painting, paved the way for those who came after them. They forged a pioneering spirit in the art world that was taken up by the Post-Impressionists and continues to this day.

(Standards: Art Connections: 1,1-2, 4, 6-7)

LESSON 1: Paul Cézanne (1839–1906)

The Story

Paul Cézanne was hard at work on a painting in his studio. He was so absorbed that he didn't hear a loud knock on his door. The visitor knocked again and finally heard a gruff "Come in." Paul didn't even look up to see who it was. He just kept on working. All around him on the floor were many completed paintings.

"Paul, what are these paintings doing on the floor? They'll get ruined," said his friend. "And someone told me that when he was painting out in the countryside last week, he saw some of your paintings left behind shrubs and trees. So much work left in the wind and rain—left to thieves, left to be trampled under foot. What is going on?"

"That is what they deserve!" muttered Paul. "They don't please me. Every morning I get up early, and I work until the natural light fades in the evening. And still I do not achieve my goals. I'm not interested in merely showing how I feel about what I see or how light changes the way things look, like your Impressionist friends. I want to show what doesn't change: the shapes of things! I want to be like an architect who puts pieces together to create a building. The rocks and trees, houses, and even the fruit in that bowl are *solid* shapes. The apples have *weight.* Here, feel!" An apple came flying through the air. "I build my pictures, and the brush strokes are my building blocks."

"So that is why some of the fruits in your still lifes appear bigger than we know they are in real life, and why sometimes objects seem to lean to one side. You're really building a construction that pleases you the way a sculptor would shape a piece of clay. You're trying to see these objects in a new way."

"Yes," replied Cézanne. "I paint standing back as far as I can from the canvas so I can see the whole and place things where I think they should be to create balance. Still I don't get it right!"

"But you are succeeding, Paul. Some of us go to the art dealers who have your pictures. We study them and talk about them. Why, just the other day, Gauguin told us that if we really wanted to learn, we should look at your pictures!"

"But they must please ME," said Paul. "I work for months on a picture. I do it over and over again. It must please ME. And so I keep on."

"But you must stop sometime. Come to dinner with us. Relax. Forget your troubles. You will return to your work refreshed. There's nothing like the company of friends to cheer up a person!"

"No, I am best left alone," growled Cézanne. "I don't behave well among people. I lose my temper and say things I shouldn't. Go, and leave me in peace."

Cézanne continued to work, more and more often alone. He didn't even live with his wife and son most of the time, though he loved and supported them. After his father's death, he moved into the family home in Provence, in the south of France, and continued to paint. Slowly his fame spread, and artists from around the world came to study with him. He ignored most of them and worked alone. And he died just as he wished—painting! One day he walked into the countryside to paint. He was caught in a rainstorm on the way home and collapsed in the road. He lay there for hours before someone found him and brought him home. The doctor told him to remain in bed, but he continued to go to his studio to paint. He died a week later of pneumonia at the age of sixty-seven.

Paul Cézanne left over a thousand paintings. You can imagine how many there would have been if he had not destroyed so many! Today these paintings hang in museums all over the world and are worth millions of dollars. Some people call him the "Father of Modern Art."

(Standards: Language Arts: Listening and Speaking 8.4)

Viewing the Art

While many of the Impressionists strove constantly to reveal the passing effects of nature, Cézanne was intent on showing nature's enduring forms and colors and the relationships between them (Murphy 1968, 7). There is no motion in the artist's paintings, but they are alive with energy. When viewing Cézanne's work, concentrate on his mature style, for which he is best known. Call attention to the shapes and the colors he used to achieve solid forms. Notice the horizontal and vertical lines in such pictures as *Orchard in Pontoise*, *Mont Sainte-Victoire Seen from Bellevue*, *View of Gardanne*, and *The Bay from L'Estaque*. View more landscapes. (See *Cézanne & Pissarro* in the references.) Do the children see the parallel brush strokes? The shapes?

Cézanne achieved depth in his pictures in ways that differed from the Renaissance painters and other predecessors. His objects overlap one another, giving the impression that the first is in front of the second. He used reds and oranges to bring objects forward and cold colors like blues and greens to move objects back. Can the children find the artist using these techniques in *Still Life with a Basket of Apples*, *Still Life with Apples and Oranges*, *Still Life with Water Jug*, *Still Life with Bread and Eggs*, and *Mont Sainte-Victoire Seen from Bibemus Quarry*? Then look at Cézanne's different use of colors in *The Bather*. Notice the shades of black on the left in the cloud formations and the white surrounding the bather's body. What effect do the children think these colors have on the depiction of space in the picture?

Point out that people have gone to visit the places in France that Cézanne painted (see *Cézanne in Provence* and *Cézanne: Landscape into Art* in the references) and have reported that the scenes are often more detailed than the ones we see in the artist's work. He did not hesitate to move buildings or trees, to represent a whole grove of trees by a single one, or to use colors such as green in a sky or blue in a tree trunk. The result contains the essential components of a scene. Look for some of these same characteristics in Cézanne's still lifes. *Cézanne in the Studio: Still Life in Watercolors* (see references) provides a fascinating look at the details in the still life paintings. Some fruits are larger than they appear in real life. Fruit bowl bases are off-center, as in *Still Life with Compotier*. Table tops slant up or down. The horizon line of a table is visible behind objects and re-emerges at a different point, as in *Still Life with Green Melon*. Colors are not what we see in nature. Yet the whole achieves the effect Cézanne intended. Invite the children to point out some of these characteristics in the pictures they are viewing. An excellent activity, especially if you have an LCD projector, is to go to http://www.metmuseum.org/explore/cezannes_apples/splash.html. It is called *Cézanne's Astonishing Apples*. The painter once said, "I will astonish Paris with apples," and he painted many pictures of them. At this site, children can listen to a story about Cézanne and how he painted a still life with apples. They can engage in activities while exploring this painting. They can also see other works by the artist. This is a truly worthwhile experience.

Finally, enjoy some of Cézanne's paintings of people, especially *Portrait of Victor Chocquet (seated)*; *The Card Players*; some portraits of his wife Hortense and son, Paul; and those of himself. Note their lack of emotion and individuality and unexpected coloring. *Cézanne: The Self-Portraits* contains wonderful close-ups in which the children can really see the colors. Again, Cézanne was more interested in form rather than spirit or personality.

(Standards: Art Connections 1.1-8; Language Arts: Viewing 9.6, 23)

Journal Writing

Paul Cézanne was a difficult man who kept to himself. Do you think this helped or harmed his work? Why? Invite the children to write about one of the still lifes they viewed. What things did they notice about it? Were there any unexpected things in the picture? If you studied the Impressionists, which one is Cézanne most like—Degas, Monet, or Cassatt? Why?

(Standards: Language Arts: Writing 1.7, 23, 33-37)

Art/Drama Activity: Composing Still Lifes

Materials

- Large reproductions of several of Cézanne's still lifes. Slides are ideal.
- Three sets of similar materials for composing a still life. Some possibilities are cloth, basket, fruits and vegetables, pitcher, bowl, and figurines.
- Paper
- Paints

Review several Cézanne still lifes together. Talk about the ways Cézanne placed his objects. Cover an object in a picture and look at the picture again. Does the absence of that object destroy the balance in the picture? After the students understand that Cézanne placed his objects to achieve certain effects, divide them into three groups. Give each group a set of objects that are similar in number and kind. Send them to three different parts of the room to compose a still life. Each group should discuss the reasons for placing objects in certain positions. After allowing sufficient time for this activity, invite the three groups to visit each other's work. What are the similarities? Differences? Effects achieved? You can stop the session here or, if there is time, invite the children to paint the still life they have created.

An interesting still life activity is described by Sabbeth (2002, 90). Have children draw the outlines of three pieces of fruit, overlapping some to show some pieces in front of others. Draw the same outline on another piece of paper. Color the fruits in one picture warm colors such as yellow, orange, and red, and the background cool colors such as blue and lavender. In the other picture, reverse the process, using cool colors such as green and plum for the fruits and warm colors for the background. Color the table brown in both pictures. Stand back and see the results. The warm-colored fruits will stand out more since warm colors advance and cool colors recede.

Another worthwhile activity, if you are comfortable with nudes, is to show the children a large reproduction of Cézanne's masterpiece, *The Large Bathers*. Supply tracing paper and invite them to trace the outline of the figures. They will readily notice that the whole piece is triangular in shape. The children may enjoy searching for shapes in other Cézanne paintings and creating pictures of their own using such geometric shapes as spheres, triangles, cylinders, etc.

(Standards: Visual Arts: 1-4.1-11; Working with Others: 1-4.1-3, 5-8)

LESSON 2: Vincent Van Gogh (1853–1890)

The Story

Joseph Roulin wiped his forehead with his large handkerchief as he walked slowly up the street. His almost-empty mail sack swung from his shoulder. Only two more stops and his mail route would be finished. Then he could sit in the café, have a glass of wine, and gossip with his friends. And he had plenty to tell them!

"Ah, my friends," he called as he entered the café, glad to be out of the hot summer sun. For even though it was late afternoon, summers in his little town of Arles in the south of France were hot indeed. "A fine day, eh? What is the latest news?" asked Joseph.

"Joseph," said a neighbor at one of the tables. "From the twinkle in your eyes, I can tell YOU are the one with some news. Let's hear it."

"You know the new painter in town, the one who lives in the yellow house on the corner—Vincent van Gogh? He's asked to paint my portrait. Imagine, me, a postman, in a real painting. We're to begin tomorrow."

"Better be careful, Joseph," said one of his listeners. "I've heard so many strange stories about Monsieur van Gogh. Do you remember that other painter who came to stay with him—Gauguin, I think his name was? The two of them used to go tramping into the countryside together to paint. But when he came in here in the evening, all Gauguin would do was complain. He just couldn't get along with van Gogh. Gauguin certainly didn't last long. He left before he even had a chance to get settled."

"True," said another. "Van Gogh is a bit strange. The other evening I saw him sitting in front of his easel wearing a crown of lighted candles on his head! He said it was so he could keep painting all night long. I watched him for a while. There he was dipping his brush over and over again into his paints and putting layers of paint on his canvas. He almost seemed angry at the painting!"

The men talked on and on until it was time for them to go home to dinner. "Good luck, Joseph," they called as they each went their separate ways. "Don't let him put globs of paint on you the way he layers paint on his canvases!" Their laughter echoed down the street.

Joseph did pose for van Gogh the next day. In fact, he posed several times, and so did his wife. Vincent Van Gogh painted several pictures of them, and of many other people in Arles: people working in the fields, men and women posing in a chair like Joseph did, and even people at the café. You can see his wonderful pictures of Joseph Rolin sitting proudly in his blue postman's uniform with its shiny gold buttons. But he looks a little uncomfortable, too, maybe because he wasn't used to so much attention.

For months Vincent painted and painted, excited by the brilliant sun and the bright colors in the sunny French town. Vincent often wrote to his brother Theo, an art dealer living in Paris, and told him about the work he was doing. He even put drawings in the letters. Vincent sent Theo pictures to sell in his shop, too—many, many pictures. Even when Vincent had to go to a hospital to rest his troubled mind, he painted over 100 pictures there. He just never stopped.

Vincent worked as an artist for ten years, in Holland, in Paris, and in Arles. In that short time he did over 2,000 paintings and drawings. But only one of Vincent's pictures was sold during the painter's lifetime, and not for very much money, either.

Theo saved his brother's artwork and his letters even after Vincent's death and never stopped talking about him. Little by little people began to find out about Vincent's work, and to admire it. When Theo's son grew up, he gave all his uncle's paintings to the Dutch government, for Vincent and his brothers and sisters had been born in Holland. The Dutch government built a special museum for them, and thousands of people visit that museum every year. Not so long ago, one of Vincent Van Gogh's paintings was sold for $82.5 million! Imagine it: The poor painter who could only sell one painting in his lifetime is now one of the most famous and best-loved artists who ever lived!

(Standards: Language Arts: Listening and Speaking 8.4)

Viewing the Art

Spend some time on van Gogh's drawings, for he considered them the root of good art. *Vincent van Gogh: The Drawings* (see references) is an excellent choice for viewing the artist's vast output of drawings. A fine activity, especially if you have an LCD projector, is to go to *How Van Gogh Made His Mark* at http://www.metmuseum.org/explore/van_gogh/intro.html. Here children can learn about the artist's life, see how a drawing is transformed into a painting, zoom in on drawings, and even make their own drawings online. This site is provided by the Metropolitan Museum of Art.

It is difficult to obtain the full impact of Vincent van Gogh's work from reproductions in books—to see the tangible layers of paint and the brilliant colors. If at all possible, try to obtain one of the films listed below. If you do use books, begin by showing van Gogh's early pictures, especially *The Potato Eaters*. Do the children notice the dark palette? The somber subject matter? Crispino (1996) has a good explanation of this picture for children. Then focus on the contrast when van Gogh discovered color. An excellent book to use for this is *Vincent's Colors* (see references). In rhyming text taken from the artist's own words, children are introduced to the many colors in these beautifully reproduced paintings.

Concentrate on the paintings done in Arles. The children will enjoy seeing the building where van Gogh lived, his simple room, his and Paul Gauguin's chairs. You may wish to read *The Yellow House* (see references), a picture-book account of Gauguin's stormy time in Arles with van Gogh.

Introduce some of the citizenry of Arles through their portraits: Ada Ginoux, Roulin the Postman. (See *Van Gogh Face to Face: The Portraits* in the references.) Talk about the weather in Arles, the intense heat and brilliant sun. When you show paintings of the countryside, be certain to include many that feature Vincent's favorite color, yellow, and focus especially on the beautiful *Harvest at La Crau*. Have the children notice the yellows and the artist's strokes, which are like dashes. (If you study Seurat, it is interesting to compare Van Gogh's dashes and Seurat's dots.) Discuss the swirls of motion in *Starry Night* and *Cypresses*. Show some of the beautiful sunflower paintings with which Vincent decorated his little house. Van Gogh did many self-portraits. Notice the intensity in the eyes, the unusual colors. Discuss the differences among the portraits. The children may be curious about the portrait of Vincent with the bandaged ear. Explain that when he was feeling especially depressed, he cut off part of his ear and almost died.

(Standards: Art Connections 1.1-8; Language Arts: Viewing 9.6, 23)

Journal Writing

Have the children write about Vincent and his brother Theo. How did that relationship affect Vincent's work? Do they have a close relationship with a sibling or a friend? How does that relationship affect their lives? Invite the children to choose one picture they especially like and write what they think that picture tells us about Van Gogh.

If you use the song "Vincent" by Don McLean, older children might wish to write a response to it.

(Standards: Language Arts: Writing 1.7, 23, 33-37; Art Connections 1.3; Music: .15)

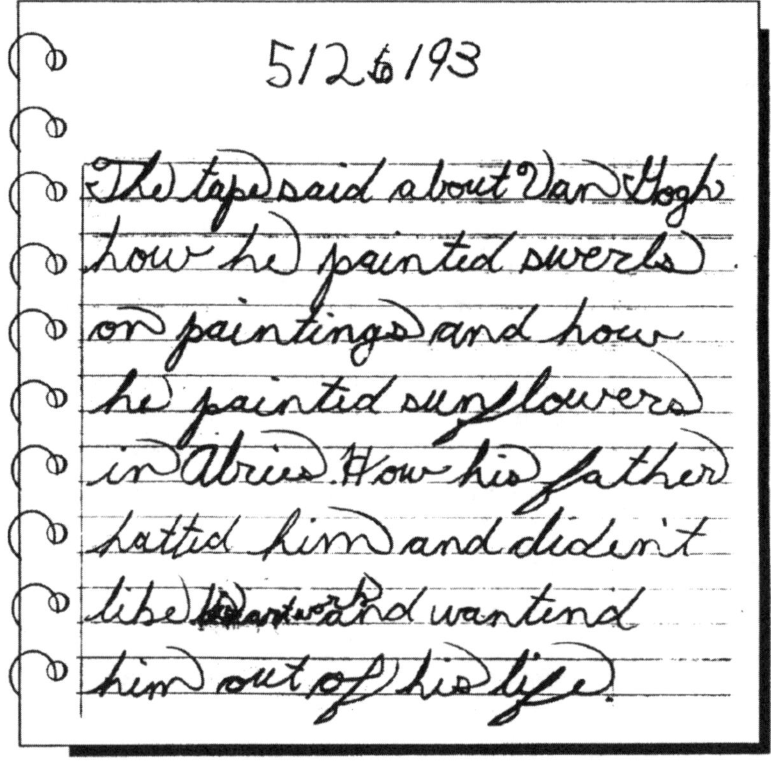

5/26/93

The tape said about Van Gogh how he painted swerls on paintings and how he painted sunflowers in Arles. How his father hatted him and didin't like [illegible] and wantend him out of his life.

Art/Drama Activity: Brilliant Yellows

Materials

- Paints, especially yellow
- Paper
- Paintbrushes

If possible, go out into the schoolyard or on a walk when the sun is at its hottest. How does its brilliance affect what the children see—trees, grass, playground equipment? When you return to the classroom, recall with the children that Vincent Van Gogh loved the color yellow, especially the brilliant yellow of the sun or the bright light of the stars. Talk about different shades of yellow and mix paints with the children to make a few. Add white to yellow to make a pale, creamy color. Add a few drops of red to make a more fiery yellow. Then invite the children to paint a picture of something they saw outside, or a scene they recall from when they were outside on a hot day, using shades of yellow. In her picture book *In the Tall, Tall Grass,* Denise Fleming uses yellow to color the sky instead of blue because she wanted the reader to feel the heat of a summer's day and for her, yellow conveyed the idea of heat better than blue. Show the children her artwork to demonstrate this effective use of yellow (see references). The children might want to make their own "composition in yellow"—a still life (featuring, perhaps, sunflowers), a scene from their bedroom, a landscape. Recall that when Van Gogh painted his bedroom, he made even the pillows on his bed yellow, though they probably weren't in real life.

(Standards: Visual Arts: 1-4.1-11)

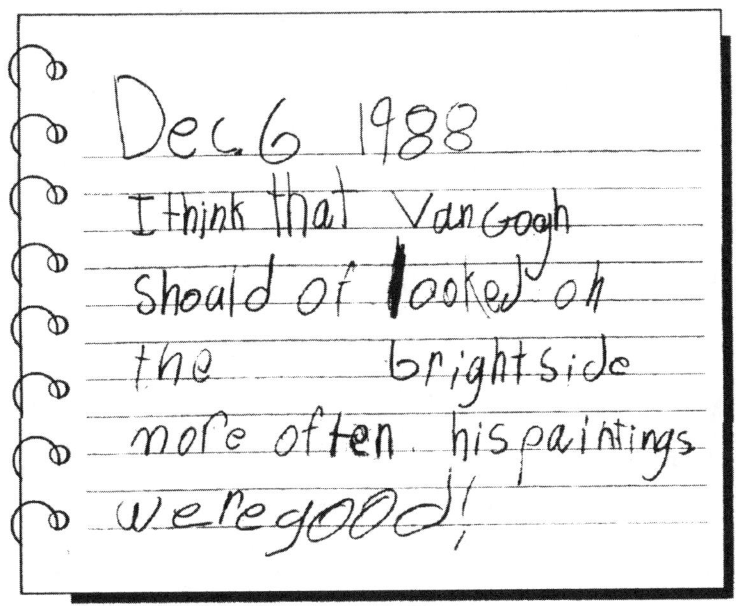

Dec 6 1988
I think that Van Gogh
shoald of looked on
the bright side
more often. his paintings
were good!

LESSON 3: Georges Seurat (1859–1891)

The Story

"Georges, come away from that book. You've been at it long enough! Aman-Jean and I are going to the exhibit of new painters—you know, the ones the critics call Impressionists. Since the Salon won't take their paintings, they are having their own exhibition. Take a break and come along!"

"In a minute, Ernest. But look at this with me first."

"Oh, you and your scientists! You read one scientific book after the other. You're supposed to be studying art, my friend. Why waste your time on science?"

"But, Ernest, I believe science can teach us so much about art. Look at this color wheel here in the book. The writer says that when you put colors next to each other, they pick up one another's colors and look different from the way they are on a page by themselves. Isn't that fascinating? Here, take a look for yourself."

"So? I still don't know what this has to do with our art studies."

"Don't you see, if I put the right colors near each other on my canvas, they can mix together. I tried mixing them myself on my palette, but all I got was black. But if I put the separate colors near each other in my picture, they will mix together in the eyes of the people looking at the picture. I'm going to try that next."

"The viewer's eyes mix the colors? That sounds crazy to me, but if it will satisfy you, try it. For now, though, come with us to the exhibition."

Georges did go to the exhibition, and he liked the Impressionists' work. In fact, he put some of his own paintings in other Impressionist shows. But he didn't want to follow their ideas exactly. He didn't want to capture just a moment or a certain light on objects outdoors. He wanted to plan and compose his paintings. For two whole years he concentrated on practicing his drawing. Then he worked on using color. He even destroyed some pictures he didn't like! His first big painting was a picture of young people swimming, for he loved the water. He made many drawings to get ready to paint this picture and was very proud of it when it was finally finished. But many people thought it was too different from what they were used to.

Seurat didn't change his ideas, though. He kept working and working at them. In fact, he made his work even more different by using small dots of paint, instead of short strokes like the Impressionists. By using dots, he thought his colors would seem to dance or vibrate on the canvas when people looked at his pictures and their eyes mixed the colors together.

Georges was a very quiet man who worked steadily from early morning until late at night, painstakingly putting small dots of color on huge canvases. He knew so much about colors that he could actually paint in the evening in artificial light, while some of his friends could only paint in natural light. They would visit him and try to get him to stop working, but he stayed up on his ladder.

"I know how to get him off that ladder," whispered Aman-Jean to Ernest one evening. "I'll pretend I don't understand what he's trying to do with those dots of his. Then he'll come down and start arguing and explaining. Once we get him off the ladder, we'll each grab an arm and take him to the café for a bite to eat." Sure enough, Ernest's plan worked, because Georges believed so strongly in what he was doing that he was always ready to defend himself.

Seurat only painted for about twelve years, but he actually became famous in that short time. The picture that made all of Paris start talking about him was a huge painting of groups of people out enjoying themselves on an island on a Sunday afternoon. Georges made over sixty practice drawings and paintings to get ready for *A Sunday Afternoon on the Island of La Grande Jatte*, and he worked on it for two years! Five years later, when he was hanging pictures in a drafty building for an exhibition, Georges caught a chill and developed a throat infection. He died a week later. He was only thirty-one years old. But even though his life was a short one, he gave us some wonderful pictures and a new understanding of how colors work together.

(Standards: Language Arts: Listening and Speaking 8.4)

Viewing the Art

Begin by showing some of Seurat's small paintings and drawings before he developed his pointillism technique. There are several pictures of peasants working that the children might enjoy. Note the similarities to the work of the Impressionists. Look at *Bathing at Asnières*. What are some of the things Seurat has done to let us know it is a very hot day? Spend a considerable amount of time on *A Sunday Afternoon on the Island of La Grande Jatte*. Two excellent books that will help with this viewing are Burleigh's *Seurat and La Grande Jatte* and Herbert's *Seurat and the Making of La Grande Jatte* (both in the references). Show the children some of Seurat's preliminary drawings and paintings. Talk about pointillism and its effects. Note all the vertical lines. How many different activities can the children discover in the painting? How many different people? How many colors can they see in the grass, the trees, the water, the clothing? Do they notice that Seurat painted his own frame around the picture? Note the more somber tones in the indoor scene called *The Side Show*. Can the children point out all the horizontal and vertical lines? There is not much movement here in contrast to *The Circus*, Seurat's last painting. He hung it for exhibition shortly before his death. What do the children think he intended to add? Note the predominance of blue. If possible, show the children Seurat's final study for *The Circus* (a reproduction appears in Madeleine-Perdrillat's *Seurat* on page 193) so they can see how he laid out his colors.

(Standards: Art Connections 1.1-8; Language Arts: Viewing 9.6, 23)

Journal Writing

Invite the children to write about the effect Seurat's pointillism technique has on them. Do they like it? Why or why not? Can they explain what he was trying to accomplish? Some children may wish to write about *A Sunday Afternoon on the Island of La Grande Jatte*. What is their favorite part of the picture? Why?

Language Arts: Writing 1.7, 23, 33-37; Art Connections 1.3)

Art/Drama Activity: Pointillism

Materials

- A color wheel
- Paintbrushes
- Paint
- Paper
- Newspaper

Children enjoy imitating Seurat's pointillism to create artwork of their own. If they are old enough for a discussion of the color wheel, talk first about how colors work. Point out complementary colors, that is, those colors that are opposite each other on the color wheel, such as red/green, purple/yellow, blue/orange. When the children apply their dots to paper, encourage them to place colors next to each other that will blend in the viewer's eye to create new colors.

(Standards: Visual Arts: 1-4.1-11)

LESSON 4: Henri de Toulouse-Lautrec (1864–1901)

(If possible, try to plan this lesson around the time of a special school or community event so the children can make posters to publicize it. This real-life activity will be quite meaningful to them.)

The Story

Four-year-old Henri, dressed in his finest outfit, sat in the coach between his parents, the count and countess de Toulouse-Lautrec, on the way to his baby cousin's christening. When the ceremony began, he shifted from foot to foot in the cold church, anxious for it to be over so the celebrating could begin. Finally, the adults lined up to sign the registry, signaling that it was time to go. Henri pulled on his father's trousers.

"Papa, I want to sign the book, too."

"But Henri, you can't even write your name yet! It's impossible."

"Then I can draw a cow in the book. Pick me up so I can reach, Papa."

Imagine, a four-year-old who could already draw animals quite well. But that wasn't so surprising, for his father and many of his relatives could draw. They were happy to see Henri pass his time that way, too. But he was not expected to make drawing and painting his career. No, he was expected to become a fine horseman, to hunt, and to care for his father's large estate.

As Henri grew older, he learned to ride so well it seemed as though he were almost part of the horse. He hunted with his father and his uncles and had a fine time. But his mother worried about him because he was small for his age and not very strong. When he was about thirteen, he slipped and fell and broke a thigh bone. The doctors set the broken bone, but perhaps because their methods then weren't as good as they are now, or because Henri's bones were not very strong, his leg never healed properly. He walked with a cane for a year.

Then one day while the family was gathered in the living room, the doctor came to visit. "Hurry, Henri, get up and greet the doctor," said Henri's father. When Henri rushed to get out of his low chair, he dropped his cane and he fell, breaking the other leg! From that time on, Henri's legs simply stopped growing, while the upper part of his body continued to grow into manhood. You can imagine how strange he looked—a person with a regular-size head, arms, and chest, and very short legs. He had to walk with canes the rest of his life, and he could never ride horses again or take charge of the family property.

What happened to Henri was very sad, but actually, some good did come out of it. He had plenty of time to devote to his art, and a few years later, his wealthy parents gave him a generous allowance so he could go to Paris to study. Henri was very smart, and he worked hard at his drawing until he got so good he set up a studio and began his career as an artist.

Henri knew some of the Impressionists in Paris and liked their work, especially Degas's. But he didn't want to follow their ideas exactly. He wasn't interested in painting pretty pictures, but pictures that told the truth about people. He wanted to use outlines for his figures, and longer strokes of his brush. Every night Henri went into the well-known Paris nightclubs with his sketchbook and chalks and drew what he saw. He drew the singers and dancers and the people in the crowd. Then he would take his drawings back to his studio and turn them into paintings. The owners and the people who came to the nightclubs got used to seeing Henri drawing at his special table every night. They liked the little man who was always full of jokes and liked to have a good time. Soon the owners began to ask him to make posters advertising their nightclubs. They could have the posters printed and hung up around the city to bring in business. Many of Henri's posters were so excellent they made the nightclubs famous. Even today we know about the Moulin Rouge in Paris because of Henri's art.

But you can imagine that being in a nightclub every night got Henri used to drinking, and in a few years he became an alcoholic. His mother was so worried about his health that she hired a man to stay with him at all times to stop him from drinking. Henri figured out a way to fool the man. He bought a special cane that was hollow inside, and every day before the man arrived, Henri unscrewed the top, filled the cane with whiskey, and screwed the top back on. Then in the nightclub, when the man's back was turned, Henri drank from his cane! But as his mother feared, all that drinking made Henri sicker and sicker. Soon he could not even paint well. He suffered a stroke and died when he was only thirty-seven. Although he had been working as an artist for less than twenty years, he left over 1,000 paintings, more than 5,000 drawings, and over 300 prints and posters!

(Standards: Language Arts: Listening and Speaking 8.4)

Viewing the Art

There are many photographs of Toulouse-Lautrec available, so begin by showing the children some of them. They will surely be curious about what he looked like. The children might also enjoy his painting of his mother, the countess de Toulouse-Lautrec, and his portrait of Vincent Van Gogh, if they have studied

Van Gogh. Show some of the nightclub paintings and portraits. A few you might select are *At the Moulin de la Galette*; *At the Moulin Rouge: The Dance*; *La Goulue Entering the Moulin Rouge*; *At the Moulin Rouge*; *Jane Avril Leaving the Moulin Rouge*; *At the Moulin Rouge*: *The Clownesse Cha-u-kao*; and *Marcelle Lender Doing the Bolero in Chilperic*. Note the outlined figures, the swirling garments of the dancers, the expressions on the faces of the patrons, the fashions of the day. Can the children find the artist in any of the pictures?

The Impressionists used natural light outdoors. Toulouse-Lautrec worked with artificial indoor light, often theatrical. How did he show this light in his pictures? Show some of the posters (see *Great Lithography by Toulouse-Lautrec* in the references), especially his most famous, *Jane Avril*. Note how a line that comes out of the musical instrument encircles Jane and returns to the instrument. As you view the posters, cover the words. Notice how off-balance they seem without the writing. Lautrec's genius was that the print in his best posters was an integral part of the whole, not something added on.

(Standards: Art Connections 1.1-8; Language Arts: Viewing 9.6, 23)

Journal Writing

Invite the children to pick a character from one of the artist's paintings or posters. What can they tell about the personality of the person from the piece of art? Would Toulouse-Lautrec have pursued his art if he had not been crippled? Why or why not?

(Standards: Language Arts: Writing 1.7, 23, 33-37; Art Connections 1.3)

Art/Drama Activity: Poster-making

Materials

- Large poster paper
- Markers, especially black for outlining and lettering
- Reprints of Toulouse-Lautrec's posters to use as guides
- Paints
- Paintbrushes
- Newspaper

Invite the children to make posters about an event that will take place in the school or community. They may work individually or in groups. Have them plan the poster beforehand. What illustration will best describe the event? What lettering will they need, and where will it go on the poster so it becomes a real part of the picture, and so the poster is well-balanced? What colors will they use to attract the attention of viewers? When the posters are completed, hang them in the lobby or halls of the school if they describe a school event. Otherwise, obtain permission to hang them in appropriate places in the community. Remind the children to remove the posters when the event they advertise is over.

(Standards: Visual Arts: 1-4.1-11)

Additional Activities

- Children love to dramatize events in the colorful lives of these artists. Some possibilities for dramatization are
  - Edouard Manet visiting Degas in his messy studio
  - The Impressionists banding together to form their own exhibit after their work is repeatedly dismissed by the Salon
  - Mary Cassatt's father refusing to allow her to study art
  - The meeting of Degas and Cassatt
  - Boudin convincing Monet to paint outdoors
  - Monet setting up his garden
  - Cézanne, the loner, who concentrates only on his work
  - Van Gogh and Gauguin in Arles
  - Seurat discovering the way colors work on each other
  - Toulouse-Lautrec drinking from his cane
- On a large map of France and one of Holland, draw in the birthplaces of different artists and where they worked.
- Create a newspaper that might have been published in the time of the Impressionists. Assume the role of critics and write about some of the Impressionist paintings. Some children can assume the role of detractors while others see something promising in this new kind of art.
- Present a slide show of Impressionist and Post-Impressionist works accompanied by poetry readings. Selected poetry titles follow in the children's book references.
- Objects in nature are not just one color. For example, grass is not just one shade of green, even in the same lawn. Clouds might have several different colors: wisps of pink, streaks of black, etc. Invite the children to look again at some Impressionist and Post-Impressionist paintings of the natural world and make a list of colors in some of the objects they see. They might want to go outside and paint something they see around the school—a flower, a tree, etc.—being careful to observe and record the different colors in their object.

(Standards: Theater: 2.1-2, 10; Geography 1.30; Language Arts: Writing 1, 3.10-11)

Curriculum Connections

Social Studies

- Study the history of France at the time of the Impressionist movement: the Franco-Prussian War, the change from monarchy to republic, etc.
- Study the old Paris and the new reconstruction of the city by Georges-Eugene Haussmann. David P. Jordan's *Transforming Paris : The Life and Labors of Baron Haussmann* (see references) is a wonderful source of pictures for this study.
- Make a time line of Impressionist painters and Post-Impressionist painters.
- Study the Industrial Revolution and its effect on French society.
- Study the fashions of the time; design hats for Parisian women of the nineteenth century.
- Find out about the popular cafés in Paris at the time of the Impressionists. Which ones appear in Impressionist paintings?
- Peruse some of the books listed in the references to find quotes from some newspapers of the time. What did critics say about Impressionist paintings?
- Mary Cassatt was active in the women's suffrage movement. Research the movement in the United States. Who were some of its leaders? What were some of the things they did to try to get women the vote? (See White 2005 and Fritz 1999.)
- World War I took place during the lifetimes of some artists in this section. Find out what caused this war, what countries were involved, the names of important generals, etc.

(Standards: World History: 34, 39.17, 50; Grades K-4 History: 4.38; Civics 1.53; Language Arts: Media: 10.10)

Science

- Study the inventions of the era: the camera, the steam engine, the electric light, the car, the airplane. (See Richter 2006 and St. George 2002.)
- Find out what kinds of flowers actually grew in Monet's garden. Plant those that will grow in your area. Design a layout for maximum beauty. (See *Monet's Garden in Art* and *Secrets of Monet's Garden* in the references. You might also compare Monet's garden with those of Van Gogh and Cézanne in books by Fell in the references.)

(Standards: Grades K-4 History: 8.38, 45)

Literature

- Read biographies of important people of this era.
- Find poems that go with some of the artists' works.
- Read the poem "Thoroughbred" by Edgar Degas. (See *Degas* by Gordon and Forge, page 73.)
- Suggest that the children, working alone or in groups, write a biography of their favorite Impressionist or Post-Impressionist artist. They can think of creative ways to present their biographies: as an alphabet book, as a poster, etc. They may want to use *Edgar Degas: Paintings That Dance, Claude Monet: Sunshine and Waterlilies, and Sunflowers and Swirly Stars* (see references) as models.
- Using such books as *Degas and the Little Dancer, Suzette and the Puppy,* and *Marie in Fourth Position* as models (see references), write a fictional story to go with a painting by any Impressionist or Post-Impressionist artist. This can be a whole group activity in which the story is printed on a chart, or the children can work individually or in small groups.

(Standards: Language Arts: Writing: 1-4.11, 20, 33-38; Reading: 6, 7:13; Working with Others: 1-4.1-10)

Music

- Find out which great composers lived during the time of these artists. (See Levine's *Story of the Orchestra* in the references for a discussion of Impressionist music and a sample CD.)
- Explore the relationship between the art and the music of this era.
- Find musical pieces that go with Impressionist paintings.
- Listen to some ballet music as you view Degas's paintings of ballet dancers. (See *Music of the Ballet* CD in the references.)

(Standards: Arts and Communication: 4.29; Music 7.4, 7)

References (for chapters 12 and 13)

Adult Books

Adriani, Gotz. *Toulouse-Lautrec: The Complete Graphic Works.* New York: Thames & Hudson, 1988. ISBN 0500091889.

This book has breathtaking, large reproductions of Lautrec's work.

Armstrong, Carol, and David Hockney. *A Degas Sketchbook.* Los Angeles: Getty Trust Publicaions, 2000. ISBN 0892366109.

Twenty-eight pages of Degas's sketchbook are reproduced in this book.

Bade, Patrick. *Degas: The Masterworks.* New York: Portland House, 1991. ISBN 0517053780.

Bade discusses the life of the artist and presents a detailed discussion of his major works. Large pictures for viewing.

Barnes, Rachel, ed. *Degas by Degas.* New York: Alfred A. Knopf, 1990. ISBN 0394589076.

Some of Degas's paintings are presented, with comments by the artist.

———. *Monet by Monet.* New York: Alfred A. Knopf, 1990. ISBN 0394589068.

Some of Monet's paintings are presented, along with comments by the artist.

Barter, Judity A., et al. *Mary Cassatt: Modern Woman.* Chicago: Art Institute of Chicago/Harry N. Abrams, 1998. ISBN 0-8109-4089-2.

This excellent book traces the artist's development through the years. It contains over 100 color prints and is a gem for viewing Cassatt's work.

Bomford, David, et al. *Art in the Making: Degas.* London: National Gallery London, 2004. ISBN 1857099699.

The authors discuss how Degas created his artworks.

Cachin, Francoise, et al. *Cézanne.* Philadelphia: Philadelphia Museum of Art, 1996. ISBN 0810940396.

More than 240 large color plates and 262 black-and-white reproductions with commentaries. Produced in conjunction with the Cézanne exhibit at the museum.

Conisbee, Philip, and Denis Coutagne. *Cézanne in Provence.* New Haven, CT: Yale University Press, 2006. ISBN 0300113382.

The authors discuss how closely related Cézanne's work is to Provence and present over 140 excellent plates for viewing.

Courthion, Pierre. *Georges Seurat.* New York: Harry N. Abrams, 1988. ISBN 0810915197.

Seurat's life is followed by discussion of forty of his best-known works. Color reproductions.

De Toulouse-Lautrec, Henri, Frederico Zeri, et al. *Toulouse-Lautrec at the Moulin Rouge.* Richmond Hill, ON, 2000. ISBN 1-55321-017-4.

The artist's keen sense of observation is evident in the large paintings in this book.

Donson, Theodore B., and Marvel Griepp. *Great Lithography by Toulouse-Lautrec.* Mineola, NY: Dover, 1983. ISBN 0486243591.

Eighty-nine lithographs in full color are beautifully reproduced and suitable for viewing.

Feigenbaum, Gail. *Degas and New Orleans: A French Impressionist in America.* New Orleans: New Orleans Museum of Art, 2000. ISBN 0-89494-072-4.

This book contains paintings done by Degas in New Orleans as well as paintings he did in Europe that are related to his connection with that city.

Fell, Derek. *Cézanne's Garden.* New York: Simon & Schuster, 2004. ISBN 0743225368.

The artist's paintings are juxtaposed with photographs of the artist's gardens. Children will be interested in views of the artist's studio.

———. *Secrets of Monet's Garden: Bringing the Beauty of Monet's Style to Your Own Garden.* New York: Friedman/Fairfax, 1997. ISBN 1-56799-463-6.

Fell discusses the different parts of Monet's garden and offers suggestions for modern gardeners.

———. *Van Gogh's Gardens.* New York: Simon & Schuster, 2001. ISBN 0743202333.

Using the artist's notes and letters, Fell photographs the fields and gardens that appear in Van Gogh's paintings.

Gallati, Barbara Daver. *Children of the Gilded Era: Portraits of Sargent, Renoir, Cassatt and Their Contemporaries.* London: Merrill, 2004. ISBN 1858942721.

These portraits are fine for viewing.

Gatto, Alfonso. *Cézanne.* New York: Rizzoli, 2004. ISBN 0-8478-2731-3.

Part of a series of small books about artists, this has a one-page explanation of each of the works it contains and is suitable for small groups.

Gordon, Robert, and Andrew Forge. *Degas.* Translated by Richard Howard. New York: Harry N. Abrams, 1988. ISBN 0810911426.

This beautiful book includes Degas's life and large reproductions for viewing.

———. *Monet.* New York: Harry N. Abrams, 1989. ISBN 0810980916.

The artist's work is discussed and represented in more than 125 color reproductions and many black-and-white images.

Herbert, Robert L. *Seurat: Drawings and Paintings.* New Haven, CT: Yale University Press, 2001. ISBN 0300071310.

Herbert examines the drawings and paintings of the artist.

Herbert, Robert L., and Neil Harris. *Seurat and the Making of La Grande Jatte.* Los Angeles: University of California Press, 2004. ISBN 0520242106

The authors discuss all the studies and work Seurat put into the creation of this painting over two years.

Hirshler, Erica. *Impressionism Abroad: Boston and French Painting.* London: Royal Academy of Arts, 20005. ISBN 1-903973-77-5.

This book contains the Impressionist paintings owned by the Boston Museum of Fine Arts. There are many of Monet's works in the collection.

House, John. *Monet: Nature into Art.* New Haven, CT: Yale University Press, 1986. ISBN 0300043619.

House explores Monet's evolution as an artist. Large reproductions.

Ives, Colta. *Vincent van Gogh: The Drawings.* New York: Metropolitan Museum of Art, 2005. ISBN 030010720X.

Produced in conjunction with an exhibit at the museum, this volume contains 400 of the artist's drawings and watercolors.

Janson, H.W. *History of Art.* 6th ed. Englewood Cliffs, NJ: Prentice Hall, 2003. ISBN 0131056824.

This is one of the most famous surveys of the major art periods.

Jobert, Barthelemy. *Delacroix.* Translated by Terry Grabar and Alexandra Bonfante-Warren. Princeton, NJ: Princeton University Press, 1998. ISBN 0691004188.

Jobert offers a fine discussion of Delacroix's work, and the reproductions are large and fine for viewing.

Jordan, David P. *Transforming Paris : The Life and Labors of Baron Haussmann.* New York: Free Press, 1995. ISBN 0029165318.

Jordan discusses Haussmann's part in transforming Paris into a modern city. Many pictures illustrate the old and new Paris.

Katz, Robert, and Celestine Dars. *The Impressionists in Context.* New York: Crescent Books, 1991. ISBN 0517065126

The authors give the history of Impressionism and the life and works of major Impressionist artists. Large reproductions for viewing.

Kelder, Diane. *The Great Book of Post-Impressionism.* New York: Abbeville Press, 1990. ISBN 0896595749.

This huge book begins with the work of the Impressionists and shows how those who came after them adapted their ideas into new styles. Hundreds of large reproductions.

Kendall, Richard. *Degas: Beyond Impressionism.* London: National Gallery London, 1996. ISBN 1-85709-130-2.

Degas's later works are featured in this book.

Kendall, Richard, ed. *Degas by Himself.* 1987. Reprint, Secaucus, NJ: Chartwell Books, 2005. ISBN 0785801669.

See the artist through his works and writings from his journals and letters.

Lemoine, Serge. *Paintings in the Musee D'Orsay.* New York: Harry N. Abrams, 2004. ISBN 081095608X.

This huge book contains more than 800 beautiful reproductions suitable for group viewing. All the artists in the chapters on Impressionism and Post-Impressionism are represented.

Machotka, Pavel. *Cézanne: Landscape into Art.* New Haven, CT: Yale University Press, 1996. ISBN 0300067011.

Machotka examines the surfaces and tones in all of the artist's landscapes. This is a wonderful book.

Madeleine-Perdrillat, Alain. *Seurat.* New York: Rizzoli, 1990. ISBN 0847812863.

The author discusses Seurat's life and works. This is a large book containing wonderful reproductions.

Mancoff, Debra N. *Mary Cassatt: Reflections of Women's Lives.* London: Frances Lincoln, 1998. ISBN 1-55670-852-1.

The paintings in this lovely little book show women in various aspects of their lives: alone, in social settings, as mothers. The colored prints are suitable for group viewing.

———. *Monet's Garden in Art.* New York: Viking Studio, 2001. ISBN 0-670-89384-6.

Along with photos of Monet and his family in the garden, this book offers paintings of the plantings in every part of this garden. This is an excellent source for showing water lily paintings.

Michels, Heide. *Monet's House: An Impressionist Interior.* Translated by Helen Ivor. Photos by Guy Bouchet. New York: Clarkson Potter, 1997. ISBN 0-517-70667-9.

There are photos of every room in Monet's house—even the clothes in his closet!

Murphy, Richard W. *The World of Cézanne.* New York: Time-Life, 1968. ISBN 0809402726.

Murphy examines Cézanne's work in light of the society in which he lived.

O'Connor, Patrick. *Nightlife of Paris: The Art of Toulouse-Lautrec.* New York: Universe, 1992. ISBN 0876636229.

Large reproductions accompanied by notes reveal Lautrec's view of Paris at night.

Pissarro, Joachim. *Monet's Cathedral.* New York: Alfred A. Knopf, 1990. ISBN 0394588711.

Large reproductions of the complete Rouen Cathedral series, including the time of day they were painted.

———. *Pioneering Modern Painting: Cézanne & Pissarro 1865–1885.* New York: Museum of Modern Art, 2005. ISBN 0-87070-184-3.

This is a fascinating comparison of Cézanne's and Pissarro's work to show how, although they are considered in two different categories, they both ushered in modern art. It is an excellent source of Cézanne's paintings for viewing.

Platzman, Steven. *Cézanne: The Self-Portraits.* Los Angeles: University of California Press, 2001. ISBN 0-520-23291-7.

This is a perfect source for viewing the artist's many self-portraits.

Plazy, Gilles. *In the footsteps of Van Gogh.* Photographs by Jean-Marie del Moral. New York: Penguin, 1997. ISBN 0-670-88250-X.

Plazy and del Moral bring readers to Holland and Provence, where van Gogh lived and worked, in this combination art, travel, and biography book.

Rathbone, Eliza E., ed. *Impressionists on the Seine: A Celebration of Renoir's Luncheon of the Boating Party*. Washington, DC: Counterpoint, 1996. ISBN 1887178309.

Impressionists such as Monet and Renoir painted many scenes along the Seine.

Rewald, John. *Cézanne*. New York: Harry N. Abrams, 1986. ISBN 0810907755.

Rewald discusses Cézanne's life and work. Beautiful, large reproductions.

Rishel, Joseph J., et al. *Van Gogh Face to Face: The Portraits*. New York: Thames & Hudson, 2000. ISBN 0500092907.

This beautiful book has 200 color reproductions of portraits painted by the artist. There are many drawings and many self-portraits as well.

Russell, Vivian. *Monet's Water Lilies*. Boston: Little, Brown, 1998. ISBN 0-8212-2553-7.

Gorgeous photographs of water lilies along with Monet's paintings and an explanation of how the artist chose the plants for his garden grace this lovely book.

Schapiro, Meyer. *Cézanne*. New York: Harry N. Abrams, 1988. ISBN 0810910438.

A brief life of the artist is followed by detailed discussions of many of his works. Large reproductions.

Smith, Paul. *Interpreting Cézanne*. New York: Stewart, Tabori & Chang. 1996. ISBN 155670464-X.

Published in conjunction with the 1996 Cézanne exhibit in Philadelphia, this work seeks to find the right way to see the artist's work.

Spate, Virginia. *Claude Monet: The Color of Time*. New York: Thames & Hudson, 2001. ISBN 0-500-28273-0.

Spate offers a complete study of the artist's work using more than 300 illustrations. There are many large prints for viewing.

Stuckey, Charles F. *Claude Monet 1840–1926*. New York: Thames & Hudson, 1995. ISBN 0865591342.

This lovely books is an excellent source of some of Monet's series paintings.

Thomson, Richard, et al. *Toulouse-Lautrec and Montmartre*. Princeton, NJ: Princeton University Press, 2005. ISBN 0-691-12337-3

This book contains the important paintings, drawings, prints, and posters Toulouse-Lautrec made on Montmartre subjects as well as paintings by his contemporaries. It has 370 color plates.

Tinterow, Gary, and Henri Loyrette. *Origins of Impressionism*. New York: Metropolitan Museum of Art/Harry N. Abrams, 1994. ISBN 0-87099-717-3.

Published in conjunction with an exhibit at the Metropolitan Museum of Art, this is a marvelous collection of paintings highlighting many aspects of Impressionist art.

Todd, Pamela. *The Impressionists at Home*. London: Thames & Hudson, 2005. ISBN 978-0-500-51239-5.

This gorgeous book affords readers the opportunity to see the Impressionists at home—theirs and their patrons'. Full-page color reproductions of the paintings of Cassatt, Monet, Degas, Manet, Renoir, and others are included.

Tucker, Paul Hayes. *Claude Monet: Life and Art.* 1995. Reprint, New Haven, CT: Yale University Press, 1998. ISBN 0300072864.

Monet's life is seen through his work.

Tucker, Paul Hayes, et al. *Monet in the 20th Century.* Boston: Museum of Fine Arts, 1998. ISBN 0-300-07749-1.

This is a catalog of an exhibition that presents the artist's work in his later years. It has a wonderful foldout section of the water lilies.

Vigne, Georges. *Ingres.* Translated by John Goodman. New York: Abbeville Press, 1995. ISBN 0789200600.

Vigne discusses the artist's work, accompanied by reproductions.

Weckler, Charles. *Impressions of Giverny: Monet's World.* New York: Harry N. Abrams, 1990. ISBN 0810911329.

Incredible photographs using the grain structure of color film show the interior of the house and the gardens at Giverny. A must!

Children's Books

Anholt, Laurence. *Camille and the Sunflowers.* Hauppauge, NY: Barron's Educational Series, 1994. ISBN 0812064097.

Based on a true story, this picture book relates how the postman's daughter met Vincent van Gogh in Arles. Some of the artist's paintings are included in the book.

———. *Degas and the Little Dancer.* Hauppauge, NY: Barron's Educational Series, 1996. ISBN 0812065832.

This is a picture-book story about Degas and his statue of the young ballet dancer.

Armstrong, Carole. *Cézanne in the Studio: Still Life in Watercolors.* Los Angeles: J. Paul Getty Museum, 2004. ISBN 0-89236-623-0.

Armstrong examines the artist's series of watercolor still life paintings.

———. *Van Gogh; My Sticker Art.* London: Frances Lincoln, 1996. ISBN 1845072154.

This exploration of Van Gogh's life and art, includes twenty-five peelable, reusable sticker reproductions of the artist's most popular paintings and clues about where to place them in the book. *My Monet Art Museum* by the same author is also available.

Bassil, Andrea. *Vincent Van Gogh.* Milwaukee, WI : Gareth Stevens/World Almanac Library, 2004. ISBN 0836856074.

Bassil combines photos and art reproductions to tell van Gogh's story.

Bernard, Bruce. *Van Gogh.* New York: Dorling Kindersley, 1999. ISBN 0-7894-4878-5.

This biography features photographs of the materials Van Gogh used to create his art as well as small reproductions of his work.

Bjork, Christina. *Linnea in Monet's Garden*. Illustrated by Lena Anderson. New York: Farrar, Straus & Giroux, 1987. ISBN 9129583144.

Linnea and her neighbor Mr. Bloom go to France to view Monet's works and his home at Giverny. See related videocassette.

Blizzard, Gladys S. *Come Look with Me: Exploring Landscape Art with Children*. Boston: Charlesbridge, 1996. ISBN 0934738955.

This book is designed to help children appreciate landscapes. Van Gogh's *Starry Night* is included.

Boggs, Jean Sutherland. *Degas*. Chicago: Art Institute of Chicago, 1996. ISBN 0-8109-6324-8.

A biography of the artist is followed by thirty-five full-page color plates.

Bucks, Brad, and Joan Holub. *Sunflowers and Swirly Stars*. New York: Grosset & Dunlap, 2001. ISBN 0448425211.

Readers learn about van Gogh's life and work through a report written by Bucks.

Burleigh, Robert. *Seurat and La Grande Jatte*. Chicago/New York: Art Institute of Chicago/ Harry Abrams, 2004. ISBN 0-8109-4811-7.

Burleigh describes the painstaking care with which Seurat prepared for and executed this painting and compares it to the work of other painters of Seurat's time. This is an absolute must for discussing Seurat.

———. *Toulouse-Lautrec : The Moulin Rouge and the City of Light*. New York: Harry N. Abrams, 2005. ISBN 0810958678.

This is a wonderful book in which the author uses both period photos and reproductions of the artist's work in the various media he used to present the author's life. Burleigh's writing is engaging and delightful.

Cassatt, Mary. *Baby Loves*. New York: Atheneum, 2003. ISBN 0689853408.

Sixteen of Cassatt's paintings depicting mothers and babies, along with two-word descriptors, are the subject of this tiny, beautiful book for young children.

Cole, Kristin N. *Edgar Degas: Paintings that Dance*. New York: Grosset & Dunlap, 2001. ISBN 0-448-42611-0.

Degas's life is presented as a report written by a young school girl. In addition to small reproductions of the artist's work, some childlike illustrations accompany the "report".

Connolly, Sean. *Paul Cézanne: Life and Work*. Chicago: Heinemann Library, 2002. ISBN 1403404984.

This biography for very young children includes photographs and reproductions of the artist's work.

Crespi, Francesca. *A Walk in Monet's Garden: Full Color Pop-Up with Guided Tour*. New York: Bulfinch Press, 1995. ISBN 0821221957.

In one pocket of this book is a booklet about Monet's garden and in the other a fold-out pop-up that reveals the plantings in the garden as well as the houses on the property. This would make a delightful addition to a study of Monet.

Crispino, Enrica. *Van Gogh*. Illustrated by Simone Boni et al. New York: Peter Bedrick, 1996. ISBN 0-87226-525-0.

This excellent book has fine explanations of many of the artist's works and information about his contemporaries and the things that were happening in France during his lifetime.

Esbensen, Barbara Juster. *Dance with Me*. Illustrated by Megan Lloyd. New York: HarperCollins, 1995. ISBN 0060227931.

This is a collection of poems about dance in nature.

Fleming, Denise. *In the Tall, Tall Grass*. New York: Henry Holt, 1991. ISBN 080501635X.

In delicious rhyming text, Fleming describes the critters that lurk in the tall grass. This is an excellent book to use to show how colors convey meaning.

Flux, Paul *Georges Seurat: Life and Work*. Chicago: Heinemann Library, 2002. ISBN 1403400016.

This biography for very young children includes photographs and reproductions of the artist's work.

Fritz, Jean. *You Want Women to Vote, Lizzie Stanton?* New York: Putnam, 1999. ISBN 0698117646.

Fritz's wonderful style is evident in this well-written account of women's efforts to win the vote.

Giesecke, Ernestine. *Mary Cassatt: Life and Work*. Chicago: Heinemann Library, 2001. ISBN 158810284X.

This biography for very young children includes photographs and reproductions of the artist's work.

Greenberg, Jan, and Sandra Jordan. *Vincent van Gogh: Portrait of an Artist*. New York: Delacorte/Random House, 2001. ISBN 0385328060.

This life of the artist begins with his boyhood and is enhanced with photographs and eight pages of color reproductions of his work.

Haas, Jesse. *Hoofprints: Horse Poems*. New York: Greenwillow, 2004. ISBN 0060534060.

Haas offers more than 100 poems about horses.

Hodge, Susie. *Claude Monet*. New York: Franklin Watts/Scholastic, 2002. ISBN 0531122263.

Small reproductions of the artist's work accompany this biography. There is information on the Impressionist palette and a glossary.

Hubbell, Patricia. *A Grass Green Gallop*. Illustrated by Ronald Himler. New York: Atheneum, 1990, ISBN 0689316046.

These poems celebrate various kinds of horses.

Isadora, Rachel. *Not Just Tutus*. New York: Putnam, 2003. ISBN 0399236031.

This is a delightful book of poetry for young children about ballet.

Isom, Joan Shaddox. *The First Starry Night.* Boston: Charlesbridge, 2001. ISBN 158089027X.

An orphan meets van Gogh in Arles and the artist leaves the boy paintings when he departs the village.

Kelley, True. *Claude Monet: Sunshine and Waterlilies.* New York: Grosset & Dunlop, 2001. ISBN 044842522X.

This biography of the artist is written as a child's school report. The cartoon illustrations are fun and readers will learn a good deal.

Kendall, Richard. *Degas Dancers.* New York: Universe/Rizzoli, 1996. ISBN 0-7893-0060-5.

In this small book a brief section of text in the beginning is followed by page after page of reproductions of Degas's paintings of dancers.

Knight, Joan MacPhail. *Charlotte in New York.* Illustrated by Melissa Sweet. San Francisco: Chronicle Books, 2006. ISBN 0811850056.

Charlotte, a fictitious daughter of a painter, who lives in Paris and has watched Claude Monet at work, travels with her family to New York, where she meets other Impressionist painters and supporters of the arts. Many artists studied in this book are included in the delightful story, along with some of their paintings and brief biographies.

Le Tord, Bijou. *A Blue Butterfly: A Story about Claude Monet.* New York: Doubleday, 1995. ISBN 0-885-31102-8.

Le Tord uses Monet's palette of only eight colors for the illustrations in this very simple story about the artist.

Levine, Robert. *Story of the Orchestra : Listen While You Learn About the Instruments, the Music and the Composers Who Wrote the Music!* Illustrated by Meredith Hamilton. New York: Black Dog & Leventhal Publishers, 2000. ISBN 1579121489.

Levine takes readers through a musical journey through the ages. The illustrations are humorous and there is an accompanying CD.

Littlesugar, Amy. *Marie in Fourth Position.* Illustrated by Ian Schoenherr. 1996. Reprint, New York: Putnam Juvenile, 1999. ISBN 0698117697

This is a picture-book story of the little girl who inspired Edgar Degas's wonderful sculpture called *The Little Dancer.*

Loumaye, Jacqueline. *Degas: The Painted Gesture.* New York: Chelsea House, 1994. ISBN 0791028097.

A group of young students make a study of Degas's work.

———. *Van Gogh: The Touch of Yellow.* New York: Chelsea House, 1994. ISBN 0791028178.

Two children and their uncle try to determine whether a painting is an authentic Van Gogh by traveling to the sites of his pictures and viewing his works in museums.

Mayhew, James. *Katie Meets the Impressionists.* New York: Scholastic, 1999. ISBN 0531301516.

When Katie goes to the museum with her grandmother, she is transported into paintings by Degas, Monet, and Renoir.

Merberg, Julie, and Suzanne Bober. *Dancing with Degas.* San Francisco: Chronicle Books, 2003. ISBN 0811840476.

This board book with rhyming text and illustrations by Degas offers very young children the opportunity to learn about his work.

———. *In the Garden with van Gogh.* San Francisco: Chronicle Books, 2002. ISBN 0811834158.

This board book with rhyming text and illustrations by van Gogh offers very young children the opportunity to learn about his work.

———. *Sunday with Seurat.* San Francisco: Chronicle Books, 2005. ISBN 0-8118-4758-6.

In a board book with rhyming text, the authors make some of Seurat's most famous works available to very young children.

Muhlberger, Richard. *What Makes a Cassatt a Cassatt?* New York: Viking, 1994. ISBN 0670857424.

Muhlberger discusses twelve Cassatt works and what makes them unique.

———. *What Makes a Degas a Degas?* New York: Viking Juvenile, 2002. ISBN 0670035718.

This is a lively and interesting discussion of the various aspects of Degas's art.

———. *What Makes a Monet a Monet?* New York: Viking Juvenile, 2002. ISBN 067003570X.

Muhlberger discusses twelve paintings and the unique techniques used by Monet in creating his art.

———. *What Makes a Van Gogh a Van Gogh?* New York: Viking Juvenile, 2002. ISBN 0670035734.

Muhlberger discusses twelve paintings and the characteristics that make them uniquely Van Gogh's.

O'Connor, Jane. *Mary Cassatt: Family Pictures.* Illustrated by Jennifer Kalis. New York: Grosset & Dunlap, 2003. ISBN 0448431521.

Claire finds out all about Mary Cassatt when she does a report on the artist for school. Cassatt's best-loved paintings are included in this picture book.

Raimondo, Joyce. *Picture This! Activities and Adventures in Impressionism.* New York: Watson-Guptill, 2004. ISBN 0-8230-2503-9.

Using the work of Monet, Renoir, Degas, Pissarro, and Cassatt, Raimondo studies one of each artist's paintings and then suggests follow-up activities. The depiction of children's artwork is especially charming.

Richter, Joanne. *Inventing the Camera.* New York: Crabtree Publishers, 2006. ISBN 0778728366.

Richter describes how the camera was invented.

Rubin, Susan Goldman. *Degas and the Dance: The Painter and the Petits Rats, Perfecting Their Art.* New York: Harry N. Abrams, 2002. ISBN 0-8109-0567-1.

In this delightful picture book, Rubin shows Degas as he studies dancers behind the scenes while they practice. More than thirty of the artist's paintings grace this book.

———. *The Yellow House: Vincent van Gogh & Paul Gauguin Side by Side.* Illustrated by Joseph A. Smith. Chicago: Art Institute of Chicago/Harry N. Abrams, 2001. ISBN 0-8109-4588-6.

Using quotes from both artists, Rubin tells the story of Gauguin's stormy time with van Gogh in Arles. A life of each artist, author's note, and bibliography are included.

Russell, Vivian. *Monet's Landscapes.* Boston: Bulfinch/Little, Brown, 2000. ISBN 0-8212-2672-X.

Photographs of the actual locations are placed alongside Monet's paintings of the scene.

Sabbeth, Carol. *Monet and the Impressionists for Kids.* Chicago: Chicago Review Press, 2002. ISBN 1-55652-397-1.

Sabbeth provides a wonderful introduction to Impressionist art and suggests more than twenty activities to help children understand its meaning.

Sagner-Duchting, Karin. *Monet at Giverny.* Translated by John Brownjohn. New York: Prestel Publishing, 1994. ISBN 3791313843.

This is an introduction to the artist's contribution to Impressionism and an analysis of his haystacks and water lilies series.

Salvi, Francesco. *The Impressionists: The Origins of Modern Painting.* Illustrated by L. R. Galante and Andrea Ricciardi. New York: Peter Bedrick, 2001. ISBN 0872263142.

Salvi sets the stage for the appearance of Impressionism in Paris.

Sellier, Marie. *Cézanne from A to Z.* New York: Peter Bedrick, 1996. ISBN 0872264769.

Information on the artist is arranged in alphabetical order.

Springer, Nancy. *Music of Their Hooves.* Illustrated by Sandy Rabinowitz. Honesdale, PA: Wordsong/Boyds Mills Press, 1994. ISBN 1563971828.

This is a collection of poems about horses and their owners' feelings about them. Some excellent poems to accompany Degas's pictures of racehorses.

St. George, Judith. *So You Want to Be an Inventor?* Illustrated by David Smalls. New York: Philomel, 2002. ISBN 0778728366.

Lively text and humorous cartoon illustrations make this book a winner.

Sweeney, Joan. *Once Upon a Lily Pad.* Illustrated by Kathleen Fain. San Francisco: Chronicle Books, 1995. ISBN 0-8118-0868-8.

Two frogs who live in Monet's garden are convinced they are the subjects in his paintings as they watch him paint every day. A fold-out reproduction of one of the artist's lily pad paintings is included.

———. *Suzette and the Puppy : A Story About Mary Cassatt.* Illustrated by Jennifer Heyd Wharton. Hauppage, NY: Barron's. ISBN 0764152947.

In this fictional story of the famous Cassatt painting *The Little Girl in the Blue Armchair,* Suzette's uncle, Edgar Degas, commissions Mary Cassatt to paint his niece's picture, and the artist includes her own dog in the portrait.

Thomson, Belinda. *Van Gogh.* New York: Harry N. Abrams/Art Institute of Chicago, 2001. ISBN 0-8109-6738-3.

In this fine biography, Thomson often uses van Gogh's own words to describe his paintings and offers works of other artists of the time as well.

Turner, Robyn Montana. *Mary Cassatt.* Boston: Little, Brown, 1992. ISBN 0316856509.

This is a very readable biography of the artist with a few color prints.

van Gogh, Vincent. *Vincent's Colors.* San Francisco: Chronicle Books/Metropolitan Museum of Art, 2005. ISBN 1-58889-155-8.

In rhyming text taken from the artist's own words, children are introduced to the many colors in these beautifully reproduced paintings.

van Gogh, Vincent, and Bruce Bernard. *Van Gogh: Explore Vincent van Gogh's Life and Art, and the Influences That Shaped His Work.* Edited by Phil Hunt. New York: DK Children, 2000. ISBN 0789448785.

This is a fine examination of the artist's life and work, including large details of some of his paintings.

Venezia, Mike. *Degas.* Danbury, CT: Children's Press, 2001. ISBN 0516271725.

This is a simple biography of the artist.

———. *Henri de Toulouse-Lautrec.* Chicago: Children's Press. Reprint, Danbury, CT: Children's Press, 1995. ISBN 0516422839.

This is a simple biography of the artist featuring some works by Toulouse-Lautrec as well as cartoon illustrations.

———. *Monet.* Chicago: Children's Press, 1990. Reprint, Danbury, CT: Children's Press, 1990. ISBN 0516422766.

Using cartoon illustrations, Venezia presents a very simple life of Monet for young children.

———. *Seurat.* Danbury, CT: Children's Press, 2003. ISBN 0516278134.

The author presents Seurat in a format that is easy for children to understand.

———. *Van Gogh.* Danbury, CT: Children's Press, 1989. ISBN 051642274X.

This very simple life of Van Gogh for young children features cartoon illustrations as well as works by the artist.

Waldman, Neil. *The Starry Night.* Honesdale, PA: Boyds Mills Press, 1999. ISBN 1-56397-736-2.

A boy meets an artist named Vincent in Central Park in New York City, and from that moment looks at his world differently. Waldman has infused his own childhood discovery of van Gogh into this fantasy, and his illustrations imitate the drawings and paintings of the artist.

Wenzel, Angela. *Dance Like a Butterfly.* New York: Prestel Publishing, 2002. ISBN 3791327364.

Children are encouraged to look at the sights and colors of the ballet and discover why Degas was attracted to it.

White, Linda Arms. *I Could Do That! : Esther Morris Gets Women the Vote.* Illustrated by Nancy Carpenter. New York: Farrar, Straus & Giroux, 2005. ISBN 0374335273.

In this picture book White tells the story of Esther Morris's efforts to get the vote for women in Wyoming.

Woodhouse, Jayne. *Edgar Degas: Life and Work.* Chicago: Heinemann Library, 2002. ISBN 1403400008.

One of a series of biographies for very young children, this book presents the artist's life, some photographs, and reproductions of the artist's work.

Audiovisual Materials

Allen, Norman. *Mary Cassatt: A Brush with Independence.* Video. Home Vision, 2005. Cat/# CAS040.

This shows Cassatt as the independent woman she was and her acceptance into the colony of French Impressionists in Paris.

Awareness Series: Modern Masters. Video. National Gallery of Art, n.d. VC120.

This video presents short studies of the works of Monet, Renoir, Degas, Cassatt, Gauguin, Cézanne, and Picasso.

Degas: At the Races. Slides and booklet. National Gallery of Art, n.d. 064.

These slides present Degas's paintings and drawings of horses and riders and are an excellent source for the viewing section of the lesson on Degas.

Degas: The Dancers. Slides and audiocassette. National Gallery of Art, n.d. 054.

This program discusses the artist's style and technique and fascination with the dance.

Great Women Artists: Mary Cassatt. DVD. Kultur, 2001. ISBN 0-7697-8096-2.

This film presents Cassatt's focus on painting children.

Impressionism. Slides and text. National Gallery of Art, n.d. 041.

These slides show the outgrowth of Post-Impressionism from the Impressionist movement.

Impressionism and Post-Impressionism. Library Video Company, 1999. V8157.

This program features van Gogh and Degas.

The Impressionists: The Other French Revolution. DVD. A&E Home Video, 2001 Cat#: AAE-70245. ISBN 0-7670-3798-7.

Focusing on the work of Renoir, Monet, Degas, Pissarro, and Morisot, this film tells the story of the revolutionary Impressionist movement.

The Impressionists Box Set. DVD. Kultur Video, 2006. Catalog Code: D1577. ASIN B000E3LCZO.

These films highlight the work of Monet, Seurat, Pissarro, Manet, Degas, and Renoir.

The Impressionists Collection. Video. Library Video Company, 1999. A0205.

Gauguin, Toulouse-Lautrec, Cézanne, van Gogh, Degas, Renoir, Manet, and Monet are featured in this video.

The Inquiring Eye: French Impressionism and Post-Impressionism. Slides, prints, booklet. National Gallery of Art, n.d. TP311.

This program presents the art and history of nineteenth-century French painting, with emphasis on the Impressionist movement.

Life & Works of Claude Monet: A Painter of Light. Video. Library Video Company, 2002. A0681.

Middle school students will enjoy this presentation of the artist's life and works. Younger children can view the video without the sound.

Life & Works of Paul Cézanne: The Art of Drawing. Library Video Company, 2002. A0695.

In addition to the artist's life and works, this video provides step-by-step instructions for drawing a still life.

Linnea in Monet's Garden. Video. Library Video Company, 1993. K9951.

This is an animated version of the delightful book listed in the children's book references.

Mary Cassatt: American Impressionist. DVD. Library Video Company, 1999. V9645.

This film presents the life and work of the artist.

Monet. Video. gettingtoknow.com, 1999. MONT0101.

Winner of the 2004 ALA Notable Children's Video Award, this video is based on the book by Mike Venezia. It combines animation and presentation of actual works by the artist. Young children will love it.

Monet: Shadow and Light. Video. Library Video Company, 2000. K2471.

Children are introduced to Monet's life and work.

Music of the Ballet. CD. New York: Metropolitan Museum of Art, n.d. N1065.

This CD contains music from some of the world's most famous ballets, including *The Nutcracker* and *Sleeping Beauty*. Sixty minutes.

Paul Cézanne: The Man and the Mountain. DVD. Home Vision, 2000. ASIN 6303317073.

This program provides views of the countryside in which the artist lived, his works, and quotes from his writings.

Post Impressionists Boxed Set. DVD. Kultur Video, 2006. ASIN B000FC2HPY.

Seurat. DVD. Library Video Company, 1999. V8173.

This film shows Seurat's pointillism technique.

Sunday in the Park with George. DVD. Library Video Company, 1986. V0213.

Older students may enjoy this film of the Broadway play centered around Seurat's painting *A Sunday Afternoon on the Island of Grand Jatte.* It stars Bernadette Peters and Mandy Patinkin.

Toulouse-Lautrec and Montmartre. DVD. Home Vision, 2004. ASIN B0007989SE.

This film examines the artist's life and work through footage of Montmartre and interviews.

Van Gogh. gettingtoknow.com, 2001. VOGH0201.

Winner of the 2004 ALA Notable Children's Video Award, this video is based on the book by Mike Venezia. It combines animation and presentation of actual works by the artist. Young children will love it.

Van Gogh: Visions of Reality. DVD. Claervue & SVE, 2005. W64DV9342.

This film presents the life and work of the artist.

"Vincent." A song by Don McLean. CD. Available on Don McLean's album, *American Pie*, from EMI Records Group North America.

Older students may enjoy this tribute to Vincent Van Gogh in which McClean sings about the artist's talent and his troubled spirit. View the painting *Starry Night* as you listen.

Vincent van Gogh. Slides and booklet. National Gallery of Art, n.d. 065.

This program uses van Gogh's drawings and letters to help viewers understand his art.

Other Materials

Boutan, Mila. *Art Activity Pack: Cézanne.* San Francisco: Chronicle Books, 1996. ISBN 0811813339.

This packet contains a booklet on the artist's life, some reproductions, an artist's notebook that provides some drawing activities for children based on the artist's work, and a large poster for children to color

———. *Art Activity Pack: Degas.* San Francisco: Chronicle Books, 1997. ISBN 0811816885.

This packet contains a booklet on the artist's life, some reproductions, an artist's notebook that provides some drawing activities for children based on the artist's work, and a large poster for children to color

———. *Art Activity Pack: Monet.* San Francisco: Chronicle Books, 1996. ISBN 0811813355.

This packet contains a booklet on the artist's life, some reproductions, an artist's notebook that provides some drawing activities for children based on the artist's work, and a large poster for children to color.

———. *Art Activity Pack: Renoir.* San Francisco: Chronicle Books, 1997. ISBN 0811816907.

This packet contains a booklet on the artist's life, some reproductions, an artist's notebook that provides some drawing activities for children based on the artist's work, and a large poster for children to color.

———. *Art Activity Pack: Van Gogh.* San Francisco: Chronicle Books, 1996. ISBN 0811813126.

This packet contains a booklet on the artist's life, some reproductions, an artist's notebook that provides some drawing activities for children based on the artist's work, and a large poster for children to color.

The Impressionist Art Game. Card game. Palo Alto, CA: Birdcage Press, n.d. ISBN 1-889613-06-1.

Children learn the stories behind artworks by Impressionist artists while they play cards.

Impressionist Go Fish for Art. Card game. Palo Alto, CA: Birdcage Press, n.d. ISBN 1-889613-13-4.

A deck of thirty-two playing cards and a guide to the artists help children learn about Impressionist artists while having fun playing "Go Fish."

Van Gogh and Friends Art Game. Card game. Palo Alto, CA: Birdcage Press, n.d. ISBN 1-889613-09-6.

Children learn about the art of van Gogh, Cézanne, and others while having fun.

Van Gogh and Friends Go Fish for Art. Card game. Palo alto, CA: Birdcage Press, n.d. ISBN 1-889613-14-2.

Children learn about the art of van Gogh and others while playing "Go Fish."

Van Gogh & Kids CD-ROM. CD-ROM. Metropolitan Museum of Art, n.d. M8128.

In this game, children need to unscramble pieces to put van Gogh's works where they belong.

Web Sites

Birdcage Press. http://www.birdcagebooks.com/lc_impart.html (accessed September 11, 2006).

This site provides links to audiovisual tours, teacher resources and other information for an examination of Impressionist art.

Birdcage Press. http://www.birdcagebooks.com/lc_vgf.html (accessed September 11, 2006).

This site provides links to audiovisual tours, teacher resources and other information for an examination of Post-Impressionist art.

Inside Art. http://www.eduweb.com/insideart/index.html (accessed March 26, 2006).

This marvelous site provides an art game. Children go inside a painting—one of van Gogh's, and other artists are available as well (Monet and Cézanne). To get out, children have to answer some questions. There's a teacher guide.

Teach Impressionism. http://www.impressionism.org/teachimpress/default.htm (accessed March 26, 2006).

There are eight lesson plans for teaching Impressionism. Activities are included.

Vincent. http://www.e-wollmann.com/the.htm (accessed March 26, 2006).

Students can listen to Don McLean's song "Vincent" by clicking on a link on this page.

Part VI
The Art of America

14 Arts of Native America

The parents said, "This has been the struggle of our People.
We have suffered but we have endured."
"Listen," they said, and they sang the songs.
"Listen," they said, "and they told the stories."
"Listen," they said, "this is the way our People live."

—SIMON ORTIZ, *The People Shall Continue*

Background Information

There is some uncertainty about when the first humans came to North America. Some scientists say they may have come as early as 50,000 years ago, following herds of animals across a broad land mass stretching between Asia and Alaska. Surely they were here 10,000 years ago, for their artifacts tell us a good deal about their lives and customs. A huge glacier covered North America over thousands of years, alternately advancing and retreating until the Ice Age came to an end about 9000 BC. Then the land bridge was submerged under water that we now call the Bering Strait, and the peoples who had come over to the North American side were here to stay.

Scientists call these early Americans "Paleo-Indians." Some thrived in the harsh climate of the north and remained there. Their descendants are the present-day Inuit living in Canada and Alaska. Others, ever on the hunt for food, spread over millennia across the continent, traveling southward even into Mexico and eastward to the woodlands of New England and the marshes of present-day Florida. Adapting to the environments in these vastly different regions, these peoples formed tribes and devised ways to survive and prosper.

The "Indians" received their name by accident, because Christopher Columbus, arriving in waters off North America in 1492, believed he had discovered a route to India and named the people he found on the land "Indians." This became a general term for native peoples, but it is more common now to call them "Native Americans." Native Americans, of course, comprise many different tribes, and rather than the generic term "Native American," they prefer to be called by their unique tribe names.

Columbus and other Europeans who came to these shores considered the people they found here to be inferior, primitive savages who needed to be civilized by their superior European selves. In reality, however, Native Americans had by the fifteenth century created highly complex civilizations, languages, customs, and spiritualities; invented many things we use today such as hammocks and snowshoes; built structures that rival the pyramids of Egypt; and developed crops such as corn and squash (see *Food, Farming , and Hunting, Science and Technology* and *Medicine and Health* in the resources). Their contributions were and continue to be numerous and invaluable, but we concentrate here on only one—their highly sophisticated and beautiful art. Although most Native Americans made baskets and pottery, there are specific arts that were intimately bound to the different environments in which the tribes lived.

Even after the land bridge was submerged, some people left Asia and came to the new continent by sled over the polar caps. They never traveled south into warmer climes but remained in the frozen lands stretching from Alaska to Greenland. Known to Europeans as "Eskimos," which means "eaters of raw meat" in their language, they prefer their own name for themselves, "Inuit," which means "real people." Life in this frozen land was harsh and difficult. Some Inuit lived along the coast and hunted whales, seals, and walrus. These animals provided all they needed for sustenance: food, clothing, and oil for light and heat. They also provided materials for artwork: ivory and bones from which the people carved beautiful figures, many of them made to please animals and entice them to offer themselves up to the hunt. Other Inuit were nomads, following herds of caribou and musk ox across the tundra.

The tribes of Native Americans who lived along the Northwest coast of the continent derived their livelihood from the abundance of the sea and the surrounding woods. The waters teemed with salmon, and the forests provided big game and magnificent cedars from which the people built canoes, houses, and items for daily living. Because the climate was generally mild and life relatively easy, these Native Americans had ample time to create works of art, and they used the abundance of cedar trees to carve replicas of the animals that gave them life. These status-conscious peoples gave away their possessions in potlatch (gift-exchanging) celebrations to broadcast their wealth, and proudly carved and painted their family histories into huge poles, known today as totem poles, which they displayed outside their homes.

When white settlers arrived in California in the eighteenth century, there were over 130,000 Native Americans already living there, speaking over seventy different languages (Griffin-Pierce 1995, 137). Food gathering for these peoples was easy because of the favorable climate, the abundance of woodlands, and the proximity to water. The Native Americans of California, especially those in the center of the region, made some of the finest baskets in the world. In addition to beautiful baskets, those in the north, where wood was plentiful, made wood carvings, houses, and canoes, while those in the south made pottery.

The Native Americans living in the Great Basin, that region stretching between the Sierra Nevada mountain range in California and the Rocky Mountains in Colorado, had to adapt to a harsh land. They faced an arid, blistering-hot desert in summer and subzero temperatures in winter, traveling from place to place hunting and gathering food as best they could. Since these peoples spent much of their time gathering food, they had little left over to produce art. There was some basket- and pottery-making, and rabbit fur was woven into warm blankets for protection against the winter cold.

The southwest area of North America includes the present-day states of Arizona and New Mexico, southern Utah, and southwestern Colorado. It is in this area that we find evidence, such as rock paintings and ancient tools, of the oldest continuous inhabitants of the continent. The Native American peoples of the Southwest include three main groups: the Pueblo, which include the Anasazi and the Zuni; the Navajo and their close relatives, the Apache; and the desert tribes including the Pima, the Papago, and the Mojave (Glubok 1971, 3).

Native American Cliff Dwellings, Arizona

The ancient Pueblo built large two- to four-storied apartment dwellings out of stones and clay on natural stone shelves on the sides of steep mountains. They dug large round rooms called kivas into the ground and used them for special gatherings and ceremonies. These people were farmers who climbed hundreds of feet daily to reach their fields.

When drought drove them out of their cliff dwellings in the thirteenth century, they moved farther south, where they continued to farm and built small villages with homes made of clay. Although there was not much time for art, the Pueblo made pottery. Their descendants, the Hopi, are known for their beautiful baskets and pottery. Most of the Hopi ceremonies were conducted for the good of the community, and Hopi artists created Kachina masks, which their priests wore in special dances to obtain much-needed rain. They also made Kachina dolls to teach their children about the sacred Kachina cult. The Yuman peoples, who lived in lands made fertile by the Colorado River, farmed corn, beans, pumpkins, and melons. Other less fortunate Yuman groups had to depend on hunting and gathering and moved constantly to follow their food sources. The Pimans lived in the inhospitable desert, where farming was impossible, and they also hunted and gathered wild plants. These peoples made beautiful baskets and some pottery. The Navajo and Apache tribes were relative newcomers to the region, arriving from Canada in the fourteenth century. The Navajo lived in round domed houses called hogans. They farmed the land and did some hunting and gathering as well. Later they became sheep- and goat-herders. Navajo women are noted for their exquisitely designed blankets, while medicine men made special sand paintings for ceremonies to cure individuals from their ills. In the late nineteenth century, the Navajo also began producing silver and turquoise jewelry.

The Great Plains comprise the land from Canada south to Texas and from the Rocky Mountains east to the Mississippi River. This is a vast, open landscape, buffeted by extremes of heat and cold. The Native Americans who lived on the plains were of two groups. Those, such as the Omaha and the Osage, who lived near the Mississippi, were farmers who supplemented their diet with the buffalo that roamed the plains by the hundreds of thousands. They lived in dome-shaped lodges made of earth. The others, like the Sioux and the Cheyenne, were nomads who followed the buffalo herds and gathered wild plants. They lived in tipis made of poles and animal hides that the women could take down and set up easily when the tribe moved. When Europeans brought the horse to America (beginning in the sixteenth century), the lives of the Plains tribes changed dramatically, for they could hunt more easily and travel greater distances. Much of the art of the Plains tribes involved the buffalo. They made elaborately decorated clothing of buffalo skins embellished with colorful beads and other rawhide articles such as containers and robes. The Plains peoples also used feathers to create elaborate headpieces for battle or ceremonial dances.

The northeastern region of America extended from the Atlantic Ocean to the Mississippi. This land of lush forests was home to the Iroquois and Algonquin tribes. The Iroquois lived in longhouses made of wood and covered with tree bark. These structures housed several families, and many longhouses formed a settlement. The people lived off the fruits of the forest, using the animals and plants for food, shelter, and clothing. They also did some farming. The Algonquins who lived among the birch forests farther north made dome-shaped wigwams and, while they did some farming, relied heavily on the animals and plants of the forest for their needs. The Northeast Native Americans also used materials from the forest for their art. They made birch bark canoes and used other woods to make masks and implements. The animals supplied hides from which the people made clothing, beautifully decorated with beads introduced by the Europeans. They also made beads from seashells.

Tribes such as the Cherokee, the Creek, and the Seminole inhabited the fertile lands of the Southeast, bordering the Atlantic Ocean and the Gulf of Mexico. The people prospered in this land with a long growing season, forests filled with game and plants, and waters teeming with fish. Sequoyah, a Cherokee, was the only person in history to create a written language on his own (see *Sequoyah* in the references). The Cherokee also had their own schools and a written constitution. The peoples of the Southeast made pottery, wooden masks, baskets, and beautiful patchwork clothing.

All of the Native American tribes suffered once Europeans came to the continent. White settlers' ever-increasing thirst for land pushed native peoples farther and farther from their homes. The now infamous Trail of Tears migration, when the Cherokee were forced to move to western lands, resulted in the deaths of thousands of people. Tribes were decimated through hunger, war, and illnesses brought by the Europeans. Still they endured, and their descendants are here to pass on to us the rich heritage and wonderful arts of their ancestors. While the art of any of the tribes would make a delightful and worthwhile study, space will permit us to linger only on pottery and wood carving here. Nevertheless, there are many books in the references that will enable you to create additional lessons about other ancient Native American arts and even some contemporary artists should you wish to do so. (See especially *The Art of Dan Namingha* for beautiful reproductions of work by a contemporary artist who is a descendant of a famous Hopi potter.)

(Standards: Grades K-4 History: 5.1-2, 6-9, 22, 31-33, 43; Art Connections: 1,1-2, 4, 6-7)

LESSON 1: Woodcarvers of the Northwest Coast

The Story

Hundreds of years ago, a young boy named Swift Runner lived on the northwestern coast of what is now the United States with his parents and his relatives' families in a very large wooden house. The ancestors of these families were among the first people to come to our continent. Each family had its own space in the house, depending on how wealthy it was. The people did not have money as we do, but they showed their wealth in the number of canoes, blankets, shells, baskets, fancy wooden bowls, or other possessions they had.

It was almost winter. The salmon had been caught and dried for food. The women had made robes of cedar bark and bearskin. There would be storytelling and dancing in the long, cold evenings ahead. But this year was even more special. Everyone in Swift Runner's village was very excited, for their chief was building a beautiful new cedar house for himself and his relatives, and he would give a huge potlatch party when it was ready. Chiefs and people from neighboring villages would be invited, and Swift Runner would be able to play with friends he had not seen all year.

For months the best carver in the clan had been making a huge entrance pole for the chief's house. The whole village had followed the carver into the forest when he went to choose the special red cedar tree for the pole. It was perfectly straight, with hardly any bottom branches, and over seventy feet tall. It took many hours for the men to bring it down, and the strength of all the men in the village to carry it out of the forest. Now the carving was almost complete. Swift Runner had often watched the artist at work. He saw him carve the human watchman with his tall hat at the top of the pole so there would be someone to guard the families inside and warn them of danger. He saw the animal figures on the pole take shape slowly under the carver's skilled hands. All of these creatures told the story of the chief's ancestors and his tribe.

Finally, the big day arrived. People who had been traveling from early morning were pulling their canoes up onto the land, and crowds began to stream toward the chief's new home.

"Hold still," said Swift Runner's mother as she helped him put on his ceremonial clothes. "You will get ready much faster if you just calm down."

"But, Mother, the potlatch is about to begin. Hurry!" And before she could stop him, he ran to find his friends, who were gathered in front of the chief's immense new pole, their heads thrown back to see to its very top. How beautiful it was against the blue sky!

"Welcome, welcome," said the chief, as he handed the head of each household a gift. Everyone received something until the chief had nothing more to give. Then the eating began. Swift Runner had never seen so much food. Everyone ate as much as he or she could so they would not offend their host. The party went on and on far into the night. Storytellers told about how the people first came to be, about how the salmon came to fill the waters and the bear to live in the forests. Swift Runner had heard the stories before, but he never tired of them. They were the stories of his people. Someday he would tell them to his children, and they to their children. He would have his own special pole carved and give a potlatch party for the villages. But for now, it was enough to listen until he could no longer keep his eyes open and his parents carried him home. (You may wish to read *Raven: A Trickster Tale from the Pacific Northwest*—see references—to accompany this story.)

(Standards: Language Arts: Listening and Speaking 8.4)

Viewing the Art

Explain to the children that wood was a main resource for artwork among the peoples of the Pacific Northwest because they lived in the midst of an immense cedar forest. This wood was a perfect material since it was soft and easy to carve, yet resistant to weather and insects. Show the children as many examples of totem poles as you can. (See *Listening to Our Ancestors, From the Land of the Totem Poles, Looking at Totem Poles,* and *Totem Pole Indians of the Northwest* in the references. There are also two Web sites about totem poles listed in the references.) Explain that these poles often told a family's history. Point out the guardian figures at the top, the pointed hats, the animal figures. What colors did the Native Americans use to paint them? How did they make these colors? What animals do you see? You may wish to read Hoyt-Goldsmith's *Totem Pole* or Jensen's *Carving a Totem Pole* (see references) before or after you look at totem poles with the children. The tall tale *Totem Tale* (see references) would also be a very enjoyable addition. If you wish, you could show the children other art created by Northwest Coast peoples. Their wonderful, cone-shaped hats with wide brims to keep off the rain are very special. There are also marvelous figures, masks, bowls, and other implements carved from wood. (See *Native American Art* in the references for gorgeous pictures of these art treasures.)

Journal Writing

Each figure on a totem pole told the story of the person's family or the tribe. They all had special meaning. In preparation for the art activity to follow, invite the children to think about their own family stories. What figures would symbolize special family events or ancestors, such as great-grandparents? Have the children make a list of such figures and symbols and what they stand for.

(Standards: Language Arts: Writing 1.7, 23, 33-37)

Art/Drama Activity: Making a Totem Pole

Materials

- A piece of balsa wood about seven inches long and three inches wide for each student
- Extra small pieces of balsa wood

- Craft knives
- Paints, especially red and black
- Paintbrushes
- Clay

If the children are too young to use craft knives, they can just draw figures on the wood without carving them. Or you can use two or three individual, small cereal boxes taped together and covered with brown paper. Open extra cereal boxes flat so the children can cut out shapes such as arms or hats and glue them on their totem poles where appropriate.

Using the information from their journal writing, invite the children to make totem poles for their families. The poles should contain figures that tell their family stories. They should first draw the figures onto the wood or cardboard. They can then cut the shapes into the material as you wish. Additional features such as arms can be glued on. Paint the pole and anchor it in a small piece of clay. Display the mounted totem poles in the classroom.

(Standards: Visual Arts: 1-4.1-11)

LESSON 2: Pottery Makers of the Southwest

The Story

Sweet Corn lived hundreds of years ago with many families in a pueblo, a home made of clay mixed with straw, in a place that is now Arizona. She was a happy young girl, full of energy and fun. Sweet Corn earned her name well, for she loved to work in the corn, digging up the earth to plant the tiny kernels and watching to keep the hungry crows away from the precious crop.

But this day she was not running among the rows of corn. She was not practicing her pottery-making either. Every afternoon until a week ago she had been working hard with her aunt to learn to make pots and bowls of clay just the way her ancestors had before her. But then her aunt had become ill and could not help her with the clay. Sweet Corn and her mother brought her bowls of corn soup to make her strong. They put cool cloths on her forehead to help her endure the blistering heat of the day. The men had even performed special Kachina dances to bring cooling rains and health to those in the tribe who were ill, but Sweet Corn's aunt had continued to grow weaker. And yesterday she had died. Already Sweet Corn missed her. So she was sitting quietly behind the pueblo filling her mind with memories of her aunt, of the hours they worked together grinding corn and working the clay. She was thinking of her aunt's beautiful clay pots—of the one that had been chosen for a special ceremony, of the ones that had been traded to other tribes, of the ones that the family used for carrying water and storing corn meal. Her mother was going to choose one of her aunt's best pots for the burial rite. Sweet Corn wondered which one it would be.

The next day, everyone in the tribe gathered to help Sweet Corn's aunt go to the Spirit World. They carried her body to the burial grounds, where a grave had already been dug. The priests did special dances while the people sang burial chants. Then Sweet Corn's mother presented one of her aunt's bowls to the chief priest. He held it high for all the people to admire and, using a small tool, cracked a hole in the middle of the bowl, then placed the bowl right over the dead woman's face.

"This woman made this bowl while she was among us," he said. "Now she will take it with her into the next world. Spirit of the woman, see, I have carved a hole for you to leave her and go out into the Spirit World. Be happy there forever."

Sweet Corn listened carefully to the priest's words. They made her feel better, because she knew her aunt would continue to live and be happy in the next life. She joined in the final chanting with a happier heart.

The next day Sweet Corn gathered some clay all by herself. She mixed it with water to soften it and added sand as she had seen her aunt do many times. When it was soft enough for her to work with her hands, she rolled the clay into long ropes and began to coil the clay ropes around and around, building up the sides into a bowl of her very own. She worked quietly, remembering her aunt's careful instructions. Soon the clay began to take shape. Sweet Corn looked down at her work.

"Aunt," she said, "you are now in the Spirit World, but in a way you are with me, too. I can remember your words and use your instructions to make bowls. I can continue your work so that our people will always have pots for their food and their ceremonies. Thank you, aunt, for passing your art on to me for the good of our people." Sweet Corn slept with contentment that night.

(Standards: Language Arts: Listening and Speaking 8.4)

Viewing the Art

Show the children as many examples of pottery made by Southwestern tribes as you can. Many of the books listed in the references have exquisite reproductions (see especially *Native American Art,* pages 123–173; *Casas Grandes and the Ceramic Art of the Ancient Southwest;* and *The Pueblo*). Notice the designs. Some are geometric, while others have animal or even human figures. Most have a cream-colored background with designs painted in red, black, and sometimes white. Some are red. The children may also enjoy seeing some Kachina dolls (see *North American Indian* in the references). *Enduring Traditions: Art of the Navajo*, in addition to the pictures of pottery, shows some exquisite Navajo turquoise jewelry. McIntosh's *Pueblo* shows some Pueblo artists, including a young boy, at work with clay.

(Standards: Art Connections 1.1-8; Language Arts: Viewing 9.6, 23)

Journal Writing

Native Americans believed that art was for the good of the people, not just an individual talent to profit a single person. What do the children think of this concept? Can they think of ways in which they or others can use a talent for the good of the group? Can they think of other artwork made for all people (e.g., Mexican murals, cave paintings, Renaissance architecture)? How are these things the same? Different?

(Standards: Language Arts: Writing 1.7, 23, 33-37; Thinking and Reasoning: 3.3)

Art/Drama Activity: Pottery

Materials

- Self-hardening clay (white or cream if possible, otherwise red)
- Reproductions of Native American pottery designs for the children to copy
- Red, black, white paint
- Paintbrushes
- Fine sandpaper

Have the children make clay bowls. Begin by working the clay so that it is soft and malleable. Then roll it into long strips. Coil the strips around a few times until the base is as large as desired, then begin building up the sides. When the sides are completed, try smoothing out the piece as much as possible so that the coils no longer show. Allow to dry and harden for several days. Sand gently and then paint designs.

Encourage the children to work quietly and contemplatively as the Indian potters probably did. You may wish to read aloud Byrd Baylor's beautiful book, *When Clay Sings* (see references), as they work.

Additional Activities

- Have a Native American feast, complete with dancing and authentic foods. See *A Native American Feast* by Penner (in the references) for information and recipes.
- Learn and play some Native American games. See *Native American Games and Stories* (in the references).
- Share some Native American literature at the feast, such as folktales and/or poetry. There are many books listed in the references to use as sources.
- Visit a museum to view Native American artwork.

- Learn some words in any of the Native American languages (see *Sequoyah* in the references). Listen to the CD that comes with *Coyote Steals Fire: A Shoshone Tale.* Children will be able to hear the Shoshone language. Also, go to http://www.nativetech.org/games/ojibwemowin/index.html to learn some Ojibwe words.
- Research the different groups of people mentioned in the background information. Illustrate your findings on a large mural, being sure to include types of houses, dress, ways of obtaining food, kind of art, etc.
- Locate the tribes the children research on a map.
- Make replicas of different types of Native American homes: longhouses, tipis, hogans, pueblos, etc.
- Perform one of the plays in *Pushing up the Sky: Seven Native American Plays for Children* (see references).
- Find out more about corn, a crop given us by Native Americans. What are some ways it is used today? Talk about its role in providing fuel (see *The Story of Corn* in the references).

(Standards: Theater: 2.1.9; Geography: 1-2.30; Grades K-4 History: 7.1-2, 6, 22, 27, 33)

Note: Curriculum connections and references are at the end of chapter 17.

15 Colonial Historical Painting

I have (God be praised) passed through the many dangers of the seas and am now at my studies with Mr. West who gives me encouragement to persue my plan of painting and promises me all the instruction he is capable of giving.

—CHARLES WILLSON PEALE TO JOHN BEALE BORDLEY, London, 1767

Background Information

For most of the Europeans newly settled there the colonial period in America was a time of intense hardship and industry. Obtaining food and shelter was the first order of business. Land needed to be cleared, crops put in, houses built. But eventually life improved, and cities and towns began to spring up. By the eighteenth century, many Americans were well established in trades. They were able to build bigger and better homes, and looked to decorate them. Architects copied the Georgian style popular in England, and the furniture within the houses they built was made by American craftsmen who copied such English masters as Chippendale and Hepplewhite.

Because the Puritans of New England were a sober group, they disdained ostentatious decoration, but they cherished portraits of family members. Since many people died young and children often did not survive beyond infancy, these portraits served as reminders of loved ones no longer present and as a record of family history. Dutch colonists, as they had in their homeland, favored portraits, still lifes, and paintings of ordinary folk engaged in their daily activities. Coming from a land in which the sea played such an important part, they loved seascapes as well. However, because they were working so hard to conquer the wilderness, they, and other newcomers to America as well, had no desire to grace their homes with landscapes.

While wealthy plantation owners in the southern colonies were able to import their art from England, those in the north looked mainly to local talent. The country was too young for established schools of art, so for many years there were no trained American artists. Some European artists came to the New World to earn their living, and they were kept busy painting portraits and other works for people eager to duplicate the amenities they had left behind. But many portraits were painted by sign painters or decorators who used stencils to emulate English wallpaper patterns. These self-taught artists, both men and women, traveled from town to town offering their skills to interested families. Most of their delightful pictures were unsigned, and many, especially those that were not portraits, have not survived. But enough have to give us a wonderful glimpse of life in eighteenth- and nineteenth-century America.

As the nation grew and prospered, Americans became more and more self-sufficient. American-born artists began to engage in formal study and to rise in prominence like their European counterparts. Eventually, Americans would establish art schools to rival those in the Old World, but in the nation's infancy, artists had to travel to Europe to study. Even in the tumultuous years of the American Revolution there were those who managed such travels—men like John Singleton Copley, Gilbert Stuart, Benjamin West, and Charles Willson Peale—who have given us portraits of all the great leaders of their day. Their work and pioneering spirit paved the way for artists who would come after them to record the people, the landscape, and the ideas of this immense and diverse country.

(Standards: Grades K–4 History: 3-4.1, 16; Art Connections: 1,1-2, 4, 6-7)

LESSON 1: Benjamin West (1738–1820)

The Story

"Father is dead, Benjamin," said his brother, Raphael. "At last his sufferings are over. We must tell the people of England that their great painter is gone."

Slowly the two young men closed their father's eyes and pulled the sheets up over his face. Then they quietly left the room to notify the authorities of the death of their father, the great painter Benjamin West. For days all of England mourned. Many lined the streets for his funeral. Then Raphael and Benjamin Jr. began the sad business of packing up hundreds of their father's paintings. They planned to travel to the United States to convince the representatives in Congress to set up a museum in Philadelphia, where their father was born, and to put his pictures there so Americans could enjoy the work of their first great American-born painter.

As they worked, they began to talk about their father. "How did he ever become an artist?" asked young Benjamin. "He grew up in a little village in Pennsylvania where there were no pictures at all. The people there were Quakers and didn't believe in decorating their houses with art."

"But remember," answered Raphael, "Grandfather's friend showed Father a picture when he came to visit, and from that moment on, Father wanted to paint pictures of his own. It was hard, because he had no materials—not even a brush—and his parents didn't believe in painting pictures!"

"Well, I'm glad they didn't stop him," said Benjamin. "They didn't even punish him when they found out he had cut fur off his cat's tail to make a paintbrush! Poor cat! I'll bet he didn't like the idea one bit!" (You might want to read *Benjamin West and His Cat Grimalkin* and/or *The Boy Who Loved to Draw*—see references.)

"No, I guess not," said his brother. "But once Father had a brush, and the Indians living in the woods nearby taught him how to use plants and tree bark to make colors, there was no stopping him. He just painted picture after picture." For days the brothers continued to prepare and crate their father's pictures and to talk about his long career as an artist.

A few weeks later, the two men boarded a ship for America. It was the year 1820, and the new country had already fought a war with England for independence and another war in 1812 to remain free of England's control. So when Raphael and Benjamin appeared before the representatives in Congress, some of the members were not happy that Benjamin West had spent his whole adult life in England, the country that had so recently been an enemy. "Why should we build a museum to honor a man who left us for England?" they asked.

"But, sirs," replied Raphael. "Our father had to leave because there were no art schools at all in America where he could study. Even as a teenager he was painting fine portraits, but he wanted to become even better. He needed to learn from the work of the great masters, so he went to Italy and then to England. The English people loved his work so much that they begged him to stay. The king of England made him his special painter, and the Royal Academy of Art made him its president. Many English nobles asked him to paint pictures for them. The years just passed, and he never had a chance to return home. But he never stopped loving America. He always asked for news of his country, especially during the Revolutionary War, which saddened him greatly. And when other American artists came to England to study, he always helped them. I can remember our house always full of struggling artists taking lessons from father. And he never even charged them for his services!"

Then one of the representatives stood up. "What these two young men say is true. My nephew went to England to learn from West, and he wrote back glowing reports of how much help he received, how inspired he was by the old man's continuing to paint huge pictures and try new things even though he was ill and in pain. Surely, an artist who was so loved and honored by Englishmen can find some honor in his native country!"

"Yes, sir," said another congressman. "What you say is true, but where is our new nation going to get money for a museum at this time? We have just built an Academy of Art in Philadelphia so our young men can study art in their own country. Let us display some of West's works there in the state where he was born."

And so it was agreed. Benjamin West's sons gave the U.S. government some of their father's pictures for display in the art school. Today many of the pictures of this great artist do hang in museums in Philadelphia and other American cities. When we look at some of his work, we will see how he changed the way painting was done in his day and why he is considered one of the great artists of colonial times.

(Standards: Language Arts: Listening and Speaking 8.4)

Viewing the Art

(*The Paintings of Benjamin West* by von Erffa and Staley—see references—is an excellent source for this viewing session.)

Begin by showing some of West's early work before he received any formal training, such as the portraits of Jane Morris and *The Death of Socrates*, so that the children can see the growth in his skill as an artist. Contrast these with such portraits as *The Cricketers, John Allen,* and *Mrs. West and Raphael West* (does this last remind the children of any Italian madonna paintings?), done after West's trip to Italy. Show some of West's early historical paintings. Some you might select are *Venus and Cupid, Paetus and Arria, Venus Lamenting the Death of Adonis, The Departure of Regulus from Rome,* and *Leonidas and Cleombrutus.* Spend considerable time on West's *The Death of General Wolfe.* When West's work, depicting Wolfe in his uniform, was unveiled, Sir Joshua Reynolds, one of the most important British painters of the day, felt that showing General Wolfe in his boots and leggings rather than in Greek or Roman clothing, as was the custom, would erode respect for the national hero. Reynolds's opinion caused a great controversy. Point out that although two painters, Edward Penny and George Romney, had painted General Wolfe in his British uniform several years before, their paintings were not as large or important as West's. The king of England was so shocked by the painting that even though Benjamin West was his court painter, he refused to buy it. Later, though, when the painting was accepted as a masterpiece, he asked for a copy of it. Wolfe was a British general who died fighting Americans. What details in the painting signal that Wolfe is a British officer? What parts of the picture indicate the connection with America? Show other historical and biblical paintings as you wish, especially the two huge paintings West completed in his later years: *Christ Healing the Sick* and *Death on the Pale Horse.* The children would also probably enjoy seeing West's self-portraits.

(Standards: Art Connections 1.1-8; Language Arts: Viewing 9.6, 23)

Journal Writing

If the children had been members of the Congress asked to set up a museum in West's honor, would they have voted to do so? Why or why not?

(Standards: Thinking and Reasoning: 6.4; Language Arts: Writing 1.7, 23, 33-37)

Art/Drama Activity: Posing and Painting History

Materials

- Large roll of paper for a mural
- Pencils
- Paints
- Paintbrushes
- Pictures of people of eighteenth- and early nineteenth-century America so children can have an idea of clothing styles
- Polaroid camera and film, if possible

Brainstorm with the children about some of the things that were going on in our country during the time Benjamin West was growing up and during his stay in England. Some suggestions are the Boston Tea Party, in which Americans dumped tea overboard in Boston harbor to protest the British tax on tea; American and British troops fighting the American Revolution; Washington crossing the Delaware; writing the Declaration of Independence; Washington being made the first president; treaties and other interactions with Native Americans, etc. Invite the children to assume roles and pose some of these scenes so that they can get an idea of how figures can be arranged to tell a story. If you have a camera, take a picture of each group's pose. Otherwise, ask the children to keep their poses in mind because they will have to draw them in a short while.

Remind the children that historical paintings tell the story of events that happened in the past. Have the children pretend that they have gone to England to study with Benjamin West and have learned how to do historical paintings. Invite them to paint pictures of some of the historical events already discussed and posed as a story of what was going on during Benjamin West's lifetime. Each group of children should paint the scene they posed, using the Polaroid picture or their memory of the scene as a reference. Assign each group a space on the mural and invite them to first draw and then paint their scene. Display the completed mural in the classroom or hallway.

(Standards: Visual Arts: 1-4.1-11)

LESSON 2: Charles Willson Peale (1741–1827)

The Story

"Sir, this letter is from your friend, Chief Justice Allen. I hope his recommendation will encourage you to help me learn to improve my painting."

"Charles," replied Benjamin West, "you are an American. That is enough for me. Of course I will help you. How I miss my country! I've been in England for seven long years, as you know. But I've made such a reputation here that I cannot leave now. Would you believe that I could not even get home to marry my fiancée? I had to bring her here instead! Welcome to my studio. I will teach you what I know."

And that's how young Charles Willson Peale, a boy born in Maryland, came to stay with Benjamin West, a boy born in Pennsylvania, who now was a talented young artist living in England. Charles studied with Benjamin for a long time. When Charles didn't have enough money to buy his own food, Benjamin invited him to eat with his large family. But then news of trouble in America reached England. The American colonists were unhappy with the British who ruled them. They didn't like the taxes the British placed on them, and they wanted to be free to make their own laws. It seemed war would break out any time.

"Benjamin, I must leave as soon as possible," said Charles. "I love art and know I still have much to learn. But I love my country more. I must go home and fight in General Washington's army."

"I shall miss you, Charles," said Benjamin. "Who will fix things around here when they break? Who will make my children laugh with his jokes and tricks? But you have learned a good deal. You're a fine artist, and I know you will do well. Write to me whenever you can and let us remain friends."

When Charles arrived home, he did serve in Washington's army, but he brought his paints along, too, and painted portraits of the people around him every chance he got. When the war ended, he continued painting, and his portraits were very popular, for he did something that was unusual for his time: He put hints in his pictures of how his subjects made their living. He put a book and quill pen in his portrait of a lawyer, a guitar in a picture of a musician, navigating instruments in a portrait of a boatman.

Yes, people bought Charles's portraits, but he was restless. There was so much more he wanted to do. The country was just beginning. The people needed to learn so many things. They needed schools, museums, and art galleries just like the people in Europe had. When Charles saw something that needed to be done, he didn't ask someone else to do it. He did it himself. So before long, he began working on starting a natural history museum and art gallery in Philadelphia. He talked the leaders of Philadelphia into giving him room for his project, and they agreed to let him use the top floor of a building that was empty. He had animals in the yard outside for people to see and enjoy. He had stuffed animals inside—animals some people had never seen before. And not only that, he painted special scenery that showed people where the animal lived when it was in the wild. One time he even went on a dinosaur dig and brought back the bones of a huge mastodon. He put the bones together and displayed the animal skeleton in his museum. He painted pictures of all the leaders of the country—men like George Washington, who became his close friend; Thomas Jefferson; Benjamin Franklin; and many others—and displayed those pictures in the museum, too. Every single man who helped form the new government of the United States had his picture painted by Charles Willson Peale.

You would think that with all the work he did, Charles would be too busy to have a family. But he actually got married three times, for two of his wives died, and he had sixteen children! He named most of them after famous European artists. Not all his children lived, but many did, and several became fine artists like their father.

Charles was so busy that the years flew by. Before he knew it, he was in his eighties. But did he sit quietly and relax? Did he let his children take over for him? Of course not. He wanted to keep trying new things. He experimented with new kinds of painting, with using light and shadow. He kept inventing things, too. One day a group of men asked him to paint a portrait of himself for his museum. Charles thought about it for a long time. He wanted that portrait to tell people the story of his life. We're going to look at it shortly.

(Standards: Language Arts: Listening and Speaking 8.4)

Viewing the Art

(A good source for all these paintings is Richardson's *Charles Willson Peale and His World*—see references.)

Show some of Peale's portraits, especially those of George Washington and other leaders the children might know about. It is quite interesting to compare the seven portraits of Washington done by Peale. When Washington sat for his portrait in 1795, both Charles and his son Rembrandt painted his picture. Compare the two. Charles's is idealized, showing a strong, determined "Father of His Country," while Rembrandt's shows Washington as the old, retired man he was. Peale did several portraits of his family members that might interest the children. Show *James Peale Painting a Miniature* (his brother); *Mrs. Charles Willson Peale* (Hannah Moore); *Rachel Weeping* (Rachel is one of Peale's wives, and the child is their daughter Margaret, who died in infancy); *The Peale Family*; and *The Staircase Group: Raphaelle and Titian Ramsay Peale*. When showing the latter, tell how Peale displayed this painting framed by an actual doorway with some steps in front of it. It was so realistic that a visiting George Washington actually greeted the boys. If you wish, read them the delightful picture book *The Joke's on George* by Tunnell (see references).

Peale also did several self-portraits the children might enjoy. The one referred to in the story, *The Artist in His Studio*, tells us much about Mr. Peale. Look carefully and see how much you can notice about Peale's life. Some things the children should see are the museum itself, the palette to represent his painting, the bird exhibits, the mastodon jaw and mounted skeleton, the taxidermy tools, and the portraits of famous leaders. Show also *The Exhumation of the Mastodon* and point out that the device being used to haul water out of the pit was invented by Peale. The story of the mastodon project is recounted in the picture book *Mister Peale's Mammoth* by Sam Epstein and Beryl Epstein, while Giblin's *The Mystery of the Mammoth Bones and How It Was Solved* is a vastly interesting account of the same project written for older children (see references). *Mister Peale's Museum* (see references) also has some fine pictures and the story of the hurdles Peale encountered as he worked to establish the first natural history and art museum in the country.

(Standards: Art Connections 1.1-8; Language Arts: Viewing 9.6, 23)

Journal Writing

Have the children write about Peale's different portraits of George Washington. How are they alike? Different? What do they say about the character of the man? What do the children feel is Peale's greatest contribution? Why?

(Standards: Thinking and Reasoning: 3.3; Language Arts: Writing 1.7, 23, 33-37; Art Connections 1.3)

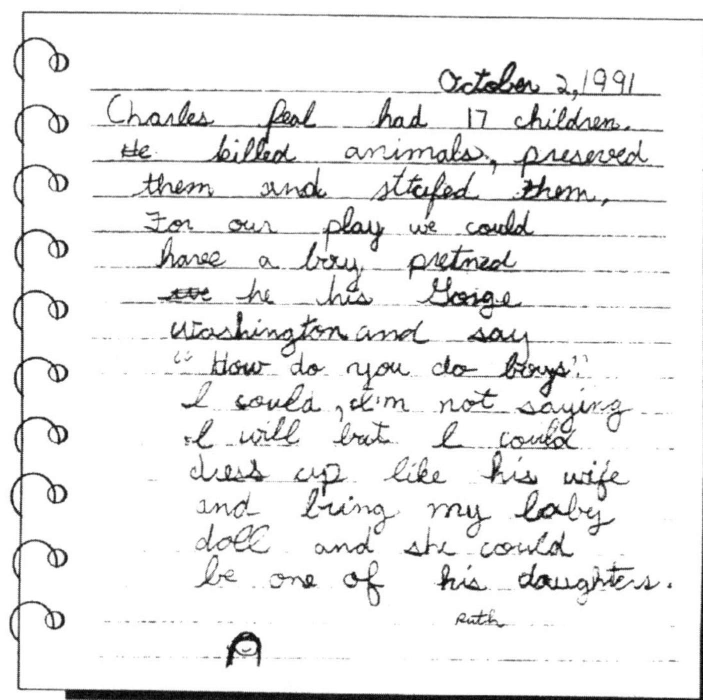

October 2, 1991
Charles peal had 17 children.
He killed animals, preserved
them and stufed them.
For our play we could
have a boy pretned
he his Gorge
Washington and say
"How do you do boys".
I could, I'm not saying
I will but I could
dress up like his wife
and bring my baby
doll and she could
be one of his daughters.
Ruth

Drama/Art Activity: Portrait Gallery

Materials

- Paper
- Pencils
- Paints, markers, or colored pencils

Pair the children. Begin by having each partner write what he or she knows is special about the other. They can interview one another if they need more information. Perhaps someone is a good soccer player, plays the piano, runs fast, loves to read, etc. Then invite the children to do each other's portraits, including in the picture some symbol indicating that person's special characteristic: a sheet of music or a piano in the piano player's picture, for example. Make a gallery display of these portraits in imitation of Charles Willson Peale's gallery.

(Standards: Working with Others: 3-4.5-6, 8-9; Language Arts: Writing: 1, 4.33, 36; Visual Arts: 1-4.1-11)

Note: Curriculum connections and references are at the end of chapter 17.

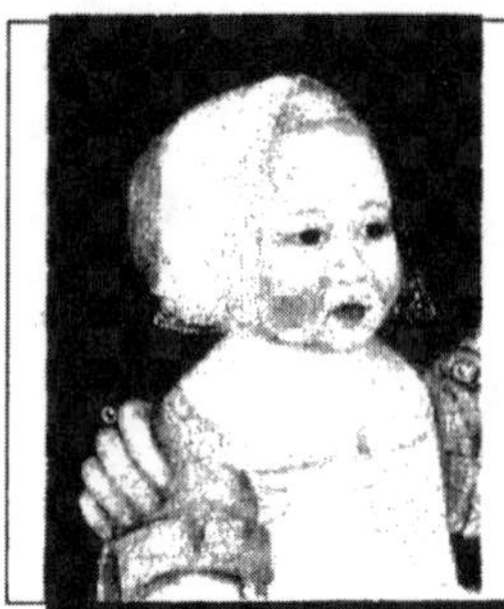

16 Anonymous American Primitives

There will always be nonacademic art so long as there are artists willing and able to create their own styles in accordance with their own instincts.

—JANE KALLIR, *The Folk Art Tradition*

LESSON

Background Information

Since it took a while after the American Revolution for artists to begin plying their craft and for their subjects to have the means or the leisure to consider home decoration, the high point of American primitive, or folk, art was between the end of the eighteenth century (about 1790) until the 1870s, when the photograph became practical and popular. We discuss folk art here as a bridge between the two centuries. "Primitive" or "folk" are not disparaging terms but ways to distinguish art that is done by untrained, natural artists. While such art was for many years considered inferior, critics now generally recognize that it has a delightfully fresh quality, and the extant pictures are highly prized. Since folk artists were not trained in the principles of perspective or anatomy, they made little attempt to adhere strictly to reality in their pictures. Their figures are rounded, the clothing giving little evidence of being draped over real flesh and bone. In fact, many even painted the torsos or clothing at home in the winter months when traveling was difficult, and then added faces when they could travel to a sitter's home. It is this abstract quality of primitive paintings that makes them valuable and charming.

Primitive or folk painters were often engaged in other work as well. They formed the ranks of the farmers, house or sign painters, carpenters, doctors, and housewives of the developing nation. They traveled from house to house, offering their services and charging very little. Many of them did not even bother to sign their works. In order to give you a larger body of work from which to choose, we treat the genre as a whole here, rather than isolate a single artist. And we concentrate on portraits of children, since these will resonate especially with those you teach. The story that follows, then, is about no particular person, but rather an account of how these folk paintings may have come to be.

(Standards: Art Connections: 1,1-2, 4, 6-7)

The Story

"Mother, I see him, I see his wagon coming down the road," cried little Sarah as she jumped up and down. "May I run down and show him the way to our house?"

"No, child," said Sarah's mother, wiping her hands on her apron. She had been baking all morning. Her hair was damp from the heat of the fire, and wisps of it escaped her cap and hung along the sides of her face. "The road is muddy from the rains. He will be here soon enough."

Sarah stood by the doorway, hopping from foot to foot in her impatience. At last the wagon pulled up in front of the house and a slim man jumped out, picked up a satchel, and came to the door. Before he had a chance to knock, Sarah's mother opened it and invited him in.

"Good day, madam. I've come to do your walls as we arranged last fall. I've brought my stencils with me and can set to work immediately. When I'm finished, your parlor will look as though it is papered in one of the finest European patterns—and without the expense!"

"Wonderful. My husband has brought in the ladder from the barn. It's set up for you in the parlor. And be sure you stop for some refreshments mid-afternoon. I've just baked some cakes."

"I'll look forward to it, madam," said the man as he began to remove his jacket and roll up his shirt sleeves.

"May I watch?" asked Sarah, looking for a hint of approval on her mother's face.

"I don't think so, my dear," her mother responded. "You'll be in the way, and you may get paint on that new dress you insisted on wearing today."

"Madam, I never splatter," said the painter. "And I'll make sure the little lady stays on the opposite side of the room. She'll be no bother at all. I'd rather like the company."

"Well, if you're sure."

Hardly able to hide her excitement, Sarah followed the stranger into the parlor and settled herself in a chair a good distance from where he began spreading out cloths on which to mix his paints. Then she watched in fascination as her mother's parlor walls slowly filled with dainty flowers. Why, it was beginning to look as grand as the big houses they saw in the city when they went in her father's wagon for supplies. She chattered away about her friend Mary, who lived only a short wagon-ride away, and about her doll, Agnes, and about how soon she would be old enough to go to the school house and do her lessons. The amused painter managed an occasional "M-m-m . . . ."

Finally Sarah's mother called them into the warm kitchen for tea and cakes. As they were eating, the man said, "You have a delightful daughter, madam. So full of life and expression. I surely would love to paint her picture."

"You paint portraits as well as designs on walls?"

"Oh yes, madam. In fact, I've done several of your neighbors, and they were quite pleased with the results. A picture of your loved one hanging in the parlor will really make it special. In fact, I could do the two of you—a mother and child portrait. Very touching."

"Well, it would be a wonderful thing to have. We've already lost two children, and no likeness of them to keep their dear faces in our memory. But we haven't much money," Sarah's mother said sadly.

"Oh, madam, I wouldn't charge much. Since you've hired me to do the parlor, I could do the portrait as well for very little more."

"Please say yes, Mother," begged Sarah. "And I could hold Agnes. You will put Agnes in the picture, too, won't you, sir?"

"If it's Agnes you want, then Agnes you shall have," he said, smiling. "She'll help you sit still for me."

And so the woman arranged to have the painter come back the following week, when she would have on her Sunday dress, to do a portrait of herself and her daughter. It was hard for Sarah to sit still for so long, but she managed. The painter worked as quickly as he could, until at last he produced the finished picture. Sarah could hardly believe her eyes. There she was, and Mother and little Agnes sitting comfortably in her lap. Her mother was pleased, too. She paid the painter and proudly placed the portrait on the mantle for her husband to see when he came in from the fields.

"I'll be off then, madam," said the painter. "But I'll be back this way again next year. Perhaps your husband will want to sit for me then." Sarah watched him pack his paints and saw him out the front door. She didn't stop waving until his wagon was a small speck in the distance.

In the first hundred years of our country's existence, there were many painters like the one in our story—men and women, too—who traveled from house to house painting portraits. These artists never went to school to study art. What they knew, they taught themselves. I did not give the painter a name in this story because most of these portrait painters never signed their pictures. We have some of their wonderful paintings, but we don't know who they were. When we look at their work, we will learn a great deal about what life was like in our country, especially for the children, over a hundred years ago. (You may wish to read *The Limners: America's Earliest Portrait Painters*—see references.)

(Standards: Language Arts: Listening and Speaking 8.4)

Viewing the Art

As you view these works, point out to the children that the men and women who did them are called primitive or folk artists because they lacked formal training. They painted what they knew to be true about people rather than what they actually saw. They were interested in the overall pleasing design of the picture rather than accurate perspective or accurate anatomy. Tell the class that while we know who did some of these paintings, there are many that we call anonymous because the artists who traveled from place-to-place painting them didn't sign their work. While viewing these pictures, invite the children to comment on all the things they learn about the children in them who lived so long ago. *Small Folk: A Celebration of Childhood in America* by Brant and Cushman and *Treasures of American Folk Art* by Rumford and Weekley (see references) are perfect for this purpose. However, there are a number of other books on primitives listed that will serve you as well. See the references for several titles. Keep a list of the playthings, pets, and other artifacts the children mention during their enjoyment of the portraits. If you use *Small Folk*, show other artworks in addition to the portraits, for example, carved playthings. This will enable the class to see children's work tools, furniture, and toys. They will need this information later during the art activity.

It would be an interesting exercise to show the children a few family and single portraits by Mary Cassatt and contrast them with the portraits done by folk art painters. *The Children of Vespasian Emerson Flye* (page 38 in *Small Folk*) and *Girl in Red Dress with Cat and Dog* (page 36 in *Five Star Folk Art*) are good choices. If you show this last painting, you might wish to read Nicholson's (1998)delightful picture book of the same name. (See references.)

(Standards: Art Connections 1.1-8; Language Arts: Viewing 9.6, 23)

Journal Writing

Invite the children to create a life for one of their favorite children in the pictures. Does the child come from a wealthy or middle-class family? How do they know this? How does the child spend his or her time?

(Standards: Language Arts: Writing 1.7, 23, 33-37; Art Connections 1.3)

Art/Drama Activity: Museum Advertising

Materials

- Paper
- Colored pencils
- Pictures for reference

Have the children pretend that they are working for an advertising firm. Their job is to create advertising for art magazines announcing the opening of a new museum dedicated to the children of the eighteenth and nineteenth centuries. Each child should write a brief ad about some of the things in the museum. To accompany the text, they can draw a child in the dress of the times, some toys that might be on display in the museum, or some tools or work instruments that might be on display. To help the children with their portraits, you might follow the activity described on page 17 of Panchyk's *American Folk Art for Kids* in the references.

(Standards: Language Arts: Writing 1-4.11, 33-34; Visual Arts: 1-4.1-11)

Note: Curriculum connections and references are at the end of chapter 17.

17 Painters of a Changing Nation

America, America, God shed His grace on thee,
And crown thy good with brotherhood,
From sea to shining sea.

—KATHERINE LEE BATES, "America the Beautiful," 1893

Background Information

Americans in the nineteenth century turned their focus inward on themselves and their growing nation. Another war with England in 1812 had convinced them that isolation from Europe was the best course, and the desire for things from the Old World, even great works of art, fell off. Instead, American artists themselves took up brush and palette and began to depict the land and its inhabitants. A people looking for escape from the drudgery of daily toil welcomed the works of the new Romantic painters, artists like Thomas Cole and the painters of the Hudson River School who rendered the beautiful landscape of the Catskills and the Hudson Valley, shrouded in dreamy mists and clouds. Realists, on the other hand, concentrated not on the land but the people, painting what they saw around them. Among them, Thomas Eakins, the great portraitist, and Winslow Homer, famous for his genre paintings of ordinary people and his poignant pictures of the Civil War, were two of the greatest American painters of the century.

The Louisiana Purchase in 1803 more than doubled the size of the United States, so that it stretched to the Rocky Mountains, tempting settlers with the promise of rich new land. John James Audubon, lured by the fascinating wildlife of the vast wilderness, became famous for his exquisite renderings of birds. George Catlin, rightly fearing that the westward migration would put an end to the Indians' free roaming on the plains, rushed to capture on canvas as many of these native peoples as possible before their way of life disappeared forever. Frederic Remington painted and sculpted American cowboys and their beloved horses. And Albert Bierstadt traveled all the way to the Rocky Mountains and brought their awesome grandeur home to New York in sketches that he transformed into dramatic paintings.

American painters were not so immersed in their own country that they ignored what was happening across the ocean, however. When the Impressionists began to shake the French art world, forcing artists to see color and light in new ways, some Americans such as Mary Cassatt, James Abbott McNeill Whistler, and John Singer Sargent joined their ranks.

American artists throughout the nineteenth century recorded the growth and diversity of a new nation. With an enthusiasm and thirst for adventure symbolic of the country itself, they worked in the cities and on the frontier, painting what they saw and felt. They founded schools of art, took their place beside the masters of Europe, and prepared the way for the century of freedom and experimentation that was to follow.

(Standards: Grades K–4 History: 5.6, 11; Art Connections: 1,1-2, 4, 6-7)

LESSON 1: George Catlin (1796–1872)

The Story

All day long Indians lined up outside the tipi where George Catlin was painting portraits. They had seen the portrait Catlin had painted of their chief, and they were so amazed they could hardly believe it. They had never seen such wonderes before, and now everyone wanted a picture. Each man felt a part of himself was in the picture, so he carried his painting carefully back to his tipi and placed it against the wall. He spent hours looking at it and wondering how the strange white man could do such a marvelous thing.

But not everyone was happy. One of the braves was jealous because the chief said he must be one of the last to have his picture done. So he squatted down where George was painting. "Ha," he said to the man who was posing for his portrait. "You are only half a man!"

"Half a man? How dare you insult a brave warrior like me! How can you say that?"

"Come look for yourself, then. This man paints only half of your face. He must think you are only half a man."

Now it was true that George Catlin was painting a profile, or side view, of his subject, so of course only half of his face was showing. But the brave felt he had been insulted. He ran out of the tipi to get his gun and fight the man who had insulted him. But when his wife saw what he was doing, she secretly unloaded his gun so that he would not be harmed, for she loved him a great deal. Her plan didn't work, though, because when the other man raised his gun, her husband could not fire back, and he was shot dead. This caused a great deal of trouble, as many in the tribe wanted revenge for their friend's cruel death.

"Oh, how horrible," moaned a heart-broken George Catlin. "I have walked thousands of miles through dangerous lands to help the Indian, and now I have caused deaths because of my pictures. I want to bring my pictures to Washington, D.C., so that the American people can see that the Indians are not savages. I want them to see the strong, noble faces of the chiefs, the beauty of the women, their colorful clothing and beautiful decorations. I want them to see how talented and special these people are. That is my dream. Now look at what has happened."

But George kept moving, traveling from tribe to tribe. He wanted to complete his work before white settlers drove the Native Americans from their homes forever. "Perhaps if people see my paintings and all the wonderful things I have collected like peace pipes and clothing, they will come to respect Indians as I do and allow them to remain on the land," he thought. For six long years George traveled and painted, and when he finally went back east to his wife, Clara, for good, he set up exhibits of his collection. He tried to convince the government to buy his paintings for the Smithsonian Museum in Washington, but Congress kept refusing. Meanwhile, George was running out of money to support his family and was growing desperate.

"I know what I'll do," he told his wife. "I'll tell Congress I'm going to take my collection to Europe and sell it there. I know the American government would never want these paintings of their own American Indians to leave the country." But Congress still did nothing. So George took his collection to Europe and held many exhibitions. Even Queen Victoria of England came and was very impressed.

Yet George didn't make enough money to take care of his wife and four children. First his young wife died, then his youngest child, little George—the pride of his father's heart. George Catlin himself was ill and growing deaf. Still the American government would not listen and buy his collection. An American man finally took it to pay off some of George's debts and stored it in a warehouse. Then George's rich brother-in-law came and took away his three daughters: "My sister and your son have died. I don't want anything to happen to these girls. My wife and I can give them a fine home and education."

George was left with no family and no collection. Most people thought he was just a fanatic and ignored him. But he didn't stay locked in a room by himself. He actually went on a long trip to South America and painted the people there—even though he was sixty years old and quite ill! At last George was too sick to continue painting and went to New Jersey to be with his three grown daughters. He had not seen them in fifteen years! They took care of him, but could not make him well. He died at the age of seventy-six, saying, "What has happened to my collection?"

When he was alive people did not understand how important George Catlin's work was. Now we know that if it had not been for his bravery, we would be missing a great deal of information about Native Americans. Although some of his collection was destroyed by rats and dampness in the warehouse, much of it has been restored. We will look at some of his paintings now, but you can enjoy the actual pictures if you go to the Smithsonian Institution in Washington, D.C. George Catlin would be pleased to know that his collection is now where he always wanted it to be.

(Standards: Language Arts: Listening and Speaking 8.4)

Viewing the Art

(An outstanding source for Catlin's paintings is *George Catlin and His Indian Gallery*. Not only are there large color reproductions of the artworks mentioned below, but there are also landscapes and excerpts from Catlin's writings. See the references.)

From the mid-1800s on, as its use became more widespread, the camera began to assume the role the portrait once had—a momentous change in how we were to preserve our history. Make use of both by showing the 1824 self-portrait of George Catlin as an incredibly handsome young man and contrasting it with the photograph of him in Brussels that is now in the Smithsonian. Talk about how the years of travel, danger, and hardship took their toll. Explain that the Indians never harmed Catlin, as they did other whites, because they sensed his respect and admiration for them. Among the many wonderful pictures from which to choose, the children might particularly enjoy *Wun-nes-tow*, *Kee-o-kuk*, *Ten-squat-a-way*, *La-doo-ke-a*, *Ha-won-je-tah*, *Tah-teck-a-da-hair*, *Tis-se-woo-na-tis*, *Ah-mou-a*, *Tal-lee*, *His-oo-san-chees*, *Os-ce-o-la*, *Mandan Medicine Man*, *Kiowa Girl and Boy*, and *Champion Choctaw Ball-Player*. Show the children the two pictures of *Wi-jun-jon* going to and returning from Washington. Tell the children how saddened Catlin was by the fate of this Indian. (He went to Washington in his distinguished native dress and returned wearing clothing that was not suitable for him and having acquired a taste for whiskey, which led to his downfall.) This picture reveals how Catlin felt about the whites' treatment of Native Americans.

(Standards: Art Connections 1.1-8; Language Arts: Viewing 9.6, 23)

Journal Writing

Because George Catlin painted such precise pictures of Indians, we know many small details of their appearance and dress. Using words instead of drawings, describe another student in the room. For example, note what shirt and pants (or skirt) is worn, the pattern of the material, if there is a belt, belt loops, or pockets and where they are, and so on. Try to paint a picture in words so that someone reading those words could actually draw an accurate picture, from head to foot.

(Standards: Language Arts: Writing 1.7, 23, 33-37)

Art/Drama Activity: Make a Book

Materials

- Paper and pencils
- Tempera paints
- Brushes
- Catlin pictures to serve as models

Catlin wrote several books about his adventures in the West and the peoples he met and painted there. Divide the children into groups to work on a similar book of their own. Have each group compose a brief paragraph or two with paintings to go with it based on the artist's work. When each group has finished and the paintings are dry, bind their pages together into a book. Decide on a title and design for the cover. Display the book on a special stand or keep it in the classroom library.

(Standards: Visual Arts: 1-4.1-11; Working with Others: 1-4.1-6; Language Arts: Writing: 1, 3-4.33-34)

LESSON 2: Winslow Homer (1836–1910)

The Story

Young Winslow Homer sat in his apartment in New York writing a letter to his family in Cambridge, Massachusetts. It was the early 1860s, and the Civil War was raging between the North and South. Winslow wrote:

"I have finally returned from the war front. While I was there, I drew many pictures on wood for *Harpers* magazine. They paid me well, but I decided to quit, since I have no stomach for war. In fact, even while battles were going on all around me, I preferred to draw the men in their camps rather than the fighting. Their faces and their emotions interest me. Now I am working on my own, and trying my hand at painting, something I know very little about as yet. I am taking a few classes and will try to turn some of my Civil War sketches into oil paintings. These along with some pictures I'm painting of people in the countryside are giving me a good deal of practice. I will submit two of my best pictures for the exhibit at the National Academy of Design. If no one buys them, I shall know that I have no talent for painting and will give it up. I think of you all often. Winslow."

"Give up painting for good?" cried Winslow's favorite brother, Charles, when he read the letter. "We can't let that happen! He has too much talent, and I know he will continue to get better and better. I must do something to get thoughts of quitting out of his head."

Then Charles, who loved the outdoors, went out for a long walk. Breathing the cool, fresh air helped him think. Three hours later, he returned, beaming. "I know exactly what I shall do," he announced. "I will go to New York and buy those paintings myself. Winslow need never know. Will you all promise to keep my secret?"

Of course, the family did, and Charles left the next day for New York. He went straight to the academy and bought his brother's paintings, refusing to sign his name or say who he was.

Winslow didn't find out what Charles had done until years later, and he was pretty angry when he did. In fact, he wouldn't even speak to Charles for a few weeks!

"Oh, come on, Win," said Charles. "It was for your own good. I know how stubborn you are. Imagine how awful it would have been for you to stop painting. Do you regret all the wonderful work you have done since then? You see, my plan worked!"

Winslow had to admit that his brother was right, for he did become an incredibly good painter. He was so good, in fact, that he became famous in his own lifetime. Reporters called him and wanted interviews for their newspapers and magazines, but Winslow ignored them. "My life is my own business," he said. "What people should be concerned with is just my art."

Then he left New York and went to England, where he stayed in a small fishing village and painted pictures of the fishermen and their wives. He began to love the sea more and more, and he realized that for the rest of his life he wanted to paint nature.

When Winslow returned to the United States, he decided to move to Maine, where he could be far away from people. "I do my best work alone," he said. He lived in Maine by himself for twenty-seven years, painting the local people, especially his handyman, and the ocean. His favorite times were when there was a storm at sea. He would put on his yellow rain slicker and stand on the cliff watching in awe as the waves rose and crashed against the rocks. He painted many pictures of these storms. Summers he would go tramping through the woods with Charles, hunting and painting the animals and scenery.

Winslow Homer made wonderful wood-block prints when he was a young man. He could have become rich doing that, but he wanted to try something different, and so he learned to paint with oils. People loved his oil paintings, but he still wasn't satisfied, so he began working with watercolors. Right up until the end of his life, Winslow Homer kept trying to paint better and better pictures. When he became very sick and went blind, Charles went to Maine to take care of him, and Charles and their younger brother, Arthur, were with him when he died. Winslow Homer was always proud that except for a few lessons about using paint, no one ever taught him art. He developed his own methods and style. Today many people consider him the best American watercolor artist who ever lived.

(Standards: Language Arts: Listening and Speaking 8.4)

Viewing the Art

Begin by showing some of Homer's early works: pictures for *Harpers* such as *Skating on the Ladies' Skating Pond in Central Park* and *August in the Country.* (See Kushner 2000.) Show some of the Civil War paintings. (Simpson's *Winslow Homer: Paintings of the Civil War* is an excellent source—see references.) Tell the children that Homer's *Prisoners from the Front* (Simpson devotes several pages to the painting and includes details as well) made the artist famous when he was still a young man. Talk about the faces of the men in the picture: the defeated Confederate prisoners, the Union officer. What are they thinking and feeling? Is the Union officer cruel? Kind? Proud? Other Civil War pictures you might choose are *In Front of the Guard-House* and *The Sutler's Tent.* You may wish to read Taylor Morrison's *Civil War Artist* (see references), which recounts an experience similar to what Homer must have gone through to get his drawings to his newspaper. Cikovsky's *Winslow Homer* is a beautiful, huge book and an excellent source for the paintings that follow (see references). The class may especially enjoy some of Homer's paintings of children such as *Nooning, Homework,* and *Country School.* Show pictures of the strong women and fishermen Homer painted in England such as *Gale* and *Watching the Tempest.* The children may be interested in knowing that Homer painted *Life Line* in New York by stringing a line on the roof and having two models pose for him. He repeatedly doused them with water until he got the look he wanted. The painting was a huge success. Show some of Homer's famous oil paintings of men and the sea: *The Lookout—All's Well, Herring Net,* and *Eight Bells.* Spend considerable time viewing some watercolors (see Unger 2001 and Cooper 1987), including scenes from the tropics and some woodland animals and scenery, the result of Homer's summer trips with his brother. Tell children the story of the *Fox Hunt.* Homer had friends bring him dead crows that he froze and used as models for the painting as he needed them. But when he pinned the frozen crows in position, they thawed out too quickly and became limp and useless. Frustrated, Homer had to scatter corn to lure live crows to fly near his home so that he could paint them from life. The ducks in *Right and Left* were painted a year before his death, and *Driftwood* was his last picture.

(Standards: Art Connections 1.1-8; Language Arts: Viewing 9.6, 23)

Journal Writing

Winslow Homer rejected the limelight and chose instead to live alone in a remote area in Maine. What do the children think of that decision? What were some advantages of Homer's living apart from people? Disadvantages? How might his work have been different had he stayed in New York? Are there times when the children work better alone? With others? When and why do they choose to be alone? If you have studied any of the Impressionists or Post-Impressionists, discuss which artists led similar solitary lives, and why you think they did.

(Standards: Language Arts: Writing 1.7, 23, 33-37; Thinking and Reasoning: 6.4)

Dec 12/4/95

Winslow Homer
he did painting for a
Magazine, but beafor
he said: I will never
work for some one
again! Then he did
pictures of boats and
children at school. When
he went to France
he learne that they used
more color. He lived
in Main and his house
was by the shore
his Mother was a water-
painter (But was not
famouse) he learned from
his mother, he became
Famouse when he was
old.

Art/Drama Activity: Watercolors

Materials

- Watercolor paper
- Brushes
- Enough sets of watercolors for the children to share
- Cloths for wiping brushes
- Water
- Watercolors by Homer to use as reference

In imitation of Winslow Homer, one of the country's greatest watercolorists, have the children make watercolor paintings. Demonstrate how the paints look different depending on how much or how little water is added to them. It would be most fitting for the children to do nature scenes, so if the weather is fair and your school has some woods or trees nearby, take a walk to get some ideas. The children might like to sketch what they see and return to the classroom to turn their sketches into paintings. At the very least, have some reproductions of Homer's nature scenes for them to use as reference.

Additional Activities

Drama

Children enjoy acting out several scenes from the lives of the artists they have studied. Some possibilities:

- Benjamin West makes a paintbrush out of his cat's tail.
- Benjamin West learns how to make paint from the Indians.
- Benjamin West helps American painters who come to England to study. Peale is one of these.
- George Washington is fooled by Charles Willson Peale's painting of his sons.
- Charles Willson Peale goes on a dig for dinosaur bones.
- Charles Willson Peale sets up his natural history museum.
- Untrained painters travel door to door painting portraits.
- George Catlin's painting of an Indian's profile causes trouble in the tribe.
- George Catlin tries to convince Congress to buy his Indian collection.
- Charles buys his brother Winslow's paintings on the sly.
- Winslow Homer tries to paint thawing crows.

Create a gallery of American painters. Paint portraits of the artists studied and include an object in the portrait that says something special about them.

(Standards: Theater: 2.1-2, 10; Visual Arts: 1.1-3)

Curriculum Connections

Social Studies

- Make a large map of North America and indicate the places in which the different groups of Native Americans lived. Can the children also locate some of the tribes George Catlin visited?
- Study the different encounters of Native Americans with European Americans (i.e., treaties, fur trading, any of the Indian wars, etc.).
- Learn about the customs of different Native American tribes.
- Learn about the first settlers to come to America. Who were the different groups? Why did they come? Place their settlements on a map.
- Learn about the American Revolution. Why was it fought? Against whom? Which Indians participated? On what side?
- Learn about the Civil War. What were the issues? Some battles? The outcome?
- What were some changes in fashions from the eighteenth through the nineteenth centuries?
- Learn some games played by Native Americans, such as Shinny, played by Navajos. (See *North American Indian Games* in the references.)
- Prepare some foods using ingredients that have come to us from Native Americans. (See *Food, Farming, and Hunting* and *American Indian Foods* in the references.)
- Learn more about potlatch celebrations, which was the subject of the story about Indians of the Northwest. (See *Potlatch: A Tsimshian Celebration* in the references.) A wonderful project would be to contact children in a school in Alaska where potlatches are still regularly celebrated and enable your students to talk to native children about this custom. Schools in Alaska have very sophisticated Internet connections since it is their link to the rest of the world, and arranging such an exchange is a much easier matter than you might think. If you want to talk to the children in real time, using such programs as Skype or MSN messenger—free downloads—you just need to keep in mind the time difference.
- Learn some Native American signs. (See *Native American Talking Signs* in the references.)

(Standards: Dance 5.7; Grades K–4 History 5, 7.2, 6, 8, 22, 27, 33, 37-39, 42, 48, 51; Geography: 1.5, 30)

Science

- Learn about the contributions Native Americans have made, for example, crops such as corn, beans, and squash as well as drought- and insect-resistant strains; inventions such as snowshoes. (See Keoke and Porterfield 2005.)
- Study the history of the horse in this country and its impact on Native American life.
- Learn about Native American calendars.
- Find out about the plants Native Americans used for healing. (See *Medicine and Health* in the references.)
- In *Seasons of the Circle* (see references), Bruchac talks about the circle as an important Native American symbol. What other symbols can the children discover? The Web site http://www.geocities.com/ctesibos/symbols/native-american.html may be helpful.
- What was medicine like in colonial times? During the nineteenth century?
- Discuss some inventions of the eighteenth and nineteenth centuries, such as the telegraph and the steam engine.
- Research some of the animals that appeared in Charles Wilson Peale's museum or Winslow Homer's watercolor paintings.

(Standards: Grades K–4 History: 8.38-41; Science 11.29, 39)

Literature

- Read biographies of famous Native Americans and others who worked with or fought against them. (See Russell Freedman 1987, 1995.)
- Native Americans are wonderful storytellers. Read some Native American folktales. Those listed in the bibliography are only a fraction of what is available.
- Read the Native American sayings collected in *Enduring Wisdom* (see references). Copy some favorites on special paper and decorate the paper with borders using symbols or imitations of the artwork of the tribe from which the saying came.
- Read *Children of Native America Today* (see references). Find out about some of those mentioned in the "People to learn about" section for each tribe.
- Read some Native American poems in *The Earth Under Sky Bear's Feet* and *Night Is Gone, Day Is Still Coming* (see references).
- Read biographies of some of the great founders of our country, and of Lincoln and the generals of the Civil War.

- Contrast the illustrations of the Civil War done by Winslow Homer with the photographs taken by Matthew Brady (See Armstrong 2005.)
- Walt Whitman was a great poet of the nineteenth century. Enjoy a few of his poems. Who were some other great writers of the times?
- Find poems to go with Winslow Homer's beautiful seascapes.
- Charles Willson Peale wrote the first known autobiography in the United States. Suggest that children write stories about themselves in imitation of him.

(Standards: Language Arts: Writing 1.9, 11, 15, 33-38; Reading: 5-7.4, 7, 10, 13, 27-28)

Music

- Learn some Native American music and dances using books from the references.
- Make Native American instruments, such as flutes and drums.
- Learn some songs of the American Revolution and the Civil War. Visit http://www.pabucktail.com/songs.htm to listen to Civil War songs, and http://www.fssd.org/PGS/PGS_Digital_Museum/music%20Folder/songs.html for Revolutionary War songs.

(Standards: Music: 7.4, 7, 15-16)

References (for chapters 14 through 17)

Adult Books

Anderson, Brook Davis, and Stacy C. Hollander. *American Anthem: Masterworks from the American Folk Art Museum.* New York: Harry N. Abrams, 2002. ISBN 0810967405.

Published in conjunction with the second major exhibition at the American Folk Art Museum in New York, this book features art from the colonial period to the present.

Benad, Ursula , and Martin Benad. *Trompe L'Oeil Today.* Translated by Ingrid Li. New York: W. W. Norton, 2004. ISBN 0-393-73130-8.

Readers discover how to create illusions in painting much the way Peale did with his staircase painting.

Brant, Sandra, and Elissa Cullman. *Small Folk: A Celebration of Childhood in America.* New York: E. P. Dutton, 1981. ISBN 0525931317.

The authors provide information about childhood in early America as well as reproductions of children's portraits and other artifacts.

Brody, J. J. *Mimbres Pottery*. Rev. ed. Santa Fe, NM: School of American Research Press, 2005. ISBN 0933920466.

This book has excellent reproductions of Southwest Indian pottery.

Cartwright, Derrick R. *Benjamin West: Allegory and Allegiance*. San Diego: Timken Museum of Art, 2005. ISBN 1879067080.

This slim book features many pictures by West and some by his contemporaries.

Catlin, George, George Gurney, et al. *George Catlin and His Indian Gallery*. Washington, DC: Smithsonian American Art Museum, 2002. ISBN 03930552176.

With 150 full-color illustrations of Catlin's work, this is a prime source of images for group viewing.

Cikovsky, Nicolai, Jr. *Winslow Homer: Watercolors*. New York: Macmillan/Hugh Lauter Levin Associates, 1991. ISBN 0-88363-891-6.

Except for a few pages at the beginning, there is no text in this book. The stars are the pictures, most full-page color prints. This is a glorious book for viewing.

Cikovsky, Nicolai, Jr., and Franklin Kelly. *Winslow Homer*. Washington, DC: National Gallery of Art, 1995. ISBN 0-300-06555-8.

Published in conjunction with the Homer exhibit, this book contains more than 200 works that span Homer's career, with commentaries on each.

Conrads, Margaret C. *Winslow Homer and the Critics*. New Haven, CT: Princeton University Press/Nelson-Atkins Museum of Art, 2001. ISBN 0-691-07099-7.

The author studies the paintings done by Homer during the 1870s. There are some charming pictures of children.

Cooper, Helen A. *Winslow Homer Watercolors*. New Haven, CT: Yale University Press, 1987. ISBN 0-89468-087-0.

This thorough discussion of the watercolors has reproductions suitable for viewing.

Craven, Wayne. *American Art: History and Culture*. New York: McGraw-Hill Professional, 2002. ISBN 0071415246.

The artworks of several artists studied in chapters 15–17 are represented in this book and cover all areas of the country. Many are suitable for viewing.

Davidson, Marshall B., and Elizabeth Stillinger. *The American Wing at the Metropolitan Museum of Art*. New York: Random House/Metropolitan Museum of Art, 1988. ISBN 0517646269.

This book depicts the artworks in the American Wing of the Metropolitan Museum of Art in New York. Many of the artists studied in chapters 14–17 are represented.

Feder, Norman. *American Indian Art*. Reprint, New York: Harry N. Abrams, 1995. ISBN 0810981327.

Feder explores various aspects of Indian art such as origins, materials used, and ecological aspects. Large reproductions.

Fussell, Betty. *The Story of Corn.* Reprint, Albuquerque: University of New Mexico Press, 2004. ISBN 0826335926.

Fussell presents the history of corn and its importance to native peoples.

Hendricks, Gordon. *The Life and Work of Winslow Homer.* New York: Harry N. Abrams, 1979. ISBN 0810910632.

This huge book on the life and work of the artist is accompanied by reproductions for viewing.

Hill, Tom, and Richard W. Hill Sr., eds. *Creation's Journey.* Washington, DC: Smithsonian Institution Press, 1994. ISBN 1560984538.

Art and photographs in the Smithsonian collection and voices of Native Americans shed light on their beliefs and traditions.

Hollander, Stacy C., et al. *American Anthem: Masterworks from the American Folk Art Museum.* New York: American Folk Art Museum/Harry N. Abrams, 2001. ISBN 0810967405.

Artworks from the colonial period to the present make up the content of this book. The first section is especially relevant to the content of this chapter.

Hoving, Thomas. *The Art of Dan Namingha.* New York: Harry N. Abrams, 2000. ISBN 0-8109-4050-7.

Namingha's abstract paintings are reproduced in large color plates.

Jacka, Lois Essary. *Enduring Traditions: Art of the Navajo.* Photos by Jerry Jacka. Flagstaff, AZ: Northland Publishing, 1994. ISBN 0-87358-584-4.

Large reproductions of modern-day Navajo pottery, jewelry, sculpture, rugs, paintings, sand paintings, and baskets fill this beautiful book.

Jensen, Vicki. *Totem Pole Carving: Bringing a Log to Life.* Seattle: University of Washington Press, 2004. ISBN 029598368X.

Jensen follows a Native American artist through all the stages of creating a forty-three-foot totem pole.

Jonaitis, Aldona. *From the Land of the Totem Poles.* Photos by Stephen S. Myers. Seattle: University of Washington Press, 1991. ISBN 0295970227.

This excellent book describes in text and pictures the Northwest Coast Indian art collection at the American Museum of Natural History and is perfect for large group viewing.

Kallir, Jane. *The Folk Art Tradition.* New York: Penguin, 1982. ISBN 0713914831.

This discussion of folk art is accompanied by reproductions suitable for viewing.

Ketchum, William C. *American Folk Art.* New York: Todtri Productions, 1998. ISBN 1880908387.

Many kinds of folk art are discussed in this book. There is a section on paintings that can be used for viewing.

Kushner, Marilyn, et al. *Winslow Homer: Illustrating America.* New York: Brooklyn Museum of Art, 2000. ISBN 0807614661.

Kushner concentrates on Homer's early illustrations.

Lipman, Jean, and Tom Armstrong, eds. *American Folk Painters of Three Centuries.* New York: Hudson Hills Press, 1980. ISBN 0933920059.

This book contains biographies and some representative works of thirty-seven artists.

Lipman, Jean, et al. *Five-Star Folk Art: One Hundred American Masterpieces.* New York: Harry N. Abrams, 1990. ISBN 0-8109-3302-0.

Four centuries of American life are represented in paintings, sculpture, furniture, and textiles.

Lipman, Jean, Elizabeth V. Warren, and Robert Bishop. *Young America: A Folk-Art History.* New York: Hudson Hills Press, 1986. ISBN 093392075X.

This history of folk art is accompanied by large color reproductions.

Macnair, Peter, Jay Stewart, et al., eds. *Listening to Our Ancestors: The Art of Native Life Along the Pacific Northwest Coast.* Washington, DC: National Geographic, 2005. ISBN 0792241908.

A companion volume to the exhibit at the National Museum of the American Indian, this book has impressive reproductions of totem poles, bowls, tools, and other artifacts of Northwest Coast peoples.

McKeever, Jill Leslie. *Mojave Pottery, Mojave People: The Dillingham Collection of Mojave Ceramics.* Photographs by Peter T. Furst. Santa Fe, NM: School of American Research, 2001. ISBN 0933452659.

This discussion of Mojave life and customs is accompanied by color photos of their pottery.

McMaster, Gerald, and Clifford E. Trafzer, eds. *Native Universe: Voices of Indian America.* Washington, DC: National Museum of the American Indian/National Geographic, 2004. ISBN 0-7922-5994-7.

In this exquisite book, Indian voices from the past and contemporary society speak about their history and their art. Beautiful, large photographs are perfect for viewing. There is a very valuable map listing where different tribes reside.

Penney, David W. *Art of the American Indian Frontier: A Portfolio.* Detroit: New Press/Detroit Institute of Art, 1995. ISBN 1565842510.

This work provides exquisite photos of Indian bead work, baskets, carvings, and more.

Penney, David W., and George C. Longfish. *Native American Art.* Southport, CT: Hugh Lauter Levin Associates, 1994. ISBN 0-88363-694-8.

This book features Native American works of art from every part of the United States and has beautiful, large reproductions.

Penney, David W., and George Horse Capture. *North American Indian Art.* New York: Thames & Hudson, 2004. ISBN 0500203776.

This introduction to the subject encompasses Indian tribes from different parts of the country and has eighty large color reproductions.

Richardson, Edgar P., Brooke Hindle, and Lillian B. Miller. *Charles Willson Peale and His World*. New York: Harry N. Abrams, 1983. ISBN 0-8109-1478-6.

Peale's biography, large color reproductions of his work, and essays by distinguished scholars fill this book. It is one of the few available sources for an extensive sampling of the artist's paintings.

Rumford, Beatrix T., and Carolyn J. Weekley. *Treasures of American Folk Art*. Boston: Little, Brown, 1989. ISBN 0821217267.

This history of folk art is accompanied by large color reproductions.

Seale, Doris, and Beverly Slapin, eds. *A Broken Flute: The Native Experience in Books for Children*. Walnut Creek, CA: Alta Mira Press, 2005. ISBN 0759107785.

The editors provide invaluable information about how Native Americans are represented in books for children.

Sellers, Charles Coleman. *Mr. Peale's Museum: Charles Willson Peale and the first Popular Museum of Natural Science and Art*. New York: W. W. Norton, 1980. ISBN 0393057003.

Sellers discusses the difficulties Peale had in establishing his museum.

Simpson, Marc. *Winslow Homer: Paintings of the Civil War*. San Francisco: Fine Arts Museum of San Francisco, 1988. ISBN 0-938491-15-6.

Simpson's study of Homer's Civil War paintings includes large reproductions accompanied by period drawings and cartoons.

Stewart, Hilary. *Looking at Totem Poles*. Seattle: University of Washington Press, 1993. ISBN 0295972599.

Stewart provides a drawing of each pole along with an explanation of the different figures on it.

Townsend, Richard F., ed. *Casas Grandes and the Ceramic Art of the Ancient Southwest*. Chicago: Art Institute of Chicago/Yale University Press, 2005. ISBN 0-300-11148-7.

Full-page color reproductions of pottery and other artwork make this a perfect choice for the viewing session of lesson 2.

Trimble, Stephen. *Talking with the Clay: The Art of Pueblo Pottery*. Santa Fe, NM: School of American Research Press, 1987. ISBN 0933452187.

This book tells the story of Pueblo pottery from the point of view of contemporary potters.

Unger, Miles. *The Watercolors of Winslow Homer*. New York: W. W. Norton, 2001. ISBN 0-393-02047-9.

Unger begins with the artist's earliest watercolors and proceeds to those done just before his death. The reproductions are excellent sources for viewing.

von Erffa, Helmut, and Allen Staley. *The Paintings of Benjamin West*. New Haven, CT: Yale University Press, 1986. ISBN 0300033559.

This chronological discussion of many of West's paintings and career has large color reproductions. It documents all of West's known works.

Ward, David C. *Charles Willson Peale: Art and Selfhood in the Early Republic*. Berkeley: University of California Press, 2004. ISBN 0-520-23960-1.

Ward discusses Peale's extraordinary achievements. There are fifty-one black-and-white photos.

Ward, Gerald W. R., et al. *American Folk.* Boston: MFA Publications, 2001. ISBN 0878465952.

The authors describe folk art and the pieces owned by the Boston Museum of Fine Arts.

Children's Books

Abby Aldrich Rockefeller Folk Art Center Staff and Amy Watson. *The Folk Art Counting Book.* Williamsburg, VA: Colonial Williamsburg Foundation, 1992. ISBN 0879350849.

This counting book utilizes works from the Abby Aldrich Rockefeller Folk Collection.

Adler, David. *Heroes of the Revolution.* New York: Holiday House, 2003. ISBN 0-8234-1471-X.

Adler offers short biographies of twelve heroes, both men and women.

Anderson, Madelyn Klein. *North American Indian Games.* New York: Franklin Watts, 2000. ISBN 0-531-20403-0.

Anderson examines the many games played by North American Indians, including shinny and other ball games, dice games, and guessing games.

Armstrong, Jennifer. *Photo by Brady: A Picture of the Civil War.* New York: Atheneum, 2005. ISBN 0689857853.

In telling the story of the Civil War, Armstrong uses the stirring photos taken by Matthew Brady at the time.

Arnold, Caroline. *The Ancient Cliff Dwellers of Mesa Verde*. Photos by Richard Hewett. New York: Clarion, 2000. ISBN 061805149X.

Arnold describes the Anasazi, who built extensive cliff dwellings and disappeared in the thirteenth century.

Ashabranner, Brent. *A Strange and Distant Shore*. New York: Dutton, 1996. ISBN 0525652019.

When seventy-two Indian chiefs and warriors were imprisoned in 1875 as punishment for raids against frontier settlements, they began to paint pictures to recapture their lost world of freedom on the Plains.

Aveni, Anthony. *The First Americans: The Story of Where They Came from and Who They Became.* Illustrated by S. D. Nelson. New York: Scholastic, 2005. ISBN 0439551447.

Aveni traces the origins of native peoples in North America and their evolution. There is a chapter on the Northwest woodlands Indians and totem poles and on Indians of the Southwest. Information on artifacts, games, and more makes this a wonderful resource.

Baylor, Byrd. *When Clay Sings.* Illustrated by Tom Bahti. New York: Aladdin Paperback, 1987. ISBN 0689711069.

In poetic text the author imagines the history of some pieces of prehistoric Indian pottery.

Bedry, Christa. *The Pueblo.* New York: Chelsea House, 2003. ISBN 0791079643.

The author tells the story of the Pueblo, who built cliff dwellings to protect themselves from enemies.

Beneduce, Ann Keay. *A Weekend with Winslow Homer.* New York: Rizzoli, 1993. ISBN 0847816222.

The painter invites the reader into his home and talks about his art. List of museums containing Homer's works.

Beyer, Don E. *The Totem Pole Indians of the Northwest.* New York: Franklin Watts, 1989. ISBN 0-531-10750-7.

The way of life and the art of peoples of the Northwest are discussed.

Brenner, Barbara. *The Boy Who Loved to Draw: Benjamin West.* Illustrated by Olivier Dunrea. Reprint, Boston: Houghton Mifflin, 2003. ISBN 0618310894.

This is a simply written biography of the artist that reveals how he became interested in drawing as a young child. How he learned to make paints from the Indians and used his cat's fur for brushes are among the incidents related in the story.

———. *If You Were There in 1776.* New York: Bradbury Press, 1994. ISBN 0027123227.

Brenner puts the reader in the New World in the year 1776. Lively presentation of major leaders and events of that year.

Bruchac, Joseph. *Between Earth & Sky.* Illustrated by Thomas Locker. Reprint, San Diego: Harcourt Brace, 1999. ISBN 0152020624.

This book of legends about Native American sacred places includes a map locating tribes and a listing of the special places. Beautiful illustrations.

———. *The Boy Who Lived with the Bears.* Illustrated by Murv Jacob. Reprint, New York: Parabola, 2003. ISBN 0-930407-61-X.

Bruchac presents six Iroquois folktales.

———. *Children of the Longhouse.* Reprint, New York: Puffin, 1998. ISBN 0140385045.

In this short novel set in a Mohawk village in the late 1400s, a twin brother and sister, well-loved in the community, make enemies of an older gang. Filled with Mohawk traditions, including a ball game we now know as lacrosse.

———. *Crazy Horse's Vision.* Illustrated by S. D. Nelson. New York: Lee & Low, 2006.

In this picture-book biography, Bruchac provides a good deal of information about Crazy Horse's youth.

———. *The Earth Under Sky Bear's Feet: Native American Poems of the Land.* Illustrated by Thomas Locker. New York: Putnam Juvenile, 1998. ISBN 069811647X.

This is a collection of nature poems from many different tribes.

———. *Four Ancestors: Stories, Songs, and Poems from Native North America.* Illustrated by S. S. Burrus, Jeffrey Chapman, Murv Jacob, and Duke Sine. New York: Bridgewater Books, 1996. ISBN 0816738432.

Illustrated by four Native American artists, the tales in this beautiful book explain the wonders of the four elements: earth, air, fire, and water.

———. *How Chipmunk Got His Stripes: A Tale of Bragging and Teasing.* Illustrated by Jose Aruego and Ariane Dewey. Reprint, New York: Puffin, 2003. ISBN 0142500216.

When Squirrel gets tired of Bear's bragging and teases him, Bear's claws transform Squirrel into a chipmunk.

———. *Pushing up the Sky: Seven Native American Plays for Children.* Illustrated by Theresa Flavin. New York: Dial, 2000. ISBN 0803721684.

Bruchac turns tales from the Abenaki, Ojibway, Cherokee, Cheyenne, Snohomish, Tlingit, and Zuni people into plays for children.

———. *Seasons of the Circle: A Native American Year.* Illustrated by Robert F. Goetzl. Mahwah, NJ: Troll/Bridgewater, 2002. ISBN 0-8167-7467-6.

A different activity and a different Indian tribe are introduced for each month of the year.

Bruchac, Joseph, and Gayle Ross. *The Girl Who Married the Moon: Tales from Native North America.* New York: Bridgewater Books, 1996. ISBN 081673481X.

This is a collection of Native American tales from the Northeast, Southeast, Southwest, and Northwest.

Bruchac, Joseph, and James Bruchac. *Native American Games and Stories.* Illustrated by Kayeri Akweks. Golden, CO: Fulcrum Publishing, 2000. ISBN 1555919790.

Master storytellers help readers learn about Native American games and enjoy their stories.

———. *Raccoon's Last Race.* Illustrated by Jose Aruego and Ariane Dewey. New York: Dial, 2004. ISBN 0-8037-2977-4.

This Abenaki *pourquoi* tale tells readers why raccoon is short and fat and moves quite slowly.

Bruchac, Joseph, and Jonathan London. *Thirteen Moons on Turtle's Back.* Illustrated by Thomas Locker. New York: Philomel, 1992. ISBN 0399221417.

This book celebrates the seasons through a collection of poems based on the legends of various Native American tribes.

Bruchac, Joseph, and Michael J. Caduto. *Native American Animal Stories.* Illustrated by John Kahionhes Fadden and David Kanietakeron Fadden. Golden, CO: Fulcrum Publishing, 1992. ISBN 1-55591-127-7.

This delightful collection of Native American animal tales is perfect for reading aloud since each one is quite short. The authors mention each tale's tribe of origin.

Bruchac, Marge. *Malian's Song*. Illustrated by William Maughan. Middlebury, VT: Vermont Folklife Center, 2006. ISBN 0916718263.

This picture book is based on the true story of a deliberate attack by English Major Robert Rogers on Quebec's St. Francis Abenaki community in 1759 and how many of the people survived thanks to a warning from a Mohican scout.

Caduto, Michael J., and Joseph Bruchac. *Keepers of Life*. Illustrated by John K. Fadden et al. Golden, CO: Fulcrum Publishing, 1999. ISBN 1555913873.

Readers discover plants through Native American stories and earth activities for children.

———. *Keepers of the Earth: Native American Stories and Environmental Activities for Children.*. Illustrated by Carol Wood. Reissue. Golden, CO: Fulcrum Publishing, 1999. ISBN 1555913857.

Native American legends and ecology activities for children. Audiocassette available.

Capek, Michael. *Artistic Trickery: The Tradition of Trompe L'Oeil Art.* Minneapolis, MN: Lerner, 1995. ISBN 0822520648.

Capek discusses the ways in which artists trick viewers into believing what they have painted is real. Peale's *The Staircase Group* and other accomplishments of the Peale family are included.

Curry, Jane Louise. *Back in the Beforetime: Tales of the California Indians.* Illustrated by James Curry. New York: Margaret McElderry, 1987. ISBN 0689504101.

This is a collection of Native American tales

Dennis, Yvonne Wakim, and Arlene Hirschfelder. *Children of Native America Today.* Watertown, MA: Charlesbridge, 2003. ISBN 1-57091-499-0.

Many different tribes, their traditional customs, where they live, etc., are the subjects of this book.

Dewey, Jennifer Owings. *Stories on Stone: Rock Art: Images from the Ancient Ones.* Santa Fe: University of New Mexico Press, 2003. ISBN 082633024X.

This picture book presents some of the rock art found in the Southwestern United States and attempts to answer questions about the ancient native peoples who produced it and what they were trying to say.

DK Publishing. *Civil War Battles and Leaders.* New York: DK Children, 2004. ISBN 0789498901.

This interesting history of the Civil War is enhanced by excellent illustrations.

———. *North American Indian.* New York: DK Children, 2005. ISBN 0756610826.

Interesting text and fine illustrations make this a good history of North American Indians. This is a good source of information about kachina ceremonies.

Englar, Mary. *The Pueblo: Southwestern Potters.* Mankato, MN: Capstone Press/Blue Moon, 2000. ISBN 0-7368-1538-4W.

This book focuses on the Pueblo Indians and how they make their pottery. It includes a recipe and a game.

———. *The Southwest Indians: Daily Life in the 1500s.* Mankato, MN: Bridgestone Books, 2006. ISBN 0736843191.

The author describes the life and activities of the Indians of the Southwest.

Epstein, Sam, and Beryl Epstein. *Mister Peale's Mammoth.* New York: Coward, McCann & Geoghegan, 1977. ISBN 0-69820-402-6.

This is a picture-book story of Peale's dinosaur dig.

Erdrich, Louise. *The Birchbark House.* New York: Hyperion, 1999. ISBN 0-7868-0300-2.

This excellent novel for fourth-graders and up is the story of an Ojibwa girl and her family and the devastation that comes when a white man brings smallpox to the community. The story continues with *The Game of Silence.*

Fisher, Leonard Everett. *The Limners: America's Earliest Portrait Painters.* Reprint, Singapore: Benchmark Books, 2000. ISBN 0761409327.

This is an excellent book to use for an idea of what America's earliest untrained painters were like.

Flood, Bo, and Nancy Bo Flood. *The Navajo Year: Walk Through Many Seasons.* Illustrated by Billy Whitethorne. Flagstaff, AZ: Salina Bookshelf, 2006. ISBN 1893354067.

Readers follow the Navajo people and their various activities through the twelve months of the year.

Francis, Lee. *When the Rain Sings.* New York: Simon & Schuster, 1999. ISBN 0689822839.

Native Americans in grades two to twelve wrote the poems in this collection.

Franco, Betsy, Annette Pina Ochoa, et al., eds. *Night Is Gone, Day Is Still Coming: Stories and Poems by American Indian Teens and Young Adults.* Cambridge, MA: Candlewick Press, 2003. ISBN 0763615188.

In this fine collection, a few of the poems are suitable for younger children.

Freedman, Russell. *Buffalo Hunt.* Reissue. New York: Holiday House, 1995. ISBN 0-8234-1159-1.

Freedman describes the importance of the buffalo to the Plains Indians, methods of hunting, and uses of the animal.

———. *Indian Chiefs.* New York: Holiday House, 1987. ISBN 0-8234-0625-3.

These biographies of six western Indian chiefs are written by a master biographer.

———. *Lincoln: A Photobiography.* New York: Clarion, 1989. ISBN 0-3955-1848-2.

This Newbery-award-winning book is THE biography of Lincoln for children, and it is fascinating reading.

Giblin, James Cross. *The Mystery of the Mammoth Bones and How It Was Solved.* New York: HarperCollins, 1999. ISBN 0-060-27494-8.

Written for older children, this is the story of Peale's discovery of a mammoth skeleton.

Glubok, Shirley. *The Art of the Southwest Indians.* New York: Atheneum, 1971. ISBN 006022066X.

Glubok provides a very simple presentation of the arts of the Southwestern Indians for young children.

Goble, Paul. *The Girl Who Loved Wild Horses.* Rev. ed. New York: Atheneum/ Richard Jackson, 2001. ISBN 0689845049.

This lovely picture-book story of a girl who loved horses so much she joined them is accompanied by a reading on CD accompanied by Indian music.

Griffin-Pierce, Trudy. *The Encyclopedia of Native America.* New York: Viking, 1995. ISBN 0670851043.

This is a very readable history of the different groups of Native Americans in North America, their customs, arts, and interaction with Europeans.

Hakim, Joy. *The First Americans.* 3d ed. New York: Oxford University Press, 2002. ISBN 0195153200.

This history of Native Americans is accessible for younger children.

———. *A History of US: Making Thirteen Colonies.* 3d ed. New York: Oxford University Press, 2002. ISBN 0195153227.

This is a delightful history of the United States from colonization to the middle of the eighteenth century.

Haslam, Andrew, and Alexandra Parsons. *Make It Work! North American Indians.* New York: Scholastic, 1995. ISBN 0590937464.

This book explores different aspects of Indian life such as clothing and suggests related activities.

Hausman, Gerald. *Eagle Boy.* Illustrated by Lee Christiansen. Seattle, WA: Sasquatch Books, 2000. ISBN 1570611718.

In this Navajo legend, a boy is carried off by eagles and learns their ways.

Henry, Marguerite. *Benjamin West and His Cat Grimalkin.* Illustrated by Wesley Dennis. Laceyville, PA: Bradford Press, 2000. ISBN 0970561806.

In this picture book, Henry recounts the story of young Benjamin West and how he made a brush from his cat's tail.

Hirschfelder, Arlene B., and Beverly R. Singer, selectors. *Rising Voices: Writings of Young Native Americans.* New York: Ivy Books, 1993. ISBN 0804111677.

This is a collection of poems and essays in which young Native Americans speak about themselves. For older children.

Hirschi, Ron. *People of Salmon and Cedar.* Illustrated by Deborah Cooper. Photos by Edward S. Curtis. New York: Cobblehill, 1996. ISBN 0525651837.

The author discusses the culture and history of the Northwest Coast Indians.

Hoyt-Goldsmith, Diane. *Potlatch: A Tsimshian Celebration.* Illustrated by Lawrence Migdale. New York: Holiday House, 1997. ISBN 0-8234-1290-3.

The Tsimshian people living in Alaska have a potlatch feast to celebrate their heritage. The pictures and story will give students an excellent idea of what a potlatch is like and greatly enhance the story told about the Northwest Indians in chapter 14.

———. *Pueblo Storyteller*. Photos by Lawrence Migdale. New York: Holiday House, 1991. ISBN 0823408647.

A young Cochiti girl describes how her grandparents make pottery story dolls in their pueblo.

———. *Totem Pole*. New York: Holiday House, 1990. ISBN 0823408094.

A young Indian boy describes how his father makes a totem pole for a neighboring tribe.

Jensen, Vicki. *Carving a Totem Pole*. New York: Henry Holt, 1996. ISBN 0805037543.

This is a close-up look at a Nisga'a artist's carving of a doorway pole and how it embodies the culture of a people. Sepia photographs.

Jeunesse, Gallimard, et al. *Native Americans*. Illustrated by Ute Fuhr and Raoul Sautai. New York: Scholastic, 1998. ISBN 0590381539.

In this First Discovery book, plastic overlays help young children learn about the history of Native Americans.

Kelly, Michael. *Native American Talking Signs*. New York: Chelsea House, 1998. ISBN 0-7910-4681-8.

Kelly explains Native American sign language.

Keoke, Dean, and Kay Marie Porterfield. *Food, Farming, and Hunting*. New York: Facts on File, 2005. ISBN 0-8160-5393-6.

The authors discuss farming methods and crops such as corn and gourds that have come to us from Native Americans.

———. *Medicine and Health*. New York: Facts on File, 2005. ISBN 0-8160-5393-0.

A cure for scurvy, sweat lodges to relieve pain—these and other ways to promote good health have come to us from Native Americans.

———. *Science and Technology*. New York: Facts on File, 2005. ISBN 0-8160-5397-9.

Indians developed hand signals, silversmithing, mining for metals, and more.

Littlechild, George. *This Land Is My Land*. Emeryville, CA: Children's Book Press, 1993. ISBN 0892391197.

The artist, a member of the Plains Cree Nation, explains some of his paintings in this beautiful picture book.

Littlesugar, Amy. *Jonkonnu: A Story from the Sketchbook of Winslow Homer*. Illustrated by Ian Schoenherr. New York: Philomel, 1997. ISBN 0399228314.

Based on a true account of Homer's visit to Petersburg, Virginia, in 1876, this is the story behind the painting *Dressing for the Carnival*.

Martin, Rafe. *The Rough-Face Girl*. Illustrated by David Shannon. Reissue. New York: Putnam, 1998. ISBN 0698116267.

This is an Algonquin version of "Cinderella."

McDermott, Gerald. *Coyote*. Reprint, San Diego: Voyager/Harcourt Brace, 1999. ISBN 0152019588.

In this Zuni tale, Coyote meets disaster when he insists the crows teach him to fly.

———. *Raven: A Trickster Tale from the Pacific Northwest*. Reprint, San Diego: Harcourt, 1993. ISBN 0152656618.

Raven uses trickery to obtain light and warmth for the people.

McIntosh. *Pueblo*. Philadelphia: Mason Crest, 2004. ISBN 1-59084-676-1.

Written with help from three Pueblos, this book shows what life is like for various Pueblo Indian groups today.

Miller, Jay. *American Indian Foods*. Danbury, CT: Children's Press/Grolier, 1996. ISBN 051626091X.

This account of Native American harvesting and preparing of foods is very simply written for young children.

Morrison, Taylor. *Civil War Artist*. Reprint, Boston: Houghton Mifflin/Walter Lorraine, 2004. ISBN 061849538X.

In this wonderful picture book, Morrison follows the activities of an unnamed Civil War artist from sketch to the newspaper office to the complicated process of getting the drawing into print.

Mott, Evelyn Clarke. *Dancing Rainbows: A Pueblo Boy's Story*. New York: Cobblehill Books, 1996. ISBN 0525652167.

Photos and text tell the story of a young Tewa Indian boy as he and his grandfather prepare to participate in a special tribal dance.

Nicholson, Nicholas B. A. *Little Girl in a Red Dress with Cat and Dog*. Illustrated by Cynthia Von Buhler. New York: Viking, 1998. ISBN 0670871834.

This is a delightful story about the little girl who is the subject of Ammi Phillips's painting *Little Girl in a Red Dress with Cat and Dog* and what her family life might have been like. The illustrations imitate folk art paintings.

Northern Band of the Shoshone Nation. *Coyote Steals Fire: A Shoshone Tale*. Logan: University of Utah Press, 2005. ISBN 0874216184.

Members of the Northern Band of the Shoshone wrote and illustrated this story about how their people obtained fire. The picture book comes with a CD of a tribe member telling the story in the Shoshone language.

Olsen, Madeline. *Native American Sign Language*. Illustrated by Ben Carter. Mahwah, NJ: Troll, 1998. ISBN 0816745099.

In addition to the Plains Indians' sign language, readers learn about their customs, family life, and crafts.

Ortiz, Simon. *The People Shall Continue*. Illustrated by Sharol Graves. Rev. ed. San Francisco: Children's Press, 1988. ISBN 0892390417.

This is a poetic history of Native Americans for young children.

Panchyk, Richard. *American Folk Art for Kids with 21 Activities.* Chicago: Chicago Review Press, 2004. ISBN 1-55652-499-4.

Folk art is explained and examples of different kinds of folk art along with related activities are provided.

Panzer, Nora, ed. *Celebrate America in Poetry and Art.* Reprint, New York: Hyperion, 1999. ISBN 0786813601.

This gorgeous book of poetry is accompanied by art prints that celebrate the 200 years of America's history.

Patent, Dorothy Hinshaw. *The Buffalo and the Indians: A Shared Destiny.* Photographs by William Munoz. Boston: Clarion, 2006. ISBN 0618485708.

Patent describes the relationship between the Indian and the buffalo, how Europeans decimated the herds, and how Indians are now bringing the animals back.

Penner, Lucille Recht. *A Native American Feast.* Collingdale, PA: Diane Publishing Company, 1994. ISBN 0-7881-6557-7

Penner offers authentic Native American recipes, including cooking techniques, manners, and customs.

Philip, Neil, selector. *Earth Always Endures: Native American Poems.* Photos by Edward S. Curtis. New York: Viking, 1996. ISBN 0670868736.

This is an anthology of poems written by members of Native American tribes from the woodlands, the plains, the deserts, and the pueblos. Accompanied by magnificent black-and-white photos.

———. *The Great Circle: A History of the First Nations.* New York: Clarion, 2006. ISBN 061815941X.

This is a carefully researched history of Native American peoples.

Powell, Patricia Hruby. *Zinnia: How the Corn Was Saved.* Navajo by Peter Thomas. Illustrated by Kendrick Benally. Flagstaff, AZ: Salina Bookshelf, 2003. ISBN 1-893354-38-5.

When the Navajo people's crops fail, Red Bird is sent to ask Spider woman for help.

Preus, Margi, and Lise Lunge-Larsen. *The Legend of the Lady Slipper.* Illustrated by Andrea Arroyo. Boston: Houghton Mifflin, 2004. ISBN 0618432310.

In this Ojibwe Tale, a young girl risks her life on a winter journey to bring herbs to her sick family.

Rappaport, Doreen, and Joan Verniero. *United No More!: Stories of the Civil War.* Illustrated by Rick Reeves. New York: HarperCollins, 2006. ISBN 0060506008.

Using primary sources, the authors tell seven stories that recount people's experiences on both sides of the conflict.

———. *Victory or Death!: Stories of the American Revolution.* Illustrated by Greg Call. New York: HarperCollins, 2003. ISBN 0060295155.

Using primary sources, the authors tell eight short stories about unsung heroes during the American Revolution.

Raymer, Dottie. *Welcome to Kaya's World.* Edited by Jodi Evert. Middletown, WI: Pleasant Company, 2003. ISBN 1-58485-722-6.

This beautiful picture book recounts the history of the Nez Perce people, beginning with a creation story and ending with the lives of the people today. There are many folktales throughout, as well as information about dwellings, clothing, artwork, and more.

Rumford, James. *Sequoyah: The Cherokee Man Who Gave His People Writing.* Boston: Houghton Mifflin, 2004. ISBN 0618369473.

This outstanding picture-book biography is written in both English and Cherokee and includes the Cherokee alphabet.

Sneve, Virginia Driving Hawk. *The Cherokees.* Illustrated by Ronald Himler. New York: Holiday House, 1996. ISBN 0823412148.

In this picture book the author describes the tribe's history, social life, arts, and situation today.

———. *Dancing Teepees.* Illustrated by Stephen Gammell. Reprint, New York: Holiday House, 1991. ISBN 0823408795.

This is a delightful collection of poetry written by Native American children.

———. *Enduring Wisdom: Sayings from Native Americans.* Illustrated by Synthia Saint James. New York: Holiday House, 2003. ISBN 0-8234-1455-8.

Sayings from many Indian tribes are collected in this book.

Sufrin, Mark. *George Catlin: Painter of the Indian West.* New York: Atheneum, 1991. ISBN 0788163426.

Sufrin offers a complete biography of the artist, with a bibliography.

Sullivan, Missy, and Deborah Schwartz. *The Native American Look Book.* New York: The New Press/Brooklyn Museum of Art, 2000. ISBN 1-56584-604-4.

This is a book of activities for children involving Native Americans.

Terkel, Susan Neiburg. *Colonial American Medicine.* New York: Franklin Watts, 1993. ISBN 0531125394.

Terkel describes the illnesses prevalent in colonial America and the sometimes outrageous remedies for them.

Tunnell, Michael O. *The Joke's on George.* Illustrated by Kathy Osborn. Reprint, Honesdale, PA: Boyds Mills Press, 2001. ISBN 1563979705.

This is a delightful picture-book story of how one of Peale's paintings tricked George Washington.

Van Laan, Nancy. *In a Circle Long Ago.* Illustrated by Lisa Desimini. New York: Apple Soup/Knopf, 1995. ISBN 067995807X.

Twenty-five stories, poems, and songs from over twenty different North American tribes fill this beautiful book.

Vanasse, Deb. *Totem Tale: A Tall Story from Alaska.* Illustrated by Erik Brooks. Seattle, WA: Sasquatch Books, 2006. ISBN 1-57061-439-3.

Figures on a totem pole come to life and then argue about their placement on the pole when it comes time to become inanimate once again.

Venezia, Mike. *Winslow Homer.* Danbury, CT: Children's Press, 2004. ISBN 0516269798.

Cartoon drawings coupled with color reproductions of the artist's life combine to offer a readable biography.

Weber, EdNah. *Rattlesnake Mesa: Stories from a Native American Childhood.* Photos by Richela Renkun. New York: Lee & Low, 2004. ISBN 1-58430-231-3.

Weber recalls her childhood on a Navaho reservation and then at an Indian boarding school. Older readers will find this a very moving account.

Wilson, Janet. *The Ingenious Mr. Peale: Painter, Patriot, and Man of Science.* New York: Atheneum, 1996. ISBN 0-689-31884-7.

This biography examines the many facets of Charles Willson Peale's talent, including his involvement in politics, his painting, his inventions, farming, and even motion pictures. Bibliography.

Yerxa, Leo. *Ancient Thunder.* Toronto: Groundwood, 2006. ISBN 0888997469.

Leo Yerza, an artist of Ojibwa ancestry, celebrates the horse through his beautiful illustrations.

Audiovisual Materials

American Art, 1785-1926: Seven Artist Profiles. DVD. The National Gallery of Art, n.d. DV330.

Winslow Homer is among the artists presented in this film.

American Art from the National Gallery of Art. Videodisc. The National Gallery of Art, n.d. LD304.

There are more than 2,600 images in this program, and each work presented includes five details. Hypercard software is an available supplement for this program that can be borrowed for nine months. The hypercard number is HC304.

The American Vision. Video. The National Gallery of Art, n.d. VC101.

This video surveys American painting from pre-revolutionary days to the beginning of the twentieth century.

Ancient Art of the American Woodland Indians. Slides and audiocassette. The National Gallery of Art, n.d. 055.

These slides explore the artwork of the prehistoric Indians of the woodland areas of Midwestern and Southeastern North America.

Awareness Series: American Art. Video. National Gallery of Art, n.d. VC125.

This video provides short studies of the major artists represented in the Gallery's collection. George Catlin and folk art painters are included.

The Far North: 2,000 Years of American Eskimo and Indian Art. Slides and audiocassette. The National Gallery of Art, n.d. 042.

This program explores the art and cultures of the Alaskan Eskimo and Athabaskan and Tlingit Indians.

Folk Arts of the Spanish Southwest. Slides and audiocassette. National Gallery of Art, n.d. 024.

These slides survey crafts produced in New Mexico and California by Native Americans.

The Inquiring Eye: American Painting. Slides, prints, and booklet. National Gallery of Art, n.d. TP312.

Available for a nine-month loan period, this program is a survey of American painting from the colonial period to the early twentieth century.

Pottery. Slides and audiocassette. National Gallery of Art, n.d. 026.

These slides survey American pottery, examining techniques and the development of forms and glazes.

Survey of American Painting. Slides and audiocassette. The National Gallery of Art, n.d. 002.

This survey includes works by Benjamin West, Winslow Homer, and Mary Cassatt, among others.

Winslow Homer: The Nature of the Artist. Videocassette. The National Gallery of Art, n.d. VC148.

This film follows Homer from his Civil War illustrations to his mature and late work.

Other Materials

First North American Dream Catcher. Usborne Press, 2005. ISBN 1-58086-800-2.

This kit contains everything children need to create an Indian dream catcher.

Zuk, Bill, and Don Bergland. *Art First Nations 1.* Art Image Publications, 1999

This kit focuses on the artistic innovation of First Nations peoples in five major geographical and cultural areas of North America: Southwest, Arctic, Eastern Woodlands, Plains, and Northwest Coast. It contains twenty prints and a teacher's guide.

Web Sites

Civil War Songs. http://www.pabucktail.com/songs.htm (accessed April 1, 2006).

Listen to Civil War songs from both the North and South.

Colonial Williamsburg. http://www.history.org/media/ (accessed April 1, 2006).

This is a really fine site. Children can see a slide show of folk art pieces, learn about life in colonial times, and much more.

George Catlin and His Indian Gallery. http://americanart.si.edu/collections/exhibits/catlin/highlights.html (accessed April 1, 2006).

View online thirty-four images that make up this exhibit and read a short biography of the artist.

Native American Technology and Art. http://www.nativetech.org/, (accessed March 28, 2006).

This site has links to many aspects of Native American art and culture. See how they prepare clay to make pottery, do bead work, etc.

North Native Symbols. http://www.geocities.com/ctesibos/symbols/native-american.html (accessed March 27, 2006).

A large number of symbols are pictured, with their meanings.

Oyate. http://www.oyate.org (accessed March 28, 2006).

This is THE site to visit when researching books and other information about Native Americans. Oyate offers reviews and ways to avoid mistakes in teaching about Native Americans and their culture.

Revolutionary War Songs. http://www.fssd.org/PGS/PGS_Digital_Museum/music%20Folder/songs.html (accessed April 1, 2006).

Listen to songs of the American Revolution.

Southern Pow Wow. http://library.thinkquest.org/3081/#intro (accessed March 29, 2006).

At this wonderful site, visitors can hear Native American songs and drums and learn about Native American dances, pow wows, etc.

Totem Poles: An Exploration by Pat Kramer. http://users.imag.net/~sry.jkramer/nativetotems/default.html (accessed April 13, 2006).

On the home page of this site, a camera pans a totem pole's full height as an instrument plays. Links lead to all kinds of information: stories connected with totem poles, humor in totem poles, basic figures, and much more. This is well worth a visit.

Totem Poles: Art of the Pacific Northwest. http://members.aol.com/Art1234567/Totemart.html (accessed April 13, 2006).

See a lesson about totem pole art, read a folktale about how Raven stole fire, and make a box connected with this story. This is a neat activity for children.

Part VII The Art of Mexico

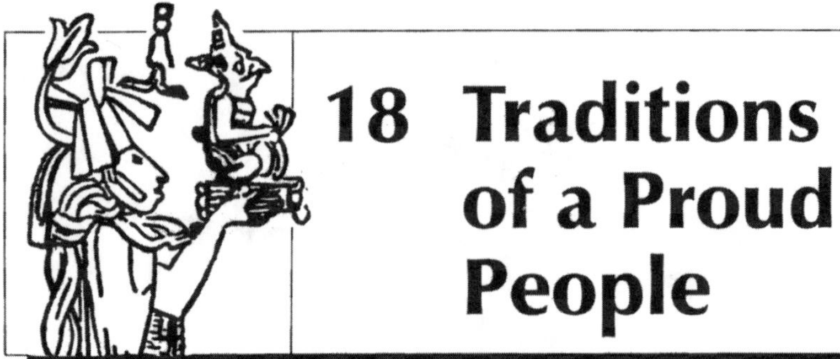

18 Traditions of a Proud People

LESSON 1: The Ancient Mayans

Of the moral effect of the monuments themselves, standing as they do in the depths of a tropical forest, silent and solemn, strange in design, excellent in sculpture, rich in ornament, different from the works of any other people . . . . I shall not pretend to convey any idea.

—JOHN LLOYD STEPHENS, in *The World of the Ancient Maya*

Background Information

The Mayans are descendants of those ancient peoples who came across the land bridge between Asia and Alaska down through what is now the United States and into Central America and Mexico at least 10,000 years ago. Their agricultural way of life enabled them to settle in one place and establish complex societies. The ancient Mayans built pyramid-shaped temples to rival those in Egypt. Without the benefit of the sophisticated measuring instruments we use today, they devised three calendars: one containing 365 days for calculating the events of daily life, one of 260 days for planning religious ceremonies and the planting of crops, and one based on the phases of the moon.

Considered to be among the most literate of ancient peoples, the Mayans made paper from fig tree bark and devised both a written language using hieroglyphs and a number system based on lines and dots. They developed the concept of zero as a place holder for writing large numbers. The Mayans were able to determine the orbit of Venus and some of the other planets and to predict accurately eclipses of the sun and moon.

Mayan society was established under strict class rules. Each large city had one chief, who usually ruled for life and passed his position on to his descendants. Other lesser rulers assisted him in his task. The priests, some of whom were rulers, were the highest class of society. They taught and organized religious ceremonies. Second highest were the wealthy families living privileged lives in comfortable homes close to the center of the city and the temples. There was a warrior class and a farming class as well. Farmers lived in simple huts, worked the land, and gave some of their produce to the wealthy. The people indicated their social status by the manner in which they painted their bodies: black patterns for children, red for married people, red and black for warriors, black and white for slaves captured in war, and blue for priests and nobles.

Most of Mayan art had to do with their religious ideas. Mayans believed that the universe was created by a supreme god named Hunah Ku. He created people, too, but several of his first attempts were unsuccessful—until he used corn as his raw material. For Mayans, corn was not only a source of their own existence, but also the staple that sustained them throughout their lives. Yum Kax, the corn god, was thus an important deity. The people devoted much of their art to the honor of their gods, creating sculptures of and temples for the different divinities, almost all of whom were related to nature, and decorations for ceremonies in their honor. Itzamna, god of the sun; Chac, god of rain; Ex Chua, god of warriors and merchants; and Ixchel, goddess of pregnancy, were especially venerated by the people. Mayan ruins and reconstructions are evidence of their sophisticated architectural and engineering skills and the incredible carving and painting done in the name of religious worship. Like the Egyptians, the Mayans sent important people on their journey into the afterlife equipped with jewelry, especially jade, and artifacts the dead would need for the next world. They also wove decorative clothing embellished with the feathers of birds that shared their tropical rain forest environment, made lovely baskets, and created ornately painted jars.

Mayan civilization was at its height ca. AD 250–900, after which, for unexplained reasons, it began to decline. Some archaeologists believe that poor farming methods may have resulted in the people's inability to provide adequately for themselves. The arrival of the Spanish in the sixteenth century effectively put an end to the way of life these ancient people had been practicing for centuries. The Spanish burned precious Mayan books, believing them to contain the work of the devil. They brought diseases that killed thousands of Mayans, who had no resistance to them. Today there are about two million Mayan people living in Mexico and Central America. While they are mostly Catholic, they still follow some of the ancient customs of their people. However, the glories of ancient Mayan civilization, with its impressive temples and wondrous ceremonies, are gone forever.

(Standards: Art Connections: 1,1-2, 4, 6-7; World History 17.114)

The Story

Over a thousand years ago, a young Mayan girl living in what is now Mexico was getting ready for a special ceremony in honor of Yum Kax, the corn god. She and her family would have to hurry, because it was almost dawn. The priests in the temple were going to reveal whether or not the time was right to begin planting. Everyone was preparing for the big event. Her father was arranging his special feathered headdress. The girl watched him place it on his head, where it seemed to reach high into the sky, showing how important he was. She watched her mother put on her most decorative garment and place huge earrings in her beautiful ears. Her brother was exercising for the game of *pok-to-pok* in which he would play that afternoon. What a difficult ball game that was! He and his teammates would have to get a hard rubber ball through a high hoop without even using their hands! If her brother's team won, the people watching the game would reward them with jewelry. She decided she would do her part to help him.

"Here," she said. "Let me tie leather cloths on your hips and arms and elbows to protect you from the hard ball." She gathered up the strips and set to work. When she had finished, her mother helped her put on special earrings and bracelets and the family, ready at last, walked the short distance into the center of the city where the temple to the corn god was located. Her father proudly carried a basket of choice vegetables the family was offering to Yum Kax.

The girl saw people gathering from all parts of the community: poor farmers and powerful warriors, as well as prosperous families like her own. The crowds, carrying their offerings, pressed into place at the foot of the temple stairs. In the darkness it was hard to see the beautiful carvings and statues that decorated the temple, but the girl knew it was a fine and fitting place in which to honor the god of corn. Finally the musicians carrying their big drums, conch shells, and flutes took up their positions, and the dancers, arrayed in their fabulous masks, placed themselves nearby. A quiet descended on the people.

As the sun slowly rose in the sky, everyone looked up to see a priest on the platform of the temple pyramid. The people began to pass up to him their offerings for the corn god and to watch silently as the priest spread out the gifts and prayed to Yum Kax on their behalf. Would the god be pleased? Would he accept their humble offerings and grant a good growing season for the corn that was to sustain their lives?

It seemed to the girl as if everyone were holding their breaths, waiting for an answer. Finally, the priest faced the crowd, raised a conch shell to his lips, and blew into it. The loud blast seemed to vibrate right through the girl's body. "My people," the priest proclaimed, "Yum Kax is pleased with your offerings. He says the time is right for planting. The rains will come in their season, and the corn will grow tall and strong and continue to give life to us all. Let the celebrations begin!"

A cheer rose up from the crowd as they made way for the dancers. The musicians began to play while the dancers leaped and whirled to the beat. The girl's father lifted her high on his shoulders so that she could see the swirling streamers and the prancing feet. At last the dancers, exhausted by their efforts, stopped and moved from the center of the crowd and the *pok-to-pok* teams took their places on the court. The ruler and his nobles sat in their special grandstand to watch while the people milled around. How proud the girl was that her big brother was a player! "May you be swift and sure and lead your team to victory," she whispered to herself as she watched him move on the court. And he did hit the ball many times, but not through the target. For two hours the weary players moved the ball back and forth, but not once did it go through the hoop. Finally, one of her brother's friends gave the ball a powerful hit with his hip and it went sailing through the hoop. The team let out a shriek of victory and went running through the crowd for gifts of jewelry. Her brother ran to their mother and gave her a beautiful jade bracelet, the reward of his achievements. How proud the family was of him!

"Now, my son," said his father, "let us relax and rest after this eventful day. It is time for the feasting." Like everyone else, they set out good food and drink. For the rest of that day and even through the night, the murmur of joyful talk and laughter could be heard. At last the sun rose once more in the sky and the sleepy people went to their homes. Tomorrow they would plant their kernels, tend the tender plants, and watch anxiously for the first ears of corn to appear—the promise of life and health.

(Standards: Language Arts: Listening and Speaking 8.4)

Viewing the Art

Begin by showing the children some Mayan architecture, done mostly to honor the gods or to provide palaces for rulers. (See Stuart 1993, Thomas 2001, and Proskouriakoff 2002.) The temples at Uxmal are especially fine examples. (See http://www.smm.org/sln/ma/ux.html for some pictures that are suitable for individual viewing.) Explain to the children that the Mayans built their pyramids of limestone rocks, sometimes hauled over long distances. They built narrower and narrower layers of these bricks, held together with mortar, and then built a temple at the top. About every fifty-two years, they built another temple over the old one, so that archaeologists have uncovered layers and layers of Mayan art.

Elizabeth Mann's *Tikal* (see references) is an excellent children's book to use to show the development of the Mayan city of Tikal in the Yucatan Penninsula. There is a fold-out page with many buildings labeled.

If the children have studied Egyptian art, compare Mayan pyramids to those of the Egyptians. Mention that the Mayans, too, buried art treasures with people so they would have them in the afterlife. If the children have studied the Greeks, ask how Mayan temples compare to Greek temples. Show the Temple of the Magician, the largest structure at Uxmal. (Day 2001, 23 has a good picture.) You may also wish to read *The Dwarf Wizard of Uxmal* (see references), a folktale connected with this temple; the nunnery (probably a school for wealthy children); the governor's palace; and the ball court. Notice the beautiful carvings, or friezes, over the seven doorways of the nunnery and the corbeled arches that are somewhat like gothic arches except that they form a straight line instead of a point on the top. (Page 63 in Braman 2003 has an excellent drawing of a Mayan arch.)

Show some carvings of statues and of hieroglyphs. Many of the carvings are statues of the gods the Mayans honored. Kings in Mayan culture were considered deities, and their importance in Mayan life can be seen not only in the palaces erected for them but also in the way they were represented in paintings and artifacts. The beautiful book *Lords of Creation* (see references) documents the origins and nature of Mayan kingship and its depiction in their art. The illustrations in this book are large and full of detail, and it is highly recommended that you try to obtain it for viewing. There are vessels, tools, jewelry, plates, and much more to delight the children and give them a real sense of what the people looked like. An interesting section on the origins of Mayan writing might prove useful for the activity below. Be sure to show a Mayan head that represents what the people considered true beauty: the sloped, pointed forehead, the large, hooked nose, ears enlarged with the weight of jewelry, and crossed eyes. Explain to the children that when babies were born, Mayan mothers pressed their heads between boards to achieve a long, slanted forehead and hung a bead from a lock of hair in front of their eyes so that their eyes would become crossed. Mayans also put clay on their noses to make them look larger. Show some mural paintings found inside palaces and tombs and paintings on pottery. Miller and Martin's *Courtly Art of the Ancient Maya*—see references—also has gorgeous color pictures of statues, carvings, and paintings.

(Standards: Art Connections 1.1-8; Language Arts: Viewing 9.6, 23)

Journal Writing

Invite the children to compare the Mayan idea of beauty with their own. Is one better than the other? Why or why not? Or ask them to consider the Mayan architectural achievements in light of the fact that they had no building machinery such as bulldozers or cranes. Why do they think the Mayan civilization declined?

(Standards: Thinking and Reasoning: 3.3; Language Arts: Writing 1.7, 23, 33-37; Art Connections 1.3)

Art/Drama Activity: Mayan Writing and Celebrations

Materials

- Pens and ink, black pencils, or black tempera paint
- Thin brushes
- Samples of Mayan hieroglyphs
- Large sheets of paper

Have the children pretend to be artisans carving hieroglyphics on a new temple for one of the gods. Explain that scholars have been trying for many years to understand Mayan hieroglyphs. Many discoveries about Mayan writing have been made by studying the writings on buildings constructed by the Mayans. The Spanish who conquered Mayan lands destroyed most of the books they found, so studying Mayan writing has been very slow and difficult. (If the children have studied Egyptian art, recall how the Rosetta Stone helped to decipher Egyptian hieroglyphics.) We now know how the Mayan writing system works and what some of the hieroglyphs mean. "A Mayan scribe put signs together to make a hieroglyph. He drew them in a glyph block. This block held a main sign by itself or a main sign with several smaller signs around it. Glyph blocks were stacked together in pairs to make the Maya version of a sentence" (Coulter 2001, 29).

Invite the children to write their names using the syllabary on pages 44–45 in Coulter's *Secrets in Stone*. Or they may enjoy using the directions on the back endpapers of the same book to write secret messages to their friends. If you have access to a blender, you can even make imitation Mayan paper by pulverizing scraps of construction paper, yarn, bits of fabric, and water; squeezing the water out; and drying the "paper" on a flat surface.

As a drama activity, the children might enjoy enacting a Mayan celebration in honor of the gods. A child can take the role of the leader, others can be dancers, others musicians, and others enthusiastic people in the crowd. They can make drums to play and/or use recorders or flutes as well.

(Standards: World History: 17.107; Music: 3.4-5, 16; Theater: 2.10)

LESSON 2: Diego Rivera (1886–1957)

To be an artist, one must first be a man,
Vitally concerned with all problems of social struggle,
Unflinching in portraying them without concealment or evasion,
Never shirking the truth as he understands it, never withdrawing from life.

—DIEGO RIVERA

Background Information

In the early 1800s, after more than 200 years of Spanish rule, Mexicans became inflamed with a desire for independence and, led by Miguel Hidalgo y Costilla, began an eleven-year struggle to that end. Mexican independence was finally declared in 1821, but so many lives had been lost and resources spent in the contest that the fledgling country was riddled with problems. In addition, Mexico engaged in repeated conflicts with the United States over what is now Texas and, in the end, was forced not only to relinquish Texas but also to sell to the United States huge chunks of land stretching to the Pacific for a paltry sum. More internal strife between the ruling conservatives and the liberals, who wanted to enact reforms in educational and job opportunities, rocked the country in the latter half of the century until, in 1877, an army general named Porfirio Diaz seized power. He brought order and control to Mexico at the expense of long sought-for freedoms, and his dictatorship lasted more than thirty years.

Diego Rivera and Frida Kahlo lived at a time when Mexico was seething with unrest as poor workers and landless farmers agitated for revolution. The revolution of 1910 deposed Diaz, but he regained control in 1913. Violence and uprisings continued until 1919, and true democracy only became a reality in 1934.

Although he was studying art in Europe, Rivera returned home and became involved in the revolution for a time. But realizing that his life was in danger and that he could do more for his country through his art, he left for Italy to study the ancient art of fresco painting. For seventeen months he examined the works of the great fresco masters and returned to his beloved Mexico once again, this time ready to tell her story on her walls. Previously, Mexican art had been "Europeanized," but Rivera and other muralists changed that: drawing on the brilliant colors of the sunny land, they depicted Mexican history for the common person in vast, popular murals.

From the early Mayan and Aztec civilizations, through the Spanish conquest, to the plight of the workers and peasants of his day, Rivera sought in his art the heart of the native peoples. Both Diego Rivera and his wife, the painter Frida Kahlo, were passionate about their native land and championed Mexico in their art. Frida dressed in Mexican Indian garb even during her travels in the United States and supported her husband in his efforts to win rights for the poor. Together they made the world more aware of their country, its struggles, and its triumphs. Today many Mexicans, especially the descendants of the Indians who once thrived in highly literate and organized societies, are still striving for a decent wage and a way out of their abject poverty. Diego Rivera's murals stand as a beacon of hope for them and for everyone who cares about equal justice for all.

(Standards: World History 35.146, 185; Art Connections: 1,1-2, 4, 6-7)

The Story

"Frida, Frida, wonderful news has just come in the mail!" artist Diego Rivera shouted to his wife. Frida was busy painting at her easel, but she put her paints aside and went to her husband.

"What are you so excited about?" she asked. Then she saw that Diego was holding a letter in his hand.

"The great John D. Rockefeller of New York City has asked me to paint a mural in the RCA building in Rockefeller Center. It is a great honor and a challenge. But it will mean staying away from our beloved Mexico even longer than we had planned. I've worked on this mural for the auto workers in Detroit for so many months already. I want to go home."

"Of course you must do that mural," replied Frida. "A few more months away from Mexico won't make that much difference." So as soon as Diego finished his work in Detroit, the two artists packed their things once again and left for New York.

After drawing sketches for the mural in the RCA building, Diego had workers set up a huge scaffold, and he began to paint. From early morning until late at night he worked, even eating his meals up on the platform. Newspaper reporters found out about the project and came with their notebooks and cameras to get stories about the famous artist at work. But then one day Diego put the face of Lenin, the Russian Communist leader, into his mural. When the reporters saw that, they wrote about it in their newspapers. The people who passed through the lobby of the RCA building saw Lenin's face, and some of them complained. Many Americans hated the ideas of the Communist politicians and were afraid they wanted to take over the world the way they had taken over the system of government in Russia. But Diego liked communist beliefs. He felt the Communists wanted to give every person a chance to earn a decent living, and so he put the Communist leader in his mural.

Finally, John D. Rockefeller himself came to visit Diego. "You must replace Lenin's face with someone else's," he told the painter. "I know that you mean well, but the managers of this building are too angry. They are saying that I'm giving you money to spread dangerous ideas. I can't have my reputation ruined."

Diego was furious. "You knew I was going to do this. I showed you my sketches and you okayed them. Now you're changing your mind. Well, I won't change my mind. Lenin's face stays in the mural."

Diego began painting more quickly than ever. He wanted to finish the job before something happened. Then one morning when he came to work, he found canvas taped over his mural. Mr. Rockefeller was waiting for him. "Go home, Diego. Go back to Mexico. America is not ready for your ideas. Nothing will happen to your mural. Just go."

Sadly, Diego and Frida packed their things and set out for home. No sooner had they left than a group of workers went into the lobby of the RCA building with sledge hammers and pounded Diego's mural to dust. When he heard the news, Diego was heartbroken.

"Frida," he said. "I wonder if it has all been for nothing. I worked so hard to study art so that I could use my talent to make the world a better place. I traveled to Europe and stood out in the rain for hours to study the paintings of the great Paul Cézanne in Paris. I worked on new kinds of art with the great Pablo Picasso. I even went to Italy to study how Michelangelo and Raphael painted frescoes on walls. And now my work has been destroyed."

"Ah, Diego," his wife answered. "That one mural no longer exists—yes—but look at all the others you have done! And the ones you will do in the future. Stay here in Mexico and paint the story of our people on walls all over the country so that all Mexicans, even the ones who cannot read writing, can read your pictures and be proud of their heritage."

And so that is what Diego did. He painted stories of the Mayan and Aztec Indians who first lived in Mexico. He painted pictures of the Spanish conquerors and of the peasants who fought in revolutions to make Mexico free. He painted pictures of farmers in the fields and women weaving baskets. He painted flowers and fiestas. He painted the stories of his people until the day he died. He even left them a museum of ancient Mexican artwork he had been collecting all his life. Today the Mexican people honor Diego Rivera as one of their greatest artists. His murals give them hope for a better future.

(Standards: Language Arts: Listening and Speaking 8.4)

Viewing the Art

The children will enjoy seeing some of Rivera's self-portraits (see Hamill 2002, 29, 181, 201; Downs 2002, 188–195.) as well as his drawings at age three of a train and at age twelve of a woman's head (Hamill 2002, 19). Diego Rivera's art extends beyond the murals for which he is famous. He ventured into Cubism and Impressionism as well. Canvases such as *Flower Day* and *Zapatista Landscape*—a good introduction to the Mexican Revolution and its leaders—are among his finest works. After showing these, reserve the bulk of your time for the murals, since those are the focus of the art activity to follow. Diego and Frida have something in common with Michelangelo. Both Diego and Michelangelo painted huge expanses, on scaffolds. Like Michelangelo, Frida painted (often) on her back. Emphasize that Rivera's murals tell stories and encourage the children to work together to discern what those stories are. Begin with the artist's murals of the ancient Indian civilizations: *Totonac Civilization*, *Huastec Civilization*, and *The Papermakers*. Some of the others you may choose to view are *The Dyers*, *The Sugar Refinery*, *The Ribbon Dance*, *Our Bread*, *Distribution of the Arms*, *Alliance of the Peasant and the Industrial Worker*, *Partition of the Land*, *The Agitators*, and *The History of Mexico*. (*Mexican Muralists* is a good source—see references.) If you can obtain the DVD *Diego Rivera: The Art of Steel* (see references), it would be a wonderful experience for the children to actually see the artist at work on the mural for the Detroit Institute of Art. What is Rivera saying about his country, about the treatment of the poor, about labor? Can the children find Diego and/or his wife in any of the murals?

(Standards: Art Connections 1.1-8; Language Arts: Viewing 9.6, 23)

Journal Writing

Rivera painted his murals to tell stories about people or issues he really cared about. Ask the children to write about something they feel is really important for people to think about. Environmental concerns, getting along with those of different races and backgrounds, or homelessness are just some of the possibilities. Tell the children that after they have written in their journals, they will share their ideas with one another in preparation for painting a mural. The mural will contain those issues most mentioned in their writing.

(Standards: Language Arts: Writing 1.7, 23, 33-37; Art Connections 1.3)

Art/Drama Activity: Mural Painting

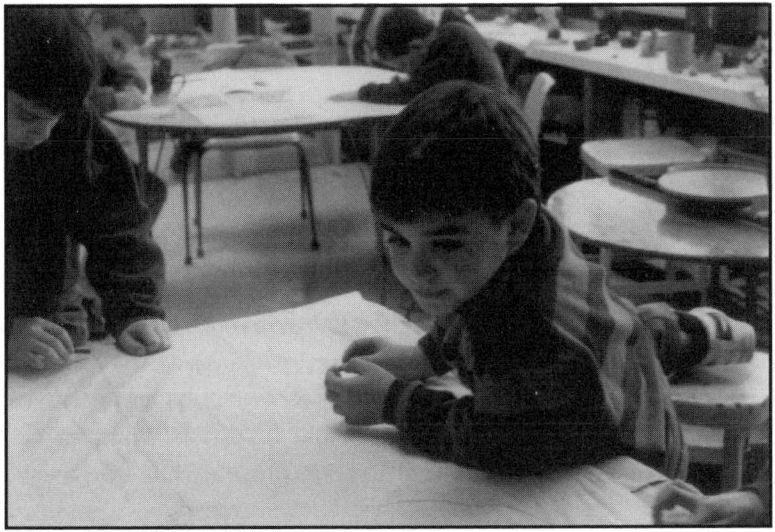

Children Working on a Mural about Protecting the Environment

Materials

- A large sheet of paper from a roll
- Tempera paints
- Paintbrushes
- Pencils
- Regular-sized paper (8½ x 11)

Begin by discussing the children's journal writing. What issues were mentioned repeatedly? Which issues do the children feel should be depicted on their mural? Will the mural have just one theme, or panels containing different ideas? When the children have decided on the content of the mural, talk about the scenes that need to be painted to illustrate their ideas. Divide the class into the number of groups necessary to paint those scenes. Each group should sketch its scene on small papers first, as Rivera did, and then proceed to sketching and then painting the mural. Display the mural in the hall or school lobby. The children might also want to use it to focus the school or another class on an activity: cleaning up a nearby lot, for example, if it's a mural about the environment.

(Standards: Arts and Communication: 3.2-5; Working with Others: 1-4.1-10; Visual Arts: 1-4.1-11)

LESSON 3: Frida Kahlo (1907–1954)

The only thing I know is that I paint because I need to, and I paint always whatever passes through my head, without any other consideration.

—FRIDA KAHLO

Background Information (See Lesson 2 on Diego Rivera.)

The Story

"Frida," said Alex as they rode home from high school on the bus together, "that was a crazy thing you and your friends did last week—riding down the corridor on a donkey! If you keep that up, they will expel you. Then how will you ever become a doctor?" But Frida didn't have a chance to answer, for at that very moment, a trolley crashed into the bus and she was thrown into the street. When Alex ran out to her, he saw that she was in terrible condition. Many of her bones seemed to be broken, but worst of all, a hand rail from the trolley was pushed right through her stomach.

"Help, get an ambulance!" Alex screamed, as he covered Frida with his jacket. At the hospital the doctors were afraid she would die, because she had broken her spine, collarbone, ribs, pelvis, and right leg—the same leg that had been weakened by polio when Frida was only six. And, of course, there was no telling how much damage the hand rail had done.

Eighteen-year-old Frida did not die, but she had to stay in bed for months, completely encased in plaster casts. How boring it became! Frida was such a bright person, and here she was, stuck in bed and unable to go to school or do things with her friends. Hoping to help, her father, who was a photographer and a painter, suggested, "Frida, why don't you try using my paints?" From that moment on, Frida changed her mind about becoming a doctor. All she wanted to do was paint. Her mother had a special easel made so that Frida could paint in bed, lying down, without moving. "Come, pose for me," she begged all the members of her family. Frida painted and painted, and the months passed. Finally she was able to get up and walk, but throughout her life pain never left her, and her body was always weak.

One day her father came home with some news. "Everybody's talking about Diego Rivera," he said. "He's painting a huge mural about our revolution. The whole town is talking about it."

"Hmmm," thought Frida, "I must see this for myself." The next morning she went to the courtyard where Diego was working, stood at the foot of his scaffold, and watched him all morning. Every day that week she went back. Now Diego liked pretty women, and he was flattered that this beautiful young girl came to see him work. Finally one day he saw that she had a large package under her arm.

"What is it you have there?" he called from the scaffold.

"Some of my paintings," Frida replied. "I want you to tell me if they are any good." Diego came down right then, even though he almost never stopped his work for anybody. One by one Frida showed him her pictures.

"Yes, these are good," said the artist. "You must keep painting."

Frida could hardly wait to tell her parents. "Momma, Poppa!" she shouted as she burst in the door. "The great Rivera thinks I have talent. Isn't that wonderful news?" From that day on, Frida was more determined than ever to become an artist. And she was determined to get Diego Rivera to pay more attention to her. She continued to watch him work, she even brought him food—until finally, they fell in love and got married. Their marriage never went smoothly, but they loved and helped each other, and respected each other's talent, all their lives.

Within a few years, Frida's work had become so famous that an art gallery wanted to exhibit her paintings. She was so ill that she couldn't get out of bed, so they dressed her in a beautiful Mexican dress and carried her and her bed to the exhibit. There she was, in the middle of the gallery, greeting all the visitors from her huge four-poster bed!

Frida died just a year after that, and Diego was heartbroken. When we look at her paintings now, they tell us the story of her life—about how much she suffered from her injuries and how unhappy she was that she could never have children. But they also tell us that she was a strong-willed, independent woman who loved her husband and her country. The Mexican people are proud that she is one of them.

(Standards: Language Arts: Listening and Speaking 8.4)

Viewing the Art

Some of Kahlo's paintings contain scenes—such as evisceration or childbirth or death—that may be upsetting to children. Be sure that the books you leave around the room do not have these in them.

Tell the children that many of Frida Kahlo's paintings are self-portraits and that many of them are sad because she had to endure so much suffering in her life.

These make interesting viewing, but at the same time, make sure to show some actual photographs of the artist. *Frida Kahlo: Portraits of an Icon* (see references) is a cornucopia of large photographs of the artist from her early childhood to one of her on her deathbed. In several of the photographs Frida is pictured with her husband, Diego Rivera, and it would be interesting for the children to see them together. *I Will Never Forget You* (see references) has some of the same photographs as well as different ones, and many are in color.

Show *My Grandparents, My Parents, and I* (*Family Tree*). Tell the children that Frida's maternal grandparents were Mexican, so she painted them over the hills of Mexico. Her paternal grandparents were from Germany, so they are suspended over the ocean they crossed from Europe. Frida herself stands in the beloved blue house she grew up in, holding a red ribbon connecting herself to her grandparents. The baby in her mother's womb is probably Frida. Frida puts a camera, symbol of her father's profession, in her portrait of him. *The Bus* is probably a reminder of the horrible accident Frida suffered when she was eighteen. Talk about the variety of people the artist put in this picture. *Frida and Diego Rivera* is a wedding portrait. What do the children notice? (the great difference in their sizes, the palette in Rivera's hand symbolizing his work, Frida's Mexican costume and the bright Mexican colors, the ribbon across the top—a typical Mexican custom).

In *Fulang-Chang and I*, Kahlo gives herself very monkey-like features. Notice her hair and eyebrows. Show more of Frida's self-portraits: *Roots, Self-Portrait Dedicated to Leon Trotsky, Self-Portrait on the Border Line Between Mexico and the United States, The Two Fridas,* and *The Frame*. From what the children know of her life, what do they think the artist is saying about herself in these portraits? Notice the decorative birds and flowers Frida painted on glass as a background for herself in *The Frame*. Frida Kahlo has been called a surrealist painter (that is, a painter whose works embody the fantastic or beyond what is real). What surrealist elements have the children noticed during their viewing of her pictures?

(Standards: Art Connections 1.1-8; Language Arts: Viewing 9.6, 23)

Journal Writing

Frida Kahlo continued to paint up until her death, in spite of constant pain and weakness. How do the children think she was able to do this? Have they ever conquered obstacles to accomplish something of which they are proud?

(Standards: Language Arts: Writing 1.7, 23, 33-37; Art Connections 1.3)

Art/Drama Activity: Self-portraits

Materials

- Mirrors (ask the children to bring in small mirrors from home wrapped well against breakage)
- Paints in bright colors
- Paper
- Paintbrushes

Invite the children to look at themselves in their mirrors and paint self-portraits. They may wish to try this in pencil first. Encourage them to look in the mirror and not at their papers and keep drawing until they have finished. They will probably be surprised and amazed at the results. They can repeat the process once they are ready to use paints, or paint over their drawing. They may wish to add some symbols in their pictures as Kahlo did, or to frame them with special decorations as she did in *The Frame*. They may even wish to include a ribbon across the top.

(Standards: Visual Arts: 1-4.1-11)

Curriculum Connections

Social Studies

- Find out more about the beliefs and practices of the Mayans. (See *The Maya* by Tamra Orr and *The Ancient Maya* by Lila Perl as well as many other children's books listed in the references.)
- Locate Mayan civilizations on maps of Mexico and Central America.
- Find out what Mayans wore, keeping in mind that different segments of society wore different clothing.
- Find out what role the jaguar played in Mayan culture.
- Learn about the tropical environment of the Mayans. What animals and plants flourished there?
- Find out about Mexico and its people. Discuss some of the problems between America and Mexico over immigration.
- Have a feast of Mexican foods (see Rivera, *Frida's Fiestas*, for recipes).
- Find out how to make chocolate and what role chocolate played in the lives of the ancient Mayans.

(Standards: World History: 17, 35.30, 32, 87, 114; Geography: 1, 2.5, 30; Grades K-4 History: 7.2)

Mathematics

- The Mayans were the first to use zero as a place holder and developed an elaborate number system. Find out about this system (see *Secrets in Stone*, pages 17 and 41 and *Technology in the Time of the Maya,* pages 36–37) and write from 1 to 50 in Mayan numerals.

(Standards: Mathematics: 9.29-30)

Science

- Find out about Mayan farming methods (see "Growers of Maize" in Perl 2005). What role did corn play in the lives of the ancient Mayans?
- The Mayans devised three calendars. Study them in class.
- What did the Mayans know about astronomy? Find the building archaeologists think might have served as an observatory.
- Read *Quetzal* by Patent (see references) to find out about this bird that is especially loved by the people of Central America and Mexico.

(Standards: Historical Understanding 1-2.1; Science: 11.29, 39, 51; Geography .39; Grades K-4 History: 7.15)

Music

- Learn about Mayan instruments. What does a conch shell look like? Can anyone bring one in?
- Make drums and other Mayan instruments.
- Play some modern Mexican music. What is a mariachi band?

(Standards: Arts and Communication: 4.1, 29; Music: 3.7, 19)

Literature

- Read biographies of the Spanish leaders who conquered the Mayans. (See *The Maya Indians* by Victoria Sherrow in references.)
- Read Nancy Day's *Your Travel Guide to Ancient Mayan Civilization* (see references) and, using the book as a model, invite the children to write a travel guide to some of the places they enjoyed most in their study of the Maya.
- Find out about Mayan folktales. Read *People of the Corn* by Gerson (see references). Read some Mexican folktales.

- Read some poems and stories in *The Tree Is Older Than You Are* by Nye (see references). The children may especially enjoy "Prayer to the Corn in the Field."

(Standards: Language Arts: Writing 1, 3-4.11, 33-34; Reading: 5-7.4-5, 7, 13, 23, 26)

Physical Education

- Learn more about the Mayan game *pok-to-pok.* Try playing it. Read David Wisniewski's *The Rain Player* (see references), a story connected with this ancient Mayan pastime.

(Standards: Physical Education: 1-2.18-19, 35)

References

Adult Books

Dexter, Emma, and Tanya Barson, eds. *Frida Kahlo.* London: Tate Publishing, 2005. ISBN 1-85437-567-9.

This book presents an overview of the artist's work. The illustrations are excellent for viewing.

Downs, Linda Banks. *Diego Rivera: A Retrospective.* Edited by Cynthia Newman Helms. Reissue. New York: W. W. Norton, 2002. ISBN 0393046095.

Published in conjunction with a retrospective of the artist's work at the Detroit Institute of Arts, this volume has 200 color reproductions and over 300 photographs and is an excellent source for viewing.

Favela, Ramon. *Diego Rivera: The Cubist Years.* Phoenix: Phoenix Art Museum, 1984. ISBN 0910407118.

Favela discusses Rivera's work in Cubism. Large reproductions.

Fields, Virginia M., Dorie Reents-Budet, et al. *Lords of Creation: The Origins of Sacred Maya Kingship.* Los Angeles/London: Los Angeles Museum of Art/Scala Publishers, 2005. ISBN 1-85759-386-3.

The authors discuss the origins of Mayan rulers and provide many beautiful illustrations containing representations of kings.

Grimberg, Salomon. *I Will Never Forget You . . . : Frida Kahlo to Nickolas Muray.* Munich: Schirmer/Mosel, 2005. ISBN 3829601212.

This book has large color photographs of Frida, some with her husband as well.

Hamill, Pete. *Diego Rivera.* New York: Harry N. Abrams, 2002. ISBN 0810990822.

This book has interesting photographs of the artist as well as reproductions of his work suitable for viewing.

Henderson, John S. *The World of the Ancient Maya.* 2d ed. Ithaca, NY: Cornell University Press, 1997. ISBN 0801482844.

Henderson traces the rise and development of Mayan civilizations. Illustrations by the author and examples of hieroglyphics.

Herrera, Hayden. *Frida Kahlo.* Reprint, New York: HarperCollins, 1993. ISBN 0060923199

The photos of Frida and Diego and large color reproductions of her work make this an excellent source for viewing.

Lowe, Sarah M, and Carlos Fuentes. *The Diary of Frida Kahlo.* New York: Harry N. Abrams, 2005. ISBN 0810959542.

Compiled during the last ten years of her life, Kahlo's diary is accompanied by 338 illustrations, 167 in color.

Miller, Mary, and Simon Martin. *Courtly Art of the Ancient Maya.* New York: Thames & Hudson, 2004. ISBN 0-500-05129-1.

This beautiful book has gorgeous pictures of Mayan carvings, statues, and paintings.

Proskouraikoff, Tatiana. *An Album of Maya Architecture.* Mineola, NY: Dover Publications, 2002. ISBN 0-486-42484-7.

Using all the available research, archaeologists have reconstructed ancient Mayan temples and religious compounds. This book presents large drawings of these reconstructions.

Rivera, Guadalupe, and Marie-Pierre Colle. *Frida's Fiestas.* Photos by Ignacio Urquiza. New York: Clarkson Potter, 1994. ISBN 0517592355.

This is a gorgeous book by Rivera's daughter that contains recipes and reminiscences of life with Frida Kahlo.

Rochfort, Desmond. *Mexican Muralists: Orozco, Rivera, Siqueiros.* San Francisco: Chronicle Books, 1998. ISBN 0811819280.

Rochfort traces the lives of the three artists through the revolutionary days and provides color photos of their major murals.

Schele, Linda, and Mary Ellen Miller. *The Blood of Kings: Dynasty and Ritual in Maya Art.* Photos by Justin Kerr. New York: George Braziller, 1986. ISBN 080761159X.

The authors present new information about the rise and fall of the Mayans before the arrival of the Spanish. Large reproductions and information on hieroglyphics.

Stuart, Gene S., and George E. Stuart. *Lost Kingdoms of the Maya.* Washington, DC: National Geographic Society, 1993. ISBN 087044929X.

The authors present an excellent discussion of the ancient Mayan civilization, with wonderful pictures of architectural sites for viewing.

Thomas, Victoria. *Books of Stone.* Photographs by David Alexander Björkman. Niwot, CO: Zone 913 Press, 2001. ISBN 0-943289-03-3.

Travel to thirteen Maya pyramids in the Yucatán Peninsula.

Wilford, John Noble. "On Ancient Walls, A New Maya Epoch." *The New York Times,* May 16, 2006, Science Times.

The author discusses the new discoveries made in ancient Mayan ruins in Guatemala.

Children's Books

Ada, Alma Flor. *Three Golden Oranges.* Illustrated by Reg Cartwright. New York: Atheneum, 1999. ISBN 0689807759.

In this Mexican folktale, three brothers who want to find wives are instructed to work together to obtain three golden oranges.

Andrews-Goebel, Nancy. *The Pot That Juan Built.* Illustrated by David Diaz. New York: Lee & Low, 2002. ISBN 1-58430-038-8.

Written in the same form as "This Is the House That Jack Built," this is the story of Juan Quezada, the most famous potter in Mexico.

Baquedano, Elizabeth. *Aztec, Inca & Maya*. Photos by Michel Zabe. New York: DK Publishing, 2000. ISBN 0756613833.

The author presents the history and beliefs of the Aztecs, Incas, and Mayas.

Bell-Rehwoldt, Sheri. *Amazing Maya Inventions You Can Build Yourself.* Chicago: Independent Publishers/Nomad, 2007. ISBN 0977129462.

Twenty-five hands-on projects highlight the amazing achievements of the ancient Maya.

Braman, Arlette N. *The Maya: Activities and Crafts from a Mysterious Land.* Illustrated by Michele Nidenoff. Hoboken, NJ: Wiley, 2003. ISBN 0-471-21981-9.

Braman explores the culture and traditions of the Maya and provides related activities. Children can make Mayan food and masks, and even write in the Mayan language.

Braun, Barbara. *A Weekend with Diego Rivera.* New York: Rizzoli, 1994. ISBN 0847817490.

The author speaks to the reader about his life and work. List of places where Rivera's work can be found.

Coulter, Laurie. *Secrets in Stone: All About Maya Hieroglyphs.* Illustrated by Sarah Jane English. Toronto: Madison Press Books/Little, Brown, 2001. ISBN 0-316-15883-6.

This book explains Mayan writing and number systems and is essential to the art activity above.

Crandell, Rachel. *Hands of the Maya: Villagers at Work and Play.* New York: Henry Holt, 2002. ISBN 0-8050-6687-X.

This beautiful picture book for young children has photographs of people going about their daily lives in a Mayan village in Belize. There is a map of Mayan lands in Mesoamerica.

Crosher, Judith. *Technology in the Time of the Maya.* New York: Raintree/Steck-Vaughn, 1998. ISBN 0-8172-4881-1.

Crosher discusses many technological advances ushered in by the Maya, including latex (or rubber) a number system, and more.

Day, Nancy. *Ancient Mayan Civilization.* Minneapolis, MN: Runestone Press, 2001. ISBN 0-8225-3077-5.

Written like a travel guide, this very enjoyable book is packed with information about the Mayans.

Ehlert, Lois. *Cuckoo/Cucú: A Mexican Folktale/Un Cuento Folklórico Mexicano.* Translated by Gloria de Aragón Andújar. San Diego: Harcourt Brace, 1997. ISBN 015200274X.

This Mexican tale, told in both English and Spanish, is the story of lazy Cuckoo, the only one who can save the season's seed crop from fire. The outstanding collage illustrations are inspired by Mexican crafts and folk art.

Frazier, Nancy. *Frida Kahlo: Mysterious Painter.* Woodbridge, CT: Blackbirch Press, 1992. ISBN 1567110126.

This biography for older readers includes some history of Mexico, including the Mayans and their art, and contains photographs and reproductions of some of Kahlo's artworks.

Frith, Margaret. *Frida Kahlo: The Artist Who Painted Herself.* Illustrated by Tomie dePaola. New York: Grosset & Dunlop, 2003. ISBN 0448426773.

A young girl with the same first name as the artist writes a report about her. The book is filled with information and reproductions of Kahlo's work. dePaola's illustrations are fine, and the decorative frames he uses would make good models for the suggested art activity in this chapter.

George, Charles, and Linda George. *The Maya.* New York: Blackbirch Press/Thomson Gale, 2004. ISBN 1-56711-738-4.

The authors present various segments of Mayan society and other interesting information about these people.

Gerson, Mary-Joan, reteller. *People of the Corn.* Illustrated by Carla Golembe. Boston: Little, Brown, 1995. ISBN 0316308544.

This is a folk story of how the Mayan gods created the people from corn. Beautifully illustrated.

Grifalconi, Ann. *The Bravest Flute.* Boston: Little, Brown, 1994. ISBN 0316328782.

On New Year's Day, following Mayan custom, a boy leads a procession over a mountain trail carrying a heavy drum and playing his flute. A beautiful picture book.

Johnston, Tony. *The Magic Maguey.* Illustrated by Elisa Kleven. San Diego: Harcourt Brace, 1996. ISBN 0152509887.

In this picture book the people in a Mexican village love the beautiful maguey plant that grows on the land of a wealthy man, and they save it from destruction.

Lieurance, Suzanne. *The Ancient Maya: A MyReportLinks.com Book.* Berkeley Heights, NJ: Enslow, 2004. ISBN 0-7660-5197-8.

Information in this book is supported by Internet links provided in the book.

Litwin, Laura Baskes. *Diego Rivera: Legendary Mexican Painter.* Berkeley Heights, NJ: Enslow Publishers, 2006. ISBN 0766024865.

This is a biography of the painter, with a few reproductions of his work.

Lourie, Peter. *The Mystery of the Maya: Uncovering the Lost City of Palenque.* Honesdale, PA: Boyds Mills Press, 2001. ISBN 1-56397-839-3.

The author describes his journey to the ruins of Palenque, Mexico.

Macdonald, Fiona. *Aztec & Maya Worlds.* New York: Lorenz Books, 1998. ISBN 1-85967-763-0.

Macdonald discusses many aspects of Mayan and Aztec life and suggests several related activities for children to do, including constructing a temple.

Madrigal, Antonio Hernandez. *The Eagle and the Rainbow: Timeless Tales from Mexico.* Illustrated by Tomie dePaola. Golden, CO: Fulcrum Publishing, 1997. ISBN 1555913172.

Five tales, each from a different indigenous group in Mexico, are told, along with an explanation of the people's history and customs.

Mann, Elizabeth. *Tikal.* Illustrated by Tom McNeely. New York: Mikaya Press, 2002. ISBN 1-9231414-05-X.

This is a well-written account of the Mayans and their construction of buildings in Tikal. It has a fold-out view of the city and is excellent for viewing.

Menchú, Rigoberta, and Dante Liano. *The Honey Jar.* Translated by David Unger. Toronto: Groundwood Books, 2006. ISBN-13 978-0-88899-670-1.

This is a fine collection of Mayan folktales. The tales are short and would make good read-alouds for young children.

Montejo, Victor. *White Flower: A Maya Princess.* Translated by Chloe Catan. Toronto: Groundwood, 2005. ISBN 0888995997.

In this Spanish folktale reset in a Mayan empire, a princess uses magic and trickery to get her parents to allow her to marry the man she loves.

Orr, Tamra. *The Maya.* New York: Franklin Watts/Scholastic, 2005. ISBN 0-531-12296-4.

Orr provides a history of the Maya, their beliefs, how they looked, and their lives today.

Nye, Naomi Shihab, sel. *The Tree Is Older Than You Are.* New York: Simon & Schuster, 1995. ISBN 0689802978.

These poems and stories from Mexico are written in Spanish and English and illustrated by Mexican artists.

Patent, Dorothy Hinshaw. *Quetzal.* Illustrated by Neil Waldman. New York: William Morrow, 1996. ISBN 0688126634.

This is the story of the quetzal, a bird found in Central America and Mexico, and its significance for ancient peoples.

Perl, Lila. *The Ancient Maya.* New York: Franklin Watts/Scholastic. 2005. ISBN 0-531-12381-2.

The chapters in this book are wonderful: "Gods and Priests," "Warriors and Traders," "Scribes and Artists," and "The Legacy of the Ancient Maya." It is well worth finding.

Philip, Neil. *Horse Hooves and Chicken Feet : Mexican Folktales.* Illustrated by Jacueline Mair. New York: Clarion, 2003. ISBN 0618194630.

This excellent collection has illustrations in the style of Mexican folk art.

Raczka, Bob. *No One Saw: Ordinary Things through the Eyes of an Artist.* Brookfield, CT: The Millbrook Press, 2002. ISBN 0-7613-2370-8.

Rhyming text for very young children helps them see the world that artist saw when they created their pictures. Several artists in this chapter are represented.

Ramírez, Antonio. *Napí.* Illustrated by Domi. Toronto: Groundwood, 2004. ISBN 0-88899-713-2.

In this lovely picture book, two Mexican artists tell the story of a Mazateca Indian girl and her little village in Oaxaca, Mexico.

Rockwell, Ann. *The Boy Who Wouldn't Obey: A Mayan Legend.* New York: HarperCollins, 2000. ISBN 0-688-14881-6.

When the god Chad steals a young boy, the disobedient child turns out to be a great deal of trouble. Rockwell gives sources for the story and the artwork and weaves a good deal of Mayan culture into this delightful picture-book tale.

Sabbeth, Carol. *Frida Kahlo and Diego Rivera: Their Lives and Ideas.* Chicago: Chicago Review Press, 2005. ISBN 1556525699.

Sabbeth presents the two biographies along with the artists' works. The activities involve several Mexican crafts.

Schaefer, A. E. *The Life and Work of Diego Rivera.* Chicago: Heinemann Library, 2003. ISBN 1403404941.

This is part of a series of books for very young children. The artist's life, some photographs, and reproductions of his work are included.

Sherrow, Victoria. *The Maya Indians.* New York: Chelsea House, 1994. ISBN 0-7910-1666-8.

This is a good source of information about Spanish conquerors and much more.

Shetterly. *The Dwarf Wizard of Uxmal.* New York: Atheneum, 1990. ISBN 0689314558.

This is a Mayan folktale about Tol who, with the magical aid of the old woman who hatched him from an egg, proves himself greater than the ruler of the city of Uxmal and takes his place as leader of the people.

Sills, Leslie. *Inspirations: Stories About Women Artists*. Niles, IL: Albert Whitman, 1989. ISBN 0807536490.

These are the lives of four female artists, among them Frida Kahlo. Some reproductions.

Sullivan, Charles, selector. *Here Is My Kingdom: Hispanic-American Literature and Art for Young People*. New York: Harry N. Abrams, 1994. ISBN 0810934221.

Latino poetry and art are combined in this gorgeous book. Many of the poems are for older children, but there are some that will interest younger ones as well.

Venezia, Mike. *Diego Rivera*. New ed. Danbury, CT: Children's Press, 1995. ISBN 0516422995.

This simple biography of the artist combines his work with cartoon drawings.

———. *Frida Kahlo*. Danbury, CT: Children's Press, 1999. ISBN 0516422995.

This simple biography of the artist combines her work with cartoon drawings.

Volkmer, Jane. *Song of the Chirimia/La Musica de la Chirimia*. Minneapolis, MN: Carolrhoda, 1992. ISBN 0876144237.

This bilingual tale from Guatemala is about the coming of music to the world.

Winter, Jeanette. *Josefina*. San Diego: Harcourt Brace Jovanovich, 1996. ISBN 0152010912.

Inspired by Josefina Aguilar, a contemporary artist working in Ocotlan, Mexico, this is the story of Josefina and how she forms in clay the many wonderful things she sees around her.

Winter, Jonah. *Diego*. Translated by Amy Prince. Illustrated by Jeanette Winter. New York: Dragonfly Books, 1994. ISBN 067985617X.

This picture book presents the life of the artist in English and Spanish.

———. *Frida*. Illustrated by Ana Juan. New York: Scholastic/Arthur A. Levine, 2002. ISBN 0-590-20320-7.

This is an outstanding picture-book biography that clearly portrays the artist's vivid creativity.

Wisniewski, David. *The Rain Player*. New York: Clarion, 1995. ISBN 0395720834.

Pik challenges the rain god to a game of *pok-a-tok* to bring rain to his people. Beautiful cut paper illustrations.

Wooten, Sara McIntosh. *Frida Kahlo: Her Life in Paintings*. Berkeley Heights, NJ: Enslow Publishers, 2006. ISBN 0-7660-2487-3.

Frida Kahlo's life with its ups and downs is told here for young people. There are some reproductions, but not many.

Woronoff, Kristen. *Frida Kahlo: Mexican Painter*. New York: Blackbirch Press/ Thomson Gale, 2002. ISBN 1-56711-594-2.

Use this biography for photographs of the artist and her husband, Diego. There are a few self-portraits in the book, but it is most valuable for the photos.

Audiovisual Materials

Ancient Maya. DVD. Library Video Company, 1998. V7157.
Students will learn about Mayan religious beliefs, hieroglyphs, inventions, the people, food, and culture.

Diego Rivera: I Paint What I See. DVD. New Deal Films, Inc., 1989. ISBN 1-878917-11-0
This film traces River's work from his early years through his murals. Much of the narration is taken from his and Frida Kahlo's own words

Diego Rivera: The Age of Steel. DVD. Kultur Video, 2001. ASIN B00000I1HR.
The first part of this film shows Rivera actually at work on his mural for the Detroit Institute of Art and the second part shows the completed mural in color.

The Life and Times of Frida Kahlo. DVD. PSB Video, 2005. LTFK601.
This film explores the artist's life and combines her artwork with photographs and interviews. If the narration is too difficult for your students, use this as a good source for viewing Kahlo's paintings.

The Lost Kingdom of the Maya. Video. The National Geographic Society, 1993. 51554.
This great video explores the Mayan ruins in Mexico and South America and reenacts some of the rituals that took place in those places. Excerpts might be useful to play in conjunction with the story about the Maya.

The Mystery of the Maya. DVD. http://www.razor3donline.com/maya.html, 2000.
Remastered from the original IMAX film, this film explores the ruins of ancient Mayan civilization.

Web Sites

Diego Rivera. http://www.fbuch.com/diego.htm (accessed April 2, 2006).
This site provides a biography and the opportunity to see many of Rivera's paintings and murals.

Frida Kahlo. http://www.fbuch.com/fridakahlo.htm (accessed April 2, 2006).
This site provides a biography and the opportunity to see many of Kahlo's paintings and murals.

Maya Adventure. http://www.smm.org/sln/ma/ (accessed May 3, 2006).
Presented by the Science Museum of Minnesota, this site provides archived photos of Mayan sites, activities, and more.

Maya Ruins. http://mayaruins.com/ (accessed May 2, 2006).
Click on various places on a map and see photographs of places connected with the Maya.

The Mystery of the Maya. http://www.civilization.ca/civil/maya/mminteng.html (accessed April 2, 2006).

This is a MUST VISIT site that includes many links to Mayan culture, beliefs, astronomy, math, and more. Visitors can see Mayan Jaguar masks and other artifacts as well.

Also see the links in Lieurance (2004).

Part VIII
The Art of the Twentieth and Twenty-First Centuries

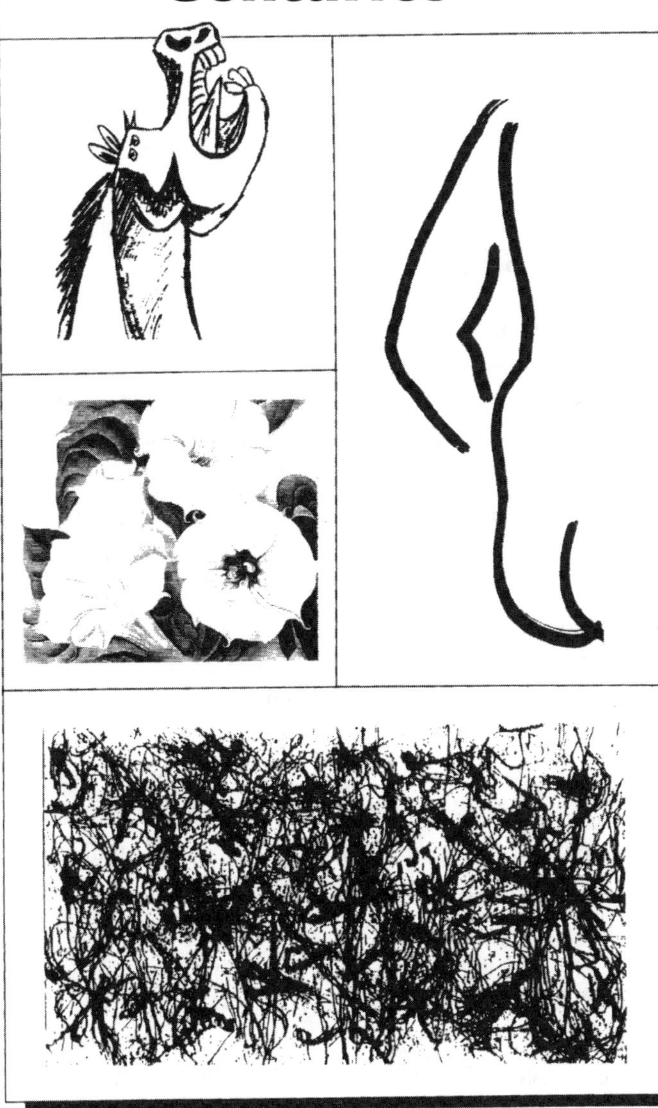

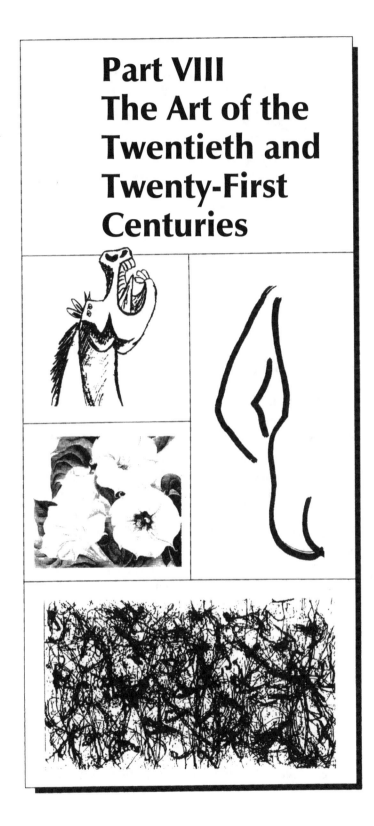

19 Five Modern Masters

Twentieth-century explorations in art have broken many boundaries. New ideas, followed by new techniques and new materials have led to new expressions in all the arts and have given us new insights into ourselves and our world.

—ROSEMARY LAMBERT, *The Twentieth Century*

Background Information

Change has occurred during the twentieth and into the twenty-first centuries more rapidly than in all the centuries that preceded them. Cell phone use has become widespread, not only for conversations, but also for written messages, photos and videos, and much more. Trains have gained speed, airplanes have taken to the skies, and spacecraft have traveled to the moon and distant planets. Inventions such as the radio, movies, television, and, most recently, computers, have made it possible to communicate almost instantly with most areas of the world. Because it no longer takes considerable time for news in the art community to spread, art movements have traveled back and forth across the Atlantic with alacrity, and this century has spawned more "isms" than any other. Perhaps, too, because the twentieth century has known the devastation of two world wars, a worldwide depression that stretched over many years, and numerous civil wars, artists have struggled more than ever to express on canvas, in architecture, and in sculpture their own and humanity's reaction to a world of constant change and turmoil. Due to considerations of space, only a few of the principal artistic trends of the century are mentioned here.

The Spanish artist Pablo Picasso initiated one of the first art movements of the twentieth century, Cubism, in which he abandoned realistic details and tried to show the different sides of objects simultaneously. Cubism, spawned from African art, had far-reaching effects on other artists as they tried to find new ways to represent three-dimensional objects in a two-dimensional space. The Fauves, led by French painter Henri Matisse, expressed themselves by using intense, unexpected colors in their works. Northern Europeans, among them Edvard Munch, communicated through their swirling lines and colors their inner emotions and turmoil in a movement called Expressionism. Frequently depicting machines, the Futurists, who had their origins in Italy, tried to deny the past while emphasizing constant motion toward the future through use of repeated lines in their work.

Building on the ideas of the Expressionists, artists such as Kandinsky and Mondrian pioneered abstract painting, a style using line, shape, and color without benefit of representation. While the Dadaists, who took their name from the French word for hobbyhorse, mocked the established art scene by their random placement of objects and by treating commonplace things as works of art, the Surrealists focused on the fantasy world of the unconscious. Max Ernst and Salvador Dali were two prominent artists from this group.

At the turn of the twentieth century, when New York City was teeming with new immigrants who often lived in the poorest conditions, a group of painters called The Eight (and referred to pejoratively as The Ash Can School) made these city dwellers the subjects of their representative paintings. Led by Robert Henri, the group included George Luks, William Glackens, John Sloan, and Everett Shinn. Ernest Lawson, Arthur B. Davies, and Maurice Prendergast eventually joined them.

The Second World War in Europe forced many artists to come to the United States, and New York became the new art capital of the world. A host of American artists such as Frank Lloyd Wright, Grant Wood, Andrew Wyeth, Alexander Calder, Georgia O'Keeffe, Jackson Pollock, and Louise Nevelson began to take their places beside the greats of Europe. Andy Warhol used objects of mass culture such as soup cans and soda bottles in surprising ways and gave rise to a new genre called Pop Art in the 1960s.

Contemporary artists are using such technologies as photography and, most recently, the computer, to push realism far beyond what we have ever experienced. Performance art is confounding viewers with its insistence on more active involvement. It is clear that as the new millennium continues its fast-paced march into the future, artists will continue to seek new ways to express their ideas about themselves and the world around them. And it is also clear that their work may initially shock and outrage us much as Giotto and, much later, the Impressionists, surprised their contemporaries.

How are we to judge this new art? What will we say to our students who complain, "It doesn't look like anything. All I see are lines and colors"? Surely it will not help to compare these works to what we might have been used to in the past. Rather, we should look, not at what they lack, but at what they have to offer. Philip Yenawine, in *How to Look at Modern Art,* offers his own criteria: "Good art sustains my interest over time, perhaps for its original appeal, perhaps for reasons that are new each time I see it" (1991, 144).

(Standards: World History: 46.100, 102; Art Connections: 1,1-2, 4, 6-7)

LESSON 1: Henri Matisse (1869–1954)

The Story

"France is at war with Germany!" screamed the headlines of the Paris newspapers. The once-lively city was plunged into gloom. Citizens, fearing poison gas attacks from the Germans, carried gas masks with them wherever they went and practiced racing to shelters for protection against bombs. "I can't go to the shelters," complained the famous artist, Henri Matisse, who was already over seventy years old. "The damp down there will make my hands cramp so badly that I will never be able to paint again! There is only one thing to do: leave France."

Henri's assistant obtained a special visa for him so that he could leave the country. He had a ticket to South America and his luggage was packed. "Let me stroll along my beloved streets one more time," he told his assistant. "Then we'll leave." Henri put on his coat and hat and set out. He had only gone a few blocks when he met another artist, the famous Pablo Picasso. "Ah, Pablo, how fortunate to see you before I go. I am about to leave for Rio de Janeiro."

"You and everybody else, Henri. Look down that road. Family after family heading for the border like refugees. Well, no one is scaring me away. I'm staying!"

"I had no idea that so many people were leaving," replied Henri. "Why the city will be empty, and if everyone leaves, what will become of France? I guess I will stick it out in my own country, too. You and I, Pablo, doing our art as best we can. Let's stay in touch."

The two artists parted. Henri got his money refunded for the tickets to South America, and instead went to southern France, where he began working once again on his paintings. But each day pains in his stomach got worse and worse until he could hardly hold his brush.

"Father, I'm taking you to the doctor, like it or not," declared Henri's daughter, Marguerite, when she came for a visit. And she did that very afternoon.

"I'm sorry, Mr. Matisse," the doctor said, after he had examined the artist. "It's cancer, and we have to operate right away."

"But my work!" said Henri. "What will become of my work?"

"You will not have to worry about your work if we don't operate," said the doctor. "You'll be dead!"

Well, that wasn't much of a choice for Henri, so of course he let the doctors operate—more than once, in fact, and he recovered. But his stomach muscles were so weak Henri could no longer stand up for very long. He had to spend the rest of his life in bed or in a wheelchair. He no longer had the energy to stand before an easel all day and paint with oil. But did he give up? Not at all! He just found a new way to do his art. Henri had his assistants paint large strips of paper in brilliant colors. Colors were always very important to Henri because they helped him express what he was feeling. Once Henri had his sheets of paper, he would look carefully at objects he loved—birds or leaves or other things in his room. He would think of places he had been, like the beautiful South Pacific where the waves splashed up on the beach. Then he would take his scissors and cut out shapes to represent those objects and have his assistants arrange and rearrange them on a wall or background until the arrangement pleased him.

People heard about Henri's new art, and everyone wanted to see it. Publishers asked him to illustrate books with his cutout shapes. The wealthy Rockefeller family in New York asked him to design a special window. Nuns in a convent asked him to do the artwork in the new chapel where they said their prayers. Henri went to the chapel in his wheelchair. He drew simple outline shapes on the walls by using a piece of charcoal fastened to the end of a long stick. And he designed beautiful stained glass windows. (It would be interesting for the children to see Matisse at work on his cutouts. Several books in the references contain photographs. A good choice is *Matisse: Cut-Out Fun with Matisse.*)

All of his life Henri Matisse tried to find the simplest lines to express himself in his art. Some people think that of all of his work—his wonderful oil paintings, his sculptures, and his drawings—he succeeded best of all as a sick old man working in the nuns' chapel. Henri Matisse died just two years later, but art lovers will always remember his wonderful shapes and colors. Many consider him one of the greatest artists of the twentieth century.

(Standards: Language Arts: Listening and Speaking 8.4)

Viewing the Art

It might be helpful to preface the viewing by talking to the children about modern art. If they expect to see purely representational art (though Matisse did not move totally away from the representational—that would come with later artists), they will be disappointed, or feel that this kind of art is inferior. Instead, it's important for them to realize that artists were trying to find new ways to express their feelings and even their fantasies. Just the way Renaissance artists discovered linear perspective and shading to represent three dimensions on a two-dimensional plane, so modern artists experiment with new ways to do the same thing.

Tell the children that as a younger artist, Henri Matisse was the leader of a new art movement called Fauvism. When the French people saw the wild colors Matisse and his artist friends used, they called them *fauves,* or wild beasts. Begin by showing the children two of Matisse's portraits of his wife: *Woman with the Hat* and *Portrait of Mme Matisse/The Green Line.* (See Klein's *Matisse Portraits* in the references.) Note the unexpected colors (multicolored background, green lines in the face). What do these colors achieve? How do the children react to them? Show other works that reveal Matisse's brilliant use of color. A few choices might be *The Joy of Life, Interior with a Violin* (Matisse was an accomplished violinist), *The Red Studio, Goldfish,* or *Still Life with a Red Jug;* then discuss them.

Matisse tried to achieve motion and solid forms with the simplest of lines. Show some sculptures and pictures that exemplify this: the sculptures *La Serpentine* and *Large Seated Nude,* and the paintings *Dance I* and *Dance II, Red Still Life with Magnolia, The Pewter Jug, The Rumanian Blouse, The Pink Nude* (if you can, show the twenty-two versions of this, to demonstrate how hard Matisse tried to get it just right), and his great mural *Dance.* Tell the children that Matisse was asked to make a mural to fit into several arches. He worked for a long time on it only to find out that the measurements he had been sent were wrong and his paintings were not tall enough. He began the whole project again!

Finally show the cutouts, those in the Vence chapel and others: *The Swimming Pool; Parakeet and the Mermaid or Siren; Blue Nude; Polynesia: The Sky; Polynesia: The Sea;* and Matisse's two versions of *The Snail.* His book *Jazz* (see references) has excellent large cutouts for viewing. (With over 800 illustrations, more than 200 of which are in full color, Schneider's *Matisse* is an excellent source for any Matisse works you wish to show. See the references.)

(Standards: Art Connections 1.1-8; Language Arts: Viewing 9.6, 23)

Journal Writing

One of Henri Matisse's first teachers told him, "You were born to simplify art." Did he fulfill his teacher's prophecy? Why or why not?

Look at one of Henri Matisse's brilliantly colored pictures for as long as you can. How do you react to it? Why?

(Standards: Language Arts: Writing 1.7, 23, 33-37; Art Connections 1.3)

Art/Drama Activity: Paper Cutouts

Materials

- Large sheets of colored or white paper
- Tempera paints
- Paintbrushes
- Scissors
- Glue

Invite the children to make cutouts in imitation of Henri Matisse. If they can, have them paint white sheets of paper from which to cut their shapes and to use as background. If they do so, advise them to make their paint strokes go in only one direction. The children can make varying shades of a color by adding more water to the paint or adding white to the color with which they are working. They may also cut their shapes from colored paper.

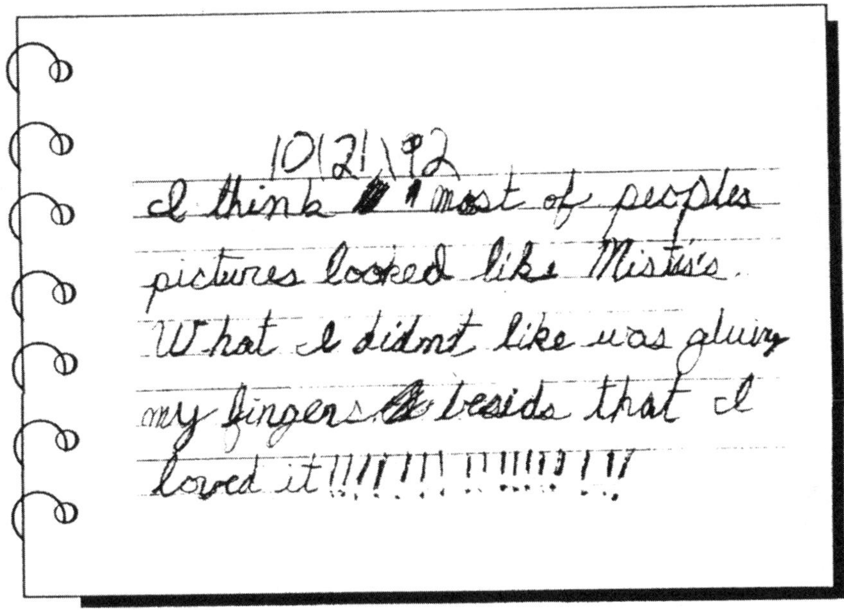

10/21/92
I think most of peoples
pictures looked like Mistis's.
What I didnt like was gluing
my fingers besids that I
loved it!!!!!!!!!!!!!!!!

As the sheets are drying, have the children experiment with color. What colors make each other vibrate or stand out? What colors look good together? They should also find an object in the room to study at length. What is its essential shape? Does it have curves, sharp angles? How does it make them feel? Or they may think of a scene they particularly like. When they are ready, they should cut out shapes to represent the object or scene. They may make repeated cutouts if they wish. It is also possible to use the shape that is left in a sheet after the cutout is removed if they cut all in one piece. These are positive and negative shapes. Arrange the shapes on another colored sheet until the desired effect is achieved, and glue them down.

You may wish to use *Drawing with Scissors* and/or *Cut-Out Fun with Matisse* (see references) in conjunction with this art activity.

(Standards: Visual Arts: 1-4.1-11)

LESSON 2: Pablo Picasso (1881–1973)

The Story

"Here, Pablo," said the young boy's father. "See if you can finish drawing this dove for me. I have to rush to school now to teach my class and haven't the time myself."

"Sure, Poppa," the boy answered. "You know I love to draw." Pablo picked up his father's chalks and went to work. When his father returned home later that afternoon, he was surprised at what he saw.

"Son, this drawing is better than I could have done myself! Here, take my chalks. From now on you will do the drawing in this family. You are more talented than I am. How would you like to apply to the art school where I teach? The entrance examination is very difficult, but I know you can do it."

"Do you mean it, Poppa? I can leave my school and study art! You know how I hate my studies. I'll never be able to add and subtract well, but drawing—ah, that is my first love."

"Yes, son, I can certainly see that. You are in luck, for it so happens that the admissions office is interviewing prospective students all this week. You shall come to the school with me tomorrow."

Pablo could hardly sleep all that night. Art school! Could it be that his dreams were coming true? The next morning he dressed carefully and went to the admissions office with his father.

"So you want to study at our school?" the director asked.

"Yes, sir, more than anything," replied Pablo.

"Well, your father tells me you have talent, but we must treat you the same way we treat all the other young people who apply here. You must first pass an examination, and it is not an easy one. You will have one month to present me with a drawing of a human figure. At the end of that time I will expect to see you here. If you are late, I shall consider it an automatic failure. All the students I am seeing this week have the same deadline. Do you think you can do that?"

"Oh, yes, sir, and I shall begin right away."

Pablo hurried home and worked all day on his figure and by evening, he had finished.

"Finished, Pablo! That is impossible. Such difficult work demands time," said his father when the boy announced at dinner that he had completed the task. But when he saw the drawing, his father had to agree that it couldn't be any better. The next day Pablo brought it to the director.

"Well, I can see you have no real interest in attending this school," the director said. "I'll take a look at what you have there, but it's obvious that anything done in such a hurry must be slipshod and a waste of my time."

Pablo, who didn't look very worried, said nothing, but handed his portfolio to the director. The room was silent for a long time as the director studied Pablo's work. Finally, the man spoke. "Are you certain this is your work—completed just since yesterday morning?"

"Yes, sir. My father can verify that if you have any doubts."

"Well, I have never seen anything like it. It is absolutely perfect! We would be honored to have you in our school."

And that's how Pablo Picasso, one of the greatest artists of all time, began his art education. He graduated from that school and went to another, but quit because he found it too boring. He didn't agree with the ideas of his teachers. Pablo was too filled with his own ideas and was anxious to try them out. So he left his family and Spain, his country, and went to Paris, France, the art center of the world. Pablo Picasso kept changing all of his life. In the beginning of his career, he was not very successful. In fact, he was so poor that he had to burn some of his pictures in the fireplace to keep warm! Other times he had to paint his pictures over one another because he had no money to buy new canvas. But little by little people began to buy his paintings. Pablo was able to paint beautiful pictures just the way painters did in the time of the Renaissance, pictures that looked exactly like the objects or people he used as models. And people bought those paintings. Pablo could have said to himself, "Well, I am successful now. I'll just keep painting like this and making money." But he didn't. He wanted to keep trying new things. He wanted to take what he saw in front of him and use his imagination to change it in surprising ways.

Pablo started a whole new style of art called Cubism, in which he was able to show all the sides of a thing or person at the same time. Imagine that! At first, people didn't like the new art. But then it began to catch on and artists all over the world began to have the courage to use more imagination in their art, too. Many new kinds of art began to develop. Pablo Picasso became so famous that crowds of people tried to follow him around and visit him in his studio. He had to have many locks on his doors! But he kept on working and trying new things right up until the day he died at the age of ninety-two! Can you believe that just a few years before his death, he did more than 300 engravings in one year? He never seemed to get tired.

So fasten your seat belts. We are going to travel through so many different kinds of artwork that you might think it was done by different people. But really, it was done by one incredible man: Pablo Picasso!

(Standards: Language Arts: Listening and Speaking 8.4)

Viewing the Art

(*The Ultimate Picasso* would be a fine source for just about any work by Picasso you wish to view with the children. Children might also like to see photographs of the artist in action as they view his works. *A Day with Picasso* has some good ones. See References.)

Begin by showing some of Picasso's representational works, especially his pictures of children, which should be especially appealing. (*Picasso The Early Years* and *Picasso's World of Children*—see references—are great sources for this viewing.) Some choices might be *Child with Dove, The Gourmet, La Soupe,* and *Paulo on a Donkey.* Explain that perhaps because he was poor and suffering himself, Picasso went through a period when he painted serious subjects in shades of blue. Two examples you might want to show are *Crouching Woman* and *The Old Guitarist.* This was followed by his rose period, during which he painted many circus types. Be sure to show *Family of Saltimbanques.* (See the film on this subject in the references.) Picasso created a sensation with his painting *Les Demoiselles D'Avignon,* the beginning of his Cubist period. Spend considerable time on this picture. (See Staller 2001.) You might wish to say nothing and have the children talk about what they see. They should notice the two figures on the right as being particularly distorted, the African masks (mention Picasso's love of African art), the many angles instead of rounded forms. What is Picasso saying about women here? Show *Three Women,* which is a less-distorted version of the same theme. Other Cubist pictures you might show are *Harlequin, Three Musicians, Factory at Horta de Ebro, Portrait of Daniel-Henry Kahnweiler,* and *Portrait of Dora Maar.* Show the first collage in the history of painting, Picasso's *Still Life with Cane Chair.* Show other Cubist collages, especially if that is the art activity you will choose later in the lesson.

Some paintings from Picasso's Surrealist period you might show are *The Kiss* and, especially, *Guernica.* Explain that *Guernica* is Picasso's response to the horrors of war. (*Kelley's Pablo Picasso: Breaking All the Rules*—see references—has a child's reaction to *Guernica.*) What are some things the children see? What is the artist saying about war? An absolutely delightful book that showcases Picasso's Surrealist work is *The Surrealist Picasso* (see references). It is filled with large color plates of paintings, portraits, and sculptures. Children will find these works whimsical and extraordinary in their stretch beyond the boundaries of reality. Some students may even want to try imitating this kind of art.

Have fun with Picasso's sculptures, especially those in which he uses found objects in novel ways. Some examples are *Woman with an Orange, Woman Reading, Woman with a Pram, Bull's Head,* and *Baboon and Young.* (See *Pablo Picasso: The Sculptures* in the references). What are some of the surprising things Picasso uses in these sculptures? What do the children think of the effect?

The children may be interested in seeing Picasso's writings in his own hand and the drawings that accompanied them. (See *The Surrealist Picasso* in the references.)

Finally, if the children have studied Matisse, it would be fascinating to show some of his and Picasso's work side by side. The relationship between the two is amazing. *Matisse Picasso* by Cowling et al. is a perfect vehicle for such a viewing. You might read the picture book *Bonjour, Mr. Satie* to accompany this part of the session.

(Standards: Art Connections 1.1-8; Language Arts: Viewing 9.6, 23)

Journal Writing

Invite the children to choose one piece of art they have viewed and write about it. What do they like about it? What is surprising about it? What do they think the artist was trying to say with that particular creation?

(Standards: Language Arts: Writing 1.7, 23, 33-37; Art Connections 1.3)

Art/Drama Activity: Art from Scraps

There are two activities that are particularly effective in a study of Pablo Picasso. Plan to do one or both, depending on the amount of time you wish to spend on the artist. Whatever you decide, it will be necessary to prepare for the activity(ies) in advance by having the children collect objects. If you intend to make a sculpture, discuss with the children what it might be beforehand. They may wish to make an animal or a building. What kinds of objects might be useful for such a project? Another possibility is to have the children assemble their objects and determine what figure emerges from arranging them. You may decide to do this as a whole class project forming one sculpture. Or you may divide the children into groups, each group creating its own sculpture.

10\14\93

I wonder why everybody says yuck or wird to somthing thats new and interesting. They did it to Pablo Picasso. I thought it was very intresting the way he drew in the church. I also thought the colors and the pictures sortof match, even thogh I've never seen a man with a blue or green face.

Activity 1: Sculpture Using Found Objects

Materials

- Objects collected by teacher and students (suggestions are old toys, screws, nails, pieces of pipe, parts of appliances, cloth, cardboard, etc.)
- Glue

Refresh the children's memories by showing some of Picasso's wonderful found-object sculptures once again. Invite the children to experiment with arranging their objects to form a figure or structure until they are pleased with the result. Glue them in place to form a permanent figure.

Activity 2: Collage

Materials

- Objects collected by teacher and students: scraps of paper, cloth, wood, etc.
- Paints
- Paintbrushes
- Scissors
- Large sheets of paper
- Colored pencils
- Glue

You may wish to study some of Picasso's collages again for inspiration. When the children are ready, have them arrange their objects on the paper in whatever way pleases them. They may use paints or pencils in their work as well. Glue everything down.

(Standards: Visual Arts: 1-4.1-11)

LESSON 3: Georgia O'Keeffe (1887–1986)

The Story

Georgia O'Keeffe wiped her forehead as she came into her small studio. It had been a busy day of teaching, and she was hot and tired, and yes, she had to admit it, discouraged. Oh, she enjoyed her teaching. It was exciting to help young people develop their talents and put their ideas on canvas as her teachers had once helped her. But being an art teacher was not what she really wanted. She wanted to be an artist. And now she felt herself caught in the trap that everyone had always told her would be set for her—the teaching trap. For in the years of her youth, it was assumed that young ladies could not become famous artists. Only men could do that.

Georgia frowned to herself. Why, it was only recently that women were even allowed to study art and draw from live models like the men were. Well, who cared about that. She'd never much liked painting pictures of people anyway. She wanted to paint objects, especially objects in nature. And her teachers had even admitted she had talent, so why was she stuck here teaching? "Let's see that talent, Georgia," she said to herself. Quickly she began to go through her stacks of finished paintings and stand them up all around the studio. Then, hands on her hips, she slowly circled the room, looking at each painting with a critical eye. After awhile, Georgia stopped her circling and sat down. "That's what's wrong," she thought. "There's no Georgia in any of these paintings. They are simply expressions of what my teachers have told me to do. Look, these represent ideas from my teachers at the Chicago Institute of Art. These are from my teachers at Columbia University in New York. But where am I? Where are my ideas, my own personal style?"

Right then and there Georgia made up her mind to do something very hard. She collected all her pictures and put them in the back of her closet. "I'll never take those out again or try to sell any of them," she said to herself. "From this moment on, I will begin all over again trying to find my own expression. No hiding behind pretty colors; just charcoal. Then we'll see whether I have the talent to be a real painter."

Right after her classes were over each day, Georgia worked on her charcoal pictures. She worked long and hard for months until she had done many of them. Then she rolled them all up, put them in a mailing tube, and sent them to her friend, Anita, in New York City. "Anita," she wrote, "these are my latest drawings. They are my attempt to find my own art, not someone else's. Don't show them to anyone, but please tell me what you think of them. I trust your judgment. If you say they are worth something, then I will continue to struggle to become an artist. Otherwise, I shall continue to earn my living teaching."

When Anita looked at Georgia's drawings, she could hardly contain her excitement. "How can Georgia tell me not to show these to anyone? They're too good to hide!" For two weeks Anita did as her friend requested and showed them to no one. Finally, she could stand it no longer; she packed up the drawings and took them to the photographer, Alfred Stieglitz. Both she and Georgia had been to his studio many times and admired his photographs. Stieglitz often helped young artists get started and ran exhibits of their work. He looked at the drawings for a long time without saying anything. Then, finally, he told Anita how much he liked them. "Georgia has great talent," he said. "She must come back to New York and launch her career!"

"Georgia," wrote Anita. "Please forgive me, but I had to show your drawings to Stieglitz. He thinks you have talent and should come back to New York. I hope you're not angry with me." Georgia wasn't angry at all. She was really delighted, and as soon as her teaching term was over, she packed up and went to New York.

When she had been back for a few months, she heard people talking about a new exhibit at Stieglitz's studio by a person named O'Keeffe.

"What does he think he's doing?" screamed Georgia to Anita. "He can't just show my pictures without my consent!" Georgia grabbed her coat and hat and went storming off to see Stieglitz. But he soon calmed her down. The people who were coming to see her drawings liked them. He had even sold one for $400!

More and more people began to find out about Georgia's unusual paintings. She painted abstract pictures, that is, pictures that didn't represent anything a person could recognize, but that showed her feelings. She painted giant pictures of flowers to get busy New Yorkers to stop and notice the beauty of nature. Soon she and Stieglitz fell in love and got married, and he continued to run exhibits of her pictures. Together they traveled to Lake George, New York, every summer where Georgia could paint the beauty of the countryside. And then she began traveling to New Mexico, where she painted the rocks and bones and wide open skies over the desert. When her husband died, Georgia moved to New Mexico for good and continued to paint there. Even when her eyesight became poor, she found ways to work with colors to express the feelings she had.

Georgia O'Keeffe fulfilled her dream of becoming a famous artist. The president of the United States gave her one of the country's highest awards, the Medal of Honor. Many other countries and colleges gave her awards, too. She became a very rich woman. But she never really cared much about these things. She continued to wear simple clothing and live very simply in her adobe house in New Mexico. Georgia O'Keeffe continued to paint almost until she died at the age of ninety-eight. By being honest with herself she achieved her dreams.

(Standards: Language Arts: Listening and Speaking 8.4)

Viewing the Art

After you have explained what abstract art is, begin by showing some of O'Keeffe's abstract works. You might wish to show them without the titles and get the children to express how the pictures affect them. Then show the titles and continue the discussion. Some good choices for viewing are the different variations of *Evening Star; Orange and Red Streak; From the Plains I and II; Painting No. 21; Music—Pink and Blue I; At the Rodeo; New Mexico;* and *Black and White.* Be sure to show some of O'Keeffe's Western pictures, since New Mexico meant so much to her. An excellent book for viewing these pictures is *Georgia O'Keeffe in the West* by Bry and Callaway (see references). Include some of her pictures of bones and note the attention O'Keeffe gives to the holes in the bones as well as to the shapes of the bones themselves. It would be interesting for the children to see the pictures that O'Keeffe kept for herself. Throughout her life, the artist kept at least half of all her paintings because she felt they were excellent examples of her work. *O'Keeffe's O'Keefes: The Artist's Collection* contains many for viewing. Finally, show some of O'Keeffe's huge flowers. (See *One Hundred Flowers* in the references.) Can the children name any of them? What does the artist achieve by making them so large?

(Standards: Art Connections 1.1-8; Language Arts: Viewing 9.6, 23)

Journal Writing

One of Georgia O'Keeffe's teachers told her that her goal should be to fill a space in a beautiful way. Do the children feel she has accomplished this? Why or why not? Perhaps they could pick one picture to illustrate their point of view.

(Standards: Language Arts: Writing 1.7, 23, 33-37; Art Connections 1.3)

Art/Drama Activity: Nature Paintings

Materials

- Large pieces of paper
- Pencils
- Paints
- Paintbrushes

Tell the class that they are going to imitate Georgia O'Keeffe by making paintings of something in nature—paintings that are much larger than the thing would actually be in real life. In that way, they can notice every single detail about the object they have chosen: its lines, shape, colors, etc. Then take the class outside and allow each child time to choose an object: a branch, a rock, a blade of grass, a flower, if they can be picked. Otherwise, you might have a bouquet of different kinds of flowers in the classroom for the occasion. When the children return to the classroom, they should spend a considerable amount of time observing the object from all angles. When they are ready, they should draw the object on their papers, being sure to fill the entire space. Finally, they can paint the completed drawing.

(Standards: Visual Arts: 1-4.1-11)

LESSON 4: Louise Nevelson (1900?–1988)

(You will need to prepare for this lesson well in advance. Ask each child to bring in a shoebox. The children should also begin collecting objects with interesting shapes: thread spools, empty matchboxes, pieces of wood, twigs, corrugated cardboard, etc., that are small enough to be arranged in the box.)

The Story

Louise sat sipping a cup of tea as she looked at her work. The sculptures that filled her studio stared back at her, silent giants in the large room. The rent was due soon, and she had no more jewelry left to sell to pay it.

"What do I have to show for all I have sacrificed?" she thought. "I gave up my marriage; I sent my son to Rochester to live with my parents and hardly see him. I even sold my wedding bracelet so that I would have enough money to go to Europe and study art. I have worked night and day on my sculptures trying to create something new. And no one will even give me a chance to exhibit my work."

The more Louise thought about her situation, the angrier she became. Finally, she made up her mind. She contacted all the artists she knew. "Whose art gallery is the most important gallery in New York?" she asked them. No matter whom she asked, the same name kept coming up: Karl Nierendorf. "Well, Mr. Nierendorf, you're in for quite a surprise," Louise muttered to herself as she straightened up her studio and arranged her sculptures in the best possible light. Then she put on her most attention-getting outfit and headed straight for Nierendorf's Gallery.

"Mr. Nierendorf, I am Louise Nevelson and I want to exhibit my sculpture in your gallery," she said as soon as she walked in the door. Nierendorf stared at her in disbelief. No one ever told HIM what to do. HE told THEM. After all, he was the most important art dealer in the city! But something about this determined woman made him agree to go to her studio and look at her work. When he did, he was so impressed that he agreed to show her work in one month! Usually, galleries took a full year to arrange for an exhibit. Louise was thrilled and worked day and night to get her pieces ready. She cleaned and repainted them and planned how they would be arranged.

When the big day arrived, Louise was nervous. Her success depended on whether the art critics and the visitors to the gallery liked her work, and she desperately needed to sell some sculptures to pay her bills. Well, the art critics did love Louise's work. They thought it was new and interesting. She was creating abstract art in her sculptures the way some modern painters were on canvas. But she did not sell a single piece! Nor did she sell anything at her next exhibit. However, galleries were beginning to notice her and offering to exhibit her work. Mr. Nierendorf even wanted to show her work again, but he died before he got the chance.

His death saddened Louise so much that for awhile, she could hardly complete any sculptures. But she knew she must go on, and she did, working long hours every day. She even roamed the streets of the city looking for things to put in her sculptures. One evening she was all dressed up for a fancy party when she saw some pieces of wood in somebody's garbage. "I can't let that great wood go to waste," she said. Before her friends could stop her, she went rummaging through the garbage to pick the wood pieces out. She saved scraps of iron, vegetable crates—anything that might be useful. Then Louise created a wonderful new show called *Moon Garden + One*. Everyone loved it so much that the Museum of Modern Art in New York City bought the most important part of the exhibit, a piece called *Sky Cathedral*. From that moment on, Louise Nevelson was famous. It had taken thirty years of hard work and many disappointments! Louise received hundreds of requests to do sculptures for buildings and exhibits. In fact, if you go to New York City, you can see some of her huge sculptures on the sidewalks in front of buildings.

Everyone looked forward to seeing Louise at her exhibits. They never knew what she would be wearing next. She was almost a work of art herself. She wore fancy hats and turbans, long, long dresses and coats made of all sorts of unusual materials, and many pairs of false eyelashes at the same time! She never seemed to lose her energy. All through her seventies she continued to work on huge sculptures, trying new materials like metal and Plexiglas™. People thought that surely when she reached eighty, Louise would not be able to continue such hard work, but she did. Louise Nevelson, in fact, worked almost to the end of her life and died of heart failure at the age of eighty-eight. Although she was born in Russia and came to the United States when she was six, we consider her one of our greatest American artists. She received all the highest awards the United States can give, and she proved that women can become just as successful as artists as men can.

(Standards: Language Arts: Listening and Speaking 8.4)

Viewing the Art

Since it is difficult to find books that feature Nevelson's work, it is highly recommended that you obtain the film *Louise Nevelson, in Process*—see references. It can be obtained inexpensively if your library does not have a copy, and it shows her at work on her sculptures. Children will have a fine idea of what the sculptures look like by viewing it. Don't let the scarcity of books keep you from studying this important artist who proves women can achieve whatever they set out to do. She was always a favorite with my students, and they loved the art activity that follows. If you can obtain *Nevelson's World* (see references), it will be all you need in print form for an excellent viewing session. It has huge reproductions as well as fascinating photographs of Nevelson herself.

Mention that we do not have many examples of Louise Nevelson's early pieces because she often destroyed them, creating enormous "barn fires." For her, it was the act of creation that was important, not preservation.

Begin by showing some freestanding works. Some choices might be *Self-Portrait, 1940;* the *Moving-Static-Moving Figures* (tell the children the viewer can actually move these figures into different positions by swiveling them on the center dowel); *Ancient City; The Circus Clown; The Open Place; Undermarine Scape; Indian Chief;* and *First Personage.* Nevelson admired African and Native American art. Can the children see any evidence of this in these pieces?

Since the art activity that follows uses them as models, spend considerable time on Nevelson's *Black, White, and Gold Environments.* Discuss the meaning of environment with the children and how they should be viewed as a whole. Be sure to include such works as *Sky Cathedral* and its variants, *Sky Columns; Homage to the World; Dawn's Wedding Feast; Chapel of the Good Shepherd; An American Tribute to the English People;* and *Dawn, 1962.* Nevelson, who was Jewish, created another variant, *Homage to 6,000,000 II,* in memory of the Jews who were killed during World War II. What do the children see in this structure that relates to its subject matter?

As the children view these environments, ask whether they see any relationships among the different niches. Are there patterns? Are there particular formations that especially express the title theme? If you wish, conclude with some transparent and metal pieces, especially her celebrations of New York, a city she loved and which she felt gave her a place in its art community.

(Standards: Art Connections 1.1-8; Language Arts: Viewing 9.6, 23)

Journal Writing

Invite the children to choose one environment they particularly like and write about it at length. What does it say to them? How did Nevelson tell a story in the way she arranged her shapes? This writing is an important preparation for the art activity that follows.

(Standards: Language Arts: Writing 1.7, 23, 33-37; Art Connections 1.3)

Art/Drama Activity: Shoebox Sculptures

Materials

- Shoeboxes
- Wood scraps

  If the school has a woodworking room, or if there is one in the area from which you may take surplus pieces, this would be ideal. A lumber yard would probably be willing to give you scraps as well. When we did this activity, we were also able to use an almost harmless tiny electric saw apparatus so that the children could shape their pieces as they wished. Second graders were able to use the machine with no difficulty or danger.

- Found objects such as empty thread spools

- Wood glue
- Cans of spray paint: black, white, and gold
- Newspapers

Have the children create a sculpture in their shoebox using the wood scraps and other objects. They should spend some time beforehand thinking about what they wish to say, and then about what objects and arrangements they can put together that will "write" their story. In this way, they will realize that Nevelson's work is not just a random placing of "junk" that reveals very little talent. The artist often said that each piece has a relationship to the other pieces in a work. Try to encourage that same thoughtful consideration in the students. When they have arranged pieces to their satisfaction and glued them down, place the boxes on newspapers and spray paint them black, white, or gold. The color decision should have been made beforehand, since it is intrinsic to the message.

Another, more difficult, option, for older children, is to have the class decide on a theme together and have each shoebox sculpture work with the others to create that theme (in which case you would need spray paint of only one color). When the boxes are completed, glue them together and spray paint the whole environment. Decide on a prominent place in the school for its installation.

(Standards: Visual Arts: 1-4.1-11)

LESSON 5: Jackson Pollock (1912–1956)

(Unless you have an art room in which splatters do not matter, it is wise to save this lesson for pleasant weather so that the children can do the art activity outdoors if at all possible. It is quite messy and can wreak havoc on classroom floors and materials.)

The Story

Dear Jackson,

"I hear you're having trouble at school. Forget about that place. Why don't you join me here in New York? If you're serious about becoming an artist, this is the place to be anyway. You can study at the Art Students League. I know you don't have much money, so move in with me until you're able to support yourself."

Jackson's excitement grew as he read his older brother Charles's letter, and he made up his mind to leave Los Angeles that very week. But when he arrived in New York a few days later and tried to get settled, he discovered that life in the big city wasn't quite as wonderful as he had dreamed back home. There were poor people on every street corner. Men in tattered clothes held out their hands for money. Others sold pencils or apples on the corner. The year was 1931. The country was in the middle of a depression, which meant that there were no jobs and people could no longer afford to pay their rent and other bills. Thousands were homeless. Of course, since money was so scarce, not many people had extra to buy artworks, so artists suffered, too.

Jackson studied at the Art Students League, but he hated living with Charles. Even though Charles was very kind to him, Jackson felt he was always watching him work. "I can't paint with Charles looking over my shoulder in the same room," he said to himself. "He's such a good artist, I'm afraid he'll make fun of my work." So he moved out to a much smaller and shabbier apartment not far away. But he was having trouble getting enough money for food and rent. He got a job as a janitor, but that didn't pay very well. Finally one day he found out that the president of the United States was starting a special job program to put people to work. Some men were building roads, others were working on bridges. Artists were hired to paint pictures to decorate government buildings. Jackson was told he could have a job if he was willing to follow all the rules. He had to work at home to paint a picture every month. And he had to go to the central office every morning and evening to punch a time clock to prove he was working. Well, Jackson hated to get up early, and it was hard for him to get to the central office by eight o'clock every day. Some days, people would see him running down the block in his pajamas to get there in time! But he kept that job for a few years.

This doesn't sound like a very good beginning for an artist's career, but Jackson Pollock did become a great and famous artist. He was only a teenager when he first went to New York, and it took many years of hard work before people began to recognize that his art was special. At first, Jackson painted pictures that people could recognize. But little by little, his paintings began to get more and more abstract. He believed a painting should tell the story of what was going on in the artist's head, not what the artist could see in front of him. As he worked on his paintings, he discovered that he couldn't get the paint on them the way he wanted just by using paints and a brush in front of an easel. So he took huge pieces of canvas and tacked them down to his studio floor. Then, instead of a palette and small brushes, he used big paint cans and sticks and big brushes to drip and pour paint onto the canvas.

At first people couldn't believe their eyes. Some asked whether this was really art. Others said that any baby could pour paint all over the place! But Jackson didn't just pour paint any old way. His paintings had a plan and a pattern. A film crew came to make a movie of him working. Reporters wanted interviews. At last, Jackson Pollock became so well known that he began to influence other artists. Some people say he was the leader of a new abstract art movement in the United States. But he did not live to continue working for long. On the way home one evening, he drove his car too fast around a curve, hit a tree, and was killed instantly. His wife, who was also an artist, took very good care of the hundreds of pictures that Jackson had painted and sold them slowly so that they would be rare and bring in high prices. His pictures began to sell for more and more money, so that today they are almost priceless. Jackson Pollock, who hardly sold any pictures while he was alive, had finally become famous!

(Standards: Language Arts: Listening and Speaking 8.4)

Viewing the Art

If the children have not had any of the other lessons in this chapter, it will be important to review with them the concept of abstract art: that it is not a representation of something we can see but is the expression of a feeling or idea through the use of line, color, and shape. (Varnedoe's [2002] excellent book contains all you will need for this viewing session. It also has great photos of the artist at work and his wife as well.)

Begin by showing some of Pollock's early, more representational work so that the children can see his development. Tell them that he grew up in Wyoming and liked people to consider him a wild cowboy. He also had a teacher in New York who painted Western scenes, so some of Pollock's first works had Western themes as well. Show *Camp with Oil Rig* and *Going West. Moon Woman Cuts the Circle* has a Native American art influence.

Before showing Pollock's abstract and "dribble" paintings, read Greenberg and Jordan's *Action Jackson* aloud (see references). This book concentrates on Jackson's creation of *Lavender Mist* (Number 1, 1950). In this way the children will come to understand that a good deal of thought went into each of Jackson's paintings and that he didn't just throw paint on a canvas haphazardly. Show *Lavender Mist* (*Action Jackson* has a good reproduction) and compare its calm and lyrical lines and colors to the more energetic and vigorous *Autumn Rhythm, No. 30.* What has Pollock done to create these differences?

Mural, 1943 is a painting Pollock did for the art patron Peggy Guggenheim, to decorate a building. Her support was a big help to him when he was starting out. What patterns do the children see in this painting? Why do the children think Pollock used "eyes" as a motif in *Eyes in the Heat*? Examine some dribble paintings in which areas of color are filled in such as *Out of the Web, No. 7* and *Convergence: No. 10.* How are they different from the paintings that are mostly swirls? Show *Blue Poles: No. 11.* What do the children see in this picture? What is Pollock trying to say? What is the children's overall impression of his painting? End by showing some photographs of Pollock at work on his canvases.

(Standards: Art Connections 1.1-8; Language Arts: Viewing 9.6, 23)

with the computer. The tools at the artist's disposal when using such programs are those that replicate the equipment we associate with artists in general: pencils, pens, brushes, etc. Adobe Illustrator and Adobe Photoshop are popular software packages that enable users of all ages, whether they use a Mac or a Windows operating system, to create computer art.

Often artists combine processes to create their work. For example, they may use the computer to provide a background for a photograph taken in the conventional manner. They may use a scanning device to scan a picture into the computer and then manipulate it to interact with computer-generated images already on the screen. Digital cameras are also playing an increasing role in computer art.

The computer makes it possible for the artist to see many different possibilities before a work is completed. It relieves him or her of the tiresome burden of scraping paint off a canvas, mixing a new palette of colors, and trying again. With the computer, a new beginning is as simple as the press of a button. In fact, special education teachers agree that the computer has enabled many of their learning and physically challenged students to become successful artists, a feat that had hitherto been impossible for them.

Because computer art is generated by a machine, some might be tempted to consider it inferior or not "real" art. However, it is now accepted that photographers, although they use a camera instead of brushes to create their pictures, are true artists. They need to consider the composition of their pictures, the effect they wish to achieve, and the best ways to achieve that effect. It is this "eye for the creative" that separates the amateur photographer from the artist. So, too, the computer artist needs to have a sense of design, a feel for the way colors work together, a knowledge of how to make the parts work together to form a perfect whole. In a word, the computer artist must transcend the tools he or she uses to create art.

The artist discussed here, April Greiman, began her career as "class artist" in her elementary and high school years, going on to become one of the foremost graphic designers of our day. She obtained her degree at the Kansas City Art Institute, where she majored in graphic design and ceramics; studied in Switzerland; then returned to the United States, where she taught at the Philadelphia College of Art, consulted for the Museum of Modern Art, and freelanced in New York. Eventually she opened her own studio, Made in Space, in Los Angeles, where she continues to accept commissions from companies both in the United States and abroad.

The landscape of the American Southwest, its subtle desert colors contrasted with the vibrant pinks, turquoises, and yellows favored by its large Latino population, greatly influences her work. An early pioneer of computer art and one of the first graphic designers to use the Macintosh, April now uses the computer in almost 90 percent of her work. She has received numerous awards and was hailed in 1993 by *How* magazine as one of the ten most influential designers of today. April received the medal of the AIGA (the American Institute of Graphic Arts), the most distinguished award in the field of graphic design, in 1998.

Computer technology changes almost monthly, and artists like Greiman can do far more intricate work of better quality now than when the field first opened up in the late 1970s and early 1980s. We can only imagine what wonders these men and women will create as the technology continues to evolve throughout the twenty-first century.

(Standards: Grades K–4 History: 8.1,3; Art Connections: 1,1-2, 4, 6-7)

LESSON: April Greiman (1948–)

The Story

The head of the U.S. Postal Service walked into his head designer's office. "Well, Carl, how are we coming along in designing a new stamp for the seventy-fifth anniversary of the Nineteenth Amendment? After all, we need something really special to celebrate the day women were given the right to vote. I'm sure people will be anxious to see what we come up with."

"Well, sir, I've hired several artists, and their ideas are starting to come in. I have an appointment with a member of Congress at the end of the week. She wants to see what choices we have before we go ahead and print a stamp."

"Fine. It looks like you're on top of things, so I'll leave you to it. Let me know what happens."

Later that same week, Carl went to the congresswoman's office with his designs. "Here are the samples we have for our new stamp," he said. "What do you think?" He laid the pictures out on her desk, and the congresswoman looked at each one slowly and carefully.

"These are nice, but they're not what I had in mind at all, Carl," she finally said. "Look—they just show portraits of dead people, like Elizabeth Cady Stanton and Susan B. Anthony. Of course, they were very important people. They did so much to help women gain the right to vote. They sacrificed their time and even their lives when people threatened to harm them. But if we put their pictures on this new stamp, then the stamp will just be like all the others—celebrating the life of a famous dead person. I want this stamp to celebrate all women! I want it to stand for their struggle to gain equal rights. I want it to say somehow that the struggle is still going on. I just don't think a picture of a dead woman will give the message we want."

"I can see your point, but what do you suggest we do? Ask the artists to start all over again?"

"No, I'd like you to hire a woman to do the design. I think a woman would have a better idea of what we would like the stamp to represent."

"A woman? But we never have women design stamps. I think that has happened only once before in the entire history of the U.S. Postal Service!"

"Well, then it's about time it happened again—especially for a stamp that's about women in the first place. Don't you agree, Carl?"

"Okay, okay, but I don't even know anyone to ask."

"A graphic designer named April Greiman spoke at the Smithsonian Institution a few weeks ago. She was very impressive. Let's track her down and ask if she's interested."

So that very afternoon Carl called April, and she agreed to design the stamp. But instead of using paint and brushes, April used the computer. The computer enabled her to layer pictures over one another to make a stamp that would capture people's attention and help them remember that we still need to make sure that all people are treated equally and fairly. It has images of the women who struggled seventy-five years ago for the right to vote alongside men and images of women today struggling for equal rights. When April's stamp came out, it was so different from any other stamp people had ever seen that it certainly did get their attention. Many people loved it. But some thought it was very strange. We've seen before that as soon as artists try something new, people who aren't used to it complain. When I show the stamp to you, you will have to make up your own minds about what you think it is trying to say and whether you like it.

April Greiman was the second woman to design a U.S. stamp. But she has done other things as well. Many companies ask her to create designs for them, too. Let's look at her work now and see the magical wonders she creates with her computer.

(Standards: Language Arts: Listening and Speaking 8.4)

Nineteenth Amendment Stamp by April Greiman

Viewing the Art

When viewing April Greiman's work, it is important to keep in mind that for the artist, space and scale are all-important. Whether she's designing a business card, the interior of a restaurant, a magazine cover, or a poster, April considers how the various components of her design relate to the allotted space. In addition, a facet of her work that will appeal especially to children is that it is rooted in a medium dear to their hearts—collage. She layers images on one another, fusing different technologies such as photography, photocopying, video, and computer, to achieve the effect she wants. It is up to the viewer to look carefully and then decide what April is trying to say and how her message affects him or her.

Color is another important aspect of April's art. In her book, *It's Not What You Think It Is* (see references), she discusses the interpretations some people give to the various colors:

- red—energy, creativity
- orange—receptivity, wholeness
- yellow—mental/emotional activity
- green—growth, balance of yellow and blue
- blue—creative expression, sincerity, patience, wisdom
- purple—royalty, vision, tranquility
- white—expansion, purity, divinity

The book *Something from Nothing* (see references) has some designs throughout the second half that show what Greiman does with color and light. The children will especially like the section on reflections and, in particular, the page entitled "Transmitting Reflecting."

As you view April Greiman's art with the children, be certain to discuss her use of space and color and her layering of images. It may be more difficult to find samples of her work than that of the other artists in this book, but it is well worth the effort. Her books (see references) are, of course, the best sources. Her designs also appear in numerous magazines. Some of the magazines are listed in the references at the end of this chapter. A few pieces you should make certain to enjoy with the students follow.

The Nineteenth Amendment stamp, which is the subject of the story. In addition to the image that appears above, there is a beautiful double-page ad featuring this stamp in the May/June 1996 issue of *Communication Arts* magazine (see references) as well as a brief article about its origin. There is also a picture of the stamp in *Something from Nothing.* Talk about the different images on the stamp, the contrast between the two groups of marchers, the buildings, colors, textures.

Vertigo (in *Hybrid Imagery,* pages 19–21). Discuss what the word "vertigo" means. Do these images convey that meaning?

Shaping the Future of Health Care poster (in *Hybrid Imagery*, pages 110–111). Greiman used Quantel Video Paintbox to create this poster and included a chest X-ray negative, photographs of a flag and an eagle, and a drawing of the symbol (known as the caduceus) for the medical profession. The hands are video clips of one of the studio designers. Do the children have any other suggestions? Where would they place these objects?

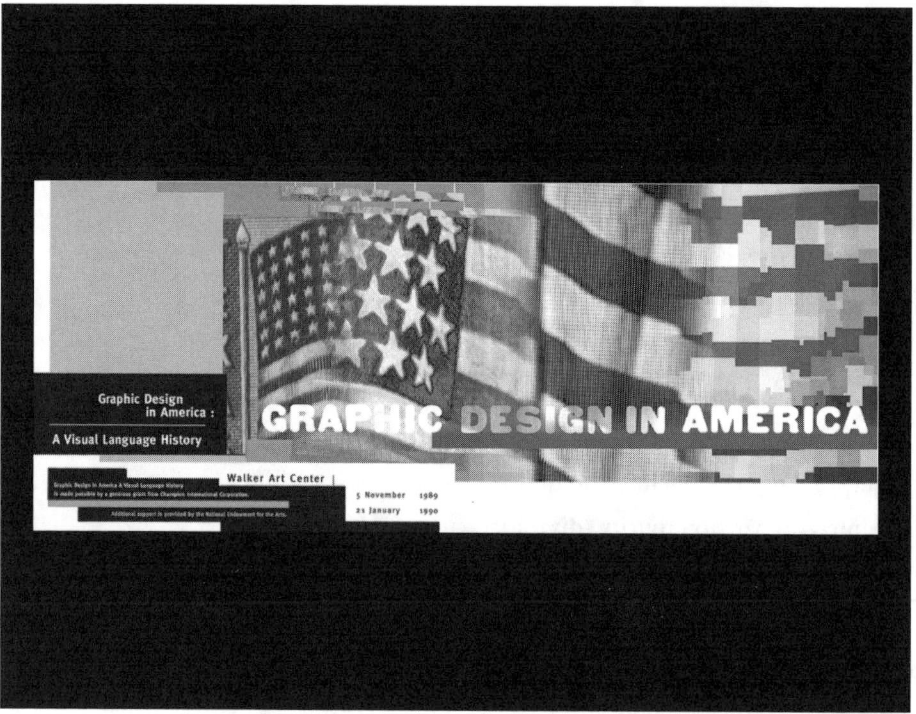

***Graphic Design in America* by April Greiman**

Graphic Design in America (see above as well as in *It's Not What You Think It Is,* pages 26–27 and also in *Something from Nothing*). Here Greiman uses four technologies to convey her message, and each technology produces its own texture: video creates a weave like that found in textiles; steel engraving yields fine, sharp lines; offset reveals a textured dot pattern; and the computer offers ever-higher resolution depending on the number of little pixel squares. Try to discover the different textures in this piece. Note how the flag seems to stand out and wave over the other layers of images. What role do the different colors play?

Follow the steps in the creation of the *Modern Poster* (*Hybrid Imagery*, pages 122–131). Discuss the shapes, the layers, the textures, the colors.

The children may enjoy the creatures that appear in *It's Not What You Think It Is* (pages 38–39, 56–57). What do they think the creatures are? Why?

Journal Writing

How is April Greiman's work different from the work of the other modern artists discussed in this chapter? How does it affect the children? Why?

(Standards: Language Arts: Writing 1.7, 23, 33-37; Art Connections 1.3; Thinking and Reasoning: 6.3)

Art/Drama Activity: Computer Pictures

Several activities are appropriate follow-ups to a study of Greiman's work.

If the children have access to computers and to art software packages, they should create their own art and designs on the computer. Young children may especially enjoy two pieces of software designed especially for them. Kid Pix Deluxe 3 and Kid Pix Deluxe 4 enable children to create their own pictures, combining sound, graphics and special effects. They can even add narration and movement to their pictures. Both are available from Broderbund Software (see references) and can be used with Windows or Macintosh. Broderbund's various Print Shop packages also enable children to create pictures and designs on the computer.

Visit a computer art studio in a local high school or college and watch computer artists at work.

Art/Drama Activity: Work with Textures

Materials

- Materials of different textures such as silk, wool, velvet, corrugated cardboard, string, etc.
- Glue
- Paper

Have children decide on a design they wish to create. Perhaps they are designing an advertisement for a class event: Parents' Night, a class play, etc. What is the mood they would like to convey with their design? Then, invite them to choose from among the various textured objects you provide, layer their choices in a way that achieves the effect they desire, and glue them onto their papers. They should pay special attention to the way in which they arrange the objects in the allotted space. They can include pencil designs on their papers as well.

(Standards: Visual Arts: 1-4.1-11; Arts and Communication: 1-3.2-5, 11)

Additional Activities

Drama

- Children have enjoyed acting out the following scenes:
  - Matisse and Picasso meet before the invasion of Paris.
  - Matisse is too ill to continue painting at an easel.
  - Picasso gets into art school.
  - Paris disputes the merits of Matisse and Picasso (see *Bonjour, Mr. Satie* by de Paola).
  - Georgia O'Keeffe decides all her paintings are no good and starts over.
  - Georgia O'Keeffe argues with Stieglitz when he exhibits her work without permission.
  - Louise Nevelson demands an exhibit in Nierendorf's gallery.
  - Louise Nevelson, dressed in one of her outlandish outfits, is interviewed at the opening of one of her environments at the Museum of Modern Art. (See a great photo on page 285 of Lucie-Smith's *Lives of the Great 20th Century Artists*—see references.)
  - Jackson Pollock moves in with his brother Charles.
  - Jackson Pollock sees the poverty and despair of New Yorkers during the Depression.
  - Jackson Pollock is filmed making one of his dripping paintings and tries to explain his art in front of the camera.
  - Head of design for the U.S. Postal Service and congresswoman confer about an artist for the Nineteenth Amendment stamp.
- Visit a museum of modern art that contains some of the work of the artists in this chapter.
- Publish a newspaper that reviews the work of the artists in this chapter.
- Have a TV talk show and interview some of the artists studied in this chapter. Plan questions that will get them to explain their work.
- In imitation of *Matisse from A to Z* by Sellier (see references), create an alphabet book about a favorite artist (or artists) from this chapter.

The illustrations in more and more children's picture books are now being generated by computer. Janet Stevens uses the computer to create her wonderful books for children. Visit her Web site with your class (see references) and see a step-by-step demonstration of how she creates an illustration. Audrey Wood is another children's book illustrator who uses the computer. To see how she creates her pictures on the computer, see her Web site in the references as well. Have children study the illustrations in the two authors' books and discuss how they were done. They may wish to write to the illustrators to obtain more information or to give their opinions of the works.

(Standards: Theater: 2.1-2, 10; Language Arts: Writing: 1-4.33-34; Listening and Speaking: 8.30)

Curriculum Connections

Social Studies

- Do some research about World War I and World War II. What caused these wars? Who fought in them? Who won? Find out about the Holocaust. (See *Where Poppies Grow* and *Six Million Paperclips* in the references.)
- Locate on a world map the countries of origin of the artists studied. For the Americans, locate the states in which they were born or worked.
- Read about the Great Depression. What caused it? What were the results? How did the government help? (See Cooper's *Dust to Eat* in the references.)
- What changes in clothing styles have taken place throughout the twentieth century? Make and illustrate a time line of male and female clothing of the twentieth century, highlighting significant styles (e.g., the flapper clothing of the 1920s). If the students can obtain clothing from relatives or other sources, stage a live fashion show.

(Standards: Geography: 1-2.30; World History: 39-41.76, 189)

Science

- Find out about important inventions of the twentieth century, such as the car, airplane, radio, movies, television, and computer. What impact has each of these inventions had on modern life? Make a mural depicting these inventions in chronological order.
- Discuss important medical advances, such as vaccines, organ transplants, antibiotics, and genetic research.
- Find out about some well-known scientists of the century and their contributions.

(Standards: World History: 46.91; Grades K-4 History: 8.41, 45)

Music

- Select examples of atonal modern music and some abstract art pieces that seem to go with it.

- Plan a musical program highlighting major musical styles of the century, such as Big Band music of the 1940s, rock and roll of the 1950s, etc. Learn some dances to go with the different kinds of music.

(Standards: Arts and Communication: 4.29; Music: 7.3-4, 7)

Literature

- Who are some of the great poets of the century? Find some poems to go with the pictures viewed during this study.
- There are some lovely quotes from Georgia O'Keeffe in *Georgia O'Keeffe: The Poetry of Things* (see references). After viewing some of her pictures, write a few sentences about each that describes them much as Georgia described her work. Decorate these sayings and display them around the room.
- Read biographies of some of the artists studied as well as some of the great figures of the century.
- Read a biography of a prominent computer genius. See the references for titles.
- Who are some of the great novelists of the century? Are any of the themes in their works echoed in modern art?
- Write a story to go with a work of abstract art studied in this section.
- Using *Henri Matisse: Drawing with Scissors* and *Pablo Picasso: Breaking All the Rules* as models, invite the children to write a report on their favorite artist studied in this unit.

(Standards: Language Arts: Writing: 1, 3-4.10-11, 33-37; Reading: 5-7.5, 13, 26, 28)

References (for chapters 19 and 20)

Adult Books

Aynsley, Jeremy. *A Century of Graphic Design.* Hauppauge, NY: Barron's Educational Series, 2001. ISBN 0764153242.

Aynsley shows the work of the century's most influential graphic designers. You may not wish to show the explicit graphic in April Greiman's section, but there is a fine biography that is useful.

Baldassari, Anne. *The Surrealist Picasso.* Paris: Flammarion, 2006. ISBN 2-0803-0509-3.

This book is devoted to the surrealist works of Picasso from 1924 to 1939. It has wonderful large reproductions for viewing. A special section at the end has the artist's writings in his own hand and should be fascinating for the children to see.

Bry, Doris, and Nicholas Callaway, eds. *Georgia O'Keeffe: In the West.* New York: Random House, 1991. ISBN 0-3945-7971-2.

There are huge color reproductions of O'Keeffe's Western paintings.

Cowling, Elizabeth, et al. *Matisse Picasso.* London: Tate Publishing/Museum of Modern Art, 2002. ISBN 0-87070-008-1.

Published in conjunction with an exhibit at both museums, this is a fascinating look at both artists' works side by side.

Dumas, Ann. *Matisse, His Art and His Textiles: The Fabric of Dreams.* London: Royal Academy Books, 2005. ISBN 1-903973-46-5.

This is an interesting look at the fabrics Matisse created, both in his paintings and actual textiles, as in the vestments he designed.

Elderfield, John. *Henri Matisse: A Retrospective.* New York: Museum of Modern Art, 1992. ISBN 0810961164.

More than 400 of the artist's works are reproduced in this book, more than 300 are in color.

Faerna, Jose Maria, ed. *Great Modern Masters: Matisse.* Translated by Teresa Waldes. New York: Harry N. Abrams, 1994. ISBN 0810946858.

This book contains gorgeous reproductions of more than sixty major works.

———. *Great Modern Masters: Picasso.* Translated by Wayne Finke. New York: Harry N. Abrams, 1994. ISBN 0810946904.

This book contains gorgeous reproductions of sixty-five art works.

Fitzgerald, Michael. *Picasso: The Artist's Studio.* New Haven, CT: Yale University Press, 2001. ISBN 0-300-08941-4.

This book contains large reproductions of the works Picasso did in his studio.

Fort, Francine, and April Greiman. *It's Not What You Think It Is.* Zurich: Artemis Verlag AG, 1994. ISBN 3764355425.

This is an excellent source for viewing Greiman's work.

Friedman, B. H. *Jackson Pollock: Energy Made Visible.* Reprint, New York: Da Capo Press, 1995. ISBN 0306806649.

This reprint of the illustrated biography of Pollock has a new foreword by the author.

Gerber, Ann. *All Messed Up.* New York: HarperCollins, 2004. ISBN 1856693902.

The author demonstrates how some mistakes made in creating designs can actually become an advantage. There is an interview with April Greiman in the last section of the book.

Gomez, Edward M., and Allison Goodman, eds. *New Design Los Angeles: The Story of Graphic Design.* Chanhassen, MN: Rockport Publishers, 1999. ISBN 1564965597.

This book features the work of major graphic designers, among them April Greiman.

Greiman, April. *Hybrid Imagery.* New York: Watson-Guptill, 1990. ISBN 0823025187.

Greiman describes her design process. Filled with reproductions of her work.

———. *Something from Nothing.* Hove, East Sussex, England: Rotovision, 2002. ISBN 2880465478.

Revel in Greiman's amazing computer designs. The stills in this book can be seen in motion at aprilgreiman.com or madeinspace.la.

Greiman, April, and Liz Farrelly. *Floating Ideas into Time and Space, the Cutting Edge Series.* New York: Watson-Guptill, 1998. ISBN 0823012018.

This book is easy reading and includes many narratives/descriptions of Greiman's projects.

Hunt, Wayne. *Environmental Graphics: Projects & Process.* New York: Harper Design, 2003. ISBN 0-942604-90-3.

This book shows some interesting graphic design projects. The children may enjoy seeing them in conjunction with their study of April Greiman.

Kay, Helen. *Picasso's World of Children.* New York: Doubleday, 1984. ISBN 0385126271.

This book is filled with large reproductions of the artist's paintings and drawings of children.

Klein, John. *Matisse Portraits.* New Haven, CT: Yale University Press, 2001. ISBN 0-300-08100-6.

This is an excellent source for viewing the artist's portrait paintings.

Lambert, Rosemary. *The Twentieth Century.* Reissue. Cambridge, England: Cambridge University Press, 1981. ISBN 0521296226.

The author presents a brief introduction to the art of the twentieth century.

Landau, Ellen G. *Jackson Pollock.* New York: Harry N. Abrams, 2005. ISBN 0810992450.

This examination of Pollock's personal life and work has beautiful reproductions.

Leal, Brigitte, et al. *The Ultimate Picasso.* New York: Harry N. Abrams, 2000. ISBN 0-8109-3940-1.

This book contains a reproduction of most of the works done by Picasso and is a fine source for viewing.

Lipman, Jean. *Nevelson's World.* New York: Hudson Hills Press, 1983. o.p. ISBN 0933920334.

This is a big, magnificent book containing huge color reproductions and discussions of Nevelson's work. It is well worth seeing if your library can obtain a copy. There are also huge photographs of the artist with her multiple false eyelashes and attention-getting outfits.

Lisle, Laurie. *Louise Nevelson: A Passionate Life.* New York: Summit Books, 1990. ISBN 0-671-67516-8.

This adult biography is not suitable for the classroom. However, there are ten pages of photographs that the children will find interesting.

Lucie-Smith, Edward. *Lives of the Great 20th Century Artists.* New York: Thames & Hudson, 1999. ISBN 0-500-23739-5.

Several pages are devoted to each of the many artists in this book. Those artists discussed in this and other chapters are represented.

Lynes, Barbara Buhler. *Georgia O'Keeffe: Catalogue Raisonné.* New Haven, CT: Yale University Press, 1999. ISBN 0-300-08176-6.

This two-volume work is over 1,000 pages long and contains more than 2,000 of the artist's paintings, watercolors, drawings, and sculptures.

Lynes, Barbara Buhler, et al. *O'Keeffe's O'Keefes: The Artist's Collection.* New York: Thames & Hudson, 2001. ISBN 0-5000-9299-0.

This book contains the paintings the artist kept for herself. The reproductions are large and there are great photographs and quotes by the artist as well.

Matisse, Henri. *Jazz.* New York: George Braziller, 1992. ISBN 0-8076-1291-X

This huge book reproduces Matisse's original cutout work, with text written by him as well. Wonderful for viewing.

McCully, Marilyn, ed. *Picasso: The Early Years 1892–1906.* New Haven, CT: Yale University Press/National Gallery of Art, 1997. ISBN 0-300-07166-3.

This is an excellent source of reproductions of Picasso's early work.

O'Keeffe, Georgia. *One Hundred Flowers.* New York: Knopf, 1990. ISBN 0-6797-3323-X.

These are beautiful reproductions of O'Keeffe's oversized flower paintings.

Percheron, René, and Christian Brouder. *Matisse from Color to Architecture.* Translated by Deke Dusinberre. New York: Harry N. Abrams, 2003. ISBN 0-8109-5582-2.

This large book has beautiful reproductions of the artist's work. The cutout work is especially striking.

Phaidon. *The 20th Century Art Book.* New York: Phaidon, 1996. ISBN 0-7148-3542-0.

This huge book devotes one page to each of 500 artists of the twentieth century. They are arranged alphabetically and there is a reproduction and a block of text for each. There's a fine picture of Louise Nevelson's *Royal Tide V.*

Pickover, Clifford A. *Visions of the Future.* New York: St. Martin's Press, 1992. ISBN 0312084811.

This is a book of essays on the impact of the computer on human life into the twenty-first century.

Rose, Bernice B., and Bernard Ruiz Picasso, eds. *Picasso: 200 Masterworks from 1898 to 1972.* Boston: Bulfinch Press/Little, Brown, 2001. ISBN 0-8212-2792-0.

Many of the works seen in this book are rarely seen in other books. There are 300 illustrations.

Rubin, William Stanley. *Picasso and Portraiture: Representation and Transformation.* New York: Harry N. Abrams/Museum of Modern Art, 1996. ISBN 0870701436.

Published to accompany the museum's exhibit, this book is a comprehensive study of Picasso's experimentation with a variety of portrait styles. It contains reproductions of hundreds of the artist's portraits and self-portraits.

Schneider, Pierre. *Matisse.* New York: Rizzoli, 2002. ISBN 0847805468.

This mammoth book has over 800 illustrations and is suitable for viewing any of the artist's work you wish to show.

Spies, Werner. *Picasso's World of Children.* New York: Prestel, 1994. ISBN 3791313754.

Spies discusses children in Picasso's art. Large color reproductions.

Spies, Werner, and Pablo Picasso. *Pablo Picasso: The Sculptures.* Ostfildern, Germany: Hatje Cantz, 2000. ISBN 3775709096.

This contains 740 works, from the small paper figures to the huge metal ones.

Staller, Natasha. *A Sum of Destructions: Picasso's Cultures & the Creation of Cubism.* New Haven, CT: Yale University Press, 2001. ISBN 0-300-07242-2.

Staller presents a thorough discussion of Picasso's Cubist art. There are fine reproductions.

Turner, Elizabeth Hutton. *Georgia O'Keeffe: The Poetry of Things.* Washington, DC/New Haven, CT: The Phillips Collection/Yale University Press, 1999. ISBN 0-300-07935-4.

Different periods of the artist's life are discussed, with accompanying reproductions and her writings.

Varnedoe, Kirk. *Jackson Pollock.* New York: Museum of Modern Art, 2002. ISBN 0870700685.

Varnedoe gives new insight into Pollock's work. The book has so many color reproductions suitable for viewing that it will likely be all you need. There are excellent photos of the artist at work as well.

Wands, Bruce. *Art of the Digital Age.* New York: Thames & Hudson, 2006. ISBN 978-500-23817-2.

Wands presents the work of over 100 artists from around the world and discusses how traditional arts have been transformed by digital techniques.

Children's Books

Antoine, Veronique. *Picasso: A Day in His Studio.* Translated by John Goodman. New York: Chelsea House, 1993. ISBN 0791028151.

A child stumbles into Picasso's studio, and the artworks come to life to talk about their master's life and art.

Balliett, Blue. *The Wright 3.* Illustrated by Brett Helquist. New York: Scholastic, 2006. ISBN 0-439-69367-5.

Readers who enjoyed *Chasing Vermeer* will get caught up in this mystery novel about Frank Lloyd Wright's architectural masterpiece, the Robie House.

Beardsley, John. *First Impressions: Pablo Picasso.* New York: Harry N. Abrams, 1991. ISBN 0810937131.

Very complete biography of the artist for children. Color reproductions.

Brackett, Virginia. *Steve Jobs: Computer Genius of Apple.* Berkeley Heights, NJ: Enslow, 2003. ISBN 0766019705.

This is a biography of the founder of Apple Computers.

Brooks, Philip. *Georgia O'Keeffe: An Adventurous Spirit.* New York: Franklin Watts, 1995. ISBN 0-531-20182-1.

This biography for older readers has a nice blend of photographs and reproductions of Georgia's paintings.

Bryant, Jen. *Georgia's Bones.* Illustrated by Bethanne Anderson. Grand Rapids, MI: Eerdman's Books for Young Readers, 2005. ISBN 0-8028-5217-3.

This beautifully written, fictionalized biography has illustrations that imitate the artist's style.

Cain, Michael. *Louise Nevelson.* New York: Chelsea House, 1990. ISBN 1555466710

This complete biography of Nevelson includes photographs and black-and-white reproductions.

Cooper, Michael L. *Dust to Eat: Drought and Depression in the 1930s.* New York: Clarion, 2004. ISBN 0618154493.

This moving account of the Depression includes interviews with those who lived through it.

dePaola, Tomie. *Bonjour, Mr. Satie.* New York: G. P. Putnam's Sons, 1991. ISBN 0399217827.

In this picture book, Mr. Satie tells his niece and nephew about a dispute that erupted in Paris over whose work was best, Matisse's or Picasso's. Great fun!

Dickins, Rosie, and Tim Marlow. *The Usborne Introduction to Modern Art: Internet Linked.* Edited by Jane Chisholm and Carrie Armstrong. London: Usborne Books, 2004. ISBN 0794509231.

The authors introduce works of modern art and provide Internet links on the subject.

Granfield, Linda. *Where Poppies Grow: A World War I Companion.* Markham, ON: Fitzhenry and Whitside, 2005. ISBN 1550051466.

This is a scrapbook about the war.

Greenberg, Jan, and Sandra Jordan. *Action Jackson.* Illustrated by Robert A. Parker. New York: Roaring Brook Press, 2002. ISBN 0761316825.

While telling Jackson's story, the authors concentrate on the creation of his painting *Lavender Mist.* This is an excellent, award-winning book and accessible for young children.

Heslewood, Juliet. *Introducing Picasso.* Reissue. North Mankato, MN: Chrysalis Education, 2002. ISBN 1931983453.

Heslewood examines Picasso's life and art in the context of his times. Photographs and large reproductions.

Hodge, Susie. *Pablo Picasso.* Milwaukee, WI: World Almanac Library, 2004. ISBN 0-8368-5601-5.

This is a fine biography for older children, with good reproductions.

Hollein, Nina, and Max Hollein. *Matisse: Cut-Out Fun with Matisse.* Translated by Ishbel Flett. New York: Prestel, 2003. ISBN 3-7913-2858-1.

Matisse is shown doing his cutouts, and children are invited to try some of their own.

Jacobson, Rick. *Picasso: Soul on Fire.* Illustrated by Laura Fernandez and Rick Jacobson. Toronto: Tundra Books, 2004. ISBN 0-88776-599-8.

This is a beautifully illustrated biography of the artist. There's a good reproduction of *Guernica.*

Johnson, Keesia, and Jessie Hartland. *Henri Matisse: Drawing with Scissors.* New York: Grosset & Dunlop, 2002. ISBN 0-448-42667-6.

The artist's life is presented as a child's report for school.

Kelley, True. *Pablo Picasso: Breaking All the Rules.* New York: Grosset & Dunlop, 2002. ISBN 0-448-42862-8.

Picasso's life is presented as a child's report for school.

Krull, Kathleen. *V Is for Victory: America Remembers World War II.* New York: Knopf, 2002. ISBN 0679961984.

Krull, a masterful storyteller, brings key players of the time into her narrative, including Rosie the Riveter and Anne Frank. Readers learn all about the causes and events of World War II.

Kucharczyk, Emily Rose. *Georgia O'Keeffe: Desert Painter.* New York: Blackbirch Press/Thomson Gale, 2002. ISBN 1-56711-592-6.

The story of Georgia's life is accompanied by many photographs and some examples of her work.

Lockman, Darcy. *Computer Animation.* New York: Benchmark Books/Marshall Cavendish, 2001. ISBN 0-7614-1048-1.

This simple explanation of how computer animation is done and how it has revolutionized the entertainment world will surely interest students.

Lowry, Linda. *Pablo Picasso.* Illustrated by Janice Lee Porter. Minneapolis, MN: Carolrhoda Books, 1999. ISBN 1-57505-331-4.

This is the simplest biography of Picasso on this list, and young children will be able to listen to a reading or even read it for themselves.

Messenger, Norman. *Imagine.* Cambridge, MA: Imagine, 2005. ISBN 0-7636-2757-7.

All kinds of play with flaps enable readers to imagine all kinds of things. Using a book like this can open their minds to the imaginative creations of today's artists.

Morales, Leslie. *Esther Dyson: Internet Visionary.* Berkeley Heights, NJ: Enslow, 2003. ISBN 076601973X.

This is a biography of Dyson, who is believed to be the most powerful woman in the field of computers.

Oliver, Clare. *Jackson Pollock.* New York: Franklin Watts/Scholastic, 2003. ISBN 0-531-12237-9.

In this biography, Oliver discusses other artist contemporaries of Pollock and the kinds of art they were doing.

Peters, Craig. *Bill Gates: Software Genius of Microsoft.* Berkeley Heights, NJ: Enslow, 2003. ISBN 0766019691.

This biography of the software guru has fine pictures.

Pfleger, Susanne. *A Day with Picasso.* New York: Prestel, 1999. ISBN 3-7013-2165-X.

Follow the artist as he works. This book has wonderful photographs.

Raimondo, Joyce. *Express Yourself! Activities and Adventures in Expressionism.* New York: Watson-Guptill, 2005. ISBN 0-8230-2506-3.

Through a variety of activities, children discover the art of van Gogh, Kandinsky, Pollock, Kirchner, de Kooning, and Munch. This book is great fun!

Ridley, Pauline. *Modern Art.* New York: Thomson Learning, 1995. ISBN 1-56847-356-7.

Beginning with Matisse and Fauvism, Ridley explains several of the "isms" prevalent in twentieth-century art.

Rodari, Florian. *A Weekend with Matisse.* New York: Rizzoli, 1994. ISBN 084781792X.

The artist invites the reader to spend a weekend with him to learn about his life and work. List of museums containing Matisse's work.

———. *A Weekend with Picasso.* New York: Rizzoli, 1993. ISBN 0847814378.

The artist invites the reader to spend a weekend with him to learn about his life and work. List of museums containing Picasso's work.

Rodríquez, Rachel. *Through Georgia's Eyes.* Illustrated by Julie Paschkis. New York: Henry Holt, 2006. ISBN 0-8050-7740-5.

This picture-book biography of O'Keeffe is beautiful and very suitable for young children.

Sabbeth, Carol. *Crayons and Computers: Computer Art Activities for Kids Ages 4 to 8.* Chicago: Chicago Review Press, 1998. ISBN 1556522894.

Using Kid Pix, Mac Clarisworks, or Windows Paintbrush, children create drawings on the computer and color them.

Scarborough, Kate. *Pablo Picasso.* New York: Franklin Watts/Scholastic, 2002. ISBN 0-531-12229-8.

This good biography contains some photos and reproductions of the artist's work.

Schroeder, Peter W., and Dagmar Schroeder-Hildebrand. *Six Million Paper Clips: The Making Of A Children's Holocaust Memorial.* Minneapolis, MN: Kar-Ben Publishing, 2004. ISBN 158013176X.

This is the story of schoolchildren who make a memorial of paperclips to understand the impact of the Holocaust.

Scieszka, Jon, and Lane Smith. *Seen Art.* New York: Viking/Museum of Modern Art, 2005. ISBN 0-670-05986-2.

While looking for his friend, Art, a youngster, finds his way into the Museum of Modern Art in New York, where he discovers a whole new kind of art. This is a marvelously creative book and highly recommended. Many of the pictures viewed are represented in the last chapters of this book.

Sellier, Marie. *Matisse from A to Z.* Translated by Claudia Zoe Bedrick. New York: Peter Bedrick, 1993.

Matisse's life is told in stories arranged using key French words in alphabetical order. An interesting and unusual presentation.

Skurzynski, Gloria. *Know the Score: Video Games in Your High-Tech World.* New York: Bradbury, 1994. ISBN 0027829227.

The author describes how electronic games and programs are created.

Stevens, Janet, and Susan Stevens Crummel. *And the Dish Ran Away with the Spoon.* San Diego: Harcourt, 2001. ISBN 0152022988.

In this version of the nursery rhyme, the illustrations are computer-generated.

Welton, Jude. *Henri Matisse.* New York: Franklin Watts/Scholastic, 2002. ISBN 0-531-12228-X.

Welton discusses the artist's different periods, and the influences on his work, in this biography. Reproductions and photographs.

Winter, Jeanette. *My Name Is Georgia: A Portrait by Jeanette Winter.* San Diego: Silver Whistle/Harcourt, 1998. ISBN 0-15201-649-X.

This is a small, beautifully written biography for young children, with illustrations that imitate O'Keeffe's work.

Wood, Audrey. *Alphabet Adventure.* Illustrated by Bruce Wood. New York: Blue Sky/Scholastic, 2001. ISBN 043908069X.

Alphabet letters help a child learn to read. The illustrations in this picture book are generated by computer.

———. *The Red Racer*. Reprint, New York: Aladdin, 1999. ISBN 0689826826.

When she is teased about her old bike, Nora tries to find a way to get her parents to buy her a new one. The illustrations in this picture book are generated by computer.

Worland, Gayle. *The Computer*. Mankato, MN: Capstone Press, 2003. ISBN 0736822151.

Worland offers a brief history of the computer for young children, discusses its impact, and suggests an activity.

Yenawine, Philip. *How to Look at Modern Art*. New York: Harry N. Abrams, 1991. ISBN 0810924854.

The author gives the reader tools with which to view and appreciate modern art. There are 137 illustrations, sixty-two in full color. Emphasizes seeing what can be learned from observation of different artworks.

Magazines

Since books about computers become dated quickly, magazines are listed as an up-to-date source of information.

Art Education
Box 1108
2317 Arlington Ave.
Saskatoon, Saskatchewan
S7K3N3 Canada
This excellent magazine is full of ideas for art in the classroom, including computer art.

Communication Arts
410 Sherman Ave.
Palo Alto, CA 94306-1826
(415) 326-6040
A large reproduction of the Nineteenth Amendment stamp by April Greiman appears in an ad on pages 6–7 of Volume 38 (2), May-June 1996 issue.

Computer Arts Magazine
Future Publishing
30 Monmouth St.
Bath BAI 2BW UK
The magazine comes with a CD-ROM that helps readers create stunning artwork, photos, animations, and 3D models.

Graphic Arts Magazine
Reed Business
8878 Barrons Blvd.
Highlands Ranch, CO 80129-2345
This is a good resource for information on graphic arts.

Web Sites

April Greiman. http://www.mkgraphic.com/greiman.html (accessed April 5, 2006).
Read about April and learn what she thinks about using the computer to create art.

Audrey Goes Digital on Red Racer. http://www.audreywood.com/mac_site/Aud_go_dig/aud_goes_dig_1/aud_goes_dig_1.html (accessed April 7, 2006).
See how Audrey Wood, children's book illustrator, created the pictures for *Red Racer* on her computer.

Georgia O'Keeffe. http://www.ellensplace.net/okeeffe1.html (accessed April 13, 2006).
This is an excellent site that provides a biography of the painter, her comments on her art, and images of her work.

Janet Stevens. http://janetstevens.com/today/index.htm (accessed April 7, 2006).
Janet Stevens, famous children's book author, talks about her work and enables viewers to watch her create a computer-generated illustration.

Madeinspace. http://www.madeinspace.la/MadeInSpace.html (accessed September 13, 2006).
At this Web site, Greiman showcases the work her studio produces.

Night Sail. http://www.bluffton.edu/~sullivanm/lapublicsc/nevelson.html (accessed April 5, 2006).
This site affords viewers several views of Louise Nevelson's huge outdoor sculpture called *Night Sail.*

Appendix: Sources for Audiovisual and Other Materials

A&E Home Video
Distributed by:
New Video
126 Fifth Ave., 15th Floor
New York, NY 10011
Phone: (800) 314-8822
info@newvideo.com
http://www.newvideo.com/nvfiction.html

AGC United Learning
150 Sherman Ave., Suite 100
Evanston, IL 60201
Phone: (888) 892-3484
Fax: (847) 328-6706
E-mail: info@unitedlearning.com

American Art Clay Company, Inc.
4717 West Sixteenth St.
Indianapolis, IN 46222
Phone: (317) 244-6871

Angel Records
c/o Angel/EMI Records
810 Seventh Ave.
New York, NY 10019
Phone: (212) 603-8600

Art Image Publications
61 Main St.
Champlain, NY 12919
Phone: (516) 298-5432

Birdcage Press
853 Alma St.
Palo Alto, CA 94301
Phone: (800) 345-2980 or (650) 462-6300
Fax: (650) 462-6305
E-mail: info@BirdcagePress.com
http://www.birdcagepress.com/

Broderbund Software
500 Redwood Blvd.
P.O. Box 6121
Novato CA 94948-6121
Phone: (800) 521-6263

Chronicle Books
275 Fifth St.
San Francisco, CA 94103

Clearvue/EAV, Inc.
6465 N. Avondale Ave.
Chicago, IL 60631
Phone: (800) CLEARVU

CustomFlix
140 Du Bois St., Suite A
Santa Cruz, CA 95060
Phone: (800) 853-6077
http://www.customflix.com/Customer/VideoShopHome.jsp

Delta Records
933 E. 86th St.
Brooklyn, NY 11236
Phone/Fax: (718) 257-2209
E-mail: ishop@deltarecord.com

Discovery Channel
P.O. Box 788
Florence, KY 41022-0788
Phone: (800)-627-9399

EMI Records Group North America
1290 Avenue of the Americas, 42nd floor
New York, NY 10104
Phone: (212) 603-8600

Film Ideas, Inc.
308 N. Wolf Rd.
Wheeling, IL 60090
Phone: (800) 475-3456
Fax: (847) 419-8933

Films for the Humanities and Sciences
P.O. Box 2053
Princeton, NJ 08543-2053
Phone: (800) 257-5126
http://gettingtoknow.com

Home Vision/Public Media Inc.
5547 North Ravenswood Ave.
Chicago, IL 60640
Phone: (312) 878-2600 or (800) 323-4222

Kazabee, Inc.
P. O. Box 391
Buffalo, NY 14226
Phone: (716) 906-1443

KingTutShop
Egypt Cyber Trade, LLC
Wilmington, DE 19809
Phone: (888)209-0862
Fax: (800) 517-9256
http://www.kingtutshop.com/index.html

Kultur International Films, Ltd.
195 Highway 36
West Long Branch, NJ 07764
Phone: (732) 229-2343
E-mail: info@kultur.com
http://www.kultur.com/

LCSI
Highgate Springs, VT
Phone: (800) 321-5646

The Library Media Project
1807 W. Sunnyside, Suite 2A
Chicago, IL 60640
Phone: (800) 847-3671
E-mail: info@librarymedia.org
http://www.librarymedia.org

Library Video Co.
P.O. Box 1110
Bala Cynwyd, PA 19004
Phone: (800) 843-3620

Main Street Arts Press
P.O. Box 100
Saxtons River, VT 05154
Phone: (802) 869-2960
E-mail: info@mainstreetarts.org

Metropolitan Museum of Art
1000 Fifth Ave.
New York, NY 10028–0918
Phone: (212)570-3756 or (800) 468-7386
www.metmuseum.org

Monterey Media inc.
566 St. Charles Dr.
Thousand Oaks, CA 91360
Phone: (805) 494-7199 or (800) 424-2593
Fax: (805) 496-6061

Museum Store Company
Phone: (888) 965-0001
http://theartifact.com/product_info.php?products_id=1774

National Gallery of Art
Department of Education Resources
4th and Constitution Ave., NW
Washington, DC 20565
Phone: (202) 737-4125
(All the materials they provide are free of charge. You pay only return postage.)

National Geographic
P.O. Box 6916
Hanover, PA 17331-0916
Phone: (800) 437-5521
Fax: (717) 633-3343

New Deal Films, Inc.
P.O. Box 2953
Corrales, NM 87048
Phone: (505) 897-9738
E-mail: info@newdealfilms.com

New River Media
4455 Connecticut Ave., NW, Suite C-100
Washington, DC 20008
Phone: (202) 363-1000
Fax: (202) 454-0662
E-mail: info@nrmedia.com
http://www.nrmedia.com/

PBS Video
1330 Craddock Place
Alexandria, VA 22313
Phone: (800) 328-7271

Questar Video
P.O. Box 11345
Chicago, IL 60611
Phone: (312) 266-9400 or (800) 544-8422
Fax: (312) 266-9523
E-mail: info@questar1.com

Rabbit Ears
P.O. Box 954
Middlebury, VT 05753.
Phone: (888) KID-TAPES or (888) 543-8273 (in US)
E-mail: info@GreatTapes.com

Razor3d.com
947 Hamilton Ave.
Menlo Park, CA 94025
Phone: (800) 339-5287
http://www.razor3donline.com/maya.html

Rice Paper Kite
1638 Jackson St.
Denver, CO 80206
Phone: (720) 249-2467
Fax: (720) 249-2615
E-mail: info@ricepaperkite.com
www.ricepaperkite.com

Scholastic Publishers
555 Broadway
New York, NY 10012–3999
Phone: (212) 505-3316 or (800) 325-6149

Sound Vision
9058 S. Harlem Ave.
Bridgeview, IL 60455
Phone: (708) 430-1255
Fax: (708) 430-1346
E-mail: info@soundvision.com

SR Publications
163 3rd Ave., Suite 122
New York, NY 10003
Phone: (888) 879-5919

The Teaching Company
4151 Lafayette Center Dr., Suite 100
Chantilly, VA 20151-1232
Phone: (800) 832-2412

Triloka Records
306 Catron St.
Santa Fe, NM 87501
Phone: (505) 820-2833

Usborne Press
Phone: (800) 611-1655
E-mail: customerservice@ubah.com
http://www.theusbornebookstore.com/

Video Universe
CD Universe
101 N. Plains Industrial Rd.
Wallingford, CT 06492-2360
Phone: (800) 231-7937 or (203) 294-1648
Fax: (203) 294-0391
http://www.cduniverse.com/productinfo.asp?pid=1713440

WGBH Boston
125 Western Ave.
Boston, MA 02134
Phone: (617) 492-2777

General Bibliography

The following art books are useful and address the subjects of more than one chapter.

General Books

Beckett, Wendy. *Sister Wendy's Story of Painting.* New York: DK Adult, 2000. ISBN 081095608X.

Sister Wendy offers her own interpretation, often spiritual, of artworks from the caves to modern times, though the emphasis is on Western art. There are more than 400 color reproductions.

Boardman, John. *The World of Ancient Art.* London: Thames & Hudson, 2006. ISBN 978-0500-23827-1.

The author explores ancient art from the time of the caves onward. Works from Egypt, Greece, China, and Africa are included in the 700 illustrations.

Fowler, Karen Joy. *Reading Women.* Foreword by Stefan Bollman. New York: Merrell, 2006. ISBN 1858943329.

Works from the Middle Ages to the present depict women reading. Teachers might use this to inspire their children to read.

Miller, Judith, et al. *Tribal Art: The Essential World Guide.* Photographs by Graham Rae. New York: DK, 2006. ISBN-13 978-0-7566-1884-1.

This book presents the tribal art of African tribes, Native American tribes, Oceanic tribes, and Mexican and South American tribes. It has beautiful color photographs and would be a good source of viewing for the chapters on Africa and the Americas.

Newton, Douglas. *Masterpieces of Primitive Art.* Photos by Lee Boltin. New York: Knopf, 1982. ISBN 0394500571.

Newton describes the artworks in the Nelson A. Rockefeller primitive art collection in the Metropolitan Museum of Art in New York City.

Perry, Claire. *Young America: Childhood in 19th-Century Art and Culture.* New Haven, CT: Yale University Press/CA: Iris & B. Gerald Cantor Center for the Visual Arts, 2006.

Children will especially love this book filled with paintings of children from all walks of life in America.

Preble, Duane, Sarah Preble, and Patrick L. Frank. *Artforms: An Introduction to the Visual Arts.* 7th ed. Upper Saddle River, NJ: Prentice Hall, 2003. ISBN 0131830902.

By looking closely at the many artworks in this book, readers are encouraged to see the joy and enrichment the visual arts can bring.

Turner, Jane, ed. *The Dictionary of Art.* New York: Grove's Dictionaries, 1996. ISBN 0195170687.

Although it is frightfully expensive, some teachers may be fortunate enough to have nearby a library that owns this exciting, thirty-four-volume set. Some 6,700 authors have contributed articles on individual artists and art periods, art conservation, and the social and political background of great art movements.

Wilkins, David G., ed. *The Collins Big Book of Art: From Cave Art to Pop Art.* New York: Collins Design/HarperCollins, 2005. ISBN 0-06-08285-1.

This lovely book covers art history from prehistoric times to the present. There are sections of art themes such as landscapes, urban art, still life, etc.

Children's Books

Adams, Simon. *The Kingfisher Atlas of the Ancient World.* Boston: Kingfisher/Houghton Mifflin, 2006. ISBN 0-7534-5914-0.

This fine atlas provides maps of ancient cities as well as information about important buildings and lives of the people.

———. *The Kingfisher Atlas of the Medieval World.* Boston: Kingfisher/Houghton Mifflin, 2006. ISBN 978-7534-5946-1.

Provided in this book are maps of medieval civilizations in different parts of the world as well as information about the people who lived there.

Blake, Quentin. *Tell Me a Picture.* Brookfield, CT: Millbrook Press, 2003. ISBN 0-7613-2748-7.

Blake arranged an art exhibit for the National Gallery London, and the same pictures are the subject of this book. They are arranged in alphabetical order and placed on the page along with Blake's enchanting line drawings. The author asks children to look for the stories the pictures tell.

Blizzard, Gladys S. *Come Look with Me: Animals in Art.* Watertown, MA: Charlesbridge, 1992. ISBN 1565660137.

Children view twelve color reproductions of pictures of animals done by different artists. Discussion questions and background information on the artists.

———. *Come Look with Me: Enjoying Art with Children.* Watertown, MA: Charlesbridge, 1990. ISBN 0934738769.

Twelve color reproductions of paintings by different artists are presented, some of whom are covered in this book. Discussion questions and background information on the artists.

_____. *Come Look with Me: Exploring Landscape Art with Children.* Watertown, MA: Charlesbridge, 1996. ISBN 0934738955.

Children look closely at landscape paintings. Discussion questions and artists' backgrounds are included.

———. *Come Look with Me: World of Play*. Watertown, MA: Charlesbridge, 1993. ISBN 1565660315.

There are twelve works of art showing people at play. Different art styles are represented.

Brown, Laurence Krasney. *Visiting the Art Museum*. Illustrated by Marc Brown. Beecher, IL: Sagebrush, 1999. ISBN 0833548549.

On a visit to a museum, a family enjoys various art periods from primitive through twentieth-century.

Catalanotto, Peter. *Emily's Art*. New York: Richard Jackson/Atheneum, 2001. ISBN 068983831X.

After her painting is rejected by a judge, Emily becomes discouraged but eventually comes to realize the true meaning of art and rekindles her passion to paint.

Cressy, Judith. *Can You Find It? More than 150 Details in 19 Works of Art*. New York: Harry N. Abrams, 2002. ISBN 0-8109-3279-2.

Children are asked to find a list of items in each famous work of art. There is an answer key in the back.

———. *Can You Find It, Too? Search and Discover More Than 150 Details in 20 Works of Art*. New York: Harry N. Abrams, 2004. ISBN 0-8109-5046-4.

Children are asked to find a list of items in each famous work of art. There is an answer key in the back

D'Harcourt, Claire. *Louvre in Close-up*. 6th ed. Translated by David Wharry. San Francisco: Chronicle Books, 2006. ISBN 0811855104.

This book contains works covered in many chapters of this book: stained glass, Greek vases, etc. They are very large color reproductions, with enlarged details of each work surrounding the page.

———. *Masterpieces up Close*. San Francisco: Chronicle Books, 2006. ISBN 0811854035.

Children can view masterpieces from the Middle Ages to the present. Many of them are discussed in this book.

Davidson, Rosemary. *Take a Look: An Introduction to the Experience of Art*. New York: Viking, 1994. ISBN 0670844780.

Davidson introduces the history, techniques, and functions of art through a discussion of different artworks.

Dickins, Rosie, and Mari Griffith. *Introduction to Art: In Association with the National Gallery, London*. Edited by Jane Chisholm. London: Usborne Books, 2004. ISBN 0794506615.

The authors present a history of art simple enough for young children to understand. There are over 160 reproductions of art masterpieces.

Florian, Douglas. *A Painter*. New York: Greenwillow, 1993. ISBN 0688118720.

Florian describes the work a male fine arts painter does, his tools, and what he tries to achieve in his paintings. For the very young child.

Gibbons, Gail. *The Art Box.* Reissue. New York: Holiday House, 2000. ISBN 0-8234-1556-2.

Gibbons describes the materials artists' use and encourages children to create their own pictures.

Glubok, Shirley. *Painting: Great Lives.* New York: Scribner's, 1994. ISBN 0684190524.

These brief lives of European and American painters include many covered in this book: O'Keeffe, Rivera, Velazquez, Vermeer.

Hurd, Thacher. *Art Dog.* New York: HarperCollins, 1996. ISBN 0060244240.

When a painting is stolen from the Dogopolis Museum of Art, the mysterious Art Dog finds the culprits. Children will love trying to recognize the take-offs in this humorous picture book on paintings they have studied.

Isaacson, Philip M. *A Short Walk around the Pyramids and through the World of Art.* New York: Knopf, 1993. ISBN 0679815236.

In presenting works from various times and places, the author discusses both the tangible and abstract aspects of art.

Janson, Anthony F. *History of Art for Young People.* 6th ed. New York: Harry N. Abrams, 2003. ISBN 0131833006.

Janson provides comprehensive coverage of the art of various regions of the world along with numerous reproductions in this classic book.

Jeunesse, Gallimard. *Paint and Painting.* New York: Scholastic, 1994. ISBN 0-590-47636-X.

This wonderful book uses overlays to discuss different painting techniques across the centuries.

———. *What the Painter Sees.* New York: Scholastic, 1994. ISBN 0-590-47648-3.

Jeunesse uses overlays, mirrors, and other devices to discuss art through the centuries, including perspective, portraits, abstract art, etc.

Katz, Susan. *Mrs. Brown on Exhibit and Other Museum Poems.* Illustrated by R. W. Alley. New York: Simon & Schuster, 2002. ISBN 0-689-82970-1.

Mrs. Brown and her class love to visit museums, and there is a poem in the book for each exhibit they see, including Egyptian mummies, Degas's dancer, the Middle Ages, and more. An interesting addition is a listing in the back of the book of unusual museums and their locations.

Kidd, Richard. *Almost Famous Daisy!* London: Frances Lincoln, 1997. ISBN 184507162X.

In this picture book, Daisy travels the world to find her favorite thing to paint. On her journey she sees paintings by Van Gogh, Monet, Chagall, Gauguin, and Jackson Pollock.

Knox, Bob. *The Great Art Adventure.* New York: Rizzoli, 1993. ISBN 0847816885.

Two children take an imaginative trip through time in a wacky museum. They visit many famous paintings, which come to life. This is an excellent book.

Kohl, MaryAnn F., et al. *Discovering Great Artists: Hands-on Art for Children in the Styles of the Great Masters*. Bellingham, WA: Bright Ring Publishing, 1997. ISBN 935607099.

Short biographies of many different artists are followed by suggestions for imitating those artists' work.

Koscielniak, Bruce. *Looking at Glass through the Ages*. Boston: Houghton Mifflin, 2006. ISBN 978-0618-50750-4.

This is an excellent picture-book story of the invention and uses of glass, from its inception in Egypt, to its use in ancient Rome, to its use in stained glass windows in churches.

Krull, Kathleen. *Lives of the Artists: Masterpieces, Messes (and What the Neighbors Thought)*. Illustrated by Kathryn Hewitt. San Diego: Harcourt Brace, 1995. ISBN 015200968X.

Krull offers brief humorous lives of different artists, including some interesting facts. Da Vinci, Michelangelo, Rembrandt, Cassatt, and others are included.

Lach, Dr. William. *Can You Hear It?* New York: Abrams Books for Young Readers/Metropolitan Museum of Art, 2006. ISBN 0810957213.

This book introduces children to great art through music as they listen for sounds of creatures and objects in paintings during musical compositions. CD included.

Lehman, Barbara. *Museum Trip*. Boston: Houghton Mifflin, 2006. ISBN 978-0-618-58125-2.

In this wordless picture book, a young boy visits a museum and becomes part of the exhibits.

McDonnell, Patrick. *Art*. Boston: Little, Brown, 2006. ISBN 0-316-11491-X.

Art lets his imagination run free and creates all kinds of art.

Micklethwait, Lucy, selector. *A Child's Book of Art*. New York: Dorling Kindersley, 1993. ISBN 1564582035.

Family words, garden words, pet words, etc., are depicted in famous paintings. Beautiful.

_____. *Children: A First Art Book*. London: Frances Lincoln, 2006. ISBN 1-84507-116-6.

Paintings of children, some created by artists studied in this book, introduce very young children to the wonderful world of fine art.

———. *Colors: A First Art Book*. London: Frances Lincoln, 2005. ISBN 1845073967.

Young children learn color concepts by viewing fine art.

———. *I Spy: An Alphabet in Art*. Reissue. New York: HarperTrophy, 1996. ISBN 0688147305.

Children study a different artwork beginning with each letter of the alphabet.

———. *I Spy Shapes in Art*. New York: Greenwillow, 2003. ISBN 0060731931.

Children look for shapes in great works of art.

———. *I Spy Two Eyes: Numbers in Art.* Reprint, New York: HarperTrophy, 1998. ISBN 0688161588.

Numbers of objects are spied in nineteen fine paintings by artists such as Botticelli and Robert Indiana.

National Gallery of Art. *An Illustrated Treasury of Songs.* Reissue. Milwaukee, WI: Hal Leonard, 1999. ISBN 0793500613.

This book contains fifty-five traditional songs, ballads, folk songs, and nursery rhymes with lyrics and musical notation. Paintings by many artists discussed in this book, including American primitives, are used throughout. A treasure indeed!

Nilsen, Anna. *Art Auction Mystery: Fine the Fakes, Save the Sale!* Boston: Kingfisher, 2005. ISBN 0-7534-5842-X.

Readers are shown four groups of forgers and, by looking at reproductions of original artworks and pictures of the same works set for auction, must discover which auction works are fakes and who the forgers were. The author has two similar books: *Art Fraud Detective* and *Great Art Scandal.* These books encourage children to look closely at paintings.

Panzer, Nora, ed. *Celebrate America in Poetry and Art.* New York: Hyperion, 1994.

A book of poetry accompanied by art prints that celebrates the 200 years of America's history. Gorgeous!

Phaidon Press. *The Art Book for Children.* Reprint, New York: Phaidon Press, 1997. ISBN 0714836257.

This art dictionary covers 500 famous artists, each receiving a page. A brief bio, a work by that artist, and an analysis of the work is provided for each entry.

Philip, Neil. *Mythology of the World.* Boston: Kingfisher, 2004. ISBN 0-7534-5779-2.

This book explores ancient and contemporary cultures by looking at their stories. Many of the cultures studied in this book are represented.

Raczka, Bob. *Art Is . . .*: Brookfield, CT: Millbrook Press, 2003. ISBN 0-7613-1832-1.

Raczka invites children to experience more than twenty paintings with all five of their senses. Very suitable for young children.

———. *Here's Looking at Me.* Brookfield, CT: Millbrook Press, 2006. ISBN 0-7613-3404-1.

Using the artists' own artwork, Raczka shows how fourteen artists see themselves through their self-portraits.

———. *More Than Meets the Eye.* Brookfield, CT: Millbrook Press, 2003. ISBN 0-7613-1994-8.

As in *Art Is . . .*, children experience paintings with their five senses.

———. *Unlikely Pairs.* Brookfield, CT: Millbrook Press, 2003. ISBN 0-7613-2378-3.

Raczka changes the meaning of an artwork by pairing it with another painting. Children might love to arrange some unlikely pairings of their own after using this book.

Renshaw, Amanda, and Gilda Williams Ruggi. *The Art Book for Children.* New York: Phaidon Press, 2005. ISBN 0714845302.

This book explores the work of thirty artists and discusses a major work for each one: Why did they create the particular work? What choices did they make in its creation? What does it mean?, etc. It is a beautiful book.

Roalf, Peggy. Looking at Painting series. New York: Hyperion. Various dates.

This series of fine books covers such topics in art as children, the circus, dogs, cats, horses, landscapes, seascapes, flowers, musicians, self-portraits, dancers, and families. In addition to discussing what is in the artist's eye when he or she paints, the author provides dates, locations, and sizes of the works presented.

Roche, Denis. *Art Around the World: Loo-Loo, Boo, and More Art You Can Do.* Boston: Houghton Mifflin, 1998. ISBN 0-395-85597-7.

Art projects for children are inspired by countries such as Mexico, Peru, Italy, Egypt, France, and China.

———. *Loo-Loo, Boo, and Art You Can Do.* Boston: Houghton Mifflin, 1996. ISBN 0-395-75921-8.

Children are encouraged to do all kinds of art projects such as sculpture, mask-making, and collage.

———. *Oodles to Do with Loo-Loo and Boo.* Boston: Houghton Mifflin, 2001. ISBN 0-618-15423-Xl.

This book is a compilation of the two previous books.

Romei, Francesca. *The Story of Sculpture: From Prehistory to the Present.* New York: Peter Bedrick, 1995. ISBN 0872263169

Children can view step-by-step presentations of different sculpture techniques. Many full-color and black-and-white photos.

Rowden, Justine. *Paint Me a Poem: Poems Inspired by Masterpieces of Art.* Honesdale, PA: Wordsong/Boyds Mills, 2005. ISBN 1-59078-289-5.

Fourteen poems are paired with fourteen works of art, many of them by artists studied in this book. This book would be perfect to share with children to inspire them to do their own poetry/artwork pairings.

Sayre, Henry. *Cave Paintings to Picasso.* Vancouver, BC: Raincoast Books, 2004. ISBN 0-8118-3767-X.

This beautiful book contains beautiful reproductions of fifty art masterpieces from prehistoric times to the present, with information on the artist and the work.

Schulte, Jessica. *Can You Find It Outside? Search and Discover for Young Art Lovers.* New York: Harry N. Abrams, 2005. ISBN 0-8109-5795-7.

Using rhyming couplets, the author asks children questions about thirteen works of art.

Siebert, Diane. *Tour America: A Journey through Poems and Art.* Illustrated by Stephen T. Johnson. San Francisco: Chronicle Books, 2006. ISBN 0-8118-5056-0.

Siebert's beautiful poems take readers on a journey to America's scenic treasures. Artworks accompany each poem.

Sousa, Jean. *Faces, Places and Inner Spaces: A Guide to Looking at Art.* New York: Harry N. Abrams, 2006. ISBN 0810959666.

Sousa provides examples of how artists use faces, places, and themselves to create art. The examples range from African masks, to Mexican pottery, to works by van Gogh.

Steele, Philip. *Middle East.* Foreword by Paul Adams. Boston: Kingfisher/Houghton Mifflin, 2006. ISBN 0-7534-5984-1.

Steele's in-depth presentation of the countries includes information about ancient trade routes, monuments, the conflicts associated with the region, and more.

Tang, Greg. *Math-terpieces.* Illustrated by Greg Paprocki. New York: Scholastic, 2003. ISBN 0439443881.

Tang asks children to find objects in twelve pieces of art and to group them in certain ways, in this excellent math concept book.

Tchana, Katrin Hyman. *Changing Woman and Her Sisters: Stories of Goddesses from Around the World.* Illustrated by Trina Schart Hyman. New York: Holiday House, 2006. ISBN 0-8234-1999-1.

These tales of goddesses include stories from African, Navajo, Egyptian, and Mayan cultures.

Thomson, Peggy, with Barbara Moore. *The Nine-Ton Cat: Behind the Scenes at an Art Museum.* Edited by Carol Eron. Boston: Houghton Mifflin, 1997. ISBN 0395826837.

Thomson brings readers inside the National Gallery of art for a day to view the work behind the scenes.

Wellington, Monica. *Squeaking of Art: The Mice Go to the Museum.* New York: Dutton, 2000. ISBN 0525461655.

Ten mice visit an art museum and go to different galleries: landscapes, still lifes, etc. Questions are posed as they and readers look at the artworks.

Wolfe, Gillian. *Look! Body Language in Art.* London: Frances Lincoln, 2004. ISBN 1-84507-034-8.

Wolfe asks children to look at the facial expressions, hand gestures, and body poses in seventeen famous paintings to determine what this body language is saying.

Woolf, Felicity. *Picture This: A First Introduction to Paintings.* New York: Doubleday, 1990. ISBN 0385411359.

There are twenty-four pictures and commentary geared to help children understand art. Small reproductions.

Yenawine, Philip. *Colors.* Reissue. New York: Museum of Modern Art, 2006. ISBN 0870701762.

The author uses nineteen works from the museum's collection to explore the function of color in art.

———. *Lines.* Reissue. New York: Museum of Modern Art, 2006. ISBN 0870701754.

The author explores with young children the function of line in various works of art.

———. *Shapes.* Reissue. New York: Museum of Modern Art, 2006. ISBN 0870701770.

The author explores with young children the function of shape in various works of art.

———. *Stories.* Reissue. New York: Museum of Modern Art, 2006. ISBN 0870701789

Readers are asked to uncover the stories told by various works of art.

Other Materials

American Art Ditto. Card Game. Birdcage Press, n.d.

Art cards have a full picture of the artwork on one side and details on the other. American art is featured.

Art Shark. Card Game. Birdcage Press, n.d.

In this card game, children make "money" by replacing fakes with original art and outbidding others at auction.

Getty Museum Close-Up. Card Game. Birdcage Press, n.d.

Children can play matching games with forty-eight cards containing pictures of works in the Getty Museum.

Grafton, Carol Belanger. *120 Great Paintings: CD-ROM and Book.* Mineola, NY: Dover Publications, 2006. ISBN 0486996778.

Children can view masterpieces from five different countries.

Great Art Close-Up. Card Game. Birdcage Press, n.d.

Children learn about great museums throughout the world by playing five different card games.

Masterworks from the Collection; The Metropolitan Museum of Art CD-ROM. Metropolitan Museum of Art. M3885.

Two hundred fifty-seven works from the museum's collection are presented, with titles by the curators. There are many supplemental works, video clips, and more.

National Gallery Close-Up. Card Game. Birdcage Press, n.d.

Children can play matching games with forty-eight cards containing pictures of works in the National Gallery of Art.

Temples. New York: Scholastic, 1996. ISBN 0590896628

This discovery box contains a book about temples, especially those of the Greeks, Romans, Egyptians, Mayans, and Japanese, and a model to help students assemble the facade of a Greek temple.

Thompson, Christine. *Art Image Early Years.* Derby Line, VT: Art Image Publications, n.d.

This art-based curriculum for preschool children consists of five packets organized around themes: shapes, colors, and stories; pets; portraits; animals; and children. Each packet contains color reproductions, a teacher's guide, and activities incorporating various aspects of the curriculum.

Watt, Fiona. *Art Ideas Pack.* London: Usborne Books, 2002. ISBN 0-7945-0119-2.
This pack contains materials and instructions for creating various kinds of art such as crayon resist and watercolors.

Title Index to Art

Due to the number of artworks cited in the text, only those discussed in some depth are indexed here.

Subject Index

About the Author

Marianne C. Saccardi, M.A., taught in public and private elementary schools for twenty years before teaching children's literature in the graduate school at the College of New Rochelle and Early Childhood Department at Norwalk Community College. As a consultant to the Connecticut Literacy Initiative AmeriCorps America Reads Project, Marianne conducted numerous literacy workshops for AmeriCorps Members. She has also served as a consultant for Broderbund Software, is a book reviewer for *School Library Journal,* and serves on the committee to select the winner of the Connecticut Book Award for illustration. She has also written a Teacher's Guide for the *Grolier Multimedia Encyclopedia.* With Marilyn Jody, she founded BookRead, a national electronic-mail system linking children, authors, and books, and co-authored *Using Computers to Teach Literature: A Teacher's Guide.* Marianne has presented workshops at the conventions of the International Reading Association and the National Council of Teachers of English. Most recently, working as an independent consultant for the Connecticut State Department of Education, she has written a literacy curriculum for entry level preschool teachers, taught an advanced literacy course, and written the script for a literacy training DVD. Her articles have appeared in *School Library Journal, The Reading Teacher, School Arts, Book Links,* and *The Constructive Triangle.*